KU-717-381

WITHDRAWN
FROM STOCK

Coláiste Oideachais Mhuire Gan Smal

155.413

Luimneach

THE CHILD'S
CONCEPTION OF GEOMETRY

THE CHILD'S
CONCEPTION OF GEOMETRY

BY

JEAN PIAGET
BÄRBEL INHELDER

AND

ALINA SZEMINSKA

TRANSLATED FROM THE FRENCH BY

E. A. LUNZER

LONDON
ROUTLEDGE AND KEGAN PAUL

1195

First published in England 1960
by Routledge and Kegan Paul Ltd
Broadway House, 68–74 Carter Lane
London, E.C.4
Reprinted 1966, 1970

Printed in Great Britain
by Lowe & Brydone (Printers) Ltd,
London

© Routledge and Kegan Paul 1960

No part of the book may be reproduced
in any form without permission from
the publisher, except for the quotation
of brief passages in criticism

ISBN 0 7100 6193 5

Coláiste Oideachais
Mhuire Gan Smál
Luimneach
Class No. 155·413 AA
Acc. No. 20320

CONTENTS

v

CONTENTS

PART FOUR

AREAS AND SOLIDS

PART FIVE

CONCLUSIONS

PREFACE

IN our earlier work, *The Child's Conception of Space*, we studied certain problems of a general nature in regard to the development of spatial concepts in young children, dealing in particular with the elaboration of projective and Euclidean concepts out of the more elementary topological notions. But the problem of spatial intuition as a whole is exceedingly complex, and we were compelled to postpone our discussion of measurement and metrical geometry. These form the subject matter of the present volume.

Geometrical measurement is a part of the elementary school curriculum. Therefore we may safely say that an analytical study of the beginnings of measurement will be of interest not only to mathematicians and philosophers but to all those who are concerned to foster an educational approach which is securely based on a knowledge of the laws of mental development. It is not difficult to see how the facts brought to light in the present study of the psychogenesis of metrical notions may some day be given a practical application in teaching.

Because the present approach is psychological rather than educational, we have deliberately avoided making any use of the knowledge which children acquire in the course of their formal education. To have done otherwise would have meant obscuring important psychological findings. Nevertheless, the fact that the responses given to our questions are spontaneous should prove an added incentive for working out their implications for education.

To ourselves as psychologists the study of how children come to measure is particularly interesting because the operations involved in measurement are so concrete that they have their roots in perceptual activity (visual estimates of size, etc.) and at the same time so complex that they are not fully elaborated until some time between the ages of 8 and 11 (depending on the amount of composition involved in the operation itself). A further point of interest is that questions of measurement are closely bound up with those of conservation, and hence its evolution presents a remarkable parallel to the growth of number.

Because the problems themselves are important, we have tried to be more than usually systematic in our mode of approach. The first part of the volume deals with spontaneous reactions to the task of measuring and with the representation of changes of position. The second part is devoted to the conservation and measurement of length. The third part deals with metrical construction of angles and curves. The fourth part contains a discussion of areas and volumes, while the last part is a summary in which we retrace the main levels in the development of metrical conceptions of space.

vii

PART ONE

INTRODUCTION

CHANGE OF POSITION
AND SPONTANEOUS MEASUREMENT

COMPLEX operations often depend on others which are more elementary. This is certainly true of measurement, which is a synthesis of two operations, one of these being the coordination of changes of position. Since this first part is designed to form an introduction to our study, we have deliberately dealt with situations in which the child's activity is as spontaneous as it can be. This should enable us to observe the way in which measuring behaviour as a whole is elaborated in the course of the child's activity. Moreover, we should see clearly how measurement implies certain other operations, not only in the context of our experimental situations but in real life. The following two chapters are therefore inductive rather than deductive in approach. The first deals with the way in which children reconstruct their own movements or changes of position by drawing on their own conceptions of the spatial field, and how, as they grow in maturity, so the latter become increasingly coordinated. The second deals with the way in which they measure, or show those more primitive kinds of behaviour which eventually lead to measurement itself; the actual situation is a kind of game in which the child is asked to make a construction which he recognizes sooner or later as one which demands a degree of precision that only measuring can guarantee.

Chapter One

CHANGE OF POSITION [1]

THE concept of change of position is fundamental for Euclidean metrics. These changes form a mathematical 'group', and can be represented in terms of a three-dimensional space structured by a coordinate system. The subject has already been touched on in two earlier investigations. The first of these was concerned with the organization of changes of position at the level of sensori-motor intelligence, during the first eighteen months of life.[2] The second was devoted to the study of spatial representation between the ages of 4 and 12[3]: we saw how younger children described changes of position in terms of end-positions only, while older children compared paths of movement. Dimensions and coordinate systems have also been investigated in an earlier work in which we showed how gradually children learn to structure their space in terms of horizontal and vertical axes and went on to trace the stages of development in the construction of a ground-plan like that of a village.[4] We have yet to study how children come to reconstruct changes of position in terms of a comprehensive system of references, or coordinate system.

A good way to bridge the gap between these earlier studies and the present researches on problems of spatial measurement is to study how children learn to use reference systems in thinking of a group of movements. This investigation should prove a valuable introduction to the study of Euclidean metrics in general.

To measure is to take out of a whole one element, taken as a unit, and to transpose this unit on the remainder of a whole: measurement is therefore a synthesis of sub-division and change of position. However, although this way of looking at it seems clear and self-evident, the process is far more intricate in fact. As often happens in psycho-genetic development, a mental operation is deceptively simple when it has reached its final equilibrium, but its genesis is very much more complex.

The idea of change of position is doubly difficult for the young child. In the first place the concept of measurement goes beyond the ability to carry out the necessary bodily movements or the ability to transpose

---

[1] Written with the collaboration of Miss Gisella Muller.
[2] *The Construction of Reality in the Child*, London, 1955, ch. II.
[3] *Les notions de mouvement et de vitesse chez l'enfant*, chs. 3, 4.
[4] Piaget and Inhelder, *The Child's Conception of Space*, here referred to as C.C.S.

3

things; it implies the representation of changes of position, and the ability to reconstruct a sequence of action comes much later than the ability to carry it out correctly. But secondly, to be able to imagine movements is not enough, for the subject must link movements to reference points. Some system of reference is implicit in the representation of any sequence of movement. An understanding of measurement demands that the several reference points are linked in a systematic whole, which implies 'coordinate axes'. This is especially true of measurements in an area or a space, ch. VII, where the subject must take account of two or more measurements simultaneously, and of angular measurement, ch. XI, where he has to note differences in direction over and above the changes of position involved.

In several of the above mentioned researches it was shown that children begin by considering a change of position in terms of the end-position only. They make no attempt to link end-point with starting-point, still less do they consider both in terms of a more embracing system of reference. We will meet this phenomemon again and again in the present series of enquiries, particularly in that which deals with the constancy of the length of an object when it is moved (ch. IV). Before analysing the way in which children build up the concept of metric space, we must return briefly to the study of movement, bearing in mind the difference between actually moving an object and describing change of position, and especially how closely linked the latter must be to a system of references (see C.C.S., chs. XIII and XIV).

We need to examine the representation of changes of position in a situation with which the subject is thoroughly familiar. It will not do to face him with a concrete problem comprising movements which are quite new to him, asking him to describe them. Not only should the changes of position themselves be familiar; the reference system of which they form a part should be one with which the subject is familiar and which he can readily envisage (unlike the imaginary village of C.C.S., ch. XIV). Accordingly the preliminary investigation deals with large-scale changes of position as against the minute and accurate ones which figure in measuring. Moreover, we shall leave out the question of measurement altogether, and concentrate on (i) the conflict between representation and action, and (ii) the necessary relation between the representation of change of position and a system of references.

By studying the way children between the ages of 4 and 10 describe a familiar walk, such as the road from home to school, or that from school to various well-known places round about, we will see clearly how they learn to describe changes of position by using landmarks and eventually link these reference points in a comprehensive system. Thus the main buildings and squares, bridges, rivers or streams (in Geneva, the Rhone and the Arve), their own school and their homes are the landmarks which go together to form a reference system, and this in turn enters into their description of changes of position.

§1. *Outline of method and results*

Children cannot be questioned below the age of 4 or 5, which is when, in Switzerland, they first enter the Kindergarten, that is, at Stage II. Even between 4 and 7 children cannot be made to stay the length of the experiment unless they become interested in the questions asked.

The subject comes into the experimental room attached to the school and is taken to the window where he is asked to point out various buildings and well-known places. This is merely to ascertain the extent of his local knowledge and sense of direction. Next, he is made to sit at a table with his back to the window and given a sand-tray with wet sand, carefully levelled off. He is also given a number of little wooden houses of various sizes, representing the school and nearby buildings, little pieces of wood representing greens, recreation grounds, public squares and bridges, and a ribbon to represent the Arve. (The experiment was carried out at a school quite close to the river.) The experimenter takes the biggest house and puts it in the middle of the sand tray, saying: "Now this is the big school (meaning the primary school as against the kindergarten). There are plenty more houses, little ones and big ones. These little bits of wood are to make bridges with and this blue ribbon is the Arve. Now I want to know about everything near the school. You put the things in the right places." (Children who are too nervous to use the models can be asked to draw it all on the sand for a start.) At the end of the first part of the experiment the subject is asked to draw a plan in the sand or on a piece of paper, showing how he would go home from school or, better still, how he would go to a place which they all know (the 'Place Neuve' which is quite close to the area shown on the sand tray). The drawing is a free drawing but the child is asked to show how it fits in with his general plan. Next the child is asked to make a drawing of the sand-model on a large sheet of paper. When he has done this, the experimenter turns the 'school building' through 180° and asks: "Now if I turn the school round like this, must we move everything else about as well or can we leave it just as it is?" The child is asked to make the necessary changes himself. With older children the entire experiment can be carried out with pencil and paper.

There are thus three related parts to the enquiry: (1) a plan of the school buildings and the principal features in the immediate vicinity; (2) a reconstruction of the route from school to a well-known landmark; and (3) changes in the location of features when the school building has been turned through 180°. The first of these has already been covered in C.C.S., ch. XIV, and may therefore be passed over in the present chapter. We shall concentrate instead on the representation of changes of position as shown by a child's reconstruction of the route from school to a given destination or as necessitated by turning the original plan through 180°. However, it is clear that both these tasks demand a system of references which is in effect a topographical schema or plan of the neighbourhood.   .

The responses made by children to this enquiry show three levels of development. During stages I and II, that is, up to an average age of 7, children produce three kinds of reaction, all of which are interrelated. (1) When dealing with a route, they think of their own actions first, as though these were some kind of absolute, and the various landmarks are fixed in terms of them, instead of vice versa. (2) Their landmarks are not organized in terms of an objective spatial whole; the links between any two are conceived of as being independent of the system as a whole; subjective considerations determine the location of the various points. (3) Subjects cannot rotate a plan through 180°, nor can they reconstruct a route in the reverse direction, because both imply operational thinking.

The next level (IIIA) is marked by limited objective coordinations of space. Children reconstruct routes, using sub-systems of reference which are not linked together as a whole. Their plan of the district is made up of several portions which are correct in themselves but do not agree with one another. In rotating the plan they reverse some of the relations required but not all. Finally, stage IIIB shows complete spatial coordination alike in the representation of a route, in the topographical schema and in the correct reversal of a plan of the school.

Development of the power to reconstruct changes of position proceeds along similar lines to that which enables young children to handle these relations at the perceptual level. We have shown in an earlier work how this is achieved by the building-up of a group at the perceptuo-motor level.[1] The present development, although many years later in point of time, conforms to the same important principle. In both, there is development away from what might be termed egocentric coordination towards objective coordination, that is, coordination which no longer hinges on the subject's own actions. Whereas earlier the subject's actions were the only reference system available for the representation of spatial reality, these actions themselves are later seen within the context of an objective system. He can therefore describe his own movements in terms of objective references which are systematically interrelated. At the level of representation, it is when children pass from an egocentric attitude to objective coordination that they build up a group of positional changes[2] and work out a coordinate system. A similar move away from an egocentric attitude and an equally remark-

---

[1] *The Child's Conception of Reality*, ch. II.   [2] French: *groupe de déplacements*.

able achievement occurs in the first eighteen months of life when children build practical groups of changes of position in dealing with concrete objects. The youngest children in the present study cannot describe changes of position as an objective group because they lack a coherent network of reference points (see C.C.S., chs. XIV and XV, sec. 5, op. vi). They are as incapable of the operation of inversion as of associative and transitive composition, as is clear from their attempts to describe changes of position, and from the landmarks they use. From their own point of view these are coordinated, but this is in terms of their own actions. When dealing with sensori-motor space we called this a 'subjective group', since from the point of view of the objects there is no group. Later, when changes of position and landmarks are coordinated and allow of inversion, there is a true group.

§2. *Stages I and II: Landmarks are uncoordinated and changes of position cannot be described*

We have said that the above experiment cannot be carried out with children under 4. However, by noting spontaneous remarks made by children aged between 18 months and 4 years as we take them for a walk, we may observe the earliest spatial reactions which lead into stage II.

JAC (1; 7), when some 100 yards away from a certain mountain chalet, shows in what direction it lies and also points out the road taken by his grandfather when he left three days previously. At the age of 1; 11 he is able to show the direction of his own home although it is half a mile away and he has his back to it. But when he starts on his way back he begins by thinking his home is still behind him, till he discovers his mistake. At 3; 3 he walks along the right hand side of a road to avoid oncoming traffic, but on the way back he goes to the left, mistaking it for his right.

L, even at 3; 11, when travelling in a car, thinks the mountains are moving.[1]

Their sense of direction is quite good, for the first child knew where his own home was as well as the road along which he accompanied his grandfather a few yards. On the other hand they are still inclined to hesitate and make mistakes when dealing with an about face which switches 'behind' to 'in front' and left to right, and even the framework of distant landmarks is for them not a stationary one.

This type of thinking along two distinct planes continues throughout stage II, and it is not until stage IIIA, when their powers of representation have become greater, that children are able to link the two together. The first plane is that of practical spatial orientation or effective action. When children are taken to the window of the experimental room they can show where they live, where the Arve is, and various

[1] See *The Child's Construction of Reality*, obs. 126, and *Play, Dreams and Imitation in Childhood*, obs. 130.

7

other landmarks they know, and if we walk home with them they manage to show the way quite well, although they can only explain each portion as they come to it. The second plane, however, which is the one we are studying, is that of true representation, which is temporarily divorced from action. Such representation occurs when children merely think out a route and the spatial relations between various well-known landmarks. Quite clearly, the step from action to representation is still quite a large one at stage II. Children at this stage can orientate themselves in a practical way, that is, in action, which means that up to a point they can even anticipate the spatial relations between one landmark and the next as they come to them; but instead of building up a picture of their environment in general as an ordered whole, they stop short at a more or less incoherent juxtaposition. Their arrangement of landmarks draws on their own personal recollections of actual journeys and on their main interests, for these helped to fix in their minds the way they went and the landmarks they passed.

The examples which follow illustrate this way of arranging landmarks, and the confusions which result.

Luc (4; 2) is taken to the window. He points correctly the direction of his own school (the kindergarten building) as well as the Arve, etc. "Where is the Salon de l'Auto?—*Over there* (he points in the direction of the Arve which is wrong).—*No, there* (this time he is right).—Why did you change your mind?—*Because that's where I live.*—(He is taken to the experimental table and asked:) Where do you live?—*You know the trams, well after the theatre* (he means the travelling circuses on the Plaine de Plainpalais) *it goes to the rue de Carouge: then the rue Dancet is there* (which is where he lives).—Have you ever been to the theatre?—*Yes, once. I saw a tiger.*—Where is the theatre?—*You know, over there, near the Prize Giving.*—What would you find near the school building?—*Trees, tennis, gardens, then yards, gardens, the little boys' playground, the big boys' playground.*—Where is the sandpit? —*Near where we play.*—Where? Show me?—(He points in the wrong direction, then corrects himself when taken back to the window.)—Where is the rue de Carouge?—(Instead of showing the shortest way he shows a round-about route which passes by his own home and describes it through the window with his arm): *You go straight ahead, then you turn there, and there, and there* (which is where he lives), *that's the rue Carouge.*" Luc is now told to arrange the things he spoke of on the wet sand tray, taking care to put them where they belong relative to each other. He produces a jumble of separate relations, set side by side, whose main features are these: (1) Several relations are incorrect because of purely subjective links (interests, etc.). Thus, where the main school building is only a few yards from the kindergarten and Luc's home is several hundred yards away, Luc leaves a large gap between the two schools and puts the kindergarten quite close to his home. (2) Although the two playgrounds adjoin one another, being separated only by a lattice-work fence, Luc puts the older boys' playground away on the far side of their school instead of in between the two buildings: he sees and hears these boys every time he goes out to play, but he pushes them off as far as possible when it comes to finding their geographical place. (3) There may be confusion between things that are conceptually similar and things that are close together (cf. C.C.S. ch. XIV, §3). Luc puts the two bridges he knows over the Arve side by side. Other objects are incorrectly arranged because of illusions arising from egocentric habits of thought. Thus, where the Salon de l'Automobile lies half-way between his home and his school, Luc puts it right by his home and even feels he must move the school further to stress its distance; because he passes the Salon on his way to school and therefore thinks it is nearer home. He does not realize that the return distance from school is as great as the distance there. Again: "Where is the Plaine de Plainpalais?— *On my way home, but not right by it* (Luc puts it some distance away but fails to place it correctly with respect to his home, his school and the Salon de l'Auto)." At times, Luc is correct in the spatial relations between two places, but when dealing with three, even apart from egocentric confusion, he fails because he cannot synthesize.

GEI (5; 11) puts the main school near the kindergarten with the two adjoining playgrounds in between, which is correct. However, while a nursery and various other buildings which have no particular interest for him, find their right place by the main school building, places which fascinate him: the football ground and "*that house with the presents*" (a general store which sells toys) are put near his own school—because they are near to his heart. Then again, he rightly puts his home near the Arve, indicated with the blue ribbon, but, in doing so, he forgets all about the school, and as a result his home and the school are shown on the same side of the river instead of on opposite sides. He goes on to put a bridge near his house (the Pont des Acacias) but all this part of the plan is opposite where it should be in relation to the whole area. This leads to inevitable confusion: "Where is the Salève?—*There, because it must be over towards the Pont de Carouge*", which is right enough when looked at from the school building, but Gei goes on to put both the Salève and the bridge in question on the wrong side of the plan, so that in the end the whole is nothing but a jumble.

MIU (6; 10) puts a number of places together in what appears to be a pell-mell arrangement: the building and corridors of the main school, the main school playground, the kindergarten playground and entrance, the gymnasium which is a separate building, and a mound of sand on the bank of the Arve. He goes on to show the Arve itself near the gymnasium without taking any notice of what preceded, while the Pont des Carouge and the Pont des Acacias are wrongly put side by side. In short, a number of places are brought together by Miu's personal interests, while others show confusion between conceptual similarity and proximity in space.

It may be noted that these subjects occasionally succeed in arranging two objects in isolation, but they fail whenever they have to synthesize two relations, that is, when three or more elements are involved. The reasons for this are quite general and have been indicated in earlier works.

First, a true relation in logic is one which can be combined with

9

others ('multiplied') while the 'pre-relations' of young children are isolated links between pairs of elements, which is why little children cannot arrange a series but simply bracket objects in pairs.[1] In spatial relations, the same difficulty may be expressed more precisely. The idea that two elements are close together is not beyond children at this level. They can even reconstruct the order in which things are situated in terms of a single dimension, although their reconstruction is intuitive, and therefore does not permit of inversion (reversing the order, C.C.S., ch. III). Multiplying orders in two or more dimensions, however, implies a coordinate system, and in a previous enquiry we demonstrated that young children do not understand coordination in several dimensions. Thus children at stage II tried to copy the schematic model of a village as if the relations involved could be expressed in purely linear terms.[2] It follows that even when these subjects are successful in showing proximity, their thought is still at a topological level: they are quite incapable of building up a Euclidean schema where the whole is coordinated in terms of a reference-system.

True enough, included in their schema are a number of juxtapositions which arise from their experience of change of position, which implies that it is not based exclusively on static proximity. Unfortunately, they distort distances because of egocentric illusions which they acquire in the course of their habitual journeys. These journeys are always seen unidirectionally, or at any rate subjects fail to equate the distance there with the distance back, so that the end-points cannot be compared. Luc's arrangement of the Salon de l'Auto and his house is but one example. A similar mechanism is at work in yet another phenomenon which is the most frequent of all. The distance between objects is dismissed altogether where these are held together by subjective interest. Thus Luc puts his school and home quite close together (to be explained partly by the frequency of this journey and partly by subjective interest) and the main school a long way away, simply because it does not concern him. Gei puts "the house with the presents" near his school, etc. Finally, conceptual similarity is mistaken for proximity in space, as is the case with the bridges which nearly all subjects put side by side because they belong to the same class of things.

The characteristics, then, of this level are these: some neighbouring places are put together in pairs, the arrangement being purely topological and lacking any coordinate system, others which do not belong together are put together because the subject repeatedly makes the journey between them, others again are so arranged because the activity

[1] See *Le developpement des quantites chez l'enfant*, pp. 223–33, and compare H. Wallon, *L'origine de la pensée chez l'enfant*, where Professor Wallon shows the general significance of linked couples.

[2] C.C.S. ch. XIV. In the experiment referred to subjects were asked to copy a model, while in this experiment they have to reconstruct the position of real objects.

10

of the subject is the final criterion. As a result, position and distance are systematically distorted by egocentric illusions engendered by action—which is not operational as is logical thought. There are indeed occasional suggestions that children at this level are groping towards the representation of a group of changes of position, as shown by the following examples. But these phenomena seem in no way to influence those described earlier.

Luc (4; 2) wished to put his house near the kindergarten, as readers may remember. The experimenter went on to ask him if that was right. Immediately Luc began to puzzle it out in quite a different way, bringing out very clearly the pattern of children's thinking at this level: "Where do you live?—*There.*—Why?—*Because I live opposite the kindergarten.*—Do you really live opposite?—*No.*—Well, where do you live?" In answer to the question, Luc turns round in his chair and looks out of the window; he points with one hand in the true direction of his home and draws a twisting path in the sand with the other. All this while he repeats to himself: "*I turn, I turn, I turn, I turn.*" Then he looks back at his hand which is still pointing in the true direction and puts the model house at the end of the path he has drawn.

Mor (5; 10) is asked to show the way from school to the Place Neuve. He immediately draws a line with a right angle bend and a slight curve at the end, saying: "*There, I have to turn. That's the Place Neuve.*" He remembers only where he starts and where he finishes and the fact that he has to go round a corner on the way. He cannot call to mind a single landmark and the journey he shows bears no relation to his plan of the school and district.

Al (6; 1) seems more advanced, for he remembers the names of several roads on the way: rue Hugo de Senger, "*a road over there*", rue Dancet, rue Pictot de Bock. But he cannot remember their order or the places where he had to turn, so that his drawing of the route is just an arc with a number of points put in haphazard to correspond with names he can remember.

Du (6; 4) on the other hand, makes a very complicated drawing of his route and one which looks very accurate, saying: "*I go straight along, I turn there, I go straight along again, I turn there, then after I keep going straight and I turn once more.*" However he does not know a single landmark for any section of the route. Indeed he regards objective references as so unimportant that on one occasion he changes round the end point and the starting point and calls "school" what he had been calling "the Place Neuve" and vice versa.

Fan (6; 7) draws a route to the Place Neuve which is practically rectilinear and starts off by recalling a number of landmarks more or less correctly: "*I go near the Rond Point, then along the road towards the Bastions, the Bastions and the Place Neuve.*" But when his drawing is finished the experimenter asks him to show the exact whereabouts of the Rond Point, and Fan puts it on the near side of the school instead of beyond it and half way to the Place Neuve. In the same way he puts the Plaine below the school instead of on the road from school to the Rond Point. With the Salon de l'Auto his error is even greater, etc. In short, the walk itself and the few landmarks which are remembered in conjunction with it are quite disconnected, as indeed are the

11

different landmarks with one another. Instead of being related, they are juxtaposed.

Gio (7; 1) produces a straight line with a right angle at either end. One represents the school in relation to the roads he follows, while the other stands for the Place Neuve. On either side of the middle section of the route he puts a circle, one of these being the Plaine de Plainpalais, and the other the Jardin des Bastions. But Gio has inverted their positions and what is more, he puts a certain road between the school and the Plaine, though this particular road is one along which he travels every day on his way to school and is really on the other side of the Arve.

These responses are interesting because they show that the recollections which help subjects to picture the route are essentially practical and even motor. It is quite true that we ourselves draw on journeys which we have actually made when thinking out the whereabouts of a town or when describing a route we followed on a mountain trip. Suppose we are asked either of these questions by a passer-by or a tourist, we cannot but be made very much aware that the use of gestures and calling a motor schema to mind are far more helpful than true representation. Above all, if we think closely, we must recognize that our own comings and goings provide the framework for our memory-images of districts and landscapes. Indeed, examples such as these provide the best proof that visual images are internal imitations of actions, the objects being imagined and the actions internalized. Remarkable in this connection is the extent of distortion to which we are liable when picturing a district. Thus those parts we have covered most frequently are thought of as much larger than they are while others seem smaller because although they too are known, they are, so to speak, less actively known. Facts such as these bear an analogy with the picture of changes of position formed by children at this level, but there is an important difference. We try to relate our motor recollections to landmarks, in order to establish direct and objective relations between landmarks, and make up a single ordered system. In so far as we succeed, we can describe any set of movements coherently, so that logical transformations are possible. The reaction of these subjects is interesting because they seem quite content with the motor or subjective element in their descriptions, so much so, that some (like Luc) do not feel any need for references, while others fail to see the need for stable relations between references.

In the process of remembering their own actions, these subjects are led to mention landmarks. But these are simply tacked on to their recollections, where by rights the motor schema should fall back on the landmarks. Accordingly, astonishing as it may seem, subjects fail to respect the true positions of landmarks and do not even preserve the order in which they come to them.

12

We are reminded of the way in which, at the same level, they describe alternative paths between two points. In an earlier experiment, children were shown two paths, one being a straight line between two points while the other was bent at various angles.[1] To begin with, they ignored everything except the end-point, so that if the end-points coincided they regarded the paths as being of the same length: only by the most gradual steps did they reach a stage where their judgments were based on the paths themselves. We see now why children, in describing a well-known journey, are reduced to recollections of a schema which is almost purely motor in character: it is because changes of position, for them, consist merely in change of final location, ending at a given point; they fail to see them in terms of an ordered system of points and intervals, of which their own journey forms a part. Children at this level do not regard changes of position as actions in space; they seem to leave space altogether at their starting point and come back to it at the end-point, and these are not linked in an ordered whole. They are interested only in their own translocation. The space in which this occurs is a secondary matter, so that the stages of their journey and the permanent and all-important sites which they pass fall into no objective order. Their order is a subjective one, dependent on their own actions.

At stage II, therefore, there is no true 'group' of changes of position. There is only a 'subjective group' which links the subject's own movements without reference to objective order in space. A similar 'subjective group' it will be remembered, was a feature of one stage of sensori-motor intelligence.[2] The most convincing proof that these subjects lack a true and objective group lies in their inability to understand inversion. Here, this operation consists in rotating landmarks as a function of a 180° reversal of plan. A similar link appeared between the sensori-motor group of changes of position (as seen in the movement of objects from one place to another)[3] and the ability to turn things round at will. The baby who is still at the level of 'subjective groups' cannot turn his bottle through 180° when he is given it back to front; as soon as he is capable of the first objective groups in dealing with movable things, he can turn it without the slightest difficulty. At the level of representation, the same is true. Where there is no group of changes of position, children find difficulty in systematically turning the plan of the school through 180°. (Only the school buildings themselves are involved together with the immediate neighbourhood.)

Here are two illustrations drawn from among the most advanced subjects at stage II:

GIO (7; 1), cited earlier, builds up the model as if he were facing the main entrance. The playground is correctly shown behind the school with the

[1] Piaget, *Les notions de mouvement et de vitesse chez l'enfant.*
[2] Piaget, *The Child's Construction of Reality,* ch. II, §2.   [3] Ibid., ch. II, §§ 3, 4.

kindergarten to the right, the nursery and tennis courts to the left and the Arve beyond the playground. He makes a mistake in putting the rue de Carouge and a certain fountain on the wrong side of the Arve, but a little chalet opposite the main entrance is correctly shown. The Salon de l'Auto and the Plaine are likewise shown in the right direction, though everything is rather approximate. Now when we start a new plan and put the school building the other way round, telling Gio to imagine himself in the playground, Gio successfully shows the playground in front of the main building, and even shows the fountains next to the playground, but after that he is lost; he puts the kindergarten on the right as it was before, and still puts the Arve and the quays on the far side of the school, etc.: "Now be careful, if the playground is here and the fountain is there, is the Arve right?—*Oh, no, it should be here* (he puts it right).—Then where should the nursery be?—*Over there, by the tennis courts* (he goes wrong again and puts them both on the left instead of on the right)." The chalet stays in front of the school, etc.

The experimenter tries to make things easier by using only one wet sand tray with the objects already arranged as in the first layout, seen from outside the front entrance to the main school. He turns the building round and puts a little lead figure on the playground side to stand for Gio himself: "Now what's happened?—*I'm in the playground.*—Good. You understand now. Now do the things stay as they are?—*Oh, no.*—Well you put them where they belong." But instead of changing the layout of the model, Gio merely takes the objects one at a time and turns them round on their own axes, without altering their position, as if the figure in the playground now sees everything as it would do if the plan had been rotated. Only the Arve is not turned: "What about the Arve? Does that remain back there?—*Yes, because you can't turn the Arve round!*"

JEA (7; 0) builds a much more sketchy plan as seen from the front entrance. He starts by going wrong over the embankment, which he puts in front of the building, and the playground, which he puts on the far side of the Arve, but he rearranges them with the playground behind the school, the embankment behind the playground, and the Arve behind that. The experimenter adds nothing but merely rotates the school building, telling him the little figure is now in the playground. He correctly alters the relative positions of the school, the playground, the quay and the Arve. However, in spite of this promising start, when asked to put in the kindergarten, the store, the nursery, etc., he consistently uses left for right and foreground for background.

Even the most advanced subjects at this stage are unable to find the correct solution to the problem of rotating the model, though they may have been fairly successful in producing an approximate reconstruction of the school buildings and immediate neighbourhood. Nor is this altogether surprising since children at the same level were unable to reverse the perspectives of a mountain range.[1] This is the same problem except that the content here is familiar to the subjects and they are asked to express the change of viewpoint in terms of changes of position.

[1] Cf. C.C.S., ch. VIII, §§ 2, 3.

§3. *Sub-stage IIIA: Representation of changes of position is partially coordinated by the use of landmarks*

At sub-stage IIIA we find the beginnings of objective grouping in the representation of changes of position, and hence also the beginnings of coordinated landmarks. The reactions of subjects at this sub-stage are interesting because of this relationship, which shows that representation of a group of changes of position is impossible unless the journeys which are described are embedded in the context of a coordinate system. As is clear from the illustrations which follow, the elaboration of a coordinate system and grouped representation of movement are interdependent. However, children at this level are unable to coordinate the system as a whole, either in describing a route or in showing the topographical relations between landmarks. The following illustrations show how they deal with the sketch of the neighbourhood.

REV (7; 10) begins his sand model by showing correctly the two school buildings and their playgrounds, likewise the fountain, the swing, the sandpit, the football-ground, the quay and the Arve. When he comes to put in the nursery and the *"dog's house"* Rev remembers that they go together, but though he corrects himself after first putting them on the right instead of on the left, he still leaves them too far away from the other features. Then he looks out of the window and adds a road *"going uphill"*, a cafe, etc., and finishes up with a new group of features on the extreme left of the model. The experimenter tells him to put in the chalet which can be seen through the window, but now he finds himself at a loss. First he puts it opposite the entrance to the main school, which is correct, then he takes it away again and puts it in with the second group, near the cafe, and that too is correct: "Where is the chalet?—*Here*, (in front of the school). *No, here*, (by the cafe).—But which is more correct?" Thus Rev's model consists of two separate sub-groups which are quite independent although each is correct in itself. The object which they have in common does not help him because he sees it first in one context and then in the other.

TRU (8; 2) has three sub-groups each of which is a consistent whole. First, he draws the school, the playground, the tennis courts, etc., all of which make up the first system. Next he looks out of the window without getting up and says: *"And now that road over there."* Since the window looks out onto the front of the school, the road in question should be shown running at right angles to the building, but Tru simply tacks it on to the nursery which is on the left of his drawing. This leads him to show a second group which consists of that road, the chalet, a road fork which he calls *"the two roads"*, etc. A third group, shown on the right, is made up of the kindergarten, the Arve, etc.

CHU (8; 7) also produces two unrelated sub-groups. One contains the school which is shown correctly together with all the buildings round about as far as the Arve; the other is made up of the Plaine, the rue de Carouge, the Salon de l'Automobile, etc. and bears no relation either to the school or to the Arve.

CLA (9; 0) provides an interesting example of a transitional level between IIIA and IIIB. He begins by drawing the school buildings, the Arve, etc., in

15

some detail. Then, after looking out of the window, he draws the rue Masbou, indicating the name of the road, and finishes up with the rue de Carouge (into which it leads), etc. However, instead of making this system agree with the first, he ignores it, which leads him to obvious contradictions. For instance, the rue de Carouge is shown between the school and the Arve, whereas, in fact, the school is in between the other two. Cla notices this and draws another plan which is consistent and inclusive.

These examples and many more are essentially similar. The same kind of grouping occurs at a lower developmental level (IIA and IIB) when subjects can actually see the countryside as they make their plan instead of being asked to build up a plan from memory.[1] Why, then, do we find two unrelated partial plans even at level IIIA, although children can now coordinate two dimensions in their drawing[2] and are beginning to show a sense of relativity in coordinating perspectives?[3] The answer, in part, is that children can solve a problem in a concrete situation before they solve it from memory. But these examples show another feature which bears on the representation of changes of position as such. Each of these partial plans can be shown to have been drawn with a particular vantage point or a particular journey in mind. The partial plans are unrelated because their authors are as yet unable to bridge the gap between one privileged vantage point or journey and the next. Unlike children at earlier stages, they appreciate objective relations between landmarks which feature in a single journey, or those which stand out from a particular vantage point, but each journey and vantage point is still unique and therefore they cannot coordinate all the features in an area taken as a whole.

As they pass from one group of features to another they make it very obvious that the order within these groups is dependent on a particular vantage point or journey. So it is that Rev looks out of the window to finish his drawing and straightaway builds up an independent plan based on that viewpoint alone: the 'uphill' road (which in fact is perfectly level), the cafe, etc. Now the first part of his drawing was based on what one might expect to see when facing the school. It is therefore diametrically opposed to the second, and corresponds with the way he goes to school each morning. The drawing of Tru suggests the same two viewpoints, but Tru draws a third group of features based on the way he went to the kindergarten the previous year. Thus he shows the road to the kindergarten as a sinusoidal curve, which is a common characteristic of drawings based on motor imagery. Chu shows one group of features belonging to his journey to school and another based on the route from his home to the Plaine, where he likes to play. Finally Cla begins by drawing one group corresponding to the journey to school and another to the journey from school, but, though their orientations

---

[1] See Piaget, C.C.S., ch. XIV, §4.   [2] Ibid., ch. XIV, §5.   [3] Ibid., ch. XVIII.

16

are opposite, the groups become intertwined and contradictory, so that he is forced to start afresh, when he finally produces a single coherent plan.

While these subjects show much greater powers of coordination than those at stage II, their topographical schema is not yet ordered as a unified whole. They fix their landmarks in sub-groups, based on a number of independent vantage points. The examples already given suggest the somewhat paradoxical conclusion that these children cannot coordinate landmarks in terms of a unified system because their own changes of position are inadequately grouped. In truth, the two groupings are mutually dependent, because changes of position cannot be grouped except in the context of a well coordinated reference-system. The following examples show the reverse dependence. Here subjects use landmarks correctly to describe changes of position but fail to arrive at a coherent and comprehensive group because their reference-systems are insufficiently coordinated.

PEL (9; 3) is asked to explain the way from school to the Place Neuve: *"Here is the school, I go along that road over there; there I turn and carry straight on.*—How do I know when to turn?—*First you come to the No. 8 tram-stop, then you reach another turning,* (he means the Rond Point) *and finally you get to the Place Neuve.*—Where is the Rond Point?—*Here,* (he points to the last turning shown).—What about the rue de Carouge?—*That's here,* (he now points to the stretch of road between the first turning—where the No. 12 tram stops at the Boulevard de Pont d'Arve—and the Rond Point). *But there are two rue de Carouges. One leads to the Rond Point and the other to the Pont de Carouge* (he now draws a second group of features showing the southern section of the rue de Carouge, the Arve and the Pont de Carouge. But this 'second' rue de Carouge is almost at right angles to the first, so that the two sub-groups cannot be reconciled although each is well coordinated in itself).—Do these two rue de Carouges come together?—*Yes, they come together near where the No. 12 tram stops, coming from the rue du Pont d'Arve."* Now it happens that this point is very near Pel's own home. He cuts the rue de Carouge in half and makes one stretch run perpendicular to the other which gives him two groups of features which conflict because these areas correspond to two quite different walks as far as he is concerned.

PAT (9; 4) produces a drawing which is correct if schematic and shows the school, the rue Dizerens (which runs at right angles to the school building), the rue de Carouge, the Rond Point, the Bastions and the Place Neuve, all of which he names. After that, however, he draws a large diamond shape to show the exact whereabouts of the Plaine de Plainpalais, and draws in several more roads none of which bear any relation to the first part of his drawing, except that he puts in a road leading from the Plaine to the Bastions.

SAN (9; 4) does a similar drawing, though his account is quite remarkable for its wealth of detail and the number of roads which he mentions by name. Nevertheless, he finishes up with three unrelated sub-groups: the route from school to the Place Neuve, the Plaine together with a large number of roads

17

nearby and, finally, the Bastions and the Treille, etc., which link up with the far corner of the Plaine but do not touch the first sub-group.

Why is it that in spite of their remarkable memory for detail, children continue to show a number of separate and unrelated journeys? San has given the answer himself. Formerly he lived at the far end of the Plaine de Plainpalais and he knew the roads in that area before he learned to know the district where he lives at present: hence there is no coordination between the two areas which he has frequented. Similarly, Pel cuts the rue de Carouge, and hence his schema, into two because he lives near the No. 12 tram stop to which he refers: the two halves of his schema correspond to the two directions in which he travels from home. And so on. These subjects cannot describe their own changes of position in terms of a comprehensive schema because their landmarks are unrelated. At the same time, they refer to landmarks in the more limited context of each sub-group, unlike children at stage II who are content with what might be called bare descriptions of movement.

It is a vicious circle. To describe changes of position objectively, that is, to build up a group which is free from personal associations, descriptions must comply with a coordinated reference-system; but to achieve such a comprehensive reference-system changes of position must be grouped. At level IIIA, we see the beginnings of these interdependent operational systems in descriptions of separate subsidiary wholes. Each of these is a coherent group of changes of position implying a coordinated framework of reference. However, when asked to produce a plan of the area as a whole, these children fail because they do not integrate all the changes of position involved, and when asked to describe their journeys they fail because they do not link all the landmarks in a single network.

Experimental rotation of the model building through 180° again results in partial success. Subjects understand the need for conversion of the plan as a whole and are no longer content to pivot the models on their own axes. But for reasons which will appear later, they cannot carry out their plan to the end.

Lav (8; 4) succeeds in rotating the relative positions of the playground, the kindergarten, the embankment and the Arve, but puts the Chalet, the roads near it and the Plaine on the right instead of on the left, and the sportsground on the left instead of the right.

Via (8; 10) rotates the sand model correctly when moving the school buildings, the playgrounds, the embankment and the Arve. But in altering a group consisting of the Salon de l'Automobile and neighbouring buildings he merely moves them from the back to the front of the tray without transferring them from right to left; likewise, the nursery and tennis courts.

San (9; 4) rotates the school buildings correctly, as also the objects near it. But in rearranging a second group consisting of the Plaine, the Salon de l'Automobile, the road from the school to the Salon and the chalet which stands on one side of the road, he moves them from back to front only, and not from right to left. This is all the more remarkable in that he rotated the main school building and the kindergarten in a left to right direction, and when he came to draw the Plaine he remarked spontaneously: *"It's on the same side as the Kindergarten, but I can't put it here* (where it should have been) *because it's over in that direction* (pointing through the window towards the Plaine from where he sits), *so I have to leave the kindergarten and then I have to turn."* He proceeds to draw an imaginary path which winds its way from the kindergarten shown on the left and finishes at the Plaine which he shows on the right of the plan. As for a third group consisting of the Pont des Acacias, the rue Caroline, etc., San becomes more and more the victim of his true position, and does not rotate it at all.

PEL (9; 3) does exactly the same. A group which consists of the school buildings, etc., is correctly rotated, one which contains the nursery, etc., is moved from back to front only, and a third which comprises the Plaine, etc., is simply drawn as he might see it through the window.

These facts are of a piece with those just discussed. The subjects concerned can rotate a limited group of objects but they are lost when they have to include further sub-groups: either they confuse the hypothetical viewpoint and their actual position or they forget to rotate in terms of both directions.

To sum up, three types of behaviour have been investigated. In all cases it has been found that children at level IIIA show the beginnings of objective coordination but are insufficiently advanced to build up a systematic whole in all its parts. It was seen when they were required to group changes of position, when asked to coordinate landmarks and when told to rotate a plan by altering their point of view. These results are in complete agreement with those given elsewhere.[1]

§4. *Sub-stage IIIB: Landmarks are fully coordinated, changes of position are represented as a comprehensive group*

As we would expect in view of our earlier investigations,[2] subjects at level IIIB can construct a topographical schema in line with a two-dimensional coordinate system, though the various intervals are not always strictly proportional to each other. Although in the earlier study subjects were required to draw a plan of a model in front of them, while here they have to build it up from memory, in both investigations complete coordination is achieved at level IIIB.

ALA (8; 3) thinks of 24 separate features and arranges them correctly. Now and again, in bringing in a new object, he is driven to build up a sub-group involving fewer relations, but each time he succeeds, almost immediately, in integrating this sub-group with the main plan. For instance, when he comes to the Salon de l'Automobile he says: *"There's the Boulevard du Pont d'Arve*

---

[1] Piaget, C.C.S., chs. XIII, XIV, VIII.   [2] Ibid., ch. XIV.

and there is the Plaine, so the Salon must be here." And for the rue de Carouge: "*There's the Boulevard du Pont d'Arve with the Place de la Poste, so the rue de Carouge must come next.*"

NIE (9; 6) succeeds in grouping 20 elements in his plan, and even more remarkably, he achieves a perfect coordination in spite of the fact that the rectangle showing the school has not been drawn parallel with the edge of the paper. The base-line for his plan is the course of the Arve, and this is shown running obliquely from the left to the top of the paper. This forms a base line for his accurate presentation of the plan as a whole.

STA (9; 10) draws a most detailed and accurate plan, but experiences a peculiar difficulty in reproducing the area of the Plaine de Plainpalais. For every detail he shows, he finds he must start anew from the Pont des Acacias, and so retrace the entire journey right up to the particular point he seeks to locate (e.g. the church, the Rond Point, etc.).

Once again, in sketching their journeys, these subjects produce a coherent whole.

POR (9; 11) traces the route from the school to the Place Neuve as follows: "*The rue Hugo de Senger, the Boulevard du Pont d'Arve, the rue de Carouge, the rue du Conseil General, and next the Place Neuve.*—Is there anything you've missed?—*Oh yes; the Bastions, there, and over there the theatre and the museum.* —Where is the Plaine?—*There. There is a path which goes that way and leads to the Sacré-Cœur. You go by there to reach the Place Neuve.*" And so on. Step by step his plan is extended as far as the Arve and he shows the direction of its flow. Thus what began as a sketch-plan of a route finishes as a general map of the district.

As a final basis for comparison, here are the reactions of three of these subjects to the rotation of the school plan through 180°.

ALA (8; 3) has no difficulty in rotating the school buildings themselves in both dimensions (left and right as well as front and rear). He goes on to put the rue Hugo de Senger above the main school and parallel with its façade. He hesitates a moment before moving the nursery and tennis-courts to the right of the drawing: "*No, the Boulevard du Pont d'Arve is this side* (shifting it to the left) *which makes the nursery here* (right)", etc.

NIE (9; 6) approaches the problem in that same systematic manner which he showed in dealing with the initial plan. First he rotates the school, then he shows three roads round it, and next he draws in the playground, the embankment and the Arve. Tackling each bit as he comes to it, he perseveres till he has rotated the whole plan of the area.

POR (9; 11) starts off by rotating the building and showing a chalet, a cafe, gardens, etc., all of which lie over against the main entrance. Then he moves the nursery from the left to the right and does the same with the tennis-courts and a house on the embankment. Next he crosses to the left of his plan and shows a block of houses together with the barracks. He draws in the Arve and the Plaine, and comes back to the school entrance, so that his sketch is now complete.

There is a marked difference between these reactions and those of subjects at lower levels. In the first place, a topographical schema is planned from the outset as a single whole and even where a subject deals with it in separate sub-groups or adds a section to his drawing, he wastes no time in making the different parts agree with each other. This coordination is achieved by means of two complementary methods. Sometimes a subject groups the several elements in terms of relations between 'sites', as does Ala; sometimes, like Sta, he selects one or more common starting points and reconstructs routes which radiate from them. The end-result is always a coordinated whole, though its coordinates need not run parallel with the margins of the paper, for the system may be based on a line drawn at a slant and representing the Arve (cf. Nie).

Changes of position are likewise described in terms of a reference-system, as indeed is the case with subjects at sub-stage IIIA; but unlike these, the present subjects use a single comprehensive group instead of a number of independent sub-groups. The difference between a comprehensive group structure and partial coordination is quite apparent. In the first place, subjects can now relate any one part to all of the remaining parts, because the law of associativity enables them to reach one and the same point by a variety of routes. For in the field of changes of position associativity amounts to detour, which is considerably harder to master at the representative level than it is at the level of action. Thus Por shows two quite separate routes which converge on the Place Neuve but there is complete harmony between them. Secondly, and here too associativity is of the utmost importance, descriptions of changes of position are reversible; in other words, children find it just as easy to imagine a route in the reverse direction as they do to reconstruct it in the first place. This same point was fully borne out in the experiment on rotation, where they were able to grasp the implications of altering the observer's point of view, including the reversal of left and right, and of back and front.

§5. *Conclusions: Coordinate systems and grouping of changes of position: Egocentric attitudes to spatial relations compared with grouping*

This introductory study covers both the elaboration of reference-systems and the progressive grouping of changes of position. In previous investigations they were treated separately.[1] Two points which emerge are crucial to the study of the growth of Euclidean metrics in children.

The first of these is that there is a close link between the child's

---

[1] For the elaboration of reference systems, see C.C.S., chs. XIII, XIV, and for the grouping of changes of position, see *Les notions de mouvement et de vitesse chez l'enfant*, chs. I–V, with special reference to chs. III and IV.

growing ability to describe changes of position as a comprehensive group, and his gradual construction of systems of references or coordinate-systems. An earlier enquiry, confined to the study of movement within a single dimension, i.e. linear movement, revealed that the operation involved in 'order of position' [1] was virtually identical with the qualitative operation involved in 'change of position',[2] since the latter was in essence merely a change in that order. However, it was stressed that change of position as an alteration in rank order implied a reference not merely to objects in position but also to a system of 'sites'.[3] The sites were conceived as permanent. They were defined in terms of objects which were themselves stationary, not being involved in change of position. The point we are making here is merely an extension of that, but since we are no longer dealing with linear order, but instead with systems of two or more dimensions, we find that reference-objects cannot be fixed without coordinate axes.

Here, too, we find a close psychological relationship between the ability of subjects at each level to build up a topographical schema and their efforts at describing a particular route. The operation involved is identical. The reference-system is qualitative, because subjects construct their plans without measuring distances and without accurate scaling. They arrive at their schema by a process of logical multiplication, where the basic relation involved is the rank-order of objects along the two coordinate axes.[4] Grouping of asymmetrical relations is achieved by logical multiplication in terms of one-one correspondence. But it is limited to sites or objects conceived as stationary and so providing a framework of reference for movement. Changes of position are also apprehended in a qualitative way, because subjects do not measure the distances which they walk. The operational system involved is still one of logical multiplication in two dimensions, but the basic relation is now a change in the rank order of a moving object or person relative to these coordinated reference points, and not the static rank-order of the reference points themselves. Nevertheless we are fully justified in referring to this process as a 'group' in the mathematical sense, because quite clearly subjects at level IIIB could measure the intervals between reference-objects and the distances involved in changes of position, even though they make no explicit reference to a particular metric system. However, grouping is more elementary than measuring, and it is by grouping that subjects construct reference-systems and itineraries involving change of position. That there should be close agreement between the two is hardly surprising since the operations are identical whether they refer to fixed points of reference or to positional changes. Moreover the mathematician can interpret the

---

[1] French: *placement.*
[2] French: *déplacement.*
[3] French: *emplacement.*
[4] C.C.S., ch. XV, §5, op. VI.

relation inasmuch as the six parameters involved in change of position are directly related to the three dimensions of a coordinate-system. A mathematician simply translates non-quantitative into quantitative terms, where the possibility of quantification is already implicit.

Now the close genetic link between groups of changes of position and coordinate systems is of the utmost importance to the present study. For there can be no measurement without a well-defined group of positional changes. It is a mistake to think that the small movements used in measurement are so elementary as not to require precise grouping, as we shall see when we come to study the way in which young children go about the task of measuring. For instance, younger children cannot use a unit measuring rule because they fail to apply it in such a way as to resume measurement from the exact point reached when they last moved it. If there can be no measurement without grouping of movements, it follows that measurement implies a coordinated space. This implication needs to be thoroughly understood; in the next chapter, for example, we shall see children who think that two towers are of equal height if their tops look the same height, ignoring altogether the heights of their bases. Unless the distances which are being measured, on the one hand, and the movements of the measuring rule on the other, conform in some degree with the demands of a coordinated system, measurement is futile, even where only a single dimension is involved.

This introductory study leads to another conclusion, which should also be stressed. The gradual elaboration of children's notions to the point where changes of position form a group and imply a reference system, is a reversal of these notions, for they began with a primitive egocentric attitude to spatial relations. This indeed is what we found in our study of the coordination of perspectives and projective relations (C.C.S., ch. VIII). Operational groupings, which are at the root both of a coherent picture of positional change and of a coordinate-system, and which therefore form a starting-point for measuring, are not themselves the outcome of a simple additive process. They do not arise from the summation of relations, each of which is valid in itself and can therefore be added to others. They are the result of a structuring of the whole which leads to a complete reversal of the type of linkage that children make. Therefore, here again, in order to understand the genetic origin of space, and more especially of spatial measurement, we need to understand how egocentric attitudes give way to grouping.

The answers given by children in the foregoing examples might well suggest that, whether in the description of change of position or in the plan of a town, development lies in the mere accumulation of patiently acquired knowledge. At four years of age, a little boy is brought to school by his mother; he is aware only of the school, of his own home, of "the house with the surprises" (i.e. the grocer's store on the corner), and of the 'theatre' (i.e. the travelling circus on the Plaine de Plain-palais); he makes up a plan of the area with the few reference-points which he is required to show, and he indicates the journeys he makes on the plan. At seven a child knows several roads; those which take him to school where he now goes by himself and those which he walks along with his family when they go for their customary walks; he can there-fore describe several fragmentary routes, and he can draw a plan show-ing a number of discrete areas. At nine or ten, a child is free as a man and can roam at will all over the town; he therefore answers all the questions satisfactorily.

However tempting this view might appear, it leaves a number of facts unaccounted for. A child of four who sees an object moving along a straight path and another moving along a path bent at an angle will judge the distance covered purely by reference to the end-point reached.[1] When dealing with a linear path, he cannot see that the distance between two points is equal in both directions.[2] If we confine our attention to the present observations, we may ask why it is that children of four to seven years old are unable to rotate a plan through 180°, although they are as familiar with the appearance of the school from the playground as they are with its appearance from the street. We may ask why, at the age of nine, Pel (§3) talks about two "rues de Carouge" simply because he lives half-way along its length. We may ask why, if he has never moved from his own valley, a mountain dweller finds difficulty in estimating distance. We may ask why it is that the concept of spatial metrics has undergone such fundamental transformations from Aristotle to Copernicus and Newton, and again from Newton to Einstein.

In short, the growth of knowledge is not a matter of mere accumula-tion, and while it is true that between the ages of four and ten, children collect a good deal of information about their district, they also coordi-nate the picture which they have of it, which is an infinitely more com-plex process of development. Bit by bit they de-centre relations which they have learnt in the course of their own actions, and transform them in such a way that they can be combined with other relations without the intermediary of the self, so that their own actions are included as mere elements within an independent system. From the egocentric point of view which characterizes action, change of position is simply move-ment in the direction of an end-point, and hence, being experiential, it is irreversible. (As between a journey from home to school, and a jour-ney from school to home, the two end-points afford no basis of com-parison.) A first step in development is the appearance of short links which connect end-points with start. These break up the primitive intuition of mere movement, and are the beginnings of reference objects.

---

[1] *Les notions de mouvement et de vitesse chez l'enfant*, ch. IV. [2] *Ibid.*

For a long time movement will be remembered as a mere motor tendency in a certain direction and reference objects will be thought of as mere adjuncts without any objective coordination, simply because the journey itself has not yet been de-centred (stage II). Nevertheless, the linking of starting-point with end-point marks the first stage in coordination and paves the way for a reconsideration of the journey itself. In time journeys will be regarded as symmetrical intervals between termini which are further linked by relations of order and change of position, these being asymmetrical. Later, a growing ability to grasp relations which are not centred on the actions of the subject will lead to an increase in the reversibility of changes of position, and in the end a clear distinction will be made between fixed references on the one hand, and moving things or people on the other. This level is reached at the beginning of stage III, when journeys come to be conceived as intervals. Egocentric relations now give way to relations between objects, and the subject at last sees himself as but one moving object among others, situated in a framework of fixed references. Thus we have the beginnings of an objective treatment of Euclidean space.[1]

Development of the power to reconstruct change of position, while it occurs several years later, nevertheless takes the same course as the earlier development at the sensori-motor level, when children come to handle changes of position in the realm of actions. To begin with, the subject sees all such changes only as they relate to the immediate ends of his own actions; in the finish, he sees his own actions themselves as part of a network of possible changes of position within a framework of fixed objects. The latter outlook is a complete reversal of the former. The egocentric view of space found in children is the first stage in the representation of change of position, just as it was the first stage in the handling of these changes, when the children were babies. But it is far from being an exact but incomplete replica of the objective view which is to come. Here, as indeed in every other realm of human knowledge, intelligence starts from an unconsciously egocentric outlook which is a very congeries of unwarranted centrings, and which hinders grouping because it leads to irreversible assimilations. The very fact of overcoming this egocentric outlook, is by definition, we may say, the first and necessary step towards the logical combination of relations (reversible composition). The process of de-centring reaches its final state of equilibrium with logical (or sub-logical) grouping and the mathematical group. In the realm of spatial conception the major categories of logical structure have the following specific character: the fundamental law of equilibrium takes the form of reversibility, allowing for the identity of any given path irrespective of the direction of motion; logical identity becomes spatial identity, that is, the product of those

[1] Cf. C.C.S., ch. XV, §5.

direct and inverse operations which enable us to give a stable and fixed position to any given starting-point; associativity makes possible the use of detour; transitivity enables us to combine the various operations of the group indefinitely.

It is no mere coincidence that intellectual representation of a group of changes of position appears at the same time as the system of references or coordinates which form their context: both are dependent on the equilibrium of the group.

Such is the form of equilibrium which marks the final stage in the process of de-centring whereby egocentric attitudes give way to grouping. It is this equilibrium which lies at the root of the apparently fortuitous temporal coincidence of groups of positional changes, as they occur in intellectual representation, and of systems of references or coordinates, to which these changes refer. The development of measurement takes place within the context of this de-centring process, as will be apparent in this study. So long as the subject's conception of space is egocentric, it remains a law unto itself, because it lacks references which are coordinated, and changes of position which are grouped. As a result, objects are directly assimilated to egocentric notions rooted in the perceptual situation, and measurement is impossible; indeed, it is inconceivable. Measurement arises out of a chain of systematic comparisons which gradually conform to the laws of coordination and grouping.

Chapter Two

SPONTANEOUS MEASUREMENT[1]

IT was assumed in ch. I that there can be no measurement, just as there can be no true representation of change of position, unless the space in which it takes place is structured by a system of references or coordinate-system. This is because, in essence, measurement is a form of movement, one which consists in placing a measuring rule against whatever is being measured and transferring it as many times as the part chosen as unit will go into the whole. This assumption may well seem exaggerated, if, to take an example, we have a mental picture of a foot rule with feet and inches already marked on it, standing upright against a wall, with no thought as to how it came to be there; and *a fortiori* if our thought is of an elementary mensural operation, such as that involved in moving a measuring rule which is taken to be constant, that is, when it is assumed that the rod does not alter in length. But a foot rule as we know it is the end-product of operations carried out in the past, which means that there is no point in studying how children use ready-made foot rules until we have investigated the way they make up their own foot rules or mensural units, even if the latter are crude to a degree and serve only a momentary purpose.

The study of these makeshift units will show that the succession of units in a continuous rectilinear series is created by an active subject who can transfer the units in the required manner, just as inches do not appear along a wall, unless there is a subject who can picture the precise changes in position involved in measuring its height. As for the conservation of length when a unit-object is moved from one position to another, the reader should not be surprised to find that little children quite fail to see this as self-evident, and, indeed, that it implies a preliminary construction (see ch. IV). Yet the conservation of length is a necessary postulate for Euclidean measurement. Moreover, it should be fairly obvious that unless one can group changes of position and relate them to a coordinated spatial framework, one cannot realize the significance of a succession of units along a vertical line, and one cannot appreciate that there must be conservation of length when a unit-object is moved. At the very least, it is apparent that the evolution of such mensural notions cannot fail to involve multifarious transformations and is worthy of careful study.

For this reason, the present chapter, which like the first is introductory,

[1] Written with the collaboration of Mme Beatrice Begert-Demetriades.

will be devoted to the study of spontaneous efforts at measurement. Given the fact that, when it has been perfected, the process of measurement carries within it a great deal that is implicit, our task must be to investigate mensural behaviour when still in a formative state, for only in this way can we hope to make a precise assessment of operations which enter into the psychological construction of measurement. The chapters that follow can then be given to a detailed and piecemeal study of these operations. It should be remembered that our study is primarily one of psychology and not of logic, even if formulations proper to the latter study may occasionally be useful in the exposition of the structure of operations which are mastered in the course of mental development. Now though it is easy enough to arrive at the conditions of measurement *a priori* by making a logical analysis of what it implies, we cannot know whether these operational conditions correspond to operations which are ever carried out in practice, nor can we know which of these latter are most important, unless we investigate the genesis of measurement in the course of children's development.

The study of spontaneous measurement raises a problem which we did not encounter in our treatment of the representation of a group of changes of position. This latter was largely a matter of transforming the motor element inherent in action to make it conform with a coordinate system; while the construction of measurement proceeds in the main from perceptual comparisons. This is not to deny that the coordination of movements also involves perception, or that there is a motor element in mensural operations, and indeed in the perceptual comparisons which precede spontaneous measurement. But it must be emphasized that for a long time children are content with visual comparison, and only later do they think of putting objects alongside each other to check their estimate, while the concept of a measuring rule which can provide a common measure arises later still. Whether measurement arises directly out of visual comparison, or whether the discovery of its inadequacy leads to measurement, we are faced with a problem in the psychology of perception; how is perceptual measurement related to operational measurement?

When we look at two objects, e.g. two straight sticks, in order to compare their lengths A and B, to decide which is greater, we perform a kind of visual measurement, known in German as *Augenmass*. This visual measurement is composed of two essential elements. The first is a virtual movement of one object towards the other, a sort of bringing-together of the two, which accompanies the actual transfer of our visual focus; this virtual bringing together we will call 'transfer'.[1] The second element of visual measurement, which arises when the objects to be

---

[1] French: *transport*. Cf. Piaget et Lambercier, 'La comparaison visuelle des hauteurs à distance variable dans le plan fronto-parallèle'. *Arch. Psychol.*, vol. XXIX, p. 173.

compared appear unequal, is a decomposition in two parts of the larger object B, so that one part is equal to A while the other is the remainder A'; there may follow a comparison between A and A' (again by means of 'transfer') which could, for example, lead to the conclusion: if A = A' then B = 2A. Thus, even in a perceptual estimate we find both sub-division and change of position, which practically amount to measurement. In general, however, perceptual measurement is inexact and merely approximative, and it is subject to illusions or systematic errors. Now an adult, though he may not be familiar with the exact nature of optical illusions, is nonetheless well aware that perceptual estimates are often misleading; he therefore treats his judgments with some reserve, particularly if the objects to be compared are very far apart or if they differ greatly in size, which amounts to the same. It is reasonable to ask whether children, too, are aware of these limitations from the outset, and, if not, how it comes about that bit by bit they learn to distrust their visual estimates. In particular we may enquire which perceptual 'transfers' seem acceptable to them and how they distinguish between permissible transfers and others which are almost sure to lead them into error. And here the relationship between measurement, grouping of changes of position and coordinate systems is apparent even in the field of perceptual comparison. For it is clear that so long as a child has no notion of structuring his space by means of coordinate axes, he is in no position to limit visual comparison in any way (which means, incidentally, that in some ways visual comparison is more accurate in young children than it is in older children and even in adults),[1] while as he learns to coordinate his space in three dimensions he acquires new ways of measuring which largely take the place of visual estimates.

We may reasonably suspect that perceptual 'transfer' can be regarded as the starting-point for the operational movement of a foot rule or of any other standard measuring rule when comparing distances, involving real movement of a common measure as against virtual transfer. The suggestion seems all the more plausible if we consider the behaviour of children when they first shed their trust in perceptual comparison at a distance: some time before they can envisage the movement of a third object serving as a middle-term, they want to bring together the objects they are asked to compare. Furthermore, if this hypothesis should prove correct, we would expect that once the operation had been encompassed, it would exert a retro-active influence on the perceptual activity which was its starting-point, just as concepts influence percepts in the field of parallelism (C.C.S., ch. XI) and angular separation (C.C.S., ch. XII, §1). And indeed we shall see that once a subject has grasped

[1] Cf. H. Würsten, 'L'évolution des comparaisons de longueurs de l'enfant a l'adulte', *Arch. Psychol.*, vol. XXXII, p. 1.

the possibility of using a movable foot rule, which is no easy achievement, the real movement affects perceptual transfer in turn. This means that from then on he has a conscious insight into the nature of perceptual transfer, and therefore makes more effective use of it. A similar question arises in conjunction with perceptual sub-division, as, it may be, perceptual estimate of the mid-point of a straight line: if the bisection of a straight line grows out of a perceptual estimate of the mid-point, should we not find that measurement exerts a retroactive influence on its forerunner in perception?

Questions such as these, arising as they do from the study of spontaneous measurement, show the importance of the link between measurement, grouping of changes of position and coordinate systems. Inevitably we are led to the hypothesis that this link lies at the root of the entire process of evolution from perceptual transfer as the sole means of comparison: bringing the objects themselves together, using another object as a common measure, and finally the construction of units to measure any distance by stepwise movement, i.e. unit iteration. To begin with, comparison of distant objects is perceptual and immediate, because representation of changes of position is still ungrouped and representation of space is unstructured by a system of coordinates. When the process is complete, and this presupposes both the grouping of positional change and the structuring of space, we find that measurement in the accepted sense is itself immediate. This implies the concept of a unit which can be repeated indefinitely in three dimensions, and this in turn grows out of an increasing mastery both of sub-division itself and of the use of movable objects as common measures.

§1. *Outline of method and results*

The subject is shown a tower made of twelve blocks, cubes and parallelipipeds. The tower is 80 cm. in height and stands on a table. He is asked to build a similar tower on another table. The instructions avoid any mention of measurement; the experimenter uses phrases such as: "You make a tower the same height as mine", or simply "the same as mine", etc. In order to prevent the subject from using similar blocks at every stage, which would result in mere one-one correspondence, the blocks he is given are smaller, but there are sufficient for him to make a tower the same height as the model. He is told to build this tower on another table which is two metres away and 90 cm. lower. This is to guard against the subject being satisfied with visual transposition. It is advisable to erect a large screen between model and copy while the subject is at work, but he is told that he can "go and see" the model as often as he wants to. The screen helps the experimenter to record actual transfer of objects and the use of common measures, while it does not hinder visual comparison by those younger subjects who know no other method. Needless to say, the subject is given many more blocks than he needs. He is also given a supply of paper strips and sticks. However, on no account is he told how to use them: only when his spontaneous efforts have been exhausted is he told to use the paper strips and sticks if he has not done so already.

The responses made by our subjects show that there are three main developmental stages, each of which is subdivided into two sub-stages. The first stage, which covers the period up to the age of 4 or 4; 6, is one in which *perceptual comparison* is the only basis of comparison between model and copy. There is no common measure, and in comparisons of height, nothing is moved except the line of vision. Visual *transfer* is thus the only basis of comparison between the two terms, and the subject does not think of actually moving one of the terms itself. Within this stage, we may distinguish two sub-stages: sub-stage IA when copies are summary and syncretic, and sub-stage IB when there is evidence of more analytic estimates.

During stage II, which lasts from 4; 6 or 5 until about 7, objects are moved in the process of measurement, i.e. there is *change of position*. Sometimes the object in question is one of the items being compared, and sometimes it is a third term, presaging the appearance of a common measure, but there is as yet no operational transitivity. At sub-stage IIA the visual transfer characteristic of stage I is supplemented by what we will term *manual transfer*, by which we mean that the objects to be compared are brought closer together, so that although the comparison is still visual, it is no longer comparison at a distance, but an appraisal of a whole made up of neighbouring objects. Sub-stage IIB is marked by an interesting development which brings out yet more clearly the waning supremacy of perception taken in isolation. Children now use an intermediary term, but this is still not an independent common measuring rule, for, instead of using a third article with which to satisfy themselves that the copy is equal to the model, these children use their own bodies: at times it is the span of their hands or that of their arms, while at others they avail themselves of unlikely seeming bodily reference-objects (shoulders, etc.), using these to transfer a distance from one object to another. Obviously such methods are a carry-over from manual transfer (IIA) just as the latter is a carry-over from visual transfer (IA and IB). Earlier the subject moved the article itself, now he transfers a grasping or enfolding gesture, involving his hand or his arms, because he hopes that such a gesture will be a measure of the length of an object after he has let it go. This mode of behaviour, characteristic of sub-stage IIB, we will call *body transfer* or *object imitation*. Imitation is the precursor of symbols and images. The use of a common measure must therefore have its origin in visual and manual transfer, inasmuch as its initial components, both perceptual and motor

31

give rise to representational images which confer a symbolic value, first, on the subject's own body, and later, on any neutral object, so that these come to stand for the original transfer.

Thus the end of stage II is marked by behaviour which stands midway between level IIB and level IIIA. Here we find that instead of using their own bodies, subjects use a *symbolic object* to imitate a size, and we see them moving this object from copy to model to compare their heights. Though this is clearly a decisive turning-point in the development of mensuration, it would be wrong to speak of it as true common measure, because the use of such symbolic objects as third terms is severely restricted. They are in fact symbolic in that they are imitations either of the copy or of the model. Sometimes, indeed, we find a third tower being used to convey the height of the first to the second. More often it is some other object having the same height as the towers themselves. This second limitation is quite general. If the third term is either larger or smaller it is dismissed as useless, because it does not occur to these subjects to mark off the length they want on something bigger, still less do they appreciate how to use a small object by stepping it along the required length.

The next important step forward occurs when intuitions, initially perceptual and later imaged, become true operations. An operational intermediate term is an expression of the general logical principle: $A = B$; $B = C$, therefore $A = C$. This insight is the distinguishing characteristic of stage III. It is heralded by the intermediate behaviour which we have just described. In effect, transfer is now operational because it is logically transitive. However, transfer is only one of the two aspects of measurement; it has bearing on changes of position because it leads to the recognition of the conservation of length despite such changes. The other aspect is subdivision, and only when this too has been mastered can one part be assigned a unit-value and so be repeated as often as necessary. Now this gradual fusing of subdivision and change in the position of a common measuring rule occurs during stage III, and it occurs in two sub-stages.

Subjects at sub-stage IIIA use a middle term which is larger than the end terms, but not one which is smaller, for the latter requires stepping more than once. Given a large rule, they mark off the required length and remember it while transferring the rule. But at sub-stage IIIB, subjects can use a smaller middle term as well as the larger one. They too make a note of the length required, but where their rule is too short, they step it along (unless they are satisfied with a visual estimate of the difference). This implies that eventually they learn to use any object whatsoever as a common measuring rule, even one which is several times smaller than what they are measuring. Such an object is stepped as often as necessary, which is equivalent to assigning a unit-value to a given length and repeating it. The acquisition of measurement is thus a synthesis of subdivision and change of position.

It should be noted that these stages and sub-stages are something more than a mere chronological succession of attainment levels, for each of them marks a reintegration of the behaviour-types which precede it, while a child at any given sub-stage is unable to compass the behaviour which belongs to the next sub-stage.

§2. *Stage I. Direct visual comparison: transfer is purely visual*

The criterion of this first stage is the exclusive use of visual comparison. It is one which may at times raise a delicate problem. Any subject, whatever his age, is quite liable to make a visual estimate when comparing heights before he sets about measuring. Whether he goes on to measure will depend on the degree of confidence which he has in his perceptual estimate; if the latter is securely based on a number of clear reference-points he may dispense with measurement altogether. Therefore we cannot say that a subject is at stage I simply because he begins with a visual estimate, or even because he does not go any further. We can say this only if (*a*) he exaggerates the reliability of his visual estimate and (*b*) he will not agree to any more accurate procedure, as may happen either because he cannot carry it out, which would apply to common measure and even to body transfer, or because he fails to see the need for it, which would apply to manual transfer.

However, two further points need to be added to make clear what is meant by this twofold criterion. First, long after they have passed stage I a number of subjects continue to be over-confident in their visual estimates though at the same time they are willing enough to use manual or body transfer; they simply claim that a visual estimate is more accurate and use it to test the accuracy of procedures which in fact are more refined. Nevertheless, inasmuch as they are willing to try auxiliary methods, they are no longer at stage I. Second, visual transfer at stage I must arise out of a mode of comparison which is so global and syncretic that the very task of copying the model presents the utmost difficulty. Thus the detailed visual comparison of stage IB is itself an immense step forward as against the primitive syncretism of stage IA, found in 2- and 3-year-olds and sometimes even in 4-year-olds: it marks the beginnings of analytic comparison. It is therefore hardly surprising that to begin with children tend to put more faith in it than it justifies, for their thinking is still vitiated by egocentric attitudes proper to perception. Nonetheless we need to separate the various factors which contribute to this tendency: above all, we need to understand why it is so remarkably resilient, being proof against all the contrary evidence which must arise in everyday experience.

We may now proceed to give a few illustrations of the kind of

33

comparison we find at level IA when children find great difficulty in copying the model tower, and when even visual comparison is still undifferentiated.

LIL (3; 10) is told to make a replica of a simplified version of the tower: "You make one exactly the same height as that one.—*Oh yes.*" She puts two blocks side by side to form a base, then adds other blocks which are smaller, and so on, saying: "*That's it . . . huge . . . huge.*—Is it exactly as high as the other?—*Well, I'll just put this little thing on . . . oh, it's getting big, it's lovely!*—Yes, but is it just as high as mine?—*Oh yes, you've only got to look.*" At this point the structure collapses. She makes a fresh start and at one point uses a block similar to one she sees in the model. "*There you are, it's the same: here's the same little block.*"

CLA (4; 1) is given the usual instructions. He spends a long time looking at the model, then carefully makes a tower of his own without looking at the model. When he has finished, he looks back to the model, breaks his up and starts afresh. The same thing happens a third time. "Is yours the same height? —*Oh yes.*" He is given a little stick: "You look with that. Can you measure? —*I can't use that stick. That one is all right.*" The second stick is a smaller one, and he places this at the top of his tower as an embellishment, saying: "*It's the same height!*"

The next illustrations belong to stage IB. The copies now point to an attempt at something more than undifferentiated similarity. There is some analysis of detail, especially of height as such. Nevertheless, transfer is exclusively visual.

NIC (4; 2) gazes at the model a long time. He makes a correct arrangement of blocks to form the base. He adds more blocks. He looks back at the model tower, and finds four similar blocks which he arranges side by side around the tower. He removes one block which is half a centimetre short. "Are they the same height?—*Yes.*—How do you know?—*I can see they are.*—You take this big stick and see if they're the same height.—*Yes.*" He takes the stick and rests one end on his tower, aiming the other end at the top of the other tower. Although the stick is not horizontal, Nic does not realize this: "*Yes. They're the same height.*"

This use of a stick as an aid to visual transfer heralds a type of behaviour which we shall see later when the tops are joined.

GER (4; 6) puts his tower together meticulously, glancing at the model several times: "Is it the same height?—*No. That one is taller* (the model).— What if we carried it across near the other? *It's both the same.*—But can you tell that without carrying it across?—*Yes.*—Here's something to measure (a ruler).—*But it isn't long enough; I can't measure.* (In point of fact the ruler is the same length as the model.)—Can you use your hands?—*I know why that one is higher. It's on a higher table.*" Still he does not measure. "Can you draw it?" He does so. "Is it the same height?—*No that one is higher* (the model).— How high should it come to be the same height?—*As far as this* (the point is an arbitrary one).—How can you tell?—*Because I've got good eyes.*"

FRAN (5; 0) looks long at the model, checks by sight as he arranges the blocks and finishes correctly. "Are they the same height?—*Yes.*—Why?—*I can see for myself they are.*—And how about this big stick? Does that help you to judge?" He puts the stick against his tower and then against the model, but takes no notice of their relative heights. "*Yours is lower. I could tell with the stick that yours is on the bench.* (!)—But what about the tower itself? Is it the same height?—*No it's lower.*"

MAR (5; 1) looks at the model and arranges his bricks differently while making his tower the same height. Now and again he checks on his progress. "Is it the same height?—*Yes.*—Why?—*Because I can see.*—Take this stick and you'll see better.—*And what must I do with it? No, they're not the same because of this* (pointing to a block which has no counterpart in the model)."

JEA (5; 3) builds his tower as Mar did. "Is it the same height?—*Yes*—How do you know?—*By looking at the blocks.*—What if I told you it isn't as high? —*I can see it's the same.*" He adjusts a crooked block without altering the height of the tower. "Can you think of a trick to see if it's the same height?—*No, I tell you it's right!* (In a peremptory tone.)"

YVE (5; 5) looks first at the tower then at the model, and then he builds. "*Can't get it. It's a bit higher, the table, and the bench is lower.*—But the tower itself, just the tower, is it the same height?—*Yes, you're right. But the blocks, my blocks, they're a little higher. The bench is lower.*" We see that he fails to establish a link between the base and the top.

BLAI (5; 8) builds quickly. He makes a mistake and corrects it on looking back at the model. "Same height?—*Yes.*—How do you know?—*By looking.* —And with this stick. Does it help?—*No. You haven't put one against your tower. But that tower is smaller, because it's lower* (being on the bench)."

AGU (5; 10) places his blocks carefully, comparing them with those used in the model. "Why do you do that?—*Because I could see they weren't the same height.*" He carries on building in the same way. "Are they the same height?— *No, because they aren't the same blocks.*" He changes the blocks. "And now? —*Yes.*—Are you sure? You can go and measure." He walks over to the model and looks at it without moving. "Is it the same height?— . . . —Can you measure?—*No.*—If we carried this one over, how would it look?—*The same height.*—Why?—*Because.*—(His tower is taken to the model.)—*It's the same height.*—And supposing we took it back, what would it be then?— *Smaller.*—Why?—*Because the table is smaller.*—But would the tower grow smaller?" He hesitates: "*No, the tower would be the same.*"

The task of copying the model, having regard to its mode of construction as well as its overall height, produces a reaction at one of two levels. At level IA, subjects like Lil and Cla are satisfied with a copy which is vague and approximate. They do not analyse the model in detail, and the blocks they use bear no correspondence with those used in the model. Because the similarity which they conceive is undifferentiated, the height of their structures is only a rough approximation to that of the model. They do not compare the towers in detail and are guided more by recollection of the model, that is, by an 'internal' model, than by genuine visual transfer. This type of behaviour is followed by level

IB, when the foundations are laid for the eventual appearance of measurement. Now children tend to analyse the model and look at it as they build their own tower. They therefore frequently reproduce its actual dimensions, and in particular its height, instead of confining themselves to its general shape. This process of analysing and making elements correspond is essential to the differentiation of visual comparison. It is in this way that the latter begins to develop.

A study by the senior author in collaboration with Marc Lambercier on the perceptual comparison of height in children and adults yielded the following conclusions: (1) With subjects 4-5 years old, experimental precision is difficult to achieve as their replies tend to be fanciful, precisely because they fail to analyse what they perceive. (2) With subjects aged 5-7 years, as indeed with adults, reactions vary according to the angular separation of the objects being compared. When they are sufficiently close for the subject to compare them without appreciable eye-movement, he simply builds up a composite whole (although even here there are certain eye-movements implying a limited transfer). But when they are further apart, the subject tries to bring the distant objects together, and thus to 'transfer' their heights. This second kind of transfer is governed by perceptual laws which are fairly precise. Thus one can establish statistically which of two elements is more likely to be transferred, when the comparison involves two objects only.[1]

An elementary comparison like those made by subjects at level IB is the product of 'visual transfer' which is a genuine event occurring in space and time. True transfer does not occur so long as both objects can be brought within the compass of an inclusive configuration, such as a partly imaginary figure made up of lines joining the tops, bases and sides of the two towers. Such a configuration is merely the result of differentiation of purely perceptual relationships. Transfer is an activity and therefore quite distinct from passive or receptive perception. It begins with the first appearance of true analysis, and is governed by perceptual laws. It is a quasi- intentional motor behaviour. We cannot speak of transfer when a subject simply allows his gaze to wander from one object to another but only when he deliberately looks across from the first to the second with the idea of comparing them, that is, when he makes a more or less conscious effort to remember something of one object when looking at the other. What is remembered may on occasion be in part a primitive image, but this is rare. More often it is simply a sensori-motor recollection, i.e. a sensori-motor schema expressing shape and size.—It should be recalled that transfer is but one variety of perceptual activity and perceptual activity as a whole comprises many ramifications (C.C.S., ch. I, sec. 1). These include active 'transposition'

---

[1] Piaget et Lambercier, 'La comparaison visuelle des hauters à distances variables dans le plan fronto-paralle', *Arch. de Psychol.*, vol. XXIX, p. 173.

(when what is transferred is a complex relation), temporal transfer and temporal transposition ('Einstellung') and various forms of anticipation—in a word, all that combining activity which enters into the perception of complex figures. Thus the part played by sensori-motor intelligence in behaviour as a whole, before the advent of language and representation, is continued throughout life by perceptual activity, albeit in the more restricted sphere of perceptual and motor behaviour.

From all this it follows that visual transfer is at once the starting point for further development in mensuration including manual transfer, etc., and a perceptual phenomenon which exists in its own right and which therefore persists at every level including the adult level. However, while it is true that it maintains its independent character alongside other modes of comparison and at the same time becomes an integral part of these, visual transfer does not remain unchanged. It is refined and enriched by the intellectual advances to which it contributes, and this retroactive influence is manifested even in the domain of perception as such. That is why, in time, a subject becomes aware of visual transfer and of its mechanism, and is therefore able to regulate it more precisely because he knows its limitations and the illusions to which it is subject. Visual transfer becomes an integral part of a system of perceptual transpositions of ever-growing complexity, and one which comes more and more under the retroactive regulating influence of operational reasoning. As a result of these transpositions even perceptions are eventually included within the framework of a true coordinate system.

In a word, we shall find that visual transfer engenders representational comparison and is therefore at the root of all measurement, while at the same time it undergoes further development in its own particular field, that of perception, because higher forms of structuring exert a retroactive influence upon it.

At level IB, visual transfer acts in isolation. In other words, it has not yet given rise to manual or body transfer, etc., from which it follows that these have not yet influenced it retroactively, so that its mechanism is as yet unrefined. Therefore the visual transfer which belongs to substage IB is a primitive and rudimentary mode of comparison, for even when judged as purely perceptual activity it is elementary in relation to the visual transfer found at higher stages.

Thus the outstanding characteristic of visual transfer at stage I is that it is unconscious: even at level IB subjects believe that they just see (Nic and Mav: " I can see." Fran: "I can see for myself") or that they just 'look' (Jea and Blai) or even that they have 'good eyes' (Ger). They are quite unaware that when two things cannot be seen simultaneously, their comparison involves a real action and is therefore open to trial-and-error. They concentrate entirely on the object and disregard the subject altogether. The subject, for them, is passive and receptive, and hence they are unaware of transfer.

Again, because the objects whose heights are to be compared are situated at different levels, visual transfer must include an element of transposition. It is not enough to transfer the points reached by the tops of the towers; what must be transferred is a relation. Thus if A is the base of the model and B is its top, while A' and B' are the base and top of the copy, the relation AB must be transferred to A'B' because A and A' are on different horizontal planes. At sub-stage IB we find that either subjects are unaware of this difference in base planes, in which case they simply compare the heights of the topmost points, or else that while they have noticed the difference in question, they do not know how to allow for it. Thus when Nic aims his stick at the topmost point of the model with one end resting on the copy, he allows it to veer markedly from the horizontal; but he is quite unaware of it and makes no effort to hold it parallel with a line joining the two bases A and A'. Ger and Agu think one of the towers is higher "because it's on a higher table" or "because the table is smaller". True, they admit that the towers would be equal if they were placed side by side, but they cannot help using the words 'higher' and 'lower' with reference to absolute height where their sole concern should be relative height. Thus transfer of relation exists only at the perceptual level, while at the conceptual level there is simply comparison of absolute height. Agu overcomes the difficulty in the end, and so marks the appearance of a higher level, but Yve resists our explanation: "Yes, you're right. But the blocks, my blocks, they're a little higher." Fran finds out that the bases are at different levels by using the stick, although he places the stick against the model only, which implies that he does not know how to measure. Nevertheless he insists, as does Blai, that his tower is lower. None of these subjects fully masters this problem of the relation between base and top. Ger comes near to its solution and Agu shows insight in the end.

We infer that these subjects believe that objects vary in height with every variation in the height of the surface upon which they stand. This conclusion may seem hardly justified in view of the limited character of the experiment. But in ch. IV we will examine what is essentially the same problem. We will show how we can take two sticks and put them side by side to demonstrate that they are equal in length, then move one forward a fraction of an inch, and subjects at this level believe one of the sticks to be larger because it projects further. Children at stage I lack a postulate which is fundamental in all measurement, i.e. the conservation of length when objects are moved, whether that movement is vertical or horizontal. The next three chapters will be given to the detailed study of conservation of length. For the present we see that our subjects fail to establish the relationship between the tops of the towers and their bases, precisely because their bases are on different planes. This fact alone shows what it is these children lack which is essential to measurement. They lack a coordinate system which alone allows the changes of position involved in measuring to form part of a group.

Since the bases and the tops of the two towers are on different planes, it is only by means of a coordinate system that the several planes can be comprehended within a single conceptual act. In the last chapter it was shown that the representation of a group of changes of position and the ability to evolve a coordinate system are complementary aspects of the same process. It is because they lack that ability that these subjects are at a loss when faced with this problem. Because they see that the towers rest on different planes, they are unable to compare them. Moreover, as will be made apparent in chs. III and IV, the conservation of length or of distance itself demands a coordinate system, because conservation involves grouping of changes of position. This explains why, even when the towers are put side by side so that the subjects see they are equal, they lose their certainty as soon as the towers are put back on different planes.

These results are particularly revealing because they show how children can still make valid comparisons although they rely entirely on visual transfer. So long as they are allowed to remain at the perceptual level, they have little difficulty in making a naive comparison which is fairly accurate. It is only when they are asked to verify their judgment that they become aware of the fact that the towers are on different planes. Thus it is only at the conceptual level that they experience failure. In effect, young children who lack the use of a coordinate system find perceptual comparisons easier than do their elders and their perceptual comparisons are often more accurate. These conclusions are borne out by other evidence. We find little children looking at pictures upside down; often they do mirror drawing. In the laboratory, we find that they are better than adults at comparing non-parallel lines which slope in different ways.[1] On the other hand they are bad at estimating the degree of slope because their spatial perception is unstructured. This explains why at level IB children prefer to rely wholly on visual transfer instead of establishing the relations between corresponding parts of the two objects. When they are made to compare at a conceptual level they are baffled by the difference in planes, as also by their inability to understand length as a relation between two extremities.

The gradual growth of a coordinate system has the effect of weakening perceptual comparison of length between objects which are either not parallel or at different heights. On the other hand, the gain in operational comparison has a retroactive effect, even on perception, and makes it more discriminating.

[1] Cf. H. Würsten, op. cit.

At stage I visual transfer operates unconsciously. Transposition of coordinated relations is impossible and errors of interpretation are therefore conspicuous by their absence. Comparison at this stage is a kind of assimilation and is unmediated either by a measuring rule or by the structurization of space. The subject is in fact unaware of space as such. He therefore has a blind faith in his visual estimate, and does not wish to know of more exact ways of measuring. Not one of these subjects tries to move the towers closer together or to measure with his hand or arm. Still less do any of them look about for something else to measure with. The mere act of looking is all they require, and, indeed, we find that their visual transfer is often remarkably accurate. They are supremely confident because they are supremely unaware of the empty space which separates the two objects. It is the subject who, by the mere act of seeing, furnishes the only link between the objects so that one is directly assimilated to the other. He therefore dispenses with the use of an objective measuring rule and with the structurization of space.

§3. Stage II. First appearance of change of position.
Sub-stage IIA: Manual transfer as an auxiliary to visual transfer

The movements involved in measuring must be integrated within a coordinate system. Such is the conclusion to which we are forced by the analysis of reactions at stage I. Without such a system, comparison is purely perceptual. Grouping changes of position provides the link between reference-points and thus enables the individual to construct a coordinate system (ch. I). So in measuring, comparisons become coordinated through changes of position.

The changes of position used in measuring are of increasing levels of difficulty. The hardest and most advanced is the use of a unit measuring system. The easiest is to put two objects side by side, making sure that they are on the same level. Such manual transfer simply makes visual transfer easier. The following examples show an intermediate mode of behaviour which links manual transfer with perceptual comparison. The subject uses a straight-edged object to bring the towers together. The straight edge is placed along the line of sight. Nic, at stage I, used a stick to aim from one tower to the other. The following subjects actually bridge the towers with the stick they are given to measure with.

SAM (5; 6) removes the screen in order to compare, he first says his is too high, then he says they are equal. He is offered a stick to help him. He uses it to bridge the tops of the two towers and shouts: *"Oh yes, they're the same!"* All the while the stick is inclined but without regard to the difference in base levels.

ART (5; 10) behaves likewise, but comes to the opposite conclusion: *"No they're not the same.—How* can you tell?—*I don't know, but they're not the same."*

BER (6; 0) begins with a visual estimate. The screen is removed: "How would you measure them?—*One could put a stick across from there to there or one could use one's hand* (to join the two tower-tops)." He lays the stick across and says they're the same, although the slope of the stick bears no relation to the difference in base-levels. One of the towers is now moved to a chair. He puts the stick back between the tops and finds that now it slopes considerably more: "*No, it's too big.*"

PHI (5; 10) says the heights are identical: "Why?—*I've looked.*—Can you make a mistake in looking?—*No.*—Can you think of another way?—*Yes* (he puts one hand over the top of each tower, but does not compare the difference between the levels of his hands and those of the two bases).—Is there yet another way?" He now says the towers could be put on the same table.

TOM (7; 1, backward all-round): "*It's not the same height because the table is higher. You can see with your eyes.*—Can't you make a mistake with your eyes?—*One could put the new tower up against the old.*—How could one tell without moving it?—*One can take a stick and put it over to join the tops.*"

This intermediate type of behaviour highlights the essence of the problem which is solved only at stage II. The subject is required to compare height AB with height A'B' where the bases A and A' are at different levels. At stage I, comparison is by undifferentiated visual transfer. The subject is unable to express a perceptual equivalence in terms of intellectual relations because he lacks a coordinate system. Here we find children who believe they have solved the problem by putting a straight stick across the tops B and B'. Is this a step forward?

It would be if the line between the bases, AA', were horizontal. Again it would be a step forward if they built up a line AA' as well as BB' and could then appreciate that the two lines were parallel. Finally, they could look on their line BB' as part of a coordinate system in which AB and A'B' are both vertical, and the angles which they make with BB' are equal to those they make with AA'.

However, their behaviour is uncomplicated by such considerations. They look at their line BB' and ignore the line between the bases AA' What is the criterion for their judgment that AB = A'B' or AB $\neq$ A'B'? Is BB' seen as a horizontal or a sloping line? Is it seen as perpendicular to the towers AB and A'B'? Such questions do not occur to these subjects. At the beginning of stage II, a child has not yet mastered the concepts of vertical and horizontal (C.C.S., ch. XIII). He cannot tell whether sloping lines are parallel or not unless they are perceptually very close together (ibid., ch. XI). Moreover he lacks a coordinate system (ch. I and C.C.S., ch. XIV) and is therefore unable to judge between one slope and another. We must assume that the bridge BB' is an attempt to reach greater precision than is possible by visual transfer. But it is an intellectual link which is of no help to them. Indeed, visual transfer alone is more effective in that conceptual analysis breaks up perceptual wholes to yield relations which are at first

41

isolated. Similar isolated relations may be found when children estimate the length of a path of movement by reference to the finishing point only (*Mouvement et vitesse*, ch. III) or when they compare lines in length with reference to one extremity only or when they select the mid-point of a line without reference to its starting point (chs. IV and V, infra.).

We have here an admirable illustration of an attempt at measurement where the conceptual basis for it is lacking. These subjects lack the ability to reconstruct changes of position as a group, they lack a coordinate system, they lack even those preliminary notions of relation which form the groundwork for such a system: parallel, vertical, horizontal, more or less inclined to the vertical or the horizontal. Nonetheless, bridging the tops is a step forward as against pure visual transfer because it is the first step in analysis. Sooner or later the subject comes to realize that this step by itself is of no value, and he then begins to consider the bases. He cannot bridge the bases at the same time as the tops. Indeed, it does not occur to him to do so, because he does not fully understand parallelism, slope and angularity, and because he lacks a coordinate system. He therefore seeks to bring the towers closer together, whence the appearance of manual transfer, as in the cases of Phi and Tom.

The following examples are of subjects who think of manual transfer but whose understanding does not extend to more advanced processes:

ANO (5; 2) uses visual transfer to begin with, but even while building his tower he puts one brick against another (both belonging to his own tower, not the model) to make sure they are the same size. He finishes his tower and goes across to look at the model: "Are they the same height?—*Yes.*—Are you sure? —*Yes, I'm sure because I've looked.*—Do you never make a mistake when you look?—*No* . . . (he hesitates).—Could you measure?—*No, I don't know how to.*—What else could you do?—*We could take it down and put it up again here* (by the side of the model).—Can you measure with your hands?—*No. I don't know how to*", etc.

DAN (5; 2) also thinks they are equal "*because I can see.*—Can you measure? —*No, I can't carry it without first taking it down.*"

CLAN (5; 3) keeps looking at the model. "*They're the same height.*—How do you know?—*You can see how high they are.*—Are you sure?—*One could carry it over there right up against it.* (This is done. He puts one hand on top of each tower in an attempt to bridge them horizontally.) *Mine is too small.*"

MOR (5; 6) repeatedly carried bricks over to the model to be sure of their size, but he does not put them against the bricks to which they are to correspond; this manual transfer of elements is therefore no more than an aid to visual comparison. When he has finished, he is given a stick "to measure with". He rests the stick on the ground (not on the table) and stands it up against his own tower, then he puts his finger on the stick to show the point reached by the top of the tower. This measure is lost on the way to the model. He now rests the stick on the bench, stands it up against the model and says: *"Mine is bigger. It's on a table."* This behaviour foreshadows a common measure. At the same time it shows why at this stage such a common measure is impossible: the initial and terminal points are unrelated; in other words, changes of position are not grouped.

NAN (6; 0) does exactly the same as Mor, but he says simply: *"It's similar."* It may be noted that both Nan and Mor fail to move the tower as a whole, although they use manual transfer when dealing with individual bricks.

CHRI (6; 1) also carries bricks across to the model, but he is less satisfied with a visual comparison of the finished towers: *"They're the same.—How do you know?—You can see.—*Are you sure?*—No, unless you carry it over, you can't see properly."*

JOS (6; 11) *"It's the same height.—*Are you sure just by looking?*—Yes, you can't go wrong.—*Can you tell with your hands?*—No, you'd have to put it there* (both on the same table).—Can you measure? Have you been shown how?*—Yes, but I only know how to measure myself: you put a ruler up here* (points to his head), *you make it go all the way down and then you look.—*And can't you measure the tower with this stick?*—No."*

SCHA (7; 0) compares each brick with those of the model as he builds his tower. When he has finished, he is satisfied with a visual estimate. "Is there another way of comparing them?*—One can take it down and build it up again here* (on the same table).—And without doing that?*—One could bring the bench nearer or one could bring this one over there."*

Manual transfer grows directly out of visual transfer since the subject brings things together for the purpose of visual comparison. But the fact that he does so points, in a general way, to a waning faith in unaided visual comparison, and more particularly, it shows that he is aware of its inadequacy when objects are at different levels. Such differences in height or in depth are common in everyday life, and it may be surmised that as children come across them and realize the difficulties in the way of perceptual comparison, so they gradually become aware of the inadequacies, and indeed, of the existence, of visual transfer.

However, the fact that these children are conscious of the difference in base levels and that, in contrast with those at stage I, they find perceptual comparison difficult in a wide variety of situations, can only be due to the beginnings of a Euclidean structurization of space. That structurization leads them to take account of the bases as well as the tops of the towers. At the same time it stands in the way of that direct and immediate comparison which ignores space altogether, and which was characteristic of stage I.

Even here, the structurization of space is only in its very beginnings. It is not until they reach level IIIB that children think in terms of an all-embracing coordinate system. However, their realization that the towers cannot be compared unless they are at the same level, suggests that they have the beginnings of notions of horizontality and parallelism. Their notion of the horizontal might refer to the floor of their room and their notion of parallelism might be limited to the special case when lines are horizontal or close together.[1] Thus, unlike children quoted earlier in this section, Clan and Jos refuse to join the tops of the towers unless they are both on the same table.

The beginnings of Euclidean structurization account for the appearance of change of position in comparison. Chri tells us: "Unless you carry it, you can't see properly." To compare the heights of two objects we must bring them together within a single framework. (Here, the objects must both be in the same horizontal plane.) The fact that the only things that are moved are the objects being compared shows that at this level children lack the power to think in terms of grouped changes of position and a coordinate system. Were they able to do so, they could utilize changes in the position of a common term to bridge the gap between the towers. Mor and Nan, who use such a common term, (the stick "to measure with") move it in a way which shows clearly that changes in its position are quite uncoordinated. Mor does not know how to establish a correspondence either between initial points (he rests the stick on the ground when measuring the copy but on the bench when measuring the model) or terminal points (he forgets where he put his finger on the way to the model). A measuring object should be laid alongside the measured and show congruence. Changes of position like those of Mor are too inexact to allow of such 'grouping'.

§4. *Stage II: Elementary use of changes of position.*
Sub-stage IIB: Body-transfer imitating the measured object

With sub-stage IIB we see the first appearance of a common term which was missing in visual and manual transfer. At these levels, as we have seen, changes of position are as yet rudimentary. Because they possess no coordinate system, children cannot so order the various terms involved in the comparison as to admit of precise spatial relations, whatever their location. In the beginning the common term is the subject's own body. This limitation parallels the behaviour studied in ch. I, §2, where the initial representation of changes of position, also occurring at stage II, was limited to the recollection of the subject's own sequence of movements.

Childish egocentrism is in essence the assimilation of objects to subjective schemata and precedes that further decentration which confers on them their full objective character. This explains why children first select their own bodies as an intermediary measure with which to com-

---

[1] Level IIA is also when children gain the idea of perpendicularity. Their drawing of a beaker partly filled with water shows the water surface running parallel with the base of the beaker, even when this is tilted. (C.C.S., ch. XIII.)

pare copy and model, rather than whatever is to hand. They measure one term against their fingers, their arm or their trunk and transfer that bodily measure over against the other term. The following are examples:

ELI (4; 6 very advanced) stands midway between level IIA and level IIB. He makes frequent use of manual transfer in building his tower, comparing his blocks with those of the model. His tower in the end stands 72 cm. high against the 74 cm. of the model: "Are these towers the same height?—*Mine is smaller because the table is lower.*—Would it still be smaller if we carried yours over by the side of the other?—*No.*—Can you measure their height (he is given the material to do it)?—*Yes.*—(Eli climbs on to a chair, puts one hand against the base of the model and raises the other in the general direction of its top. He drops his hands and holds the chair to climb down. He then runs over to his own tower and holds one hand towards the base and the other towards the top. Thus he makes no effort to conserve the height he measures.) *Mine is smaller.*—Can you measure their width?—*No.*" This behaviour is not so much a true act of measuring as a gesture to indicate height.

RYS (5; 7 advanced) also uses manual transfer to build his tower and on one occasion he puts an open hand against two bricks to compare them. When he has finished he is asked if the towers are the same height: "*I don't know.*— Go and see.—*There, that one* (the bottom brick of the model) *is obviously* [*sic!*] *big all over* (he puts his hand over the edge of the cube feeling its width and height at the same time, then goes across and does the same with his copy). *It's shorter. I must fill the holes* (he adds more bricks).—And now?—*It's taller. No, it's the same height.*—Can you measure them?—*No, because my hand would have to come down* (he moves his hand horizontally from the top of his copy towards the model, and then shows how the line between the tops slopes downwards). *No, I can't measure them because the chair is lower. Do you see what I mean?*—Is there nothing you can do about it?—*No.*" He is told to make a drawing the same size as the model. To measure it he says: "*I could put the line up against the tower* (manual transfer)." But he goes on to use his fingers to compare the details. The result leaves him dissatisfied: "*But I did measure.*—Well?—*Yes but I closed my fingers* (and lost track of the size in the process of change of position)."

BRU (5; 11) also uses both manual and body transfer, transferring bricks and measuring with his fingers. In the finish, he brings the completed tower nearer and uses his fingers to compare corresponding parts of the model and copy. "Does it change the height of the tower if you carry it on to a higher table?—*Oh no, it stays the same height.*"

COUR (6; 5) carries bricks across to compare them with those of the model. When he has finished his tower he asks if he can build it again by the side of the model: "*I don't know if they're the same height because the table is higher but if I do it again over there I can be sure.*" He uses two fingers to measure each part of the model, transferring the measures to the copy: "*It's the same.* —What about the height of the whole?—*I can't do that because I have to drop my hand* (as Rys). *I must go on like this* (taking one part at a time)."

DOM (6; 5) carries bricks to the model to compare their size. When he has finished he puts one hand over the top of the model and the other against its base. He keeps his hands at this distance and so transfers the height to his copy. Still not satisfied, he goes back to the model and climbs on to a chair: "*I'm not big enough. I got to be the same height to see properly.*" He uses his own body as a yardstick, putting one finger against himself at the level of the base and joining his head and the top with a ruler. He then goes across to the other tower and repeats this manœuvre : "Could you do it another way?— *I could use my arm* (holding it against the two towers in turn).—What about this brick?—(He holds the brick at the level of the base of one of the towers, and holding one hand aloft, he transfers this height to the other tower.)"

The next few cases still show a predominance of body transfer, but these do in the end hit upon the notion of an independent common measure, however inadequate and non-operational. They represent an intermediate level like that which will be studied in §5.

TIS (6; 6) holds each brick close to the model and measures its height with two fingers. He follows this procedure throughout: "How can you tell whether it's right?—*I can bring them together.*—What if you don't do that?— *I can take a stick. If it's straight* (i.e. horizontal when held across the tops) *that means they're the same height.*" He finds the stick is sloping, but he uses a strip of paper to join the bases, and ascertains that the stick and the paper are parallel: "*When they slope the same way* (when the oblique lines are parallel) *the towers are the same height.*—Is there yet another way?— *Yes, you can make a mark on this bit of paper* (held vertically)." Tis tries this last method but fails because he does not measure from the base. It remains that, after first using manual transfer, body transfer (his fingers) and the parallel alignment of the tops and bases, he reaches the notion of an independent common measure.

LOU (6; 6) "*They're the same.*—How do you know?—*I've seen.*—How can you be sure?—*I could take away the screen so as to see better.*—What else?— (He puts one hand to the top of the tower and the other to the base and walks away; but finding that his hands have moved he begins all over again.)— Aren't you liable to go wrong that way?—*No.*—What about this (a stick which is too short)?—(He stands it against his tower and tries to move it horizontally while maintaining it in an upright position, ignoring the difference in base levels.)"

BER (7; 2) uses his fingers to measure the bricks used for the base and carries a few across to lay them against those of the model. Having completed his tower, he holds his hand up to the top and tries to move it horizontally to the model: "*It isn't the same height because that* (table on which it stands) *is lower.*—Are you sure, the way you went about it?—*Yes, because I kept the size.*—Where?—*In my head.*" Next he puts one hand to the top and another to the base and transfers the height to the other tower, keeping his hands in the same position. Half way there he cries: "*Oh, that's no good!*" He now constructs a rule made up of two sticks and transfers the height with a fair degree of success. Yet when asked to compare widths, he holds the sticks vertically either side of the model and carries them across in the belief that he can keep them the same distance apart!

46

These examples show how the transition from manual transfer to a common measure comes about through the initial discovery that the subject's own body can be used as a common term. While most subjects use outstretched fingers and arms, Dom who uses his whole body, marks a point on his legs to correspond with the base of the tower, his head corresponding with the top.

However, the subject's own body is not an independent middle term in the full sense. Body transfer begins as an extension of manual and even of visual transfer. Whenever an object A is compared with another object B, and whenever a thing is measured, there exists an intermediary element, though it would be incorrect to call this a middle-term. Its function is to act as a link between A and B and to conserve them during the process of comparison. This intermediary element is at first bound up with the subject's own activity. In visual transfer, the intermediary element is the eye-movement, which is successful in so far as it links A and B, but quite inadequate in conserving their respective sizes. Manual transfer follows hard upon. Here the intermediary element is the hand movement used in bringing the objects together. If these are reasonably solid, manual transfer successfully conserves their sizes, but unless they are sufficiently flat to be laid right up against each other, it is no more than an aid to visual transfer. At level IIB this intermediary element, while still bound up with the subject's own body, becomes differentiated and we see it in the form of gestures used to imitate an object and transfer its size. During stages I and IIA the intermediary element, although present, is still undifferentiated. Its differentiation at stage IIB is the forerunner of an independent middle term.

We have to consider, first, how this differentiation comes about, second, how far it assists conservation of size, and third, how it affects earlier forms of transfer which have not been abandoned at level IIB.

The use of gesture in manual and visual transfer makes the transition to its differentiation as body transfer a relatively easy step. Even at stage I, children may be seen using their hands and fingers in an imitative manner when making a visual estimate, and H. Delacroix regarded this as the beginning of so-called automatic imitation. A number of subjects move one hand up as they try to evaluate the height of a tower with their eyes. H. Würsten,[1] reporting an experiment on children's estimates of the length of lines, noted how children of 5 or 6 often spread their fingers under the table, as though to help them in what is strictly visual transfer. The close tie-up between eye-movements and imitative movements appears in drawing and is important throughout that period in the development of symbolic thinking when the signifier is still imitative in character.[2] Body transfer at sub-stage IIB is itself a natural development out of manual transfer. The movement used in

[1] Op. cit., pp. 80 ff.　　　[2] Cf. Piaget, *Play, Dreams and Imitations in Childhood.*

taking hold of the tower passes into an imitative movement which sur-rounds the object or merely indicates boundaries whether in height or depth. In our youngest subject at this level (Eli, 4; 6) the relationship is still obvious. Eli merely climbs on to a chair and embraces the copy lengthwise, then does exactly the same with the model. He makes no effort to keep his hands at the required distance while walking from one to the other. The very same movement in his case functions as a descriptive gesture subserving visual transfer, as a symbolic adumbra-tion of manual transfer, and as a bodily third term, imitative in charac-ter, passing between the objects being measured. The movement is less ambiguous in the next example: Rys spreads his hand against the brick he wants to measure. Brun and Cour, who simply spread their fingers, show a further differentiation. In Dom, who measures the height of the tower with his whole body, measuring behaviour has become so differ-entiated that we see him marking limit points on his head and legs. In Tis, Lou and Ber imitative gestures have been further differentiated so that they can be transferred to a symbolic object, whether a stick or a strip of paper. Here we see the beginnings of a common measure which is no longer tied to the subject's own body.

Where the differentiation is least apparent, the conservation of length in the process of transfer is little better than in visual transfer. Subjects like Eli are unaware that conservation presents any kind of problem. They seem to think a gesture indicating an interval can be repeated at will, and show exactly the same dimensions. Rys is far more circum-spect. He is not satisfied with his transfer of width, because he may have closed his hand on the way. Both he and Cour refuse to compare the two heights by moving their hand from the top of one to that of the other, because the motion would not be horizontal. Ber sees the differ-ence in base levels but thinks he can transfer a height "in his head", without so much as an imitative hand movement. But when he tries to transfer a distance by holding his two hands at a constant interval he admits he is beaten: "Oh, that's no good!" Thus, in the main, subjects at level IIB learn to be critical of body transfer as a method of conserv-ing distance, which is why they try to transfer detail rather than overall dimensions.

It is of some importance to understand why they are thus critical, because this attitude is bound up with the growth in-spatial understand-ing at this level. In transferring an imitative movement a child becomes much more aware of horizontal and vertical axes than in visual transfer. The mere fact of standing upright or lying down brings no such ad-vances, because the child does not seek to establish the spatial relations between his body and the surrounding objects or between the objects themselves (C.C.S., ch. XIII). He is driven to establish these spatial relations by the very fact of body transfer. When he seeks to transfer

48

dimensions by imitative gesture, he is compelled to pay attention to holding himself upright and keeping his hands horizontal, and he must refer to the towers, the tables and the floor as criteria. Hence, with the exception of cases like Eli and Lou which are transitional, subjects at this level are better aware than were those at earlier levels, both of the horizontal axis and of the difference in base levels.

A practical notion of the horizontal and vertical axes, an intuitive appreciation of parallelism, a more accurate estimate of slope and angularity, an effort at conservation of size in change of position—these form the necessary groundwork for a system of coordinates and the grouping of changes of position at the level of representation, and all these are elaborated at sub-stage IIB. We have seen the child's insight into horizontality. A clear appreciation of parallelism may be seen in the remark of Tis when he links the tops and the bases and says: "When they slope the same way, (when the oblique lines are parallel) the towers are the same height." Immediately before, he bridged the tops with a stick, saying: "If it's straight (horizontal) that means they're the same height." Thus Tis shows that he has some appreciation both of horizontality and of parallelism, and also that he can make a workable estimate of the degree of slope.

At this level such insights are still intuitive in character. They become coherent and operational only at stage III (cf. C.C.S., chs. XI–XIII). At level IIB they are not linked together to form a whole, as they must be if the subject is to group changes of position and to form a coordinate system. When the medium of measurement is still body transfer, change of position must always be approximate, but even older subjects like Tis, Lou and Ber, who discover an independent third term, are far from changing its position in such a way as to establish precise congruence. They cannot use change of position to overcome the problem of different base levels. Tis measures from the ground instead of from the base of the tower; Lou's stick, which is too short, is moved horizontally in an upright position and he does not think of stepping it along the tower to measure; Ber manages to measure its height with two short sticks (though he too does not step his measure, but sets about the task in a way which recalls "the making of an ad hoc instrument"), in measuring its width he merely holds the sticks parallel and apart. Thus at this level, whether body transfer is used or whether the subject begins to use an independent third term, the changes of position which he effects are still far from admitting of that mobile composition which is essential to conservation of the length of the measuring object and its congruent alignment with whatever is being measured.

Nevertheless, the new-found insights into horizontality, parallelism and slope have a retroactive influence even on visual transfer. Perceptual comparison is affected in two ways. First, it undergoes refinement in that visual transfer is extended to more complex relations, because even perceptual space shows greater structurization as a result of fresh intellectual insights. Second, the subject is more conscious of the limitations of visual transfer. Thus, at sub-stage IIB, we find hardly any who still believe that they can establish a precise comparison between two objects some distance apart simply by looking at them in turn.

However, imitative or body transfer derives its main importance from the fact that it provides a continuous transition to the discovery of independent middle terms. We have seen that body transfer arises as a continuation of those imitative movements which are a natural accompaniment to visual and manual transfer and assist in comparison. Now characteristically, imitation passes over into imagery, and the image itself is no more than interior or interiorized imitation.[1] Thus representative images are acquired as a result of those imitative movements which enter into body transfer. The image is then linked to a symbolic object which is made to stand for one of the terms of the comparison. When this step has been taken, that object becomes an independent middle term, i.e. a common measure at the intuitive level. This last step may be compared with the analogous development in symbolic play: a child first imitates a person or an action, then projects his imitation onto a symbolic object to which he attributes his own imitative powers.[2] So, in the development of common measure, we see imitative powers being conferred on symbolic objects like the strip of paper, the stick or the two sticks held together, which are made to imitate one of the towers by Tis, Lou and Ber, in order to transfer its size to the other. Indeed, in the case of Ber, when transferring width, he makes the two sticks behave exactly as his arms would have done.

The fact that, at the intuitive level, the common measure still has a symbolic function, provides a clear illustration of the difference between intuitive and operational thinking. We may therefore consider a few cases which are transitional between level IIB and level IIIA. They stand midway between the intuitive measurement of stage II and the operational measurement of stage III. The examples which follow, though somewhat more advanced than those of Tis, Lou and Ber, cannot yet be classified unreservedly as belonging to a higher stage. They illustrate what is the decisive turning-point in the evolution of true measurement.

§5. Transitional development between levels IIB and IIIA: gradual discovery of an independent middle term

Towards the end of sub-stage IIB a number of subjects (Tis, Lou and Ber) after first using body transfer, i.e. imitating the objects, went on to make use of independent middle terms. Other cases at the same level

---

[1] For a fuller discussion, see C.C.S., chs. I, II.
[2] *Play Dreams and Imitation in Childhood*, pt. II.

no longer have recourse to body transfer (or at least they no longer begin with it). To all appearance, they proceed straightway to an independent common measure. Nevertheless, for two reasons, they belong to a zone which is transitional between stage II and stage III (levels IIB and IIIA). They also show the continuity between imitative behaviour and the use of an independent middle term. First, the common measure, or *tertium comparationis*, begins by having a clearly symbolic function, giving rise to imitative behaviour which falls considerably short of operational transitivity: thus the middle term may be a third tower, or its use may be accompanied by imitative movements, etc. Second, and related to this, measurement is successful only in the limiting case when the middle-term, because it is a symbolic object, is of exactly the same height as the tower which it is made to represent. When it is either taller or shorter its use is still inadequate. It is only when it proves an exact copy of the size of the tower that it is successfully used in comparison.

The analysis of the way in which children come to discover the use of a middle term is sometimes complicated by the experiences they have had. Many subjects, while still belonging to stage II, have learned how to measure; others have seen adults measuring. In these and similar cases, it is easy to distinguish between external and internal factors, because the child assimilates whatever he is shown to his own schemata of representation and only remembers what he understands (that is, apart from mere parrot-wise verbal reproduction). Thus he discovers the need for an independent common measure only when, towards the end of sub-stage IIB, he senses the difficulty of transferring sizes by spreading his fingers and arms. Following are a number of examples.

PAV (5; 1) builds a tower by comparing bricks visually. "Is it the same size? —(He goes across to see and adds two bricks.) *Yes.*—Can you measure it?— (He takes a stick which is longer than the tower and stands it up against it.) *And now what?* (Without waiting for an answer he goes to the model and stands the stick against it.) *Yes, it's right.*—How did you find out?—*There's a bit short on this and a bit short on that. It's the same.* (He has not measured the two differences or marked the top of the tower on the stick.)—Could you use this brick for measuring?—*No.* (Pav now builds a third tower using bricks of different sizes, making it the same size as his, and carries it over by the side of the model.) *They're the same height* (after making an adjustment)."

HEN (5; 4) merely looks at the model as he builds his copy, saying: "*You can't see very well from a distance.*—Is it the same height?—*Yes.*—How can you tell?—*The bench is too low, but I can still see.*—Can you measure with this stick (longer than his tower)?—*Yes.* (He marks the length of his tower but loses track of it on his way to the model which he measures nonetheless.) *It's the same.*—What about using this little stick?—(He stands it vertically at the foot of his tower and proceeds to raise it along the entire length of it, an imitative gesture. He does the same against the model.) *Yes, it's the same height.*"

NEL (5; 6) likewise confines himself to glancing at the model as he builds his copy, but he is not certain they are equal. "What should you do?—*Measure them.*—What with?—*With a ruler* (note the effect of learning).—What about this (a strip of paper of the same length as the model)?—(He measures the model without troubling about his own:) *Yes, it's right.*—Are they the same height?—(He now measures the copy.) *The other* (model) *is bigger.*—What about this (a stick which is shorter than the model)?—(He lays it against the two towers in turn and, seeing his copy is taller than the stick, says:) *Mine is bigger.*—You said the tower is smaller measured with the paper and bigger with the stick?—*Yes.*—Well, then?—(Seems unconcerned)—What about this brick?—*It won't work.*—And this (the strip of paper which is the same length as the model)?—(He measures them both, adds a block to his tower to make them equal and says:) *They're the same.*—What about this (a longer strip of paper)?—(He measures his tower.) *The paper is longer.*—And this (a shorter strip of paper)?—*It won't work.*"

DEN (5; 9): "Is it the same height?—*Yes, because I did it the same* (he checks on a brick he forgot).—What should you do to be sure?—*Take this card and put it over there* (seeing the screen is the same height as his tower).—What else could you do?—*I could break up the tower and build it up again near the other one.*—What else?—*I could use my arm* (he holds it along the length of the tower, but finds it too short).—What about this (a ruler)?—*No it's too small.* (He now builds a third tower the size of his copy, using miscellaneous bricks:) *I have to put it against the other.*—Good, I'll help you. (The experimenter takes this tower to pieces and builds it up by the side of the model, deliberately altering the order in which they are placed; the overall height is found to be identical with that of the model:) Are they the same height?—*No, those two bricks belong on top, not at the bottom.* (Den fails ro realize that lengths A + B and B + A are equal! He is offered a long stick and refuses it.) *It's too big.*—(A short ruler. He stands it against the foot of his tower and, like Hen, makes an imitative movement with it but he raises it to the top of the tower and lowers it again to its foot. He does the same against the model:) *It's all right.*"

TRA (5; 10) merely looks at the model while building and is unsure of the result: "Same height?—*Don't know.*—What should you do?—*Take this card.* (He takes the screen and places it alongside the two towers in turn, finding that all three lengths are identical.) *It's the same height.*" But he refuses any stick which is either longer or shorter than the towers, as well as the paper strips. The only other solution he admits is "*to put both towers on the same table and do this with my hand* (put it across the tops to see if the line is horizontal).

LAU (6; 1) merely looks at the model to begin with but soon finds this difficult owing to the difference in base levels. He carries bricks across to compare them more closely, and later stretches his arms to span the tops of the towers. But he goes on to say "*The table comes this high*", showing the point on the model corresponding with the base level of the copy. He now stands against his tower and looks for a reference point on his own body (his shoulders) but thinks better of it and finds a ruler to measure the two towers. He succeeds because the ruler happens to be the same length as the towers.

When asked to measure with a longer ruler, he judges the difference by eye and loses his reference point in the process. He therefore bridges the tops and uses another ruler to bridge the bases, noting that the rulers are parallel: *"It's the same height because they slope the same."* When given a shorter ruler he measures his tower and uses his own hand to make up the difference.

AN (6; 2) measures first by eye and then by hand but is still not satisfied: *"I don't know.—*Why?—*Because my hand keeps dropping."* He tries to use the rulers but succeeds only when the ruler is the same height as the towers. He cannot mark a reference point on a long ruler and he fails to step a short one correctly.

WEB (6; 4) begins by standing midway between the two towers and looking across from one to the other: *"First I look at this one, then at that one, I'm sure it's right."* Later, however, he is less confident. He manufactures a common measure using two unequal sticks the total length of which is equal to the towers.

FROM (6; 10) begins by carrying individual bricks nearer the model, but even as he builds his tower he says: *"I need a ruler."* He takes a ruler and builds the tower to the exact height of the ruler! To compare the towers in width he uses two sticks which he tries to hold apart at a constant distance (cf. Ber, §4).

ARI (6; 11) looks alternately from one tower to the other then finds the procedure inadequate *"because this one is on a lower bench".* He takes a stick which is longer than his towers and marks its height with his finger. But he moves his finger when he moves the stick, and his attempt at measuring is successful only when the ruler is the same length as the tower.

REN (7; 5) wants to *"bring the other one across"* and goes on to build a third tower the same height as his own. He uses 17 bricks to build this and, when rebuilding it alongside the model, he counts out the bricks and builds them up in the same order. Finally, he uses two sticks held end to end saying: *"I have to carry the sticks over and see if it reaches the same height."*

MAI (8; 4) also builds a third tower but in doing so he chooses bricks carefully to correspond with those of the model. His common measure is therefore a replica of the model.

These intermediary cases are highly instructive. They show the first beginnings of a stage of development the final equilibrium of which is the transfer of height by means of a common measure, where conservation is assured by means of coordinated reference points. But while, at this earlier level, the body transfer of stage IIB leads to the discovery of a movable common term, the field of application of this latter is still not generalized.

We may note in the first place that the common term appears at the end of sub-stage IIB in an intuitive form. It is symbolic or imitative in character and thus shows a striking continuity with the imitation of body transfer. Thus a child often moves a stick up and down his tower as he might move his arms (Hen and Den), while others either build a third tower in its entirety or else erect a column of bricks (Pau, Ren, Mai, etc.), showing that they cannot make abstraction of the height of a common term, and feel that an object can only be used in this capacity if its general appearance is similar to that of the objects being compared. Given two objects A and C, the child uses a middle term B which is an image of A and C. B is a symbolic substitute which helps him to imagine C against A or A against C. It is not yet generalized to a point which admits of the deduction: If $A = B$ and $B = C$ then $A = C$. Thus the middle term retains its perceptual and intuitive character and falls short of operational transitivity.

The semi-perceptual character of such intuitive image-making is borne out by sundry details of behaviour. Nel makes contradictory judgments analogous to those which we find in perceptual estimates: he finds his tower is smaller than the model when using a strip of paper which is the same length as the model, but when he uses a short stick he thinks his tower is taller. Here we may see both the contrast effect and the relativity of measure and measured which are characteristic of perceptual relations.[1] Again, measures of height are often at a higher level than those of width, because it is easier to measure width simply by using one's hands and very much easier to transfer it—since our arms happen to grow at the same level instead of one above the other! Here too, there is an analogy with visual comparison where horizontal comparisons are likewise easier than vertical ones.

The middle-term at this level has been called intuitive because it is imaginal, imitative and semi-perceptual. Hence the child is unable to use it successfully unless it is approximately the same length as the objects being measured. He demands a certain similarity between all three terms. Given a common measure which is longer or shorter, he fails because it is unlike the terms being measured. Intuitive transfer passes into operational measurement only when the subject can carry out genuine operations. That level has yet to be reached.

The geometrical properties of measurement are such that without the ability to represent a group of changes of position and a coordinated system of reference there can be no operational transitivity as expressed by the formula: $A = B$; $B = C$; therefore $A = C$. Measurement is something more than mere logical deduction. If we disregard the problem of subdivision and the assumption of a measuring unit, we may say that to begin with, measurement is the expression of two equalities $A = B$ and $B = C$. These equalities become transitive because the middle term B is a movable one, but unless changes in the position of B are so grouped as to admit of reversible and associative composition, implying a multi-dimensional system of reference, they will not lead to the equation $A = C$. When these conditions are not fulfilled

---

[1] See *Psychology of Intelligence*, ch. III.

even measurement in a single dimension, here, the height of two towers, is fraught with difficulty.

First of all, there is the difficulty of finding a stable reference-point and keeping to it while transferring a measure. With a stick which is longer than the towers Pau makes a visual judgment of the discrepancy. Hen and Ari indicate a reference point but lose track of it, Lou finds a reference-point by eye and loses it, An cannot envisage it, From does not think of applying to the width of his tower a method which he uses in gauging its height. Positional changes in the common measure B are entirely lacking in reference points if $B > A$ or $> C$. Measurement is successful only when B is already equal to A and C.

Turning to the changes of position themselves, we note three limitations. A number of subjects have difficulty in seeing that they must move the middle term from A to C. Thus Pau lays the middle term B against his own tower A, and asks: "And now what?" Only then does he take it to the model C. Nel stretches the paper against the model C, ignoring his own tower A, and says, "Yes, it's right." When the middle term is shorter than those being compared, children often move it up and down these. They behave as though the length of these were a function of the end-point and beginning point of this motion, making no attempt to count the number of times the measure goes into the measured. It is not only the notion of a unit measure which is wanting, it is also a group of changes of position and a system of reference points. Finally, a number of subjects (cf. Den) erect a tower of blocks to correspond with one of those being compared, and go on to try and re-erect them in the same order beside the other tower, behaving as if the sum of equal parts did not always result in the same total or as if the distance AB were not equal to BA. In the case of Nel the resultant confusion leads to his failure to admit the conservation of length.

If, at this level successful use of a middle term occurs only in the limiting case when $B = A = C$, it is not only the intuitive nature of transfer which is at fault, but also the inadequacy of representation of changes of position. Alike in the sphere of their own movements, when changes of position are large (cf. ch. I), and in that of measurement of smaller objects, children fail to organize the relations between these changes and to link them to a system of reference-points. They cannot organize these relations because distance and length are not seen by them as intervals between a succession of points arranged in an ordered sequence. They think only in terms of the two extreme points.[1] It is therefore no accident that they can show the congruence of lengths if these are already given as equal, but are unable to equate limited portions of unequal wholes. Moreover, without a reference-system, it is impossible to organize relations between intervals, so that those children

---

[1] Cf. *Les notions de mouvement et de vitesse chez l'enfant*, ch. III.

who cannot even fix on the necessary reference-points in a single dimension are even more at a loss where two or three dimensions are involved.

It has been shown that at the end of stage II imitative and symbolic representation leads to the discovery of a middle term as a basis of comparison, but also that this discovery alone is not sufficient for measurement to be operational. The changes of position involved need adequate representation in terms of a group which allows of associative and reversible composition. This in turn demands a network of co-ordinated reference points. Unless these conditions are present subjects will fail to move a unit measure stepwise. Such iteration which corresponds to the equations: $A + O = 1A$; $A + A = 2A$; $A + 2A = 3A$, etc., presupposes that the successive positions of A are subject to additive composition $A + A + A \ldots$ and that the reference points for the correct placement of A in successive positions are adequately fixed.

§6. *Stage III: Operational common measure. Sub-stage IIIA:*
Transitive congruence without iteration of units

Stage III marks an advance on stage II and also on the intermediate level treated in the last section because children are now in a position to use any long object as a common term. They no longer require either that it should look like the things being measured or that it should be identical with them in length. It may be longer or shorter. During sub-stage IIIA, they use one which is the same length or one which is longer: if it is shorter they fail because they cannot yet handle the concept of a unit. On the other hand when the middle term is longer, they organize its changes of position more effectively than heretofore and begin to coordinate reference-points. However neither their organization nor their coordination is sufficiently flexible to enable them to subdivide a length into a number of equal parts and thus to step a unit measure, knowing that its successive positions may be added. Nevertheless they do try to find some solution even when the middle term is short: they combine it with another length, or with the length of their hands, etc. But iteration as such is still absent, and the use of additional props is clumsy. This is in marked contrast to their sure and operational handling of a measure which is too long. Here they mark a reference-point which shows the difference exactly. Thus comparison is operational but only at a qualitative level, i.e. they compare lengths in a systematic way, and even use subdivision insofar as they add partial lengths to form a total and regard this as invarient, but they do not use one such subdivision as a unit to determine all the others and their total. Thus changes of position as between the parts themselves have not as yet been mastered.

On an average an understanding of how to use a yard-stick which is too long occurs spontaneously at about the age of 7, as only then do the intuitive transfers of level IIB achieve an equilibrium by becoming transitive and reversible. True, there are children of 6 who can measure. But such cases are exceptional and the behaviour is limited to the precise conditions in which it has been demonstrated. Measurement is not generalized. It occurs only in the precise conditions in which it has been learned, and a subject who is asked to measure a drawing may say: "I've forgotten that", which is the language appropriate to learned material. On the other hand, when measurement answers to genuine development, irrespective of whether it has been discovered or taught, it is assimilated and generalized to cover new fields.

WAG (7; 2) to begin with, is satisfied with a visual comparison: "*I look at both together and I can tell.*—Can you look at both together?—*No, but immediately after! You could take a ruler and measure them.*—Which is more reliable, looking or using a ruler?—*A ruler, because you put your finger where it comes to. You could look if the table were the same height. As it is, a ruler is better.*—(He is given a ruler longer than the tower and he places it exactly parallel with it.) Does it matter whether it's straight or whether it's leaning a little?—*Yes, because this way the tower is bigger* (i.e. if the ruler is inclined, the length to be marked off is greater). *You have to mark off the length* (he marks it off with his finger and transfers it to the model). *It's right.*—What about the width?—(He measures it exactly the same way, holding his ruler some way up the tower but parallel with the base)." Given a shorter ruler, he uses his hand to make up its length to that of the tower.

ROB (7; 4) measures the height exactly with the large ruler by placing his finger at the appropriate point and noting the number he finds, which is 33 (he is using a metre ruler with the zero uppermost, so that his 67 cm. tower comes against the 33 cm. mark). Given a short ruler, he judges the discrepancy by eye without stepping his ruler. Given a long stick and a short one he does the same. "What about this brick?—*It's too small.*—Can't you count how many times it goes?—(He steps it in a rough and ready fashion, without well-defined reference points. After counting 13 steps, he repeats the process against the model.)—Is it right?—*No, because it was 33 with the ruler.*"

ERN (7; 5) likewise, succeeds with the long ruler and fails with the short one. "*It can't be done. It's too short.*—Is there no way round that?—*You can do it if it's too long but not if it's too short.*"

JAC (7; 6) measures details by eye then carries his tower across and takes it back again: "Is there another way?—(He measures the details with his fingers)—What about the whole thing?—(He tries the cardboard screen.) *No it's too small* (but he takes a long ruler and measures them correctly).—What about using a short ruler?—*I can do it if my hand is big enough* (he makes up the discrepancy with his fingers). *I prefer using the long ruler because it's easier. I can just mark off the right length.*—Can you do it with one of these bricks?—*No. I'd need a lot of them.*—What about a big one?—(He measures with the brick and uses the span of his hand to make up the deficiency.) *It won't work. My hand keeps moving.*—Couldn't you lay the brick against it several times?—*No because I couldn't do the same with the other tower.*"

Rob (8; 4) goes through each of the lower levels in turn: *"It's the same height because I looked at it carefully, just as if it were near the other one* (!)*"*, then *"You can take it to pieces and put it up again next to that one."* Then he transfers the height of the tower by holding his hands apart, but comments: *"I may go wrong, because I move my hand even when I don't mean to."* He goes on to measure them correctly with a long ruler though he cannot do so with a short one.

Two points should be noted. First, the use of a common measure brings about operational equilibrium at a qualitative level: qualitative, because there is as yet no iteration of a unit of measure. Second, earlier ways of measuring are themselves modified by this newly acquired behaviour.

At level IIB the middle term is imaged or imitative because perceptual and intuitive transfer are still subject to the accretions of sensation and symbolic imagery. It is when these accretions are sloughed that transfer becomes reversible and hence operational. Here as elsewhere, operational reversibility is an end-state of dynamic equilibrium, which comes about as a result of adjustments which are first perceptual, then intuitive. They derive from the interaction of assimilation and accommodation at the representative level.

Geometrical thinking has reached a new stage of development as compared with the intermediate level of §5. It is new because the reference system is organized and there is grouping of changes of position. Without these there might be congruence but congruence could not be transitive. Even at level IIB subjects formed intuitive notions of horizontality, parallelism, and slope which enabled them to link the difference in base levels with a line joining the tops. But representation of changes of position based on reference points was still inadequate. Hence measurement with a common term, B, was successful only in the limiting case where B was equal to A and C, the two towers. Even when B was longer than A they could not mark a point on B to delimit a portion equal to A. But at level IIIA, the notions already referred to become synthesized. They form a reference system which enables changes of position to be sufficiently grouped to allow of transfer of congruence. Wag achieves a synthesis of two actions by marking off a reference point on a long ruler to indicate a portion of B which is equal to A, and then carrying B carefully to C, taking care to hold it parallel because otherwise "the tower is bigger". In comparing widths he does exactly the same, taking care to hold his ruler horizontal and to keep constant the distance from the reference point to the end of the ruler. It is this synthesis which enables him to measure accurately in three dimensions, albeit without unit iteration. The partial configuration made up by the two towers with their differing base levels and the middle terms is coordinated so that changes in the position of the latter from one tower to the other are grouped. Only thus can there be a precise judgment A = B and B = C, therefore A = C. (This should not be taken to imply that for this subject the whole of surrounding space is likewise coordinated.) Although the subject is still unable to move a short ruler stepwise (iteration) he can use a ruler for measuring by adding a length which will make it equal to the tower. Moreover this process is reversible and associative: thus Ern uses small bricks to make his ruler up to the length of the tower but, unlike Den in §5, he has no qualms about assembling ruler and bricks in a different order, because he knows that an overall length is equal to the sum of its parts whatever their order.

We may note that the partial coordination achieved at this level in the development of measuring corresponds to an analogous partial coordination in the representation of a group of changes of position (ch. I). But there is one important difference over and above the difference in scale. When a child is dealing with changes in his own position with reference to fixed objects like buildings and crossroads, he need not concern himself with the size of the moving term, nor are there any reference-points on this term itself. But the present experimental situation involves both an external and an internal reference-system. The external or stationary system is less complex than the ground-plan of a village or district, though it is complicated by the different heights at which the towers are erected. But the moving term, which is the middle term carried from one tower to the other, constitutes a further internal reference-system. The child must take its size into account by marking off a point which corresponds with the top of the model tower. The difficulty inherent in the representation of changes of position in measuring arises directly out of the need to coordinate both systems of reference at the same time. It is overcome at level IIIA, which is when the partial coordinations were achieved in the situation studied in ch. I.

Here too, there is still only a partial coordination, since it does not yet allow of the systematic stepwise movement of a short and arbitrary unit length. Not only is the child at this level unable to think out such a procedure on his own, he cannot be accurate in his use of reference-points, even when told what to do (cf. Rob). Indeed there are other obstacles in the way of successful iteration, as is shown by the peculiar reaction of Rob who compares 13 units as measured with a single brick with the 33 units marked on the metre stick, as though the units involved were identical or even comparable!

It is instructive to compare the development of measuring with that of number.[1] Why, one may ask, does a child whose understanding has reached a point where he is able to use a common measure at a qualitative level, fail in building up a true metrical system by iteration of a unit

---

[1] See Piaget, *The Child's Conception of Number.*

length? Because his conception of length is transitive, and he can co-ordinate changes of position using precise reference points, he can transfer relations of congruence. Thus he has at his disposal both essential components: first, changes of position are adequately grouped and demarcated to permit the transfer of congruence; second, there is qualitative or intensive subdivision of the form $A + A' = B$; $B + B' = C$, etc. This latter is shown by his ability to make up a short ruler to the required length, using additional component lengths, and by his willingness to regard an overall length as independent of the arrangement of its parts. To achieve metric iteration, he has only to apply one of these subdivisions to all the others, when, by transferring congruence and keeping in mind its transitive character, he will arrive at a solution represented by the formula, if $A = A' = B'$, etc., then $A + A' = 2A$ $(= B)$; $B + B' = 3A$ $(= C)$, etc. Measuring is no more than an operational synthesis of subdivision and change of position which is achieved when subdivisions are equated by applying one subdivision against each of the others. Since he has mastered both subdivision and change of position, it may well be asked why he cannot synthesize them.

We may remember that number presents a parallel operational synthesis of the addition of classes and the seriation of terms, and there the synthesis is achieved simultaneously with its component processes. Moreover these component processes are themselves analogous to those of subdivision and change of position. Additive grouping of classes $(A + A' = B; B + B' = C$, etc.) has the same structural form as the summation of parts to yield an overall length, while seriation of the form $A \longrightarrow B \longrightarrow C \ldots$ etc. is a grouping analogous to the grouping of order and change of position.[1] Number is a group which arises through the fusion of two groupings, addition and seriation, just as the metric group springs from two parallel groupings: subdivision (with summation of parts) and change of position. In the case of number the appearance of its logical components, also at level IIIA, leads to the whole number series, generated by the iteration of a unit, 1, i.e. $1 + 1 = 2$; $2 + 1 = 3$, etc., which is mastered immediately the child has acquired its logical components. Why in the case of measuring do we find it otherwise?

The qualitative measuring of level IIIA which consists in transitive congruence differs from a true metrical system only in that the latter involves changes of position among the subdivisions of a middle term in a metrical system (one such subdivision is chosen as a unit of measurement and applied to the others), whereas in qualitative measuring one object in its entirety is applied to another. This distinction defines the difference between operations which are intensive and those which are

---

[1] Cf. C.C.S., ch. XV, op. II, in §§ 3, 4 and 5, showing that change of position (déplacement) is a special case of order of position (placement).

extensive or metric (see C.C.S., ch. XV, §3). Yet its psychological difficulty is not immediately apparent. On closer analysis, we may see that the synthesis of a metrical system is beset by intuitive obstacles which do not affect the synthesis of number. A number is like a class or a series in that it is a collection of discontinuous objects, so that when a child has mastered the addition of classes and seriation these two operations can be synthesized. He then regards objects as being both equivalent in terms of class membership and distinct in terms of the order in which they are enumerated, i.e. as numerical units. But in the realm of measurement, although subdivision and change of position are analogous groupings to the addition of classes and seriation, there is no automatic synthesis. This is because length is continuous and not composed of discrete units. It can indeed be subdivided as we have seen,[1] but the portions arrived at are immobile because they are connected so that it is difficult to compare them. The realization that successive segments of a straight line are congruent therefore demands a greater degree of abstraction than the establishment of congruence between two separate movable objects. This is why the metric unit is not mastered until level IIIB while operational transitivity at a qualitative level occurs at level IIIA. The order in which these operations are acquired confirms the order of genetic succession which we have seen to hold between "intensive" operations and extensive or metrical operations (C.C.S., ch. XV, §6).

In conclusion, we may note how the intellectual achievement of level IIIA exerts a retroactive influence on more primitive modes of comparison. Visual, manual and body transfer are still in evidence in their own right as approximations existing alongside and preceding measurement as such. Thus subjects use their hands for body transfer—but they realize that their "hands keep moving" (Jac), etc. But it is in visual transfer that the progress is at once most striking and theoretically important. Thus Rob is himself aware of transfer and accurately describes its mechanism, when he says: "I looked at it carefully just as if it were near the other one." Later, the evolution of operational transitivity brings about a quasi-transitive structuring of visual transfer. Thus Piaget and Lambercier,[2] in their study of children's judgments of size and distance found that older children use middle terms when making visual comparisons between near and distant objects. If A is a near object and C is a distant object while B represents one or more intermediate objects interpolated between A and C, then children who have not reached operational transitivity are liable to see A = B; B = C, yet they see A > C; children of 7 + on the other hand, who can deduce

---

[1] See also C.C.S., ch. V, for a more detailed study.
[2] Piaget et Lambercier, 'Transpositions perceptives et transitivité operatoire dans les comparaisons en profondeur', *Arch. Psych.*, vol. XXXI (1946).

A = C, eventually come to see them as equal (albeit after some delay, which points clearly to the retroactive effect of operational thinking on perception).

§7. Stage III. Operational common measure. Sub-stage IIIB: Evolution of a metrical system by unit iteration

It is through trying to use middle terms which are too short that children discover unit iteration. Having established a transitive relation between the terms being compared, they now find that differences between terms are likewise transitive. Let B_1 and B_2 be the two towers and let A be a short middle term (i.e. A < B) while A' is the difference $B - A = A'$. Qualitative measuring had reference only to B_1 and B_2 together with a third term which was equal (B_3) or greater $(B_3 + \ldots)$. The remainder was left out of account and only the congruences $B_3 = B_2 = B_1$, were kept in mind. At sub-stage IIIB, A is applied against A'—it is used to measure A'. Measurement is so far generalized as to include remainders, which means that it now involves different portions of a single whole. Thus if it is found that A' = A then the differences are declared equal, so that A = A' and B = A + A' = 2A whence $B_1 = B_2$, since both amount to two units A (or, if A' = 2A then B = 3A, etc.).

Of the following examples, the first two are transitional between levels IIIA and IIIB:

Igo (7; 1). "*It's the same height.*—How do you know?—*I can see it is.*—How would you make sure?—*By putting one up against the other.*—What if you can't do that?—*I've got to measure* (he takes a strip of paper to transfer the required height). *It's the same.*—Can you use this (long ruler)?—*It's too big* (he marks off the difference and compares the mark with the top of the other tower). *It's right.*—Can you use this (short ruler)?—*It's too short* (he marks on the tower the point reached by the ruler and measures the remainder with a stick, then he transfers the overall height).—Can you use this (little brick)?—(He moves it stepwise up the tower, marking each position with his thumb.) *It goes 13 times* (he does the same against the other tower): *It's the same.*" Finally he is asked to draw a line equal to the towers and uses the short ruler as a unit, counting 1 + 1 + 1 = 3 which leaves him with a fractional length which he transfers in addition to the three units.

Ful (7; 9) reacts likewise. When given the little brick he starts by building a tower of similar bricks, so as to transfer it as a middle term: "What if you only have one brick?—*I can move it* (he turns the brick over on itself against his copy and transfers the number of rotations to the model, which is equivalent to counting the number of sides taken as units)."

Chri (8; 3) says: "*You have to take their measurements.*—How?—(He uses a long stick to measure height and width.)—What about using this (small brick)?—*That's easy.* (He turns it over and over on its 4 equal sides, measuring his own tower by rotating it 13 times. When measuring the model, he simply moves the brick stepwise from base to top, and marks off 13 unit lengths.)"

WAL (8; 6) measures first with a long stick and then with the small brick used as a unit: "Will you get the same result with the brick as you do with the stick?—*Yes* (smiling).—How many times will the brick go into the stick as far as that mark?—*Thirteen times, like the tower.*"

The gain in understanding may be described as follows. At sub-stage IIIA, subjects often make up a discrepancy by holding some other object in prolongation of a ruler if this is too short (as do Igo and Ful, using the short ruler and a stick). But that behaviour does not amount to unit iteration: it amounts to the construction of an *ad hoc* middle term with juxtaposed parts, implying no more than the summation of intensive or qualitative subdivisions. At sub-stage IIIB the middle term A is itself applied as often as necessary against the discrepancy between its own length and that of the tower, which implies iteration of its length taken as one unit. The brick is taken as 1A and the difference $B - A = A'$ is shown to be equal to 12A, whence $B = 13A (= A + A')$, and these 13 units are then transferred to the other tower. Thus it is clear that the evolution of a metrical system by unit iteration derives from the synthesis of subdivision and changes of position which occurs when the latter are applied to subdivisions as against entire objects (i.e. they involve the unit A and the length A' which represents the discrepancy between the part-length A and the overall length B).

Operational fusion of subdivision and change of position demands both the accurate representation of a group of changes of position and the use of a system of precise reference points to distinguish successive subdivisions. The reference points act as coordinates for the changes in the position of the unit measure, while these in turn provide a mathematical measure of length. We note how Chri after rotating his unit brick along his own tower, moves it stepwise along the model and readily equates the number of quarter-turns with the number of steps, thus showing that he has a thorough understanding of change of position. Reference points, too, must be accurate if successive subdivisions as measured by a unit length are to be contiguous yet not overlapping. This internal reference system, together with the external reference system described in the last sections, enables the subject to build up a network sufficiently coordinated to envisage the changes of position involved in measuring. It is the final stage of a gradual developmental process which begins with stage I. At every stage there is progressive coordination both of reference systems and of changes of position. Complete coordination of the former leads to subdivision and the end of this evolutionary process is its fusion with change of position.

§8. *Conclusions: the representation of changes of position and problems of measuring*

The significance of the findings reached in ch. I and their bearing on the genetic analysis of measuring should now be apparent. At stage I representation of changes of position consists simply in recalling the subject's own actions. It amounts virtually to a set of bare sensori-motor schemata. Possible reference objects are centred on the subject's own movements, and indeed on the arrival points alone. Hence instead of viewing his own movements in terms of coordinated reference objects, he shows a systematic egocentric distortion of space. A continuous developmental process leads to the reversal of these conditions. At level IIIB a subject can reconstruct his own changes of position adequately in conformity with the laws of mathematical "groups" and in terms of external reference objects. These in turn are systematically coordinated. Henceforward, his conception of space includes himself as one moving object among many. Changes in his own position are integrated within an objective spatial group and therefore comparable with other forms of movement.

Measuring itself, which forms our main concern, is first and foremost a change of position, whether it be the moving eye which makes a visual comparison between distant objects, or the movement of a common measure or a yardstick which effectively links them to each other. There-fore, all that has been learnt of change of position applies to measuring. The representation of large scale changes of position was studied precisely because it is seemingly remote from measuring. The analogy between the way in which subjects reconstruct their walks in a town and their spontaneous attempts to measure two little brick towers is all the more striking. At the beginning of the developmental process measuring is visual comparison or visual 'transfer'. The belief that the towers can be compared in terms of the beginning- and end-states of their eye-movements, or in terms of the latter alone, while the extent of these movements and possible reference-systems are totally ignored, shows a clearly egocentric attitude to space. This is further confirmed by the way they ignore the difference in base levels and concentrate on the absolute height of the tops, because for them the end-points alone are important. At the end of the process, at level IIIB, measurement consists in the iteration of a unit measure. This unit measure is a middle term whose positional changes are grouped in terms of two linked reference-systems, an external system made up by the towers with objects in their immediate vicinity and an internal system made up by reference points on the middle term itself. Here too, the final stage is a reversal of the egocentric visual stage. The subject's own movements as instanced by visual, manual and body transfer are gradually decentred. Their function is taken over by a middle term. In the process measuring becomes objective, operational and coherent. Egocentricity gives way to grouping. At the same time objects now form part of a spatial framework which includes the subject's own movements. The framework is stationary and coordinated while the subject is seen as one moving object among many.

Throughout this development there is a functional continuity which links the various methods of measuring from visual comparison to operational metrics. At the same time, primitive methods persist alongside those more advanced but are themselves modified by them.

Little children at stage I have an exaggerated confidence in visual comparison; their measuring may be summed up with the words: I look and I see. That faith is undermined when they come to notice a difference in base levels. As a result the two perceptual fields are brought together by manual transfer (sub-stage IIA). When they are required to compare them without moving them, they go through the motions of manual transfer. They accommodate their hand movements to the size of the towers, imitating their height. Thus they are in the process of discovering a natural middle term to supplement their existing stock of intermediate elements, eye- and hand-movements. Through body transfer (sub-stage IIB) they reach the idea of a common measure. Because body transfer is inaccurate, sooner or later they reject it. But the image born of imitation gives rise to the symbolic object. This object is symbolic because it is still to some extent a copy of the things being compared, but it is also a common measure independent of the subject's own body (intermediate phase bridging levels IIB and IIIA). Intuitive transfers which now make their appearance are gradually regulated, with the result that they achieve operational reversibility. This implies transitivity at a qualitative level (sub-stage IIIA). When transitivity is extended to include relations between separate parts of an overall length, the evolution of a metrical system, consisting in unit iteration, is completed (sub-stage IIIB).

More advanced ways of behaviour have a retroactive influence on primitive ways of perception and action. In the first place, the gradual evolution of a group of changes of position at the level of representation makes for greater coordination of the subject's own movements. In the second place, visual transfer undergoes a transformation when it gives rise to more advanced ways of comparing and measuring. While to begin with visual transfer knows nothing of the transfer of relations and is not integrated in a coordinated system, it gradually comes to comprise the transfer of increasingly complex relations, and these in turn are organized in terms of coordinate axes which are increasingly stable. This explains the paradoxes found in the study of children's perceptual comparisons. While little children are better at judging the length of lines showing different slopes because they lack perceptual coordinates, older children are better at judgments of size when they can use transitive relations, because organized operations which belong to thought have a retroactive influence on perceptual activity and because coordinate systems are so far generalized as to include perceptual phenomena.

While the development of grouped changes of position at the level of representation and the evolution of coordinate systems are the two processes which underlie the growth of measuring behaviour, there are a number of problems which are specific to measuring as such and these will form our next subject matter. Changes of position as such have been adequately dealt with in ch. I and in *Les notions de mouvements et de vitesse*, chs. I–V; coordinates have been covered in C.C.S., chs. XIII–XIV and ch. XV, §5. The present chapter is designed to introduce problems specific to measurement, i.e. Euclidean metrics.

Foremost among these is the problem of conservation of length and distance. The successive modes of comparison we have outlined constitute a progression towards the conservation of length in spite of change of position. How is such conservation finally achieved? To answer this in detail we must first study the conservation of distances as such, next that of length with change of position, and finally that of successive segments forming a continuous straight line which are then separated to form a broken line. Only then will we be in a position to show the exact relation between conservation of length, which springs from operations which are qualitative though they involve a coordinate system, and one-dimensional measurement.

The next four chapters are devoted to the study of conservation of length which is the fundamental prerequisite of all measuring. Next will come the relations between linear measurement and the measurement of areas and solids. We have already seen how measurement of width is not immediately identical with that of height. We may ask in a more general way what are the steps involved in measuring areas and solids, and once again we must begin with their conservation. Finally, bearing in mind the study of angular separation in C.C.S. and the present findings which link measuring with the representation of changes of position and coordinate systems, we shall examine the measurement of angles and the representation of curvilinear forms (in their relation to metrics and movement).

PART TWO

CONSERVATION AND MEASUREMENT OF LENGTH

THE first part of this work was devoted to a study in broad outline of how children coordinate changes of position and how they measure. This wider context needs to be borne in mind in the more detailed analysis of Euclidean metrics which follows.

The first problem, here as elsewhere, is that of conservation. We cannot measure the length of one object without moving another, the length of which we know will not be altered by its movement. Does conservation antecede measurement or is it the outcome of measure? If it is prior, what are the relations between the operations of conservation and those of measuring? To answer these questions we must first study the conservation of distance and length at a qualitative level and only then pass on to examine how they are measured. The experimental situations will need to be more structured so that the various processes involved can be clearly delineated instead of, as hitherto, allowing subjects to select whichever method suits them.

Chapter Three

RECONSTRUCTING RELATIONS OF DISTANCE

BEFORE analysing the conservation and measurement of length we need to study how children judge distances and how they achieve their conservation. It may be that common usage makes no sharp distinction between the concept of distance and that of length. But psychologically they point to two quite different situations which become interdependent only as a result of a gradual development. We must therefore study them separately. On the one hand, there is the question of the linear size of objects like sticks or the paths along which we walk. We shall use the term 'length' to denote this kind of size. The term 'length' will therefore refer to the size of filled space, i.e. to objects as such. 'Distance' will be used to refer to the linear separation of objects, i.e. to empty space. Psychologically, the problems of distance are different from those of length, though logically, they are interdependent, since distance is the length of an interval and length is the distance taken up by an object. However, as psychologists, we may ask whether children recognize their interdependence from the outset, and, if not, how they come to its realization.

Because the concept of distance denotes intervals or empty space, it is one whose study should prove rewarding not only for problems of measurement but for examining how children reconstruct Euclidean space as a whole. Where this concept is present, children will view space as a common medium containing objects and spatial relations between objects. Such relations will evolve to a point where coordinate systems are achieved and a metrical system becomes possible. When it is absent, space as a medium common to several objects will be uncoordinated. There may still be ideas of spatial relations within separate objects or isolated shapes, but there can be no understanding of measurement.

The building-up of notions of distance enables children to pass from elementary topological relations to those of Euclidean space. The notion of distance is therefore crucial to the emergence of relations which are essential both to the development of measuring and to the elaboration of coordinate systems. As was demonstrated in ch. II, these processes are interdependent. In C.C.S., chs. I–V, children were shown to have a grasp of elementary topological relations long before they were able to reconstruct projective and Euclidean relations. The former are concerned only with the spatial properties of single shapes while the latter comprise any number of shapes within a common spatial

69

medium. The present study of the development of Euclidean metrics must therefore begin with an examination of the growth of the notion of distance, because this provides the necessary conditions for the emergence of space as a common medium out of primitive topological intuitions. Without this common medium there can be no measuring.

It might be argued that the notion of distance is given by perception. Or again, it might be said that if the notion of distance is taken to mean something more than vague and undifferentiated perceptual estimates, then such a notion must depend on measurement instead of the other way round. It is our belief that the reconstruction of distance constitutes a problem which is separate both from that of perceptual distance and from that of measurement, and that it is itself a condition of measurement. Again and again it has been found that even perceptual relations of long standing are not a sufficient condition for their reconstruction at the level of representation. Thus in C.C.S., ch. VI, it was shown that while children are able to perceive straight lines ready-drawn at quite an early age, they are unable to construct projective straight lines until much later (about 7 years), although the task is based on perceptual 'aiming'. Reconstruction[1] implies the operational coordination of perceptual behaviour. Hence representational distance may be quite different from perceptual distance. If children cannot reconstruct a straight line before 6; 6 to 7; 6, there is every reason to think they will also be unable to reconstruct distance inasmuch as a distance is a rectilinear interval between two points.

The question whether representational distance must be based on measuring is one which can only be decided by psychological experiment. There are no *a priori* grounds for stating that it must be so. If A, B and C are known to be successive points on a straight line, then, without measuring, we may deduce that the distance AB is shorter than the distance AC. The deduction follows from a knowledge of the order of points ABC and an understanding of the distances AB and AC which, being intervals, are symmetrical relations, but which correspond to the order of points, an asymmetrical relation. Again, it follows that distances AB and AC will remain constant as will the relation AB < AC, however many terms X, Y, etc., are interpolated between A and B or between A and C.

It is this problem of the conservation of distance when new terms are interpolated which will be studied in this chapter. Alongside this study we shall examine children's understanding of the symmetrical character of distance: AB = BA. Subjects who site A, B and C in a common spatial medium will find no difficulty in solving these questions. But

---

[1] I have used the terms 'reconstruct' and 'represent' as equivalent, for the French *représenter*—E.L.

they will prove baffling to those who cannot relate objects to one another in terms of an independent spatial reference-system, and whose understanding is limited to topological relations of neighbouringness and of order, because they know nothing of straight lines or co-ordinates. From the primitive topological standpoint, the relationship between two objects is altered when a third object is introduced between them because children lack the notion of an empty space with invariant geometrical properties. Nor will the identity $AB = BA$ appear self-evident at every developmental level. Children whose thought is intuitive and irreversible will see nothing in common between order AB and order BA, a disparity which is exaggerated by siting A and B on different horizontal planes. The notion of distances presupposes that space is isotropic. Perceptual space is far from isotropic, and there is nothing to show that the representational space of very young children is any different.

§1. *Outline of method and results*

Two lead figures, or two trees, identical in height, are first set out on a table at an interval of approximately 50 cm. To give the child an idea of what the problem is about and of the language which will be used, he is asked to state whether they are 'near one another' or 'far apart'. It is important to avoid any reference to movement or distance travelled, a consideration which applies equally to the study of length. The figures should remain in the same place throughout the experiment. If the subject is in any doubt about this point the trees should be used instead. When the child has replied that they are 'near' or 'far apart' a cardboard screen is gently placed between them. The screen is a little higher than the figures, and these remain in their previous positions. The child is then asked whether they are still as 'near' or as 'far apart', depending on his previous reply, and he is pressed to give a reason. One subject said the distance had altered but would have remained unchanged had there been a hole in the 'wall'. Accordingly a window was added to the screen and the question aimed at the conservation of distance was asked both when it was open and when it was shut. Next, the screen is removed and replaced by a large cube which is higher than the figures. Once again the subject is asked whether the distance has remained unchanged. The situation may be further varied by interposin several bricks which are lower than the figures and form a 'fence' between them, or by covering the whole interval with low bricks to make a 'carpet'.

The question of symmetry is raised by asking quite simply: "Is it as near (or 'far', using the child's own formulation) from there to there (AB) as it is from there to there (BA)?" The experimenter runs his finger along distances AB and BA to avoid any misunderstanding. Next the

71

figures are replaced by two more, one of which (B) is twice as high as the other (A). The child is now asked if, as they face each other, B is as near to (or far from) A as A is to B. Finally, one of the figures (their size is immaterial) is raised 50 cm. above the level of the table so that they are now at different levels. Any mention of climbing up or down is avoided. Again the child is asked whether AB = BA.

Children's responses to these various questions fell into three stages, the third stage being reached about the age of 7. Nearly all children aged under 6, and some even older, believe that the distance changes when a third object is introduced between the figures or trees. The vast majority think the interval is less: "They're nearer than before." A few believe it to be greater, but always because they are thinking of movement. When they think only of the distance they all agree that this is less. The only exception occurs when the interval is covered with the 'carpet' of small bricks. The explanation is as follows:

During stage I, which lasts up to about 4–5 years, the two intervals separated by the screen cannot be brought together in a single whole, so that the introduction of the screen puts an end to any distance relation between A and B. The subject considers only a part of the whole with which he began, and finds that the distance is less. When the figures are at different levels, he fails to establish any relation between them and simply judges their distance from his own person.

During the second stage, which lasts on an average from the age of 5 to that of 7, the subject allows an overall distance between A and B whatever the intervening objects. But it is significant that during a sub-stage IIA, the overall distance is thought to be less when the screen is introduced because the space taken up by the screen itself must be subtracted. The width of the screen cannot be part of the distance separating A and B because it is now filled space and not empty! When the figures are at different levels, the subject responds in a way which shows that his conception of space is still not symmetrical at sub-stage IIA: it is bound up with the effort involved in crossing it.—Sub-stage IIB yields two distinct modes of response, both intermediate. Either there is non-conservation of distance when a screen is interposed but a difference in levels does not alter the symmetry of the relation, or symmetry is denied while conservation is recognized.

Beginning with stage III, which rarely appears before the age of 7, there is conservation of distance in spite of interpolated objects and the relationship is symmetrical in spite of the difference in levels.

Thus the notion of distance becomes operational at the same time as that of a straight line (C.C.S., ch. VI, §1) and, more important, when operations of order are generalized and form a reversible grouping (C.C.S., ch. III). Since it may be assumed that the conservation of distance is essential to that of length, these responses will now be examined in detail, because this development heralds that of measurement as well as Euclidean notions in general.

§2. *Stage I: Absence of overall distance*

The characteristic of stage I is that children do not bring together the two distances AS, BS (A and B representing the figures and S the screen) so that the distance relation between A and B ceases to have any meaning when the screen is interposed. Moreover, distance is asymmetrical when A and B are on different horizontal planes, and sometimes even when they are on the same plane:

THO (4; 2). The screen is placed in position between the two figures: *"They're nearer.—Why?—*(No reply.)*—Look at them carefully. Are they nearer than before or the same?—Nearer* (pointing to the distance AS).— And like this (screen removed)?—*Further."*

"And is it the same from here to here (A to B) as it is from here to here (B to A, without screen and at the same level) or nearer or further?—*This way is further* (AB).—Why?—*It's far.—*What about from here to here (BA), is it just as far?—(No reply)." It is obvious that he fails to understand the question and thinks only of their respective distances from himself.

"And now, like this (B 50 cm. above A), is it as far from here to here (AB) as it is from here to here (BA) or not?—*This way is further* (indicating B).— Why?—*Because the other is higher."* He is judging from his own point of view. "What about these (short A, tall C)?—*This way it's further* (AC).—Why?— *Because he's big and the other one is little."*

CLAI (4; 9). The intervening space is covered with a carpet of bricks: *"They're near.—*(A few bricks removed.)*—They're still near.—*(Space left empty.) And this way?—*They're far.—*(Space filled.)*—Very near.—*(One brick only.) Are they near one another or far apart?—*Far apart.—*(Brick removed.) —*Further.—*(Screen.)*—Nearer.—*Why?—(No reply.)" These judgments are consistent although they are still unexplained. The apparent reduction of distance when the screen is interposed is presumably the result of his inability to compose distances. On the other hand, the intercalation of little bricks which are lower than the figures again leads him to think the distance is shorter, but this time because filled space is seen as shorter than empty space. "From here to here (AB, objects removed) is it near or far?—*Far.—*And from here to here (BA)?—*Far.—*The same as the other way?—*No.—*Why not?— (No reply. The question is not understood.)"

SZI (4; 11) replies like the others but states explicitly: *"It's further when the screen isn't there, because when it is, it's only half as far."* Plainly, there is no composition.

DEN (4; 11). Two trees: *"They're far apart.—*And now (screen introduced) is it just as far?—*No, it's less far. This one is by itself and that one is by itself too."* Thus the overall relation of distance between A and B disappears with the interposition of the screen "But aren't they far apart, like they were before?—*No, they're near the screen."*

When the figures are at different levels, distances are unequal, because figure B is 'further' (from the subject himself). The experimenter insists that he wants to know about the relations AB and BA. Den explains: *"It's not as far this way because the man at the bottom is looking at the feet of the one at the top and the man at the top is looking at his eyes . . . It's further for the man at the bottom because it's higher."* His remark shows that he has begun to establish a relationship between the two figures themselves, but it is asymmetrical and not symmetrical.

These responses may seem less interesting than those of stage II. But they merit careful study, if only to bring out clearly the way in which they differ from stage II. At stage II there will still be denial of conservation, but the partial distance from the first object to the screen, AS, and that from the screen to the other object, SB, will be brought together as one whole.

We note first, that children at stage I cannot join the two intervals AS, SB and so obtain an overall distance ASB. Why not? In the first place, because intuition is always irreversible, with the result that operational composition is also impossible, which means that once a thing has been broken into parts the subject cannot reconstruct it as a whole.[1] However the intuitive conditions may be such as to reinforce that irreversibility or they may render it inoperative. In the present situation irreversibility is reinforced both by the child's notion of distance which is expressed by the terms 'near' and 'far', and by the perceptual appearance of the set-up. Distance is empty space, i.e. an interval which is free from solid objects; the moment such an object S is interposed between A and B there is no distance relation between them. The only distance relations are AS and BS which cannot be composed because the object S is in the way. Den makes this clear when he states that "this one is by itself and that one is by itself too" and adds even more unambiguously that "they're (A and B) near the screen (S)" and hence cannot be near to or far from each other! As was made clear in an earlier discussion of the priority of topological relations over Euclidean relations (C.C.S., chs. I–V), children at stage I reason in terms of proximity rather than by means of relations which extend to non-neighbouring objects. When the figures are joined by a carpet of low bricks, the responses foreshadow the next stage; thus Clai maintains that the figures are further apart when the space between them is empty than when it is partially filled by bricks.

Finally, to come to the symmetrical property of distance, AB = BA (without intervening objects), we must distinguish two situations. If A and B are on the same horizontal plane, children simply fail to understand the question whether the distance from A to B is the same as that

---

[1] See *The Child's Conception of Number*, ch. VII. A logical whole B cannot be compared with a part of itself A, because once B has been removed, intuition knows only the remainder A'.

from B to A because their notion of relations of order is not a reversible one. Elsewhere, we have described a child in the process of discovering the symmetrical nature of intervals. At 6; 7 the child spoke of equality in terms of contradictory asymmetries: "Lausanne is much further than La Sage and La Sage is much further than Lausanne." The child was then asked to measure a distance in both directions AB and BA and said: "But that's what I meant! It's the same!" [1] During stage I, that is, up to the age of 4–5 years, children think of distances in a given order, be it AB or BA, and are unable to compare these distances with what they might be in the reverse order. On the other hand, if one of the endpoints is higher than the other, either because it is taller or because it is situated on a height, the comparison may be meaningful, but the meaning is a direct function of that asymmetry: distance seems greater in an upward than in a downward direction (*Le mouvement et la vitesse chez l'enfant*, ch. IV, §1). Den provides a clear instance of this response. But most subjects judge the distance of the objects from themselves, and so fail altogether to compare AB and BA.

§3. *Stage II, Sub-stage IIA: Non-conservation of overall distance, distance relations asymmetrical*

At stage II we see the central core of the problem. Children can compare the reciprocal distances between A and B even with the interposed objects S; nevertheless they maintain that the overall distance composed by the summation of AS and BS must vary with thickness of S. At the same time a difference in height between A and B produces the belief that the distance between them is asymmetrical:

KEL (4; 6). Two figures; screen already in position: "Are they near together or far apart?—*They're near.*—Near what?—(He moves his finger across from one to the other, passing it over the screen.)—And now (screen removed)? —*They're further, because before you put the thing in between.*—Why are they further?—*Because now they're looking at each other* (a reply which makes sense only if taken to mean that the space between them is now empty).— And now (a cigarette packet used as screen)?—*They're nearer.*—Why?— *Because you put the box there.*"
ANO (5; 3). Two figures; no screen: "*They're near together.*—(Screen:) Are they as near as they were?—*They're nearer.*—(Window in screen open:) And like this?—*They're further, because there's a hole in it.*—Why are they further?—*Because before this thing* (window) *was shut.*—(Experiment repeated.)—*It's nearer when you shut the door.*—And with this (cigarette box)?—*It's nearer because it's thicker.* (!)"
DEL (5; 6) no screen: "*They're far apart.*—(Screen:) Are they as far apart now?—*They're not far apart.*—(Window open:) And like this?—*It's far with the door open.*—(Cigarette box)?—*It isn't far because there's a wall.*"
Large figure A and small figure B, without screen: "Is it as far when this

[1] Cf. *Play, Dreams and Imitations in Childhood*, p. 265.

man looks at this one (indicating AB) as when this one looks at this one (indicating BA)?—*No.*—Why?—*It's further for the little one because the big one is taller.*"

LIN (5; 11). Interval filled with bricks: "*They're far apart.*—(One brick removed.) Are they as far now?—*They're further.*—Why?—*Because you took one brick away. There's more room.*—(Two bricks removed.)—*Further still.*—(Empty space.) And this way?—*Much further.*—Then it keeps changing?—*Yes.*—(One brick replaced.)—*It's nearer.*—(Brick removed)?—*It's further.*—(Screen)?—*It's nearer.*"

Two figures on the same plane, both the same size: "Is it as far when (A) looks at (B) as when (B) looks at (A)?—*That one (A) has got to look further: there's more space.*—Why?—*That one (B) is further and that one (A) is nearer.*" (Lin is judging from his own point of view although he understands the question perfectly.)

Two figures, both the same size but at different levels: "Is it as far when this one looks at the other as when that one looks at him?—*It's further this way* (looking down) *because he's higher and that makes him bigger.*—(Large and small figures, both on the same plane.)—*It's further this way* (from the larger to the smaller figure) *because he's bigger.*"

GIN (5; 11) shows a rare response in thinking of the empty space as less. At any rate, he starts that way, because he is influenced by thoughts of movement: "(Two figures. Space filled with bricks.)—*It's far.*—(One brick removed.) And this way?—*It's nearer.*—(Bricks removed one at a time; each time Gin replies:) It's nearer. (One brick replaced.)—*It's further because you've put the brick back.*—Why?—*Because you put the brick there . . . Oh, no! It makes it nearer when you put the brick there.*—Why?—*Because there's less room.*—(All bricks removed.)—*It's further, because now it's a long way.*—And if I put in this cardboard screen, is it as far as it was?—*No, it's a little shorter.*—(Screen removed.)—*It's a bit bigger.*—(Experimenter and subject with a chair between them:) Are we as far apart as we were?—*Yes . . . no, it's less.*—Then the space between us changes?—*Yes, because you put a chair there.*" Initially, Gin thinks in terms of the length of the journey involved, but he suddenly changes his mind, and thinks of the empty space ("room"), which grows less when solid objects are interposed.

Two figures, both the same size but at different levels: "*It's further for the one underneath.*—Why?—*Because he looks up.*"

FRI (6; 0) makes his reasons quite explicit. Without the screen the figures are "far apart".—(Screen in position.)—*They're still far apart, except for one tiny bit there where the screen is* (indicating the width of the screen)." Symmetry: "*This way* (upwards) *it's further.*"

FIS (6; 1). "Are they near together or far apart (without screen)?—*A bit far.*—And if I put this screen in, is it just as far?—*No, it's nearer.*—Why?—*It separates them.*—Then are they as far apart as they were, or not?—*Nearer.*—And with this (cigar) box?—*It's nearer because it's thicker.*—And with this bridge (wide but open underneath).—*It's further than with the box.*—And like this (space empty)?—*It's far.*—And with this screen?—*It's nearer.*—Why?—*Because there's this* (indicating the width of the screen).—(Several objects interposed.) And like this?—*It's nearer.*—(Interval filled with bricks.)—*Still*

76

nearer.—Nearer than when there was nothing?—*Yes.*—Why?—*Because it's more full."*

Distances AB and BA, with B raised. *"It's further to look from below* (AB). —Why?—*Because it's going up, and that way* (BA) *it's going down.*—If I put a stick in between them, would it be the same size going up and coming down (A and B spanned with a ruler)?—*It's bigger going up."*

FRAN (6; 2) also says: *"It's far between them"* when the space is empty, and *"It's nearer"* with the screen interposed.

Figures A (blue) and B (red) both the same size and on the same level: "Is it the same when (A) looks at (B) as when (B) looks at (A)?—*No, it's further for the blue man* (i.e. AB which corresponds to the subject's own viewpoint).— (B raised.)—*It's further for the man on top."* However, with A and B spanned by a stick Fran says: *"It's bigger for the man at the bottom."*

BOR (6; 2) begins by thinking in terms of movement, like Gin. With the window in the screen open, he says: *"They can pass now. It's nearer."* But later, with the screen removed, he changes his ground: *"It's further, because there's more room* (empty space)," etc.

DIV (6; 4). Without screen: *"They're far apart.*—(Screen.)—And like this? —*They're nearer.*—(Bricks added.)—*A little nearer.*—(Interval carpeted with low bricks.)—*Further."*

Two figures, A and B, the same size and at the same level: *"This one* (A, nearer the subject) *has further to look.*—And that one?—*Oh yes! It's the same!* —(B is raised)—*It's a little nearer for the one on top.*—Why?—*Because it's further for the one at the bottom. He has to lift his head up."*

MAR (7; 0). Without screen: *"They're far apart.*—(One brick.)—*They're nearer one another.*—Why?—*Because you put a brick there."*

A and B at the same level: *"It isn't the same* (AB and BA): *it's further for the red one* (A, nearer the subject).—What about the other one?—*Oh yes! It's the same!*—(B raised.)—*It's further for the one on the mountain, no, for the one at the bottom.*—And like this (large and small figures on the same plane)?—*It's further for the little one.*—Why?—*Because he is little."*

Although these children find difficulty in making explicit the subtle relation which they are establishing, in the main their responses are perfectly clear.

Unlike children at stage I, these construct an overall relation of distance between figures A and B, instead of being confined to separate relations between each of the figures and the screen S. The general character of their reasoning makes this distinction clear: thus Fis explains that the screen 'separates' them, therefore they're 'nearer'; or again: "They'll still be far apart, except for one tiny bit there where the screen is" (Fri), etc. Often the subject expresses himself in a way which makes the overall nature of the relation explicit: "It's far between them," says Fran, while Mar says: "They're nearer one another, because you put a brick there." The establishment of an overall distance relationship between A and B by combining AS and SB is not necessarily indicative of an operation. An intuitive link is sufficient since

A, S and B are all seen together, while SB is in direct prolongation of AS, and moreover, A and B remain stationary throughout.

However, although they recognize an overall relationship between A and B in spite of its subdivision into AS and SB, they are quite sure that the introduction of the screen S alters the distance between the end-points A and B. Nearly all believe that the distance AB, far from increasing as might be expected, is reduced by an amount equal to the width of the screen! Gin and Bor are alone in maintaining initially that the screen makes the distance greater, but they are then thinking in terms of the walk which it would involve: the interposition of the screen necessitates a detour while without it "they can pass" (Bor). We should make it clear that before we had learned to understand the part played by topological relations of proximity and order in children's reconstructions of space (C.C.S., chs. I–V), and more especially, before we discovered how children's notions of change of position depend on their notions of order (*Les notions de mouvement et de vitesse*, chs. I–V), we expected all of them to respond in a manner similar to Gin and Bor. Yet these subjects themselves changed their minds after a while, and came round to the standpoint of the others, saying that the distance grows less. The reason is as follows: distance is an interval between objects in a given order, but since an interval can only mean empty space, the introduction of a screen reduces that interval because it occupies space equal to its own width!

The explanation given by Fri and already quoted is unambiguous: "They're still far apart, except for one tiny bit there where the screen is," the "tiny bit" being the thickness of the cardboard screen to which he points. Many more subjects give the same reply in less explicit terms. Fis harps on the thickness of the objects: the interposition of the box makes him say: "It's nearer because it's thicker," while several little bricks elicit the reply: "It's still nearer . . . because it's more full." Gin himself, after he has changed his mind, says: "It makes it nearer when you put the brick there . . . because there's less room." Lin too says: "They're further because you took one brick away. There's more room."

Distance is equated with 'room' or empty space as opposed to the dimensions of objects which occupy space. It is a dimension of intervals and not of objects in position. Responses to the opening and shutting of the window in the screen provide an admirable illustration. Thus Del says: "They're not far apart" when the window is shut but "it's far with the door open". All are in agreement on the point, as though the presence or absence of a thickness of cardboard could modify the length of a straight line drawn from A to B! For these subjects a straight line drawn through a hole constitutes a greater distance because the space is empty throughout its length, while one which runs through a screen is shorter, because only those portions which are free are qualified as 'near' or 'far'.

An object situated among others may itself be described as 'long' or 'short', wide or narrow, etc., these being relations of length. At the same time it may be 'far' from another object or 'near' it, these being relations of distance. But the latter apply only to empty 'room'. They do not qualify objects occupying space. Hence at this level, there is no composition between distance and length. Therefore the first problem is why distance and length remain uncoordinated. Its solution depends on the answer to a second problem raised by the responses of these same children: why are distances asymmetrical even when they are limited to empty 'room'.

Even when the figures at A and B are identical in size and on the same plane subjects at sub-stage IIA often deny that the distances AB and BA are equal. Yet, unlike those at stage I, they understand the question. The reason can only be that, from the subject's own point of view, the order AB, from 'near' to 'far' cannot be compared with the order BA, from 'far' to 'near'. The responses of Div and Mar show the moment of insight when the discovery of the reciprocal relation between A and B leads to the reversibility of their order, AB passing into BA, and to the equality of distances AB and BA. But when A and B are at different levels all the children at this sub-stage refuse to admit that distance AB is equal to BA. Some, like Fis, believe that 'it's further to look from below because it's going up", while others, like Fran, think "it's further for the man on top, because it's higher". The same is found when the figures differ in size on the same horizontal plane): "It's further for the little one," says Mar, because he himself is looking up. . . . When the figures are at different levels, Fran goes so far as to maintain that a stick held between them is "bigger for the man at the bottom", which at once illustrates the effect of non-conservation of distance on that of length.

We are now in a position to understand the non-composition of distance and length, the non-conservation of distance taken by itself, and also its asymmetry. All three phenomena derive from the same basic reason: the two groupings, order and change of position, are both incomplete; being as yet non-operational, they do not admit of composition or of reversibility in all circumstances. Length, which is a property of objects in position, and distance, which is a property of 'room', are heterogeneous ideas to children at this level because they lack the notion of a common space which includes both. As was seen in chs. I and II they lack a coordinate system to which they might refer objects which occupy 'room' on the one hand and unoccupied space or empty 'room' on the other. The first stage in the construction of such a system would be the recognition that even though solid objects may be placed in various positions, each of them must occupy a 'site' which remains constant regardless of whether it is filled or empty, and is therefore comparable with empty 'room'. However, as we have noted more than once,[1] it is only by grouping relations of order and change of position simultaneously that children discover that objects which are moved leave behind them stationary 'sites'. This discovery leads them to conceive of space as a container or reference system which is independent of its content. The grouping is not complete until about the age of 7. At the present sub-stage, subjects make judgments of the length of objects in terms of the order (or 'position') of their boundaries while judging distances in terms of intuitive intervals between objects. They do not compare lengths and distances because they lack a general grouping of order and change of position. Their failure to perceive an identity between the sites of objects and the empty spaces also leads to their non-conservation of distance (and length, cf. ch. IV). Lacking the grouping, they lack the reversibility which characterizes it, and therefore look upon an interval AB between objects in a given order as different from the same interval between the objects taken in the reverse order BA.

§4. *Stage II. Sub-stage IIB. Type A: Non-conservation of overall distance. Distance relations symmetrical*

Subjects at sub-stage IIB, type A, like those at sub-stage IIA regard distance and length as heterogeneous, distance referring to empty space and length to solid objects. Therefore the interposition of a screen S between end-points A and B leads to the non-conservation of distance AB. On the other hand, they now understand the symmetrical character of the interval and recognize the equality of distances AB and BA.

BER (5; 7, advanced). The figures are "*far apart.*—And if I put the screen in?—*They'll be less far.*—Why?—*Because the screen is in between.*—Have they moved?—*No.*—And this way (screen removed)?—*They're further.*—And now (screen replaced)?—*It's less far.*—Why?—*If there were a little window in the cardboard it would be the same thing* (as the screen removed)." It was this spontaneous remark by Ber which led to the introduction of the window in the screen with the replies already noted: It is "further" with the window open and "less far" with the window shut because the thickness of the cardboard must be discounted!

Reciprocal distances: With figures A and B, both the same size and on the same plane: "*It's the same both ways.*—Why?—*Because they're opposite one another.*" B is raised. A number of questions were asked but are omitted here for the sake of brevity. Then: "Is it far when (A) looks at (B)?—*It's high.*—And when (B) looks at (A)?—*Well, it's low.*—But is it far or is it near?—*It isn't far, it's middling.*—And when (A) looks at (B)?—*It's middling. It's all the*

---

[1] *Les notions de mouvement et de vitesse chez l'enfant*, chs. III and IV, also ch. I supra.

same.—(B is raised further.)—*It's still higher and still lower.*—What if (B) threw a rope at (A) or (A) at (B)?—*It's just as far both ways, but that one's head will be tired* (A): *still, it's just as far because they're looking in the same way.*"

CRA (6; 3). Figures A and B separated by a row of large bricks which are taller than the figures: "*They're far apart.*—(One brick removed) Is it as far now?—*No, it's further because you've taken one brick away.*—(All the bricks are removed.)—*It's further still, it's very far.*—(One brick replaced.)—*It's less far.*"

Reciprocity on a horizontal plane: "*It's the same* (from A to B or B to A).— (B raised.)—*That one* (A) *has further to look.*—And the other one?—*That's further too. It's the same thing.*"

NAV (6; 8). Two trees A and B: "*It's far.*—(A brick midway between them.) —*It changes with the wall.*—How?—*It isn't as far now.*—Why not?—*It's less wide.*—From one tree to the other?—*Yes, it's less far because the brick is wide.*"

B is raised: "*It's the same thing* (from A to B as B to A) *because it's the opposite way round.*" Reversal of direction here produces symmetry.

PER (6; 4). A screen is placed between the trees: "*It's a little less far than it was.*—Why?—*That much less* (showing the thickness of the cardboard with two fingers).—What if I remove it?—*It's the same as before.*"

A and B at different levels: "*It's the same distance.*" (AB = BA).

With regard to the conservation of distance, these subjects respond exactly as do those at level IIA. Ber, for instance, to whom we owe the idea of inserting a window in the screen, volunteers the remark that the thickness of the screen shortens the distance but "if there were a little window in the cardboard it would be the same thing", i.e. there would then be conservation of distance. Per uses his fingers to show the thickness of the screen saying: "That much less." Nav replies, "It's less far because the brick is wide," etc. As before, distance is defined by empty space and any solid object reduces it by its own width.

However, although these subjects show no progress in the conservation of distance, they all recognize the symmetry of intervals. Whether or not A and B are the same size, and whether or not they are on the same horizontal plane, they are aware that AB must equal BA. How is this to be explained? The reply of Ber is illuminating: the distances are equal because the figures "are opposite one another". Where there is a difference in levels the lower figure finds it more difficult to look across because his "head will be tired", but the distances are still equal because "they're looking in the same way". These simple formulations express a genuine discovery. At levels I and IIA children allow their own viewpoint to interfere with those of the objects concerned. They therefore claim that the distance AB must be greater than BA, because, as they look at the objects, they see them in the order AB. As soon as they are free from that egocentric confusion they can adopt the viewpoint of A and B simultaneously, and so they find that the distances are equal, precisely because the figures "are opposite one another". Even with a difference in levels, a child will discover that the figures "are looking in the same way", overcoming an initial subjective accretion derived from movement, which is expressed by his reference to the fatigue experienced by the lower figure who has to crane his neck.

§5. Stage II. Sub-stage IIB. Type B: Conservation of overall distance. Distance relations asymmetrical

Subjects belonging to type A are those who discover the symmetrical nature of intervals AB and BA before the conservation of the distance AB with the screen interposed. Those belonging to type B make these discoveries in the reverse order: at sub-stage IIB, they recognize the conservation of distance AB with screen interposed, but they fail to admit it when B is higher than A and they are asked to compare the distances AB and BA:

ROB (5; 6, advanced) begins with a response of type A: *"They're nearer* (with screen interposed).—Why?—*Because the box hides it* (a fraction of empty space).—(Screen removed.)—*They're further again.*—(Screen replaced.) —*Oh no! It doesn't change at all! It's always just as far because it's the same distance!*—Why?—*Because they haven't moved!"*
Figure B higher than A: *"It's further this way* (BA).—Why?—*Because one of the figures is at the bottom and the other is at the top.*—Why aren't they the same (indicating AB and BA)?—*Because it's not the same distance.*—What if we measured this distance (AB) with one stick and that distance (BA) with another?—*The little man on top would need a bigger stick."*
GAS (5; 11). Interval lined with bricks; one brick removed: *"It's the same because you haven't moved either little man backwards or forwards.*—(A second brick removed.)—*It's the same,* (etc.)."
A and B facing each other on the same horizontal plane: *"They're both the same* (AB and BA).—(B is raised.)—*The one on the mountain, it's nearer for him. It's going down. It's further for the one at the bottom. It's going up."*
PIC (6; 6). With or without screen: *"It's always the same.*—Why?—*They stay where they are."*
A and B at different levels: *"The one at the bottom has more to do. It's further.*—Why?—*Because he lifts his head up.*—And if I put two trees there (lower tree at A and upper tree at B), is it just as far from (A) to (B) as from (B) to (A)?—*No. One's at the bottom and one's at the top. It's further going up.* —Why?—*It's difficult climbing.*—And if we measured (AB and BA) with sticks?—*It's longer going up."*

These subjects recognize the conservation of distance between points A and B, regardless of interposed objects, before they admit the symmetrical character of the clear interval AB = BA. Conservation of distance without symmetry is incomplete insofar as it is limited to only one of the two possible directions. On this point Rob is explicit: AB in an upward direction and BA in a downward direction are "not the same distance", and the figure at B "would need a bigger stick" than the figure at A to measure the interval between them.

As earlier, the asymmetry is due to the fact that evaluation of distance is contaminated by dynamic considerations. This should not be taken to mean that distance is thought of as movement on the part of the objects. Thus Pic says merely that the lower figure has "more to do . . . because he lifts his head up". When the figures are replaced by trees he still maintains that distance AB is greater than BA on the grounds that "it's difficult climbing". Here the effort involved is that of the spectator as virtual participant. The distance relation is assimilated to egocentric schemata connected with the subject's own actions, with the result that its order is irreversible.

If these subjects are so immature in their inability to recognize the symmetry of intervals, how, it may be asked, do they come to realize the conservation of an overall distance with objects interposed. In general their replies consist of statements to the effect that the figures have not moved forwards or backwards, that they remain stationary, etc., a fact which was appreciated by younger subjects at levels I and IIA who did not deduce the composition of distance and length. This question will be considered in connection with stage III, where the replies are similar.

For the moment we note that though the conservation of an overall distance and the symmetry of intervals are interdependent concepts at stage III, that is, when notions of order and change of position have become fully operational, the existence of two types A and B, each belonging to sub-stage IIB, proves that, initially, these concepts develop independently. A similar finding was noted in connection with the concepts of succession and duration in a study of the child's construction of time.[1] Here, the symmetry of intervals depends on the reversibility of relations of order, while the conservation of overall distance depends on such relations being simultaneously applicable to distances and lengths. Thus at the level of intuition, there can be progress in one of these without corresponding progress in the other. The following section will show that they are synthesized at the operational level.

§6. *Stage III. Conservation of distances*

Responses of children at stage III show the conservation of distance between two stationary objects A and B, whatever screening objects are interposed, while the distance is recognized as being the same in both directions AB and BA. Stage III is reached on an average about the age of 7, although of course some children are more advanced and others retarded, the distribution being normal.

[1] *Le développement de la notion du temps chez l'enfant.*

The first two examples are intermediate and illustrate the very real difficulty experienced by children in realizing that the dimensions of solid objects are a part of distance.

FRO (6; 9). Screen in position: *"They're far apart.*—(Screen removed.)— *Now it's nearer.*—And now (Screen again removed)?—*It's further.*—(A third figure between the original ones)?—*It's as far as it was. If you put a door in the cardboard* (the screen used is without one) *it would be just as far, because then they could see one another and cross towards each other.*—And without a door? —*It isn't as far. Yes it is, because they can go round."*

Symmetry, with or without difference in levels: *"It's the same both ways because they can stand on the top or at the bottom."*

NIC (7; 4). Initial responses are the same, then: *"No, it's exactly as far, because you haven't moved them."*

Symmetry is judged correctly.

The following are true instances of stage III:

SYL (5; 2, advanced). Without screen: *"They're far apart.*—(Screen interposed.) And like this?—*It's all the same. It makes no difference when there is a wall.*—(Door opened.)—*It's still the same because you haven't moved them."*

Symmetry on the same horizontal plane: *"It's the same (AB = BA) because they haven't moved.*—(B is raised.)—*It's further because he's gone up.*— But how about from (A) to (B) and from (B) to (A)?—*It's always the same between them. It's always this much* (holding his arms out to show the distance)."

GONS (5; 11, advanced). With or without screen: *"They're always the same distance apart because this* (screen) *can't make them move forward.*—(Door is opened.)—*It's still the same. This* (lower level) *can't get any lower."*

LEP (6; 10). Screen introduced: "Is it as far as it was or not?—*Yes, you see the little men are still on the same line. They haven't moved.*—(One brick interposed.)—*It comes back to the same. Bricks can't make the little men move!*— (Door open or shut.)—*One way they're looking at each other, the other way they can't see each other, but they're just as far."*

Horizontal symmetry: "(AB = BA)?—*Of course, it's the same thing.* (He laughs at the ridiculous question.)—And if I put this one up there?—*The man at the bottom must go this way and the other just the opposite. It's just as far!"*

PER (6; 11). Without screen: *"Yes, it's the same, because these two halves make the same (AE + EB = AB), because the cardboard can't move them!"*

Symmetry: two trees at different levels: *"It's the same: the trees stay where they were!"*

WAG (7; 3). Screen: *"It's the same because they haven't moved."* Symmetry with difference in levels: *"They think it's further going up, because it's a big mountain. When the one at the bottom looks at the other, it's further because it's very high. But it's a long way for that one too, when he looks right down to the bottom. It's the same both ways."*

Smaller figure A and larger figure B on the same horizontal plane: *"The little man's got little eyes so he thinks it's a long way, but it's the same thing. What's more, you could change them round and put the little man there and the big one here, so it's the same thing."*

GRA (7; 5). Screen: "*It's the same because you haven't moved them.*" Symmetry, with difference in levels: "*It doesn't matter how high you put them: it'll still be the same.*—But a little girl told me just now that it's further going up.—*When they look at each other, these two, it's always the same.*"

GREG (7; 6). Screen: "*It's the same, but they can't see each other any more. They haven't moved, you just put something here. There's less* (empty) *space between them, but it's still just as far.*—(Interval filled.)—*There's no* (empty) *space left, but it's still just as far.*" Symmetry is judged correctly.

MAR (7; 6). Screen: "*It's always the same.*—Why?—*Because there's the same space* (empty and full)."

AUB (7; 10). "*You didn't move the little men. Even if I put more bricks in, it's still the same distance.*"

These responses show an operational notion of distance. A variety of reversible compositions can be achieved by the summation of intervals or by the reversal of symmetries. They provide admirable confirmation of conclusions which were suggested by our analysis of the difficulties experienced at an earlier stage (end of §3). Distances are symmetrical intervals which are extracted from groupings of asymmetrical relations of order of position and change of position (change of order or serial position). This step becomes possible when these operational groupings have been accomplished at a qualitative level.

It is clear that the development of notions of distance is independent of any measuring behaviour. When that development is complete, distances can be measured, but no measurement is possible until the subject has convinced himself of three points: (1) a distance AB is not altered by the interposition of additional objects S_1, S_2, etc.; (2) an order AB may be reversed, giving BA, without disturbing the identity of the distance AB = BA; (3) if S lies between A and B then AS < AB. An understanding of these three points must antecede Euclidean metrics, because these deal only with identities and relations between part and whole while measurement deals with relations between one part and another, e.g. AS and SB.

From a purely qualitative (i.e. intensive not extensive) point of view, distance implies:

(1) Relations of linear order: Distances from point A to points B and C along an overall distance AC can only be appreciated if the order ABC, or its inverse CBA, remains undisturbed. Relations of order are derived psychologically from reversible operations of "positioning". They are independent of projective and metric coordination, and are grouped about the age of 6; 6 to 7 years, after the ground has been prepared by the most elementary topological intuitions (cf. C.C.S., ch. III).

(2) Symmetrical relations of interval: Relations of order are asymmetrical (A precedes B, B precedes C, etc.). But given such a grouping of asymmetrical relations, a grouping of intervals can be extracted, and these relations are symmetrical: if B lies in the interval between A and C, then it must also lie in the interval between C and A. Intervals therefore form a series AB, AC, AD, etc., in which each successive term includes all those which precede it, while each, taken separately, is symmetrical.

The child at stage I cannot construct such a nesting series and is unable to connect more than one interval. He reasons about AB if there is nothing between them, but if a term S is interposed, he thinks only on the new intervals AS and SB, while completely losing sight of the overall interval AB. During stage II, children think in terms of AB, even when S is interposed, but, except for type B of sub-stage IIB, they deduce that (AS + SB) < AB, because they think of an interval only in terms of empty space. Thus, they too fail to realize that an interval is a relation between two points which is independent of whether the space between them is empty or filled. Again, except for type A of sub-stage IIB, they do not understand the symmetrical nature of interval relations so that these continue to be asymmetrical, like relations of order or positioning. Only at stage III do children appreciate that an overall interval AB is equal to the sum of its parts AS + BS and that all intervals are symmetrical. We have to consider how they arrive at such conservation of the whole. The interval relation is not sufficient to account for a system of distances with conservation, because an elastic line ASB could be expanded and contracted and still yield AS + SB = AB, which is independent of Euclidean distance. There must therefore be other conditions.

(3) The first step from the notion of a topological interval to Euclidean distance is the ordering of interval relations in a straight line. The distance between A and B is something more than the sum of the intervals between A and B because the line formed by the series from which they are extracted is further defined by the notion of rectilinearity. But although this distinction is not a primitive one (cf. C.C.S., ch. VI) it is still not enough. In addition, relations of distance, which apply to empty space, and those of length, applying to solid objects which fill space, need to be reduced to homogeneous terms.

(4) Therefore the essential condition is that a rectilineal order and a rectilineal series of nesting intervals should be such as to comprise both empty space and the length of solid objects. Only when such a common spatial medium has been evolved is there a guarantee that distances will remain unaltered. Without such a homogeneous framework not only must distances vary with the interposition of solid objects between identical end-points, but objects themselves change in length when they

change in position (see next chapter). Thus distances and lengths can only be compared and remain invariant in terms of a fixed reference system, providing a common medium which remains stationary and is independent of changes of position. This does not yet imply a co-ordinated reference-system, for that comprehensive framework is achieved only at level IIIB as was shown in C.C.S., chs. XIII and XIV and again in the first two chapters of this book. The construction of distances which remain invariant in the context of a stationary framework marks only one stage in the evolution of coordinate systems. Distance relations are at first linear or unidimensional. The final achievement of coordinate systems depends on the extension of such relations to several series, all of which are coordinated in two or three dimensions.

How do children arrive at the homogeneity of distances, characterizing empty space, and of lengths, which qualify objects, implying rectilinear ordered series and rectilinear nesting intervals? Their responses at stage III show this process clearly. Intervals and relations of order no longer refer to movable objects as such together with the empty space between them. They refer instead to stationary 'sites' which remain unchanged when objects are moved. An argument which recurs continually is that the interposition of a screen or a brick cannot 'move' the little men or trees (Lep. Per, Syl, Gra, etc.) or 'make them go forward' (Gons), etc. Younger subjects were well aware of this and they too did not believe that, when a screen modified the distance, it was because the terminal objects were made to move. If distance is held to be invariant because the terms remain stationary, this must be because distance is now conceived of as a rectilinear interval between ordered 'sites' which make up a spatial medium comprising both objects and empty space, where, earlier, it was thought of as an interval which excluded solid objects. Greg shows this clearly when he says: "There's less (empty) space between them, but it's still just as far." Mar is even more explicit in his statement that "it's always the same . . . because there's the same space", and the word 'space' is correctly used to denote a homogeneous framework common to empty spaces and solid objects.

If we bear in mind the operations involved in the construction of distance we find no difficulty in showing how children pass from relations between objects to relations between 'sites'. Up to stage III change of position is a change of order or 'positioning', and has reference only to the objects themselves. It ignores the space which is travelled and even the relation between the start and the finish; only the finishing point matters (cf. *Les notions de mouvement et de vitesse*, chs. III and IV, and ch. I of this book). The establishment of a relationship between starting points and finishing points brings with it the concept of intervals which are travelled. Armed with this concept, children learn to compare positional changes in terms of fixed reference points instead of regarding them merely as changes in the order of movable objects. Every movement must therefore imply a distinction between movable objects and fixed sites. The latter maintain unaltered their relations to reference elements while those of movable objects are changed. The generalization of operations concerned in order and change of position therefore explains how interval relations come to include 'sites' as such, whether occupied or free, and are no longer limited to empty 'room' (a phrase favoured by subjects at stage II). Thus symmetrical relations of order and of length are brought under a single head.

Before this operational generalization, the child's space was virtually split in two heterogeneous entities instead of forming a homogeneous common medium. On the one hand, there were objects, or filled space. These were characterized by form, by intuitive notions of length, etc., and by being subject to changes of position with respect to one another. On the other hand, there was empty space which formed the intervals between objects. This intuitive notion of empty space contained the germ of the operational notion of distance, but it entered neither into the representation of change of position nor into that of length. There could be no conservation of intervals so conceived because distances were modified whenever a solid object was interposed. Even the distance between stationary objects was so modified because these were not thought of as fixed reference points for changes of position. The generalization of operations of order and change of position coordinates these heterogeneous entities, i.e. filled and empty space, not by simple fusion which would be absurd but by means of a *tertium* which comprehends both. This is the system of 'sites' which may be either occupied by objects or free, and these in turn are fixed by means of elements considered stationary.

Thus intervals become distances when they are referred to fixed sites. The true notion of distance is therefore a relation between objects expressible in terms not of changes in their position but of the stationary sites which they occupy. It therefore implies the organization of a spatial framework as a medium or container which is partially independent of its content. This shows the progress represented by the notion of distance when compared with concepts of interval and order characteristic of topological space (which consists in relations of neighbouringness to one object alone or between the several parts of a complex object). Distance implies relations between independent objects situated *in* space, and this *space* or sommon medium is then the true object of geometry. Projective space was shown in an earlier work (C.C.S.) to begin with the construction of straight lines and of perspectives, which required that topological relations of order be referred to specific "points of view", and which therefore heralded the comprehensive coordination of all points of view within a permanent whole. Similarly, distance requires that topological relations of order and of interval are referred to a system of fixed 'sites', and heralds the construction of a coordinate system and of notions of metrics, i.e. the organization of the spatial field by reference axes. These coordinates are not achieved until later (level IIIB), as is true also of Euclidean metrics and of the grouping of changes of position in more than one dimension. But the concept of invariant and symmetrical linear distances is the first step in that development, for it implies the recognition of space as a container, no longer as split into contents, or filled space, and absence of content, or empty space.

Chapter Four

CHANGE OF POSITION AND
THE CONSERVATION OF LENGTH.
LENGTH AND DISTANCE

UNDERLYING all measurement is the notion that an object remains constant in size throughout any change in position. The movement of an object appears as a congruent transformation of spatial shapes; the transformation is congruent because the length AB of an object which is moved remains identical with itself. Topological and projective notions, like those of affinity and similarity, are not enough to bring about this conservation. When children evolve topological nesting series by reuniting parts and reforming the original whole (A + A′ = B, etc.), they realize that a collection of elements remains the same collection even after its parts have been re-arranged. An example would be changing the segments of a length of string or elastic. These segments always make up the same object, although it can be tied in a variety of knots, or stretched, or contracted (cf. C.C.S., ch. V). But this conservation of wholes does not imply that of length or distance. The perceptual and intuitive universe of little children is subject to constant deformation and is thus much closer to the elastic and contractile space of topology than it is to the invariants of Euclidean space. Later, the coordination of perspectives from different points of view enables the subject to reconstruct the order of parts in any direction, e.g. from left to right or from right to left. However, even now, the apparent length of these parts varies continually in the process. How, then, do children attain the concept of invariance of size, which is essential to metric space?

The foregoing study of the construction of a notion of distance yields an important clue. The length of intervals between objects, i.e. their distance from one another, is determined by a system of sites which forms an independent medium, and is itself defined by elements which are considered to be stationary. But what happens when objects are moved? Without measurement and metric coordinates, how can a child identify the positions which are vacated by their original objects and re-occupied by others?

The answer lies in the conservation of length when objects undergo change of position. If, in the course of movement, objects changed their length in an arbitrary manner, there could be no thought of a stable spatial field to act as a medium and reference system; and hence there would be no stable distance relations between objects. Conversely, the notion of distance, which allows the construction of a stable and homogeneous medium, also brings about the conservation of length in the course of positional change. That conservation is assured only if the site of an object maintains a constant size (i.e. its distance relations) when it is left empty, and the size of a site which was previously empty is not altered when it is occupied by an object. The overall effect is that for each newly filled site there is a corresponding site which is newly empty and vice versa, which implies conservation alike of the distance between objects and of the length of objects when moved.

In order to demonstrate this process, this chapter presents a study of the way in which children reason about two sticks one of which is subjected to a change of position with respect to the other. It will be shown that, when their thought is still at a level where the notion of distance is unformed, children will first say that two sticks are equal, then they will watch one being pushed forward a little way, and they will say that stick has grown larger than the other. On the other hand, when their thought has reached a level where distance is conceived as stable and symmetrical, they recognize the conservation of length although the object has undergone a change of position.

However, before proceeding to an account of that experiment, we must ask the question whether estimating the length of an object by the interval between its boundaries is not itself the end-stage of a developmental process. For it may be that length, like movement, is first thought of only in terms of two extremities, or even exclusively in terms of the most distant point. In order to answer this problem a preliminary study was undertaken in which subjects were asked to compare a straight line with an undulating line. The lines were of different lengths but they began and finished at the same points.

§1. *The length of lines and the coincidence of their extremities*

A child is presented with a short straight stick made of wood or clay and a long undulating thread made of plasticine shaped like a 'snake'. The ends of the plasticine are made to coincide with those of the stick. The objects are arranged side by side, a few millimetres apart, with their end-points in exact alignment. The subject is first asked to compare other straight lines to see whether he can estimate whether or not they are equal in length. He is then asked to compare the lengths of the two objects. To begin with, questions are limited to the form: "Are they the same length or is one longer than the other?" If the subject says they are equal he is made to run his hand along the two lines and the question is then repeated. If he persists in saying they are the same, the question may be put in a form which draws attention to the path of movement:

if there were two ants, or two little men, and they walked along those lines, which would they find longer? Finally, the child is shown what happens when the 'snake' is straightened out, when he readily admits that the snake is now longer than the other stick, whereupon the snake is twisted back to its original shape, and the original question is repeated.

Of approximately a hundred children who were given these questions, 84 per cent of those aged 4; 6 and younger gave incorrect replies, while only 15 per cent correctly recognized the inequality of the two lengths. (6 per cent of replies were devoid of meaning.) Of those older than 5; 6, 90 per cent of replies were correct and only 10 per cent incorrect. By and large, it may be said that at stage I the length of a line is estimated solely in terms of its end-points, without reference to its rectilinearity or its departure therefrom (a finding which agrees with the fact that, at the same stage, children are unable to link partial distances to form an overall distance; cf. ch. III, §2). During sub-stage IIB (when our subjects showed the incomplete beginnings of intuitive composition of distance, length is differentiated from the order of position of the end-points of the two lines. At sub-stage IIA, the responses are intermediate between those of level I and those of level IIB.

At stage I, subjects continue to think the straight line and the 'snake' are identical in length, even after running their finger along them and even when they have seen the snake straightened out before being twisted back to its original shape.

LIQ (4; 0) can answer correctly about the equality or inequality of straight sticks. He is shown the straight stick alongside the curvilinear shape: "Are they the same length or is one longer than the other?—*Both the same.*—And if two little men walked along here and here (showing their respective paths)? —*It's just as long both ways.*—Try it with your finger (he runs his fingers simultaneously along the two lines). Is it really the same length?—*Yes.*—And this way (snake straightened)?—*It's longer.*—(Snake twisted again.)—*It's the same as the other* (the stick)."

MOT (4; 2): "*This one is shorter* (snake).—Why?—*It's twisted.*—What if two little men walked along these two roads?—*This one would have a longer journey to make* (stick) *because it's quite straight.*—Try it with your finger (he does so).—*That one is longer* (the stick).—(The snake is straightened out:) And this way?—*It's longer* (the snake).—(Original shape.)—*Now it's the same as the other* (stick)."

THER (4; 6): "*They're both the same length* (indicating the end-points).— What if an ant walked along these two things, would it have further to go one way than the other?—*It would have further to go on the stick.*—Why?— *Because the* (straight) *stick is even longer.*—Run your finger along them (he does so). Which way did you go further?—*That way* (snake).—Then which is longer?—(He hesitates and makes no reply.)—(Snake untwisted:) Which one is longer?—*The snake.*—(Twisted snake.) And now?—*It's the same as the stick.*"

RUF (4; 6): "*They're the same length.*—Why?—(He puts his fingers on the end-points without replying.)—And if two little men went for a walk like this?—*This way* (stick) *it's a longer walk, no, it's the same.*—Try it with your finger.—*They're both the same.*—(Snake untwisted.)—*It's longer.*—(Retwisted.)—*It's the same.*"

At sub-stage IIA the subject thinks the curvilinear shape is longer after the suggestion of movement (whether this is experienced with the fingers or merely conjured by the idea of the little men walking along the two paths). But static inspection of the shape still produces the judgment that they are equal, a judgment to which the subject may revert even after thinking in terms of movement.

FROH (4; 6): "*They're the same length.*—If a little man walked along these two paths, which is further?—(Froh runs his finger along them without prompting.) *That one* (curvilinear).—Which one is bigger?—(After some hesitation he points to the curvilinear shape.)—(Snake stretched out.)—*It's bigger.*—(Snake retwisted:) Is one of them longer?—*No, they're both the same length* (indicating the end-points)."

PEL (4; 6): "Is one of them longer than the other?—*That one* (curvilinear) *is smaller.*—And if two little men walk along these paths?—*That* (straight) *one is shorter.*"

BUH (4; 6): "*It's the same length. That one's like that one.*—And what if two little men walked along them, is one path shorter?—*Yes* (the straight path).—Why?—*The other's got turns.*"

LOS (4; 11): "*They're the same length.*—And if two little men walked along these two roads?—*That* (undulating) *road is longer because it's got a lump.*"

SYL (5; 2) allows at first that they are equal, then without prompting says: "*This one* (snake) *is bigger when you pull it out. But it's the same size when it doesn't jut forward.*—What if I make a couple of ants walk along these paths?—*It's longer here* (snake)."

AND (5; 3): "*It's the same length.*—And if two little men walked along these sticks?—(He runs his fingers along them without prompting) *That one* (snake) *is longer.*—(Snake straightened.)?—*Yes, it's longer.*—(Snake retwisted.)?—*It's the same length* (indicating the end-points)."

It is clear that at levels I and IIA, the length of a curvilinear shape is purely a function of its end-points, or, to be more exact, of its furthest extremity. It would be incorrect to state that at stage I the length of a line is undifferentiated from the rectilinear distance between its extremities. Thus, in ch. III, it was shown that at this level, distance was ascribed only to empty space and was therefore heterogeneous as against the size of the objects. In particular, distance was shown to be asymmetrical. In other words, distance is not yet a relation between the extremities of a line, because it is thought of solely in terms of words like 'near' and 'far'. Distance therefore tends to be an estimate of the point furthest removed from the subject (without reversibility). Again, the experiment which follows and which consists in showing children two sticks of identical length, but with one projecting slightly as against the other, makes it clear that, initially, such comparison is a function solely of the order of the furthest extremities. Hence the present responses cannot be attributed to lack of differentiation between distance and length. There is simply lack of composition both of distance and of length, and both are judged in terms of their furthest extremities. The child notes that the end points of the two lines coincide and simply ignores the internal composition of those lines, one of which is curvilinear while the other is straight. He makes the judgment that they are identical in length because his criterion is one of order.

During sub-stage I, children are insensitive even to criteria associated with movement. They assert that the paths walked by the little men will be the same length, and some are unmoved even by the experience of running their fingers along them. This is because estimates of change of position are also made at first with reference to the positional order of points on a route, as was shown elsewhere. Often, they go so far as to claim that the straight line is longer (Mot, Ther and Ruf), as if its being 'twisted' made the snake shorter relative to the straight stick and not only relative to its own length when straightened. When the snake is stretched, they all agree that it is longer than the straight stick, because it projects further. But when it is twisted back to the curvilinear shape, it once again becomes the same length as the straight stick. At level IIA that judgment is modified by the idea of movement. But the static estimate is still one of equality, and often, after a kinaesthetic judgment of inequality, a subject reverts to a judgment of equality by simple inspection (Froh, Syl and And).

Of the examples which follow, the first is intermediate while the remainder belong to sub-stage IIB, the level of correct response.

Pɪᴄ (6; 6): *"They're the same size.*—Can the shape of this one or of this one be changed?—*No.*—If an ant walked along them (the experimenter runs his finger along the two paths) which would be shorter?—*This way* (straight line). —Why?—*It's less far for the ant.*—Then it isn't the same size?—*No, if you put the snake out like this* (straight line) *it would jut out."*

Mᴏʀ (4; 10, advanced): *"The zigzag is longer.*—Why?—*Because it goes zigzag.*—What can you do to see if it's longer?—*You can go: zig!* (he straightens it out)."

Tɪɴ (5; 6): *"The snake is longer.*—Can you show me why?—*Yes* (he straightens it)."

Dᴇʟ (5; 7): *"If you undo that one, it's longer."*

Tɪʀ (6; 0): *"The snake is longer. If once you put it straight it'll be longer."*

Cᴏɴᴢ (6; 6): *"This one is longer because it's all twisted. If you put it straight it will be longer."*

Aɢ (7; 0): *"That one's longer because it's twisted."*

NIC (7; 0): "*The snake is longer because to do a thing like that* (i.e. make a curvilinear shape) *with the other, you'd need a longer bit.*"

Thus, from sub-stage IIB onwards, when intuitions are more articulated, the two lengths are correctly judged because children are aware of the intervals or segments which lie between the two extremities, these being zigzags or undulations in the case of the snake and rectilinear segments for the stick. However, the persistence of intuitions of order appears in the fact that, initially, the judgments are still expressed in terms of the end-point. Pic thinks of what the snake would be like if straightened and sees that it would 'jut out'. Later the possible transformations of the two shapes give rise to explanations concerned with the intervals as such (cf. especially, Nic). These in turn foreshadow the qualitative composition of stage III, which is prior to quantitative metrics.

§2. *Comparisons of length. Two straight lines staggered. Stage I and Sub-stage IIA: Non-conservation of length*

The main experiment consisted in showing the subject two straight sticks identical in length and with their extremities facing each other; one of the sticks was then moved forward 1 or 2 cm. (the sticks being approximately 5 cm. long), and the subject was asked to say once again which of the two was longer or whether they were the same length. At all levels, the sticks were judged equal before staggering. After that change of position, subjects at the first stage maintain that the stick which has been moved forward is longer, thinking only in terms of the further extremities and ignoring the nearer extremities. This response lasts into sub-stage IIA. Between levels IIA and IIB we find a series of transitional responses, beginning with perceptual regulations and passing from intuitive regulations to operations, when conservation of length is assured (stage III).

Following are examples of levels I and IIA:

RUF (4; 6). Before staggering: "*They're the same length.*—(One stick is moved.)—*It's bigger because you pushed it. The stick is longer.*"

KEL (4; 6). Before staggering: "*Same size.*—(After staggering)?—*That one is longer.*—Why?—*Because you pushed it.*—(Experiment repeated:)—*That one is longer because you pulled it back* (meaning "forward").—And this way (with one in prolongation of the other)?—*They're nearly the same size because you've pulled them both back.*—(One of them is moved further away)?—*It's even longer because you've pulled it back.*"

BUH (4; 8). Before staggering: "*They're the same length.*—(After staggering:) *That one is bigger.*—(The other stick is moved further.)—*It's that one which is bigger.* (Sticks arranged at an acute angle.)—*They're the same.*—And now (right angle)?—*That one is bigger* (i.e. the stick which has been moved

95

perpendicularly).—And now (parallel but staggered)?—*That one is longer* (the stick which projects)."

ZUR (4; 9): "*They're the same length.*—(One is pushed forward.)—*That one is bigger.*—Why?—*I don't know why.*—(Experiment repeated.)—*This one is bigger.*—And now (arranged in a T)?—*That one* (vertical) *is bigger* (a familiar perceptual illusion).—And this way (right angle)?—*This and this are the same.*—And now (parallel but staggered)?—*No, that one is bigger* (= projects)."

MAN (4; 9): "*They're the same.*—(One only is pushed.)—*That one is smaller* (= the nearer of the two).—(Situation reversed.)—*That one is bigger*", etc. (The stick which is moved is always judged bigger; the line of vision may be either from left to right or from right to left.)

RAB (4; 11): "*They're the same length.*—(After staggering:)—*One is longer and the other is shorter.*"

SKI (5; 0). After staggering: "*That one is bigger.*—(Staggering reversed.)—*That one is bigger because you moved it.*—And this way (in prolongation)?—*They're both bigger because they're like this.*—(Acute angle.)—*Both the same size.*—(One stick is placed on the edge of the sheet of paper and parallel with it while the other is placed at 45° to the first and touches it midway.)—*That one* (at an angle) *is bigger.*—Why?—*To make them both the same you have to put a bit on there* (= lengthen the stick lying parallel with the paper to a point which would coincide with the projection of the other)."

WET (5; 2): "*They're the same.*—(Staggered.)—*That one is bigger because you moved it forward.*—And this way (in prolongation)?—*They're both bigger.*"

NAV (5; 5): "*The same size.*—(Staggered)?—*That one* (lying back) *is smaller because it doesn't touch there* (= the extreme point of the further stick)."

HER (5; 6): "*That one is bigger because you pushed it.*—(Acute angle.)—*The same.*—(Right angle.)—*Still the same.*"

AND (5; 1): "*That one is bigger because you moved it forward.*"

KEL (5; 8): Responses identical: "*That one is bigger because you pulled it.*—(Sticks restored to their original alignment.)—*They're the same size but they could get bigger* (if pulled out of alignment)."

CHAT (7; 0): "*They're the same.*—(Staggered.)—*The one behind is longer* (but he points to the end which projects in the other direction)."

These initial responses are of considerable interest because they show how, in comparing these lines, younger children are concerned exclusively with the order of their end-points. Because that criterion is a topological one the lines are liable to expand or contract, without conservation of Euclidean length. It might be argued that the question is misunderstood, and that the words 'long' and 'short' are used in a special sense, differing from our own usage, and denoting the order of end-points instead of the intervals between them. But the problem of interpretation would still remain unsolved. The key fact is that younger children do not take account of both ends simultaneously, which means that they are quite unconcerned with intervals of length between these end-points. Whether or not the question is understood correctly, they fail to arrive at the conservation of length (just as they failed to arrive at the conservation of spatial distance in ch. III). This is why their judgments of length have no Euclidean significance and are still bound up with primitive topological intuitions of spatial order.

Again, it may be said that these subjects constantly invoke movement and that change of position is the key concept of Euclidean space. However, in the first place, changes of position, as conceived at levels I and IIA, lead to non-conservation of length. Hence the movements which they invoke are not Euclidean changes of position. The conservation of size must be evolved from its very beginning, during the stages which follow, before there can be Euclidean metrics. In the second place, the replies quoted here to questions of length are exactly paralleled by similar replies made when subjects were asked to estimate how far an object had travelled in undergoing a change of position.[1] Just as paths of movement were thought of exclusively in terms of the point of arrival, without reference to the point of departure and the interval between them, so, here, the lengths of objects themselves are found to change as a function of their end-points without reference to intervallic length.

The reasons offered by these children may be rendered thus:

(1) The majority of them follow the moving stick with their eyes, concentrating on its leading extremity, and so ignoring the other extremity which is progressively withdrawn. The stick is therefore judged to be longer than the other because it gradually outdistances it. Because at this level change of position is conceived purely as a change of order, the relative length of objects undergoing such change must be judged to vary with the order of their leading extremities.

(2) A number of subjects concentrate their attention on one side only of the moving stick, instead of following the movement as such. Once again, they ignore the fact that previously the sticks were equal and seeing that one projects beyond the other they judge that stick to be longer. This may be the stick which is moved or the stick which is stationary, depending on which end they focus their attention.

(3) For others, the judgment that the stick is longer follows automatically from the fact that its position has changed, and they do not even trouble to examine its point of arrival. Two sticks in prolongation of one another are both judged to be longer, simply because both have been moved.

(4) A rare mode of response is to concentrate on the trailing edge of the moving stick. In this case that stick is judged to be shorter, because one segment is lacking, since the subject is unaware that the segment is made up at the other end.

These responses may seem strange. They are less remarkable if we bear in mind the topological character of representational space in

[1] *Les notions de mouvement et de vitesse chez l'enfant*, ch. III.

children at these levels (C.C.S., chs. I–V), the absence of reference systems (ibid., chs. XIII–XIV), and above all the exact parallel provided by the non-conservation and asymmetry of distance relations (ch. III). While any of these findings, taken by itself, would certainly seem far-fetched, the complete agreement between them is some proof of their authenticity. What we would suggest is that non-conservation of length is attributable to the absence of an independent reference system to provide a spatial framework for moving objects. Children who fail to establish paired relations between the two extremities of a moving object, will also be unable to link objects to reference elements. They cannot therefore take into account stationary 'sites' as distinct from moving objects. Without such a stationary medium which is essential to the intercomposition of distances and lengths (cf. ch. III), judgments of the latter can be expressed only in terms of the relative positions of their leading or trailing extremities. These are static relations of order in which one stick is judged to be longer than another because it projects beyond it.

§3. *Comparisons of length. Two straight lines staggered.*
Sub-stage IIB: Intermediate responses

Sub-stage IIB shows every kind of intermediate response between those previously noted and correct replies. However, the latter, when they occur, are the outcome of progressive regulations and are not yet operational in character.

PEL (4; 10). Extremities coincide: *"They're both the same.*—(Parallel with slight staggering.)—*That one* (which projects) *is longer.*—(Two equal sticks each measuring 7 cm. are substituted for the 5 cm. sticks and arranged so that their extremities coincide.) Is one of these two sticks bigger than the other?—*No they're the same size.*—(Slight staggering though relatively less than before:) And now?—*They're also the same.*—The same as before?—*They're bigger than this way* (without staggering) *but the two of them are the same size.*—And like this (parallel but oblique)?—*They're also the same.*—And those (two 10 cm. sticks with extremities coinciding)?—*They're the same.*—And like that (staggered 1 cm.)?—*They're longer than before but the same size."* Does "longer than before" mean that each stick has grown or that the shape outlined by the pair is longer? Probably the subject does not distinguish between the two senses of the phrase; on the other hand, he admits that the sticks are equal because a projection of 1 cm. is relatively less as between 10 cm. sticks than it was for the original 5 cm. sticks.

FROH (5; 0). Two sticks 7 cm. long with extremities in alignment: *"They're the same size.*—And like this (staggered 1 cm.)?—*I think so* (making certain by replacing one against the other!) *Yes, the same.*—And like this (one stick at 45° to the other and touching it midway)?—*No, that one* (oblique, which projects beyond the other) *is bigger.*—And these two (5 cm. in alignment)?—*The same.*—And like this (staggered 1 cm.)?—*Yes. . .* (verifying by realigning!) *Yes, they're still the same size.*—And like this (perpendicular and touching the base at its mid-point)?—*No, that one is bigger* (the perpendicular).—Why?—(No reply)."

MIL (5; 6). Two 5 cm. sticks in alignment: "*They're the same.*—(Staggered 1 cm.)—*You pulled it, so that one is longer.*—(Staggering reversed.)—*Now that one is longer.*—(The sticks are realigned and then drawn apart simultaneously a distance of 1 cm. to the left and 1 cm. to the right respectively.)—*It's the same, the strips aren't any longer.*—(Sticks in prolongation:) And this way?—*When you pull both of them they're the same length, but if you only pull one, that one is longer.*"

GROS (5; 6) responds initially to a stagger of 1 cm. with the reply: "*That one is bigger because you put it like that.*" However, faced with a variety of angular presentations of the test objects, he judges all of them as equal except for the right angle: "*That one is longer* (the side running parallel to the edge of the table)." Then with the strips re-aligned in parallel with a stagger of 1 cm. he finally says: "*They're always the same size. To make one bigger you have to add a bit of wood there.*"

PER (6; 0). Staggered: "*That one is longer.*—(The other strip is drawn the same distance in the opposite direction:) Are they the same length or not?—*No, they're both longer. That one is longer there* (to the right) *and that one is longer there* (to the left).—Then are they or aren't they the same length?—(Hesitating:) *Yes.*"

GIG (6; 0). In alignment: "*They're the same.*—(Acute angle.)—*Also the same.*—(Stagger of 1 cm.)—*That one is longer because you lifted it.*—Is it really longer or does it just look longer?—*It's really longer.*—(Both sticks drawn 1 cm. in opposite directions.)—*It's the same size because you moved them both.*"

LED (6; 8). 1 cm. stagger with sticks lying parallel: "*That* (trailing) *one is smaller because you put it smaller.*—(The other is drawn in the opposite direction.)—*They're the same, but that makes it smaller.*—(In prolongation.)—*They're the same but you pulled a bit.*"

LEP (6; 10). Stagger with sticks parallel: "*That one is longer because it looks as if that one is shorter, but if you look at the other one it seems longer.*—What if you look at both?—*Then they're the same.*—(Stagger increased to 3 cm.)—*That one is longer and that one is smaller because if you look at a ship a long way off it looks small but if you bring it nearer it's the same size again.*—(Stagger reversed.)—*It's always the same.*"

LOB (7; 2). After the usual type of response ("*That one is longer*", etc.) he ends by saying: "*It looks longer, but it's the same thing after all.*"

LAC (7; 4). Two strips in alignment: "*They're the same.*—(Stagger of 1 cm.)—*That one is bigger. No, the one left behind, the one you didn't move.*—(Stagger increased.)—*One of them's a bit bigger* (but he still cannot decide which).—(Prolongation.)—*They're both the same but a bit nearer.*—(Right angle.)—*The same.*—(Parallel but with each drawn 1 cm. in opposite directions.)—*It's the same size when you pull them both.*—And if you only pull one?—*They're both bigger* (in terms of one extremity: showing first where one projects to the right and then where the other projects to the left).—And really?—*They're the same.*"

Taken as a whole, these intermediate responses throw a flood of

99

light on the whole gamut of transitions which lead step by step from the non-conservation of earlier levels to the operational conservation of stage III.

A number of such transitory steps may be discerned:

First: Regulations of a purely perceptual kind. In origin, these are independent of the judgment as such, but they influence judgment in the direction of equality. Thus, Pel is less convinced of the inequality of the test objects when their absolute size is greater which makes a stagger of 1 or 2 cm. relatively less: hence, Pel judges 5 cm. staggered sticks as unequal while recognizing that pairs of 7 cm. and 10 cm. sticks are equal.

Second: The second step may be called intuitive regulation and relates rather to the decentring of attention than to that of perception. Thus Per and Lep notice that when one of the strips is longer on the right, the other is longer on the left. Their response marks the beginning of a relationship between the two paired extremities (i.e. the four extremities taken in pairs), as against an intuitive centring on the leading extremity. But, even where the subject ends by recognizing that the sticks are equal, he may not judge them equal to what they were before. Per, for example, claims that "they're both longer", presumably because he fails to differentiate the elements forming the couple and the overall shape produced by both sticks together. Lep, on the other hand, also using this method, apparently achieves conservation of length. However, it is an intuitive conservation which depends on comparing the apparent change in the size of the strips with that of distant objects in projective vision, which regain their original size as they draw nearer.

Third: Somewhat more advanced is the intuitive regulation shown by Mil, who recognizes the conservation of length when both sticks are moved simultaneously in opposite directions, but fails to recognize it when the change of position is applied to only one.

Fourth: A number of subjects, like Froh, come nearer still to operational reasoning. They note that the sticks are equal when arranged in exact alignment, and then, because they are not sure whether that equality is maintained when one of the sticks is staggered, they realign it to convince themselves of that conservation! Their action testifies to the genuineness of the uncertainty felt by children as to the conservation of length when objects undergo a change in position. However, their method of verification does not imply operational reversibility, and is no more than an empirical or intuitive return to the starting-point. Reversibility is foreshadowed but not yet complete, as is proved by the responses of Froh who uses the method to convince himself of the equality of the sticks, but immediately denies that equality when he sees one stick lying at an angle of 45° from the mid-point of the other.

Fifth: Finally, conservation is discovered. After first believing that the length of objects really changes, a number of subjects are finally persuaded by mutually compensating contradictory intuitions (as elicited by variations in the size and relative position of the test objects) to dissociate the reconstruction of reality from perceptual or intuitive appearance. Thus Lob ends by saying: "It looks longer, but it's the same thing after all." and Led: "They're the same but that makes it smaller." Only the afterthought of Led: "They're the same but you pulled it," suggests the logical and necessary character of conservation which belongs to stage III. For the rest, the acceptance of conservation remains somewhat tentative.

Why do these subjects not regard conservation as logically necessary? They are willing to compare differences in length resulting from a given set of positional changes with those produced by others. It is these comparisons which lead to increasing compensation of an intuitive nature. In the end they guess at conservation, without basing this notion on an exact composition of the spaces left empty by the change in position of the test objects and the corresponding spaces which are occupied: they do not realize that in every change of position these two factors are mutually compensating. Their thought does not yet embrace a system of fixed sites and deals only with the transformation of objects. That limitation precludes the operational conservation of length. It does however, admit of an intuitive conservation of relations of equality, which anticipates operation and may even come near to it.

§4. *Comparison of length. Two straight lines staggered.*
Stage III: Operational conservation

The characteristic of stage III is that there is composition of stationary sites as well as of moving objects. Hence conservation becomes logically necessary and is no longer a mere hypothesis.

SOL (6; 7). Two sticks with a stagger of 1 cm.: "*It's always the same length.* —How can you tell?—*There's a little* (empty) *space there* (difference between the leading extremities) *and there's the same little space there* (difference between the trailing extremities)."

SCHA (6; 10). Two sticks staggered: "*It's the same as before.—Why?— They've grown the same both sides* (indicating equal differences between extremities at the front and back).—And like this (with one stick perpendicular to the other in the shape of a T)?—*This one is turned this way and one the other way, but they're both the same length.*"

DIM (7; 0). Stagger: "*They're both the same but they're placed differently.—* How can you tell they're the same?—(Indicates the interval between the leading and trailing extremities)."

REL (7; 6): "*It's the same length but one has been moved.*"—Adding: "*You pushed one but they stay the same.*"

CAL (7; 7): "*They're still the same, they can't grow!*" With various arrangements: "*They're always the same length and they'll always stay the same.*"

101

The experimenter persists in showing possible modifications, until, like Leibnitz, Cal invokes both the principle of sufficient reason and the wisdom of the Almighty: *"Because God doesn't want to make them shorter. He could if He would but He doesn't want to!"*

As is true of all similar problems of conservation (conservation of discrete collections, of quantities of matter, of weight etc.[1]) its final solution appears to rest simply on the recognition of identity: "They're always the same length," says Cal, "because they were the same before," and adds: "they can't grow". Cal is not aware that until stage III is reached, children are continually led by appearances and actually think the objects grow and contract. However, the apparent simplicity of the relation of identity is even more misleading in the present case than in the conservation of material quantities. In neither instance is identity the true foundation for correct reasoning. An elastic substance does not change in itself but its length alters. The question is why there is conservation of length as such. The problem cannot be solved by arguing that some solids are inelastic because the notion of inelasticity or conservation of form is itself the end-stage of a developmental process and not a perceptual given. This is clearly shown by the responses of stages I and II as well as by the whole range of topological intuitions which characterizes earlier stages in children's construction of space, and in which there is no conservation of size but only of proximity, enclosure, order, etc. Initially, therefore, children conceive of objects as being subject to deformation and the problem is to explain inelasticity and not to use this concept as an explanatory hypothesis.

As is frequently the case, the youngest subjects who are in the process of achieving the correct solution or who have recently arrived at it show signs of active reflexion, and thereby give an answer to the problem. When there is conservation of length, the subject himself sees the change of position as a change of positional order as is shown by the remark of Dim: "They're both the same but they're placed differently." A change of position may mean one of two things: it may refer merely to the changed spatial relations between objects, in which case either or both may undergo expansion or contraction (stages I and II), or it may refer to a system of 'sites' which exist independently of positional changes because they are fixed in relation to invariant elements (axes or objects considered as stationary). The latter meaning is essential to the conservation of length. Only thus can Sol explain that conservation by pointing out that the space left empty at the rear extremity of the test-object which is moved is equal to the space now occupied by its forward extremity, so that a difference favouring the leading extremity of the moving object (A) is exactly compensated by one which favours the trailing extremity of the

[1] See Piaget and Azeminska, *The Child's Conception of Number, and* Piaget and Inhelder, *Le développement des quantités chez l'enfant.*

stationary object (B). The replies of Scha and Dim are similar. Their mode of argument implies that when an object undergoes a change of position the empty sites which have previously been occupied are equivalent to sites which were previously empty and are now filled, so that the overall length of the object remains constant.

Thus, there can be no conservation of length, any more than of distance, unless there is a reference system which provides a common medium for all objects, whether moving or stationary, and this in turn implies that there must be composition as between objects and their parts, and empty sites. The result, as was shown in ch. III, is that notions of length and distance become comparable, because both are based on the appreciation of order and interval between sites. Such sites, whether empty or filled, form the essential framework of all metrics. The conservation of length, taken by itself, is similar to that of distance in that it leads both to measurement and to a comprehensive coordinate system, although it appears earlier.

Chapter Five

THE CONSERVATION AND
MEASUREMENT OF LENGTH[1]

CONSERVATION of length when objects undergo a change of position does not yet imply any understanding of Euclidean metrics. A judgment of equality between sites which become vacant in the course of changes of position and those which are newly occupied does not entail subdivision or the construction of a unit of measurement. How do children pass from qualitative conservation to the measurement of length? The detailed analysis of that transition must be preceded by a further study devoted to the conservation of length in which the subject is asked to compare the lengths of equal objects, some of which are rectilinear while others are bent at various angles. In ch. IV, §1, we reported an experiment in which children were asked to compare two shapes of unequal length, one of which was curvilinear while the other was rectilinear, but with the pair so arranged that their extremities coincided. This experiment was followed by another in which the test-objects were both rectilinear and equal in length but their arrangement was staggered. The question remains how children will respond when asked to compare two objects which are identical in length if these are first presented as rectilinear shapes in exact alignment, and then one of them is distorted in one way or another. Will the conservation of length be delayed in this situation, or will this special situation and measurement in general prove tractable as soon as conservation has been achieved? More generally, what is the process leading from conservation to measurement? The present experiment, like that of spontaneous measurement in ch. II, deals with problems of measuring, but the situation has been so devised as to take into account what has since been learned of the role of the coordination of sites in the conservation of distance and length.

The nature of metrical operations and their relation to the conservation of length will be analysed more fully. The question so far considered was the way in which children evolve a reference system in terms of which to reason about changes in the position of objects. However, it has already been shown that two systems of reference are involved. The first is a structuring of the spatial field as a whole, including the objects being measured and that which is used as a measure. This overall structuring leads eventually to the use of coordinate axes to

[1] Written with the collaboration of Mlle Lily C. Tsien.

act as a general reference system. The second system of reference is achieved through the use of precise reference points both on the objects measured and on the measure. The subject applies a yardstick or a part of one against whatever he wishes to measure and relates these internal reference-points to the external reference-system. From the latter point of view, the organization of references depends on subdivision of space and of objects. Whereas the three previous experiments stressed the part played by the external reference-system, it is subdivision which assumes importance in this. Measurement will therefore be studied as a synthesis of change of position and sub-division, while the conservation of length will be shown to consist in a qualitative co-ordination of the two operations.

SECTION 1. CONSERVATION OF LENGTH
WITH DISTORTION OF SHAPE

By way of introduction children may be presented with the following situation. Between twelve and sixteen matches are arranged in two parallel rows, with the matches end to end in each row and the two rows in perfect alignment and only 1–2 cm. apart, so that their equality is obvious. One of the rows is then modified by the introduction of angles: thus, the matches may be arranged in a series of zigzags or at right angles to one another, etc. One or more matches may be broken in two to prevent the subject from simply counting the elements and force him to reason in terms of the overall length of the row. The question is always whether the two lines are still the same length. If the subject cannot understand, the experimenter may suggest to him that two ants are walking along the rows and ask him whether they have the same distance to cover.

However, the crucial technique consists in asking the same questions using two strips of paper each 30 cm. long and about 1 cm. wide (or even less if this is found to be too wide for the precise meaning of the questions to be clear). The subject is first asked to assure himself that the two strips are identical in length. One of the strips is then cut first in two parts, then in several, and these are arranged in a variety of ways: one long strip and a shorter strip forming a right angle, two equal strips set at various angles, several very short strips arranged in an arc, etc. The aim is to establish whether there is conservation of the overall length. (Our examples will show how inaccuracies in construction do not prevent subjects at higher stages from "arguing correctly with bad illustrations", as indeed is true of all geometrical reasoning. Such inaccuracies do not account for errors in argument made at earlier stages.) The second part of the experiment consists in asking the subject to verify his judgment by giving him a number of cardboard strips of different lengths and asking him to measure. This part was carried out irrespective of whether the subject had shown a grasp of conservation in the earlier part of the experiment.

Questions about the strips of paper, like those about the rows of matches, may be asked either in terms of 'static' length or in terms of distances travelled. The answer is not always the same in both cases and the two languages should not be confused. The difficulty of using the first (static length) is to make the subject understand that what is required is the overall distance of the paper strip and not the rectilinear interval between its extremities, which obviously varies. The experimenter is therefore frequently compelled to use expressions which imply movement, though he should take care to gloss over the kinetic aspect and to use terms like 'road', 'path', etc.

These experiments were carried out on 59 subjects aged between 4 and 9, and produced three levels of response: conservation is lost when the strip is modified (stages I and IIA); intermediate responses (sub-stage IIB); necessary conservation (stage III).

§1. *Levels I and IIA: No conservation*

When strips of paper are used, responses showing no conservation are all very similar, but when matches are used there are two types of response although the difference between them does not directly concern notions of space: younger subjects fail to recognize any conservation whatsoever, even when they can count the same number of matches in each row; older subjects are influenced by number and therefore show a beginning of conservation, but this is lost if the change in shape is excessive or if one of the matches is broken in half.

CHA (4; 0). Five matches in parallel alignment with five more: "Is it the same length from there to there as from there to there or are they different?— *The same length.* And like this (the right-hand row is re-arranged in a series of zigzags)?—*No.*—Which one is longer?—*I don't know which but they aren't the same.*—Is there the same way to go?—*No.*—Is one a longer road to go?— *Yes, there* (indicating turnings), *no, that one* (straight row), *because it's long. Here it's nearer the end* (zigzag row, showing relation between extremities).— And like this (one row straight and the other straight for the first half but finishing with two very obtuse angles formed by the last three matches)?— *A little bit more here* (row containing angles).—(One match added to that row.) —*Like that it's the same.*"

Two straight strips of paper: "*They're the same length.*—And like this (with one lying oblique, the strips meeting to give the outline of a roof)?— *It's the same because it's the same size.*—And like this (both strips oblique with one in prolongation of the other)?—*Also.*—And now (one strip straight and the other lying parallel except for the last quarter which is turned at a right angle.)—*Here* (shape showing an angle), *there's less to walk because the road is shorter.*—Show me the two roads with your finger.—(He runs his

finger along both strips from end to end.)—Are they the same length?—
No, the second one (with angle) *is shorter.*—And like this (straight lines, one
unbroken, the other formed by five segments in line)?—*The same.*—(The
five segments rearranged in zigzag formation.)—*The* (straight) *line is longer.*—
Show me the paths with your finger.—(He indicates both correctly but insists
that the straight path is longer.)—(Other zigzags.)—*It's still that* (straight)
one which is longer.—Why?—*It would be the same if that came as far as there*
(a point in alignment with the straight row and in prolongation of the zigzags).—After first demonstrating that the strips are identical when unrolled,
a short length is added to the zigzags:) What if we add this bit?—*It's the same.*
—Why?—(Shows the alignment of extremities.)—And now (one strip forming
a set square and the other in zigzags but with extremities coincident.)?—*The
same.*—And like this (strip A forms a straight line, B forms a series of zigzags
ending with a long additional curved strip. The extremities of A and B are
in alignment but B is very obviously longer). Is one of them longer?—*Yes,
that one* (A) *is longer.*"

Nos. (4; 11). Two straight lines in alignment: "*They're the same length.*—
And like this (inverted V)?—*Also.*—And like this (obtuse angle of 135°, both
strips oblique to edge of table)?—*Also.*—And now (asymmetrical set-square)?
—*Still the same length.*—And now (with set-squares perpendicular to each
other)?—*Also.*—(One set-square held constant, the other altered by shorten-
ing one limb and lengthening the other.)—*No, that one* (with unequal sides)
is longer (because higher) *because this road is shorter* (equal sides).—And this
(a right angle compared with the outline of a staircase)?—*Here* (staircase)
it's longer (indicating where the extremities project)."

MAR (5; 0). Five matches forming a straight row and in parallel alignment
with five others: "*It's the same length.*—Why?—*Because there are lots of
matches.*—Can you count them?—*Not very well.*—And like this (five matches
in a row facing four in a row with the fifth at right angles)?—*There* (straight
row) *it's longer.*—(Two zigzags one of which projects at both ends:) Show
me the roads which the two ants would go along.—(He runs his finger along
them).—Are the roads the same length?—*No. Here it's longer.*—(One match
added to the more contracted shape:) How many matches are there. Can
you count them?—*One, two . . . six.*—And these?—*One . . . five.*—Good.
Then are they both the same length or not?—*Yes.*—Why?—)Points to
extremities)."

Jo (5; 1). With strips of paper responds like Ros: length is judged in terms
of the extremities. With matches, initial responses are again similar. Jo goes
so far as to call two paths the same length when one is made up of 5 matches
and the other of 8 although he has previously counted them "*because it makes
the same length.*—Why?—*There's one there and one there* (indicating the
alignment of extremities)." However, when the discrepancy is further increased by aligning a straight row of four matches with eight matches
arranged in a series of right angles, Jo calls this path "*longer.*—Why?—
Because it does this (indicating bends)." Conversely, even when the matches
are coloured in pairs with one red, one blue, etc. in each group, and these
are arranged so that the paired colours correspond in each row, he calls a rectilinear arrangement of four matches longer than one which is slightly curved.

He goes so far as to call a straight row of four matches longer than one of seven arranged in the shape of the letter G which is identical in length but which ends with a match turned inwards. But four matches in a straight line are judged shorter than seven showing curves: "*Here it's longer because there are turnings.*" Finally, five matches in a straight line are again judged longer than five in a zigzag formation.

JAN (5; 10) makes similar responses in the main, but his treatment of number is slightly more advanced when matches are used as test objects. Two straight rows, each of five matches, in parallel alignment: "*It's the same length.*—And like this (both outlines forming right angles with two matches in one limb and three in the other)?—*Also.*—And like this (one outline made up of right angles and the other in zigzag formation)?—(He counts.) *Also the same because it's four and four.*—(The experimenter breaks two matches in half. Four whole matches are arranged in the shape of a right angle and the remainder form the outline of a staircase:) And like this?—*Here it's longer. There are eight of them: that's more.*—Yes but to walk along, is the road longer, or are they the same?—*It's longer.*"

There are many more cases all of which are similar. What are the factors which produce the loss of conservation? Children do not abandon their judgment of equality just because they feel like it. When conservation is possible they adhere to it; like Nos, who recognizes conservation when straight lines are symmetrically oblique, when they form an angle of 135° without appearing symmetrical from his point of view and even when the strips are arranged in the shape of two set squares perpendicular to each other. In other words, conservation of length is recognized whenever the change of position does not involve internal distortion or cause one shape to project beyond the other. Conversely, when there is internal distortion of a shape, a variety of factors tend to bring about non-conservation of length. Of these, some are specific to younger children while others are present at any age. However, older children overcome these by the use of reason, which younger children do not.

(1) First, a factor which plays an all-important part is the point-of-arrival and, later, the relation between the point of arrival and the point-of-departure. It is a factor which is familiar from an earlier study (*Les notions de mouvement et de vitesse chez l'enfant*, ch. III). Initially, children will consider one path to be longer than another, even where the conception is static, if its further extremity (point of arrival) projects beyond the other, and this judgment is made without any consideration either of nearer extremities or of detours, angles or curves. This mode of response is apparent in many of the foregoing examples. The point need not be elaborated as it is familiar from ch. IV. Again, when the origins of two lines are in alignment, the one which projects further is judged to be longer even if the other is more circuitous. The latter mode of response determines replies given throughout the foregoing examples,

except where the order of the further extremities is counterbalanced by one of the remaining factors. Thus Jo at first thinks only of the order of end-points, but when the detours are exaggerated (eight matches in zig-zag formation as compared with four in a straight line) the 'detour' factor becomes determining.

(2) The 'detour' factor therefore works in an opposite direction to the first. Jo expresses it twice: he points to a detour with the words: "because it does this" to explain why the line is longer and later remarks plainly: "because there are turnings". But though a subject may occasionally infer correctly that a path is longer because its route is circuitous, two other factors seriously limit the initial effectiveness of this factor. In the first place, it operates only when children are thinking of change of position in dynamic or motor terms (i.e. in terms of physical or psychological movement). It appears when they think in terms of speed or of the time taken in rounding a bend but it has no bearing on the geometrical properties of the path, i.e. on its length as such. It makes a considerable difference in this connection whether questions are asked in terms of movement or of length: in terms of the latter, circuitousness seems to play very little part. In the second place, when the subject is asked to think in terms of static imagery and not of movement, he resists the idea that a line can be longer because of angles and curves unless these detours are exaggerated. Thus Jo, as we saw, allowed that a zigzag path made up of eight matches was longer than a straight path of four, but still maintained that four such matches made up a longer path than seven arranged in a G or a C. Smaller detours are therefore insufficient to create an impression of greater length as compared with straight line paths. This conclusion is corroborated by the findings reported in ch. IV, §1.

(3) A third important factor acts in a way which reinforces factor (1) and therefore weakens factor (2). This factor is concerned with pri-vileged rectilinear segments. If two lines of equal length are arranged so that their extremities are in alignment and one of them contains a rectilinear segment longer than any possessed by the other, it will be judged longer, as a whole. Thus Cha (end of enquiry) maintains that a straight line is longer than another containing zigzags and curves although they span the same distance. Nos maintains that one line featuring a right-angle is longer than another because the sides of the first are more unequal than those of the second so that one rectilinear segment is longer, etc. This factor is evidently related to the absence of composition in the judgments of young children shown in ch. III, where they failed to reconstruct an overall distance out of two partial distances, even by perceptual or intuitive linkage. Because that com-position is lacking, the subject is guided by the longest rectilinear seg-ment, with the result that a straight line between points A and B may be

thought longer than a circuitous or a zigzag path between the same points, despite the well-known (albeit circular) definition of a straight line as the shortest distance between two points!

(4) Finally, at a certain level, the number of segments or elements may influence the estimates, although its role is equivocal. The youngest subjects lack the concept of number and even the ability to observe plain and visible one-one correspondence so that their judgments of length are not influenced by the number of elements. Mar himself counts five matches in one row and six in another but still judges them to be equal because their extremities are in alignment. But at level IIA the number of elements begins to be operative. Thus Jan equates two quite different outlines because each is composed of four matches. But breaking the matches or cutting the paper strips into unequal lengths leads to an item by item count of the elements, with complete disregard for their respective lengths!

The last two factors, being those concerned with privileged segments and the number of elements, both stem from faulty subdivision, overall length being either determined by privileged elements or regarded as a collection of segments independently of their individual lengths. On the other hand, the first two factors, which relate to the part played by end-points and detours, point to a lack of differentiation, first as between intervals and the order of end-points, and second, as between change of spatial position and the physical correlates of movement (speed or time). Change of position is looked upon as merely a change of order, while initially, kinetic notions of speed and time are independent of these considerations.[1] Hence the lack of differentiation shown in these intuitive notions is essentially due to the failure to integrate relations of order with those of interval. Since errors in subdivision are themselves errors of interval relations, all of the factors accounting for non-conservation may be subsumed within the general problem of differentiation and coordination as between interval and order relations. It is true that, at lower levels of thinking, length and distance are heterogeneous notions because the latter concerns intervals of empty space while the former is an attribute of solid objects, and is not yet recognized as having the characteristic of an interval. But this is not true at the operational level, because parts of objects resemble relations of interval in that they are symmetrical and form nesting series. The problem of conservation of length is therefore one of integrating notions of intervals (parts of objects) with those relating to order and change of position. Hence, whether the question is one of length or one of distance, the difficulty at the initial levels, I and IIA, always results from the lack of coordination between subdivision and order.

A series of objects in linear formation can be viewed either as a

[1] Cf. *Les notions de mouvement et de vitesse chez l'enfant*, ch. VI et seq.

nesting series of parts, each successive part containing all those that precede it and being itself contained in that which succeeds it, or as a set of intervals between ordered points. Adding the first segment a to the next a' yields $a + a' = b$; b itself added to the next segment b' yields $b + b' = c$, etc. Understanding conservation of length is a matter of understanding that the sum $a + a' + b' = c$ or $a + a' + b' + c' = d$, etc. remains constant whatever the initial order of positions a, a', b', etc. and whatever the changes in that order. The problem is why subjects at levels I and IIA do not recognize these identities and how they come to regard them as necessary.

It is clear that these identities and the underlying conservations cannot be appreciated when there is no conservation of length. It was shown in ch. IV that at these levels even one straight stick is thought to grow longer or shorter when it is staggered in relation to another. Therefore in the series now being considered even the single element, a, a' or b' will tend to vary with the changes in position that follow their initial alignment. However, that point need not be laboured here. The problem of non-conservation of the overall length would remain even if there were conservation of partial lengths.

The difficulty for younger children lies in reconciling subdivision or interval relations and order of position or order relations. We may take a series of segments $a_1 + a_1' + b_1' + c_1' = d_1$ arranged in a straight line and another series $a_2 + a_2' + b_2' + c_2' = d_2$ arranged in a zigzag formation. When factor (1) is predominant, the subject merely notes that the series d_1 projects beyond the series d_2, or that its furthest extremity (which is also the further extremity of c_1'), is further than that of d_2 (which is also that of c_2'). He overlooks the equalities of the subdivisions and thinks only in terms of the extremities d_1 and d_2. Conversely, factor (2) may be predominant, as will happen in exceptional cases when the comparison lies between a series d_1 and another considerably longer series, for instance, g_2, so arranged that its extremities are in alignment with those of d_1. In such cases, particular detours are responsible for an apparent increase in the overall length of g_2. The sum of its parts seems longer than that of d_1 not because of the correspondence or lack of correspondence between component segments of the two series, but because of the arrangement of parts of g_2 in the shape of angles or bends. These detours, considered in isolation, suggest that movement of objects from one extremity to the other of the series will be more time-consuming. While factors (1) and (2) tend to a distortion of sub-division by considerations of order and change of position, factors (3) and (4) mean that order is overlooked because subdivision is faulty. Thus factor (3) consists in exaggerating the importance of particular long segments as compared with others which are shorter, while factor (4) consists in counting each element as a unit, regardless of its length. In both, there is faulty-subdivision which leads the subject to falsify relations of order and change of position in the series as a whole, and to neglect considerations of movement. In every case, subdivision on the one hand and order and change of position on the other are not synthesized and relatively undifferentiated. It is this lack of coordination between its two fundamental aspects which accounts for the non-conservation of a qualitative linear series. The above analysis leads to two important conclusions: first, qualitative conservation will appear as and when there is coordination of subdivision and order of position, and second, measurement of length will be possible when there is complete operational interpenetration between subdivision and change of position.

§2. *Sub-stage IIB: Intermediate responses*

Two levels of intermediate response may be discerned between non-conservation as observed at earlier levels and the operational conservation proper to stage, III. During the first of these, subjects oscillate between non-conservation and conservation without resolving their dilemma. During the second, however, conservation is achieved by a process of trial and error. Following are a number of examples:

JEA (6; 3) checks that two strips of paper are equal in length, and recognizes the equal lengths of two different L-shaped lines, one of which has equal limbs while the second has one limb more than twice the length of the other: "Are these two lines (experimenter runs his finger along them) the same length?—*Yes, because they're the same thing, because there are two bits.*— But why are they the same length?—*Because they were the same before and then you cut them and turned them round.*—And now (the longer limb of the second L shape is cut in half and turned so that the figure looks like a staircase with two right angles)?—*This one* (staircase) *is longer.*—Why?—*Because there's more paper, because you put a bit more on.*—Did I put any more on?— *No.*—If these strips were made into straight roads, would one be longer than the other?—*The same because they're the same bits.*—(This reply is verified, then the two straight strips are again altered, the first to form a broken line with acute angles and the other a line broken by two right angles.)—*That one* (right angles) *is longer because there's further to go.*—Why?—*Don't know* ... *because that path* (acute angles this time) *is longer and the other is shorter.*— But were the strips the same length before, weren't they?—*Yes.*—And now?— *Also ... Don't know ... No, that one* (acute angles) *is longer.*"

Matches in two straight rows each containing five: "*They're the same because there's five and five.*—And like this (straight row and staircase)?— *It's still the same because it's still five and five. It's still just as far.*—(One match broken and the bits laid end to end.)—*It isn't the same any more because you've broken one.*—But is one of the roads shorter than the other?—*Yes, that one, because it has seven bits and this one has five.*—And if I break more matches?—*It'll be longer still.*—And if I lay them out straight like this (two straight lines)?—*That path* (with broken matches) *will be longer.*"

112

Yo (6; 8). Two straight strips of paper known to be equal are altered to form L shapes, one with equal limbs and the other with limbs markedly different: *"That one* (unequal limbs) *is longer because the other isn't so far to go.*—Have I taken any bits away?—*No.*—Have I added any bits?—*No.*—And like this (the longer limb of the second L is broken to form another angle)?—*This one* (two limbs equal) *is longer and the other is shorter.*—Will these two little men (now placed at the beginning of each line) have the same way to go to the end or not?—*It looks as if they'd have the same way to go.*—Why?—*Because before they were the same way.*—And like this (two kinds of zigzag?—*It's the same way to go.*—And is one road longer than the other or not?—*Yes, that one* (with fewer turnings)."

MIC (6; 9) sees that two straight strips of paper are equal when laid parallel, and again says they are equal when laid penpendicular to each other: *"because these two paths are still the same size.*—And like this (shapes with equal and unequal limbs)?—(Runs his finger along the two outlines.) *That one* (unequal limbs) *is longer because this side is longer than the other.*—And if two little men walked along these two roads, would one way be longer or not?—*They're the same length.*—Why?—*Because they were the same before and then you cut them.*—Then why did you think that one was longer?—*It looks longer because this side is longer than the other.*—And like this (two zigzags with unequal segments)?—*They're both the same length because they were the same before you cut them.*—And now I've cut them?—*They're not the same length any more."*

REN (6; 2) differs from the previous subjects in that he no longer oscillates between non-conservation and conservation without reaching any conclusion. Both he and the next two subjects gradually decide on conservation. After seeing two straight strips of paper and noting that they are equal, he first denies that they are still equal when both are folded into L shapes, of which one has fairly equal and the other more unequal limbs: *"They're not the same length* (running his finger along them).—Aren't they the same distance to walk along?—*Oh, yes, because there* (one of the unequal limbs) *one's big and there* (the other limb of the same L) *one's little, and there and there* (two limbs belonging to the other L) *one's little and one's big.* (Reasoning based on compensating differences between paired limbs.)—And like this (two different zigzag arrangements)?—*No, not the same . . . Oh, yes, it's the same length because they were the same length before."*

PAU (6; 6), like Ren, starts out by deciding that the two L shapes differ in length: *"It's a longer road here* (indicating the long limb)." But later: *"No, they're both the same, because before the papers were cut they were the same length.*—And like this (widely different zigzag arrangements)?—*The same because they were the same before.*—Will they always be the same even if I go on cutting them?—*Of course."*

HEN (7; 2). Asymmetrical L shapes: "Is it the same either way?—(Hesitating.) *It's the same* (re-arranging the segments as two straight lines) *because you cut them.*—And like this (2 lines, each with two right angles but different segments)?—*That's a longer road and that one will have less far to walk.*—Why?—*Oh no: that one has a little corner missing; it would be shorter if it weren't like that* (= if the other side had not one section too many). *If they both walk together, it'll be the same way for both.*—Why?—*Because you cut bits of paper the same size.*—And like this (increasing the number of angles and the difference in length of segments)?—*Here it's longer because it bends* ... *Oh, no, it's the same because they were the same length to begin with.*"

The procedures used in the discovery of conservation of length are essentially similar to those which appear in the evolution of any other invariant in the field of mathematics and physics (logical and numerical collections, quantity of matter, of weight, etc.). The subject may return to the starting-point, either by overt action (like Hen who rearranges the segments in a straight line) or mentally ("they were the same to begin with"), or he may find that the transformations and changed relations are mutually compensating. However, this new dawn of reversibility in subdivision (straight line cut into segments) and in order and change of position (varying arrangement of segments) means that they are now increasingly coordinated. Thus a few subjects (like Jea) are led by changes in position to imagine that the number of subdivisions has actually increased, but then change their minds after mentally re-integrating the parts in their original whole. They thus effect a reconciliation between subdivision and change of position. Other subjects like Yo are misled by the number of angles, thinking that the strip has grown longer because of its change of position, and they change their minds when they remember that the individual parts are still what they were and only their arrangement has altered. Subdivision is now flexible enough to allow of confirmation by considerations of order and change of position and vice versa, where earlier, the initial irreversibility of both kinds of intuition prevented their coordination.

§3. *Stage III: Operational conservation*

The idea of necessary conservation, which entails the complete co-ordination of operations of subdivision and order or change in position, is accomplished at stage III. This stage was found to have been reached by one subject in ten of those aged 6–7, by half of those aged 7; 0–7; 6, and by three-quarters of those aged 7; 6–8; 6.

MAR (6; 2). Two strips of paper equal in length are arranged as dissimilar L shapes: "*They're also the same length. You cut them, but they're still the same size, only now they turn round.*—(Further complications added.) Is it still the same length?—*Yes, because you cut it, but it's still the same size.*—And like this (a large number of zigzags)?—*Yes, because before when they were straight, they were the same size . . .*"

CEL (7; 2). Shapes made up of two and three right angles: "*It turns round, but it makes the same length.*—(Paper replaced by matches.)—*It turns round but it's still the same number of matches.*—(More complicated outlines.)—*You've changed them round but it's still the same way.*—(A number of matches broken.)—*It's the same way because there's still the same number of matches. They're broken in half but it's still the same length."*

ALF (7; 6). Paper strips with angles: *"It looks as if this one is bigger but it isn't bigger. It's the same length because this strip was the same length as the other.*—(Various angular shapes compared with two segments at right angle.) —*The same because here there are lots of little paths and there there are two big ones, but it's still the same length.*—Why?—*Because they were the same size to start with. They stay the same."*

When subdivision is coordinated with operations of order and change of position, conservation is assured. Earlier it was shown that a series of nesting parts of the form $a + a' = b; b + b' = c; c + c' = d$, etc., is not initially subject to conservation. Not only will each part, a or a' etc. be thought to expand or contract as a result of change of position, but the overall lengths, b, c, d, etc., will be misjudged under the influence of the factors outlined in §1. These were the order of the positions of extremities, the number of angles, the role of privileged segments and the number of segments. In ch. IV, it was shown that conservation of segmental length was assured when notions of order and interval were generalized to apply to sites and not limited to filled space. The problem of conservation is more complicated when it concerns the overall length of a series which may be cut and subdivided in a variety of ways, because there tends to be mutual interference between notions of subdivision and re-union of parts and those of order and change of position. In other words the two kinds of intuitive behaviour are still undifferentiated and uncoordinated. Conservation of overall length depends on such differentiation and coordination, which can only be achieved at the operational level: inasmuch as they are differentiated the two operations are independent but because they are coordinated the subject can, if need be, draw on one to support the conclusions suggested by the other. The differentiation with which we are concerned is merely an extension of the growing differentiation between relations of interval and of order discussed in chs. III and IV. Differentiation and coordination are both impossible until the operations involved are related to sites. Thus Cel's remark, "You've changed them round but it's still the same way", implies this distinction between movable objects and fixed sites. By implication Cel refers both subdivisions and relations of order and change of position to a permanent system of fixed sites which is independent of movable objects. The beginning of stage III is marked by the simultaneous appearance of conservation of overall and of partial lengths. Both types of conservation imply a reference system. In the measure that this system has been elaborated, the subdivision and summation of parts give rise to invariants which are independent of their initial order and of changes in that order.

The explanation is simple enough. So long as a child does not base his judgments on a system of references external to the objects being judged (e.g. the table or card on which the test objects are set out) his estimates of interval and length are necessarily a function of the order of end-points. The end-points may be the extremities of individual segments or those of the overall series which he is asked to judge. Consequently subdivision (or the nesting of intervals or partial lengths) is undifferentiated from intuitions of order which are given by the relations between extremities and vary with each re-arrangement of the objects. The result is non-conservation of length. But when he finds that he can base his judgments on an external system of references (the edges of the table or of the cardboard sheet on which the test-objects are arranged) he relates nesting intervals as well as positions and changes of position to a comprehensive spatial framework which is no longer limited to the varying configurations of the test-objects. He now argues in terms of sites which function as fixed reference points. Therefore he is able to differentiate subdivision and relations of order (including change of position), and the operational conservation of length is assured.

Both operations (subdivision and ordering) are still at a qualitative level, and their mutual coordination which follows automatically on their differentiation means simply that they are complementary. Consideration of subdivision suggests that of order of position and vice versa, but when one is active the other is dormant; they do not function simultaneously as a complex grouping. Measurement, however, implies the complete fusion of subdivision and change of position, which is why there is a slight time lag between the level of qualitative conservation of length and the achievement of metrics.

SECTION II. MEASUREMENT OF LENGTHS

The previous section showed how operations concerned with subdivision and the summation of parts are at first undifferentiated from those involving order and change of position, and how the resultant instability of nesting series brought about the non-conservation of length. The achievement of both kinds of grouping, subdivision on the one hand and order or change of position on the other, led automatically to conservation because both the parts and their sums had become independent of their order and of changes in their order. However the analysis of spontaneous measurement (ch. II) showed that operations of measuring consisted in a synthesis of generalized subdivision (selecting a unit-length) and change of position (applying a unit length).   The next problem must therefore concern the relations between this eventual synthesis and the differentiation and coordination of complementary qualitative groupings.

The technique is a direct extension of that used already. The subject is again asked to judge between strips of paper in a variety of linear arrangements, involving right-angles, acute angles, etc., but these are now pasted on cardboard sheets. When he has given his replies, saying they are equal or that one is longer than the other, he is shown a number of movable strips and asked to verify his judgment: "Have a look with this and see if you're right. Try and measure", etc. Later, he is given short strips of card 3 cm., 6 cm., sometimes 9 cm. long (these lengths corresponding with those of segments on the mounted strips). The experimenter himself may apply the 3 cm. card two or three times along the mounted strips, beginning with the point of origin, and explain that a little man is walking along a road and these are the successive 'steps' he takes as he walks. Thus the idea of measurement is given in terms of 'steps' and the subject is simply asked to finish by himself what he has been shown.

§4. Levels I and IIA: Comparison by various procedures before transitivity and measurement

It is difficult to isolate each successive type of response, as was done in the earlier study of spontaneous measurement, when using a technique which consists in suggesting various ways of measuring and providing the means to carry them out. However the analysis of ch. II is sufficient in that connexion and the present technique was devised specifically to study the role of conservation of length. Levels I and IIA show a mixture consisting of a wide variety of responses which have only negative characteristics in common. The construction of a unit of measurement is impossible and the same is true even of qualitative operational transitivity in using a common term.

PER (4; 0) still uses visual comparison to the exclusion of all other procedures, a characteristic of stage I (from 2 till about 4 years of age). When shown various linear arrangements, he makes judgments of longer and shorter by simple inspection and rejects all the strips of paper and cards he is given to measure with: "Can you be quite certain just by looking?—Yes.—Doesn't it help to put this on there and this on there?—No.", etc. The 'steps' procedure fails completely.

GUS (4; 11). An L-shaped line with limbs a and b (b > a) compared with a V-shaped line with limbs a' < b', but a' > a. "That's a longer way.—Can you make sure (offering a strip of paper)?—Yes (laying the strip along a') It's smaller (i.e. the strip is shorter than a'. Then Gus lays it along a:) It's bigger (i.e. the strip is longer than a). This path is longer (examining it in detail, to see if he is right; Gus has no confidence whatever in his measuring).—Isn't there a better way of seeing if you're right (offering a 3 cm. card)?—(He slides the measuring card along the line, as if it were a little man walking.) Yes, it's bigger.—Could we find out how many steps the little man will take? Look: one step, two steps, three steps (applying the unit measure and marking each limit with a point).—(He slides it along again, but with a vague suggestion of stages and putting his points in at random.)—And on the other line.—(He does the same on the first shape.)—Do these steps help you in finding out if it's longer?—*No.*—Then why did you do that?—*Because he goes along.*"

PIE (5; 6): "Will you measure these two lines?—*Yes* (he runs his finger along them).—But couldn't you do it just a bit better?—*Yes* (he spreads his fingers and applies them to the two lines, but with complete lack of precision). —Look: we'll find out how many steps he'll have to take (demonstrating the first three and marking their limits).—(Pie continues but without taking any notice of the end-point reached at each step. In effect he merely imitates the movement instead of applying a unit measure by summating equal subdivisions.)"

OD (6; 1) thinks that a line which measures 7 units and is made up of a long straight segment with a short one perpendicular to it is longer than another line, also of 7 units but with an acute angle. He is offered a 6 cm. card with the words: "Look: use this and tell me if the two lines are the same length.—(He slides the measuring strip along the lines without measuring them.) *That one* (with right-angle) *is longer.*—And if this little man takes steps along it like this (demonstrating the first three steps)?—(He continues the length of the first outline but ignores the other.) *Yes, it's longer.*—And that one.—(He does the same against the other, but ignores the limit reached at each 'step'.) *The first one is longer.*" He is now shown two more lines of which the first has six large segments, three of them being equal in length, while the second line is shorter and bent at right angles. Od takes the large measuring strip and applies it to three segments in the second line without considering the first. "*This line is shorter.*—Why?—(He lays the large strip against the long segments on the first outline.) *This one is big because it has six strips* (six unequal segments).—Are the strips the same size?—*No.*—Do they all count the same?—*Yes.*—Doesn't it make any difference if some are bigger than others?—*No, that one is bigger because it has six steps.*—(The experimenter draws two straight lines one made of six short segments, the other of six long ones.) Which of these is bigger?—*That one is smaller because the steps are short and here they're long.*—Then what about these lines (the test-lines)?—*That one is bigger because there are six steps!*" (A wasted explanation.)

BLU (6; 1) thinks that the outline of a set square measuring 7 units is longer than an acute-angled line measuring 8 units: "*It's longer.*—Will you make sure (strip of paper)?—(he applies it to the long segment on the first figure.) *That one is bigger.*—Is that enough? Isn't there something else you should do? —*No.*—What did this paper tell you?—*That that one* (the first outline) *is bigger.*—Shouldn't you do something with the other one to find out which is bigger?—(He lays another strip of paper on one of the segments of the other outline.) *Yes . . . It's smaller because the paper is shorter* (having failed to compare the two strips of paper and even to measure the second segment on each shape)."—The experimenter now produces the unit-measure and demonstrates how the little man would take the first two steps along the first line: "Look, one step, two steps. Couldn't we find out this way if one road

118

is longer?—*Yes* (he continues). *Three steps, four steps. It's the longer one.*—Can you tell that already without measuring the other?—*Yes.*—Supposing you tried it there (second outline).—(He moves the unit measure along it, and then puts pencil marks in arbitrarily without ensuring that the intervals are equal.)—How do these pencil marks help?—*Because they mark it, and then you can tell he's walked.*—Do they help you to know whether one of the roads is longer?—*Yes. Here there are three points* (first outline).—And here (second outline)?—*Five.*—Then which one is longer?—*This one* (the first). —Why?—(No reply)."

MAR (6; 2). Two L-shaped lines both measuring 8 units, but one with nearly equal sides, the other very unequal. "*That one* (the first) *is bigger, because it has two long sticks and that one has a long one and a short one.*— (He is given the choice of three measuring strips 3 cm., 6 cm. and 9 cm. in length.)—(He lays the 9 cm. strip along the long segment of the second L, the 6 cm. strip along one segment of the first L and the 3 cm. strip along the short segment of the second L.) *There.*—Does this help you to find out if one road is longer than the other?—*Yes: that one* (the first) *is longer.*" He is then offered the unit measure and shown how the steps are taken. Mar applies it and tries to count, but the limits and intervals remain arbitrary: "Would it help you to have several?—*Yes* (he covers both lines completely with unit cards and without counting them, says:) *That one is bigger. That's all I can say.*"

DOR (6; 4) compares two lines which are equal in length one being broken by a right, the other by an acute angle. He is shown how to measure by applying a unit measure, i.e. using the 'steps'. Dor continues with passable accuracy, counting the steps: "*Six steps. It's bigger! Should I do it on the other one too?*— But how can you tell that one is bigger if you haven't tried it out on the other? —(He now measures the steps on the second path, but less accurately, adds a few arbitrary marks in the middle of the steps which seem too long and then counts them). *Nine steps. It's that one which is bigger!*"

REN (6; 3), comparing two shapes bent at right angles, applies the unit measure, counting each step as he moves the card, but without marking the limit reached at each step. The experimenter shows him how to mark these points with a pencil and he repeats the process, though inaccurately. Later he refuses to measure two slightly more complex shapes because he confuses the steps with the visible segments which are obvious: "*On that one there are three big steps and three little steps. It's longer.*—Try the cards anyway.—(He puts unequal cards along each of the two paths and says:) *Six and four!*"

ARI (7; 2) also applies measures of different sizes along the two outlines. Finding that the cards on the second outline do not quite cover it he says: "*That one is bigger because it has that bit over* (= the remainder which has not been measured!)"

LOU (7; 8) measures two broken lines by "steps" as demonstrated: "*That one is longer because there are more steps here.*—Very good. How about these (outlines made up of six and four segments)?—*That one is longer* (counting the segments).—Are all the steps the same?—*No some are big and some are little.*—Do the big ones and the little ones count the same?—*No.*—Can you measure them?—(He applies the 3 cm. units to the first outline and the 6 cm.

units to the second.) *Ten steps here and four steps here. That one is longer.*—
Are these steps the same size?—*No, some are big and some are little.*—Can
you measure this one with little ones?—*Yes* (applies the smaller unit). *Nine
here and eight here.*—Well?—*There's one step less to go here, so it's smaller.*—
Could you find out by using big steps just as well?—*Yes, if he takes big steps
they're both the same.*"

These elementary responses to a measuring situation are quite unambiguous. They are also in agreement with all that has been learnt in
section 1 of the non-conservation of length at levels I and IIA. The main
reason for non-conservation was shown to be the lack of differentiation
between subdivision and order (or change) of position. Being undifferentiated, they are not complementary to one another and remain
uncoordinated. Hence they do not participate in the construction of a
single overall spatial framework which comprehends both empty sites
and the various arrangements of objects in space. In the same way, the
above illustrations, which show how and why children are incapable
of measurement, point once again to the lack of coordination between
the two varieties of intuition, for measurement demands their operational synthesis.

The present experiment does not deal with spontaneous measurement
(which was studied in ch. II) but with children's capacity to assimilate
procedures suggested by the experimenter. There is therefore less variety
in their responses. These may be classified under one of two heads.
Either there is change of position of the unit-measure without adequate
subdivision, or the object to be measured is subdivided, in which case
the unit measure itself is not applied correctly. If one were to compare
these responses with those of ch. II, subdivision without change of
position would no doubt correspond with the earliest kind of responses,
for it is based exclusively on articulation which is perceptually obvious
and on eye-movements ("visual transfer") which help the subject to
compare the two outlines. Conversely, change of position without subdivision corresponds with those imitative movements (leading from
"manual transfer" to "body transfer") which appeared when subjects
used their own body and its movements as an embryonic common
measure. But here, the techniques of measuring are offered ready-made,
the question being simply how far a child will be able to understand
and assimilate them, which must depend on his intuitions of length, and
in particular on the presence or absence of conservation. Therefore the
two types of response are contemporaneous. What they show is simply
that the child cannot coordinate his intuitions of subdivision and order
of position because the two are not sufficiently differentiated to be
complementary to one another.

Where there is change of position without subdivision, intuitions of
movement carry the day. The most elementary form of this response

is for the subject to run his finger along the two lines and make a motor comparison (cf. Pie's intuitive behaviour). In this form there is no subdivision whatsoever. Only slightly more advanced is the form which consists in transferring a succession of changes of position made with the subject's fingers. Here there is a beginning of subdivision. A slight advance on this consists in transferring a span or the width of two or three fingers: all these response types are limited because subdivision is still approximative, there being no definite marks to guide it. It is remarkable that when the experimenter offers the subject a set of cards which could be used as units of measure, or as general common measures, the same responses appear once more. Gus (4; 11) slides the card along the line as he might have done with his finger, and then, when the experimenter has demonstrated how the steps should follow one another, he slides it again, this time in irregular stages, and then puts pencil marks arbitrarily to show the limits reached by these successive segments. The same response is made by Pie, Od, etc. Evidently, when these subjects use change of position to help their judgments, it is always at the expense of subdivision, which is either altogether absent, or arbitrary in character.

In the second type of response subjects begin with subdivision and neglect change of position. Its most elementary form would seem to be exemplified by Blu, whose initial subdivision is incomplete, i.e. inexhaustive. He lays a strip of paper along one part only of a single outline, without even covering that part completely, and thinks this is enough to judge between two outlines. Later, he lays another strip along part of the second outline and again passes judgment on the relation between the two, still without comparing the two measuring strips or the second parts of the test outlines. What Blu calls measuring is simply comparing two outlines by splitting each one separately into privileged sections, without transferring these sections from one outline to the other or comparing them with each other. When, later, he is shown how to measure by successive steps, Blu counts steps of different sizes in the two outlines. Mar also measures the outlines by comparing parts of one with parts of the other as if measurement consisted simply in duplicating an outline by stressing the existence of parts and so assisting visual comparison. Because there is no change in the position of a common measure, the subdivision is internal to each outline and the only link between the outlines is provided by eye-movements. Thus Dor, having split the first outline into unit-steps asks with all innocence: "Should I do it on the other one too?". He has not realized that the role of a unit of measurement is that of a common measure, so that changes in its position allow an exact comparison between different shapes.

In the first type of response the subject merely moves the measur along the line, as if movement by itself were an intuitive guide to length, and subdivision were unnecessary, while in the second type the subject makes intuitive sub-divisions (i.e. without considering the overall length and with a false stress on perceptually privileged sections) but does not move the measuring unit from one segment to another or from one outline to the other. Either way, measurement is obviously impossible. These response-types show clearly that measurement must begin with the synthesis of change of position and sub-division, which means (1) that for a middle term to be a common measure, it must be moved from one outline to the other, and (2) that one section must be applied to other sections (and equated with them by congruence or substitution, and so take on the role of a unit of measure.

(1) The absence of any idea of a common measure, at the initial level, is abundantly clear from the foregoing responses. It follows directly from non-conservation. Measurement begins with the comparison of A and B by means of an intermediary M, which can be expressed as: $A = M$; $M = B$; therefore $A = B$. This transitive composition entails that M is equated first with A and then with B, and this can only be done by moving M from A to B. At this stage there is so little differentiation between subdivision and order of position that A, B and M can be equated only if they have the same shape and the same position (in which case there is no need for a common measure because their equality is given by perception). If they differ in shape, their dimensions too may be thought to vary with the change in position. Therefore, at this level, children have no idea of a common measure, even aside from the construction of a unit. They do not move a middle term M from one to the other, and, instead, they measure A and B separately, because the change in the position of M would tell them nothing, as its conservation is not assured. Because subdivision and order of position are not differentiated, subdivisions are altered by change of position, and because there is no conservation there can be no operational transitivity.

(2) If what has been said is true of the relations between two shapes, it is true also of the internal relations of a single shape. Here, too, there will be no change of position and one section will not be applied to the remaining sections and used as a common measure to compare the various sections. True metrics depend on this intercomparison of sections, because the idea of a unit demands it. Let us imagine a figure A which is made up of sections a and a', and another figure B consisting of b and b'. If a child merely compares a and a' to two strips of card, m and m' ($m + m' = M$), notes that $a = m$ and $a' = m'$, and then applying m and m' to B, finds that $m = b$; $m' = b'$, he will deduce: $A = M$; $M = B$; therefore $A = B$. But this deduction does not imply a metric or even an extensive operation; it is simply a generalization of qualitative (intuitive) transitivity combined with operational com-

position and so ensuring conservation. True measurement by units involves comparing a with a' and only secondarily, with m, m', b, b', etc. This comparison must involve changes in the position of a, or its equivalent, which is transferred to a' etc., so that the sections are equated to one another or to their own second order subdivisions. This is what is meant by the synthesis or fusion of subdivision and change of position, because the *unit* of measurement is movable and equated with each subdivision, while in qualitative comparison the length of a part is compared only with the overall length of the whole. The operation of true metrics is expressed by the formula $a = a'$; therefore $A = 2a$, and not simply by $a < A$; $a' < A$.

At this level, the conception of a unit is still very remote. Children count subdivisions without caring whether or not they are equal, which is an essential condition of a unit. Thus Od, having learnt (not discovered) how to use the strip of card in order to mark successive 'steps' which the 'little man' would take along one of the paths, simply counts unequal segments on the other line as so many 'steps'. He admits that the steps are different ("some are big and some are little"), but counts them as if they were homogeneous units. Ron does likewise. Lou, even at 7; 8, measures the two lines with unequal strips, and admits the strips are not equal, but is satisfied that he can compare the overall lengths by simply counting the strips. He has so little idea of what is meant by homogeneous units that he maintains the outlines are different in length when measured with short cards, but they would be the same length if measured with 'big steps'!

Transitive composition is impossible because there is no conservation of length, and the use of a unit measure is impossible because there is no operational synthesis of subdivision and change of position. Non-conservation is the result of lack of differentiation between subdivision and positional change, and hence of lack of coordination between them. Conservation and transitivity are thus shown to be the first and essential conditions for the complete synthesis of subdivision and change of position as required by the notions of a unit and of true metrics. The findings of ch. II are borne out in what follows: transitivity is discovered before measurement, and the construction of a measuring unit is the final stage in the developmental process.

§5. *Sub-stage IIB: Intermediate responses*

While in ch. II the responses of subjects were spontaneous, here the subjects are being required to avail themselves of ready-made common measures and units. The problem is how far they can assimilate these intellectual tools at varying stages in the conservation of length. At levels I and IIA, subjects had no notion of conservation and consequently they failed to understand the concept of a middle term and that of a unit. At sub-stage IIB conservation is dimly perceived, and children at this level also begin to understand transitivity in a common measure, and later, even the role of a measuring unit. But their understanding is reached by a lengthy process of trial-and-error and falls short of operational composition. It is interesting to observe that a glimmering of transitivity appears at a level when the idea of a unit is totally absent, as is apparent in the first two examples.

CLAU (6; 2) compares a line shaped like a set square with another made up of five equal segments at right angles to one another: *"It's the same length. —Why?—Because I can see.*—Could you make sure by using this? (The experimenter shows him how to make 'steps' and he takes the card.)—*One, two,* etc. (continues to count on A up to five, and applies the same technique to B without further prompting). *They're the same."*

However, although the suggestion leads to an understanding of transitivity, the idea of a unit is still absent. Two other outlines are produced, and Clau is offered the choice of a 3 cm. card and one of 6 cm. Clau uses the 3 cm. card to measure one outline and the 6 cm. card to measure the other, concluding: *"That one is smaller.*—Why?—*Because the steps are shorter.*—Can't you do the journey in big steps?—*Yes.*—Well?—(He now measures the first line with the 6 cm. card.)—Is it shorter?—*It's the same.*—How many of these steps (3 cm.) are there in this (6 cm.)?— . . . —Look. (Experimenter places two 3 cm. cards on one of 6 cm.) Now if you measure this line (the first shape) with this (3 cm.) card, will it be the same as the other or smaller?—*Smaller."*

JAC (6; 3) also applies the technique to the second shape without further prompting and concludes that the two shapes are equal. But he too shows failure to grasp the idea of a unit and his notion of transitivity is still intuitive. He measures two more lines using a 3 cm. card for one and a 6 cm. card for the other and concludes that the latter is *"shorter.*—Why?—*Because there are fewer steps.*—Look. Are some of the steps big and some of them little?— *Yes.*—Well?— . . . —(The experimenter lays two 3 cm. cards on one of 6 cm.) Do you see?—*Yes.*—Then are these roads the same length or not?—*No. That one's shorter."*

GIS (6; 5) is beginning to see the role of a unit. He starts by sliding the 3 cm. card along the two lines which he is required to measure, as was done at earlier levels: "Can you tell that way?—*No.*—What should you do?— *Count the steps.* (The first two steps have been demonstrated earlier.)—*Try.*— (He measures five steps on the first line and then six on the second without further prompting.) *This road is longer.* (Showing an understanding of transitivity.)—And these two (the outline shape of a staircase with some long segments and others short, and another shaped like the teeth of a saw)?—He measures the second shape with the 6 cm. card and moves to the first but finds that his card is too long for the short segments. He ignores this, puts in arbitrary marks and says:) *Six and six: it's the same.*—Are you sure?— *Quite sure.*—Are all the steps the same size?—*No.* (He measures them once more, this time counting two short segments for one long one.)—What are you doing?—*I'm counting this as half.*—Do you think it's exactly half?— *Yes, I've seen it is* (he applies the unit inaccurately on two segments which are not in immediate succession). *That makes one* (which he 'saw' perceptually, but cannot yet verify by measuring)."

EAN (7; 3) is transitional between level IIB and stage III. He compares two broken lines each consisting of two segments, and judges by eye that the larger segment of the first is equal to the larger segment of the second but that the smaller segments are unequal: *"There and there* (larger segments) *it's the same, but this* (shorter segment on second line) *is bigger than this, so this one is larger.*—Can you measure like this (one step, two steps, etc.)?—(He continues, measuring both lines.) *It's four and five: this road is longer.*—What about these two (two saw-edge shapes)?—(He measures one with the 3 cm. card and the other with the 6 cm. card.) *One is 6 and one is 4. Here it's longer.* —Doesn't it make a difference that the steps aren't all the same?—*Oh yes, that's right.*—What should you do?—(He measures both with the 3 cm. card.)—And what about these two (two more outlines)?—*Here it's bigger, because there are more turnings.*—(He is offered the 3 cm. card and the 6 cm. card and measures both with the 3 cm. card.) *That's 8 and this is 7* (correct).— And with the other?—(He uses the 6 cm. card to measure one outline and the 3 cm. card to measure the other.) *That's 4 big ones here and 7 little ones there.* —Well?—(He compares the two measures without prompting.) *That* (6 cm.) *makes two like this.*—Well?—(Counts in 3 cm. units:) *That makes 8 and 7.*"

These intermediate responses are marked first by the growth of coordination, and later, by the beginnings of a synthesis of subdivision and relations of order and change of position. When the subject is asked to apply a card in successive steps, he is now able to break up the path into successive segments, and can move the standard card in a definite order, relying on reference marks which are fairly accurate. The initial demonstration helps the subject to achieve a measure of coordination and to understand how to use a common measure. At an age when, left to himself (ch. II), he would be using his own body as a middle term the present experimental procedure enables him to realize in some measure the transitivity of relations of equality or inequality. However this learnt understanding does not immediately lead to subdivision in terms of homogeneous units. Both Clau and Jac count 'steps' without caring whether they are of equal sizes, and Clau still believes that two shapes can be the same size measured one way and different sizes measured another way, which points clearly to the intuitive and pre-operational character of his understanding of transitivity. Gis and Ean, on the other hand, very nearly understand the function of a unit of measurement, but they achieve this only by a gradual process of trial-and-error. They are on the verge of operational composition but cannot be said to have mastered it.

§6. *Stage III: Operational measure*

With coordination between subdivision and order of position, conservation of length is achieved. The operational fusion of subdivision and change of position now becomes a possibility. It takes the form of systematic measuring, but there is a slight time lag before this is achieved. While conservation, and hence qualitative transitivity, are achieved at a mean age of $7\frac{1}{2}$, measurement in its operational form (i.e. with immediate insight and not by trial-and-error) is only achieved at about 8 or $8\frac{1}{2}$. The time lag is particularly interesting because here the technique of measurement is demonstrated to the subject and not left entirely to his initiative as in ch. II. It confirms the hypothesis of a difference in kind as between qualitative operations and those which are truly metrical.

Au (7; 4) compares two broken lines each made up of two linear segments: *"This road is longer because this bit is the same as that one* (the two larger segments) *and that one is bigger than this one* (smaller segments).—Are you sure?—Yes, quite sure* (he measures with his finger without prompting).— Here (strip of paper), see if you're right.—(He finds the length of one of the longer segments, marking it on the paper, and then applies it to the corresponding segment on the other line.) *It's the same.* (He then measures the larger of the remaining segments and applies it to the other, showing the discrepancy.) *It's much bigger."* Two more shapes are produced one of which has more zigzags than the other: *"That one is bigger.* Why?—*Because the line would be longer if it were straight.—*Why?—*Because it has more lines* (= segments) *and that one has fewer.—*How many?—*3 and 5.*—Are they the same size?—*No, not quite* (he measures). *This line is twice that* (continuing). *That makes 5 and 6* (units)." He is now shown a fresh pair of shapes together with the 3 cm. and 6 cm cardboard strips. He measures the segments of one shape which are unequal: *"Oh, two of these things* (= segments) *make a big one, and this* (3 cm. unit) *is half of that* (6 cm. unit)." He goes on to discover that one of the lines is longer because it measures 3 units and 3 half units as against 4 units.

Xav (7; 9). Two lines broken by acute angles: *"That one is bigger.*—Are you sure?—*I have to see the difference* (taking a strip of paper with which he measures them and then showing the difference).—And these two (outlines shaped like staircases with unequal segments)?—*That one is longer.*—Are you quite sure?—*I have to make certain.* (Given the 3 cm. and 6 cm. cards, he measures the long segments with the 6 cm. card and the shorter ones with the 3 cm. cards.) *That's half* (putting a mark half-way down the 6 cm. card). *That's 5 against $3\frac{1}{2}$* (correct)."

Wil (8; 2). Initial responses the same. He is given two broken lines with unequal segments and applies the 6 cm. and 3 cm. cards on a number of segments, then says: *"This way is longer.*—Why?—*The three little lines make one and a half* (6 cm. units) *and then there are three big lines.*—How could you tell one and a half?—*Because I put the big measure there, it's just two little ones.*—How much longer is this path than that?—*Half a line."*

Col (8; 3) measures two broken lines with the 9 cm., the 6 cm., and the 3 cm. cards: *"I see this* (9 cm.) *is two of that* (6 cm.), *no, it's that and that* (6 + 3)." He then selects the 3 cm. card as his sole unit of measurement *"because two little ones make one medium one and the medium one with a little one make one big one."* He then measures accurately each segment.

All these subjects have achieved operational conservation of length and initial demonstration was unnecessary. Their success is therefore not merely one of assimilating the demonstration of 'steps'; instead they are almost immediately able to use the standard measure without any explanation. Then, almost unhesitatingly, they compare unit lengths, and discover both that the small unit is a third or a half of the other, and also that the segments of the test-lines are likewise reducible to multiples of the 3 cm. unit. Subdivision is therefore generalized when it can be rendered in terms of a single movable unit. This generalization implies that it has become fused with change of position because the part which enters into each of the mensural wholes can only function as a unit by successive applications, i.e. through changes of position which are determined by precise reference points.

The ready-made standard measures used in this experiment together with the demonstration of 'steps' which a man might take along the test-lines might seem to lead inevitably to the idea of a metrical unit. Yet even in this situation a true understanding is reached only by subjects at stage III, who evolve the idea on their own. At earlier levels, the combination of suggestive material and demonstration brought about intuitions only, and although these were more advanced than those which had been realized in spontaneous measurement (ch. II), they still fell short of a complete operational handling of measurement. The present experimental conditions tended to obscure the difference between level IIIA (common measure without a metric unit, resulting from qualitative operational transitivity) and level IIIB (use of a metric unit). But they show a clear time lag between the achievement of conservation of length (itself an expression of qualitative operational transitivity) as studied in section I, and that of measurement as such, as analysed in the present section.

Chapter Six[1]

SUBDIVIDING A STRAIGHT LINE

THE study of children's spontaneous behaviour in a measuring situation (ch. II) revealed that the notion of a metric unit is evolved only at level IIIB and depends on the previous mastery of qualitative operational transitivity (level IIIA) and on the coordination of changes of position at the level of representation, itself a function of a system of references. The ensuing detailed analysis of that development showed that the coordination of changes of position involved in measuring and the elaboration of a reference system were alike impossible without conservation of distance and length. That conservation is therefore an essential condition of measurement, and in ch. III and IV it was shown that its achievement, both in respect of stationary distances and of the length of moving objects, was dependent on the simultaneous coordination of positional changes and sites. Ch. V then dealt with the relations between conservation of length, transitivity of relations of equality or inequality and the understanding of measurement. The method consisted in presenting problems of conservation of length and of measurement separately, using paired lines, some of which were straight and others bent. The aim was to lay bare the parts played by subdivision, or grouping of intervals, and relations of order and change of position, and to demonstrate their importance to the genesis of conservation and qualitative transitivity, and also to that of metrical units. The underlying unity of this development has been made apparent. On the one hand, the conservation of length was shown to be the product of coordination as between subdivision (or nesting interval relations) and order of position (i.e. relations of order and of changes in that order), (chs. III, IV and V). As a result of that coordination, these two qualitative groupings, which had previously been undifferentiated for want of external reference elements, now became complementary to one another, through a comprehensive reference-system. On the other hand, the measurement of length was shown to be the outcome, not of a complementary relation between subdivision and change of position, but of their operational fusion. Thus a metric unit was shown to be essentially a part which could be applied to the remaining parts of the same whole, through changes in the position of equivalent middle terms. The whole itself could then be expressed as a multiple of that unit.

However, in the last experiment, the subdivision was suggested to the

[1] Written in collaboration with Mme Renate Schaffrin-Kersten.

subject by the segmentation of the test-lines, so that the choice of a unit was to some extent imposed by the structure of the test-objects. That experimental procedure was dictated by the need to study questions of conservation. In order to complete the investigation of the development of metric operations, the next experiment reverses the technique. Children are asked to locate a particular segment on a straight line using a variety of measuring techniques which stand midway between spontaneous measurement, as studied in ch. II, and the deliberate suggestion of ch. V.

Given two straight lines $A_1 C_1$ and $A_2 C_2$ which may or may not be parallel, the subject will be asked to find a point B_2 along $A_2 C_2$ to correspond with a point B_1 on $A_1 C_1$ such that the segment $A_2 B_2$ equals segment $A_1 B_1$. The problem is similar to one discussed elsewhere[1] (which itself drew on the present findings) in which the subject was shown a given journey along a straight line and asked to show a journey of equal length on a broken line. However, apart from the fact that, here, both lines are straight, the central problem is different in the two experiments. The earlier study was mainly concerned with the dissociation of the idea of distance covered on a journey, which is an interval, from an insistence on the point of departure, and, even more, on the point of arrival. The present concern is the development of measurement as such. The study is complementary to that of the previous chapter and is not directed to the specific question of the part played by the point of arrival.

§1. *Outline of method and results*

Two straight lines $A_1 C_1$ and $A_2 C_2$ (or $A_2 D_2$ if the second line is longer than the first) are represented by lengths of string attached to nails. A bead is threaded to each and placed at A_1 and A_2, that is, at the beginning of both lines. The child is told: "The bead is a tram travelling along its track. My tram is going this far (moving the first bead from A_1 to B_1). I want you to make your bead do a journey which is just as long as mine, one the same length, etc. Now you see I'm doing this journey ($A_1 B_1$), how far will have I to go on your track ($A_2 C_2$) to do a journey the same length?" This is followed by a series of questions which are here presented in order of difficulty. However, it is best to begin by asking question 2 and not to revert to question 1 unless the subject shows that he cannot understand.

(1) The two strings $A_1 C_1$ and $A_2 C_2$ are parallel and identical in length (30 cm.). The various points on both lines are in direct alignment, so that to find B_2 the subject has only to show a point on $A_2 C_2$ immediately facing B_1.

---

[1] *Les notions de mouvement et de vitesse chez l'enfant*, ch. III.

(1b) Arrangement as before, but the subject is now asked to begin from the opposite end to the experimenter.

(2) $A_1 C_1$ and $A_2 C_2$ are again equal and parallel but they are arranged with a slight disalignment (about 10 cm.) so that A_2 is no longer in alignment with A_1.

The journey is shorter than the ruler provided to the subject, so that he can mark off a distance equivalent to $A_1 B_1$ with his finger and apply it to $A_2 C_2$.

(2b) As above, but the subject must start from A_2 if the experimenter starts from C_1, and vice versa.

(3) Arrangement as above, but distance A B is longer than the child's ruler (the threads having been lengthened to 50 cm.).

(4) As above, with A_2 staggered (to the right) in relation to A_1, but the two threads $A_1 C_1$ and $A_2 D_2$ are unequal in length.—Two variations may be introduced: A B may be longer or shorter than the ruler and the child may be asked to begin from the corresponding end or the opposite end to the experimenter.

(5) Three threads are used: $A_1 D_1$, $A_2 C_2$ and $A_3 D_3$. The points of departure A_1, A_2 and A_3 are not in alignment and do not form a straight line (e.g. A_2 may be more staggered than A_3 with reference to A_1). $A_1 D_1$ and $A_3 D_3$ are equal in length but $A_2 C_2$ is shorter.—Variations as in 4.

(6) $A_1 C_1$ and $A_2 D_2$ are unequal and not parallel. Any of the previous variations may be introduced.

Whatever the arrangement, the subject is free to use a wooden ruler (blank), a stick (also unnumbered), strips of paper (without lines or squares), threads of various length and a pencil.

Corresponding with the levels already discovered, the following responses were made to these six situations. During stages I and IIA, children immediately solve question 1 (but not 1b). In other words, they have no difficulty in seeing that two paths $A_1 B_1$ and $A_2 B_2$ are equal in length so long as the points of departure A_1 and A_2 are in alignment. But as soon as these are staggered, the children are lost. They do not know how to transfer the distance $A_1 B_1$ to the other string $A_2 C_2$ and they simply put B_2 opposite B_1, without worrying about the inequality of intervals so obtained. As we found in the earlier study (*Mouvement et vitesse*, ch. III) change of position is thought of only in terms of the point of arrival. Later, during sub-stage IIB, children solve question 2 intuitively (i.e. simply by looking at the two lines), and fail in accurate measurement, except when this is achieved by trial and error. At the beginning of this sub-stage they fail in the remaining problems, but later their measurements are empirically coordinated although complete operational understanding is still absent. Finally, at stage III all three relations are understood.

§2. Levels I and IIA: length of travel determined by point of arrival

The key feature of all responses at these earlier levels is that children fail to conceive of the length of a journey as an interval between the point of arrival and the point of departure but think of it only in terms of the former (cf. ch. IV).

MIR (4; 6). Quest. 2: "If you're going to make just as long a journey with your little train as I am with mine ($A_1 B_1$), where will you go to when you leave there (A_2)?—*Here* (opposite B_1).—Is that just as far as this ($A_1 B_1$)?—*Yes.*— Show me the journey I make and the journey you make.—(He indicates $A_1 B_1$ and $A_2 B_2$).—Which of these two journeys is longer?—*That one* ($A_1 B_1$). —Yes, that's quite right. Well make yours as long as mine.—*I don't know how.* —Look. This time I'm only going a tiny bit of a way (from A_1 to immediately below A_2). You do the same little journey with yours, the same length.— *But it's there already!*—(Problem 1 is now introduced.) You see I'm going from there to there ($A_1 B_1$). Where should you move to, to go the same length? —(Mir moves his bead correctly several times for different positions of B_1.)— (The experimenter now turns to problem 1b.) Now we're going to change the game. I'll do this ($A_1 C_1$), I'll go up with my little train and you go down at the same time (indicating $C_2 A_2$) but you must go the same length as me. Now I'm going from (A_1) to (B_1). And you?—*This far* (placing B_2 immediately below B_1).—Look, this time I'm only going a very small journey (putting B_1 very near A_1). What about you? How far will you go to do the same little journey?—*There* (again putting B_2 below B_1 which results in a large discrepancy between the distances covered $A_1 B_1$ and $C_2 B_2$). Which of us two has done a bigger journey?—*They've both done the same length journey.*— What if we both went off the same way now?—(Indicates correctly that $A_2 B_2$ is equal to $A_1 B_1$.)—That's right. Now you've made as big a journey as me. But watch what I'm going to do (the second string $A_2 C_2$ is moved a little beyond $A_1 C_1$, while keeping the beads in their original positions B_1 and B_2, so that $A_2 B_2$ is still equal to $A_1 B_1$). Are the two journeys still the same length? —*No.*—Which one is longer?—*That one* ($A_2 B_2$ which is now staggered in relation to $A_1 B_1$).—Why?—*Because it's longer.*—How do you know it's longer?—*Because you unhooked it.*—But they were the same before and they haven't been changed. Why has one suddenly grown longer than the other?— *Because . . . I don't know."* Finally, the experimenter sets out from C_1, slightly to the left, that is, nearer, and above C_2: "Look, I do this journey ($C_1 B_1$). Where will you go to do the same length?—*There* (putting B_2 below B_1).— But show me the two journeys with your hand.—(Indicates correctly $C_1 B_1$ and $C_2 B_2$.)—Well which is longer?—*That one* ($C_2 B_2$; yielding to the implied suggestion).—Can you make as long a journey with my little train?—*No.*— Why not?—*Because I'd have to undo the pins* (which hold the string).—Well, you can do what you like.—(He alters the pins and places $A_2 C_2$ immediately below $A_1 C_1$, then shouts:) *Now (!) my journey is longer!* (Showing he hadn't really believed this although he had measured them by hand).—And can't you do as long a journey with my little train?—*Yes* (placing B₁ above B₂). *It's the same length now!*"

MIC (5; 6) likewise, for problem 2 puts B₂ below B₁: "Is it the same bit of the journey?—*Yes.*—Why?—*Because it's got to be where the other one is.*— But look (showing him how to measure the distances with his fingers). Who's made a longer journey?—*You.*—Well, you do the same journey.—(He moves his bead beyond the point below B₁, but immediately brings it back, saying:) *It isn't the same: I've done more.* (He again puts it below B₁ and says he is satisfied.)" Problem 1: puts B₂ below B₁: "Why?—*The journey is the same size as yours* (which is correct).—And like this (moving one of the strings without interfering with the bead, which brings him back to problem 2)? Are these lengths the same (the experimenter indicating their extent with his fingers)?— *No* (he brings B₂ back below B₁).—And like this, which of us has done more of the journey?—*Both the same, because we're at the same* (point)!" The experimenter tries to make him measure with a stick but he takes account only of the points of arrival.

PIE (6; 3). Problem 2: "If I do that journey there (A₁ B₁), where should you go to do the same length journey?—*There* (below B₁), *it's the same length journey.*—What do we do if we want to find out if it's the same length?— *Because we think.*—How?—*Because if it isn't the same length, you've got to turn both of them round and the other's got to get to the same bit as the first.* (He moves the beads back to A₂ and a point immediately above A₂, and is surprised to find that point does not coincide with A₁!)—*The blue tram can't do the same journey* (B₂ A₂) *as the yellow tram* (B₁ A₁) *because the yellow one's string is longer.* (They are the same length but staggered.) But look aren't these two strips (A₁ C₁ and A₂ C₂) the same length?—*Yes, but one is further than the other.*—Well, then, if I do this journey (A₁ B₁) where do you go to do the same length journey?—*There* (B₂ below B₁).—Is this (A₁ B₁) the same length as this (A₂ B₂ below B₁)?—*Yes.*—How can you make sure?—*Because I know.*—You take these (rulers and sticks) and see if they help you to measure. —(He puts his ruler over B₁ and the point immediately below it on A₂ C₂. Finding that his bead is not exactly below B₁, he says:) *It's not quite the same. I have to push it back a bit* (adjusting the bead below B₁).—Show me with your finger all the way we've both gone.—(He does so.)—Do you think these journeys are the same length?—*No, that and that* (extremities A₁ and A₂) *aren't the same length because that one* (A₁) *and that one* (A₂) *are pushed here.*— Well, if I do this bit here (A₁—below A₂), where do you go to do the same length journey?—*It's there. They're both the same* (since the bead at A₂ is already below B₁).—But I've moved mine forward a bit, and you haven't moved at all.—*No, because this string* (A₂ C₂) *is pulled over more than that one.*—Now, listen carefully. You told me the two strings were the same length?—*Yes.*—That means we could have them like this (problem 1)?— *Yes.*—Now if I do this journey, where would you go to do the same journey? *There* (correct).—Good. Now I'm going to put the strings back where they were (problem 2). Is it still right (string moved without altering beads)?— *No. The yellow one* (B₁) *must be pushed back there* (above B₂).—And now are the two journeys exactly the same?—*No, because the two strings are different.* —But you've just told me they're the same length?—*Yes.*—What if I put the string like this ($A_2 C_2$ oblique: problem 6)? Now I do this journey ($A_1 B_1$): Where do you go to do the same journey?—(He looks at them and places his bead at B_2, a distance which appears equal to $A_1 B_1$, as judged by eye.) Good. But how can we tell if it's right? Is it exactly the same length journey? —*Yes* (studying them carefully). *But your train should come here* (above B_2, though $A_1 C_1$ is at an acute angle to $A_2 C_2$).—Why?—*Because like this the two journeys are the same length.*—But you told me these two journeys ($A_1 B_1$ and $A_2 B_2$ as initially placed) were the same, and now you push my train all the way here (above B_2): is that also the same length?—*Yes.*—How can we tell if that's right?—*We've got to measure from the yellow one to the blue one* (laying a ruler across B_1 and B_2).—And like this (with B_1 in first position), would that work too?—*Yes but you've got to put them this way* (B_2 now moved below B_1, which makes $A_2 B_2$ one fifth as long as $A_1 B_1$!).—And if we measured?—(He again lays the ruler transversely across B_1 and B_2.)—But are those two the same length ($A_1 B_1$ and $A_2 B_2$)?—*Yes, but in another way.*—What do you mean by 'in another way'?—*Because this string is like this and that one is like this* (indicating angular divergence. Of his own accord he adds:) *If the blue one went there* (to a point B_2 in alignment with C_1) *the yellow one would have to go right to the end* (C_1).—Would that mean they've done the same length journey?—*Yes.*"

MEY (6; 10) is slightly more advanced than the previous subjects and is nearing level IIB. Problem 2: "If I go from here to here ($A_1 C_1$, being the entire length of the string) where should you go to do the same length journey?—*From there to there* ($A_2 C_2$).—And if I go from there to there ($C_1 A_1$)?—*Like this* ($C_2 A_2$).—Very good. Now if I only go a little way ($A_1 B_1$)?—*There* (putting B_2 below B_1).—Is that just the same length?—*Yes* (showing alignment of B_1 and B_2).—And if I only go there (B_1 now in alignment with A_2)?—(Studies them and hesitates.) *You've got to take out the pins and move the string to the end* (re-aligning the strings).—But I've done this little journey (from A_1 to a point above A_2) and you've got to do a bit as long as mine.—(Moves his bead a little way beyond A_2.)—Is that the same length? —*No.*—Which journey is longer?—(He is torn between $A_2 B_2$ which projects beyond B_1 and $A_1 B_1$ which is obviously longer.) *That one* ($A_1 B_1$).—Then what can you do to make that one do the same length journey?—*We must move the pins* (eliminating the disalignment of extremities)."

Problem 1: correctly solved. 1b: "Now, we'll change it round. I go from here (A_1) and I go up, but only this far (B_1). You're going down from there (C_2). Where will you go to do the same length?—*There* (B_2 below B_1)— Which of us two has done a longer journey?—*It's the same.*—Show me with your hands who has done more.—*Me* (correct).—Yes, and what if you're going to do exactly the same bit as me?—*Then you'll go here* (C_1) *and me here* (A_2).—Listen. We'll both travel together. I do this ($A_1 B_1$). And you?— (Stops below B_1.)—Who's done more?—*Me.*—But you've got to do the same length as me. (The experiment is repeated several times and each time he makes the same response.) Now if we put it here (B_2 the same distance from C_2 as B_1 from A_1), would that be right?—(Hesitating.) *Yes* (accepting suggestion).—Can we measure them correctly with this (graduated ruler)?— (He takes it and lays it so that figure 20 coincides with extremity C_2: figure 13 then falls on B_2. He then lays figure 13 over B_1 without troubling to make the end of the ruler coincide with A_1 and says: *Yes, it's the same length.*" Finally problem 2 is reintroduced and Mey immediately places B_2 below B_1: "Is your journey the same length as mine?—*No, but I couldn't go any further because the string* $(A_2 C_2)$ *is in front of that one* $(A_1 C_1)$."

Three factors enter into these elementary replies, all of which are familiar from previous chapters and the study of estimates of a path of movement. The relations between them must now be examined in more detail. They are:

(1) Initially children judge inequality of length between journeys simply as a function of points of arrival.

(2) They do not think of lengths as coherent systems of nesting intervals (or parts).

(3) They cannot apply the same length twice and use measuring instruments purely as a means of verifying the alignment or coincidence of points of arrival.

(1) The problem of judging equal journeys illustrates more clearly than any other the initial contradiction between interval and order or between length and change of position. The facts reported in ch. III showed distance to be an (empty) interval between limits arranged in a given order. Initially, the intervention of solid objects in a previously empty interval brought about its non-conservation; at a later stage, distance was held invariant because there was composition of partial intervals and, more especially, because operations governing the order of position were eventually referred to stationary reference-objects and included both movable objects and empty sites within their purview. Next, the facts quoted in ch. IV showed length to be a (filled) interval between limits arranged in a given order. These might be the boundaries of an object the length of which was compared with that of another. Initially, there was non-conservation of length when one of these was subjected to a change of position, that is, when the order of its extremities was altered. Length came to be held as invariant when there was composition of partial lengths to form overall length, and when order and change of position were referred to fixed elements in a system of sites which might be empty or occupied at any time. Finally, the length of a path of movement, which has relevance both for the experiments of ch. V and for the present experimental situation, is an interval (or a segment of an overall distance) between successive positions of an object. Because the length of travel is a function of the positional order of points of arrival, its conservation and measurement is assured only when these are related to points of departure, and when both are linked to a system of references and fixed sites (now empty and now occupied). Moreover, intervals between points of departure and arrival must allow

of composition of parts, as given by their order of position and by changes in that order. Composition of paths of movement must take into account both the subdivision of intervals and the successive positions of moving objects. It entails a synthesis of all aspects of these two classes of operations (formerly, intuitions) as revealed in chs. III–V.

The foregoing examples of the earliest level of response show, first, the familiar predominance of intuitions of order preventing composition of subdivisions or intervals, and, second, an exclusive interest in points of arrival so that length is judged without reference to points of departure, let alone to the intervals between both. Subjects are asked to make "as long a journey" on $A_2 C_2$ as $A_1 B_1$: one and all, they move their bead to a point below B_1, irrespective of the staggered arrangement of A_1 and A_2 and regardless of glaring discrepancies between intervals $A_2 B_2$ and $A_1 B_1$. For these subjects, the length of travel is not an interval between points of departure and points of arrival. It is judged solely in relation to the order of these latter, that is, how 'far' one bead has moved as against the other.

This mode of response (which appeared again and again in the earlier study of movement) excludes any sort of measurement, because the latter must refer to the whole of each path, $A_1 B_1$ and $A_2 B_2$, and not merely to the coincidence or lack of coincidence of points of arrival, B_1 and B_2. Moreover, it leads to a contradictory judgment even at a qualitative level, because the part $A_2 B_2$ is judged equal to the whole $A_1 B_1$. For in the arrangement of problem 2, $A_1 B_1$ consists of two parts, a section extending from A_1 to a point immediately above A_2, and another which corresponds exactly with $A_2 B_2$. It is true that subjects do not judge distances as such but, rather, the order of points of arrival, but, both here and in ch. IV, they continually make false inferences about length based on these judgments. It is not that they ignore intervals completely, but that these are not differentiated from relations of order and change of position. Failure to differentiate springs directly from failure to regard points of departure as of equal importance with those of arrival and from the inadequacy of composition of parts.

(2) The experimenter moves his bead along the straight line $A_1 C_1$ from A_1 to B_1. As a result, $A_1 C_1$ is divided into two segments or partial intervals, a_1 ($= A_1 B_1$) and a_1' ($= B_1 C_1$), while the whole journey is represented by their summation $a_1' + a_1 = b_1$. The child is asked to find a similar partial journey, a_2 ($= A_2 B_2$) on a line $A_2 C_2$, representing a total interval, b_2; he must therefore neglect the interval a_2' ($= B_2 C_2$). To find a_2, he must understand the inverse operation, $b_2 - a_2' = a_2$, or at least he must be able not only to systematize relations of positional order (and change), but also to compose parts. The two kinds of composition are different because subdivisions or parts refer to intervals

while order and change of position refer to end points. At the same time they can be coordinated with each other. These initial responses prove that young children may have limited intuitions about both but they cannot coordinate them because they cannot differentiate them, and without that coordination, neither is complete in itself.

Children do judge intervals as such: they make estimates about distances and length, which constitute nesting series of parts. Their judgments are not confined to the positional order of extremities, as is clear not only from the facts reported in ch. III, but from sundry observations made in the foregoing sessions. Judgments of interval are made whenever children are asked to make an estimate by using their hands. Even Mir (4; 6), in these circumstances, admits that $A_2 B_2$ is longer than $A_1 B_1$, when B_1 is immediately above B_2 and A_1 is in front of A_2, although he is not sure about this until A_1 and A_2 are made to coincide: "Now my journey is longer!" he cries, quite forgetting that he has said it already only a few moments before. Again, both Pie and Mey agree that the overall distances $A_1 C_1$ and $A_2 C_2$ are equal in spite of their staggered arrangement (though Mey revises his judgment). Thus these subjects do not invariably estimate lengths by points of arrival, with consequences that are rigid; on occasion, when the experimenter insists on points of departure and intervals (e.g. by asking them to measure by hand), they take these into account also. However, though even young children may find it quite easy to think of intervals and even, however sketchily, of subdivisions, when the extremities, A_1 and A_2, and C_1 and C_2, are in exact alignment, these considerations do not help them to more articulated intuitions when the lines are staggered. Under these conditions, they conflict with intuitions of order, and subdivision is still undifferentiated from these instead of being distinguished yet coordinated with them. Staggering lines $A_1 C_1$ and $A_2 C_2$ demands a more complex subdivision than that entailed by two pairs of segments, $a_1 + a_1' = b_1; a_2 + a_2' = b_2$, to which reference was made earlier. To equate a_1 and a_2 (i.e. $A_1 B_1 = A_2 B_2$) two additional segments must be considered. These are, first, that part of $A_1 C_1$ which lies between A_1 and a point immediately above A_2 and which may be called O_2 because it is anterior to a_2 ($A_2 B_2$); and, second, that part of $A_2 C_2$ which lies between C_2 and a point immediately below C_1 and which may be called O_1 because it is posterior to a_1' ($B_1 C_1$). The complete subdivision of segments comprised between A_1 and C_2 then becomes: $a_1 + a_1' + O_1 = O_2 + a_2 + a_2'$. Subjects at this level cannot equate a_2 with a_1, and their corresponding remainders a_2' and a_1' because they fail to appreciate the equality of distances or empty intervals O_1 and O_2. In other words, they cannot compare differences which arise out of the staggered arrangement. To achieve this kind of subdivision they would need to order all the limiting points, including points of departure as well as those of arrival, and, within this system of order and change of position, they would need to take account of empty sites as well as filled spaces. Conversely, they could not achieve that articulation of intuitions of order without having also achieved a complete subdivision of intervals. The two classes of intuition are therefore both incomplete because they are not coordinated with each other, and they are uncoordinated because they are not even differentiated.

(3) The measurement of the two paths of movement $A_1 B_1$ and $A_2 B_2$ (or segments a_1 and a_2) demands even more than mere coordination of subdivision and order of position. It entails their synthesis or operational fusion as expressed by changes in the position of a unit-part, their equality being verified by congruence. It is therefore not surprising that subjects at this level are not only oblivious of the need to measure but also unable to carry out the operation involved. Some, like Mic, use the ruler only to verify the alignment of points B_1 and B_2 (which is reminiscent of subjects quoted in ch. II, §3 who measured the towers by linking their tops). Others, like Mey, apply the ruler lengthwise to $A_1 B_1$ but are content to verify points of arrival only without caring about points of departure!

§3. *Sub-stage IIB: Intermediate responses*

At level IIB subjects show an advance both in systematizing relations of order and change of position and in subdivision. They begin to coordinate points of arrival with points of departure and no longer judge the equality of distances only in terms of the former. They also begin to understand the composition of segments. These related developments herald the beginnings of measurement and enable children to evolve an operational notion of length at a qualitative level.

Of the following illustrations of responses at level IIB, the first two are intermediate and fall between sub-stage IIA and sub-stage IIB:

UDE (6; 7). Problem 2: "Where will you go to do a journey the same length as $(A_1 B_1)$?—(Moves bead first to a point below B_1, then a little further, and lays ruler oblique from B_1 to B_2.)—Why do you do that?—*Because there* (C_1) *it's further than there* (C_2) *and that's* (A_2) *less than that* (A_1), *so I've got to put my train there* (B_2) *instead of there* (below B_1).—(Experimenter now moves bead from C_1 to a new position B_1—problem 2b—: subject to begin from A_2.)— (Ude moves his bead near B_1, but a little short as if he had started from C_2, then lays his ruler obliquely across C_1 and C_2 and gradually moves it to the beads, trying not to alter its inclination.)—Why are you doing that?—*To measure the length.*—Show me your journey and mine.—(Indicates $C_1 B_1$ and $C_2 B_2$, saying:) *This* $(A_2 B_2)$ *is a long way, and this* $(C_2 B_2)$ *is a short way. You left that big bit* $(A_1 B_1)$ *and your train did that little bit* $(C_1 B_1)$, *so my train must do this little bit* $(C_2 B_2)$. *That's because it's like this:* (A_2) *is longer* (= less far) *than* (A_1) *and* (C_2) *is shorter* (= nearer) *than* (C_1).—(The experimenter

137

begins again from C_1): But you've got to start from the other side (A_2). You didn't understand before, did you?—(Moves bead nearer A_2.) *It's because you did this bit* ($C_1 B_1$), *mine must do this* ($A_2 B_2$, measures with fingers.)—Is that right?—*Yes.*—Can't you measure it better?—*No.*—(Experimenter measures with a stick, using two fingers to mark C_1 and B_1 and applies this measurement to $A_2 B_2$ with Ude looking on.) Is that right?—*No* (tries to measure himself, but marks only B_1, applying that mark to B_2 and ignoring points of departure!)."

MAN (6; 11). Problem 1 solved immediately. Problem 2: moves his bead below B_1 then pushes it beyond B_1 and indicates $A_1 B_1$ and $A_2 B_2$ using both hands: "*They're the same.*—Is there something you can do to make sure it's exactly the same distance?—*I can take the stick and measure.* (Takes a stick which is shorter than $A_1 B_1$ and lays it between A_1 and B_1 leaving a gap at either end. Ignores the point of departure and uses his hand to make up the distance to B_1. Applies the stick to $A_2 B_2$, again ignoring A_2. Applies hand measurement on near side of stick.)—Is that right?—*No, I must put the tram here* (below B_1). *No here* (advances it arbitrarily).—Right?—(Measures $A_1 B_1$ with a longer stick this time, still ignoring A_1. Lays the stick against the string and puts his finger opposite B_1. Applies this point against B_2, ignoring A_2 and says:) *This time it's right!*"

MAD (6; 10). Problem 3 (with strings staggered and equal as in problem 2, but longer, so that the rulers are too short for the journeys): "If my train goes from here to there ($A_1 B_1$) where will you go to do the same length journey, starting from there (A_2)?—(Examines the four points A_1, C_1, A_2, C_2, then puts his bead below B_1 and moves it on a little.)—Why do you put it there?— *I saw that that's longer* ($A_1 C_1$ staggered in relation to $A_2 C_2$), *so I moved mine in a bit because my journey* (to a point below B_1) *was shorter* (than $A_1 B_1$). —Is it the same length now?—(Measures with hands, by first holding them perpendicular to $A_1 C_1$ and then obliquely across to span $A_1 A_2$ and $B_1 B_2$.) *It looks as if my train has gone down further, but it's really right, because this* (A_1) *begins further* (= on hither side) *and that* (A_2) *only begins here.*—Can you make certain more accurately?—(Measures $B_2 C_2$ with his ruler, marking both limits, and moves the ruler to the vertical projection of these points on $A_1 C_1$, so that one mark falls between B_1 and C_1 and the other beyond C_1. He now moves the experimenter's bead to the edge of the ruler, then puts it back and looks at it, saying:) *This* (mark on ruler above C_2) *is outside that* (C_1), *because this bit* (C_2) *is further than this bit* (C_1) *and that* (B_2) *is further than that* (B_1) *also.*—Well?—(Lays ruler against B_2 but perpendicular to $A_2 C_2$. Compares distances, saying:) *It looks as if this train* (B_1) *is behind that one* (B_2) *but it isn't because the bit that's missing here* (from B_1 to B_2) *is the same as that bit there* (from C_1 to C_2). (Tries to verify his statement by laying his ruler from B_2 to C_2 but again fails to apply his measure correctly to $A_1 C_1$ and moves it perpendicularly.)"

"This time I'll start from there (C_1) and you'll start from here (A_2). Now I'm going to do this bit $C_1 B_1$ as far as here. Where will you go to do the same bit?—(Estimates the correct point for B_2 with reasonable accuracy and then uses the ruler to measure remainders $B_2 C_2$ and $B_1 A_1$. He then tries to measure $C_1 B_1$ and $A_2 B_2$ directly, but finding the ruler too short, makes a rough estimate of the remainder saying:) *It's the ruler and then this much* (indicating discrepancy)."

Problem 2b (with start at C_1 and A_2): Estimates the position of B_2 and moves bead, then measures $A_1 B_1$ with stick, and is about to measure $A_2 B_2$ but hesitates. Measures $B_1 C_1$ and is then at a loss what to measure on $A_2 C_2$: "What are you thinking about?—*Whether to move my train backwards or forwards.*—Where should you measure from?—*You started there and I started here, so I've got to measure from there* ($C_1 B_1$) *and there* ($A_2 B_2$: he does this successfully.)—Could you measure from there (A_1) and there (C_2) as well?—*Yes, you could look at it that way too.*—What about this one ($A_3 C_3$ forming a shorter line: problem 5)?—*Yes.* (Measures $B_2 C_2$ to form an estimate of the required distance $A_3 B_3$, ignoring the fact that this was correct when the lines were of equal length, $A_1 C_1$ and $A_2 C_2$, but is no longer correct when they are unequal, $A_2 C_2$ and $A_3 C_3$.)"

JEA (7; 2). Problem 2: Places B_2 below B_1 then moves it by eye to a position which is approximately correct. He then takes the ruler, measures $A_2 B_2$ and $A_1 B_1$, and adjusts B_2 accordingly.

Problem 3: "Now I'm going to do this long journey ($A_1 B_1$). Where will you go?—(Makes an estimate for B_2.)—And can you make sure?—(Lays one end of the ruler on A_1 and marks the other end with his finger, then applies the ruler again and finds that he can reach B_1 by duplicating the length of the ruler exactly. But in measuring $A_2 B_2$ he merely lays one end of the ruler at A_2 without marking the other end and then lays it opposite B_2, ignoring the point of departure. In effect his second measurement is clouded by the two unknowns: ($A_2 X$ and $Y B_2$.)—Is it right?—*Yes, I've measured it.*—And if I go back here (A_1), where must you go to do the same distance?—(He measures a segment from A_1 to a point above B_2 and $A_2 B_2$, saying:) *No, that's no good, it's too short here* (having forgotten that the lines are staggered).—Now look. We'll start again from here (A_1 and A_2) and I'll go there (B_1). Where will you go?—(Moves his bead to B_2 and now measures $A_1 B_1$ and $A_2 B_2$ correctly.) *It's right.*—Good. Now we'll start from (A_1) and (C_2).— (Moves bead to a point B_2 but again measures $A_1 B_1$ and $A_2 B_2$).—But do you remember where we set out from?—*Yes, there and there* (C_2 and A_1).— Are these the same distance ($C_2 B_2$ and $A_2 B_2$)?—(Hesitates: No reply.)— Well let's start again from here (A_1 and A_2).—(Measures correctly.)—And like this (from C_2 and A_1)?—Measures $A_1 B_1 = 20$ cm. $+ 4$ cm., then turns the ruler round and measures 20 cm. $+ 4$ cm. on $C_2 B_2$.)"

MIE (7; 4). Problem 3: Places B_2 below B_1, then moves it forward gingerly: "How shall we know if that's accurate?—I could take the ruler (which he lays against $A_1 C_1$ using A_1 as starting point but ignoring the other end; he then applies it again from an arbitrary starting point and notes that B_1 coincides with figure 6. He repeats the manœuvre against $A_2 C_2$, arranging it so that B_2 coincides with figure 6!)" Problem 2 (where the distance travelled is shorter than the ruler): locates B_2 with a fair degree of accuracy, then measures $A_1 B_1$ and $A_2 B_2$ correctly and adjusts B_2 accordingly.—The experimenter re-introduces problem 3 (where the distance travelled exceeds the length of the ruler): Mie begins by placing B_2 below B_1, then judges it more or less correctly. As before, he measures them without noting the limit reached by the first application of the ruler: "How do you know that the ruler came so far?—*By looking at it.*—Is there a better way of going about it?—*Oh, yes. I could put my finger on the string to show me where I should put the ruler the second time.* (He rectifies the error, and adjusts B_2 correctly.)" Problem 2b: $A_1 B_1 = C_2 B_2$ measured correctly. Problem 3 once more, this time with a long path of movement for $A_1 B_1$: he places B_2 where he thinks it should go, then measures $A_1 B_1$ (twice the length of the ruler) and $A_2 B_2$, "Would we get the same result by measuring the little bit at the other end $(B_1 C_1)$ instead of the long bit?—*Yes it's the same because this and this* $(A_1 B_1$ and $A_2 B_2)$ *are the same length.*—What about the two strings $(A_1 C_1$ and $A_2 C_2)$?—*Yes, they're the same too.*" But he continues measuring $A_1 B_1$ for all positions of B_1.

These intermediate cases are highly instructive. Ude and Man are less advanced than the others, and fail to achieve transitivity even at an intuitive level. Nevertheless their response shows considerable progress when compared with that of level IIA. (1) Instead of confining their attention to the point of arrival, they take the point of departure into account as well. This means that they are aware of the interval involved in change of position insofar as it represents a change of order. (2) That awareness leads to a second feature of their progress in that they begin to subdivide the line and relate the segments to its overall length. Ude, for instance, compares $C_1 B_1$ with $A_1 B_1$ and $C_2 B_2$ with $A_2 B_2$ and then compares the four segments in pairs. In other words he establishes a relation between the two paths of movement and the remainders ("You left that big bit"). Initially, the equality of $A_1 B_1$ and $A_2 B_2$ is established by a qualitative procedure. The ruler is used to reproduce the inclination of $A_1 A_2$ and $C_1 C_2$ between B_1 and B_2. Hence the segments $A_1 B_1$ and $A_2 B_2$ are equal because they form opposite sides of a parallelogram. Measurement is still absent. Instead there is one-one correspondence which heralds the logical multiplication of relationships (together with a beginning of intuitive extensive quantification). However, (3) their ability to conceive of changes of position in terms of points of departure and arrival and to subdivide with some intuitive insight into nesting relationships also enables them to imitate measurement when given a demonstration (Ude) or even to initiate it themselves (Man). But both these subjects show their immaturity by confining their attention to the point of arrival and ignoring the point of departure. This peculiar mode of response lasts practically throughout substage IIB. Thus the operational synthesis of change of position and subdivision is more complex than their individual coordination. Measurement, implying the beginning of such a synthesis, is as yet hesitant. Here earlier modes of response are still in evidence although they have been outgrown in problems of change of position or of subdivision taken separately and even in those which involve their qualitative interaction. More advanced subjects like Mad, Jea and Mie arrive at correct measurement by a process of trial and error. While Ude and Man are unable to synthesize the subdivisions and positional changes of a measuring object, Mad, Jea and Mie provide a demonstration in slow motion of how that synthesis is gradually achieved. In so doing, they pinpoint the details involved, and their successful response confirms the lessons that may be gleaned from the failure of Ude and Man.

Mad, Jea and Mie prove, by the manner of their responses, that they are fully capable of correct reasoning at a qualitative level. In evaluating changes of position they take account of the point of departure as well as the point of arrival, while they clearly understand that a total path of movement may be viewed as the sum of adjacent partial distances. But this insight is intuitive and lacks both the precision and the generality to admit of operational composition. Therefore, when required to measure, some subjects, like Mad, concentrate on the element of subdivision to the neglect of change of position, while others, like Jea and Mie, do the reverse. Only towards the end of the enquiry do all subjects achieve an exact standard of measurement by synthesizing the two mechanisms. Mad, who is over-impressed by the element of subdivision, responds as did Ude before he finally measures. He puts B_2 ahead of B_1 and uses his hand to ensure that $B_1 B_2$, $A_1 A_2$ and $C_1 C_2$ are all parallel. This reasoning fulfils exactly the twin requirements of change of position and subdivision. But it is still at a qualitative level and the organization of elements is an intuitive one. When he comes to measure, he uses subdivision alone and neglects change of position. Thus he measures $B_2 C_2$ instead of the distance covered by his bead, $A_2 B_2$, which shows that he understands that AB and BC are both parts of a nesting series AC. But instead of moving his ruler horizontally to compare his measurement of $B_2 C_2$ with $B_1 C_1$, he applies it to a section of $A_1 C_1$ and an extension vertically above $B_2 C_2$. As a result the limits indicated on his ruler fail to correspond with anything material to his problem. Though he evidently appreciates his quandary he cannot extricate himself from it by moving his ruler in a lateral direction along $A_1 C_1$, and instead, he begins to consider further subdivisions while still failing to synthesize them with change of position. Only after the experimenter reintroduces problem 2, which is easier, does Mad achieve such a synthesis and so gain an insight into measurement, although this is limited to the particular problem. Even this achievement is preceded by further-trial-and-error.—Jea and Mie show the reverse difficulty. They can move their rulers horizontally to coincide with points which are material to the problem, but their summation of successive intervals is faulty because their subdivision lacks coherence. They forget to indicate the exact points reached in successive applications of their ruler, and as a result, a portion of the distance is measured twice over. Because there is no clear demarcation of segments, change of position itself becomes crude, so that Jea and Mie think only of the point of arrival and ignore the point of departure. Only when Mie recognizes the need for precision in demarcating segments does he achieve a synthesis of subdivision and change of position, and so master the problem of measurement (in solving problem 3).

Thus, however simple it may appear to us, the art of measuring originates from a highly complex operational composition. Children cannot understand measurement until they can simultaneously subdivide a length into nesting segments and compare these segments with one another by change of position, either mentally or in practice. Before these operations are fused, subdivision can only be qualitative because positional changes are not generalized, and these in turn are qualitative because they are not accurately applied to partial segments. With operational synthesis (or with intuitive synthesis as shown at the present level) any two lengths can be expressed in terms of each other by using units and fractional parts. Length can therefore be rendered in terms of a series of equal intervals which can be applied to each other indefinitely, and space itself thus appears as a homogeneous *quantum*. Such a state of affairs is foreshadowed at the intermediate level IIB, while it is fully realized at stage III when operational thinking brings about an equilibrium to regulate notions which, at this level, are still intuitive in character.

§4. *Stage III: Operational measurement*

Subjects at stage II (level IIB) achieved the discovery of measurement only after a lengthy process of trial-and-error. Nor was the procedure generalized (e.g. from problem 2 to problem 3). The function of measurement was still only a secondary one. Measurement was used to verify a judgment reached on an intuitive basis, whether by visual estimate, or by using hands, etc. Thus metrical composition remains empirical throughout stage II. During stage III it becomes systematic and operational. The latter development shows two phases. Subjects at level IIIA achieve only a qualitative transitivity in their use of a common measure. Where the measuring stick is equal to the distance required or longer, success is assured, but when it is shorter, they simply prolong it by using supplementary lengths. At level IIIB, the newly acquired concept of a unit enables them to apply an iterative stepwise movement to a short ruler.

RAY (7; 10) illustrates level IIIA. Problem 3: He gradually moves B_2 beyond B_1, saying: "*I think it's right now.*" As the ruler is too short, he measures $A_2 B_2$ by using his hand as well as the ruler, then in measuring $A_1 B_1$ he uses a strip of paper to prolong the ruler, checking $A_2 B_2$ in the same manner, and so achieving an accurate reproduction of the distance given:

"We'll do a longer journey (B_1 nearly at C_1)." The subject thinks awhile, and begins to measure $B_1 C_1$. But he reconsiders the problem and proceeds to measure $A_1 B_1$ using every available prop (ruler, strip of paper, pencil) to achieve the required length by juxtaposition. Suddenly he drops this complicated method and simply uses the pencil to measure remainders $B_1 C_1$ and $B_2 C_2$: "(Experimenter:) Why do you do that?—*Because it didn't go all the way* (to C_1). *It left that little bit* ($B_1 C_1$), *and the pencil can do that.*"

Problem 4, with the strings unequal so that $A_1 C_1 > A_2 C_2$, a fact which he is left to discover for himself: $A_1 B_1$ is made to exceed the total distance $A_2 C_2$ so that it is impossible to reproduce it. "(Experimenter:) You do a journey the same length as mine on that string ($A_2 C_2$).—(Ray makes an estimate for B_2 then measures $A_1 B_1$ and compares the remainder $B_1 C_1$ with $B_2 C_2$. He proceeds to measure $B_1 C_1$ and $B_2 C_2$ and uses his measurement to place B_2. Thereafter he measures $A_1 B_1$ and $A_2 B_2$ by juxtaposing strips of paper, a pencil, etc. Finally he says:) *This journey* ($A_1 B_1$) *is longer than that* ($A_2 B_2$).—Can't you make it right?—*No, that* ($A_1 B_1$) *is bigger than this string* ($A_2 C_2$). *This string is longer* ($A_1 C_1$), *so I can't do the same journey.*—Good. Well let's have the strings as they were (problem 3 with the strings the same length).—(He measures $B_1 C_1$ using a strip of paper in prolongation of his pencil.)—(The experimenter adds a short length of string (problem 5) and moves his bead along $A_1 C_1$:) You do the same journey on the other two strings.—(He measures $B_1 C_1$ and transfers his measurement to $B_2 C_2$ to find B_2, then measures $A_1 B_1$, transferring the measurement to $A_3 B_3$.)—Why do you measure like this (remainders $B_1 C_1$ and $B_2 C_2$) the first time and like this (actual trajectories $A_1 B_1$ and $A_3 B_3$) the second?—*Because this string* ($A_1 C_1$) *is longer than that one* ($A_3 C_3$). *These two* ($A_1 C_1$ *and* $A_2 C_2$) *are equal but that one* ($A_2 C_2$) *looks longer because it's pushed over that way* (towards C_2), *but it's shorter there* (A_2).—What if I start from here (C_1) and you start from there (C_2)?—(Correct response.)"

Vod (7; 11) is a typical instance of level IIIB. Problem 2: Vod takes the stick of his own accord, measures $A_1 B_1$ and compares the measurement with $A_2 B_2$. "Good, now what if I do this long section (problem 3)?—*It's a bit harder but we've got this as well* (a strip of paper; which he stretches in prolongation of his stick to measure $A_1 B_1$ and $A_2 B_2$—a response at level IIIA) —Could you measure it with less trouble?—*Yes, like this* (taking the stick alone and applying it twice, leaving a fraction which he marks off with his finger).—What if I go this far (nearly to C_1)?—*Ah, then I make it easier still* (measures remainders).—What if I start here (C_1) and you start there (A_2)?— (Measures correctly by applying his stick several times.)—Could we measure like this ($A_1 B_1$ and $C_2 B_2$)?—*Yes, that's right also.*—What about this (problem 5)?—*You have to measure this* ($A_3 B_3$) *because the string is shorter.*"

Bed (8; 7). Problem 3: "*If you go there* ($A_1 B_1$) *then I must go here too* ($A_2 B_2$. He measures the distance by hand and then by ruler, using several applications.)—And if I put (B_1) near (C_1)?—(Measures remainders straight away.)—Why do you just measure that bit?—*Because it's the same length, the strings are.*—Now I'll start here (A_1) and you start there (C_2).—(Measures $A_1 B_1$ and finds it to be 17 cm.) *I can't start here* (C_2) *at 1, I have to start at 20. Oh no, I've got to turn it round like this* (reversing the ruler). *I start at 1 underneath and finish at 17.*—(Problem 5.)—(Measures $A_1 B_1$ and $A_3 B_3$ applying his ruler to successive segments.)—What if you measured this (remainders $C_3 B_3$ and $C_1 B_1$)?—*No, they're not the same size. This string is shorter so you can't measure from the end.*"

Children at level IIIB differ markedly from those at more primitive levels. They make less use of· intuitive perception and greater use of reasoning. The latter develops through a phase of qualitative composition to one of metrical operations. When this last phase is reached, earlier responses are also modified. Thus it emerges from them yet affects them retroactively.

At stage II, subjects move their bead by visual estimate and, unless specifically told to do so, they see no need to measure (unless it be by hand, cf, ch. II). Measurement, to them, is merely a check. At stage III, children will make a visual estimate only if the problem is too easy, and sometimes as an anticipatory response. The essential means of determining B_2 is now measurement. It is significant in this connexion that subjects at stage III invariably measure $A_1 B_1$, which they must reproduce, before measuring $A_2 B_2$, while those at level IIB quite frequently measure their estimate of $A_2 B_2$ and then compare that distance with $A_1 B_1$, to see how well they agree.

Again, at stage III, subjects faced with a fresh problem immediately apply any operational compositions they have just learnt, while those at stage II make what amounts practically to a fresh start with every question asked.

In order to ascertain the degree of insight into subdivision, questions were asked which bore on the relation between the distance travelled $A_1 B_1$ $(= a_1)$ and the remainder $B_1 C_1$ $(= a_1')$: could the subject make use of the nesting relation, $a_1 + a_1' = b_1$? At level IIB, subjects who fix B_1 by measuring $B_1 C_1$ do so because they find it easier to start from the nearer point C_1. They do not look on their solution as an indirect way of measuring $A_1 B_1$. But at stage III, children are constantly aware of the composition: $a_1 = b_1 - a_1'$. The difference in approach is shown in their response to problems 4 and 5, involving strings of unequal length. Ray's replies, and especially those of Bed, are in marked contrast with the wrong solutions given at level IIB (e.g. Mad, at the end of the enquiry).

Their handling of change of position is likewise different from that shown at level IIB. The latter represented an advance over previous levels in that subjects took the point of departure into account as well as the point of arrival: therefore, seeing that A_2 lay beyond A_1 they moved B_2 beyond B_1. However they did so only after first placing their 'train' below B_1, and seeing the resultant discrepancy. Such empirical trial-and-error behaviour is absent at level III (apart from a residual hesitancy shown by Ray) when points of departure and points of arrival are coordinated at once. In other words, subjects now move their bead immediately to a point which out-distances the experimenter's by the amount of disalignment existing between the two lengths of string.

The achievement of metrics at stage III depends on a twofold equilibrium between subdivision and order or change of position. The first phase (level IIIA) is marked by the successful handing of change of position where the measuring rod is equal to or greater than the objects to be measured. Where the measure is shorter, a number of objects may be juxtaposed to make up the length required, and the whole will then be used as a common measure and applied to the test objects. Thus, coordination is as yet qualitative, and this alone, together with transitivity in relations of congruence, is sufficient to yield: $A_1 B_1 = M$ (or a portion of M); M (or a portion of M) $= A_2 B_2$; therefore $A_1 B_1 = A_2 B_2$. Juxtaposition is expressed by: $A_1 B_1 = (M_1 + M_2 + M_3$ etc.); $(M_1 + M_2$, etc.) $= A_2 B_2$; therefore $A_1 B_1 = A_2 B_2$. Even such qualitative composition requires that either the measuring rod or the measured object be broken up in some way, and the subject needs to take into account the points of arrival and departure for each partial distance. The second phase (IIIB) is marked by the repeated application of a measuring rod, when this is found too short. Such iteration (M; 2M; 3M; etc.) constitutes a true metrical operation. However, all behaviour belonging to stage III shows a distinct improvement as against that of stage II in that there is no longer any overlapping of segments, and changes of position are applied to one or more measuring rods and determined by precise reference points. The twofold operation which consists in subdividing a whole and applying parts to each other seems so natural—because to us it has become habitual—that it might have remained unnoticed but for its non-appearance at earlier stages. We need to remind ourselves of the responses of subjects like Mad at level IIB who subdivide satisfactorily but fail to handle change of position in applying their subdivisions to another distance, and those of subjects like Jea and Mie, also at level IIB, who handle changes of position effectively but fail to determine precisely the limits reached by successive applications of a measuring rod. These responses indicate that the apparently simple behaviour of stage III represents a most difficult coordination (level IIIA) or synthesis (level IIIB) as between subdivision and change of position, by which their equilibrium is finally achieved.

There is nothing natural in subdividing a length where the parts are not perceptually given, nor is it natural to alter in thought the relations of positional order which govern a nesting series of segments as given to perception, in order to apply these segments to each other. In the present experimental set-up, AC is broken into the two portions AB and BC by the bead. Even here, subjects at levels I and IIA overlook the

145

whole, AC, and fail to regard the interval AB as a part. But it is quite another matter to break up AB into a number of abstract segments, as given by successive momentary positions of a ruler or a strip of paper. Moreover, such segments are at first indissociably linked with the line AC in which they occur, while measuring involves altering their position and applying them elsewhere by means of equivalent common terms. In other words, the subject must think of them not as concrete portions of $A_1 C_1$ but rather as abstract parts common to $A_1 C_1$, $A_2 C_2$, and also to the common measure. Such generalization involves robbing segments of all their material associations so that they may be common to all objects and infinitely mobile.

Thus measurement is increasingly removed from the qualitative properties of a part and likewise from concrete change of position, so that finally a part may be conceived as common to all wholes because change of position itself is generalized. This twofold generalization is effected in two phases: level IIIA, where there is qualitative coordination of subdivision and change of position, and level IIIB, where there is synthesis or operational fusion of the two, which yields a new kind of operation, that of Euclidean metrics, which comprehends both.

§5. *Conclusion. The Qualitative coordination of subdivision and change of position and their operational synthesis as shown in unit iteration*

A discussion of the precise relation between these two levels of operation should provide an apt conclusion to the present chapter and also to the second part of this work. However, it may be advisable to recapitulate briefly the chronology of levels IIB, IIIA and IIIB, as already described in ch. II and again in chs. III–VI, as the sequence of responses may seem a trifle complicated.

The study of spontaneous measuring behaviour in ch. II yielded a framework for the more detailed analyses of chs. III–VI. These were designed to lay bare the processes involved in the construction of invariants of length and distance and at the same time to analyse the elaboration of measuring behaviour in more structured experimental situations. Nevertheless the matrix provided by ch. II was found sufficient for the findings of these more detailed investigations. At level IIA spontaneous measurement is limited to 'manual transfer', whereby the objects being compared are brought together by hand. Level IIB sees the first appearance of a common measure, and this takes the form of the subject's own body which is used as a middle term between the objects. Such behaviour, termed 'body transfer' shows a beginning of intuitive transitivity. The transitivity is more pronounced at the intermediate level which follows, when a third object, which imitates those under comparison and is of comparable size, may be used as a transitive middle term. At level IIIA, the middle term may be larger than the model, and transitivity has become operational by virtue of the precise handling of qualitative relations of equality (congruence). These in turn depend on the coordination of subdivision and change of position.

The above sequence provided the framework for the studies of chs. III and IV, these being concerned, first, with the conservation of distance (empty intervals) and the effect of the intercalation of fresh elements, and second, with the conservation of length (filled intervals) and the effect of moving the test objects. In both enquiries, conservation was absent at levels I and IIA, at level IIB it was dimly perceived, while at level IIIA it appeared in an operational form. This last was seen to be dependent on the coordination of operations of subdivision and change of position at the qualitative level, and this in turn implied their extension from the linear dimensions of movable objects to those of fixed sites. Yet this coordination still falls short of metrics because the two operational systems are as yet qualitatively distinct and they are coordinated only in the sense that they complement each other. Operations of order (and change of position) govern the grouping of asymmetrical relations of order as applied to a succession of objects and their extremities. Those of interval govern the symmetrical interval relations between such ordered points. The iteration of units is unnecessary to conservation of distance and length because these two complementary 'groupings' suffice.

In ch. V, the foregoing qualitative construction was seen once more in the conservation of length when straight lines were broken at various angles: again, conservation was achieved at level IIIA, and here too, the qualitative coordination of subdivision and change of position did not entail metric synthesis. In section II of ch. V the problem of measurement was broached once more, using the same apparatus. But whereas in ch. II measurement was unprompted, in ch. V the subject was offered ready-made cards (1, 2, or 3 units in length) and he was even shown how to use them by measuring paths of movement in 'steps'. Moreover, the first two or three steps were demonstrated by the experimenter who applied the card to be used as a metric unit. While this technique yielded a slight gain in performance level as compared with the spontaneous responses of ch. II, the gain was intuitive and subjects at level IIB only began to see the possible function of a common measure (qualitative transitivity) and failed to appreciate unit iteration: although they counted the 'steps' as shown, they overlooked differences in their size. Metric iteration was not finally mastered until stage III, a year later on an average than qualitative conservation. In spite of the distortion of results produced by the initial demonstration, the experiment showed clearly the difference between simple coordination of operations of subdivision and change of position which is qualitative, and their operational synthesis as implied by true metrics.

The technique employed in ch. VI stands midway between the unstructured task of ch. II and the imitation and suggestion which appear in ch. V. The stages shown in ch. II are given detailed confirmation: a gradual coordination of subdivision and change of position takes place throughout level IIB, but it is still empirical, and progress is achieved by trial-and-error. Because of the experimental conditions, there is a slight lowering in the age of success as compared with unprompted measurement. At level IIIA operational coordination is achieved at a qualitative level, and subjects can use measuring rods equal to or greater than the objects being measured, or they may juxtapose shorter measuring rods. At level IIIB there is operational synthesis as shown in unit iteration.

How does qualitative coordination differ from metric synthesis with regard to one-dimensional measurement of distance and length as treated in part II? Operations of order and change of position determine asymmetrical relations between points on a line, these being the order of those points and changes in their order. Operations of subdivision determine enclosing or nesting series, these being symmetrical relations constituted by intervals between ordered points. The latter may be objects ordered in a series, or parts of an object the boundaries of which are likewise ordered. The two operations are complementary but distinct. Both are applied to empty sites and fixed reference elements as well as movable objects. Thus subdivision governs nesting (part-whole) relations of distance and length, while change of position governs the several positions and changes of position of the various points involved.

So long as these operations remain purely complementary, each taking the form of a qualitative (intensive) grouping and each being distinct from the other, partial lengths continue to be seen either as indissolubly fixed in the context of the whole, or else as completely divorced from that context by the fact of positional change. Yet there is conservation of the whole because there is grouping of operations involved in adding and subtracting partial lengths. Moreover length A, known by correspondence or congruence to be equal to B is also known to be equal to C if B = C (qualitative transitivity). But the several partial lengths which form part of the same whole are not applied to one another for the purpose of comparison. Therefore the part fails to become a unit, both because subdivision is not generalized to cover transitive relations between successive portions of a given length and because change of position is not generalized to cover comparison of parts.

The construction of a metric unit thus involves a twofold generalization. True measurement of distance and lengths begins when the subject recognizes that any length may be decomposed into a series of intervals which are known to be equal because one of them may be applied to each of the others in turn. Generalized subdivision therefore gives rise to measurement because it enables the subject to think of a unit as forming part of any number of wholes, i.e. as an elementary common part. But generalized subdivision cannot be achieved without generalized change of position because the former implies that the unit-part may be applied hypothetically to an indefinite number of wholes. Thus the notion of an elementary unit which may be applied indefinitely in a continuous and contiguous series of changes of position involves the operational synthesis of subdivision and change of position. Unit iteration achieves this generalization by fusing the two into a single operation. Subjects at level IIIB who apply the same measuring rod several times over are in effect doubling and trebling the partial length with which they began. The second length differs from the first only by virtue of the difference of position. Additive grouping of subdivision and additive grouping of changes of position are synthesized when the several parts are conceived of as equal without being identical. Their individual distinctness derives solely from their order but each successive part is deemed to be worth one unit.

An arithmetical unit is a similar element in a synthesis of a class and an asymmetrical relation, i.e. number. But unlike the unit of number, that of length is not the beginning stage but the final stage in the achievement of operational thinking. This is because the notion of a metric unit involves an arbitrary disintegration of a continuous whole. Hence, although the operations of measurement exactly parallel those involved in the child's construction of number, the elaboration of the former is far slower and unit iteration is, as it were, the coping stone to its construction, for at level IIIA measurement is still qualitative.

PART THREE

RECTANGULAR COORDINATES, ANGLES AND CURVES

HAVING studied the growth of measuring operations in a single dimension, we now turn to an examination of that same development where two or three dimensions are involved. One group of relations arises in considerations of area and volume. Thus in part four of this work, subjects are asked to divide areas and volumes and to double them, etc.; they also show how far they realize the conservation of such measures when objects are transformed in various ways. However that study cannot be undertaken without a preliminary enquiry as to the way in which children set about measuring straight lines forming the boundaries of plane or solid shapes as against the measurement of areas and solids themselves. At the same time we will consider how they discover the metric properties of various curves, which again involve two or three dimensions. Part three is therefore devoted to a study of the growth of understanding in relation to the measurement of angles and curves.

Ch. VII is introductory and deals with children's responses when required to locate a given point in two or three-dimensional space. Development is complete when subjects coordinate their measurements using rectangular axes. Ch. VIII then deals with angular measurement in general and covers in particular the relations involved in understanding that the sum of the angles of a triangle is constant. Ch. IX is concerned with the metric properties of curves and contains an analysis of the discovery of a number of simple geometrical 'loci'. Finally, in ch. X we examine the representation of three of the more elementary "mechanical curves". That investigation concludes our study of the genesis of Euclidean notions in the realm of angles and curves (although Euclid himself refused to recognize mechanical curves as forming part of geometry!).

Chapter Seven

LOCATING A POINT IN
TWO OR THREE DIMENSIONAL SPACE[1]

HAVING observed how children locate a point on a straight line by measuring the distance from its origin to the point in question, we will now study their responses when asked to locate a point in two- or three-dimensional space. We shall be led to two important conclusions. (1) Sooner or later, children measure in two or three dimensions by means of paired measurements along the two axes of a right angle. Therefore, later in part three, we study angular measurement as such. (2) Children cannot locate a point in two or three dimensional space without first evolving a coordinate system. The importance of rectangular coordinates was made abundantly clear in our study of the construction of Euclidean space as a whole (C.C.S. chs. XIII, XIV), and again in the present enquiries in conjunction with the grouping of changes of position (ch. I), relations of distance and length (chs. III and IV), and finally measurement itself (ch. II). Here the problem of rectangular coordinates re-appears in metrical terms.

§1. *Outline of Method and Results*

The simplest technique would have been to ask children to determine distances between the intersections of two or three straight lines presented in two or three dimensions and various points on these lines, the latter being selected at random. Subjects would thereby be required to measure along two or three lines instead of only one. However, while such an enquiry might have been a direct continuation of that undertaken in ch. VI, it could hardly have shown anything new. If a child can transfer a given length from one straight line to another he can also transfer it from two straight lines to two more, or from three straight lines to three more. If, on the other hand, he fails when only one pair of lines is involved, it is a waste of time to complicate the problem further. We have therefore sought a technique whereby the subject himself must construct lines in order to locate the point required. In other words he must select their orientation and also measure them. This problem is far more illuminating for it links questions of measurement to those of coordinate systems. We make it easier by having the axes suggested by straight lines which form the outline of the area or space

---

[1] Written with the collaboration of Mme Renate Schaffrin-Kersten.

in which the required point is to be determined, particularly as the elaboration of horizontal and vertical axes as such has already been studied in C.C.S., ch. XIII.

To find a point in two dimensions, the subject is given two sheets of plain white paper, identical in size. The first (S_1) is placed at the top right-hand corner of the table, the second (S_2) at the bottom left. S_1 contains a point P_1 shown in red about half-way between the centre of the rectangle and its upper right-hand corner. The experimenter simply asks the subject to draw, in red, a point P_2 on the other rectangular sheet S_2, in exactly the same place as point P_1 on S_1, so that if the two sheets are superposed P_2 will fall over P_1. The paper is semi-transparent writing paper and the subject can verify the coincidence of P_1 and P_2 by putting one sheet over the other. As in the previous investigation he is given a two decimetre ruler, stick, strips of paper and lengths of thread to find P_2. In the following account A_1, B_1, C_1 and D_1 are used to refer to the bottom left (A), bottom right (B), top right (C) and top left (D) corners of rectangle S_1, and A_2, B_2, C_2 and D_2 refer to the corresponding four corners of S_2.

In ch. VI the bead (little tram) was movable and its position was gained by movement from its point of origin. Here P_1 is a stationary point so that the subject does not know what to measure or where to measure from. The situation therefore provides an excellent medium for the study of spontaneous reactions to a problem which requires measurement in two dimensions. The problem is simply to make use of measurement in locating a point in an area, not to measure an area. Thus it involves logical multiplication of measurements as given by rectangular coordinates. We analyse the genesis of a purely logical system before the growth of arithmetical multiplication, as applied to areal measurement. Because the subject must orientate his own measurements, using the sides of rectangle S as axes, these observations enable us to determine, stage by stage, how measurement comes to be coordinated in two dimensions.

The technique used to determine a point in three dimensions is described in §7, together with the stages revealed in the solution of that problem. Age levels for the latter will be seen to agree fairly closely with those which emerge in two-dimensional measurement.

During stage I (until about 4 years to 4; 6) children make no use whatever of the material provided. Instead of attempting to measure, they simply find P_2 on S_2 by visual estimate. This is true even of level IIA, though now subjects may use rulers and sticks as aids to perception: their judgment is still a visual one. The estimate may be fairly accurate, or it may involve errors of logic. Thus, P_2 is often located on the side of S_2 opposite to that on which P_1 is situated in S_1. During sub-stage IIB, subjects begin to measure. Needless to say, the deficiencies already observed at this level, in linear measurement, are again apparent. Moreover, children are satisfied with one measurement only; usually the ruler is laid oblique from one corner of the rectangle or from some other prominent point. At the beginning of this sub-stage, this does not seem to mean that subjects wish to take both dimensions into account. They simply look for a convenient point of departure, and choose point C because it is the only well-defined point on BC and CD, but they take little account of the inclination of their ruler.[1] Later in the same sub-stage, subjects try to preserve the inclination of $C_1 P_1$ when applying their ruler to S_2. This form of measurement is still one-dimensional but it shows a beginning of awareness that two dimensions are involved. Being transitional, it is taken to represent an intermediate level between sub-stage IIB and sub-stage IIIA. At stage III, subjects understand the need to take both dimensions into account. The final solution of the problem is achieved in two steps. At the beginning of sub-stage IIIA, subjects start with a single oblique measurement, but show an increasing realization of the importance of the angle at which this is drawn. Gradually, they decompose its inclination and express it in terms of two separate measurements along different axes. However, although this discovery is crucial, it does not lead to the immediate coordination of length and width. It is followed by a great deal of trial-and-error behaviour. Thus children often try to coordinate an oblique line with a horizontal or a vertical line, the latter being selected because it is parallel to the sides of the rectangle. Others draw straight lines in the required directions but do not know how to bring them together, i.e. they fail to join them in a right angle. At level IIIB, the two measures are finally coordinated.

These stages correspond in broad outline with those already established in linear measurements. The two developmental processes exactly parallel one another in point of time, as far as levels I, IIA, IIB and IIIA are concerned (apart from differences due to variation between individuals). Level IIIB, in two-dimensional (and also in three-dimensional, §7) measurement, coincides with the spontaneous elaboration of coordinates (C.C.S. chs. XIII and XIV). Measurement in a single dimension is achieved somewhat earlier. Thus linear measurement is mastered at the beginning of sub-stage IIIB (that is, on an average, between 8 and 8; 6) while the remaining forms are not realized until the age of 9 or 9; 6, i.e. well into sub-stage IIIB. Nevertheless, the synchronous appearance of so many of these behavioural forms is of considerable interest.

[1] For the problem of estimating inclination at stage II, see C.C.S., chs. XI–XIII.

§2. *Levels I and IIA: The point is located visually. Measuring devices are either not used at all or used perceptually and inappropriately*

At levels I and IIA, P_2 is located by visual estimate. Its height is usually correct, but it is often shown on the wrong side. Superposing the two sheets leads to the discovery of errors and inaccuracies, but subjects fail to deduce the necessity for measurements. At stage I they are limited to visual perception. At level IIA, they agree to try the material they are given, but they use it merely as an aid to perception instead of measuring with it.

JIM (4; 4, stage I): "Can you make a little red point on the other sheet in exactly the same place? If we put your sheet on this sheet, your point should be just here, on this one.—*I can't do it* (he puts P_2 to the right of the rectangle, like P_1, but lower and also nearer BC).—Let's see if that's right (superposing S_2 on S_1).—*No, I've got to put it here* (higher).—You see, that's better. (Offering guidance.) But it's still not quite the same place. Can you use this to see (placing ruler near P_1)?—*No* (pushing aside the material and putting in another point by eye.)" etc.

MIC (5; 6, level IIA) takes the ruler and lays it about half way across the longer sides of S_2 and at a slight slant. He then looks at P_1 on S_1 and makes an estimate for P_2 which he puts in at about the right height but to the left of the ruler (P_1 is on the right of S_1). After superposing S_2 on S_1, Mic puts P_2 to the right, having once again laid his ruler about the vertical median of S_2. He superposes it once more and finds that P_2 is still not exactly right: he therefore makes a third estimate, without using the ruler. Finally, he lays the ruler oblique from B to CD, about the middle. But he still puts in P_2 by visual estimate, and inaccurately too. After a fifth and a sixth attempt, all similar, he cries: "*It's that point there* (P_1) *which keeps moving about!*"

MART (6; 10) makes an estimate for P_2 and puts it at about the right height though too close to BC. The experimenter suggests that he use the material. Mart takes a bead and puts it first on P_1 and then at about the same place on S_2 before drawing P_2. He still finds by superposing that P_1 and P_2 fail to correspond, but he spurns the ruler and sticks: "*I don't need those things.*" He continues to estimate and the experimenter interjects: "Try measuring with the ruler, won't you?—(He now lays the ruler horizontally across S_1, and a little below P_1, and then puts it a little lower over S_2. Again he makes an estimate for P_2 and puts it the same distance along the ruler but not quite high enough).—Did the ruler help?—*Yes, I measured it better.*"

JAC (6; 11) ignores the fact that S_2 is not in line with S_1 and puts in P_2 in exact alignment with P_1 so that P_2 is now near the bottom of S_2 while P_1 is in the upper half of S_1. Moreover P_2 is drawn in the left half of S_2. The experimenter superposes S_2 on S_1: "Is that right?—*No* (but he makes the same mistake a second time).—And now?—*It's a little too low* (raising it).—Are they all right now?—*Oh, I've got to put it there* (moving it to the right).—Will that be right?—*It may be too high.*—Wouldn't you find it easier using this (material)?—*I could take the ruler and measure* (laying the ruler horizontally from P_2 to P_1, so that, once again, he puts in P_2 in the lower left-hand sector of S_2).—Is that right?—*No, it's wrong. I've got to measure like this because otherwise it's too low* (he lays the ruler oblique, cutting S_2 at point C, and makes an estimate for P_2 near the edge of the ruler)."

All these subjects make visual estimates for P_2, whether or not they use any of the measuring material as a perceptual reference point. They might well have taken both dimensions into account and fixed P_2 in relation to its height and its distance from the vertical sides of S_2, while still confining themselves to visual approximation instead of transferring the relevant distances. However, it is clear that these subjects can estimate in terms of both dimensions only if they are not conscious of them. Their most successful approximations are the result of undifferentiated and not of analytical estimates (and even these are liable to errors of reversed symmetry etc.). As soon as they try to correct the inaccuracies of such global judgments by analysing the relations in two dimensions, they begin to oscillate between one and the other and cannot reconcile them (see Jac. in particular).

Young subjects find it difficult to articulate the relevant intuitions and their use of perceptual references at level IIA serves merely to confirm that difficulty. Most of them lay their ruler or their stick on S_2, i.e. on the rectangle which should reproduce the point at the required position instead of placing it over P_1 on S_1. Mic and Mart both cut S_2 in half, with the ruler approximately parallel to the base or the height of the rectangle, but Mic goes on to put P_2 on the wrong side of the ruler while Mart puts it too low. Jac merely lays it horizontally between P_1 and P_2, which amounts to the same response as that made without the ruler at the beginning of the enquiry.

It was shown in earlier chapters that children at these levels cannot subdivide lengths correctly and fail to establish a correspondence between the order of points when two sticks are staggered. Here, again, there is a systematic difficulty, even in the field of perceptual intuition. They cannot subdivide the area in terms of two dimensions, and they cannot coordinate the relevant points because the two rectangles are staggered in relation to each other. Their failure may be attributed not so much to their inability to coordinate the two dimensions as to their inability to think operationally in terms of grouped relations, or even to articulate spatial intuitions.

§3. Sub-stage IIB: Beginnings of measurement.
Measurement is one-dimensional

At level IIB, children supplement perceptual judgment by primitive measurement. Some use their hands while others make use of common terms. Their shortcomings echo those already seen in the measurement of length. In addition, they confine themselves to a single measurement by which to fix point P_2 within the area S_2. That measurement may be horizontal or oblique, in which case they take no notice of the angle of the ruler. Hence they do not arrive at an unambiguous result.

MAD (6; 11), a subject whose responses have been noted earlier in ch. VI, §3, begins with a careful study of P_1 and S_1. Next, he takes the stick and measures from P_1 to C_1 (top right-hand corner of S_1), by placing one end of the stick over P_1 and marking C_1 with his finger. This measurement is then applied to S_2, but he now starts from B_1 (bottom right) so that P_2 is inserted in the lower right hand sector of S_2. He goes on to check the equality of $C_1 P_1$ and $B_2 P_2$ by holding his fingers apart (which to him seems more convincing!). "If I put this paper (S_2) on that (S_1), will the two points be touching?—*Yes* (he tries and sees they are not, so he begins to rotate S_2 so that they will). *It's not right. I thought it was only the same place this side you wanted* (showing the right hand side of the rectangle and thereby admitting that he had ignored the height of P_1)." He then tries an estimate for P_2, and after putting his finger over the point, he uses his hand to measure $C_1 P_1$. Before drawing in P_2, he hesitates, not knowing where to measure from on S_2: he tries measuring from C_2, but ignores the fact that P_2 is too high although $C_2 P_2 = C_1 P_1$: "Will that be right now, if we put this sheet over the other?—*Yes.*—(S_2 superposed over S_1.)—*Oh no. It's not the same.*" A further attempt follows, in which Mad tries to find a different reference point and hits on a small hole made by a drawing pin along the top of S_1: "*I'd rather measure from this hole to that point* (he measures from the hole to P_1, using the ruler and marking both limits with his fingers. Then he applies this distance to S_2 where he finds a corresponding pinhole, but again he ignores the slope of his ruler).—*Is that right?*—(S_2 superposed on S_1.) *No, I've got to start there* (return to $C_1 P_1$ and $C_2 P_2$ but continued failure to take slope into account).— Why do you measure from the corner?—*Because I can't do it any other way.*— (By way of suggestion, the experimenter lays the ruler horizontally between P_1 and BC on S_1:) And this way?—(He again measures an oblique distance.)"

ORG (6; 7) makes an estimate for P_2 and draws it. He then takes the stick and lays it across from P_1 to P_2 to verify his estimate. This procedure satisfies him until S_2 is superposed over S_1. He now measures $P_1 C_1$ (top right), using the stick and two fingers to mark both limits. In transferring this measurement, he begins from C_2 but ignores the slope of the stick. On superposing once more he finds that the new P_2 is "too low.—Will you do it just right.—(This time he simply uses his fingers to measure $C_1 P_1$ and $C_2 P_2$. This technique carries greater conviction at level IIB!)—Don't you want to use anything?— (He takes the graduated ruler and measures $C_1 P_1 = 2$ to 10, then fills in P_2 by visual estimate and measures $C_2 P_2 = 1$ to 10, and is wholly satisfied.)— Look (S_2 over S_1).—*This time it's too high.*—Don't you think we should measure it differently (ruler laid horizontal)?—(He studies the new position of the ruler, then begins again from C and ends by discovering) *It's too far to the right.*—And the other way?—(He lays the ruler horizontal but turns it back to an oblique position.)—Would it work like that (horizontal)?—*Yes* (measures from P_1 to $B_1 C_1$ then inserts P_2 and measures P_2 to $B_2 C_2$, estimating the required height. Even now he again measures $C_1 P_1$ and $C_2 P_2$).—

Why do you start that way again?—*To see if I'm right.*—(S_2 superposed.) —
It's wrong.—Is that all we can do?—*Yes.*"
   MOND (7; 2) inserts P_2 by estimate. "Is that right?—*No.*" Given the material,
he lays the ruler oblique from A_2 (bottom left) to P_2 (as estimated). "Is that
right?—*No.*—Try to measure it better.—(He lays the ruler horizontally over
S_1 from P_1 to BC then transfers it carefully to S_2, trying to keep a mental note
of the number reached on S_1. However, not only is the height inaccurate but
he forgets the length. The process is repeated several times and not once does
he measure the height.) *It won't work* (he ends by again measuring the oblique
distances $A_1 P_1$ and $A_2 P_2$ without troubling about the slope)."

   As compared with earlier levels these subjects show an improvement
in perceptual intuition. Their estimate of P_2 is approximately correct
and takes both vertical and lateral dimensions into account. However,
in measuring by ruler (and even by hand) they cease to take account of
both. To achieve this, they would need to dissociate them and coordinate
them operationally and this they cannot do (cf. Mad who begins by
measuring without reference to height, as against Org and Mond whose
visual estimates are more satisfactory). The contrast between judgment
and measurement at this level finds its parallel in children's estimates of
length. They were able to subdivide and to evaluate changes of position
with some accuracy, but only within the limits of direct intuition. In
measuring, they failed to co-ordinate the two.
   A second feature of these responses at level IIB is the way in which
children try to control their judgments by using a ruler as a middle
term between S_1 and S_2. Indeed, they frequently measure distances on
S_1 before drawing P_2 in S_2.
   In spite of these two advances the response is still imperfect. Difficulties inherent in the measurement of length are again to the fore. In
essence, these result from lack of coordination between subdivision and
change of position (cf. Org and Mond). However, from the standpoint
of measurement in an area, these responses show that measurement, here
seen in its infancy, begins by being one-dimensional. When required to
fix a point on a rectangular area, subjects take note of only one interval
of distance instead of taking separate vertical and horizontal measurements. Some measure from a corner of the rectangle but fail to determine the slope of their ruler so as to reproduce it in their second
measurement (Mad, Org and Mond, initial and final attempts), while
others measure horizontally and ignore the height of the points P
(Mond, intermediate response). These aspects of their behaviour are
significant and merit the following comments:
   At this level children lack a coordinate system whereby they might
orientate measurements in two dimensions. Hence, when required to
fix a point on a plane, they take only one measurement. The development of insight into horizontality and verticality and, more especially,

the construction of topographical schemata have been considered at some length in C.C.S., chs. XIII and XIV. These studies point to the difficulties involved in coordinating positions and distances as functions of two dimensions, showing why this is a late achievement. However, the present experimental conditions are such as to invalidate an explanation in these terms, for here, the relevant axes are already given by the sides of the two rectangles (and the subject is not required to scale his representation as in C.C.S., ch. XIV). Again, the subject is repeatedly encouraged to measure, and his problem is simply to fix one point and not to determine reciprocal relations between several. Given that the perceptual intuitions shown by these subjects reproduce the relevant distances with some accuracy, taking both dimensions into account, why do they fail when measuring, behaving as if they were quite unable to coordinate them? On the face of it, it would seem a simple matter to take two measurements, parallelling the heights and widths of the rectangles.

The answer is that coordination of measurements in two dimensions presents the same difficulties as the synthesis of subdivision and changes of position in a single dimension. (From an intuitive point of view, the situation is further complicated by the fact that these difficulties appear twice.) In our study of children's measurements of length, it was shown that subjects at this level cannot construct nesting series of parts, while preserving the invariance of the whole, and at the same time use this subdivision to effect appropriate changes of position in a third term. The reconciliation of subdivision with relations of order and change of position was not mastered in dealing with a simple straight line. Its achievement is necessarily more difficult where two dimensions are involved. The problem no longer arises at an intuitive or perceptual level (although during stage I, it was not solved even perceptually), because all the relations can be apprehended in a single 'gestalt'. But as soon as the subject is required to break up the perceptual whole and take separate measurements, he is unable to fix a point in a rectangle without (1) subdivision and (2) a system regulating the order and changes of position. Subdivision enters into the need to select which partial lengths should be measured out of all the possible straight lines which might be drawn from point P to any other point in the rectangle S. A system regulating the order and changes of position is implied by the necessity to realize the order of points given by the stationary lines of the rectangles and the successive positions of the ruler. A coordinate system, even though a qualitative one, requires the imposition of spatial order in two or more dimensions between the several elements, and also demands a systematic nesting of partial intervals between such elements. Since subdivision and spatial order are implied even in qualitative and spontaneous coordinate systems, the further requirement of

160

measurement makes these twin operations even more indispensable, for measurement has been shown to consist in their mutual synthesis. Hence, subjects at this level have the utmost difficulty even in linear measurement because they lack that operational synthesis. The present task of fixing a point in an area is doubly out of their reach:—(1) They cannot orientate their measurements without a qualitative coordinate system, which in turn implies the coordination of subdivision and change of position in at least two dimensions (as against their operational synthesis, cf. ch. VI, §5). (2) The two measurements themselves imply the synthesis of a twofold subdivision and a twofold system regulating changes of position. The duplication of this synthesis, arising out of the two dimensions, presents no difficulty when metric operations have been mastered, when measurement is no harder along two dimensions than along one. But at a level where children still proceed by trial-and-error and progress is measured by the articulation of their intuitions, duplication makes the task more difficult.

Since our subjects cannot coordinate two measurements, they are satisfied with only one, which may be horizontal (because horizontal measurement is easier than vertical) or oblique, in which case they measure from a corner of the rectangle. The oblique measurement is more common and seems to suggest that subjects have an intuition of the two dimensions involved without being able to coordinate two measurements: they select an oblique orientation as a half-way term between the vertical and the horizontal. While the possibility of such an intuitive insight cannot be ruled out, there can certainly be no conscious intention, since, unlike subjects at the next level these make no attempt to preserve the inclination in transferring their ruler. However, it seems simpler to account for the predominance of oblique measurements by reference to the necessity to begin measuring from a point which is unambiguously given in perception. The corners are the only points which stand out on the horizontal and vertical sides of the rectangle and notions of horizontality and verticality are themselves embryonic at this stage. Subjects therefore choose the uppermost corner as a reference point, much as others at the same sub-stage drew a line across one of the corners of an inclined vessel to show how the water would lie in such a container (C.C.S., ch. XIII, §4) because their notion of horizontality was still imperfect. The particular slope which they use in measuring is therefore without significance. Children's drawings of parallel sloping lines and their efforts to anticipate affinitive transformations of a rhombus (C.C.S., ch. XI) all show a similar failure to deal with inclination in a systematic manner.

We are led to conclude that the one dimensional measurement shown at this level ignores all inclinations and angles, including the angle made by the ruler with the sides of the rectangle. Children measure unidimensionally, simply because they have not yet worked out a coordinate system and cannot measure in two dimensions. The first angle they master is a right angle, and so we find that at subsequent stages children take one measurement in height and another in width, and coordinate the two.

§4. *From Level IIB to Level IIIA: Transition to two-dimensional measurement*

The type of response noted in the preceding section is followed by a series of intermediate response patterns. Children still measure from P_1 to one of the corners of S_1, but they now try to preserve the slope of their ruler while moving it to S_2. Later they break up the single measurement and measure horizontal and vertical distances separately.

DIZ (6; 10) begins with an estimate for P_2 but finds by superposing S_2 on S_1 that this is not entirely satisfactory. He then lays his ruler from the top left hand corner of S_1 across P_1, and moves it gingerly to S_2 in a series of short steps, trying to maintain the same slope. However, he is not wholly successful. "Is it right now?—(S_2 superposed on S_1.) *No, not yet.* (He tries again, and interestingly enough he no longer lays his ruler across from D_1 but from a point on $C_1 D_1$ which is nearer to P_1, though still not vertical. Once more he tries not to alter the slope of his ruler while moving it to S_2.)" Diz is beginning to move from oblique measurement to vertical measurement.

COL (5; 8, advanced) is more successful in dissociating the two dimensions. He too begins by making an estimate for P_2, and when he finds this method unsatisfactory he measures the distance $C_1 P_1$ (i.e. from the top right-hand corner) and applies it to $C_2 P_2$ without worrying about the slope of the ruler (i.e. a typical IIB response). But when he sees that this method also fails to produce results, he cries: "*Oh, it's because it was like this* (slope of $C_1 P_1$) *and not like that* (slope of $C_2 P_2$)". He measures $C_1 P_1$ again and tries to maintain the slope of the ruler unaltered while moving it to S_2. When he fails he asks: "*What did you do?*" He measures $C_1 P_1$ again and this time he tries to indicate the slope of the stick by marking the point where its uppermost edge cuts $C_1 D_1$. (The ruler is fairly wide so that when one corner is laid on C_1 the upper edge cuts $C_1 D_1$ and the lower edge cuts $A_1 B_1$). He then lays the corner of the ruler on C_2 and finds the point on $C_2 D_2$ which corresponds with the mark made on his ruler. For all that, he is still unsuccessful in his measurement of P_2, so he tries once more, this time marking the point where the ruler cuts $A_1 B_1$. When this fails he complains: "*It's you who are marking it wrong!*" The experimenter reassures him. Again he lays the end of his ruler on C_1, and now he tries to ensure that its slope will be reproduced by drawing a line on the ruler itself running right along its length! He looks at it carefully and says: "*I need this too,*" adding a row of little hooks or arrows all pointing to P_1: "What are you putting those in for?—*To make sure the line is on the right side and that the point* (P_2) *won't be there or there* (either side of the line)." Again he finds that he has failed. He now takes a double decimeter ruler and measures horizontally from P_1 to the right vertical side of S_1 ($B_1 C_1$). He applies this distance to S_2 but neglects the height of his ruler. Having marked P_2 he cries: *"Oh, it's too high! I've got to measure its height."* This time he measures the height and width separately, each time laying the end of his ruler on P_1. But he fails to indicate the points where it cuts $C_1 B_1$ and $A_1 B_1$. Thus when applying what he takes to be the two measured distances to S_2, in effect he is simply making an estimate for P_2. At last he gives up all attempt to measure and draws in P_2 by visual estimate.

Rod (7; 2) begins with a visual estimate for P_2, then lays the ruler more or less horizontally from P_1 to $B_1 C_1$ and applies the distance to S_2. He decides that *"It's still not quite right; there's a little bit missing there* (in height, i.e. between P_2 and upper side $C_2 D_2$).—Is there anything else you could use (indicating the apparatus)?—*Oh, Yes!* (He uses the ruler along with a stick and a strip of paper so that their combined width all but fills the space between P_1 and $C_1 D_1$, although all three are laid horizontal. Rod simply guesses at the gap in height and applies his compound yardstick to S_2).—But why did you take those three things?—*To make it thicker* (indicating their combined width).—Wasn't the ruler all right by itself?—*No, because it couldn't go any further* (in height).—Couldn't we do it another way (experimenter gently moves the ruler to a vertical position)?—*Yes, like that* (laying the three objects side by side and vertical and estimating the distance from P_1 to the edge of the ruler).—Can't you do it using the ruler all by itself?—(He measures horizontally from P_1 to $B_1 C_1$.)—But haven't we seen that won't work?—*Oh, yes, it's too low; I've got to measure it this way* (measures height and horizontal distance)."

These transitional responses highlight the psychological preconditions of two-dimensional measurement. Unlike those considered hitherto, they bear witness to the discovery that a one-dimensional measurement, cannot be used to determine a point on an area, if it is taken at random. If a single measurement is to be used between that point and another already given, e.g. a corner of the rectangle (as against a point somewhere along one of the sides, which the subject must determine for himself), then the slope of the line of measurement must be held constant. Diz realizes the necessity almost immediately, while Col, having failed in his first efforts to solve the problem, expressly formulates the principle under discussion. The question remains: how is the inclination to be held constant? A train of unsuccessful attempts at answering this question leads eventually to the next stage: instead of taking one measurement, as at level IIB, children decompose the relationship, finding that two measurements must be taken and coordinated with each other.

In the foregoing examples, the simplest solution is that of moving the ruler in short steps, keeping the inclination uniform throughout. This may be described as an attempt to solve the problem of two-dimensional measurement by using change of position without subdivision. Diz tries, by taking several short steps, to move his ruler from

S_1 to S_2 without altering its orientation. Col's solution is even more amusing. Hoping to copy the direction of the ruler as well as its length, he draws the former on the ruler like an instruction for its correct handling, "Fragile, this side up"! By drawing a reference line on the very object which he is going to move, he shows more unmistakeably than all the subjects of C.C.S., chs. XIII and XIV taken together, that a system of references or coordinates is still quite absent. The changes of position needed for measurement remain divorced from the spatial context in which they occur. There is no general system embracing moving objects and stationary sites, as determined by reference points. He even adds a series of directional arrows, suggesting a motor-car which carries its own road signs instead of meeting with them en route!

However, while children may first try to use changes of position by themselves, and even to divorce them from their spatial context, they find themselves compelled to use reference points, and in so doing, they begin to subdivide the areas under comparison, and later to decompose their oblique measurement. Thus they arrive at a way of measuring which implies a recognition of horizontality and verticality, or, more generally, rectangular spatial coordinates.

The record of Diz illustrates these beginnings of subdivision and decomposition. Having tried and failed to reproduce the slope of his ruler, he alters it to a nearly vertical orientation in order to achieve a more exact parallelism between its successive positions.

Col, with his patient efforts to maintain the slope unaltered, eventually arrives at a genuine dissociation of measurement in two dimensions, but the two measurements are still uncoordinated (i.e. there is no logical multiplication of linear relations): after the directional arrows have failed, Col like Diz, is driven back to one-dimensional measurement: while Diz measured a vertical distance, Col measures the horizontal. But unlike subjects at the beginning of stage IIB, Col realizes the significance of the problem of the slope of $C_1 P_1$, and after measuring the horizontal distance of P_1 from the edge of the rectangle, he tries to fix its height; he fails only because he forgets to mark reference points on his ruler. Rod measures horizontally from the start, and eventually widens his measuring rod "to make it thicker", to a point where he is able to take the height of P_1 into account!

Level IIB begins with one-dimensional measurement which is oblique simply because subjects need a fixed reference point, and find it in one of the corners of the rectangle. The present subjects go beyond and understand the need to maintain the slope of their measurement unaltered. Because they fail, they abandon changes of position divorced from their spatial context, and use a reference system based on the sides of the rectangle, which implies a beginning of subdivision. Hence, instead of using a ruler in an oblique position as in their earlier attempts

164

at one-dimensional measurement, they substitute for the angle a system which implies two measurements or, as in Rod's case, a single twofold measurement. The two measures are perpendicular to each other, because one, being horizontal is a measure of width while the other, being vertical, is a measure of height. Nevertheless these subjects are as yet unaware of the necessity for two-dimensions in the subdivision of areas and for their perpendicularity, as is shown by their failure to coordinate the two measures with one another.

§5. *Sub-stage IIIA: Empirical discovery of two-dimensional measurement*

Having analysed the first stage in the decomposition of an initial oblique measurement, we may now consider how children eventually discover two-dimensional measurement, a discovery which is initially the outcome of trial-and-error behaviour.

GAL (7; 8) takes the ruler straight off and measures from the lower left hand corner A, to point P_1, but finding that he cannot readily maintain the slope of his ruler he measures the vertical distance from P_1 to $A_1 B_1$ and transfers that measurement to S_2, still ignoring the lateral intervals involved. Once more he finds that P_2 cannot adequately be fixed and so he measures the distance from P_1 to the vertical side $B_1 C_1$ with his ruler almost horizontal but not exactly perpendicular to the side. Applying this measurement to S_2 he finds that he still cannot fix P_2. He measures the vertical distance again, checking his procedure: "Is that right?—*No.*—What should you do?—*I must measure this way* (horizontally). *Oh, I know how to measure! I've got to do this* (horizontal hand movement) *and this* (vertical movement) *to find the height.*" He measures the distance from P_1 to $B_1 C_1$, applies his measurement to S_2 and keeps his finger over the point reached. He then measures the height of P_1 from the base $A_1 B_1$ and applies this measurement to S_2. To link the two measurements he carefully moves his finger vertically downwards until he is level with the height as measured, then marks P_2. S_2 is superposed over S_1, and he can now see that his procedure was satisfactory. "What about putting another point in the same place as this one (Q_1 = a new point)?—(He measures first the height and then the lateral distance of Q_1 and again succeeds in coordinating his measurements by the same method.)" Yet, odd though it may seem, when the experimenter marks a third point R_1 and asks innocently: "Could you do it by taking just one measurement?" he tries to measure $P_1 R_1$ and apply the result to S_2.

GEO (7; 11) first marks his estimate for P_2, and then measures the oblique distance $P_1 C_1$, applying it to S_2: "Will that be right (the question is put before the rectangles are superposed)?—*No, because here it's like this* (indicating the slope of $P_1 C_1$) *while here it's too narrow* (indicating the angle $P_2 C_2 B_2$). *It's wrong because it doesn't slope the same.*—What should you do?—*I've got to measure from the edge* (taking an oblique measurement from the lower portion of $B_1 C_1$ to P_1 and trying to preserve the slope of the ruler when applying it to S_2)." He changes his mind before marking P_2 and begins afresh by measuring first $P_1 C_1$ and then the horizontal distance from P_1 to the side $B_1 C_1$. He applies both measurements to S_2 and marks P_2. "Is that right (rectangles superposed)?—*No, it's too low, I've got to be accurate* (he tries again).—Is it right this time?—*No.*—How about trying it another way?—*Yes, I could measure that* (horizontal distance to BC) *and then that* (vertical distance from AB) *to see how that will work.* (He measures the horizontal distance but fails to mark the point reached. He then measures the vertical distance and finally repeats his measurement of the horizontal. However, when he comes to put in P_2, he forgets his reference points.)—Is that right?—*No. It's too high and too near the corner* (C_2)." He now measures the depth from CD to P_1, followed by the lateral distance from P_1 to BC. Applying the vertical distance to S_2, he uses his finger nails to scratch a horizontal line across the point reached. Finally, he marks P_2 on this etched line by applying the measurement obtained from P_1 to BC).—"Is that right now (as it is in principle, although the result is marred by inaccuracy in execution)?—*No, it's too low.* —Why do you measure twice?—*So as to get this and this* (making horizontal and vertical gestures with his arm).—Is it all right to measure it like this (experimenter indicates various perpendicular pairs of measurement all of which are equally admissible)?—*Yes, it's the same* (he uses his own method a second time and finds it correct).—Do you need to take two measurements?— *It may be better to do it this way* (oblique distance $P_1 C_1$) *because it's easier to remember the number.*—Can you get it right with just one measurement?— *No. I got it with two. When I did it with one it was over to one side. If you're good at keeping figures in your head, you're better off with two measurements.*"

SUZ (8; 3) asks straightaway: "*Am I allowed to measure?*" and immediately measures $P_1 C_1$ (oblique) together with a vertical measurement from P_1 to the upper edge CD. However, when applying his finding to S_2 he uses only the oblique measurement, and then, on discovering that this is not enough, he measures both again and applies both to S_2. This time he mixes up his measurements. He now proceeds to measure first $P_1 C_1$, then the vertical distance from P_1 to CD and finally the horizontal distance to BC. After first trying to apply the oblique measurement to S_2 by maintaining the slope of the ruler, he applies the remaining measurements and, with a little trial-and-error, he finally succeeds. "You measured in three different ways. Can it be done with just two measurements?—*I don't know.*—What about these (oblique and horizontal)?—*Maybe.*—Or these (horizontal and vertical)?— *Yes, that's right too. It's the same thing.*—Would you like to try?—(He tries using oblique and horizontal measurements but without success, then, using only the vertical and horizontal, he succeeds.)—Is it better that way?— *Maybe.*"

Like subjects at earlier levels, these children begin with an oblique measurement, but they are quicker to realize the difficulty of holding constant the slope of their ruler. They soon discover the need to take two separate measurements. At first they take one oblique measurement together with another which approximates either to the vertical or to the horizontal. After a period of trial-and-error which may be long or short, they finally hit upon the essential discovery which marks off stage III from level IIB, that is, the two measurements must be perpendicular to one another. In the end, they consciously perceive the need for perpendicularity as between the two measures. Thus Gal, in a flash of insight, exclaims: "Oh, I know how to measure! I've got to do this (horizontal) and this (vertical)."

At sub-stage IIIB there is no trial-and-error and subjects immediately coordinate two rectangular measurements. The trial-and-error shown at level IIIA, following on a preliminary breakdown of the oblique in terms of two non-perpendicular measurements, facilitates our analysis of the way in which the need for rectangularity is gradually appreciated. When he finds that a single oblique measurement is not enough, Gal adds a vertical measure. Next he takes another nearly horizontal, but still not perpendicular either to his preceding measure or to the side BC. Only then does he understand that he must take two coordinated measures, with the clear realization that they must be at right angles to each other and that they must parallel the sides of the rectangle. Geo likewise uses a horizontal measure alongside his original oblique measurement. For a time he is satisfied with these measures which form an acute angle. After much trial and error his consistent failure to reproduce P_1 with any accuracy leads him to the idea of rectangular coordination. Unlike these, Suz tries three measurements of which one is oblique, one horizontal and the third vertical. Eventually he drops the first of these. This variation in its mode of discovery is a clear indication that rectangularity is an equilibrium. Paired measurements gradually tend towards this orientation however they may differ initially. How is that equilibrium achieved?

Some subjects, like Suz, seem convinced of its universality only by the fact of its success. But Gal understands the principle before applying it, while others again, like Geo, seem to discover that they are on the right track while they try it out (cf. the way in which Geo scratches in a horizontal line with his finger before taking the corresponding measurement). The fact that subjects at this level discover the principle by trial-and-error proves that neither the experiment nor the discovery are independent of their own action. In effect, what they discover is how to coordinate their behaviour. Earlier attempts at solution culminated in an effort to maintain unaltered the slope of a single oblique measurement involving change of position without subdivision. Since these subjects coordinate their behaviour in such a manner as to attain rectangularity between two measurements, their achievement represents an important development. They have in fact established a twofold one-one correspondence between the lengths measured on the two rectangles. Vertical measurement admits of an infinite series of parallel lines between the vertical sides of the rectangles while horizontal measurement gives rise to another series paralleling the base and top. When Gal moves his finger to the intersection of the two measurements, he shows that he realizes that each measurement defines an infinite series of equal and parallel lines and that P_2 is fully determined by the intersection of one line from each series, these being perpendicular to one another.

Thus rectangular coordination is chosen because it ensures one-one correspondence in terms of the two dimensions involved. This coordinating principle serves as the starting-point for coordinated axes. Children at level IIIA, having realized the possibility of measuring in two dimensions, learn readily enough to construct rectangular coordinate systems. However it is only their overt behaviour which reveals such a system. Their reflexion concerning that behaviour is as yet pre-operational, as is shown by the detailed protocols adduced for each subject. Although each one of them has realized in practice the need to take two measurements and has discovered how to coordinate them perpendicularly, at one time or another they all aver that a single measurement is sufficient in principle, as though in using two they had acted against their better judgment. This alone is sufficient proof that children at this level have not yet interiorized two-dimensional measurement, and so lack an operational schema by which their actions may be planned from the start. The latter development occurs only at sub-stage IIIB, which is when children evolve a coordinate system without guidance (C.C.S., chs. XIII, XIV).

§6. *Sub-stage IIIB: Operational grasp of two-dimensional measurement*

Unlike those we have studied above, subjects at level IIIB immediately measure the height of the point and its lateral distance from one side of the rectangle. There is no hesitation and they readily explain their action, which is thus operational in character.

PAY (8; 9) immediately measures the vertical distance from P_1 to the top of the rectangle $C_1 D_1$ together with its horizontal separation from the side $B_1 C_1$. Both measures are correctly repeated on S_2. "Why did you measure like that?—*To know where to put the point, in this direction and in that one too.*—What if you simply took one measurement?—*It wouldn't work. I'd be too high or too low or too far* (from $B_2 C_2$)."

DERB (9; 2) takes the ruler at once, saying: "*You've got to measure the height and width* (which he does correctly).—Do you need two measurements?—*Yes, otherwise I'd put my point too low.*"

DOM (8; 10) was examined by an alternative technique which was used as a counter-check. Two rectangular sheets of paper were laid on a table. They were not in direct prolongation of each other. On one sheet the subject saw a matchstick lying oblique to the edges: his problem was to place another matchstick in a corresponding position on the second sheet.[1] Dom says at

---

[1] This technique gave results which completely parallel those described in §§2–6. Visual estimate is followed by one-dimensional measurement from a corner of the sheet,

once: "*Oh, I've got to measure it.*" He places the ruler along one upright edge of the first sheet and runs a strip of paper horizontally from the top of the match to the ruler: this gives him two measurements at right angles to one another and enables him to fix a point corresponding with the upper end of the matchstick. The experimenter interrupts: "Could you have done your measuring without the strip of paper?—*Yes.*" He takes the following measurements using only the ruler: (1) a horizontal measurement from the top of the match to the nearer side of the sheet; (2) a vertical measurement from the top of the matchstick to a horizontal line joining its lower end to the right edge of the paper; (3) a vertical measurement from the lower end of the match to the lower edge of the paper, and (4) a horizontal measurement from the lower end of the match to the right edge of the paper (this line having served as a reference for the second measurement). The four measurements together form a system of perpendicular straight lines.

The difference between the present responses and those of level IIIA is at once apparent. These subjects do not begin with a single measurement only to discover the need for a second dimension after a period of trial-and-error. From the outset, they realize the logical necessity to take both dimensions into account and their measurements are straightaway coordinated so as to be at right angles to one another. As Pay puts the matter: "(I need) to know where to put the point in this direction and in that one too." The oblique measurements which appeared at an earlier stage now give way to rectangular coordinated measurements. The latter are appropriate because they derive from the need for a double one-one correspondence. Thus the present behaviour is operational in character. Before the facts are given in actual experience, they are engendered by structured anticipatory schemata. These are (1) a schema of logical multiplication i.e. a table of double entries corresponding with the two dimensions, i.e. a qualitative reference system; and (2) the same structure in metric terms, i.e. a true coordinate system in which the quantitative measurements find their place as they become known.

§7. *Measurement in three dimensions: Conclusion*

One cannot but be impressed by the fact that three-dimensional measurement is exactly synchronous with measurement in two dimensions. This synchronization points to the great psychological importance of operational grouping. There is a slight time lag between the achievement of successive levels in one-dimensional and two-dimensional measurement, although the lag is so slight that the difference is only as between the first and second parts of identical sub-stages, at each behavioural level. But as between two-dimensional and three-dimensional measurement, there is no time lag whatsoever. The reason must

etc. However, at earlier stages the technique had the disadvantage of suggesting only a parallel alignment between the two matches. At level IIIB, the added complication that two pairs of coordinated measurements are necessary adds interest to this technique.

surely be that one-dimensional measurement is a synthesis of additive logical groupings (subdivision and change of position) while measurement in two or three dimensions depends on multiplicative logical groupings (subdivision together with order of position in two or three different directions). Hence, once a child has mastered the grouping of such multiplicative spatial relations, he can coordinate three series as easily as two. However, it should be stressed that the psychological equivalence of two- and three-dimensional measurement derives from the fact of grouping. From the intuitive point of view, the problem of fixing a point in a volume seems much harder than that of fixing a point on an area (the question of areal and capacity measurement is quite different and will be discussed in Part IV). Our method of enquiry is as follows: The subject is shown two identical open boxes; a short length of wire, fairly rigid, is nailed in a vertical position to the wooden base of one box only; a small bead is fitted to the upper end of the wire. The subject is required to identify the position of the bead with reference to the sides of the box, these being higher than the bead itself. The other box is empty, but the subject is provided with another bead, a two decimetre graduated ruler, strips of paper and lengths of wood, string, wire lengths, rigid like that of the model, scissors to cut the wire and drawing pins with which to nail it. He is merely asked to produce an arrangement identical with that of the model, so that the second bead corresponds exactly with the first.

At levels I and IIA, children do not think of measuring the relevant intervals and simply judge by eye. The following account is an example of sub-stage IIA:

CLAD (5; 6) selects a length of wire which is greater than the model, puts the bead over the end and pins the wire down on the same side of the box as the wire on the model, although the correspondence is inexact: "Is your bead in just the same place as mine?—*No, it's too long. I've got to take it off and cut the wire down* (he changes to another wire, still judging by eye.)—Is it right now?—*Yes.*—How do you know?—*I've guessed.*—Isn't there something we could measure in there?—*No.*—Why not?—*Because it's like that* (indicating height)."

At level IIB not more than one or two measurements are taken, and these by simple congruence without metrical subdivision:

SAV (7; 6) estimates the required length of wire and cuts it off, pinning it on the appropriate side of the box: "Is that right?—*No.*—(He adjusts the height of the bead and replaces the wire but this time he pins it on the wrong side.)—Is it exactly the same as mine?—*Oh no* (putting it back on the correct side). *It's a little too long.*—What should you do?—*I've got to measure it* (applying a strip of wire against the wire in the model and then pinning it to the other box at a point which he judges to be right without attempting to measure it).—Is that quite right now?—*Yes.*—Is there nothing else you ought to measure?—*I don't know.*"

GER (7; 8) reproduces the model in great detail, but entirely by eye, and finally says: "*Mine looks bigger than the other.*—Then try doing it just right.— (He measures the height of the wire and affixes it by eye.)—Have you put it in exactly the same place?—*No, I've got to measure it* (measures from the foot of the wire to the nearest side of the box and pins it to agree with that single measurement).—Are you sure it's right now?—*Yes, it's right.*—Is there nothing else you could measure?—*Oh yes, the other side* (taking another measurement, this time to the side opposite the one chosen earlier so that the two measurements are in direct prolongation).—And now have you done all you should?—*Yes.*—Quite sure?—(He begins all over again but continues to ignore the third dimension.)"

Children at level IIIA eventually succeed in measuring in three dimensions but only after trial-and-error:

EVEL (8; 3) begins by copying the model by eye. "Is that right?—*Yes.*—Is this one exactly the same as the other?—(He measures the wires and, finding his own to be too short, he corrects his error.)—Is everything right now?— (Measures the distance to the wire from the left side of the box as he faces it and moves his own wire to correspond. He then finds that the distance to the near side of the box is different and accordingly takes a measurement in this third dimension. However, in applying it to his own box, he lays his ruler at an angle.)—Is that right now?—*No, not yet* (adjusting the wire so that the ruler is perpendicular to the nearside of the box)."

Finally, at level IIIB, children take their three measurements without preliminary trial-and-error:

BEA (9; 1) takes the ruler straightaway and measures the distance from the foot of the wire to the left of the box saying: "*I could do it from the other side if I wanted.*" After making a provisional mark on the bottom of the box, he measures the distance from that mark to the right hand side. Without any hesitation, he measures the distance from the wire to the near side and makes this measurement agree with those already known so that the point where the wire is to be pinned is fully determined. Only then does he measure the wire itself and place the bead in position. "Is that right?—*Yes, it's all there now.*"

The above responses are in complete agreement with those recorded earlier. Measurement in three dimensions, like that in two dimensions, shows a continuous development from stage I to level IIIA. In the end, it involves three separate constructions.

(1) The earliest responses are purely perceptual in character. There is no systematic subdivision of an area or a solid. The earliest measurement (level IIB) is a pure change of position. The object being moved is conceived without reference to a stationary spatial context. Direction and inclination seem to be regarded as properties of moving objects in an absolute sense. The ensuing analysis allows children to construct an

171

organized reference system in which key points are ordered in terms of the two or three relevant dimensions. Intervals between such points are then seen as forming parts of nesting series, while the series themselves are increasingly coordinated as development proceeds. All these qualitative operations dealing with order of position and subdivision lead in the end to a comprehensive reference system which involves coordination (see ch. VI, §5) of both types of operation. In two- or three-dimensional measurement the system may be described as a qualitative coordinate system (cf. C.C.S., chs. XIII, XIV).

(2) Measurement at the beginning of level IIB is one-dimensional (and inadequate even in one dimension). This is because children cannot subdivide and are unable to coordinate their notions of order of position. They therefore "transfer" not distances alone but inclinations as well. Development in metrics during the ensuing sub-stages is simply a process whereby children learn to guide the movements of their yardsticks by using ordered and stationary reference elements together with an increasingly systematic subdivision which is applied not only to the area or solid but also to the yardstick itself. This developmental process eventually enables children to master the problem of measurement in two or three dimensions. Their newly-constructed measuring schema is now dovetailed to a coordinate system with its rectangular axes. Thus the coordinate system ceases to be purely qualitative and becomes quantitative also. Measurement in an area or a solid is a synthesis of groupings, like linear measurement (ch. VI, §5). Subdivision and change of position are not merely coordinated so as to be mutually complementary, they are synthesized in a single operation. As a result, the system of coordinates ceases to be merely a system of ordered points and nesting intervals in two or three dimensions; it becomes a two or three-fold series of unit distances. Planes and space itself are thereby converted into metric *quanta*.

(3) Both the earlier coordination and the later synthesis take on a precise rectangular structure because logical multiplication of one-one correspondences in two or three dimensions, although a qualitative operation, demands such a structure, just as much as metrical operations which imply systematic changes in the positions of unit lengths. The perpendicular arrangement of coordinate axes results from the need to define the relations between the two or three sets of one-one correspondences which go to make up the two or three dimensions. A two- or three-dimensional coordinate system, whether qualitative or metric, can therefore be conceived as a table or network with double or treble entry, the columns, rows and layers being disposed at right angles to each other.

Chapter Eight

ANGULAR MEASUREMENT [1]

AS we showed in the last chapter, before children can coordinate measurements in such a way as to fix a point in an area or a solid, they need to evolve a system of one-one correspondences with axes perpendicular. In other words, rectangular coordination depends on the principle of one-one correspondence. The measurement of angles (portions of a plane defined by two straight lines as against four)[2] depends on the principle of one-many correspondence. This conclusion may be familiar from C.C.S., ch. XII, where we studied similarities and proportions. Here we tackle the same problem in relation to the *measurement* of angles and triangles.

Angular measurement will be studied in three sections. Section 1 is devoted to the study of development in measuring open angles (acute and obtuse). Section 2 deals with the measurement of triangles. The last section is concerned with the study of how children gradually discover the characteristic metric property of the angles of a triangle, that they can be arranged in the form of a semi-circle, and hence that they total 180°.

SECTION 1. MEASURING ANGLES

The subject is shown a drawing (see Fig. 1) of two supplementary angles ADC, CDB, and is asked to make another drawing exactly

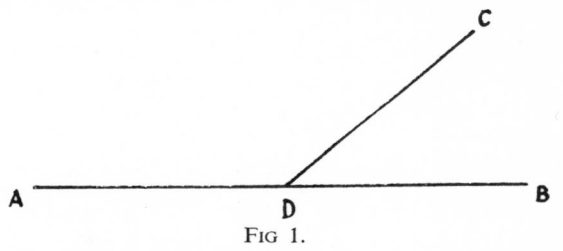

Fig 1.

similar. He is not permitted to look at the model while he is drawing, but he may study and measure it as often as he wishes while not actually

---

[1] Written with the collaboration of Mlles C. Odiniak, U. Galusser, Ch. Matthey, M. D. Nestobescu and L. Muller.
[2] Louis-Betrand defines an angle as the overlap of two half planes bounded by the arms, while Veronese sees it as the set of rays included by the arms (F. Enriques, *Encycl. Math.*, III, 1).

engaged on his own drawing. This requirement is met quite simply by having the model behind the subject. The latter is provided with rulers, strips of paper, string, cardboard triangles, compasses, etc., all of which may be used in measuring. The enquiry is repeated three times in all, the drawings being similar in each case.

Throughout stage I (up to 4–5 years) and sub-stage IIA (up to about 6 years), children were found to copy the drawings by visual estimate. There was no attempt at measurement. Subjects at level IIB measured AB or CD or even both. But these were one-dimensional measurements (and inadequate inasmuch as the essential subdivision of AB into segments AD and DB was neglected). No effort was made to measure the angular separation, and no account was taken of the slope of CD except in terms of visual judgment. Level IIIA was marked by two developments: AD and DB were measured separately and subjects measured the length of CD and tried to maintain the slope of their ruler in reproducing it. At level IIIB, subjects finally measured AC and CB to fix point D and thereby ensure the correct inclination of CD. A number of subjects at level IIIB and nearly all at the beginning of stage IV measured the distance CK, i.e. the perpendicular from C on AB. This measurement alone suffices to fix point C so that it is unnecessary to find the intersection of the distances AC and CB.

§1. *Levels IIA and IIB: Angles not measured*

Children at stage I and sub-stage IIA, being unable to measure an ordinary straight line, make a poor showing when required to measure two lines AB and CD, as well as the angle between them. Even at level IIA visual judgment reigns supreme, there being no measurement whatsoever.

JEA (6; 5) starts by drawing a horizontal line AB together with an upright CD, almost perpendicular to and bisecting AB, all by eye: "Is that right?—*No, it's not good.*—If there's anything you want, you can use whatever you find on the table.—*No, I don't need anything* (he produces another drawing, this time with the angle too acute).—Wouldn't you get it better with the ruler?—*No, I can draw a straight line without a ruler.*—What about measuring? —*No, it's difficult with a ruler.*"

NID (6; 6) draws a horizontal line AB and a line CD which joins AB at a very acute angle and nearly at point A. "Is it right?—*Not quite* (he starts afresh, making CD shorter, but without troubling about its slope).—(A second model.) What about this one?—(He goes about it in a similar manner producing a drawing with angle CDB too obtuse.)"

These responses show how children at level IIA (and *a fortiori* at stage I) not only make no attempt to measure the angles involved or to estimate the slope of CD, but seem to ignore these factors altogether. However, the present findings are in complete agreement with those of

C.C.S., ch. XI (affinitive transformations of a rhombus), and with the observations made by Würsten dealing with *perception* of inclination.

The next level, IIB, is marked by two behavioural gains. Level IIB is when children are first able to construct a rhombus intuitively (C.C.S., ch. II) while their response to affinitive transformations is intermediate (C.C.S., ch. XI). Now subjects show that they are aware of the slope of CD inasmuch as their drawings take it into account, although it is still a visual estimate. At the same time children begin to measure the length of lines.

DRE (7; 3) after sketching two lines with his hand, takes the pencil and draws AB and CD without measuring them. "Is it the same?—*Yes* (but on careful inspection he changes his mind and makes a fresh start. This time he measures AB with thumb and forefinger).—I've given you anything you may need to measure.—*I don't need anything.* (Nevertheless he takes a ruler and measures AB, transferring the measurement to his own drawing. But CD is drawn without any measurement.) *I'm doing it right and still it won't work.*"

MAR (7; 4) uses the ruler in drawing AB and CD but only to keep these lines straight. "All right?—*It's no good.*—What do you need to make it just right?—*I've got to measure it* (measuring AB and CD). *It's still not the same* (the angle is too acute). *Mine is too long.*—But you measured it, didn't you? —*Well, it isn't too long but it's too thin* (i.e. the angle is too narrow).—Can you correct that?—(He measures it again and produces a second drawing, altering the slope of the ruler for CD. But this time the angle is too obtuse.) *It won't work. I don't know why not.*—Maybe you made a mistake?—*No, I measured it right. Maybe your drawing is wrong* (!)"

IRE (7; 4) looks at the models saying: "*I need a ruler to do those, so as to draw the lines right* (as indeed he does, but without measuring them. He then finds his copy is incorrect and therefore measures AB and CD but continues to ignore the position of point D). *That's funny. I've measured it right, but it still won't work!*—Why not? Isn't there something else you might measure?— *No. I've measured that* (AB) *and that* (CD) *and that's all there is* (!)."

GIS (7; 5) draws his copy without using a ruler, putting D too near to A and making the angle too narrow: "Is that right?—*No.*—Why not?—(He makes a fresh drawing, still showing the same errors.)—Don't you need a ruler?—*I could measure the model and then draw it, using the ruler* (measuring AB and reproducing it). *No that's no good. I've forgotten that* (CD. He now measures CD and reproduces the measurement but ignores the exact position of D on AB)."

ALF (7; 5) copies the drawing without measuring it. "*It's not right, because mine is too much this way* (angle too narrow).—Can you do one better?— (Altering the angle.) *No good* (he measures AB and CD). *It won't work.*— Why not?—*I don't know.*"

PIE (7; 6) draws the lines first and then measures them: "*It's no good.*— Why?—*Because mine leans over too much.*—Can you do it right?—*Yes.* (Pie measures AB and plots point D without measuring its position on AB. He then measures CD and reproduces the length without crossing point D.)—

Why did you put a mark there (D)?—*I made a mistake.*—But maybe you need that point?—*No, I'm quite sure I don't.*"

RAY (7; 6) measures AB but not AD. He estimates the position of D and marks it, then measures CD and reproduces it from this point. "Why did you put that point in?—*To know where to draw this line. But mine leans over too far because the ruler did.*—Well, do it right.—(He tries again, without success.)"

DEN (7; 7) first draws the figure entirely by eye, then measures AB and CD: "Is that right?—*No, I measured it wrong* (making a second attempt).—All right now?—*No, but I don't know why not. I measured it very carefully.*—Isn't there something else you could measure?—*No, there are only two lines, and I've measured them both.*"

One-dimensional measurement at this level is familiar from preceding chapters. Subjects use either their hand or a common measure if this is longer than whatever is being measured. Within these limitations their measuring is fairly accurate. But they cannot decompose an interval in terms of an operational schema, subdivision being limited to what is intuitively given in the perceptual figure. The last point is fully borne out by the way in which all subjects measure AB and CD which are perceptually given as straight lines in their own right, while none of them measures AD or DB, which would enable him to fix the point D where CD touches AB. Instead, these children find the point D by simple inspection. They differ from one another only in that some draw CD without first plotting point D, while others, like Pie and Ray, plot D by inspection before drawing CD.

Their attitude to the angle of incidence may seem extraordinary. Perception is fairly accurate, as is shown by the fact that subjects are critical of their own drawings after these are made. But although they can judge whether CD is correctly inclined to AD when their drawing is complete, they are quite unable to reproduce the slope of the model, let alone measure it.

At level IIIA, children try to copy a slope by holding their ruler steady while moving it from the model to their own copy (in ch. VII it was found that even towards the end of level IIB children adopted this procedure in reproducing an oblique measurement which they had made when trying to define a point in a rectangle). However, although this approach seems simple if somewhat ineffective, it implies an understanding of the notion of parallelism between sloping lines. Now the earlier study of *The Child's Conception of Space* showed that such an understanding develops only at level IIIA. It is, of course, superseded at level IIIB when the inclination is referred to rectangular coordinate axes. Thus there is nothing surprising in the fact that at level IIB children seem unaware of the possibility of reproducing a slope and show only a perceptual and somewhat vague recognition of discrepancy between two sloping lines.

176

By the same token they are quite unable to measure the angle as a two-dimensional relationship between the lengths of two sides and their linear separation. Although they measure two separate lines AB and CD, their measurement is strictly one-dimensional. Seeing that the model is composed of two lines, they do not even consider measuring anything besides the two lines in the figure. Spontaneous remarks made by some of these children are revealing and often amusing: "I'm doing it right and still it won't work." (Dre, having measured and reproduced the lengths of AB and CD), "It won't work. I don't know why not . . . I measured it right. Maybe your drawing is wrong!" (Mar, finding his angle "too thin", and discovering that CD "isn't too long", a case of projecting his own point of view—intellectual egocentricity), "That's funny. I've measured it right, but still it won't work . . . I've measured that (AB) and that (CD) and that's all there is." (Ire, implying that angular separation as such is not measurable!), and finally: "There *are* only two lines and I've measured them both!" (Den).

Den's remark effectively sums up the horizon of level IIB: AC, BC and the perpendicular from C on AB are not perceptually apparent in the drawing, therefore they do not exist! All that may be said to exist are the lengths of AB and CD while their slope and angular separation do not. Hence children at this level cannot measure an angle. They cannot envisage subdivision and change of position when these are not actually given and at the same time they lack a coordinate system as well as the ability to establish a two-dimensional one-many relationship.

§2. *Level IIIA: Subjects try to copy the slope thus showing insight into parallelism but they cannot measure angular separation*

In one-dimensional measurement, children at level IIIA are able to coordinate subdivision and change of position. A period of trial-and-error leads to the beginning of measurement. The synthesis of subdivision and change of position which makes mensuration possible appears quite soon after, i.e. at the beginning of level IIIB, or at around 8 or 8 : 6. In two- or three-dimensional measurement we find a transitional level midway between IIB and IIIA. At this level, children substitute a single oblique one-dimensional measurement for the two separate measurements required by the problem. In repeating this measurement they try not to alter the slope of their ruler. At level IIIA they begin to decompose their oblique measurement, finding by trial and error that it is more convenient to take two measurements perpendicular to one another.

However, in the case of supplementary angles, development is slightly less rapid than in two-dimensional measurement where the coordinates are rectangular. In so far as the problem demands one-dimensional measurement its solution is indeed practically complete. Children no longer find point D by inspection. Subdivision is more precise and so

177

they measure either AD or DB or both. But although the origin of CD is correctly reproduced they cannot fix its slope by making the appropriate measurements, these being either the two lines AC and CB or the perpendicular distance CK to the line ADKB. Instead, they simply measure CD and try to maintain the slope of their ruler in applying the measurement to their own drawing. At level IIIA, the same type of response also occurs when subjects are asked to draw a triangle similar to a model (C.C.S., ch. XII, §3).

HEL (7; 10) measures AB and inserts D by inspection. He then measures DC and moves the ruler to his own drawing. "*It won't work.—Why not?— Because I carried the ruler wrong.* (Measures AD.)—Why do you measure that?—*Because I've got to know where to begin this line* (DC. He draws this line but is still not satisfied with its slope). *No good.* (He tries again, seeking not to alter the slope of his ruler.) *I've measured it wrong and I went wrong when moving my ruler.*"

REV. (8; 3) measures AB and AD "*to get it more right*". He then measures CD and transfers the measurement to his own drawing, trying hard to keep the ruler at a constant slope. "*It isn't right because I was very careful about the slope of my ruler when I moved it, but I didn't measure it right.*" Rev seems to think he was more accurate in transferring the slope of CD than he was in measuring it!

LIL (8; 5) measures the bare line AB and estimates point D. He then measures CD but says: "*It won't work.*" He then studies the problem carefully and measures AD, DB and CD. "*The first drawing was wrong so I wanted to do it better.*—And now?—*Maybe I moved that line* (CD) *wrong. I don't know.*"

SUZ (8; 6) measures AB and estimates point D. He measures DC and produces his first drawing. "*It's no good* (he begins again, measuring AD). *It still won't work.*—Why not?—*I moved the ruler wrong* (indicating the slope.)"

ROS (8; 6) begins in a similar manner, then moves the ruler to his own drawing without turning it, trying to maintain its slope "*to make this leaning side.*"

ED (8; 7) begins likewise and evolves a method of his own which shows that he too is anxious to maintain the slope. He draws the beginning of CD on the ruler itself, as if the latter could serve as a "transfer" to transfer the angle. "Why are you doing that?—*Because I need the length and the slope as well and I can't get that.*—Why do you need the slope?—*Because this line* (CD) *isn't straight up, so I've got to do it the way it is.*"

Unlike children at level IIB, these subjects are not satisfied to measure only the two straight lines in the drawing. They are aware that DC can only be plotted if the point D and the angle are determined accurately. The first task is no problem to them and they simply measure AD or DB. But the slope of the line is more difficult. In order to determine this, they would need to find the angular separation by measuring AC or BC or they would need to draw the perpendicular from C on AB.

These children whose ages range from 7 ; 6 to 8 ; 7 (confining ourselves to those whose records are given above) are at level IIIA. In other words they are beginning, by trial-and-error, to discover the technique of measuring in one, two and even three dimensions. Yet these same children are baffled by the problem of measuring an angle and their efforts at solution do not go beyond more or less successful attempts to maintain the slope as such. The same procedure was used by subjects at an intermediate level, between IIB and IIIA, when the problem was one of two-dimensional measurement (ch. VII, §4).

A study of this parallel will throw some light on the present difficulty. Although there is a superficial similarity between the behaviour of the subjects in ch. VII, §4, and those quoted here, these responses are not identical, as indeed is shown by the difference in age and developmental level. Where the children were asked to reproduce a point in a rectangle, the oblique line from the point to the corner of the rectangle was not given in the figure. It was one which the subject himself introduced because he was unable to decompose the measurement in terms of horizontal and vertical distances. Hence he made this oblique measurement and then moved his ruler to another shape nearby, using an intuitive and quasi-perceptual form of parallelism. Here, however, the line CD is already given together with its slope. Hence there is nothing untoward in that the subject should try to reproduce that slope. But what are the intellectual schemata at his disposal? These have been traced in C.C.S.: the children cannot yet equate angles by superposition and simply decide that triangles are similar or dissimilar by examining whether the sides are parallel or not (C.C.S., ch. XII, section 1, §3); more generally, having recently mastered the concept of a straight line, as shown by their ability to construct such a line by aiming or else by maintaining a constant direction (C.C.S., ch. VI), they utilize the concept in forming notions of parallelism between lines irrespective of whether these are oblique or vertical or horizontal (C.C.S., ch. XI). Hence the behaviour of these subjects when reproducing the slope of CD may be said to be governed by the notion of parallelism. Children at this level are as yet unable to determine a slope with reference to rectangular coordinate axes and they cannot understand that two angles may be equated by superposing one on the other (in the present experiment they are provided with cardboard triangles with which to measure the slope of CD but they fail to make use of them). Therefore they try to maintain the slope of their ruler as they move it in an effort to ensure the parallelism of the two lines by simply preserving a given direction of their measuring stick. Others at level IIIA behaved in precisely the same manner when asked to reproduce similar triangles (C.C.S., ch. XII, §3).

Why, it may be asked, do these subjects not measure distances AC and BC and so find the angles ADC and CDB? The answer is that they do not assimilate the figure they are given to a system of angles (indeed the figure was shown deliberately so as to permit of its being considered as a problem of angular measurement while not imposing that solution; we therefore rejected a figure consisting of one angle in favour of two supplementary angles). What they see is a sloping line with one end meeting a horizontal line at a given point; they do not see two angles to be measured as such. Therein lies the interest of their response, an interest which would have been lost had they been asked to measure an angle as given. What we see here is in agreement with the findings of C.C.S. regarding the qualitative elaboration of angles. The fact that there are two supplementary angles accounts for the slight time lag between the behaviour of subjects in dealing with the present problem and their solution of measurement in two dimensions: there is no such time lag in the measurement of triangles (section II).

§3. Level IIIB: Measuring angular separation

At level IIIB, children can equate angles by superposing one on another and are able to construct qualitative similarities as between two triangles differing in size (C.C.S.). In dealing with the present problem, they see the figure as a system of angles. Therefore they measure AC and BC which determine the sizes of the two supplementary angles, and sometimes measure the distance from C to a point K on AB perpendicular to point C. The following are examples, the first instance being intermediate between levels IIIA and IIIB:

GAL (8; 6) begins without measuring but is dissatisfied with the result. He therefore measures AB and CD and produces another drawing: "Is that right? —*No, mine is straight and it should slope that way more.*" He measures AD and plots point D, then draws DC trying to preserve the required slope. Again he studies his drawing and says: "*I must have the distance from there to there* (BC)." He measures AC and CB and alters DC, having found a unique position for point C.

PIE (8; 10) immediately remarks: "*To do that drawing I need to use a triangle.* (He takes one of the cardboard triangles provided and tries to apply it to the figure but abandons it on finding that it does not coincide with the angle CDB). *That's no good; so I have to use two rulers* (to form an angle: he measures AB and DB and draws these, then uses one ruler to measure DC and the other to measure AC. Thus he finds angle ADC by a double measurement).—Why did you take two rulers?—*Because it's easier.*—Could you do it with one ruler only?—*Yes, but I'd have to measure this first* (CD) *and then that* (AC) *to find that point* (C) *so it's quicker with two rulers.*"

LAU (9; 0) measures AB, marking D on his ruler as he does so, then, after drawing the base line ADB he draws the beginning of CD on the ruler itself (as did Ed at level IIIA, the behaviour of Lau being a residium of that level) as well as a line at right angles to it. However, when he finds that the angle he draws is too sharp, he measures the vertical distance CK (being the perpendicular from C on AB), and so finds a unique position for point C by combining this measurement with DC.

MIC (9; 3) produces a first drawing after measuring AB, AD and CD in that order. *"That's no good. I've got to change that line* (DC). *I'll measure this distance* (AC)." He makes this measurement coincide with that of DC and so fixes point C correctly.

JAC (9; 5) measures AB and AD then draws the line AB, marking point D. He then measures the distance AC and plots a provisional point C. After measuring CD he adjusts DC and AC to find the correct slope of the former: "Why did you measure that line (AC) which doesn't exist?—*But I need that line to find the slope of this one* (DC)."

REN (9; 8): *"To do that drawing I need that line* (AC).—Why?— *Because I know where that line* (DC) *begins but I don't know where it ends* (C).—Can't you measure it?—*No, because measuring it will only tell me how long it is, but I have to know how much it slopes as well."* He measures AC and DC to find point C.

LEC (9; 7) measures AB and AD, draws AB, and plots point D, then measures DC and moves his ruler, trying to keep its slope constant (as at level IIIA): *"No, that's not the same.*—Why not?—(He studies the distance AC formed by the angle ADC and replies:) *It's because that length is greater on my drawing than it is on this one.* (He measures AC and corrects his drawing.)—Why did you measure that (AC)?—*To find out how far my line should slope. I have to see how much that one slopes* (DC) *and, to do that, I have to know how far it is from here to here and from here to here* (AC and BC). *But I just took this one* (AC) *because I've already measured this* (AD) *and this* (DB)." In other words he measures the angle ADC and realizes that this is sufficient to determine the supplementary angle CDB.

WIL (9; 10) measures AB and AD, then draws AB, plotting point D. He proceeds to measure DC, but even as he transfers his measurement he exclaims: *"Oh, I need that length there* (AC) *and that length* (CB).—Why?— (He measures AC and says:) *I don't need to know that* (CB).—Why?— *Because it comes to the same* (adjusting AC and DC)."

Some of these cases are intermediate between levels IIIA and IIIB (Gal, Lau and Lec). These children make a discovery which recalls the way in which others in ch. VII found how they could decompose a single oblique measurement and so made two measurements in separate dimensions. The notion of parallelism is found to be inadequate in that they are unable to maintain a constant slope. The children then note that, by using CD together with AC or CB (Gal and Lec) or else with the perpendicular CK (Lau), they can be sure "how far it should slope". The remaining subjects succeed without initial trial-and-error. Immediately on seeing the figure, they assimilate it to an angular or even a bi-angular schema (Wil and Lec, despite the initial trial-and-error). They realise that by measuring the angular separation of ADC, they automatically determine the supplementary angle CDB "because it comes to the same", in Wil's words. Thus, because the figure is assimilated to a system of angles they automatically recognize the need to measure angular separation, which is why they measure those distances which are easiest to repeat, these being AC or BC.

It is quite instructive to compare these findings with what we already know about similar triangles (C.C.S., ch. XII) and about measurement in two or three dimensions (ch. VII, supra). The latter is a matter of rectangular coordination, but in spite of this important difference there is a close connexion between these various aspects of children's behaviour at this level. In the first place, we have to recognize that the measurement of an angle is no less a two-dimensional operation than the definition of a point in a rectangular plane area. This fact does not depend on whether we agree to accept a two-dimensional definition of an angle such as the overlap of two half-planes bounded by its arms. It is just as true even if we choose a one-dimensional definition like Veronese, who defined an angle as the set of all rays radiating from the common vertex and bounded by the two arms. The measurement of an angle still implies a special kind of coordination between the length of the arms and the distance which separates them. These two measurements cannot be oriented in the same dimension and for that very reason they are sufficient to close the area comprised by the arms of the angle. (This will happen whatever point we happen to select to coordinate the two measurements since what we are concerned to establish is the ratio of these distances and not the distances themselves.) But although the measurement of angles is a two-dimensional operation, it is not governed by the principle of one-one correspondence, which describes the matrix of rows and columns of a rectangular coordinate system. As we noted in our discussion of the way in which children discover the principle governing similarity of triangles at the same level, IIIB (C.C.S., ch. XII, section 1), when a series of successive parallel lines is drawn between the arms of an angle at increasing distances from its vertix, the constancy of the ratio of these lines to the arms of the angle depends on one-many correspondence and not on one-one correspondence, because each successive line will correspond with an appropriate distance in units along one or other of the arms. Measurement in terms of such a coordinating scheme of one-many correspondence is achieved at level IIIB and not before. But that is also when one-one or rectangular coordination is mastered. That these two different developments should coincide makes this a crucial turning point in the elaboration of operational intelligence.

§4. *Stage IV: Use of a right-angle in measuring angular separation*

If we continue by putting the problem to children beyond level IIIB and ask those who have reached stage IV which marks the evolution of formal operations we find that they tend to reject such measures of angular separation as AC or CB to measure angles ADC and CDB in favour of the perpendicular CK drawn from point C on ADKB. In other words they use the measurement which figures in the calculation of the tangent. We have sought to establish why this should be. Following are examples of children at the beginning of stage IV; the first of these being intermediate in that the subject uses both methods.

Rol (10; 4) measures AB, then studies DC saying: "*I can't copy that line because it isn't straight* (i.e. vertical)." He then measures AC and DC to determine point C, and checks his finding by measuring CK. "Is that right?— *Yes, but I'll do it again* (he makes a second copy, this time measuring only CK and omitting AC). *It's easier this way, and I can do it quite quickly.*"

Mar (10; 6) measures AB followed by point D, then CK and DC. He then draws in DC "Are you sure that's a true copy?—*Yes.*—Shouldn't you take any other measurements?—*Well, I can measure this* (interval DK on line ADKB), *but since this point* (K) *must be on the same line as* (C) (i.e. the perpendicular from C on AB) *I don't need to.*"

Mir (10; 8) measures AB and AD followed by DC but instead of drawing DC he plots a provisional point at C and then draws a line from C perpendicular to AB (CK). He measures this line and then finds where the vertical distance coincides with DC. "Why did you do it that way?—*I didn't know where to draw this line* (DC). *I knew where to begin* (D) *but not where to end. This way I can tell where this point* (C) *comes on this* (CK), *so I can do it quite easily.*"

Lov (10; 7) measures AB and AD, then measures a line DK' perpendicular to AB, K' and C being the same height above AB, together with the horizontal distance CK'. He then draws ADB, DK' and K'C, in that order, and checks that DC is the same length on both drawings, which he finds to be true. "Why do you need that point (K')?—*To know the middle* (intersection) *of these two lines* (DK' and CK').—How did you find it?—*I put this point immediately above point* (D), *and then I found the distance from* (D) *to* K') *and from* (K') *to* (C)."

Jac (10; 8) measures AB and AD and a line perpendicular to AB drawn from point B and ending at K". He then measures CK" (parallel with AB) and so draws line DC. "Why did you do it that way?—*To get this point* (C) *right.*—Is there no other way of doing it?—*Yes, I could do the same with either side* (i.e. a perpendicular on A) *but it's exactly the same.*"

The children themselves explain why they choose to measure the angle by dropping a perpendicular to the shorter of its arms: it is "easier" as Rol puts it, implying that he has chosen a convention, to measure in terms of rectangular coordinates than it is to take measurements at random. At level IIIB, children have gained an understanding of two kinds of coordination; rectangular axes which enable them to establish one-one correspondences between ranked points and to find the distance between such points in two or three dimensions, and one-many correspondence which enables them to construct similar triangles and to group measurements of the arms of an angle as a function of distances between them. In measuring an angle by dropping a perpendicular to the shorter of its arms, these children effectively integrate one-many correspondences within the framework of a rectangular coordinate system. Without knowing it they are on the verge of measuring angles in terms of the relation between the perpendicular CK and the arm DC (sine) or DK (tangent). Merely by substituting arithmetical multiplication and division for logical coordination and applying it to the distances as measured, they could calculate the sine and tangent of the angle. Naturally enough, they are satisfied with qualitative coordination between these measurements; in other words the relations involved, although expressed in metric terms, are subjected to a process of logical multiplication, whether one-one or one-many, which is qualitative and not quantitative. Nevertheless, the introduction of a perpendicular measurement is highly significant. Given the present experimental conditions, perpendicular measurement does not predominate until stage IV, because it demands a higher degree of imaginative construction than measuring AC and BC. However, the example of Lau is proof that perpendicular measurement may occur at level IIIB. The following sections will show that such measurement is quite general at level IIIB when children are asked to measure a triangle.

SECTION II. MEASUREMENT OF TRIANGLES

Measurement of a triangle may seem a more elementary problem than that of an angle, because it is a closed figure. The subject no longer needs to select an appropriate measurement to determine angular separation. From the standpoint of the necessity for one-many correspondence between relevant measurements the construction presents only one difficulty (once the child has passed beyond the stage of trial-and-error as revealed in his attempt to construct triangles by adjusting the three sides to each other): finding the height of the triangle in relation to its base. Yet the following observations make it clear that responses develop in the same way whatever the task, angular measurement or measurement of triangles. Although the model he is asked to reproduce in easier in the latter case, because its intuitive appearance is more complete, the subject has the same difficulty in intellectually decomposing and recomposing the distances involved, and he therefore passes through the same developmental phases.

We used a technique which was itself quite similar to the first. The triangle reproduced in figure 2 (with only the continuous lines ABC shown) is put on a table behind the subject. He is given a sheet of plain white paper and asked to make an exact copy of it. Various aids are provided such as graduated double-decimetre rulers, sticks and strips of paper.

Children at levels I and IIA do not measure the figure at all. They simply copy it by eye. Those at level IIB measure the three sides one at a time, i.e. their measurement is one-dimensional. Hence they fail to define where the three lines meet, and the angles are inaccurate. At

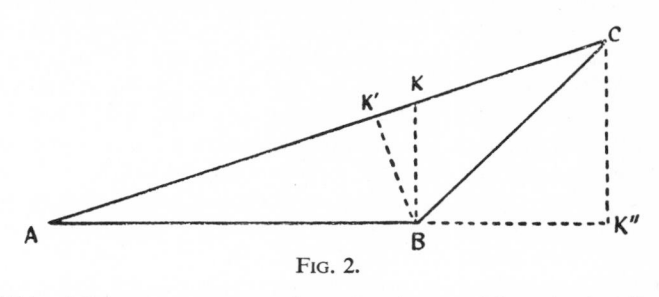

FIG. 2.

level IIIA, children try to reproduce the slopes of lines by holding their ruler at a constant orientation. They are able to adjust the three sides to each other by trial-and-error. At level IIIB, subjects measure the height of the triangle in addition to the three sides. Finally, at stage IV, they make constructions of their own outside the limits of ABC (K'').

§5. *Levels IIA and IIB: Measurement is absent altogether or is confined to linear measurement of the three sides without coordination between them*

We begin with two examples of level IIA: there is no attempt at measurement.

TA (6; 5) draws the triangle without even using a ruler: "*It's not good.—* Why?—*Because I started it wrong. I started with this one* (AB. In his second attempt he draws BC before AB). *It's still not good. I know where I should start: there.* (This time, he begins with the uppermost side AC. He produces a triangle, but one which is quite different from the model.) *I've tried it all, and it won't work.—*Why not?—*I don't know.—*Couldn't you do it better by using a ruler?—*No, because the line I have to draw is not straight* (indicating the perimeter of the triangle) *but the ruler is a straight line.*"

HEN (6; 6) draws a triangle twice without measuring and complains: "*It isn't good.—*Well, what can you do to make your drawing the same as this one?—*I'll try again.* (He tries once more, without success, and says:) "*I don't understand what's wrong.*"

These initial responses are most interesting. The reader will recall that at stage I (i.e. up to about 4 years of age), children cannot copy a triangle at all. What they draw is a closed curve which is indistinguishable from their drawing of a circle (C.C.S., ch. II). But at sub-stage IIA children learn to differentiate between triangles, circles, squares and rectangles. Thus both Jea and Hen produce triangles in this situation, which is what we may expect since they are both over 6, and therefore approaching the end of level IIA. But that is the limit of their success. The triangles they draw are all acute-angled and most are isosceles. Thus even from the purely qualitative point of view, they are unable to coordinate the subdivisions of the figure (its three sides) with their slopes. Failure is most conspicuous in their dealings with BC. When even qualitative coordination is lacking, there can be no thought of measurement which we have shown to be a synthesis of subdivision and change of position. Even more striking is the refusal of Ta to use the ruler because he sees a contradiction between the ruler as a straight line and a triangular outline. Instead of measuring, he tells us *a priori* that all measurement is one-dimensional, and therefore inapplicable to such things as triangles!

This limitation shows clearly at level IIB, when children begin to make one-dimensional measurements although these are still intuitive and incomplete, as we saw earlier. Measurement is incomplete because there is incomplete synthesis between subdivision and change of position, while measurement in two dimensions is altogether absent and children simply take one measurement, often an oblique. So also in reproducing supplementary angles they measure the sides and not their angular separation. In reproducing a triangle these children measure each of the sides in succession, but they fail to reproduce their inclinations and are therefore at a loss to know where to make them meet. What is quite remarkable is that, in their drawings, the three lines do not meet at all. The first of the examples which follow is the record of Dre, an intermediate case who has already been quoted in §1.

DRE (7; 3) draws a triangle beginning with the base line AB; followed by AC and BC (with an acute angle at C): "*It's not right.*—Why?—*You've got to start there* (C).—Why?—*Because that line* (AC) *is not straight* (i.e. neither vertical nor horizontal. He tries and fails, once more).—Can you do it another way?—*I don't know how.*—Suppose you used the ruler.—(He measures AB, AC and BC, but now AC and BC do not meet when he reproduces their lengths.) *I've tried it with the ruler and it doesn't work.*—Why not?—*I don't know.*" He continues trying, and whenever he draws the triangle without measuring it his lines form a triangle, but when he tries to reproduce his measurements, they do not meet at C.

TRE (7; 4) measures AC and draws it, then CB, and finally AB: "*It's wrong* (the gap is now at B)! *This must lean over more* (indicating AC. He tries again). *I don't know why it won't work. Each time I've measured all the sides. There's something wrong* (AB and CB fail to meet at B). *This line* (AB) *has got to be quite straight* (i.e. horizontal) *so it can't meet that one.*—Have you measured everything?—*Yes, I've measured the three lines and that's all there is.*"

MAR (7; 4) measures first AB, then CB and AC: "*It's not right. This line* (AC) *is too short in my drawing.* (It's length is correct but the line fails to meet

AB.)—Why?—*I've measured it wrong* (he now measures first AC, then CB, then realizing that if he measures AB his line will be too long, he simply draws a straight line BA without measuring it).—Shouldn't you measure that line (AB) as well?—*No, it's a straight line so I can do it without measuring* (!)— But why is it shorter than on that one?—*I don't know.*"

JAN (7; 5) measures AB and AC: "*It's no good!* (He tries again, beginning with AC then AB and finally BC.) *It's still no good, because I measured that one first* (AC. He tries again, beginning with BA). *It's no good. That line* (BC) *is too far on my drawing.*—Why?—*I don't know. I shouldn't begin with* (BA). (He tries once more starting with another side.) *It's still no good. I don't know why, but it isn't right.*—Have you measured everything?—*Yes, that's the only way to measure.*"

GIS (7; 5) Similar trial-and-error: "*It won't work. It's always the same. It isn't my fault: I've measured it right.*"

RAY (7; 6) measures AC and CB then exclaims: "*It's not right. That line* (AC) *is too long and that one* (CB) *must be like that* (indicating the backward slope and beginning his measurements again). *It's nearly right. It's not quite right because I haven't measured it right.*—Are you quite sure you haven't measured it right?—*Yes, it's too long. It's because I didn't look at the numbers carefully.*"

ALF (7; 6) measures AC and CB and finds his sides fail to meet as he goes to reproduce AC: "*This line* (AC) *leans over too far in my drawing.*—Well try again.—(Same result.) *I don't know why, but it won't work. I've measured all the lines and it won't work. It's the only way you can measure.*"

These responses form an exact parallel with those made to the problem of angular measurement, but with the odd hypothesis that the measurements must be taken in a particular order, as though their sum were not commutative or even associative!

As in the problem of angular measurement, younger children do not realize that the inclination of the sides demands an additional measurement. They imagine that by simply measuring the three sides they will find that these meet automatically, and they are so certain of this that their conviction remain unshaken until their experience has shown time and again that it lacks foundation. Evidently they have forgotten their earlier difficulties in graphic construction. Between the ages of 3 and 5 children learn to draw triangles and make the sides meet by trial-and-error. For a long time they continue to draw them so that their lines do not slope correctly and therefore fail to meet as they should. (C.C.S., ch. II, and ch. I dealing with perceptual activity as shown in haptic exploration.) But, at level IIB their perceptual and intuitive powers are such that drawing a triangle presents no problem, and what is more, unlike children at level IIA, they succeed in drawing an obtuse angled triangle. Indeed, from the age of about six, children can even copy a diamond accurately at an intuitive level (C.C.S., chs. II, XI). However, when a child tries to lend a greater precision to his drawing of the triangle by measuring its sides, he shows that his concept of a triangle is an intuitive whole such that its unity falls apart so soon as any of its parts is subjected to a separate analysis: if he measures each side separately, they no longer meet! His articulated intuition of a triangle consists of sides which are related to each other in a rigid way so that they simply complement one another. The sides of the triangle have no determinate 'inclination', because inclination is not separated out in their consciousness in the form of a mobile property which can be conserved in its own right. At level IIB, a child no sooner isolates one side of the triangle to measure it, than he ignores its position and concentrates entirely on its length, with the result that the intuitive whole is destroyed. He lacks the ability to compose the three lines by coordinating subdivision with order and change of position. Because the whole is not structured in terms of a mobile and reversible operational grouping, the inclinations of the three lines and their intersections cannot be systematically coordinated. The problem of drawing a triangle is particularly revealing in this connection: the children cannot understand why their efforts are unsuccessful as is shown by their comments, "I don't know why it won't work. . . . I've measured all the sides . . . that's all there is," Ray and Alf, who are the only ones to mention the slope of the lines, fail to conclude that their method of measuring is too limited.

Many of these children, who find that they cannot copy the triangle successfully by measuring the three sides and that the last two sides do not meet as they should, imagine that they will be more successful if they perform the same operations in a different order. A child who begins with AB ends with a gap between BC and AC, and imagines he should have begun with BC; but when he tries to do this he ends with a gap between AB and AC, so he tries again, beginning with AC. When asked why the order is important, he replies like Jan: "I don't know, but I shouldn't begin with (BC)." While the fact that they think the order of measurement is all important is understandable, it still points yet again to the synthesis of subdivision and order and change of position as the essential prerequisite of measurement. Here there can be no synthesis because the two notions are not even adequately differentiated. The belief that the three sides will meet if measured in one order but not if the order is changed implies confusion between change of position which is not commutative and summation of parts which is, and failure to recognize that both groupings are associative.

§6. *Level IIIA. Measurement of inclination and angles is discovered by trial-and-error*

In dealing with the problem of copying supplementary angles children at level IIIA tried to hold their ruler at a constant slope while applying their measurement to their own drawings (§2). When copying a triangle, they show the same response, either by itself, as in the first of the following examples, or, more often, together with trial-and-error aimed at making the sides meet. For the essential difference between this task and the earlier one is that here the three sides in the model do in fact meet. Towards the end of sub-stage IIIA, children no longer try to maintain a constant slope with their ruler but simply adjust the three measurements to one another by trial-and-error. The first three examples are of the first type:

VAL (8; 6) measures BC and tries to reproduce the slope of his ruler, then does the same with AC. AB is drawn horizontally as measured, but BA and AC fail to meet at A: "*It's no good. Perhaps I've made a mistake: I haven't measured it right.* (He tries again, with meticulous attention to detail, but still meets with failure.) *Oh, I keep forgetting that I must measure it just right.* —Is that the only way you can go wrong, to measure the length badly?— *Yes, because I'm careful about my hand* (i.e. the constant slope of the ruler) *when I move the ruler across.*"

BED (8; 3) measures and copies first AC then BC and finally AB, being careful each time to maintain the slope of his ruler. There is a gap at B: "*I've got to make it lean over like that* (BC on the model). *I've got to measure it leaning over. I've got to be careful about how it leans.*" After two further attempts, both unsuccessful, he measures CB again, but instead of drawing it he marks B provisionally and then does the same with AB. Then he studies the interval between these points and tries again until the gap is shortened and finally eliminated. He then constructs a second triangle using the new method throughout: "Why do you do it that way?—*It's easier to do a point like this because I can correct it, but a line is harder to correct.*"

JUL (8; 6) measures and copies in the order AC, BC and AB trying to preserve their inclination. He too ends with a gap: "*No good.*" He tries, and fails, again. He now measures AC and makes a pencil mark at C: "Why did you do it that way?—*To get the point right. I must get it leaning over right so I've got to try it out like that.*"

The developmental process is identical with that shown in the problem of angular measurements: measurement of length (level IIB) breaks up the unity of the figure as given intuitively, therefore the subjects must re-unite the sides by introducing new relations in place of the articulated intuitions of level IIA. Hence we find that they now pay attention to the slope as such which is first thought of simply as an instance of parallelism (Val, and initially, Bed and Jul). However when this method fails they discover a solution by trial-and-error and find the apex of their triangle by repeatedly adjusting the two measured sides. The subjects to be quoted next use only this method. They first copy the base line, then they adjust the remaining two sides until they find the point where they meet exactly without alteration in length:

HEL (8; 3) first measures and copies the base line AB, then measures AC and BC and by applying these measurements from A and B and trying various inclinations, eventually finds their meeting point at C. "Why did you do it that way?—*Because these lines lean over which means that I've got to make them lean over the same.*—Is there another way of doing it?—*No.*"

SOL (8; 8) measures AB and draws it, then measures AC, plots a point C and measures BC, plotting another point for C, remarking: "*It isn't right yet.*" He continues by bringing the two points closer together until they coincide. Given another triangle to copy he proceeds in the same way. "Why do you do it like that?—*To get them leaning over right. I mean to get the triangle right.*—Is there another way of doing it?—*No, I've got to measure the lines right and then make sure they lean over the right way.*"

GER (8; 9) draws the base line AB, then measures AC and BC and combines these measurements to make them coincide at C. "Why do you do it like that?—*Because the lines aren't horizontal. They lean over, so I've got to look at them until I get mine leaning over the same.*—And you couldn't do it another way?—*Well, I could copy the lines the way they are* (indicating their slope) *but this way it's more accurate.*"

WAL (9; 0) measures AB "*because it's quite horizontal*" then measures AC and BC saying as he does so: "*It's very difficult to get them to meet at the same point* (he adjusts them bit by bit).—Can you do it another way? Maybe an easier way?—*No, because it's right like this.*—Are you sure?—*Yes, because the lines are very different, I've got to do it this way.*"

We note that there is a growing precision about the way in which relations are coordinated. The beginning of sub-stage IIIA marks the first conscious recognition of inclination, while at the end, with Wal, the problems of construction are anticipated, which foreshadows level IIIB. Measurement of three sides combined with adjustments to achieve triangularity corresponds to the solutions offered at level IIIB in the problem of angular separation (§3). The difference lies in the fact that in the case of a triangle the three sides to be adjusted are all visibly apparent in the model. It would hardly be correct to call this behaviour an instance of two-dimensional measurement. It corresponds exactly to the first attempts at decomposition seen at sub-stage IIIA in ch. VII.

§7. *Level IIIB: The height of the triangle is measured in addition to its three sides*

Anticipating their problem as did Wal, the most advanced subject at the preceding level, children at sub-stage IIIB immediately decompose the triangle to arrive at a height perpendicular to one of the sides in addition to a length for each side. Thus all the relevant dimensions are ascertained in a systematic manner without trial-and-error.

JAC (9; 4) measures the base line AB, followed by BK drawn perpendicular to AB. Measuring AC, he draws it to pass through K (AKC) and simply joins CB without measuring it: "Why do you need that line (BK)?—*Because,*

by doing that line, I can tell exactly where to put that point (C). —How?—
Because all I have to do then is to measure the line (AC). —Couldn't you
measure it right away?—*No, because I wouldn't know how far it should lean
over."*

GEL (9; 8) measures and draws AB and then measures BK′ perpendicular
to AC as it will be. Then, measuring AC, he adjusts it to form a right angle
with BK′. Finally, he joins CB. "Why did you measure that (BK′)?—*To know
where to draw my line* (AC) *because that point* (K′) *must be just right on* (AC).
—Couldn't you do it another way?—*No, because it isn't enough just to measure
the lines* (the three sides)."

JEA (9; 9) draws the base line AB then measures BK perpendicular to it and
joins KA. He then measures KC and draws it in prolongation of AK.
Finally he joins CB: "Why did you measure that line (BK)?—*To know the
width* (i.e. the height of the triangle).—Why did you measure (KC)?—
Because I needed that line. The other half (AK). *I did just like that* (by joining
the two end points). But why did you have to measure (KC)?—*To get that
point* (C) *and join it to* (B)."

NAD (9; 11) measures and draws AB then plots K′ in the model: "Why do
you do that?—*To know the width.*—Do you need to?—*Yes, the triangle is
crooked and if I know the width I can make it lean over the right way."*

LOD (10; 0) immediately asks: "*Can I measure that distance* (BK)?—Yes.
Why?—*Because otherwise I won't know how high to make it.*—Why?—*Well,
I can measure how long they are but I have to know how they lean over as well,
otherwise I can't do the drawing properly, because that line* (AC) *leans over
so I don't know where to put this point* (C).—And if you draw that line (BK)
are you sure of getting the point (C) right?—*Yes. That point* (K) *has got to
be on the line* (AC). *Then, if I measure* (AC) *I know it all."*

These responses are interesting for two reasons. First, children now
feel the need for measuring in more than one dimension, as indeed they
do in the earlier problems of finding a point in a rectangle or measuring
an angle. By measuring the height of the triangle as well as its sides,
they effectively coordinate their measurements in terms of an anticipating operational schema. That schema argues a general principle of
one-many correspondence as does the schema which governs the
measurement of angular separation. Both of these appear at level IIIB
which is also marked by the first appearance of one-one correspondence
(ch. VII). Second, we note that in copying a triangle children measure
its height at level IIIB. They measure a perpendicular to one of its sides
(more correctly, either of its longer sides). Thus BK is perpendicular to
AB and BK′ to AC, the longest side of the triangle (and therefore con-
ventionally described as its height). Both lines figure in the calculation
of the sines or tangents, BK for angle CAB and BK′ for angle ACB.
The use of these measurements argues a general coordination as in the
case of angular measurement. However, when the problem is a closed
figure this behaviour appears somewhat earlier, at level IIIB, and not
at level IV as in the preceding section.

191

§8. *Stage IV: Perpendicular construction lines are drawn outside the figure as given*

Although in measuring a triangle children begin to establish its height at level IIIB, at or about stage IV they spontaneously introduce construction lines which did not appear before. Children of 9 or 10 measure perpendiculars within the figure as given (level IIIB), but children of 10 or 11 and over usually seem to prefer to establish K″C, which lies outside the original triangle. K″ lies on the prolongation of AB where it meets the perpendicular from C. This construction does not argue a different coordination from that of level IIIB, but it argues a greater freedom from the limitations of what is perceptually given, and as such it is typical of the beginnings of formal thought:

Lou (10; 7, cf. §4) measures and copies AB and immediately draws its prolongation, indicating point K″, and saying: "*This point has got to be on the same line.*" He then measures BK″, plotting K″, and goes on to measure and draw the perpendicular K″C. AC is now ruled in without further measurements: "Why did you measure (CK″)?—*It's the height, so I need it.*—Why?— *To get the slope right.*"

Calv (10; 9) measures CK″ straight off, saying: "*I have to know its height to copy it exactly.*—Why?—*Because if I know its height I can draw it accurately.*—Why?—*By getting this point* (C).—Are you sure it's right?—*Yes, because this line* (K″C) *is at right angles to that one* (AK″) *and that's how I get this point right.*"

Mad (10; 11) laughs: "*I can't copy it exactly without putting in some more lines.*—Why?—*I've got to draw a line there and one there* (indicating BK″ and K″C on the model).—Why?—*Once I have that line* (K″C) *that's all I need and I can do it quite easily* (he measures AC, AB and K″C, continuing AB to K″ and produces his copy).—And why do you need (K″C)?—*Because that's the height and by knowing the height I know where to put* C."

Mad gives an explicit statement of the principle which governs the use of construction lines: to make an exact copy of a figure one must put in lines which do not exist! The statement contains the germ of a whole epistemological theory. Briefly, it shows how mathematical operations enrich an object by conferring on it additional properties which stem from coordinated action on the part of a subject, and are not taken direct from the object as given. This is a principle which operates throughout the developmental sequence from stage I to stage IV, but its operation is unconscious at the levels of action and intuition because younger children project their own constructions on the object. Formal thought, on the other hand, is aware of its own constructive role, because the whole course of development which leads up to it serves to divorce it from action, and because it marks a stage at which the subject has gained full control over his own thought processes.

§9. *Measurement of an irregular polygon*

In order to check these findings, a number of children at the various levels were presented with an irregular polygon and asked to copy it. The figure is unlike any they are likely to encounter in their school work but it can be decomposed as a number of triangles (Fig. 3). The responses agree well with those given in previous tasks, measuring a triangle or supplementary angles, although complete success appears somewhat later. At level IIA, children do not measure and their copies are grossly distorted:

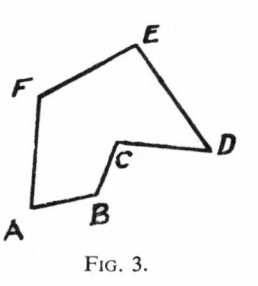

Fig. 3.

RIC (6; 2) draws **AB, BC, CD, DE, EF** and **FA** in that order without measuring any of them: "*It's not good.—*Why?*—I started it wrong* (he begins again at A but proceeds in an anti-clockwise fashion, ending with **BA**). *That's no good either. I can't do it. It's a funny drawing. I don't know how to draw it properly.*—Should you use a ruler?*—No.*—Can you measure?*—Yes* (applying a ruler). *No, it won't work. I can't measure properly.*"

At level IIB, children measure each line but they ignore its orientation with the result that their figure ends with a gap:

SIM (7; 1) first measures **FA** and **FE**, then **AB, BC, CD** and **DE**. He smiles and says: "*It won't work. I've measured all the lines but I can't do this drawing:*—Look at it carefully.*—I might have measured it wrong* (trying again). *No, I've been ever so careful this time and I kept my finger on the ruler where I measured all the time.*—Why?*—Maybe I started the wrong way. You should begin here* (AB).—Why?*—That's the straight* (i.e. horizontal) *line.*"

GUS (7; 2). The behaviour is similar, but in the end he abandons measurement altogether, and simply copies the drawing fairly correctly: "Why aren't you measuring any more?*—When you measure it you only get the straight lines and not where to put them. It's where I put them which was wrong so I don't have to measure for that.*"

The awareness shown in the last remark heralds level IIIA, when children try to conserve slope as such:

DEL (8; 3) measures each line in turn trying to maintain the slope of his ruler as he copies it because: "*It's got to be in the same position.*—Couldn't you measure something else?*—No. I've measured all the sides very carefully. Now I've got to be careful about where I put them in.*—Can't you measure that? *—No! You can't measure that! You've just got to be careful about how it leans over and I may have gone wrong about that.*"

BER (8; 4): "*To do mine exactly the same I've got to measure each side and make it lean over the same* (he tries). *It's not right. Either I measured it wrong or I went wrong when I moved the ruler.*"

RIE (8; 6) ends with a gap in his figure and says: "*I don't know how to do it, but I know I measured it right and I know I moved my ruler right.*—Well, can you do anything else?—*No, I can't. It's very difficult copying its position* (i.e. its inclination)."

These responses are of course quite characteristic of the beginnings of stage III when children are aware of slope and parallelism but are still unable to effect a rectangular or triangular coordination and orient measurements by one-one or one-many correspondence. But at level IIIB children decompose the figure into a series of triangles and measure distances which are not shown as lines on the model. However their decompositions and recompositions are inadequate to the present problem because its solution demands measurements external to the figure itself.

EAN (9; 10) measures AB, AF and FB to produce the triangle ABF. He also measures triangles BCF and FEC but not CDE, since he measures only CD and ED and not BD or CE, and consequently he fails to reproduce point D correctly.

THER (9; 11) measures the same distances as Ean and also CE. His figure is correct except for the triangle CDE, which cannot be drawn without BD: "Have you measured every distance?—*Yes, there aren't any more points for me to join.*"

Finally, at stage IV, children solve the problem because they no longer scruple to measure BD, external to the figure:

JOS (10; 9) immediately breaks up the figure into four triangles, measuring all the intervals including BD: "Why do you split it up like that?—*To know where to rule my lines. If I get the triangles right, the figure is bound to be right, if I have all the lines the right length and leaning over correctly.*" His drawing is successful.

ROB (10; 11) splits the figure into a number of triangles and adds two external construction points, K in prolongation of AF giving a right angle FKE and K′ in prolongation of KE giving a right angle EK′D. Thus triangle EK′D assures the correct slope of ED and triangle FKE that of FE, given the measurements of KE, EK′, FK and K′D: "Why did you do it that way?—*Because it's not enough just measuring the lines if I'm to put them leaning over right.*—But why did you put in (K′) which isn't on the model?—*Because I must have it so as to know where to draw* (DE)."

There is a remarkable synchronization as between the stages which appear in the task of copying this irregular polygon and those which figure in the copy of a triangle. Here, too, we note how freely construction lines are used at stage IV, the level of formal thought. The fact that measurement is dependent on development in reasoning is even more apparent in the progressive solution of the above task of copying an irregular polygon than in the previous problems of copying angles or a triangle. The reasoning may be seen in the form of coordinations and unconscious synthesis and, eventually, of deliberate deduction as well,

SECTION III. THE SUM OF THE ANGLES OF A TRIANGLE

If measurement implies a complex operational coordination, or a chain of reasoning, whether explicit or implicit, then the stages in measuring angles and triangles should have their counterpart in the development of reasoning about metric relations since these are founded on the growth of understanding in measurement. The well-known property of the angles of a triangle, that their sum is always 180°, suggests an interesting technique to analyse the whole genetic sequence whereby the construction of measurement leads into mathematical reasoning about metric relations. In presenting the problem, care was taken to avoid such verbal formulae as "the sum of its angles", and instead of using the abstract notion of 180° we spoke of a semi-circle which can be seen or envisaged intuitively.

The use of a concrete mode of presentation made it a simple matter to put the problem to children of all ages from 4 or 5 to 11 or 12, in order to analyse the responses at each of the levels which figure in the measurement of angles and triangles. The child is simply asked to predict what the angles of a triangle will look like if cut with scissors and rearranged in the shape of a half moon. He may be shown that in this or that instance they form a semi-circle and the enquiry is pursued to see whether he will generalize the solution to differently shaped triangles.

Two slightly different techniques were used alternately, each with different subjects. In the first the emphasis was on empirical discovery and generalization while the second technique was aimed more at revealing anticipation and deduction, with rather more stress on the abstraction of angles from the figure. In the first technique the subject is presented with three dissimilar right-angled triangles, of different sizes, but with the angles already cut in sectors so that they can be rearranged in the shape of a semi-circle. He is first told to pick up and replace the angles of one triangle to help him to deal with the abstraction of the angle. Next, two of the angles are put side by side and he is asked to predict what they will look like when the third angle is put to them. He does so and finds they form a semi-circle. The procedure is repeated with the other right-angled triangles, followed by three equilateral triangles (4 cm. 10 cm. and 32·5 cm.) three isosceles triangles (with bases 9, 16 and 50 cm. and heights 2·5, 4·7 and 14 cm. respectively) and three different scalene triangles. In order to enable the experimenter to pass easily from one series to another in accordance with the needs of the enquiry, all these triangles have their angles ready cut-out, so that the only problem for the child is to predict what shape they will assume when arranged side by side. Occasionally, the experimenter may suggest permutations of the three angles to see if the child realizes that such a change in order leaves their sum unaffected. Alternatively he may suggest taking an angle from another triangle and substituting it for one that belongs to the triangle with which the child is dealing, to see if he realizes that an angle from one triangle will not usually make up a semi-circle when put alongside two angles from a different triangle. Finally, a drawing of a very elongated triangle was introduced and as the enquiry proceeded the drawing was elongated more and more to see how far the subject could generalize his findings.

In the second technique, the child is shown a triangle similar to that used in section II, and asked to imagine what the 'corners' will look like if put together. The triangle is intact. Only after the child has made a reply, he is shown another similar triangle, with its angles already cut, and told to put them together. Wherever possible, the child is asked to make a prediction before seeing the result and he is encouraged to try various solutions until he discovers the answer for himself either by reasoning or by actually putting the angles together. This procedure is repeated with five other triangles of widely different shapes and the experimenter sees how far the subject can generalize.

These techniques gave rise to the following results: At level IIA children cannot abstract the angles as such and they cannot predict their sum. To them the original angles are 'roofs' and their re-arrangement is a 'half-moon' and the two are utterly heterogeneous. When considering the re-arrangement of angles they concentrate on their number and ignore their angular shapes. Even after seeing for themselves that their sum is a semi-circle, they do not generalize this result. They even fail to see that simply altering the order of their arrangement will not affect their sum, i.e. there is no conservation. It may happen that a result which was observed in one experiment is transferred to another, which makes it look as if the subject is generalizing, but in fact this is mere economy of thought and not true composition. At level IIB, permuting the order of the angles no longer affects their sum. But the very fact that children reason more means that they are less apt to make hasty generalizations, and as a result they are less sure that the angles of a different triangle will also sum to 180°. At level IIIA, children begin to generalize and are nearer to discovering the general law. But whereas induction and deduction are complementary processes in the adult, at this level they frequently conflict, because generalized composition does not go hand in hand with analysis if the latter is at all superficial. Hence responses of children at this level often seem less accurate than those given at stage II. At level IIIB children discover the law, but only by gradual inductive steps, while at stage IV the law is conceived as both universal and necessary.

§10. *Stage II: The relevant relations are not understood*

At stage I, children cannot predict that the angles of the first triangle, which they see already cut, will make a semi-circular shape. When they discover that this is so, they still fail to generalize the finding. At times there is a transfer of response from one triangle to another, but this is mere economy of thought and not generalization based on genuine composition. Even at level IIA, children are uncertain whether the angles of a triangle will still form a semi-circle if their order is altered.

FUL (5; 6) puts together three ready-cut angles taken from a right-angled triangle and sees that they form a semi-circle, although he failed to predict it: "What if I put these two corners together (taken from a second triangle) and then put the third corner alongside, what will these make?—*They'll make a half-moon as well.*—What if I do the same with the corners of that triangle (another right-angled triangle but much larger)?—(Indicates a figure less than 180°.)—Why will it be less?—(No reply.)—(Experiment.)—*Oh, it's the same!*—Now what if I take this corner on this side and put it over on that side instead of this one and put this one over here?—*It'll be bigger.*—Are you sure? —*No, it'll be a half-moon.*—Why?—*No, it will be more.*—And what if we put the corners of this figure together (a trapezium)?—*They'll make a whole circle because there are several large ones.*—And the three corners of this one (a small equilateral triangle).—*They'll make a half-moon and a little bit.*— Why?—*These two little corners make a half-moon.*—(Experiment.)—*Oh, no! It's a half-moon!*—And if I change these two round (as before)?—*A half-moon leaning over . . . I don't know.*"

RUF (5; 8) puts two angles of a triangle together: "And supposing we put the third one there as well?—*It'll make a circle.*—Why?—*That one will go right round.* (Demonstration.) *No, it's a bit of a circle, half.*—And the corners of that one?—*They'll make a bit of a circle, like the other.*—What if I put the four corners of this one (trapezium) together?—*They'll make a bit of a circle too.*—Look.—(Experiment.)—*Oh no, it's a whole circle.*—And if I take the four corners of this one (square)?—*They'll make a circle too.*—And the three corners of this one (isosceles triangle)?—*A half-moon.*—Why?—*Because there are three little cards.*—(Experiment.) Now, what if I change these two round (permuting two angles).—*It'll be bigger.*"

Clearly, even when these subjects predict that a 'half-moon' will result from the juxtaposition of the angles of a new triangle, their prediction is a case of simple transfer based on economy of thinking. The prediction itself is not constant (cf. Ful who predicts "A half-moon and a little bit" for a small triangle), and may be extended to a trapezium as well as a triangle (Ful). It is still far from being a necessary law as is quite clear from the fact that children believe the 'half-moon' will grow bigger or smaller as the order of the angles is permuted.

At level IIB, children admit that the semi-circle will remain constant when the angles are permuted, but because their intuitions are more articulated, they are less readily satisfied with simple transfer, and as a result, they are less sure that each new triangle will still yield 180°.

LIP (5; 11) puts the corners of a triangle together. "What will you end up with?—*I don't know. This* (more than a semi-circle).—Now look.—*It's a half-moon.*—And those two (larger triangles)?—*I think they'll make this* (less than a semi-circle).—And this one (right-angled triangle with which he is busy)?—*It will make half.*—Why?—*Because you can see it.*—And if I change two corners round?—*The same.*—And this one (a trapezium)?—*I don't know. This* (semi-circle).—(Experiment.)—And this (isosceles triangle)?—*A circle, but not quite* (but still > 180°).—Look.—(Experiment.)—*Oh no, it's a half.*"

SHE (6; 4) finds that the first triangle yields a "*half moon.*—What if we do the same with this one (a large right-angled triangle)?—*The same. No, more than half.*—(Experiment.)—*No, it's half.*—And that one (a small right-angle triangle)?—*A half-circle . . . No, more*", etc. "What if I take this corner and change it round with that one?—*It'll be smaller, because it's the other side.*—Why?—*No, it'll be the same.*—And like this (a different permutation)?—*Still the same.*"

RYS (6; 10): "Supposing I cut out all the corners of this triangle and put them together?—*They'll make a house, because it's the roof of a house.*—Try it with that one (ready cut).—*It makes half a balloon.*—(Another triangle.) And that one?—*Another roof of a house.*—Try.—*Oh, it's another half a balloon.*—And that one?—*That will be bigger,*" etc.

There is little progress as compared with level IIA. The semi-circle is now unaffected by permutation of the angles (although She is hesitant about this) but the sum is not seen as necessary or generalized to all triangles. When the second technique is used (as it was with Rys), the angles are not abstracted and the child quite fails to predict what their juxtaposition will yield.

§11. *Level IIIA. Relations begin to be educed*

Reponses at level IIIA are more interesting because children now try to envisage in detail the effect of uniting the three angles and are no longer content with a global prediction. This development corresponds with other reactions previously seen at the same sub-stage, notably their understanding of similarity (C.C.S., ch. XII, §3), their partial success in measuring triangles (§6 of this chapter) and in general the attention which children now pay to inclination of lines. Moreover, the experimenter can now ask children to draw what the angles will look like beforehand (instead of asking them to choose from ready-made drawings) and can even ask them to make a fresh drawing for each prediction. As a result we find a revealing conflict between the detailed representation of angles and the generalization reached from previous constructions. It is a conflict which remains unresolved at this level.

TCHA (7; 3) stands midway between level IIB and level IIIA in that he can abstract the angles as such but has considerable difficulty in geometrical composition. His first prediction is of three little triangles base to base (like three roofs): "*Oh, they're not touching. There* (he makes them touch at the apices but the sides still fail to meet, so that the drawing looks like a cloverleaf).—Look (the experimenter assembles the first two angles).—*Oh, like a cake!*—Well you put in the third angle.—(Drawing it > 180° he finds his error.)—And that one (a right-angled triangle)?—*There's the big one* (right angle) *the little one and the other little one* (< 180°, but with an isosceles right-angled triangle he ends with 180°).—Look. (Experiment.)—*It's right.* —And that one (scalene)?—(Draws it < 180°.)—Look.—(Experiment.)— *Another half-circle.*—And that one (equilateral)?—(Again draws it < 180°)." etc. Generalization is therefore absent.

YVE (6; 10): "I put these two corners together. What will it look like if I add the third one?—(Draws the three angles as more than a semi-circle.)— Look.—(Experiment.)—*Oh, it's a half-moon.*—And that one (a large right-angled triangle: Experimenter assembles the right angle together with an acute angle): What will happen when we add the third angle?—*It will be leaning over.* (He draws it as less than a semi-circle and corrects his drawing after seeing the experiment.)—What about that one (medium in size)?—(Again he draws it as less than a semi-circle and again he finds his error).—And that one (small and equilateral)?—*It won't be straight* (again < 180°).—(Experiment.)—*Oh! That's a half-moon too.*—What about that one (equilateral)?— *I'm looking and thinking . . . I think so, as well: I'm looking at that one and that one* (drawing two angles, then exclaims:) *They're all half-moons!* (Generalization is complete, but only momentary as is clear from what follows.)—What if we put the corners of this (diamond) figure together?—*That'll be more. It will be a circle.*—Complete?—*Just a little bit missing* (he draws an angle of about 345°, then finds his error by experiment).—And that one (square)?— *A full-circle.*—Sure?—*Just a little bit missing.* (Experiment.) *No, a full-circle.* —And that one (a rectangle)?—*It will make a circle.*—Are you sure?—*Yes.* —And that one (a large equilateral triangle)?—*A little less than a half-moon.*— (Experiment.)—*Oh, yes! It's a half-circle.* And that one (scalene)?—*A half-moon.*—And that one?—*As well.*"

DREI (6; 10). The second technique is used. He tries to think what the three angles will look like when assembled and produces a drawing something li!.e a triangle with re-entrant angles. He is shown the angles already cut and accurately predicts that they will form a half-circle. "*Maybe like this, but I'm not sure.*—(Experiment.)—Is it right? . . . What about that one (a right-angled triangle)?—(Draws it > 180°.)—(Experiment.)—Is that right?—*No.*—What about that one (equilateral)?—*I don't know* (drawing the angles > 180°).— (Experiment.)—*No. It's a half-moon again.*" With the next triangle (scalene and greatly elongated) he is in error again but for the fifth triangle he draws a semi-circle, saying: "*It's always the same!*"

SAU (6; 11), in spite of his tender years, quickly grasps the principle. While simple transfer is a factor, there is also some evidence of reasoning by making compensatory allowances. "(Two angles of a right-angled triangle assembled by experimenter:) Suppose I put on the third?—*It'll make this* (producing a

199

drawing of about 170°).—Look.—(Experiment.)—*Oh, no! Half a circle.*—
And that one (a large equilateral triangle)?—*Less than half. Oh, no. A half-circle because this corner is smaller than the one in the other but that corner is bigger so they'll make the same.*—And that one (scalene)?—*Another half-circle because this is a big angle but that one is very little.*—And that one (a rhombus)?—*A circle because they're all the same size.*—And that one (isosceles triangle)?—*A half-circle.*—What if I change this corner with one from another triangle?—*More than half a circle, because it's bigger.*"

NIC (7; 1): "I put these two corners side by side. What will they look like if I add the third corner?—*A half-circle.*—And that one (right angled-triangle not greatly different)?—*Less than half-circle.*—Why?—*Because the corners are smaller.*—Look.—(Experiment.)—*Oh no! A half-circle.*—And that one (equilateral)?—*Less than half a circle.*—Why?—*Because they're smaller.*—(Experiment.)—*Oh! it's a half-circle again.*—What if I move the corner round?—*It will be less . . . No, it won't change it at all.*—What about that one (scalene)?—*A half-circle again.*—And that one (a trapezium)?—*A whole circle, because they're big.*—And that one (a diamond)?—*As well.*—And that one (a right-angled triangle)?—*A circle . . . Oh, no! A half circle.*"

BAR (8; 0) notes that the angles of the first right-angled triangle produce "a half-circle.—What about that one (smaller but similar)?—*They'll be less because that one is smaller.*—Look at this corner.—*It's bigger.*—And that one?—*It's medium.*—Well?—*It'll make a half-circle as well.*—What if I move this angle round (permuting the outside angles)?—*It'll still be a half-circle because you're only moving it round.*—What about that one (equilateral)?—*It will make a half-circle.*—Why? Are you saying that because you've seen two, and so you think this one will be the same?—*Yes.*—Well will that one (large isosceles) make a half-circle as well?—*No, because this corner is too big.*—Well?—(Experiment.)—*Oh, yes. Because these two are the same.*—What about that one (scalene)?—*A half-circle as well.*"

CHRI (8; 1) finally succeeds by induction in always predicting "*a half-circle.*—What about that one (scalene but greatly elongated)?—*More than half a circle*", but thereafter he continues to generalize correctly.

PEY (8; 10) generalizes successfully until presented with a somewhat flattened isosceles triangle. "*No, that won't go, because the biggest corner is different from what it was.*—Look.—(Experiment.)—*Oh yes, because one is big but two are small.*" Thereafter his induction remains constant.

The above records are interesting because of the reasoning process which they reveal. Unlike children at stage II, these subjects reason about the angles as such. It is true that they find considerable difficulty in imagining what angles will look like when they are brought together if they have never seen this done in practice, as happens when the second technique is used. Then they imagine them base to base like a series of roof-tops, or apex to apex like a clover (cf. Tcha), or as an irregular shape like the triangle with re-entrant angles drawn by Drei. But all these are representations of angles re-arranged and not miscellaneous shapes like the house imagined by Rys at level IIB. When the first technique is used and they are first shown a set of angles assembled correctly and asked quite simply to predict what other compositions will yield, they reply very differently from children at stage II. The latter simply count the angles and transfer empirical findings, anticipating that shapes with three angles will produce semi-circles and quadrilatrals will produce circles. In so doing, they ignore the size of angles in each case, for the simple reason that they cannot even make qualitative comparisons between angles when comparing similar or dissimilar triangles. As against this, children at level IIIA make an effort to compare the new angles each time they are shown a fresh triangle, despite the fact that they have already seen one or more sets of angles assembled to yield 180°. Because they make a genuine effort to compare angles they often seem less advanced than children at stage II. That is because they no longer guess at the answer but try to construct it without side-stepping difficulties (cf. Yve: "I'm looking and thinking", a remark which bespeaks his rejection of global transfer).

However these first mental constructions show a crucial defect which is in line with all that we already know of level IIIA (inclination is understood, as is the notion of parallelism but similarity of triangles is not yet verified by superposing angles; in measuring a triangle, its height is not considered as such). These children do not think of the triangles (at least in the first instance) as figures consisting of three angles the sizes of which are mutually dependent: they simply add the angles as given and fail to grasp that as one is increased so the others must be diminished. As a result, when presented with a triangle which has one very acute angle or one very obtuse, or a right-angled triangle, their attention is apt to be centred on the arresting angle and they temporarily neglect the other two.

A second fact militates against this. It is the growing generalization of previous findings which invariably show the angles of a triangle to sum to a semi-circle. The detailed study of individual angles conflicts with induction, which is as yet not dependent on such analysis. Thus at level IIIA, children are not satisfied merely to predict a semi-circle: they try to justify their prediction, i.e. to generalize in terms of a genuine composition instead of indulging in simple transfer as at stage II. It is here that we find compensation and the notion of interdependence between the angles of a triangle. In order to explain to themselves how in spite of their contrary prediction, the angles of a given triangle yield a semi-circle, while at the same time making an effort to generalize by induction to deal more effectively with later instances, children turn their attention to the angles which they left out of account in concentrating on an unusual angle. They then find that if one angle in the given triangle is much greater than a corresponding angle in one they met earlier, the remaining angles are correspondingly smaller. However, at this level, the supplementary relation between the angles of a triangle is not yet generalized once and for all. It is a finding which is slowly reached by comparing each fresh triangle with those already encountered.

The understanding which results may be swift as in the paradoxical case of Sau, who seems partly to be influenced by immediate transfer like children at stage II, but who, unlike those, has discovered the principle of compensation ("because this corner is smaller than the one in the other but that one is bigger so they'll make the same").[1] With others, generalization may be very slow, and is particularly liable to fail when the triangle has a very acute apex, as the other two angles then look like right angles (and children therefore reason that the sum is > 180°). This fact alone is proof that while children's understanding of the compensatory relations between the angles of a triangle involves true composition, it is still inductive and not deductive. Compensation as a general principle is attained solely by way of comparisons between the angles of different triangles. They do not yet grasp that a figure containing three angles cannot exceed 180° because if it did the triangle would contain two right angles, its sides would be parallel and they would never meet to form a third acute angle.

Not until stage IV do we find some appreciation of this internal necessity. Level IIIB which precedes it differs from level IIIA only in that inductive generalization is almost instantaneous and no longer gradual.

§12. Level IIIB. The law is generalized

As compared with level IIIA, sub-stage IIIB may be distinguished in that inductive generalization is now complete, so that it takes place more quickly and often unhesitatingly. If we look ahead to stage IV, however, we note that there is as yet no awareness of deductive necessity. Thus at sub-stage IIIB, children recognize the law as universally applicable but not as logically necessary.

GAM (8; 2) first draws the three angles but is at a loss as to how to combine them. Later, when he has learnt how to assemble angles he foresees that the three together will form "*a half-moon.—*That's right. A good guess. What about this one (equilateral)?—(He draws the three angles juxtaposed forming > 180°, but remarks.) *It's really a half-moon but I've drawn it badly.*" He continues to predict semi-circles for each triangle but always by composition.

SCHA (9; 3) after finding that the first triangle yields a semi-circle, still thinks another which is very low in relation to its base will yield less than 180°, being misled by the acute angles. On making the experiment he says: "*It's the same as before. It's small here but it's bigger over there.*" An isosceles triangle with large equal angles and the third very acute leads him to anticipate

[1] Cf. C.C.S., pp. 322 ff., for the analysis of similar triangles.

more than 180°, because he sees two angles as very nearly right angles (as at level IIIA). However, the experiment in this instance makes him generalize for all cases: *"It's always a semi-circle.*—What about that one (which is even more elongated)?—*That one too."*

HAU (9; 3) generalizes after two initial failures: *"It'll make a semi-circle.*— Why?—*This angle is smaller than that one* (in previous instance), *but that one is bigger.*—What about this (a very tall isosceles)?—*That one is harder. It's a little more than a semi-circle.*—Look (experiment.)—*It's always a semi-circle.*—What about that one (even more pointed)?—*That's a semi-circle.*— What about that one (even more pointed)?—*That's a semi-circle. Oh no. Those two corners make a semi-circle by themselves, so it's more. No, it's always a semi-circle.*—Why?—*Because this one* (at the top) *gets smaller each time."*

AUG. (9; 8) sees two angles of a right-angled triangle juxtaposed and fore-sees that with the third *"it will be a semi-circle.*—What about that one (a larger right-angled triangle)?—*They'll be less because this angle isn't as big. The angle at the top is bigger but they'll still be smaller together.* (Experiment.) *Oh, no, it's a semi-circle because the right angle is one and a half times as big as that one and the other one makes it up.*—What about that one (a smaller right-angled triangle)?—*The same as the other: the big one is worth two and the little ones half each.*—And this (a small equilateral)?—*Maybe that'll be a half-circle as well: because they're the same corners* (i.e. they are equal to one another).—And that one (top angle fairly acute)?—*Still a semi-circle because one of these two angles may be a little smaller than the other and that's where you put the corner from the top.*—And will these others make a half-circle (showing the remaining triangles all together)?—*Yes, they always do."*

BRO (9; 11): *"What will you have if you put the corners side by side?*— *Another triangle.*—Draw them.—(He makes them all larger.) *A circle.*—Take them and find out.—*Half a circle.*—And this other triangle?—(He corrects his drawing several times, then says:) *Half a circle.*—Did you know it all along?—*Yes.*—What about that one?—(He draws it > 180° but says:) *Half a circle* (correcting the drawing).—*And that one?*—*I don't know yet . . . Half a circle* (with great assurance).—Why?—*I'm sure of it!"*

MAR (10; 0): *"It makes a semi-circle.*—And that one?—*That'll make more because this corner is big.* (Experiment.) *Oh, no! Because the other one is smaller.*—(Trapezium?)—*A whole circle.*—(Diamond?)—*Another circle.*— (A small scalene triangle?)—*A semi-circle because this corner is like a sixth of a circle and the others make up the rest.*—And that (isosceles very acute at the top)?—*More than a semi-circle, because these two angles by themselves make a semi-circle . . . Oh, no. They're not quite straight and the angle at the top makes up the difference.*—And supposing I made the sides as long as this (30 cm.)?—*It would still be a semi-circle."*

There is complete continuity of development as between level IIIA and level IIIB as is clear from the initial doubts of Scha, Hau and, in part, of Aug, all of whom begin by comparing each successive instance with those that went before. Nevertheless, these children are more advanced in two ways. In the first place, at some point in the enquiry they establish a relation between the three angles of every triangle considered by itself. In other words they look on these angles as part of a system of complementary relations. Thus Aug assigns numerical values to the angles of a right angled triangle in comparing them, and extensive values to those of a scalene triangle ("one of these two angles may be a little smaller than the other and that's where you put the corner from the top", in other words, the smallest angle is equal to the difference between the other two). This development leads to a second point of difference. There is no longer a conflict between the composition of the angles of a triangle and the inductive generalization as there was at level IIIA. On the contrary, the induction itself which leads the subject to believe that the angles of any triangle will yield a semi-circle provides an anticipatory schema which guides the composition of the angles of new triangles. This much is clear even in the record of Gam although his reasoning is still implicit, it appears again in the final conclusions of Scha and Hau. In the records of Aug, Bro and Mar, the principle becomes explicit in spite of their momentary doubts.

Thus the tendency to compare the angles of a triangle in their own right no longer conflicts with the tendency to generalize inductively, as at level IIIA. They are now reconciled, whence the discovery of a universal law: "They always do." But although the law is conceived of as quite general it is not yet regarded as logically necessary. The present level is characterized by the ability to compose similarity between triangles by superposing angles and to coordinate measurements of angles and triangles. Such concrete operations make induction possible, and the generality shown here is its crowning achievement. Only at stage IV do children begin to see the logical reason for the geometrical law.

§13. Stage IV. Formal necessity

It is difficult to find an exact criterion for the boundary between level IIIB and stage IV. Needless to say, we cannot expect all children at 10 to 12 to demonstrate the theorem (and subjects who had tackled the problem in their school work were omitted from the investigation). All that we can look for is an indication of when "always" becomes "necessarily", which means that a law which is generalized intuitively is seen as governed by necessary reason. Following are a number of instances, the first two of which are transitional between level IIIB and stage IV, while the last two suggest the beginnings of an insight into the possibility of logical demonstration.

BAD (10; 3): "Can you guess what these three angles will make when put together?—A semi-circle.—And that one (equiangular)?—Three-quarters of a circle. Oh no! A semi-circle.—And this little fat one (isosceles with the top angle very obtuse)?—A semi-circle.—Why?—Because there's this big angle and then the two little ones.—Could there be a triangle with angles which don't

make up a semi-circle?—*No. Never!*—What about these three angles (>
180°)?—*Yes, but they're not from the same triangle.*—What about this
(trapezoid)?—*A circle because you've got two right angles then an acute angle
and an obtuse angle.*—What about this (very sharp isosceles triangle)?—*A
semi-circle.*—What if I made it even longer!—*It will always be a semi-circle:
the angles are the same, only different in size* (confusing similarity with equality
of their sum)."

ROL (10; 9). First triangle: *"A semi-circle.—Why?—I don't know.—*And
that one?—*Another half circle.*—And that one (very elongated isosceles)?—
Another semi-circle.—Why?—Because the bigger it is here (the equal angles)
the smaller it is here (third angle).—And if we keep making it larger?—*It's
always a semi-circle because the angles* (at the base) *aren't quite right angles, and
the point makes up the difference."*

JEQ (11; 4) assembles three angles: *"A semi-circle.—Why?—I can't tell
you, it's because the angles are smaller than they would be if they were right
angles . . . You'd need four; three angles wouldn't meet* (if they were greater
than 180°).—And that one?—*I can't say in advance* (preparing to assemble
the angles). *It's another semi-circle. I'm beginning to think it's always a semi-
circle. With three angles you can't have a full circle because you'd need angles*
(two or three) *bigger than a right angle: you'd need a further stroke* (side).—
And that one (isosceles with very obtuse angle)?—*One big and two thin; a
semi-circle again! I want to try again* (in thought) *with that one* (even more
obtuse-angled). *Yes, still the same because there's an enormous angle at the top.*
And this one (very pointed isosceles)?—*A semi-circle again! These two angles
aren't quite right angles, they're made up by the one at the top. Two right
angles would make a semi-circle.*—And if we made it so long that it reached
the cellar?—*It's always the same if the lines are quite straight."*

DOB (11; 10): *"A semi-circle.—*And that one?—*If you take three angles
from a triangle they're bound to make a semi-circle.—Why?—I can't say.—*
What about these (three angles assembled without letting him see the
trickery)?—*Oh? . . . But they're not from the same triangle.*—How can you
tell?—(Indicates a right angle and an obtuse angle.)"

It is obvious that these children do not know in advance the theorem
which deals with the sum of the angles of a triangle. Yet they discover
unaided that, whatever the angles taken separately, their sum is constant
and they realize that this relationship is a necessary one. It is clear from
the records that if they see the relationship as necessary, it is because
they look on the angles of a triangle as forming a system of complementary parts, and, going beyond this, find that these parts cannot
include two right angles. Bad, who stands midway between level IIIB
and stage IV, cannot say so explicitly, but the fact that he (like the
others at this stage) has no difficulty in seeing that three angles which
sum to more than 180° cannot belong to the same triangle is indicative
of his general awareness. Rol comes near to expressing the formula
more precisely in analysing the very sharp isosceles triangle, saying that
the angles at the base "aren't quite right angles". Jeq realizes that if the

angles summed to more than two right angles the figure would require a further side to close it. He knows, too, that if the angles at the base of a pointed isosceles triangle were right angles, they would form a semi-circle by themselves, so that the figure would cease to be a triangle, having two parallel sides, and two angles which no longer required "one at the top to make them up". Dob, likewise, realizes that three angles which sum to more than 180°, cannot be taken from a single triangle because they include a right angle and an obtuse angle.

The way in which children begin to see the lawfulness of this relationship gives a clear indication of the connection between rectangular coordination (or multiplication of one-one relations, see ch. VII) and triangular coordination (multiplication of one-many relations, ch. VIII). The sum of the angles of a rectilinear three-sided figure must always equal two right-angles (or a semi-circle) and if these angles sum to more than 180° the figure must be four sided and will contain four angles equivalent to four right angles. That, in essence, is what these children express and they thereby show that they understand both the difference and the relationship between one-one and one-many co-ordination. Thus, if distances are coordinated in terms of one-one correspondence, they give rise to rectangular figures (or rectangular references). The alternative is to correlate distances in terms of two dimensions at once by making each distance along one axis correspond with a specific distance along the other so that both increase as their separation increases (the latter being measured by the perpendicular opposite to the vertex). This way of coordinating distances give rise to triangles. We saw how at level IIIB and IV, children use two perpendicular measurements both in fixing a point in an area and in establishing the size of an angle in relation to the vertical distance between its arms, or the base of a triangle in relation to its height. Perpendicular measurements were chosen in both sorts of problems, yet these children understood that in the problem of the rectangle they were dealing with a figure or a system of right angles, while in dealing with the angles and the triangle they were establishing slopes. By their understanding of the similarity and difference which obtain between the two modes of coordination, children begin to appreciate that the angles involved in a triangular system must sum to half those involved in a rectangular system, since the latter is simply a matter of parallel lines drawn in one-one correspondence along the two dimensions of the system or of the figure, while the former involves slopes, implying increasing vertical linear separation between two arms of an angle with increasing distance from the vertex, so that correspondence is no longer one-one but one-many.

The development of reasoning as studied in section III raises the following problem. What is the nature of deductive composition and how does it enable children to group the operations used in estimating angles and adding them so that they end with the universal law, that the sum of the angles of a triangle is constant? The problem is general, for there are many other cases where a series of actions which begin by being empirical finally gives rise to a necessary deduction, as though the action of the subject eventually transcends the real world although initially it is purely experimental.

There would indeed be a contradiction if action were simply a matter of manipulating objects as given and extracting or abstracting characteristics in order finally to compose these operationally. But our earlier study of similar triangles (C.C.S., ch. XII) showed that an angle was not an object ready-given, nor yet a characteristic to be abstracted from solid objects or physical reality as such. An angle is a system of relationships determined by the progressive separation of two lines as they proceed from a common vertex. The relations which arise from their gradual separation are essentially the same thing as one-many correspondences. Angles exist only in a context of straight lines, and therefore they are not ready-given in nature, any more than straight lines themselves. Straight lines are relations born out of particular ways of organizing perception, or at a higher level, out of the action of aiming or maintaining a given direction. They are not abstracted from the object; they are added to it as a result of these actions. Angles likewise, are constructed in the course of action before giving rise to operations; they are not abstracted from the object like heat or weight.

Even in the perception of angles, the activity of the subject consists in establishing relations by one-many correspondence. Thus the study of perceptual illusions in angular figures shows that when he estimates an angle, the subject compares two parallel lines which he selects at random but which usually consist of one near the vertex and another near the limit of the lines on the figure: thus the gradual separation of the arms is always seen in terms of the ratio between the shorter and the longer of the two parallels, although the schema as a whole may be more or less mobile in any particular case.

Here, then, is the starting-point for these relations which eventually take the form of operational multiplicative grouping by one-many correspondence. Thus wherever the subject is concerned with the determination of angles, from perception to intellectual operations and from visual estimate to successful measurements, there is always a real activity of the subject and it always has the same characteristic structure, although there is a progressive increase in its precision.

It follows that adding two angles or measuring an angle or even recognizing the equality of angles in similar figures is always an action and therefore admits of trial-and-error or empiricism. But the experimental behaviour is only partly comparable with induction as applied to the physical properties of an object. For here the trial-and-error, the experiment, and the induction relate to the actions of the subject upon the object, and not to the object alone. Thus children learn by experience that they cannot build a triangle with three angles greater than 180° or a 'half-circle'. But the experience is of their own actions far more than of the object. It is true that these actions tell the subject something about the object, because they are accommodated to it, but the object is essentially no more than an aliment or support to the action. It is assimilated to the schema of the subject's action and offers no resistance: it demands new accommodations only in the measure that the actions themselves betray poor internal coordination. It is true that when the subject succeeds in constructing triangles and in composing their angles in the form of a semi-circle he learns something about the object. He learns that there is a physical space constituted by the interactions of macroscopic solid objects but he also learns that there is a geometrical space created by such actions as constructing triangles and assembling angles. Physical space is at first not differentiated from the space of action, but the latter is present from the outset, for it is not the properties of objects as such which determine geometrical space but rather the assimilation of objects to the schemata of the subject's actions.

That is why, although the actions of children in constructing and comparing angles are experimental at first, and include a good deal of trial-and-error behaviour which we expect in the earlier stages, they yet eventuate in a reversible operational grouping, so coordinated as to yield universal generalizations which are deductive and necessary and which therefore transcend experience. The elaboration of these groupings at stage IV is proof in itself that elements which derive from the subject's action must have been present from the outset. Moreover, the fact that actions which give rise to angularity eventually form a deductive system of grouping is proof that the behaviour is not random. It derives from the need to coordinate actions, which is the most general characteristic of all intelligent activity. As we have shown repeatedly in the course of this chapter, the construction of angles demands a specific kind of coordination wherever it occurs, be it in the realm of qualitative similarity or in that of metric elaboration. One-many correspondence is one of the most general categories of coordination. It precedes even serial quantification (e.g. judgments of similarity) and it certainly precedes metrical quantification (e.g. measuring angles and triangles or finding the sum of the angles of a triangle). One-many multiplication of asymmetrical relations is represented in a non metrical form as one of the eight kinds of grouping manifested by logical intelligence.[1]

[1] See Piaget, *Classes, Relations et Nombres* (Vrin, 1942, ch. X).

Chapter Nine

TWO PROBLEMS OF GEOMETRICAL LOCI:
THE STRAIGHT LINE AND THE CIRCLE[1]

IT is of some interest to follow up our study of development in the construction of angles by considering certain other figures which children learn to construct by means of measurement as their understanding of Euclidean space is elaborated. The figures we shall consider are loci, that is to say, they are defined in such a way that all points of the figure have a property in common which is not possessed by any point outside the figure. The study of loci is interesting because the subject cannot construct such figures without making a generalization based on an action or an operation which is indefinitely repeated. He must therefore recognize a principle of recurrence which is as fundamental in geometrical reasoning as it is in arithmetic. In studying loci we analyse a general problem of reasoning, just as we did in our study of the sum of the angles of a triangle. The present chapter touches on questions of perpendicularity, bisection and circularity, and is therefore correctly placed between the analysis of angles (ch. VIII) and that of curves (ch. X).

§1. *Outline of method and results*

Two relations were studied. (1) The locus of points equidistant from two points A and B is a straight line which cuts the line AB perpendicularly at its mid-point. (2) The locus of all points equidistant from a given point is the circumference of a circle drawn about that point as centre.

The second problem introduces curvilinear measurement. In presenting the problem, concrete methods were used as far as possible. The child was asked to show where a series of children should stand in order to be the same distance ('just as far') from a point A on which stands a target, an agate marble which children use as a 'jack' when playing marbles. The rules of fair play demand that they should all be 'exactly' the same distance from the target, but different subjects may be more or less precise in the way in which they determine the points required.

The first problem may be studied by one of three techniques: (1) We imagine one boy standing at A and another at B: where shall we put the target so as to be the same distance from either? The question is

---

[1] Written with the collaboration of Mlle Ursula Galusser.

explained further if the child fails to understand its generality, i.e. that he is required to indicate all the places where the target might be put. (2) There is a tree at A and another at B. Where can you stand so as to be the same distance from either tree?[1] (3) For the youngest subjects the experimenter stands or sits on the far side of a table: the child is handed a number of marbles and asked to put them the same distance from himself and the experimenter. These three questions are repeated as often as necessary to elicit spontaneous generalization before attempting to provoke it. Having answered the questions in this form, the child is asked to draw all the possible positions. If he says the marbles are on a line, he is asked whether the points can touch, and how far the line can go. These questions recall those in C.C.S., ch. V, dealing with the notions of continuity and infinity.

The problem of a rectilinear locus suggests an interesting generalization in the case of older subjects. Instead of limiting the question to equidistance from two points, the problem is extended to cover equidistance from several points A and A', B and B', C and C', etc., where points A, B, C and D lie in a straight line, and points A', B', C' and D' lie at corresponding distances in another line at right angles to it. The locus of points equidistant from A and A', B and B', etc., is then the bisector of the angle.

Needless to say, whatever the question, the child may be asked whether there are any other points outside the line he has indicated which might equally satisfy the necessary conditions. This counter-check is essential to ascertain the real understanding of the subject.

The following responses were observed. At stage I the notion of equidistance has no meaning. It is discovered at stage II, but it is not generalized until level IIIA when the notion of 'loci' as such may be said to arise.

Stage I lasts until the age of 4 or 5, or even $5\frac{1}{2}$ in exceptional cases. It provides an interesting analogy to the development of the notion of distance (ch. III) and to the elaboration of measurement of length (chs. IV and VI). Little children conceive of distance simply as an empty interval instead of as a symmetrical relation between two points. Therefore there is no conservation of distance when solid objects are interposed within the empty space. It is not surprising in view of this that equidistance has little meaning since distance itself is not a stable notion. Moreover, estimates of length are initially made on the basis of points of arrival, so that two lines which are judged equal when put side by side are judged unequal when they are staggered. Little children fail to establish relations between points of arrival and points of depar-

---

[1] This question, like several others, can be put in the form of a drawing. The trees at A and B are represented by crosses and the child is asked to put several boys in by marking points at the same distance from A as from B.

ture. This, too, renders it impossible for them to make adequate judgments about equidistance, since they cannot establish relations between the several lengths separating individual players from the target. As a result we find that at stage I, children do not assimilate a point of equidistance to the mid-point between A and B and instead, they indicate a point at random, without regard to the distances involved. Sometimes they go so far as to draw an imaginary line in space to indicate that the point must be somewhere between A and B. As for the circle, they simply put the marbles around a centre at A without taking any notice of equidistance.

Stage II (from 5 to 7 on the average) falls as usual into two sub-stages and these correspond to quite distinct levels in the construction of 'loci'. In the problem of the circle, subjects at level IIA do not measure distances from its centre but simply arrange the 'children' either in a row or else in an irregular ring without discovering for each point the point which is symmetrical to it in relation to the centre. As for the straight line, they find the point of equidistance unaided in the particular case of the mid-point between A and B, this perceptual estimate being fairly accurate. Outside of this special case they are successful. The locus is therefore limited less to a single point or to a few points nearby. Sometimes children try to repeat their actions but in so doing they forget about equidistance. When presented with the problem of the bisector children fail to find even a single mid-point in relation to a series of paired points. They either look for the mid-point between two points alone, or else they produce irregular and random intervals between the various marbles. Thus this level shows a general inability to perform logical multiplication, and children never see more than one point which satisfies the requirements of the problem.

On the other hand, during sub-stage IIB, generalization begins to appear, albeit by way of simple repetition of behaviour, that is, by an empirical method which is a form of reproductive assimilation and does not yet constitute a genuine iteration of actions. Children discover the point of equidistance between two others, but the discovery is preceded by errors which recall the previous level. Moreover, they have an inkling of the 'locus', but this is achieved by extending the method used in placing the first (central) marble and by placing one marble behind another in a continuous line following the same direction. They do not consider points which are symmetrical to these with reference to the mid-point. There are occasional errors in equidistance, and these seem to result from their over-emphasis on continuing in a chosen direction, to the neglect of a careful return to the point of departure.

Stage III, the final stage, begins about the age of 7–8. Children now find an infinite number of points to satisfy the condition of equidistance. These points form a line or continuous figure. However, although the points are infinite in number and continuous with each other, infinity and continuity do not as yet derive from composition based on a more refined concept of the nature of a point. Such composition occurs only at the stage of formal thought (11–12). Here there is simply unlimited iteration of a technique to yield a succession of points equidistant from A and B (or from A alone). The iteration is interesting because it is an elementary type of reasoning, reasoning by recurrence, and is found at the stage of concrete operations. Children first find a number of points which are in fact equidistant. But in doing so, they find, for each new point, that point which is symmetrical about the mid-line AB (or the mid-point A). This development is new and important. After a number of repetitions, they try to see whether a point much further from the centre (or from those already discovered) still satisfies the requirement of equidistance from two points, and finding this to be true, they generalize immediately to the whole line.

§2. *Stage I: The notion of equidistance has no meaning*

Children at stage I simply put marbles around the given point without constructing a circle because they do not understand equidistance. They do not even put the marbles between themselves and the experimenter, because their notion of distance is not a constant relation and their judgments of length are made without reference to the point of departure.

VAL (4; 2): "You put this marble so that it's just as far from you as it is from me, and then we can roll our marbles at it.—(He puts it close to himself.)—But you watch. We've got to play, etc. It must be just as far for you as it is for me, otherwise it's too easy for one of us, etc.—(He puts it between the 'contestants' but nearer himself.)—Is it far from you?—*No, near.*—Far from me?—*Yes.*—Well put it where it will be just as far for both of us.—(He moves it near the experimenter.)—But is it far from you now?—*Yes.*—Well put it just as far for both.—(Replaces it near himself)", etc.

CYR (5; 3): "You've got to put it . . . etc.—(He places it to his right, much nearer himself than the experimenter and not in between them.)—Is it just as far for you and me?—*It's further for you.*—Quite right. Well, put it just as far.—(He puts it between the two, but quite close to himself.)—*That's better* (indicating that it now faces both himself and the experimenter).— But is it the same for you and me?—*No* (placing it further from himself and to the right so that it is about 40 cm. from himself and 80 cm. from the experimenter).—Is it just as far for both of us?—*Yes, the same* (moving it a little further from himself but further still from the experimenter)."

Circle: "I'll put the glass marble here.—All the children (giving names of his own friends) will now aim and throw their marble at it. But they must all be just as far away.—Where shall we put them to make it just as far for all of them and just as easy?—(He puts the first one 20 cm. away, the next on the far side but 80 cm. away, the third to the left, 40 cm. away, the fourth to the right, likewise about 40 cm. away, the fifth near the first, 15 cm. away, the sixth near the second and likewise 80 cm. away, the seventh to the left but about 1 m. 30 cm. away, the eighth also to the left, about 1 m. 50 cm. away, and the ninth and tenth even further.)—Look at these (3rd and 4th). Is that right?—*Yes, it's just as easy for both.*—Why?—*Because.*—What about that one (5th)?—*It's easier because he's nearer: it will go straight there.*—And is it as far from there (10th, 2 m. away) and from there (1st, 20 cm. away)?— *Yes, it can go like this* (indicating the direct path from the tenth to the centre). —What about that one (6th) why did you put it there?—*Because there's space there* (again indicating that the direct path to the centre is unimpeded)."

NID (5; 5). Circle: he arranges them in a ring around point A but at varying distances: the first facing himself, 60 cm. away, the next on the other side, 20 cm. away, the third to the right, 50 cm. away, the fourth to the left 30 cm. away, the fifth, sixth, seventh and eighth in between these but not equidistant from the centre, and the ninth and tenth much further.—"Why is the second one there?—*Because it's better in front.*—And why is that one there (8th)?—*Because there are big spaces* (between the others).—And is the tenth as near as the others?—*Oh, no, it's wrong* (placing it a little nearer).—And if all the children held hands what shape would they make?. . ."

"Now put that marble so that it's just as far for you and me and then we can play, etc.—(He puts it to his right, far from the experimenter.)—What if we have a lot of marbles to aim at?—(He scatters them around the table between himself and the adult without regard for distances.)—Is that right?— *Oh, I understand now: it's between us!* (placing one marble exactly between himself and the experimenter).—Can we put down more marbles which will be just as far for both of us?—*No.*—Would that one do (a little to the left, but equidistant)?—*No.*—Is it just as far for both of us?—*No.*"

The problem of a locus can have no meaning since the subjects fail to understand the concept of equidistance.

Probably any one of these children could find the mid-point between two others with a fair degree of accuracy. Had the experimenter begun by saying, "Put your marble between us, exactly half-way between you and me", there would be no problem, because the mid-point of a straight line is a perceptual datum. Its determination is not a problem of intelligence because eye-movements and perceptual adjustments are adequate. But where children are asked to find one (or more) points at an equal distance, "just as far", from the experimenter and themselves, we find that at stage I it does not occur to them that this condition is most obviously met by the mid-point. The record of Nid is typical. He tries every conceivable solution and scatters marbles at varying distances from the experimenter and himself, then suddenly realizes that the mid-point will produce the answer and cries: "Oh, I understand now, it's between us!" Not only do the restrictions of perceptual equilibrium compel him to think that the only point "between us" is the mid-point but he denies that a point slightly to the left of the mid-point can also be equidistant. The reason is that Nid is well able to make perceptual judgments of distance but has no intellectual notion of distance. This is neither surprising nor contradictory to those who are familiar with the facts given in ch. III.

Even more significant are the responses to the question of the circle. Since he is called upon to put some ten points around a marble, the subject naturally puts them in varying directions so that the original marble lies at the centre of a rough ring. One might suppose that the perceptual configuration of a circle is strong enough to impose equidistance here, even where the mid-point between two others is not discovered. But Cyr produces what is not a circle but a fortuitous collection of points around a centre, not unlike the pattern made by a poor shot firing at a target: yet he thinks all the players have an equal opportunity to take good aim if they 'face' the marble and no obstacles intervene, as if the points on the circumference of a circle were not related to its centre by radii forming uncrossed straight lines. Hence equidistance for him is defined by the collection of all possible rectilinear paths: he excludes positions which would involve one player standing behind another. This is because he regards distances as empty space (ch. III) which leads him to think of equidistance as likewise defined by freedom from obstacles regardless of length. Nid likewise arranges his points in a ring around the centre and he, too, puts one in front, one behind, one to the left and one to the right, then the remainder in spaces left empty. Yet even when asked what shape the children would take if they held hands he does not think of a circle. Like Cyr he was concentrating on the emptiness of intervals between the agate marble and the players while building his ring and ignored their equidistance. To sum up, at stage I children may be familiar with the mid-point of straight lines and with circular shapes in the realm of perception but this knowledge is of no help in finding the locus of equidistant points.

§3. *Stage II: The locus is gradually discovered because equidistance is understood*

In studying the responses made at stage II we can follow step by step how children elaborate the notion of the 'locus' by generalizing equidistance, as first noted in the mid-point when two references are given, or as noted in a cruciform configuration when only one point is given so that the true locus is the circumference of a circle. In the latter case, the first glimpse of equidistance may even be given by a pair of points. The first examples are of sub-stage IIA, where, to begin with, there is no generalization whatsoever.

Zur (4; 6), asked to find a point as distant from the experimenter as it is from himself, selects the mid-point. "Are there any other points which are just as far for both of us?—*No.*—Try to find some more.—(He places a marble over a little mark which he discovers on the wooden surface.)—Is that right?—*No.*—Is there somewhere else? . . ."

Two trees: he places the first boy on the mid-point: "Are there any other places?—(He disperses others at random.)—Is that all right?—*No.*" Thus there is equidistance for Zur only at the mid-point. His other placements are arbitrary because they are merely a gesture of compliance with instructions, based on a complete lack of understanding.

MAR (5; 3): "Now we'll each try and hit this marble. To make the game a fair one we must put it so that it will be just as far for you as it is for me.— (He draws a line in the air between the experimenter and himself.) *There* (too near to himself). *Oh, no! Here, that's right.*—How can you tell?—*It's in the middle.*—Look, here are some more marbles. You put them where they will be just as far for you and me.—(He adds two marbles on either side of the first and touching it.)—Can you put any more down?—*No, there isn't room.*— Would these do (two points which are both equidistant from the players but a little further from the mid-point).—*That's wrong, because it's like this* (indicating the line from the marble to the players) *instead of being like this* (straight line between the contestants. He thinks a while, then removes the two marbles he has just added leaving only the one at the mid-point). *That one is right, it's in the middle.*"

Two trees A and B: he makes a point midway between them and two more, half-way between each of the trees and the mid-point. He now shows the distance separating A from the first mark and points to the second saying: "*It's in the middle.*" Then he points to the distance from B to the mid-point and indicates the third one saying: "*That's the middle too.*" Finally he points to the first and says: "*That's really the middle.*—Could we put some more down and have them just as far from both trees?—*No, there isn't any room left.*"

The circle: the experimenter places a marble in the middle of the table and tells the child to put the boys so that they will each be 'just as far'. Mar makes up a row of nine, almost in a straight line on one side of the centre and another of six, roughly parallel, but on the opposite side. Then he adds another on the right, half-way between the two rows: "Are they all just as far from the marble?—*Yes, that one* (in the middle of one of the rows) *is better. It's right near.*"

LUC (5; 9) can be considered as approximately the same level as Mar. He puts his first marble half-way between himself and the experimenter, his second at a quarter of the distance, and his third at three-quarters: "Is that all right?—*Yes. This one* (the second) *is just as far for me and that one* (the third) *is just as far for you. Oh, no! That's wrong!* (He removes them and puts about fifteen more one after another, packing them tightly round the mid-point.)" Asked to put boys at the same distance from two trees he disposes five at approximately equal intervals to one another but oblique to the mid-point and hence at different distances from the trees. Next the experimenter arranges two rows of trees, A B C and A' B' C', at right angles to each other— telling the child to put marks at equal distances from each pair of trees: he places the first approximately mid-way between C and C', i.e. on the bisector, but the remainder are packed in a tight ring of 7 around this one, which is the same solution as in the first problem.

215

The circle: he places six marbles at approximately equal distances from the centre but without realizing that they form a circle, since they are spaced and the intervals between them are deliberately kept constant.

GER (5; 8) is a little more advanced. In addition to the mid-point he finds two more which are equidistant both from the centre and from the two contestants (the experimenter and himself). However he adds a fourth and fifth marble at the same interval, one to his own right and the other to the right of the experimenter. These are no longer equidistant from the contestants: "Why did you put them in (2nd and 3rd)?—*There's one on the right and one on the left and it's just as far for both.*—What about these (4th and 5th)?—*It's just as far and that's the only way there's room.*" The intervals between the marbles finally gain the upper hand over their distance relative to the players. The action of reproducing a constant interval between marbles is repeated over and over again although the procedure is unnecessary and indeed contradicts the continuity of a 'locus'. The idea is imposed by the interval between the players and the first marble which is in the middle.

Circle: first an irregular arrangement about the centre then an approximate equalization of distances.

JAC (5; 3) is more advanced than Ger for although he begins by placing a marble at the mid-point, he goes on to put four more to the left of the mid-point, at regular intervals but close together. Next he puts one to the right. "What would you do if you had a lot of marbles?—*I'd put them all along* (pointing to the left).—But they've got to be just as far for you and me.—*All along both sides.*" On the face of it this would seem to be a far-reaching generalization, but the remainder of the enquiry proves that his reply was more in the nature of a perseverative prolongation of the series he had begun, without consideration of equidistance relative to the players. The marbles which should be placed equidistant from trees A and B are arranged so that the first, the fourth and the fifth are not in fact equidistant although they are between the two (the fourth is a little nearer to A and the fifth a little nearer to B).

Circle: the first four marbles form a cross (the second was a little nearer the centre than the first but the error was made good). But the fifth which is placed in between two others is much further from the centre and the remainder are disposed at equal intervals in such a way that the circle turns into an ellipse. These others are put down unwillingly because left to himself Jac would have stopped at five.

LI (5; 7), asked to put marbles at equal distances from two players, first places one nearer to himself, then moves it to the centre: "Supposing I give you some more to put down just as far for you and me?—*Like this* (he constructs the series 7, 5, 3, 1, 2, 4, 6 in their numerical order which shows the beginnings of spontaneous symmetry)." His solution to the problem of the two trees is identical. Li stands on the verge of level IIB.

Circle: the marbles are loosely arranged about the centre, but later he imposes a measure of regularity and ensures approximate equidistance.

WI (6; 4) is at the same intermediate level as Li. He succeeds in constructing a row of six marbles equidistant from the players and nearly symmetrical in form. However, when presented with two rows of players A, B, C and A',

216

B′, C′ forming a right angle,[1] he marks only a single point to begin with, midway between C and C′. Later (like Luc) he puts others in a circle around this one. The experimenter suggests a point further away but equidistant from the players in each pair. He understands: *"Oh, yes, they can all see.—*Well, continue . . ." But he puts his marbles perpendicular to the bisector instead of along it.

The remaining examples belong to sub-stage IIB. The gradual progress already shown is carried further and in the end there is generalization of equidistance for all positions in these 'loci'.

PIE (6; 10) begins like children at level IIA: he puts four marbles in line between himself and the experimenter: "What if you only have one marble?— *I put it in the middle. Now it's right for both of us.—*What about the others?— (He now spaces the marbles at regular intervals, to the right of the mid-point as he sees them, but equidistant from the players.)—How far can you go?— *It's like a procession . . . right up to the edge of the table. Then it's too far."* This reply shows clearly the beginnings of generalization.

Two trees: the marbles are first put one beside each tree. "Are they just as far from both trees?—*Oh, no! Well in the middle, then.—*And the others?— *Quite near* (placing a few at regular intervals). *Oh, you can go on putting them further away each time!"* Here again there is a further instance of generalization, although in the present case it is limited to one side (and not symmetrical).

Circle: he finishes with an ellipse but the marbles are fairly close together.

DUB (6; 8). Arranging boys to be equidistant from two trees: *"In the middle.—*And the next one?—*Underneath* (maintaining the equidistance).— And the next?—*Underneath that.—*And after that?—*It continues* (putting down a few at equal intervals and fairly close together).—How far?—*Up to the end of the paper.—*Would they still be the same distance from both trees? *—Yes.—*And if we had many sheets of paper?—*We could go on putting children."* Thus Dub accepts the suggestions but his generalization extends only to one side.

CHEV (6; 0), on the other hand, thinks of both sides. To begin with he places his marbles at regular intervals between himself and the experimenter. The enquiry then passes to the question of the trees, and he puts one boy in the middle, another above and a third below, while preserving their equidistance. "What if we put in more?—(He continues the series on both sides.) —Can we put some more in the gaps?—(He begins to do so, then says:) *No, it would touch that point and then it would look like the same point."* Here there is generalization and symmetry, but not continuity.

PIL (6; 10). Two trees: he too begins by putting points at equal intervals between A and B. Then he makes them equidistant, spacing the points and later interpolating others: "What would it make if you went on?—*First a whole lot of strokes and then a long line.—*And if you went on after that?— *It would go a long way, but not as far as the mountain."*

Circle: he places six correctly then says: *"They'll make a circle."*

EG (6; 8). Two trees: he places one point in the centre and says: *"I stick*

---

[1] The question is here put in terms of marbles and players, but the drawing is no different from that used when it took the form of two rows of trees.

another by the side of it (continuing at irregular intervals).—What sort of a drawing will you end up with?—*A line.*—How far can you go?—*To the end of the table.*—And on to the grass?—*Yes.*—Any further?—*Yes, right on to the end.*" This example leads into stage III.

As we pass from one example to the next we see the progressive generalization which takes place. Zur, our first subject, allows equidistance only to the mid-point; Eg reaches the concept of a continuous and infinite line. Although the development is gradual there is a break between sub-stage IIA and level IIB, for only at the latter level do we find trial-and-error leading to spontaneous generalization.

The beginning of stage II marks the discovery of equidistance. This understanding has its roots in more developed notions of distance and length, as shown in chs. III and IV. However the geometrical locus of a point equidistant from two others A and B is the perpendicular bisector of the line AB, and our youngest subjects allow of equidistance only at the mid-point itself. Zur is persuaded by the experimenter to put more marbles on the table, but their placement is so arbitrary (e.g. he puts one marble on a little mark in the wood) as to make it abundantly clear that for him equidistance is limited to the mid-point: generalization is absent. If we bear in mind the responses made at stage I we must regard this as natural. The discovery of equidistance is too recent, the notion itself too precarious, to admit of generalization. How then does generalization come about?

The first widening of the concept appears in a response made by a number of children who seem to think of the mid-point as comprising several positions and who therefore put a number of marbles close up against the one on the mid-point. Although this can hardly be called generalization, it is a move in that direction. Thus Mar puts two marbles touching the one in the middle, and Luc eventually places fifteen all round it. A study of their overall behaviour reveals that there are two reasons for this response. These are quite distinct although they bear on each other. First, children lack the concept of a point: for them the middle is a small area and they exploit this lack of precision by thinking they can put several marbles on the one spot. Later, they may remove them (Mar) or push them close together (Mar and Luc). The very fact that they push them closer shows that the reason must be as stated, for when there is generalization the marbles are invariably spaced to begin with. Second, there is the idea that an action which was successful may be repeated. This notion marks the very first step in generalization. The subject discovers that the mid-point is equidistant from the two trees or two figures and believes that by reproducing the same lengths, he will find other points nearby which are also equidistant. That the tendency to repeat the initial action is indeed operative is proved by the fact that children soon reproduce the interval they find, beginning from the mid-point, or else from one of the figures or trees. This behaviour shows a true generalization, although they forget that the point must be equidistant from both A and B. Thus Mar, in solving the problem of the trees, puts a number of marbles at equal intervals, although their distances from the trees are by no means equal. This he calls putting points "in the middle" as against "really in the middle", showing that the idea of generalization is present in spite of the error in its realization. Luc does the same and also displays another common example of false generalization when he places three marbles between two players, at a quarter, half and three-quarters of the distance between them.

The next step is shown by Ger. He too reproduces his initial action but Ger is aware of the difference between true and false generalization. Ger puts his second and third marbles at equal distances from the first and equidistant from the players, but the fourth and fifth are at equal distances from the mid-point but no longer equidistant from the players. Like Mar and Luc, he simply repeats his first action and the interval so realized, but unlike these, he knows when generalization is correct ("It's just as far for both") and when it is not ("It's just as far, and that's the only way there's room").

With Jac, we find immediate and correct generalization, but generalization is incomplete. It has its roots in repetition of his initial action, but he anticipates the equidistance between marbles and players instead of first placing the marbles and then forming a judgment. How is this progress achieved? It occurs only in the problem of the two contestants. When asked about the two trees, Jac's response is still at the earlier level: his points are regularly spaced, with one in the middle and the others at unequal distances from the two trees. Thus generalization begins with the repetition of an action. At this stage the repetition is global in that the most obvious features of the initial action are repeated. At a later stage these will be eliminated and only one feature (equidistance) will be retained, thus preparing the way for complete generalization or reasoning by recurrence. All our young subjects reproduce their initial action by maintaining a constant interval between their own marbles in spite of the fact that this symmetry is not required by the problem since they are merely asked to place them at equal intervals relative to the players. Because this feature is more obvious, they frequently forget about equidistance. True generalization only occurs when the subject can select that feature which requires to be generalized from all those other characteristics of his action which could be reproduced. A child at the level of Jac is able to make that selection in some cases, but not in others (as here, the two trees). Generalization of equidistance therefore implies an anticipatory act of choosing which directs the generalizing activity.

With Li, we find such selective and oriented repetition from the outset. Global repetition of the action has been outgrown. But even Li places his marbles at equal intervals. Nevertheless these are now equidistant from the players or trees. Even more significant, we now find the beginnings of symmetry about the mid-point, which marks the next sub-stage.

During level IIB, development occurs in three directions: (1) there is generalization of symmetry (2) there is generalization leading towards the notion of infinity (at either end of the bisector) (3, and most important) generalization tends towards continuity, first by narrowing the intervals between marbles or points, and later by interpolating others in these spaces. These generalizations are all related but very gradual, so that in our examples we can follow their development in detail.

Pie might seem at first to belong to level IIA and less advanced than Li. Thus Pie begins incorrectly and completes only one side of his row. Moreover his marbles are still spaced at regular intervals. But he shows more insight, for in the end he discovers that he could continue indefinitely, right to the end of the table, and later: "further away each time". What began as repetition of an action now suggests true iteration. Dub reaches a similar level, but without the initial errors and in his case generalization in one direction is immediate. Chev achieves symmetry from the start which means that there is generalization in both directions. Even more significantly, while Chev begins by placing his marbles at regular intervals, he goes on to interpose others in the spaces, although he does not achieve continuity. Pie achieves continuity by gradual stages, having started with equal intervals. Finally, Eg shows generalization without equal intervals and has no difficulty in envisaging both continuity and the possibility of infinite iteration in both directions.

Generalization in the problem of the circle is similar in spite of the difference in content. At level IIA children begin by using equal intervals and soon forget the need to maintain equidistance from the centre (Mar, and, in part, Jac). Continuity is not achieved at this level (Luc, Jac with his cross, Li, etc.) but is progressively mastered during level IIB (from Pie to Pol).

However where the locus is the bisector of a right-angle (which means that the problem of the two trees is generalized and the question deals with two rows of trees) success is not achieved either at level IIA or at level IIB. Thus Wi's solution is no more adequate than that of Luc. Both subjects arrange their marbles in a circle, and although Wi later forms them in a line, his line is perpendicular to the bisector. At the level of intuition this question is more difficult because it raises a problem of logical multiplication. While the operations of addition and multiplication are equal in difficulty the corresponding intuitions are not, because logical addition is simply a matter of repeating the same actions.

When the problem does not involve multiplying relations, the repetition of actions becomes selective and directed at the end of level IIA. Because the repetition is cumulative and not tautological, it generates iteration which is a special kind of generalization. The latter is twofold: there is symmetrical prolongation of the line at either extremity and there is interpolation leading to continuity. Thus at level IIB, children have a practical understanding of geometrical loci, and are handicapped only in that they have not yet elaborated the formal concept of a point (see C.C.S., ch. V).

The discovery of loci marks the beginning of a type of reasoning by recurrence which is characteristic of the stage of concrete operations, i.e. of stage III. Expressed in general terms, reasoning by recurrence takes the following form: if, in a given structure, two adjacent points are found to satisfy the same conditions, then these conditions will be met by all the points in that structure.

This type of argument is instanced by the problem of the circle (locus of points equidistant from a given point A) and by that of the straight line (locus of points equidistant from two points A and B). It is remarkable that children as young as those at level IIB should require only a little preliminary experimentation when faced with these problems. Then, having discovered by repetition one or two points which are in fact equidistant either from A or from both A and B, they quickly generalize the equidistance to include all points on the circle or the straight line (long before they have any precise notion of a point, i.e. without formal recognition of continuity). This suggests that reasoning by the elementary principle of recurrence follows naturally on iteration or directed repetition of actions.

This finding has some bearing on epistemology. Poincaré held that recurrence was a special kind of reasoning, entirely *sui generis*, and peculiar to mathematics. According to this view, this type of reasoning depends on a whole complex of *a priori* judgments (in particular on the intuition of pure number). Logicians, on the other hand, argued that recurrence is a natural outcome of seriation: in a series generated by a 'hereditary law', the 'heritage' is always transmitted from one term to the next. The present findings support the latter thesis. Almost as soon as children can reproduce the action of finding equidistant points in a directed and selective manner, they see their way to continuing indefinitely in that iteration, being certain about the conservation of equidistance. We should perhaps add that the mastery of iteration does not imply the same facility with other kinds of seriation.

It may be argued that this behaviour is a case of perseveration, having its roots in economy of thinking, like predicting the sum of the angles of a triangle (ch. VIII). This hypothesis must be rejected for two reasons. First, these young children are quite unable to generalize without some trial-and-error, and the correct solution is achieved only if there is correct selection. Those characteristics of the initial action which are relevant to the elaboration of a geometrical 'locus' are retained, and those which are accidental, as is the equality of intervals between points, are rejected. Second, there is a long period of intuitive trial-and-error which leads to the discovery of iteration and reasoning by recurrence at the end of sub-stage IIB. The acquisition is gradual but it very soon attains operational equilibrium, for by the beginning of stage III children can anticipate the full generality of the solution in their very first replies.

§4. *Stage III: Immediate and operational construction of 'loci'*

Throughout stage III, and including level IIIA, children start out from a correct presupposition, one which makes it possible to generalize the relation of equidistance. Needless to say, there is still a certain amount of experimentation in order to discover what form any particular locus will take. But there is never any doubt that what is sought is a series of points having certain characteristics in common. For about the age of 7 or 8, children master concrete operations and these admit of reversible composition. Therefore children now select hypotheses in answer to the problem and direct their behaviour accordingly, using anticipatory schemata:

PLEI (7; 0). The trees: "*In the middle.*—Let's put in another child.—*There* (above).—And another.—*There* (below. Without further suggestion he continues by drawing a series of points in both directions). How far can we go on?—*Right up to the edge of the paper.*—And if I brought some more paper?—*We could go on to the end.*"
The two contestants: "*They'd make a line* (drawing a series of discrete points)."

MIC (7; 3): "We want this marble just as far for you as it is for me. Where should we put it?—*In the middle.*—And these others?—*We can go on putting them further and further away* (placing 1, 2, 3 and 4 on the right).—How far can we go on, remembering that they must always be the same distance for both of us?—*To the end of the world.*—And the other side?—*Yes* (placing 5, 6, and 7), *to the other end of the world.*—What would I see, if I were up in an aeroplane and were looking down at it?—*If I put them close together they'll look like a straight wall.*"
Two trees: identical response, but symmetry is immediate. The experimenter indicates a distant point: "Is that the same distance from both trees?—*Well, look* (drawing lines between the point and the trees and showing that these are equal)."
The experimenter now presents two rows of trees at right angles to each other and evenly spaced: "Now we want them all to be just as far from each

of these two trees (indicating the trees in pairs).—(He first puts two points, one at X and the other at Y, such that XC = YC'.)—But these children are playing with the same marble, not two.—*Oh, yes* (he puts one point some distance away and equidistant from the members of each pair).—Can you put a lot in?—*I can go on and on* (putting a series of points along the bisector). —What about the other side (of the vertex of the angle formed by the six trees)?—(He lays a few marbles.) *Well, so long as the children turn round that way, we can easily put them the same distance* (from the paired trees)."

The circle: He first makes two straight lines which are symmetrically disposed about point A, then exclaims: "*Oh, but they won't be the same distance to shoot.* (He therefore starts to put marbles in pairs, equidistant and symmetrically disposed about the centre. At the third pair, he stops). *A circle!*"

MER (7; 3). The response is almost identical, but for two or three false starts. For the two players, he puts three marbles on either side of the centre: "What if I gave you many?—*I could make a long straight line, as long as the world if I had a lot of marbles.*"

Two trees: again he replies, "*As long as the world.*" With two rows at right angles, each made up of eight trees, he first puts one marble equidistant from the first and second, then another equidistant for the second pair, then another for the third pair. Then he places two more marbles near the first two trees, ignoring equidistance, but removes them of his own accord. "Can we put any more down?—*No.*—What about here (a point further away on the bisector)?—*Oh, yes, of course! We can put a lot* (indicating the line of the bisector).—What about the other side?—*Oh, yes, that's all right too. It's just as far as well.*"

Circle: he produces two parallel rows, then immediately corrects them to a circle.

EXT (7; 9), for two trees, immediately produces a row of points symmetrically disposed about the mid-point. "Are there many points?—*There, all over* (indicating a straight line). *You've got to put them in a line right up to the edge of the paper.*—What if these were flat stones and we could build them up one above the other, would they still be just as far from the two trees?— *Yes, we'd have a wall right up to the sky.*"

Two rows of trees at right angles; three marbles placed along the bisector: "What would this look like if we saw it from an aeroplane?—*A line up to the edge of the paper.*—And the other side?—*The same.*—How far?—*As far as you like.*"

MIN (8; 2) first places fourteen marbles, all equidistant from a centre at A, then says: "*If the children held hands, they would form a circle.*"

For two players, he first places a few marbles then concludes that they would form a straight line. For two trees he does likewise. "Can one continue a long way?—*Yes, as far as one wants.*"

Two rows of trees at right angles: after a few careful trials he says: "*All I need to do is draw a straight line then I won't go wrong.*"

HEL (8; 6). Two trees: after a few careful trials he continues rapidly without stopping to make sure. "How far can you go while keeping it just as far from both?—*To the end of the world.*—How many points can you put in?—*They make a straight line.*"

For the circles: a few points placed with some care, then: *"It's a circle."*

All the responses at this stage are alike. This is true also of stage IV which differs only in that children show a more refined notion of a geometrical point, as noted elsewhere (C.C.S., ch. V).

KIM (11; 9). Two trees: he marks a few points then says: *"It's a straight line."* Two rows at right angles: he measures the first two points then says: *"It's all right anywhere so long as it's in a straight line in either direction."*

We note that, beginning with stage IIIA, our subjects show two fresh developments as compared with those at stage II. First, there is immediate generalization of the relationship of equidistance to cover all the points on a straight line which is therefore seen as both continuous (insofar as that notion is understood at the stage in question) and unlimited. This behaviour may be called immediate reasoning by recurrence. Second, having discovered this solution for simpler problems, they extend it and apply it to the bisector of an angle formed by two rows of trees (a problem which remains unsolved at level IIB).

The second development would appear to show a turning-point in the construction of operations. If the set of points equidistant from two points A and A' forms a straight line (a discovery made, however gradually, as early as level IIB) it would seem self-evident that the same holds good for B and B' or C and C'. When the same straight line will satisfy the conditions for all the paired points the conclusion would seem even more inevitable. Yet the problem is not solved at stage II, and for two reasons. The first obstacle to its solution is a perceptual one, which proves that reasoning at this stage is not yet operational. The line which they would need to construct is not parallel either with the row A B C or with the row A' B' C'; it is the bisector of the angle between these rows, and this makes for added difficulty (cf. C.C.S., ch. VI, sec. 1). However the principal difficulty lies in the fact that the solution is one line and not three! It involves the interaction of relations or logical multiplication, and hence these younger subjects are at a loss. Their inability to deal with these operations is proof that their solution is still intuitive and not yet fully operational. At stage III, the problem is solved quite readily, since it is always put after the question of only two trees.

But the most important achievement at this stage is reasoning by recurrence as such, which is no longer the outcome of prolonged trial-and-error but now takes the form of an anticipatory schema which ensures generalization. The child simply determines a few points in the series and immediately concludes that all the points on a circle or a straight line must have the same property, for the entire series can be built up by taking points immediately adjacent to each other. These children have barely achieved the level of concrete operations enabling them to determine metrically whether points are at a constant distance from point A or equidistant from A and B. Yet they generalize that equidistance to any point of the series forming the circle or straight line and even feel the intrinsic necessity of their mathematical reasoning. This is the most important and unexpected result of the enquiry. It is proof that reasoning by recurrence is the direct outcome of iteration of operations, as argued in §3, although iteration itself is specific to mathematical operations, for in pure logic iteration amounts merely to tautology. But it also proves that an operation which admits of iteration is different in kind and not merely in degree from empirical or inductive intuition, even if historically, the operation is only the end-state of a developing intuition, with the reversible equilibrium characteristic of all such end-states. Psychologically, this finding is of the utmost importance. The discovery of geometrical loci, as studied in the present chapter, is the finest example of the direct transition from induction which is empirical and intuitive to operational generalization which is deductive. The end-stage is reasoning by recurrence, that model of mathematical deduction which has been so brilliantly expounded by H. Poincaré.[1]

[1] This transition also occurs earlier here than in the problem of the sum of the angles of a triangle, where complete mastery is delayed until stage IV.

Chapter Ten

REPRESENTATION OF CIRCLES, MECHANICAL AND COMPOSITE[1] CURVES

IN the last chapter we saw how the simplest curve is constructed, that is, the circle. However, the method we used is not the only method available to the child in elaborating such shapes, for the notion of 'locus' can be appreciated by him only in its most elementary applications. In order to study the circle further and to advance to the construction of more complex curves, we need to use a more direct intuition of movement than was necessary for the study of equidistances. Especially appropriate are those curves known as 'mechanical curves'. These were well-known to the Greeks but paradoxically omitted from Euclid's geometry because they cannot be drawn with ruler and compasses alone. In this chapter, the last in Part III, we shall study how far children learn to understand how, by following paths of movement, we can construct circles, spirals and cycloids. A study of the last two curves should prove all the more rewarding in that it provides an opportunity of carrying a stage further the enquiry which began with the circle, since they introduce problems which cannot be solved before the level of formal operations. The present study in the field of geometrical generalization therefore corresponds with the research into the sum of the angles of a triangle (ch. VIII). Questions concerned with spirals and cycloids require the level of formal operations because they involve two reference systems instead of one. If a cylinder is slowly rolled about its axis while an ant is made to walk down its length, keeping throughout to whatever portion is uppermost, the total movement so described will be a spiral. Similarly, if we were to attach a lantern or a red disc to the rim of a cartwheel in motion, the lantern or disc would describe a cycloid curve (i.e. a series of hoops). For a child to predict what curves will result, he must mentally combine the rectilinear movement of the ant with the circular movement of the cylinder, or the circular motion of the red disc with the forward motion of the wheel. In either case, we have two simultaneous movements each of which must be referred to its own coordinate system. In order to reconstruct the total motion the observer must determine a few points and then generalize from them, as in the case of the loci in ch. IX, but the problem is more difficult because it requires the synthesis of two separate paths.

[1] Written with the collaboration of Mlles U. Galusser, J. Nicolas and N. Bellière, and M. R. Mallet.

§1. *Summary of methods and results*

Children were asked a number of questions. These were only loosely related to each other but were so designed as to enable the experimenter to deduce from the answers how far children can construct a curve derived from simple rotary movement (a circle) or from the composition of two simultaneous movements.

Question 1. A wooden disc is made to move round its own axis, the disc being pinned to a sheet of paper with a needle passing through its centre. A short pencil is fastened to a point on its circumference. The child is asked to predict what kind of a line the pencil will draw when the disc is rotated (i.e. a circle).

This experiment is followed by variants in which the pencil is fastened to a corner of a square or an angle of a triangle and these are rotated on an axis.

Question 2. The disc is stood upright and made to roll along a table while the pencil draws a path on a sheet of paper which is perpendicular to the table top. The subject must predict the shape of the line when the pencil is fastened (*a*) to a point on the circumference, (*b*) to the centre of the disc, and (*c*) to a point taken anywhere between the centre and the circumference. The problem involves the three possible forms of a cycloid: (*a*) a series of hoops (Fig. 4), (*c*) truncated hoops, and (*b*) a straight line (the limiting case).

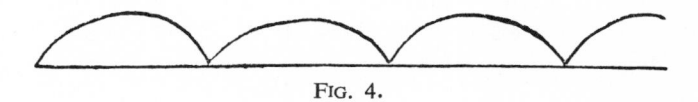

FIG. 4.

Question 3. A wooden cylinder is made to turn horizontally about its axis. The child is told that an ant is walking along a roller. The ant has walked in an inkblot and so we can follow its path along the roller. In practice the cylinder is covered with white paper and the path is drawn by a pencil point mounted in such a way that it can be made to move along the uppermost part of the moving roller. The child must predict the path taken by the ant (*a*) when the roller is stationary and the pencil moves forward (i.e. a straight line), (*b*) when the ant or pencil is stationary but the roller rotates (i.e. a circle), and (*c*) when both move simultaneously (i.e. a spiral). In the last case the relative speeds may be varied as required.

Question 4. The previous question has this complication, that the subject must not only reconstruct a composite movement but has also to envisage what the paper will look like when opened out and spread in a single plane.[1] Although in practice it is not impossible to disentangle

---

[1] For a study of such problems, the reader is referred to C.C.S., ch. X.

the two factors, it was thought advisable to include a further problem, again involving the reconstruction of a composite movement, but simpler. The shapes to be predicted are a series of curves, ranging from a straight line to an exponential curve, depending on the relative speeds of two movements. The apparatus consists of a small rectangular wooden board with a slot cut out of it parallel with the shorter sides. The board is moved lengthways, i.e. in prolongation of the longer sides, while a toy snail is made to move down the slot. The snail is fitted with a pencil point and drawn by a wire. The child is asked to predict the path taken by the snail. The correct prediction would be an oblique line where the board and the snail move at the same speed, but relative speeds were varied according to the requirements of the situation.

Question 5. Further to the problem of the ant moving on a revolving cylinder, the child may be asked to show what path the ant would take if it moved along the axis of rotation. Here the problem is to ascertain whether he realizes that a straight line pivoting about its own axis remains a straight line, and more particularly, that a straight line is the only line which remains unaltered by rotation on its own axis, a proposition which may be familiar as the definition given by Leibniz. However, it is difficult to gain an unambiguous answer because when a child is asked to think of a straight length of tubing and gives the correct reply, his response may be no more than the static representation of the tubing.

Following is a brief outline of the kind of reply made to these questions as children progress from stage I (4–5 years) to stage IV (formal thought):

Throughout stage I we find that children are unable to imagine movement as such in advance of its occurrence. They simply make a pencil mark, which may be a point or a short stroke. More often, they draw the object at rest, instead of showing what path it describes when in motion. It may be that they see their point or stroke as the result of movement, intending it as the point of arrival, but movement itself cannot be represented at all.

Responses given during stage II fall naturally into two sub-stages, A and B. During sub-stage IIA, children begin to imagine the curves described by objects in motion, but for question 1, they cannot differentiate the curve described by a simple movement from the outline of the object itself. They imagine that the path of a square when rotated will itself be square, etc. Questions 2 to 4 are even harder, and here the child is unable to differentiate curves resulting from simple movements (i.e. a circle for the rotating disc, a straight line for the forward movement of the ant and the snail), from curves which are produced by composite movement (for the movement of the disc, ant or snail needs to be combined with another movement, one which relates to an external reference system, this movement being that of the wheel or the cylinder or the board). Thus, in answer to question 2, children now draw a circle or a series of circles (often discontinuous) instead of a cycloid, for question 3 they produce a straight line instead of a spiral, and for question 4 a vertical line instead of an oblique. At sub-stage IIB, children differentiate the curve described by an object in simple motion from its static outline. Where the movement involved is composite, there is a growing differentiation of curves resulting from simple motion and those produced by composite motion. In answer to question 1, they predict that a pencil fastened to an object rotating on a pivot will draw a circle whatever the shape of the object. Passing to questions 2 to 4, we find a number of interesting compromises between simple and composite movements. Thus, although the cycloid is always represented as a series of circles in juxtaposition, these may be drawn as ellipses in order to coordinate the movement of the disc on its own axis with its change of position (displacement) relative to the table. The spiral is often shown as an oblique line, which is a compromise between the forward movement of the ant on the cylinder and the rotary movement of the cylinder itself.

During stage III (beginning at 7–8 years) children gradually reach the correct solutions, although these are preceded by trial-and-error. We may distinguish a sub-stage IIIA when some of the questions but not all are answered more adequately than at stage II, and another, IIIB (beginning at 8–9 years), when all the questions are correctly solved, although success is still preceded by hesitation and error. At stage IV (formal operations) the correct replies are given from the outset and there is no overt trial-and-error. Occasionally we find precocious subjects who are able to do this as early as 9 years of age, and conversely, we find others less gifted who continue to be uncertain even after the age of 12. As a control experiment, the same questions were put to a number of adults, and it was found that here, too, the solution was sometimes imperfect.

§2. *Stage I: Children cannot reconstruct even a circular curve of movement*

A number of subjects were interviewed and found to be at the upper end of stage I. Their drawings of circles, squares and triangles were different from each other even if unsuccessful. They were asked a few of the questions from 1 to 4, with special emphasis on question 1. The following examples illustrate the initial difficulty of the problem.

REN (4; 2). The experimenter rotates the disc on its axis before fastening a pencil to its outer rim: "Look, this pencil will make a mark on the paper. I'm going to turn the wheel. Would you like to draw what the pencil will do? —(He draws a circle.)—(The pencil is now moved to the centre.) I'm going to make a hole in the middle and put the pencil through the hole. Now show me the drawing it will make when I turn the wheel.—(Draws another circle.) —Look.—(He copies the point, showing no surprise at the fact that his previous drawing was wide of the mark.)—Now watch. I'm going to put my pencil on this point (triangle). Then I'm going to turn it like this (demonstrating). You draw me what the pencil will do.—(He tries to draw a triangle but cannot close it.) *A bell!*—Watch what the pencil has drawn.—*It turns.*— (The experiment is repeated from another angle.) What will the drawing look like this time?—*Like this* (the triangle).—Watch.—*A ring!*—Now what will the drawing be like if I put the pencil on another point and turn it round?— (Again he draws a vague triangular shape.)"

Ren is introduced to the question of the snail (question 4), with the board remaining stationary. Once again, the problem of communication is considerable. "You see this snail. He's shut up between these walls so he's got to move along like this (demonstrating: the little boy then takes the snail himself and moves it up and down its groove). Can you draw me the path it has made?—*Yes* (producing a small black circle instead of a straight line).— What's that you've drawn?—*The snail.*—Watch (showing the straight line). Try it this time. (The experiment is repeated with a fresh sheet of paper). Can you draw me the path?—(Again he draws the snail.)"

MARL (4; 8). The rotating disc: (The question is the same as for Ren, but the experimenter draws a little cross on the disc where he fastens the pencil.) Marl draws a cross.—"Watch.—(Surprise.)—(The disc is given a quarter turn:) Show me where the cross is now.—(He points correctly.)—How did it go to get there starting from over there?—*Don't know*", etc. The experimenter passes to the square: "Show me the drawing my pencil will make when I turn this round (rotating the square).—(Draws a point.)—Watch (Marl sees that it has made a circle). Now I'm going to turn it just a little (quarter turn). Can you draw me what my pencil has done now?—(He draws a little line which is vaguely straight.)—And now (a full circle)?—(He draws the square.)" For the problem of the snail he first produces a short stroke, and then he too draws the snail itself.

There is every indication that these children are unable to form any representation of a curve of motion as such. Ren repeatedly sees the drawing made by the pencil as it rotates, yet he consistently fails to draw any lesson from his experience, and invariably draws the object itself (the circle, the triangle or the snail) with perfect equanimity. At level IIA children may produce similar drawings, imagining that the pencil will reproduce the outline of a circle or a triangle as it rotates. But here the explanation is different. Ren cannot imagine a path as described by an object in movement which is why he simply draws the object itself. The same is true of Marl (who draws a cross to indicate the pencil, and later the square and the snail), but Marl shows more insight in two ways: he draws a point to indicate a pencil mark and, more significantly he produces two short strokes, one for the square when given a quarter turn and one for the path of the snail. These strokes are a first attempt at representing a curve of movement, and as such they herald the beginning of stage II. It is difficult to be certain as to their significance. What we know of the way in which children first conceive of change of position (cf. *Les notions de mouvement et de vitesse chez l'enfant* and chs. III and VI of the present volume) leads us to believe that the strokes are intended to represent the result of change of position, i.e. the point of arrival. However, it may be that they are no more than symbolic abbreviations. Whatever the interpretation, it is clear that the curve of movement is not represented in its entirety. We conclude that the ability to foresee such a path is beyond children at stage I. The reason is not far to seek. We know that movement is conceived at first as a kind of translocation. Children think in static terms, focusing their attention on the point of arrival (sometimes on the point of departure). They tend to ignore the movement involved in a change of position[1] which is why the very idea of a path of movement does not enter their minds.

§3. *Sub-stage IIA: Children draw a path of movement but cannot differentiate between one curve and another*

Unlike those at stage I, children at sub-stage IIA can form a representation of a path of movement. Even if they cannot do so under all circumstances, they can in the particular conditions set up in our experiment, where a pencil is made to leave a permanent record of its own path. When the pencil is fixed to the rim of a circular disc they grasp the notion of circularity in its path, albeit at an intuitive level. But when it is fixed to a square or a triangle and made to rotate, they continue to believe that it will draw triangles and squares. Needless to say they cannot differentiate between composite and simple motions as they are required to do for questions 2 to 4:

Bu (5; 2). Question 1. The circle: "What sort of a mark will be made by my pencil when I turn the ring (the experimenter rotates the disc with the pencil point off the paper)?—*A ring!* (He draws a circle.)—(The experimenter moves the pencil down to the paper and rotates the disc.) Look:—*A big ring!* —Now I'm going to put the pencil between the middle of the disc and the rim (fixing it near the centre at a spot marked by a small cross). Now what mark will it make?—*It will make a cross also.*—(Demonstration.)—*Oh, a little ring!*"

Rotating square: "What kind of mark will my pencil make it I put it at this point (angle) and then turn it round like this (indicating rotary movement)?—*A square.*—What if I fix my pencil half-way between the point and the middle?—*A tiny little circle.*—(Demonstration: Bu notes that he is right.) —And if I put it back at the point?—*A square.*"

Question 2. Cycloid: "What kind of a drawing will the pencil make when I roll the wheel along like this (demonstrating the entire movement using

[1] The child, like Aristotle, thinks of movement not as a state of things but as a transition from one state of rest to another.

a blue point as reference mark instead of a pencil)?—*A ring.*—Watch once again (repeating the motion).—(He draws a second ring 1 cm. away from the first.)—But tell me. How does the little blue point get across from your first ring to your second?—*It's got to roll along* (and he draws two more rings on a line)."

Question 3. Spiral: for the rotation alone he foresees a circle, and for the straight line movement "*a line*". When the experimenter shows him the two movements combined and tries to elicit a response he replies: "*One line each side*", and draws a series of parallel straight lines.

CHRI (5; 3). Question 1. The circle: "*It makes a ring* (before seeing the pencil track).—Why?—*Because there's a ring there.*—What if I put my pencil in this hole in the corner of the square over here (the experimenter rotates the square without the pencil before inserting it in the hole), how will the pencil go this time?—*It makes a square, but I can't do squares* (but he draws one all the same).—Watch (demonstrating).—*Oh, no. A ring.*—Now what will happen if I put it on this point?—(He draws another square.)"

Question 2: The experimenter rotates the upright disc with the pencil away from the paper: "*It will do a ring.*—But the wheel keeps turning.—(He now draws two circles some distance apart, representing the wheel at the beginning and end of the motion.)—And how does it get from there to there?—(He draws a series of circles between them.)" (See Fig. 5.)

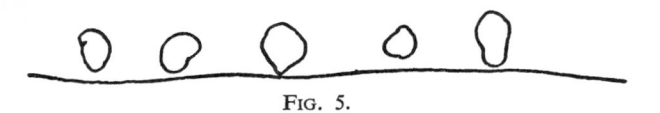

FIG. 5.

MIC (5; 2). Question 1. "Look. If I turn this ring (showing the movement) what do you think the pencil will do?—*Something* (he draws a circle not quite complete, thus showing clearly that he is trying to draw the path of motion and not the object.)—Watch (experiment).—(He draws a circle.)" Square: "Now how will the pencil go (demonstrating the movement without the pencil)?—(He draws a square.)—Watch (experiment).—*A ring!*—Why? —*Because.*—But why did it do a ring?—*Don't know.*"

Question 4. Snail: "What mark does it make along the path as it goes?— (He draws a horizontal straight line.)—Now, what if I move the board like this while he crawls, what path will he do now?—*Straight along* (drawing the same line again).—But what would happen if I pulled the board this way while he goes straight ahead, will he still make the same mark?—*Yes.*—Well, what path will the board follow when I move it without the snail?—*Like this* (the same line again)."

HUR (5; 2). Question 1. Circle: "*It will do a wheel* (drawing a circle).— And what will it do if the pencil is nearer the middle?—*A wheel* (drawing a smaller circle inside the first. Thus the topological relation of enclosure between the two paths is accurately foreseen. However, the remainder of the interview makes it clear that the diminution of the circle is not yet conceived in metric terms).—What drawing will it do if I put it even nearer the middle?—*It will be bigger* (drawing a third circle which is larger than the

232

second).—One of the other boys told me it would be smaller. Was he wrong? —*No*."

Question 2. The cycloid: a simple circle.

ER (5; 6). Question 1. Circle: "*A ring.*" Square (the question having been postponed until the end of the enquiry to exclude perseveration): "What will be the drawing left by the pencil when I turn this round?—*A square.*—Watch (demonstrating).—*Oh! A ring.*—Why won't it do a square?—*Don't know.*"

Question 2. Cycloid: The question is first asked with the pencil in the centre of the disc: "When I turn this wheel what will the little point in the middle be doing?—*A ring also.*—Now watch carefully. As it goes along does it do a ring (moving the wheel without producing the pencil track)?—*A point.*— But isn't it moving?—(Hesitating) *Well, a ring, then.*—Watch (demonstrating). —*It's making a line.*—Why?—*Because the pencil isn't turning.*—Now I'm going to put the pencil here (at the circumference).—*It will do a ring.*—Watch (demonstrating the movement without the drawing).—He draws a rough circle followed by a thread-like line to indicate the forward movement: Fig. 6).—You draw what it will do along the road (rotating the wheel).—(He draws three spaced circles.)"

Question 3. Spiral: "You watch me move the pencil along the (stationary) roller. What will the pencil do?—*It makes a rail* (drawing a straight line).—Now this time I'm turning it (causing a spiral movement)?—*It will do a ring now* (drawing the cylinder as a rectangle and putting a little circle in the centre)."

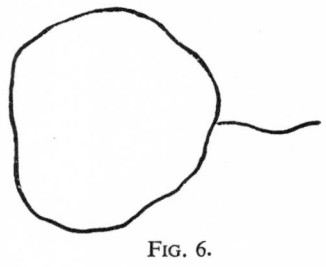

FIG. 6.

MUL (6; 4). Question 1. Circle: "What mark will my pencil make?—*A ring.*—And if I put it between the middle and the outside?—*Still a ring.*—Smaller or bigger?—*The same ring, the same size.*—And if I put it right in the middle? —*A little ring, smaller* (drawing a little circle instead of a point)." Square (the question being put at the end of the enquiry): "What will it do if I turn it like this (demonstrating without the pencil)?—*A square.*"

Question 2. Cycloid: "*It will do a ring.*—But what will be the path drawn by the pencil? Watch (demonstrating without the pencil track)?—*Well, another ring* (drawing a second circle with a gap between them).—What will it do if I put it in the middle of the wheel (straight line)?—*Still a ring.*—And when I put it half way between the middle and the wood?—*A ring again.*"

Question 3. A spiral: the cylinder is rotated with the pencil held in one position: "*It will do a ring* (correct)—Now the pencil will move along (with the cylinder stationary).—*It will do a line.*—That's right. Now this time I'm going to make both of them move (demonstrating with the pencil track). What will it do now?—*A line like this.*—Like it did when the roller didn't move at all?—*Yes.*"

PAG (5; 3) is a little more advanced than the others in his understanding of the cycloid. Question 1. Circle: "*It will make a ring.*—And in the middle?— *A little ring.*—Why will it be smaller?— . . . —Supposing I put it half way between the rim and the middle?—*Then it will be bigger than the last one but smaller than the first.*—You're quite right. Tell me why. . . ." Square (end of enquiry): "What will the pencil track look like?—*A square.*—What if I put the pencil half way between the middle and the edge?—*A little ring.*—And right in the middle?—*A tiny little ring.*—And here?—*A square."ₜ*

Question 2 (Cycloid): "What kind of a mark will my pencil make when I fix it to the rim of the wheel?—(He draws a series of circles in juxtaposition.) —And what if I put the pencil right in the middle?—(Smaller circles in juxtaposition.) *Smaller rings.*—And on the rim?—*Like this* (large circles in juxtaposition).—Watch (demonstrating). Did you do it right?—*Yes."*

Question 3. Spiral: he draws a circle for the stationary pencil over the moving roller, and straight lines for the moving pencil with the roller stationary or in movement: "Is it the same as when the pencil moves forward and the roller is quite still?—*Yes."*

JEA (5; 10) is also a little more advanced. Question 1. Square (here asked at the beginning to verify the result): "When my pencil goes round with that thing what path will it follow (demonstrating without the pencil track)?—*A square.*—And if I put it near the middle?—*A smaller square.*—Watch (demonstrating).—*Oh! A ring!*—What will happen when I put it further in? —*It will do another ring.*—Now what about this one (a triangle with the pencil fixed to the vertex of an angle)?—*A ring.*—And if I put it nearer the middle —*A little ring."*

Question 2. Cycloid: "*A ring.*—Supposing I put my pencil in the middle?— *A line* (grasping this construction!)."

Question 4. Snail: "*A stroke.*—Now what will happen if I pull the board along like this?—*A stroke again.*—Just like it was before?—(Hesitating.) *No, smaller* (indicating the beginnings of differentiation)."

These cases are a clear step ahead of those at stage I in that they try to draw the path of an object in motion instead of the object itself. The only exception is the small cross drawn by Bu, a residual response from the previous stage. For the rest, they understand that if a pencil is fixed to a moving object it produces a line representing a curve of motion. The broken circle drawn by Mic when reproducing the incomplete revolution of a disc is a clear case in point. Equally telling is the fact that those children who are more advanced can foresee that a pencil nearer the centre of a rotating object (question 1) must produce a shorter path than one attached to its rim. Their replies are a clear indication that these curves are intended to represent paths of movement and not stationary objects, as was true of children at stage I.

The difficulty raised by problems of simple circular motion (question 1) lies in that children need to dissociate the outline of a rotating figure from the curve described by its movement. If the figure is a circle there appears to be no problem, and subjects realize that the pencil will describe circles whether it is attached to the circumference of the circle or to some point within it. But when a square is rotated about an axis which runs through the centre, children fail to grasp that a pencil situated at one of its angles will still describe a circular path.

Even when the subject sees the square in motion and watches the pencil as it moves (before seeing the tracing on the paper), he cannot resist the impression that the tracing must be a square because the object is a square. To understand the reason for their failure, we must refer back to the replies given by children at this level when asked to solve problems of 'loci' (ch. IX). Correct solution requires an understanding that if a figure such as a square is rotated about an axis then any point on that figure, e.g. an angle, must describe a circle. But this understanding demands the realization, implicit or explicit, that the distance from the moving point to the centre is constant. In other words it implies the recognition of a 'locus' based on the equidistance of the centre from all points on the curve described by the point in rotation. The previous study showed how at level IIA notions of a locus and of equidistance in general are unformed and totally lacking in precision. The experience of rotary movement is no substitute for an understanding of loci, because unless there is equidistance relative to the axis of rotation, the movement itself is not necessarily seen as circular. Hence we are not surprised to find that children imagine that the path of movement will resemble the outline of the square. The error reflects some confusion between rotary movement and following an outline. Because there is no conservation of equidistance, we find a systematic error in replies to question 1 on rotary movement, and it recurs throughout substage IIA. Additional proof may be seen in that most of these children fail to understand the result of the experiment even when they see it. Thus Chri watches the pencil draw a circle from one angle of a square, but proceeds to draw a square as before when the experimenter inserts the pencil in a different angle. Mic and Er see that the pencil track is circular but are at a loss when asked the reason. Only Jea, having noted that rotation of a square produces a circle, succeeds in generalizing the result to the case of a triangle.

Because distances are not related to reference centres, curves of rotary movement are not referred to the axis of rotation. Hence the representation of movement is inadequate even when the movement is simple. Inevitably, composite movements which involve rotation (cycloids and spirals) and even those made up of two straight lines (question 4) are more difficult to represent. In both cases we find that children ascribe one and the same curve to the total composite movement and one of its constituent movements. Moreover this is often an imperfect representation even of the latter for the reasons already given.

In the case of cycloidal movement, children cannot resist the notion that a wheel which turns must engender a circle because the wheel itself is circular. The fact of its forward movement is simply shown by drawing several circles, sometimes spaced and sometimes in juxtaposition. The first circle represents the initial position and the remainder show further positions reached in the course of movement. (Chri at first draws only two circles representing points of departure and arrival, and requires further prodding before inserting more circles in the empty space between them!) The response is analogous to that of stage I: a part of the movement is not reproduced at all! The comparative regression is due to the greater difficulty of questions of composite movement. As for the simple movement involved in a composite cycloid curve, while all the subjects correctly show the curve of a wheel about its own axis as circular, hardly any realize that the centre describes a straight line, i.e. simple displacement. (The exception is Jea who comes nearest to sub-stage IIB.) Mul draws its path as "still a ring", while Pag draws a series of small circles in juxtaposition which are still unmistakeably circles although much smaller than those he drew for a point on the rim.

In question 3, subjects realize that the ant moves in a straight line when the cylinder is still, and likewise that a stationary pencil leaves a circular track when held against a rotating cylinder. It is when the two movements are composed that they fail. Some children represent the ant's path on the moving cylinder as a straight line, others as several lines in parallel, these being viewed as successive sections in a rectilinear path. Even question 4 fails to elicit a response indicative of composite movement although the composing movements are both rectilinear. Children draw identical lines for the snail's path whether the board is stationary or dragged sideways by the motion of the board, ignoring altogether the change in direction. A few go so far as to draw identical lines for the simple movement of the snail, the simple movement of the board and the composite movement of the two together (cf. Mic who draws three horizontal lines all approximately the same length). We are again reminded of the characteristic limitations of this level which spring from the inability to determine slopes and the absence of rectangular coordinates.

All of these results depend on two factors which are clearly linked. In the first place, children are unable to form a representation of relative movement, insofar as this depends on the composition of two simple movements.[1] The three problems, based on cycloidal, spiral and oblique movement (questions 2–4), are posed in such a way that these children are well aware that two movements are involved in each: the rotary movement of the wheel and its progression along the table top, movement of the ant and rotation of the cylinder, vertical movement of the snail and lateral movement of the grooved board. But even from the purely kinematic viewpoint, and quite independently of their geometrical equivalents, the constituent movements do not blend in

---

[1] This point has been discussed in an earlier work: Les notions de mouvement et de vitesse chez l'enfant, ch. V.

children's minds to form one composite movement. Similar results were found in our earlier study of relative movement where only the kinematic aspect was under consideration. Subjects were shown a snail crawling along a board while the board itself was pulled either in the same or in the opposite direction. At this level, they could not understand how two movements starting from the same point and oriented in the same direction could be added together in estimating time and distance. Yet that problem was considerably easier, since here the two movements are heterogeneous instead of being homogeneous and in the same direction. Thus the progress of the wheel, the rotation of the cylinder and the movement of the board are presented as absolute movements while the motion of the lantern suspended on the felloe and those of the ant and snail are relative to the former. The first obstacle to correct solution is therefore kinematic. But this limitation derives from another which is geometrical.

Relative movement may be viewed as the result of two elementary motions, but this conception implies a double system of references. One system is internal to the moving support while the other links it with the stationary field. Curves of composite movement cannot therefore be constructed without reference to internal and external coordinate systems. Combining two systems of coordinates is a second order operation and presupposes formal thinking. At stage II, little children cannot even construct one coordinate system with organized reference points and stable intervals in one or more dimensions. Even curves of simple movement elude their grasp as is evident from their representation of rotary movement. They lack clear notions of distance and the ability to coordinate distances. Hence they are unable to recognize equidistance which underlies the construction of such curves. Therefore any clear notion of composite or mechanical curves is quite beyond them. Thus the limitations in their powers of kinematic representation are closely bound up with parallel limitations in geometrical thinking.

§4. *Level IIB: First attempts at differentiating curves of simple and composite movement*

Level IIB shows two new developments. Circular paths now begin to be shown correctly, being differentiated from the outline of a rotating object. Similarly, curves of composite movement are somewhat more differentiated than they were.

RUT (5; 1) stands midway between levels IIA and IIB. The experimenter drew a cross on the edge of the disc and in one corner of the square used in question 1: Rut draws the successive positions of the cross and gradually finishes with a circle in both examples.

Question 2. Cycloid: to begin with he draws a circle; later he draws elongated circles because he sees the red spot on the wheel moving forward and wishes to distinguish between rotation on an axis and cycloidal movement.

NÉ (5; 4). Question 1. Circle: *"A ring.*—And what will happen if I put the pencil in the middle?—*A straight line.*" Square: "If I put my pencil in at this corner and turn the square, what kind of a line will it make?—*A square.*— Do you really think so?—*No, it will do a thing like this* (drawing the square on end like a diamond).—Watch (still rotating the square without letting the pencil mark the paper).—*No, it will make a square all the same.* (Pause: he thinks.) *Oh! A ring* (without having seen the pencil track).—Why a ring?— *Because it keeps turning. It's not the same as when it's standing still."*

Question 2. Cycloid: *"A ring.*—Look at it again as it moves along.—*No, I still think it's a ring.* (A level IIA response)."

Question 3. Spiral: he draws a circle when the pencil is held still, and a straight line when the cylinder is still while the pencil moves forward, both replies being correct: "Good. This time we will move them both together. What will happen when I move the pencil along and turn the roller at the same time?—(He draws a chain of little circles, as in Fig. 7.)"

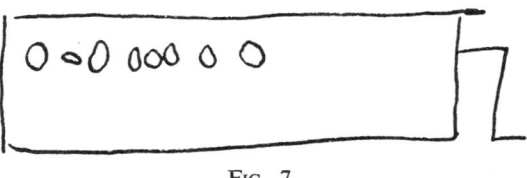

FIG. 7.

ZEE (5; 4). Question 1. The square: *"It will do a little point.*—But what if I turn the square round and round?—(He draws a few more points then cries:) *A ring* (demonstrating with his hand) *because you're turning it and then it draws.*—And what if I put the pencil nearer the middle?—*A smaller ring."* Circle: "And if I do it with this ring?—*Maybe it will do a ring like this.*—And if I put the pencil right in the middle?—*A tiny ring or a point."*

Question 2. Cycloid: "What will my pencil do if I move the wheel along? —*A line* (straight line).—Why?—*Because it goes straight along* (thinking of the path taken by the wheel on the table).

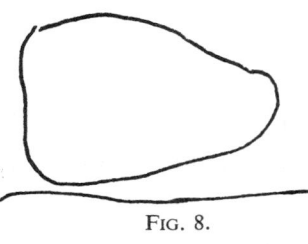

—Watch (turning it without marking the paper).—*Well, like this* (an ellipse).—And if I put the pencil through the middle?— *It will do the same* (again an ellipse)" (see Fig. 8).

PAL (5; 5) replies in similar vein to question 2 (the cycloid). He correctly shows a circle when the wheel is rotated on its own axis. When it is made to move

FIG. 8.

forward along the table, he draws a straight line. Then, as he studies the red spot, Pal draws a convex curve beginning at the bottom but stopping short at its peak. "And then?— . . . —Watch it again." He looks at the apparatus with great care, then draws a similar arc but continues with a slight downward curve ending with a short horizontal stroke. The drawing is a clear attempt to compose the circular and straight line movements, and Pal simply draws them side by side because he cannot combine them to form a cycloid. Question 3 (spiral) is answered at the level of a straight line.

Ros (5; 6). Shows the reverse pattern of partial success and failure. For question 2 (cycloid) he simply draws a circle, but for the spiral (question 3) he first draws a line parallel with the sides of the cylinder (shown as a rectangle), and then an oblique line running diagonally across it.

Marc (5; 6). Question 1. Square: "*The pencil will do a square* (turning the card himself, with the pencil off the paper). *No. It does a ring because it goes round in a ring.*" Circle: "What will the pencil do when I turn the ring?—*A ring, no a square* (afraid of being deceived by the shape of the object!).—Why a square?—*No, it's a ring.*"

Question 2. Cycloid: Series of contiguous circles.

Question 4. Snail: for the snail's path he produces a vertical line and for the board a horizontal line in direct continuation of his first line. When the two movements are combined he does not hesitate: "*It will do this!*", and he draws a long undulating line as though the movement of the board did no more than cause the snail's movement to waver in its original course!

Ley (6; 4). Question 1. Circle: "*It does a little ring.*—And when I put the pencil between the edge and the middle?—*A smaller ring.*—And right in the middle?—*A tiny little ring.*"

The square: "*It does a ring or maybe a square.*—(The experimenter demonstrates the movement without the drawing.)—*No, it's still a ring.*"

Question 2. Cycloid: "*It does a little point each time. The wheel goes round all the time, it touches the table and makes a point* (drawing a straight line with three heavy points at regular intervals to indicate the points where the pencil touches the table).—Just watch (moving the apparatus without marking the paper).—(He again draws a straight line with a heavy mark, then a large circle, saying:) *It's like the wheel only bigger* (and he draws an even larger circle, open, and marks three heavy points at regular intervals along its horizontal diameter, thus combining both his previous drawings in one).—What will the pencil do if I put it in the middle of the wheel?—*It goes flat the whole way* (i.e. a straight line), *you see, the hole is in the middle, so it does a straight line.*—And if I put it somewhere between the edge and the middle.—*It won't go straight all the way.*—And if the wheel turns in the air (i.e. on one spot?—*A ring.*—And on the table?—*You can't draw it.*"

Question 3. Spiral: He merely draws a straight line.

Bal (6; 6). Question 1. Square: "It will do an oval (drawing a fine oval).—And if I put the pencil somewhere between the outside and the middle?—*It does a ring.*—And if I put it on the edge (halfway down one side instead of at one corner, as at first)?—*It will do a square.*—Watch (demonstrating).—*Oh, a ring!*—Now watch this one (demonstrating with the pencil fixed at a corner).—*Oh, that's a ring too!*"

Triangle: (With the pencil on the

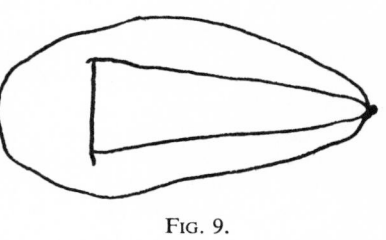

Fig. 9.

239

edge.) "What will it do?—*A rectangle* (drawing a good rectangle).—And if I put it somewhere between the middle and the edge?—*It does a half-circle.* —And on the point?—*An oval* (see Fig. 9).—And like this (taking another point within the figure)?—*A square, I think.*—Watch (he is shown the tracks made by the pencil in each position).—*Oh, a ring! Another ring! A ring!*" Circle: "*It does an oval.*—And if I put the pencil inside?—*A little ring.*"

Question 2. Cycloid: "All rings (drawing a series of circles: see Fig. 10).— And if I put my pencil somewhere between the edge and the middle?—*It will do smaller rings . . . Oh, no! Bigger ones.*"

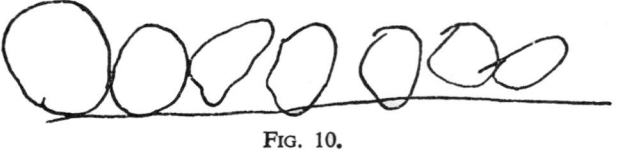

FIG. 10.

Question 4. Snail: he draws a vertical line for the snail moving on its own and a horizontal line for the board moving with the snail standing still. When the two movements are combined he draws an oblique line (although its orientation is incorrect).

ZBI (6; 6). Question 1. Square: "*It does a ring.*" When the pencil is inserted near the centre he draws a circle within a square "*because it keeps turning*", but when the pencil is attached at one of the four angles "*it does a square*".

Question 2. Cycloid: A series of circles in juxtaposition.

Question 4. The snail's motion is shown as a vertical line and that of the board as a horizontal line. Composite movement is first shown as another horizontal line "*because the wood moves and so the snail has got to move the other way*" (i.e. horizontally).—But both are moving at the same time.—*Then it does a cross* (drawing a long horizontal line with a short vertical line running through the centre of it)."

NID (6; 6). Question 1. Square. "*It does a square.*"

Five months later she first draws an arc and continues with others, ending with the whole circuit shown as an oval: "*It does a ring.*—And if I put my pencil here (at another angle)?—*Then it will do a square, no, a ring.*—Make up your mind.—*It does a ring because the other made a ring.*—But the pencil isn't in the same place, is it?—*I think it's a ring* (a long pause: the experimenter rotates without making an impression on the paper). *Yes, I'm sure it's a ring.*"

Question 2. Cycloid: a series of small circles in juxtaposition. Five months later she produces a chain of contiguous semi-circles open at the top (i.e. a cycloidal curve but upside down), then she draws points at intervals, and finally a series of broken horizontal strokes, which she ends by joining together to form two parallel lines.

Question 3. Spiral: She draws a rectangle for the cylinder with a long line running down the middle and parallel with its length and a chain of small discontinuous circles cutting across this. In other words, she tries to show both movements in juxtaposition instead of composing them: "But I'm making both of them move at the same time.—*It does a thing like smoke* (drawing a series of straight lines roughly parallel and close together. Evidently she imagines these as being fused when the rotary movement is rapid as is the case with retinal fusion)."

Question 5: "Imagine an ant going in at this little hole here in the middle and coming out at the other end (along the axis of rotation).—*It goes quite straight.*—And if I turn the drum?—*The ant turns as well* (drawing an arc with a fairly pronounced curve)."

Question 4. A vertical straight line represents the snail's path and a horizontal line that of the board. When the movements are composed she replies: "*He starts by going straight but then he goes a round about way* (drawing first an undulating line, then a straight line ending with a downward curve). *I know how it works: it does a half circle* (first drawing an arc, then reverting to the vertical line curving towards the lower end)."

MAY (6; 6) and HAE (6; 8). Question 4: The snail's path is shown as a vertical line, that of the board as a horizontal line, and the composite movement as two straight lines at right angles.

FRED (6; 9), again in answer to question 4, shows the composite movement as a horizontal line, shorter than the first: "*It does the same* (as it did with the board in motion) *but shorter.*"

CUM (6; 11) shows the same composite movement of question 4 as a vertical line (like the snail's path alone) but one which has a slight curve in the middle before resuming a straight course.

VAL (6; 8). Question 1. Circle: "*It does a mark all the way round, a ring.*" Square: he draws a square standing on an angle and begins to draw another to indicate that it has now rotated to the next angle, but stops and says: "*Oh no! It does a ring.*"

Question 2. He draws a true cycloid at once, with semi-circles in juxtaposition. However, the enquiry proves that Val has not really understood but merely intends a series of circles representing successive positions of the wheel and draws them as semi-circles in an attempt to reconcile them with the straight line representing the path of the wheel on the table. Thus his comment is: "*It keeps doing rings.*—Are those rings you've drawn?—*They're not quite rings because that's the track along the road* (i.e. the straight line he has drawn below the semi-circles).—And what will happen if I put my pencil half-way between the outside and the middle?—*It does rings* (drawing circles this time, first discontinuous, then in a continuous series).—And when the pencil is right in the middle?—(He draws a straight line: correct.)"

Question 3. Spiral: first a series of semi-circles as for the cycloid, then an undulating line. The ant's path by itself and that of the cylinder alone are shown correctly as a straight line and a circle.

LOT (6; 10). Question 1. Circle: "*It does a ring, because it keeps going round.* —And with this square?—*It's still a ring, because it goes round this way, so it goes by everything* (i.e. it does not follow the outline of the square)."

Question 2. Cycloid: the first reply is a series of discontinuous circles. After studying the pencil closely (the point being off the paper), he draws a series of arcs on a straight line but they are still discontinuous. "Why have you left holes in between?—*Because that's empty space.*"

Question 4. Snail: the composite movement is at first shown as a plain vertical line. After seeing a complete demonstration he understands that the line will slope further with increase in the speed of the board and less as this decreases, when it tends to the vertical.

GEO (8; 0, backward). Question 1. Square: he draws a square at first, then he follows the path of the angles as it rotates and finds it to be circular. The triangle produces a circle at once, but when he is shown a triangle with a very acute angle he regresses and again draws a triangle.

Question 2. Cycloid: he draws a large semi-circle but prolongs it below the level of the starting point so as to complete the circle: "Does the wheel go underneath the table?—*No.*—Well, what about it?—(He draws a smaller circle, such that the greater part of it is above the line representing the table but a section is still beneath it. Not satisfied, he draws a very small circle, wholly above the table top.)—But what is the path of the lamp?—(He draws a semi-circle but is unable to continue.)" See Fig. 11.

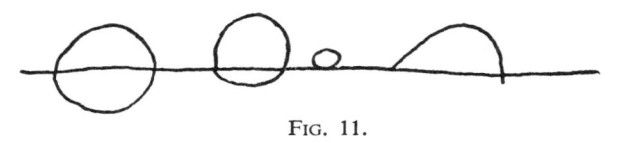

FIG. 11.

The large number of illustrations we have cited is deliberate. They are interesting for the light they shed on the representation of movement by geometrical curves (question 1) and on the growth of differentiations as between curves of simple and composite movement (questions 2 to 4).

When faced with a figure rotating on its own axis, every one of these subjects goes through a more or less prolonged sequence of trial-and-error and all of them eventually discover that an angle, when rotating, describes a circular path. The process which leads to this discovery is itself of considerable interest. We note that these subjects are aware of the danger of confusing the curve of movement with the outline of the figure which moves. Marc and Zee, having found that the square describes a circle, are afraid of making a mistake with the circle, which is why Zee is so cautious in his remark: "Maybe it will do a ring", and Marc, misled by the analogy with the square, decides that the path will be "a ring, no a square"! Yet with all their initial awareness and caution, several still find difficulty in differentiating the curve of rotary movement from the static outline of the figure. The majority arrive at the form of a circle by way of successive approximations: thus a child may be seen drawing several points or a number of short curves while slowly rotating the square or the triangle which means that the full circular form is achieved only later, by extrapolation. This procedure brings out admirably the importance of equidistance from the centre and therefore shows how the two methods of constructing a circle are elaborated in step with each other. Thus children at level IIB went through the same preliminary trial-and-error when discovering a circle by way of the 'locus' which it defines (ch. IX, §3). A number of subjects, it is true, are immediately led to the idea of a circle as they watch the rotating square or triangle, simply because the circle is the simplest closed curve (and for these subjects equidistance of the angle from the pivot is implicit rather than explicit). But there are several who conclude only that the path in question must be some kind of a closed curve, precisely because they do not trouble to conserve the equidistance. Bal, who suggests that the rotating square gives rise to an oval curve, is a case in point (but Pie, also at level IIB, gave an analogous response in deciding that the set of points equidistant from a common centre would form an ellipse, ch. IX, §3). Nid, likewise, draws a number of arcs and joins them up in a very passing oval, calling it a 'ring'. We must conclude that whatever the differences between the problems studied under the heading of 'loci' and those dealing with curves of movement, the experiments give rise to similar solutions at level IIB, with similar preliminary trial-and-error, and for the same reason: children lack an immediate operational concept of equidistance. Nevertheless we find that, in the end, these children reach the correct solution in both cases.

Parallel with the intuitive approach to simple movements at level IIB, leading, in some cases, to correct representation of the curves involved, children now begin to differentiate between simple and composite movement. Every one of these subjects tries to compose the two constituent movements entering into the composition of at least one of the three composite curves: cycloid, spiral, or oblique straight line (question 4), so that his solution for the composite curve is different from either of those he gave for the constituent movements. Their attempts to differentiate and reconcile these movements deserve fuller consideration, but the central finding is that these occur at the same time as the first correct solutions to problems of simple movement (rotation and linear movement).

As regards the method of reconciling these movements, we note the following: the most immature of these subjects is Rut and he merely draws an elongated circle for the cycloid to indicate that the wheel moves forward as it turns. The same is true of Zee. Geo, who is still immature in spite of his years, begins by drawing a semi-circle (for the wheel which rotates and moves forward at the same time), but he has no idea how to go on: he imagines that a wheel in rotation describes a circle but he realizes that a series of circles would be inaccurate as a description of the forward motion. His solution is to continue below the line of the table, which brings him back to his starting-point! Eventually he falls back on the solution of children at level IIA, as also does Val (who begins with a true cycloid, but for the wrong reason). Pal draws a semi-circle which turns into a straight line. His drawing is a juxta-position of the constituent movements instead of a composition. Juxta-position is again apparent in the solution of Ley: a row of points to mark the places where the pencil comes in contact with the table, and a circle to indicate the revolution of the wheel. Nid draws these points first as horizontal strokes, and then as continuous lines. He draws two lines in parallel because he wishes to suggest the forward movement of the wheel at its summit and also at its base. Lot comes near to the correct cycloid. Later he draws a series of arcs, but these are now spaced to suggest the simultaneous rectilinear progression of the wheel on the table.

For the spiral, all these children solve the two simpler problems: they realize that when the roller is stationary the ant moves in a straight line and when the ant marks time on the moving roller, its path is a circle. The composite movement leads to a variety of solutions. Né draws a row of contiguous circles, Ros draws an oblique line diagonally across the roller; Nid produces a series of parallel lines close together (and designed to fuse into a whole "like smoke" when the roller moves quickly); later she draws a single straight line cutting across a row of circles (juxtaposing the constituent movements); Val's solution is an undulating line, etc. The easiest problem of composite movement is that where a snail moves vertically while the board on which it moves is pulled horizontally. Even here, children produce similar faulty solu-tions, and more often than not, the constituent movements are shown in juxtaposition instead of being composed. Thus Marc draws a long wavy line, Zbi draws first a horizontal line, then a cross, Nid produces a wavy line, followed by a straight line curving slightly at the bottom, and finally an arc. May draws a right angle, Fred, a horizontal stroke which is shorter than that drawn for the movement of the board alone; Cum's solution is a vertical line with a nick in the middle, etc. Bal alone draws an oblique line, and this slopes the wrong way. Lot who draws a vertical line, understands that the slope of the oblique line will change with the relative speeds of the snail and the board—after he has seen the pencil track.

All in all, we find each of these subjects beginning to differentiate curves of composite movement from curves of simple movement, while none of them achieves their true composition. In some cases we find juxtaposition pure and simple, in others the constituent curves are mixed up in various ways. Operational construction of composite curves is still absent. However, the mode of attack is identical for prob-lems of composite and simple movement. In either case, we find children first making a series of intuitive anticipations, then drawing these together, and so making an unequivocal intuitive judgment. This final solution is correct and quasi-operational in the case of simple movements, but in that of composite movements it is inadequate and barely differentiated.

The similarity of their approach to the two kinds of problem may be taken as proof that children do not reconstruct curves of motion by immediate insight at an intuitive level. These curves are the outcome of a prolonged period of elaboration. Their gradual construction shows many links with the successive generalizations found to occur in problems of 'loci' (ch. IX). Apart from the fact that the construction of a circle may be broached with either method, we find that in problems of 'loci' as in those of curves of motion, children at level IIB begin by plotting a few points and go on to join them with varying completeness to form a curve of a sort. Full generalization is not achieved in problems of loci, just as operational rigour is lacking in those of curves of movement.

The parallel between these problems is self-evident, yet too often adults seem to think that drawing a curve to represent movement is simply a matter of visual representation or of 'sensory intuition'. They forget that if imagery intervenes in these problems, then like all imagery it is a continuation of schemata which are in part motor and become interiorized imitations. These schemata themselves are governed by anticipatory notions and assimilatory reconstructions. But these notions in turn are pre-operational before they become general and operational in character. Anticipatory notions and intuitive reconstructions cannot lead to the adequate construction of curves of motion where spatial relations are as yet uncoordinated and Euclidean notions of space have not yet been elaborated. Only at the operational level do these conditions obtain, when metric relations of distance and length, of slope and curve, enter into the definition and differentiation of curves of movement. These relations have no precise meaning for the child except in the measure that he can think in terms of reference systems which, sooner or later, imply precise coordinate axes. The system is simple enough for a circle conceived as a curve of rotary movement, for it involves no more than a set of equidistances from a central pivot about which a figure is made to revolve (question 1). But the key notion is equidistance from a central reference point, and equidistance implies distance itself, which is elaborated only very gradually (ch. III). As for composite movements, these all present the same added complication, in that they imply two coordinate systems, one absolute (to all intents and purposes) and the other relative. The double system of reference is implied by the oblique line of question 4 no less than by the mechanical curves of questions 2 and 3. Because the system of reference is doubled, the need to coordinate spatial relations when constructing curves of motion is obvious in these problems. But that condition underlies the operational construction even of elementary curves, where it is less obvious.

§5. *Stage 3. Levels IIIA and IIIB: Immediate construction of simple curves; composite curves constructed empirically and by degrees*

As they reach the age of 7 or 8, children no longer hesitate when faced with the problem of a rotating square or triangle. They see immediately that a pencil inserted in an angle must describe a circular path, as indeed, they solved the problem of equidistance with like assurance in our study of 'loci' (ch. IX, §4). Curves of composite movement are solved more gradually by trial and error. Here we may distinguish the two levels IIIA and IIIB, for during the first of these only one or two of the questions 2–4 are correctly answered, while during the second all three are solved, for now the subject makes use of an anticipating schema which he alters in the light of the experience gained by successive approximations.

Following are examples of level IIIA:

MAR (7; 1) immediately draws a circle as the path of a pencil in one corner of a rotating square (question 1). "What would happen if I put my pencil further in?—*It would do a smaller ring.*—And if I put it half-way down one side?—*A large ring.*—And right in the middle?—*A little point.*" Triangle: "*It will do a ring again.*—Couldn't it do a triangle?—*No, a ring.*—Why?— *Because it keeps going round.*"

Question 2. Cycloid: Mar first draws a series of circles in juxtaposition but explains that the first one turns clockwise and the second anti-clockwise and so on alternately. But after one look at the pencil as it describes the first arc (without marking the paper), he draws a series of contiguous semi-circles (which represents a compromise between the circles drawn previously and the elongated arcs of the cycloid curve): "Supposing I put my pencil in the middle of the wheel?—(He draws a series of arcs which are lower and more elongated, being a true representation of the curve of movement).—And right in the middle?—*They'd be smaller still* (drawing another series, curving only slightly). *Oh, no! it would do a* (straight) *line.*"

Question 3. Spiral: his solution is simply an oblique straight line.

Question 4. He has no difficulty in discovering the oblique path (correctly oriented) which arises from the composition of the snail's motion with that of the board.

GIS (7; 11). Question 1: solved immediately.

Question 2. Cycloid: the first drawing shows circles in juxtaposition, the next is a garland made up alternately of arcs and loops as in Fig. 12, because

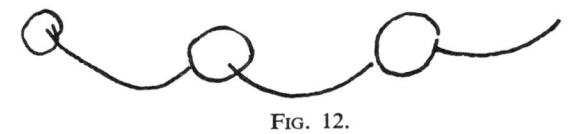

FIG. 12.

"*when the wheel goes round the pencil comes back again and then it goes forward again*" (which would be true if the pencil were fixed to the far end of a radial

246

bar which projected beyond the felloe).—"And if I put my pencil right in the middle of the circle?—*The point stays in the middle. It goes forward but it doesn't change* (in height). *It keeps going straight, it does a* (horizontal) *line.*"

Question 3. Spiral: he draws a straight line for the movement of the pencil itself and a circle for that of the roller, when the pencil is stationary. The composite movement is shown as a discontinuous chain of circles joined

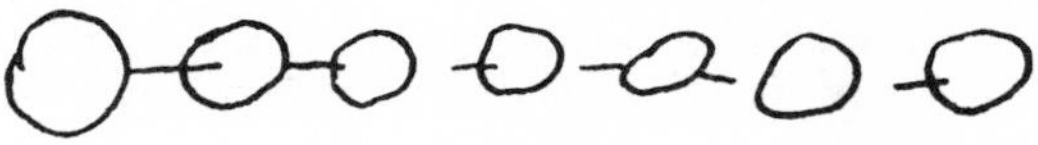

FIG. 13.

by straight lines. This solution (see Fig. 13) is at level IIB, being a juxta-position of the rotary and linear movements instead of a composition which would yield a spiral curve.

BAG (8; 2). Question 1. Correct. Question 2. Cycloid: he first draws a straight line, pointing out that the rim of the wheel must leave a linear track on the roadway. When shown one revolution of the wheel without the pencil track, he realizes that its path is cycloidal and is aware that when the pencil is in the centre of the wheel its track is linear "*because it just goes forward* (without turning)." Question 3: "*It will make a mark all round it.*" He draws a series of discontinuous circles.

PER (8; 5). Question 2. He finds the true solution (a cycloid) after watching the pencil over a single revolution of the wheel (without seeing its track). His first approximation was a circle.

Question 3. He fails to discover the spiral, and instead he produces a set of drawings not unlike those of Gis: first a straight line parallel with the cylinder, then an oblique line, and finally a line which begins straight and then curves abruptly tending to a circle around the cylinder.

DESP (8; 7) first draws the cycloid as a series of incomplete hoops each merging into its neighbours as though seen in perspective, and then reaches the true solution. But the spiral is drawn as a sloping line, and increase in the speed of rotation is differentiated by the simple method of drawing it more quickly!

SCHA (8; 3). Question 2. Cycloid: he begins by drawing circles which are not even continuous: "*It will keep doing rings.*—Look at it carefully (with the pencil off the paper).—*The ring touches the edge* (drawing a large arc which is too long and extends over all this first set of 'rings').—Look at it again.— *Oh, like this* (a correct cycloid)."

Question 3. Spiral: he draws a straight line down the length of the cylinder then comments: "*It will do a sloping line* (oblique but rectilinear).—And if I turn it quickly?—(Another oblique parallel with the first.) *The same.*—And if the ant moves quickly and the roller turns slowly?—*It will be nearly flat* (correct)."

LEP (8; 5). Question 1. Solved immediately. Question 2. Cycloid: He begins with a semi-circle and continues it as a sinusoidal curve, then brings it back again as though to form a circle. Then he exclaims: "*No, that's wrong* (to be more certain he draws three circles juxtaposed and points to the upper segments, saying:) *This part goes out, or else it would come back to the same*

247

place (and again he draws a sinusoidal curve, but points to the lower portion, saying:) *Then it comes back again. It goes round on itself once . . . No that's wrong. It doesn't go round on itself, it goes forward all the time* (and he finally draws a correct cycloid!)—And the point in the middle?—*It goes quite straight because it stays in the middle all the time.*"

Question 3. Spiral: he draws an oblique line straight off. "And if I turn it faster?—*It will be more sloping.*"

PEL (8; 6) discovers a cycloid by starting with an arc and filling in the rest of the curve bit by bit, by induction. But he wrongly suggests that the central point follows an undulating path.

Question 3. Spiral: here Pel is more advanced than the previous subjects and shows three quite separate paths for varying speeds of the roller: with the roller stationary, the ant moves in a straight line, "*it tries to go straight but it goes crooked* (follows an oblique path) *when the cylinder turns round*", and "*if the roller goes quickly, it goes underneath and comes back again*" (to the starting point—his drawing is a circle). In other words, Pel fails to construct the spiral curve and jumps from an oblique line to a circle, as though the cylinder were suddenly revolved at infinite speed.

MAR (8; 10) discovers the cycloid quickly by generalizing from his first approximation which is an arc. "And the middle?—*A straight* (horizontal) *line.*"

Question 3. The spiral is drawn first as "*a ring at the beginning, then a line, then another ring*", the two movements being juxtaposed. But his next solution is an oblique line, and finally he reaches a truer idea than the preceding subjects, his last drawing being a spiral of a sort, but one drawn with straight lines at right angles to each other.

Question 4. The composite movement is resolved straight off.

Question 5. "*It does a straight line.—And if I turn it?—Still a straight line.*"

BLAN (9; 3), unlike the others, is more nearly correct for the spiral than for the cycloid. Question 2 is answered by drawing first a chain made of linked circles, and then by a garland with alternate loops and arcs. After seeing the complete demonstration he comments: "*I thought it went round each time. . . . I thought it had to go back the other way.*"

Question 3. His first drawing is a gently curving line (not a straight line but an arc), and this is continued as a vaguely sinusoidal curve (Fig. 14), but in the end he discovers the spiral curve:

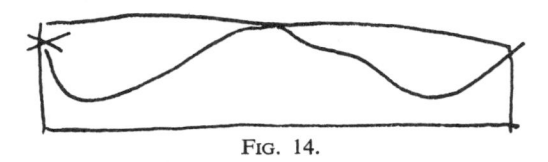

FIG. 14.

"*It does curves because it keeps going round . . ., it goes like a snake winding himself round a tree.*"

Question 4. Resolved without difficulty.

GRIN (9; 5). Question 2. Juxtaposed circles followed by a wave of the hand to indicate the way in which the red spot (on the felloe) follows a path which is different from his static representation, as it moves from circle to circle. He then draws a correct cycloidal curve.

Question 3. First he draws a series of straight lines inclining more and more to the vertical as the speed of the roller is increased. Then he draws parallel and equidistant arcs like a set of bracelets. Asked what happens behind the roller (i.e. in that part which is concealed), he replies: "*It's the same. It's always one turn further on.*" Yet his representation falls short of the spiral form, for the circles are discontinuous.

COT (9; 8). Question 2. He draws a garland with loops: "*It comes back a little but not all the way, and then it goes on again.*" But in the end he produces a true cycloid saying: "*It keeps going forward, so it can't come back.*"

Question 3. First he draws zigzags like those of Mar, but then he makes the segments curve and finally arrives at a true representation of the spiral curve.

The remaining examples belong to sub-stage IIIB. These subjects succeed in finding the true solution to all the problems, instead of one or two, but they show the same hesitancy in their approach, albeit in varying degrees.

STUT (9; 0). Question 1. The square (with the pencil in one angle): "*It draws a ring because when you turn it, it's bound to go that way* (drawing a square with arrows at each corner pointing in a circular direction).—What about the triangle?—*That will be a ring again.*—The same size or would it be smaller or larger?—*A little larger.*—Why?—*Well you can see the part* (i.e. the distance) *up to the pin* (pivot).—Well what would happen if I put the pin here (nearer the angle with the pencil)?—*The ring would be smaller.* And if I put the pencil in the middle?—*Just a point.*"

Question 2. Cycloid. He draws a series of hoops on a straight line straight off. The hoops are a little too nearly semi-circular. "*It's bound to go that way because it can't go backward.*—Some other boys draw it this way (looped garland).—*Yes, that's possible.*—Which is right?—*This one* (looped garland). —Look at it carefully (moving the apparatus without marking the paper).—*No, it's like this* (a perfect cycloid).—And if I put my pencil in the middle?—*It does a line like this* (horizontal line).—And if I put it near the middle?—*Little rings* (in juxtaposition). *No, a line like this* (a cycloid with flattened arcs)."

Question 3. He begins by drawing oblique straight lines but in the end he arrives at a spiral curve. Question 4. "*The snail is forced to go off the track* (in an oblique path).—And what if the snail moves slowly while the board moves quickly?—*It draws a line a little curved* (i.e. something like an exponential curve, which would be true of accelerated movement)."

NYF (9; 10). Question 2. Cycloid: he draws a garland with loops which decrease in size as the wheel moves forward, suggesting an object in perspective. "Why does it keep getting smaller?—*I should have drawn them the same size.*—Watch (demonstration without the pencil track).—*No, it doesn't do that. I made it go backwards.* (He draws a circle to represent the wheel when stationary, and then another twice as large, saying:) *because it goes round twice* (but the lower half of the circle is shown below the level of the table. Nyf corrects the error by drawing semi-circles above the line and eventually produces a true cycloid).—And if I put my pencil half-way between the outside and the middle?—*It does this* (a series of small discontinuous circles. Then he laughs and draws another cycloid with flattened arcs).—And in the middle?—(Another cycloid corrected to a straight line.)"

Question 3. Spirals: he draws an oblique line, but one which is continued on the far side of the cylinder (see Fig. 15). "What would it look like if I took

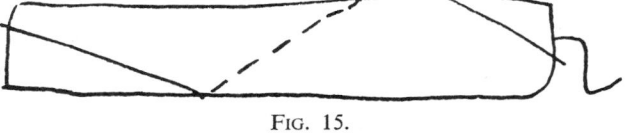

FIG. 15.

the paper off and opened it out?—(He draws a series of circles in juxtaposition, without moving his pencil from the paper, but immediately corrects this to a spiral).—And if I turn the roller quickly?—*Then it would be tighter* (drawing a screw thread with a shorter 'pitch').—And if I move it more slowly?—(He draws a thread with a wider pitch)."

SCHO (10; 5). Question 2. His first drawing is a looped cycloid (Fig. 16). "*It's because the wheel keeps coming back. Oh, no. That's wrong because the pencil*

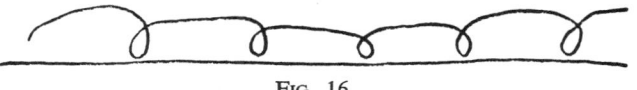

FIG. 16.

stays in the same place when it turns. The wheel doesn't come back (drawing a correct cycloid).—What if the pencil is in the middle?—*It does a straight line because the circle keeps going forward.*"

Question 3. First he draws a close zigzag pattern, then a sinusoidal curve, and finally a spiral together with a good representation of the developed surface. He alters the 'pitch' correctly according to the speed of the roller.

It is clear from these examples that there is true generalization at stage III. The problem of a rotating figure presents no difficulty, whatever its shape. Even at stage IIIA, children are immediately aware that the curve of movement is a circle. Their success is paralleled by their understanding of the same curve as the locus of points equidistant from one reference-point (ch. IX). The parallel is fully explained by the fact that the path of a rotating figure is circular only by virtue of the equidistance from the axis of rotation. Thus the spatial relations involved are identical whether the problem is posed as one of 'locus' or as a curve of movement. Mus is well aware of the underlying principle, as he shows when he alters the diameter of his circles in line with variations in the interval between the pivotal pin and the pencil. Stut makes the point explicit, saying: "Well, you can see the part up to the pin". In other words, he makes an estimate of the radius, being the distance between the centre (pivotal pin) and the circumference (pencil point).

When faced with 'mechanical' curves or curves of composite movement, children usually find it easier to construct a cycloid than a spiral. But this is not true of all children, which is why the finding cannot be stated as an absolute formula to determine the boundary between levels IIIA and IIIB. Thus, a few subjects like Blan are more advanced in their solution of the spiral than in that of the cycloid. Generally speaking children at level IIIA solve the cycloid by more or less prolonged trial-and-error but fail to construct the spiral. Their behaviour points to an anticipatory schema which, however inadequately structured, gives it direction. The subject usually starts from an assumption of circularity; if he is particularly circumspect, he imagines the curve as an arc or a semi-circle. Following that assumption he may take one of two courses. Either he tries to free himself from preconceptions governed by the shape of the static figure by defining several points along the curve and then interpolating, or he anticipates that the movement as a whole will take the form of a looped garland. In the latter event, he believes that the pencil doubles a part of its track at each turn of the wheel, which would be correct if the pencil were fixed in the line of the radius beyond the circumference of the wheel. Less frequently, we find the total curve imagined as a series of incomplete hoops which merge with one another like those of Dest, or, as with Scha, an arc which becomes more and more elongated and is then differentiated in the form of a series of hoops, or even a sinusoidal curve like that drawn by Lep. Whatever the individual variations, throughout stage IIIA we find a progressive generalization starting from a few fixed points. The generalization may be cautious and inductive or else it may spring from a quick overall hypothesis which is subsequently corrected by comparing it with observed positions of the pencil in movement.

The generalization which we observe is operational but still inductive. In other words it carries no appreciation of logical necessity. This inductive character emerges more obviously in the problem of spiral movement, which is why this problem brings out more clearly the process underlying the construction of these curves. With few exceptions, the responses given by children at level IIIA form a graded series. The series begins with the mere juxtaposition of constituent curves, i.e. the straight line movement of an ant on a fixed cylinder and the circle drawn by a pencil poised above a rotating drum. This form of reply may be seen in the example of Gis who draws a series of circles linked by dashes. Mus and Per combine the movements to form an oblique line, but Per's line shows an abrupt transition to circularity, and his level is still comparable with that of Gis. Bag draws a series of discontinuous circles: he too is still at the level of what might be termed static synthesis. Scha still draws the curve as an oblique line but he begins to fuse the two movements when considering changes in their relative speeds. He realizes that the slope of the line varies according to whether the roller or the ant moves the faster. Lep is still at the same level, but Pel differentiates these curves depending on the relative speeds: a straight line, a circle, and an oblique curve. With Mar, we reach the first attempt at a spiral, drawn by him as a series of zig-zags. Grin anticipates a series of circles but Blan and Lot discover the true spiral curve.

Problem 5 was difficult to put over, but the following results may be mentioned. Mar understands at once that the axis of the cylinder retains its linear form as it rotates, while Nid at level IIB thought of its path as altered to a gentle curve. Thus at level IIIA children not only realize that a straight line is given by aiming, that it is the only line which does not alter in form with change in perspective, and that it is given by continued motion in any one direction (three conceptions discussed in C.C.S., ch. VI), but they also appreciate that it is the only line which does not alter in shape as it rotates on its own axis.

Problem 4 is easier than the spiral. With the snail and the board moving at the same speed the problem was solved straight off even at level IIIA. But when one or the other was made to move more quickly, there was still considerable uncertainty, even when subjects had previously been successful with the speeds equal.[1] A typical example is that of Stut who drew a curved oblique line as though the movement had been accelerated.

At level IIIB the question of the spiral is no more difficult than that of the cycloid, but both still give rise to preliminary experimentation before their solution is finally achieved. However, unlike children at level IIIA, those at level IIIB construct some kind of overall figure straight off: for the cycloid this may be a series of arcs and loops or even of hoops (instead of an isolated curve or a single circle), for the spiral, a zigzag pattern or a sinusoidal curve (instead of alternate circles and straight lines). Thus we may rightly speak of an anticipatory schema of the composite movement, where previously there was only a vague orientation to guide the course of trial-and-error. Induction has proceeded to a point where it is almost deductive, although it still lacks the stamp of necessary implication.

The development of generalization from the youngest children at level IIIA to those at level IIIB, where each one of our questions is answered all but fully, is a gradual one. It is an effort at composition which parallels that which gave rise to the construction of simple curves representing rotation, although harder because the movement itself is composite. A careful survey of the preceding paragraphs must make it apparent that the growth of operational generalization is itself a func-

---

[1] Even at 12 or 13 a number of subjects cannot solve this problem without prolonged trial-and-error.

tion of the succession of stages in spatial coordination. This growing coordination enables our subjects to define the points which they observe in terms of a double reference system: one reference system for the pencil on the wheel, the ant on the cylinder, or the snail on the board, and another which relates the movement of the wheel, the cylinder and the board to the stationary environments. The actual observations made by children at levels IIIA and IIIB are exactly the same as those made by younger children at levels IIA and IIB. Every subject sees the same facts and each is allowed the same freedom to experiment, because in every case the experimenter runs through the whole movement without the pencil track. Yet if older children succeed better, it is not simply that they are better able to coordinate points which all have observed: they are better at observation. As they watch the demonstration they can note salient facts because they can relate them to coordinate systems which they themselves construct in order to make the most of their observations. Observation itself can imply a reference system, one which is partially elaborated at level IIIA and more fully at level IIIB, but which is still inchoate at stage II. That is why the constituent movements are considered successively at stage II, while at stage III they begin to be thought of simultaneously. If this were more than a beginning, there would be no trial-and-error, as will be clear if we pass to a few examples of stage IV, when this twofold coordination is immediate.

§6. *Stage IV. Immediate and deductive solutions. Conclusions*

Although level IIIB marks the completion of coordinate systems, it is only at the level of formal thought that a subject can fuse two systems in a single whole. Therefore only at stage IV can the child be said to dominate the problem of relative movement. By no means all children of 11 or 12 succeed with the question of the cycloid or the spiral. But apart from a few outstanding exceptions we do not find rapid solutions before that age. Following are three examples:

WIN (9; 8, advanced) draws a true cycloid straight off. "How did you know?—*I imagined it.*—Watch (demonstrating the movement for the first time and without the pencil track).—*That's right. I can see that's what I've drawn.*—And if I put the pencil half-way between the centre and the circumference?—*The steps will be smaller* (i.e. the hoops will be lower).—And right in the middle?—*Then it's just a straight line because the middle stays in the same place all the time.*"

Question 3. Spiral: he draws a series of parallel arcs at regular intervals. "What happens behind.—(He joins the ends of the arcs.)—And if I turn it more quickly?—*The spaces will be closer.*—And if I do it slowly?—*The thread will be coarser.*" His choice of words shows that he is familiar with mechanical constructions.

VAN (11; 10). Cycloid: "*It will do half a large circle* (but in his drawing, the arc is correctly elongated). *As it goes forward, so it makes it much bigger.*" He continues with a series of arcs, is a little undecided as to whether to draw loops, but soon decides against them.

For the spiral his immediate response is a series of equidistant arcs which he joins to form a spiral curve. For the snail, it is an oblique line with variation in slope according to the speeds involved.

OBE (12; 11). Cycloid: "*It will do semi-circles* (drawn as elongated arcs). *As it turns, they're bigger because the wheel goes forward.—Why don't you get loops here* (drawn by the experimenter)?—*Because when the pencil goes round it always stops at the table.*"

Spiral: "*It does a screw-cut.—And if I turn it faster?—There'll be more turns.—And if I go more slowly?—The thread will be coarser.*" [1]

Geometricians might cite these replies as examples of immediate 'intuition' of curves of movement. Yet even at level IIIB children could not construct these curves promptly, and we may well ask what sort of 'intuitions' are elaborated so gradually and are conspicuous by their absence through the first two stages. There can be no question of a simple faculty. On the contrary, the construction of curves of move-ment is closely linked with the operational elaboration of Euclidean Space as a whole.

The child at stage I cannot even understand the question. Because his intuitions of geometry are still tied to objects in their static configura-tions, he cannot conceive of a curve as the representation of movement. We may add, from evidence brought forward in C.C.S., chs. I and II, that even in his static intuition, he is limited to the topological proper-ties of a figure, to the neglect of Euclidean and projective properties. Now we can see the reason for these limitations: a figure cannot be Euclidean unless there is conservation both of the whole and of its parts when subjected to change of position. The child at stage I can move both his own body and outside objects, but his actions are global and he lacks any intuition of the path of movement. Only points of arrival register in his consciousness, to be joined at a later stage by points of departure, but both are static positions, while change of position, as a dynamic term, is left out of account.

At the beginning of stage II, the child shows some intuition of the path of an object when rotated. The experimental set-up helps because by mounting a pencil on the moving object we draw attention to the possibility of drawing its path as such. So also in ch. I we found that children at stage II begin to reconstruct their own changes of position,

---

[1] It should be stressed that not all children of this age give the same clear answers. Kan (12 ; 2) draws a lopped garland for the cycloid while the composite movement of the board and snail is shown as juxtaposed horizontal and vertical lines.

when thinking back on the daily journeys they make. However, the child who seeks to reconstruct a path of movement or an itinerary is faced with the same set of difficulties whether the changes of position are his own or those of a geometrical object. As already shown in ch. 1, §2, we cannot reconstruct the path followed by a change of position (or construct a curve of movement, which is the same thing) without relating every salient point on that path to a system of fixed landmarks, which also serves as a reference system for the distances and angles involved, etc. The reference system is made up of fixed elements and their interrelations. In chapter 1 we saw how young children tend to rely on personal schemata based on their own actions when trying to construct a curve of movement (although the curve in question is merely a walk which they take every day). These subjective schemata are given quasi-absolute standing and landmarks or reference objects met with on the walk are defined in terms of them, instead of the other way about. As a result the landmarks themselves are tied to a rigid and egocentric viewpoint, they are not organized in terms of an objective whole, and they do not admit of reversible operational coordinations. Exactly the same problem is met in these experimental situations, and the child at level IIA fails to understand that a corner of a square or triangle, when rotated, follows a circular path. He does not start from a point of reference, whether the axis of rotation on the moving figure, or the fixed point on the table corresponding to it (although this point is clearly indicated by the pin about which the card is made to revolve). Therefore the child may look at the object as it revolves and yet be quite unable to reproduce its curve of motion. For since he has no reference system, he is bound to treat the movement as an absolute, whose reference points are subject to its own motion, which means, of course, that the curve of movement is assumed to follow the outline of the figure, a square or a triangle. Only when the path is perceptually given in static form as occurs with the rotating circle, does the child at level IIA succeed in reproducing it. Inevitably, when reconstructing composite movements (questions 2–4) he confuses the total resultant paths with their constituent curves, since these alone are apparent in static outline.

At level IIB we find anticipation of simple curves beginning to appear at an intuitive level. Curves of composite movement are also differentiated up to a point. If there were a faculty to provide for the representation of movement by imaginal intuition, we might say that it becomes manifest at this level, because the static intuitions of stage IA now give way to intuitive anticipations or articulated intuitions. However, there can be no gain in postulating a specific faculty to explain this behaviour. To speak of the evocative power of an image or of its symbolic function is to neglect the fact that images are a form of interiorized

255

imitation and therefore imply motor accommodations, which is why they are suited to the intuitive anticipation of movement. If imagery is more effective at level IIB, it is because the motor component of imagery is more differentiated and not because of any development in the sensible properties of images. Before this level, imagery is always static because it is confined to the reproduction of perceptual movements involved in the decomposition of static outlines. At level IIB, images can be used to form intuitive outlines of curves of movement because they now draw on perceptual movements which are no longer limited to the outline of the moving figure but begin to seek some reference outside of it, although full coordination is still lacking. In other words, the subject can detach his attention from the figure as a figure and focus it on its rotation as such. Because he has no clear idea of which relations are relevant to the curve of movement he still makes many mistakes in establishing the equidistance of a revolving point from the pivot. Exactly the same process is at work when he begins to differentiate composite curves.

Before stage III, notions of movement are still bound up with imaginal intuition (although they frequently go beyond the merely perceptual or symbolic element of imagery). At stage III these notions free themselves of limitations inherent in perception and become concrete operations which are reversible and admit of a variety of compositions. Thus, at 7 or 8, notions of movement are sub-logical operations of order and change of position (parallelling logical seriation).[1] As a result, movements are grouped by reference to stationary sites and fixed reference objects, as shown in chs. I, II and IV. This enables children at level IIIA to construct a circle as that curve which describes rotary movement by noting the equidistance between successive positions of a moving point (which might be the angle of a revolving square or triangle) and the fixed pivot. But composite curves involve more than this elementary coordination and imply two further constructions. These are first, the establishment of relations between selected points in a path of movement and reference elements which are grouped in a two- or three-dimensional coordinate system (as elaborated at sub-stage IIIB), and, second, the fusion of two coordinate systems, one relative to the moving object, and the other an absolute framework. Such fusion can occur only at the level of formal operations, i.e. at stage IV. Curves of composite movement do not arise directly from imaginal intuition but imply a twofold schematic construction, and the operational experimentation of level IIIB, so far from being determined by intuitive imagery, is constantly directing intuition through increasing generalization.

Only at stage IV, when deduction is immediate, is there veridical

[1] See C.C.S., ch. XV.

imagery from the start. If we chose to forget all that has gone before, we might suspect the operation of a pure spatial intuition, retaining the imaginal properties of all intuition, yet subject to deductive synthesis. However the close relationship between the final stage in the representation of movement and those that preceded is sufficient to prove that there is no one simple faculty involved. Deduction itself is foreign to intuition and is no more than a shorthand expression for all the coordinations involved in the construction of curves of movement, simple and composite, with their reference to single and double coordinate systems. The lengthy process of construction is now telescoped in a swift act of understanding. It is true that imagery is more adequate to the construction of sub-logical operations (i.e. internal relations within a continuum) than to that of logical relations. But if imagery enters into the representation of curves of movement even at stage IV, it does not initiate and guide it. It is simply a symbolic expression for operations which do. (The symbol itself has its origin in motor behaviour.) Operations which are reversible and admit of composition may depend on the interplay of individual imaginal symbols and collective signs but they are not reducible to mere imagery.

PART FOUR

AREAS AND SOLIDS

IN part three, we saw how the organization of coordinate reference systems is essential to the elaboration of Euclidean motions of space in all its aspects, including such problems as the definition of a point in two or three dimensions, the measurement of angular separation and the construction of curves in accordance with their mensural properties. Having mastered the two kinds of spatial coordination, one-one or rectangular and one-many or triangular, the child is in a position to deal with relationships between areas and solids. Part four is devoted to the study of those operations. The operational construction of areas and solids raises a new psychological problem, over and above those encountered in measurement in two or three dimensions. To define a point in an area or in a solid, the subject takes two or three measurements and coordinates them by reference to a two or three dimensional framework. By using a two- or three-entry table, he establishes one-one correspondences between seriated points in each of two or three dimensions. The fact of measurement transforms relations of order of position into metric relations, but the operations involved are of logical multiplication. By contrast, the calculation of area or volume implies mathematical multiplication of metric relations. The concept of an area of six square units involves something more than the construction of a table consisting of two unit intervals in one dimension and three in another, allowing a point to be accurately located in one of six cells. The area of a rectangle measuring 2 units by 3 units is given by the mathematical formula $2 \times 3 = 6$ *square* units, and square units are units of area, not lengths in two dimensions. Likewise, solids are the product of mathematical multiplication of three metric variables, the result being a given number of *cubic* units.

We must therefore ask what is the relation between the metric coordinate systems studied in part III and Euclidean notions of area and volume. We know that these notions depend on mathematical multiplication but we do not know whether they arise at the same time as the construction of coordinate systems or whether they are a later development. If they arise later we must ask why there should be a time lag. To answer these questions, we undertook a number of enquiries. We begin by examining operations of addition, subtraction and simple subdivision in the field of areas (chs. XI, XII). Later we consider the problem of doubling an area or a volume (ch. XIV).

Chapter Eleven

THE CONSERVATION AND MEASUREMENT OF AN AREA AND SUBTRACTING SMALLER CONGRUENT AREAS FROM LARGER CONGRUENT AREAS [1]

WE might begin, as we did in our study of the understanding of distance and length, by asking whether little children think of an area as a stable attribute which may be conserved even while the shape of an object is altered. This question must be answered before we study the metric relations involved. To find how this kind of conservation is constructed we adopt our usual method of showing children an area which is made up of sub-areas organized in one way, and then altering the apparent structure of the whole while they look on. Does the whole remain invariant in spite of the rearrangement of its parts? Later on we shall ask how the parts themselves are compared with one another at different ages, and how their comparisons eventually give rise to metric operations.

However, before making either of these investigations, we began by an enquiry as to the composition of areas. In other words, we tried to discover what notions children might have of equality as between two areas which could be made congruent by re-arranging their parts. In making this preliminary enquiry we hoped to introduce the topic in a natural way, while breaking the monotony of keeping too rigidly to a particular experimental sequence.

SECTION I. SUBTRACTING SMALLER CONGRUENT AREAS FROM LARGER CONGRUENT AREAS

According to a well-known Euclidean axiom, if two equal parts are taken from two equal wholes, the remainders will also be equal. This investigation seeks to determine whether the proposition appears axiomatic at any age, and if not, why not, and how the identity is constructed. To begin with we note that its construction implies the conservation of area. If the area B_1 is composed of parts A_1 and A'_1, and the area B_2 is likewise composed of A_2 and A'_2, then supposing $B_1 = B_2$ and $A_1 = A_2$ we may deduce that $B_1 - A_1 (= A'_1) = B_2 - A_2 (= A'_2)$.

[1] Written with the collaboration of Mlles L. Du Pasquier and H. Pitsou.

But this is true only if A and A' are assumed to be constant quantities throughout the operation and B is taken throughout as the actual or virtual resultant of the addition: A + A'. While the questions deal with adding or subtracting parts, the underlying purpose is to study conservation—both of parts and of wholes. The ability to analyse a whole in this way is a prerequisite to measurement because when measuring an area we assume, as we do for all measurement, that partial units are conserved and can be composed in a variety of ways to form invariant wholes.

§1. *Outline of method and results* (see Fig. 17)

A child is shown two identical rectangular sheets of green cardboard measuring approximately 20 cm. × 30 cm. and told these are two meadows. The experimenter puts a tiny wooden cow beside each meadow, telling the young subject that the cow has that much grass to eat. Next, he brings in a little wooden man telling the child this is the farmer. The child first notes that the two fields are exactly "the same size". If need be, he puts them side by side to make sure, so that he realizes that the two cows will each have the same amount of grass to

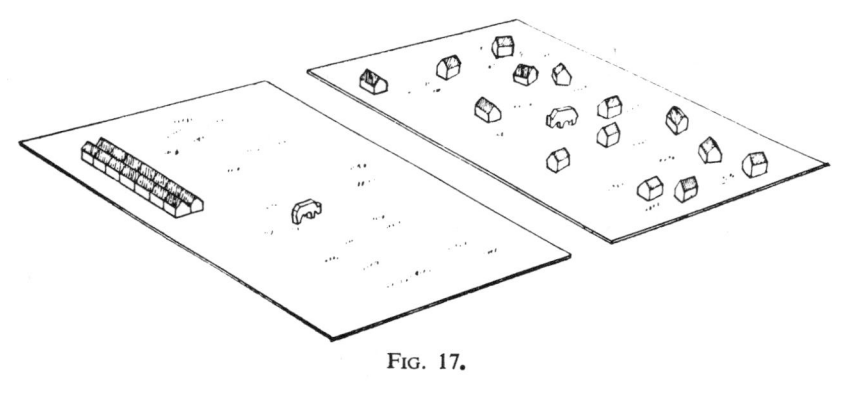

FIG. 17.

eat. Then he is told that one of the farmers has decided to build a house on his meadow: the experimenter puts a little wooden house on the green card (this might be 1 cm × 2 cm. in plan); alternatively, he uses a cube (or a parallelopiped) to stand for the farmhouse. The subject is then asked whether the two cows still have the same amount of grass to eat, and naturally, every child replies that the cow in the meadow without the house has more to eat, while the other cow loses the grass which might have grown on the area occupied by the house. The experimenter must be careful at this stage to impress the notion of area by using such phrases as: "more or less space for grass", or "green space", as opposed to "the space of the house", etc. Later the phrases may be shortened and he can speak of "more green" and "less grass". Naturally, the only things coloured green are the surfaces of the two cards.—Now the other farmer decides to build a farmhouse as well: the experimenter produces another house just like the first (showing the subject that the houses have equal bases, and they are equal in all other respects, while if cubes are used, the cubes are identical) and asks whether the two cows will still have the same "green space" or "grass", etc. Again, every child replies that they have. The necessary character of Euclid's axiom seems to be evident at all ages.

But even this second question can be varied by transforming the arrangement and thus introducing the central problem. Either the two houses are first placed in corresponding parts of the meadows (these being laid side by side and parallel on a table), in which case the experimenter later moves one house and asks: "What about like this? Do the cows still have the same amount of green?"; or else the second house may be placed in another part of the meadow from the start. Usually the positions are as follows: the first farmer puts his houses in the middle of the meadow, his first house being somewhere near the centre while the others are spaced; the other farmer builds his houses up against one another in a corner, leaving the greater apparent space for pasture land. Either way this question ends with one farmhouse in the middle of one meadow and one in a corner of the other.

For the third question, the first farmer builds another house in the middle of his meadow and away from the first house while the other farmer builds another house butting against his first, and the subject is asked: "Will the cows still have the same amount of green?" or ". . . grass to eat?" There may now be differences in the application of Euclid's axiom and older children will tend to accept as self-evident the fact that a meadow less two houses is invariant in area regardless of where the houses are situated while younger children will be deceived by the arrangements. In any case, the experimenter continues patiently introducing further houses in each meadow, always spacing them in the first meadow while placing the others close against one another. If the subject seems at all hesitant it is advisable to go on, even up to fifteen or twenty pairs of houses (each exactly like its opposite number). We have found subjects who apparently seemed convinced of the axiom with fourteen pairs and suddenly failed with fifteen because the perceptual configurations were now too dissimilar so that the appearance of more meadowland in the second meadow was somehow irresistible.

The results are exactly analogous with those obtained in experiments dealing with the compositions of length in one or two dimensions. During stage I we find it difficult to pursue the enquiry, but at stage IIA children are obviously interested, yet they refuse to admit that the remaining areas are equal, often at the very first pair of houses. Here there is no trace of operational composition, and judgment is based entirely on perceptual appearances. At level IIB we find a complete range of intermediate responses: up to a certain number of houses the subject admits that the remaining meadowlands are equal; beyond that number the perceptual configurations are too different. Here there is intuitive articulation in varying degrees, but not operational composition. At stage III, however, and even at level IIIA (usually at $7\frac{1}{2}$ but sometimes as early as $6\frac{1}{2}$-7 years), children recognize that the remainders are always equal, relying on an operational handling of the problem which convinces them of the necessity of their reasoning.

§2. Level IIA: Judgments based on perception without operational subtraction and addition

Up to the age of $5\frac{1}{2}$ or 6, the question is answered simply by inspection and at an intuitive level. Children have no difficulty in recognizing that the green spaces remaining are equal so long as the arrangement of houses in the two meadows is identical. Any variation as between the two arrangements leads to an immediate denial of equality, although as we pass from younger to older subjects, there are variations in the configurational difference which leads to the impression that the green spaces are unequal.

GAR (4; 10). A brick (parallelopiped) is placed on B_1 (the first meadow), and another on B_2 in the same relative position: "Is there as much green left in this meadow as there is in this one?— *Yes, it's the same.*—And like this (one in the centre of B_1 with the length of the brick parallel with the length of the meadow, another at one end of B_2 and laid breadthways)?—*No, there's more green left here* (B_2).—Why?—*Because there's all this left* (free space).—And like this (two bricks spaced on B_2, one centrally on B_1)?—*There's more left on this one* (B_1, correct).—And like this (two bricks in corresponding positions in each meadow)?—*The same.*—Why?—(Indicates that the green space is the same shape in both meadows.)—(The two bricks are now spaced on B_1 and jammed in a corner of B_2.) Is there the same amount of green left?—*No, there's more green left here* (B_2).—Why?—*Because these houses are touching and there's lots of green left.*—But isn't there some extra green here (between the bricks on B_1)?—*Yes.*—Then there's more green left one side than the other?—*There's more here* (B_2).—Supposing I cut out all the green left on both sides (cutting out green paper and putting it over the green areas on each card), could I take the green left on this one (B_2) and put it over the green part left on this one (B_1)?—*There's more bricks here* (on B_1, referring to their perceptual arrangement, because in fact each meadow contains two!). *there'd be more green there* (B_2).—And like this (putting together the bricks on B_1 and spacing those on B_2)?—*There's more green here* (B_1) *because they're all close together.*—And like this (with the same arrangement in both)?—*It's the same amount of green.*—And like this (with the houses on B_1 at right angles

264

and those on B_2 in line along one side)?—*There's more green left here* (B_2).— And like this (almost as before, but with a little green space between the bricks on B_2)?—*There's more green here* (B_1).—(The interval is now reduced on B_2).—*It's the same.*—(Interval increased very slightly.)—*There's more green here.*"

Doc (5; 4): "(One brick only, same arrangement)?—*There's the same amount of green left.*—And like this (one in the middle of B_1, the other along one side of B_2)?—*Like this also.*—(Two bricks on B_1.)—*There's more green here* (B_2) *because there's only one brick* (correct).—And like this (two bricks spaced on B_1 and two together on B_2)?—*There's the same green left because there are two houses each side.*—(Three houses on B_1, two on B_2)?—*There's more green here* (B_2) *because there's less bricks.*—(Three houses on each in similar arrangement)?—*It's the same amount of green.*—(Three, together on B_1, spaced on B_2)?—*There's more green left here* (B_1) *because they're all close together.*—Watch this (the experimenter takes two bags each containing 16 blue cubes and arranges both sets in equal squares of 4 × 4 cubes, so that Doc can see that they are congruent, then he lays the first set on B_1 and the other on B_2). Aren't they the same?—*Oh, no, because here they're right up together* (reasoning for the measure exactly as she did for what was measured!) —(The experimenter removes the cubes and puts the bricks back on the meadows in like arrangement.) What about like this? Is there the same amount of green left?—*Yes.*—And like this (with three bricks in line on each, the line being oriented lengthwise on B_1 and breadthwise on B_2)?—*There's more green here* (B_2)."

We might have shown a whole series of cases all at level IIA, as the level was easy to identify either by the number or by the arrangement of houses or blocks to be subtracted from the green areas. But all these responses are similar to those we have given. They show an almost imperceptible gradation in the complication necessary to persuade the subject that the remainders are unequal. (1) Where only one brick is used, A_1 on B_1 and A_2 on B_2 ($A_1 = A_2$) with remainders A_1' and A_2', Gar denies that these remainders are equal if the arrangement of A_1 differs from that of A_2. (We call A_1' the green space left on B_1, that is the difference between the total area B_1 and the area of the blocks A_1, and A_2' the green space left on B_2.) Doc, together with most subjects at this level, is prepared to allow that the remainders are equal when only one element is taken from each, whatever its position, i.e. if $A_1 = A_2$ and both consist of one element only, then $A_1' = A_2'$. However, although the conclusion could be stated in an operational form: if $A_1 = A_2$ and $B_1 = B_2$ then $B_1 - A_1$, $(= A_1') = B_2 - A_2(= A_2')$, the reasoning is not operational as is shown by the fact that if A_1 and A_2 are made larger or if more bricks are used in different arrangements, the intuition ceases to be correct. (2) When two bricks are used ($2A_1$ and $2A_2$) the subject naturally allows that $B_1 - 2A_1 = B_2 - 2A_2$ so long as the arrangement is identical in the two cards, but if there is the slightest discrepancy between their arrangement, he often denies that the remainders are equal. In other words, these children make a direct comparison between the remaining green areas A'_1 and A'_2, ignoring the fact that both result from subtracting equal parts from equal wholes. Hence, they allow that $A'_1 = A'_2$ only if these appear to be equal to their perception; if their appearance is unequal, younger subjects do not construct the equality. However, others like Doc who are more advanced reply correctly for two elements as they did for one. (3) Nevertheless, if three objects are used ($3A_1$ and $3A_2$), they start from the beginning once more. When the arrangement is similar they recognize equality in the remainders, where the bricks are close together on one card and spaced on the other they deny it. (4) Others, again, have no more difficulty with three bricks than with two, and are misled by appearances only when four are used. (5) The same may be true beyond four. (6) The experimenter may try to correct the error by giving the child a common measure to prove that the remainder $A'_1 = A'_2$. He cuts up green paper and puts it over the free spaces, or he covers these with unit cubes, using equal numbers for the two cards. Doc shows how the demonstration has no effect (aside from the fact that children at this level lack the notion of a common measure, as has been amply demonstrated earlier): he denies that the 16 cubes which cover A'_1 completely are equal to the 16 which cover A'_2 because the former are "right up together" and the others are not: in other words, the perceptual appearances are dissimilar! He uses the same procedure for estimating the measure as he did in determining the measured, which is not unexpected, but which precludes any thought of measuring areas at this level (or indeed lengths). (7) Even the number of bricks nA_1 and nA_2 is not constant for a given n. Thus Gar says simply: "There's more bricks here" when comparing $2A_1$ with $2A_2$, simply because the former are closer together (cf. *The Child's Conception of Number*, chs. III and IV).

However, although the relevant Euclidean axiom is not appreciated at level IIA and the reasons for this are clear, we cannot ignore that these subjects recognize identity up to a certain point. Thus up to a certain value of n, which varies from one subject to the next, they realize that $A'_1 = A'_2$ if $B_1 = B_2$ and $A'_1 = B_1 - nA_1$ and $A'_2 = B_2 - nA_2$, even though for higher values of n they cease to recognize the equality. We may take Doc as an example: he is misled by perceptual appearance when $n = 3$, that is, when three bricks are arranged differently on B_1 and B_2, but when $n = 2$ he resists the perceptual suggestion of difference. Others are misled with two bricks but not with one, and others still resist the suggestion with three but are misled with four, etc. What kind of composition enables these subjects to recognize the equality up to a point without generalizing beyond that point? It cannot be due to perceptual appearance, since it is this which betrays them when composition fails. Nor can it be operational composition, since there is no generalization. We speak of intuition as simple when the subject evokes a static image which resembles what might be given as a percept, and articulated when the representation admits of elementary transformations while still not possessing the mobility, reversibility and generalized character of an operation. But articulated intuitions usually belong to level IIB (and they do here, as is clear from the study of children who show gradual progress to what is nearly but not quite an operational level, §3). These results are especially instructive (like the experiments dealing with the order attributed to elements made to rotate in a fixed sequence[1]) because they show the almost imperceptible gradation from failure of all composition, through intuitive composition, at first simple and later articulated, to operational composition. Each new brick which can be added without disturbing the recognition of equality marks a step forward in development, until the point is reached when the solution is generalized to all possible situations. Developmental sequences such as these illustrate most clearly how operational systems are end-states which display a characteristic equilibrium only after they have gradually evolved out of their earliest beginnings in sensori-motor behaviour, which underlies all symbolic representation.

Elementary compositions like these, which occur at level IIA, are brought about by quasi-perceptual anticipations or reconstructions, and as such, they precede those which are intuitive or imaginal. Gar (towards the end of the enquiry) is asked to compare two pairs of bricks while the experimenter moves the bricks of one pair together or spreads them further apart. When the arrangement of both pairs is similar, he agrees that the green areas remaining (A_1' and A_2') are equal. Where it differs even slightly for the two cards, Gar judges the green areas as unequal. But when a very narrow gap is left between the bricks on one card while those on the other are touching, he admits that the remaining areas are equal. Here the subject sees the difference but he anticipates the possibility of closing the gap. We may say that he perceives that effect in advance, to indicate that the process is a kind of virtual perception due to the anticipation which is inherent in the perceptual activity itself, as distinct from true intuition. Perceptual anticipations are the natural forerunners of intuitive anticipations. The difference between them is that the former are no more than fleeting sketches while the latter are endowed with some degree of permanence either by imagery or by symbolic representation. Similarly, intuitive anticipations undergo further development until they acquire the reversible mobility of operations which represent the final equilibrium of the entire developmental sequence (stage III).

[1] *Les notions de mouvement et de vitesse chez l'enfant*, ch. I.

To recapitulate, at level IIA children begin to form intuitive compositions, but are still far from operations. Under certain conditions they perceive and conceive the collections of bricks A_1 and A_2 as equal in B_1 and B_2, and likewise the remaining areas A_1' and A_2'. But the conditions themselves are a limiting factor and these are dependent on laws of perceptual configuration, however tempered by anticipations of perception or intuition. Beyond that limit, these primitive compositions have no part and we find no constancy either in the sum of the collection A or in the remainders A', so that equal parts taken from equal wholes no longer yield equal remainders. Logicians might argue that children still do not directly contradict Euclid's axiom, since although the parts are equal to start with ($A_1 = A_2$), when subtracted from equal wholes ($B_1 = B_2$) they lose their equality, which is why the remainders are also unequal ($A_1', \neq A_2'$). But this is to force an incorrect interpretation of children's reasoning. Because they cannot maintain the invariance of the subtrahends, the minuends and the remainders, the operation of subtraction, like those of addition and composition, has no meaning for them. For subtraction and addition are reversible operations (or, better, form one reversible operation) and it is the reversibility itself which both implies conservation and is implied by it.

§3. *Level IIB: Intermediate responses. Stage III: Operational composition*

Level IIA provides a whole series of responses, as equality of remainders may be recognized up to any number of houses, 1, 2, 3 . . . n but is always denied beyond that number, i.e. for 2, 3, 4 . . . $n + 1$ houses. The critical number at which the reasoning of the subject regresses, n, differs from subject to subject. But there comes a time when all of them begin to have doubts, and wonder how the mere fact of moving around the bricks of A_1 and A_2 on the areas B_1 and B_2 can alter the size of the remaining areas A_1' and A_2'. Mobility, as we saw, is a quality which grows at every stage in this development, but it is this particular phase of more mobile articulation which, for us, defines level IIB (6 to 7 years). Following are four examples of which the first is transitional from level IIA (suggested in the first part of the enquiry) to level IIB (suggested by the third) while the others show increasing mastery of the relevant relations.

VIN (6; 0). Two bricks close together on B_1 and one at each end of B_2: "*There's more green left here* (B_1).—And like this (one brick only in the same relative position on each card)?—*Now there's the same left.*—And like this (moving the brick on B_2)?—*It's the same. You've put it that way, that's all.*—And like this (two adjacent on B_1 and spaced on B_2)?—*There's less space left here* (B_2).—And like this (narrowing the gap on B_2)?—*It's the same now.*—And like this (narrowing the gap still further on B_2 and spacing the bricks on B_1)?—*There's more space left here* (B_2).—And like this (the bricks are spaced on both, but the arrangement is different)?—*It's the same.*—And now (further spaced on B_2)?—*More space here* (B_2)."

The experimenter then passes to one of the experiments on conservation to be described in section II, a number of square cut-outs being assembled in various ways to see if the subject thinks the area or 'space' remains constant. Vin's replies are similar, being typical of level IIA. But at a certain point he is faced with three squares which form one half of a rectangle and three which form the other, the first three being spaced but not the second, and when comparing this arrangement with a complete rectangle he says: "*It's really the same, but there's still more space here* (the spaced set)." This reply is intermediate between level IIA and level IIB.

The experimenter then returns to the original questions and Vin now answers differently. Seeing three blocks together at the bottom of B_1 and three at the side of B_2, he says: "*There's the same amount of green left.*—And like this (with the blocks on B_2 laid near the centre and somewhat askew)?— *There's the same amount of green.*—And like this (spacing the blocks on B_2)?— *There's more green here* (B_2).—What makes the green less?—*The houses. Oh, it's the same.*—Why?—*Because it's always three houses. You just put them that way.*—And like this (four, touching on B_1 and spaced on B_2)?—*It's less here* (B_2). *Oh, no. It's the same because there's four houses on both.*—And like this (spacing them even more)?—*This time there's less green. Oh, no! It's the same.*—But I'm talking about the green that's left over. Is that the same space for both?—*It's a little less. Oh, no! . . . Yes . . .*" etc.

LOU (6; 1). A brick on B_1 and one on B_2: "*There's the same amount of green left.*—And like this (altering the arrangement)?—*It's the same.*—And now (with two bricks on each, differently placed)?—*There's the same amount left.* —Why?—*Because it's the same two squares.*—And like this (together on B_1, spaced on B_2)?—*It's the same because there are two houses on each meadow.*— And like this (with three bricks laid one against each of three sides of B_1, and three spaced in the middle of B_2)?—*It's the same . . . No, there* (B_1) *it's more, the green is.*—Watch. (The experimenter moves the cows around the remaining meadowland on both cards.)—*It's the same, because there are three houses each side.*—(Two bricks are added to each card and the five on B_1 are put together while those on B_2 are spaced.)—*It's the same, because there's the same number of houses each side.*—(Two more are added, giving seven spaced against seven together.)—*It's still the same.*—(Two bricks on B_2 are spaced even more.) Do you think we could cover all the green part here (B_1) with the green part here (B_2)?—*No, there's more green here* (B_1).—Why?— . . ."

HEX (6; 4) does not equate the remaining surfaces to begin with, even when only two bricks are used, but, after a few changes of position have been introduced, he solves this problem. With three bricks he refuses to admit that the spaces are equal except when the lay-out is identical, but even when both sets are laid end to end, and those on B_1 are put against one edge while those on B_2 are inset from that edge a little way, he thinks the remaining area is greater on B_1. Again after a few changes of position, he recognizes that the remainders A_1' and A_2' are equal whatever the lay-out. The same hesitancy recurs with four bricks, and here, too, the solution is reached after the

269

changes of position. The process is the same for five objects, etc. In other words Hex succeeds in generalizing the equality of remainders for any number of bricks after seeing a series of positional changes and finding out that these changes do not alter the free space which is left, yet he does not generalize from one number to the next.

JOR (6; 6) answers correctly straight off for two bricks and for three "*because the houses are the same*". The experimenter then puts 12 bricks all together at one end of B_1 as compared with three sets of 3 in different parts of B_2 with three more spaced on their own (after showing him the two sets of 12 side by side to prove that they are equal): "Is there the same amount of green left on these two meadows?—*Of course it's the same, because you put the same houses on both: you just arranged them differently.*—Now supposing I cut out the green bits on this meadow and then the green bits on this one and put one lot on the other would I be able to cover them over completely?—*No, there's less here* (B_2).—Why?—*Oh, no! It's exactly the same.*—Will the two cows have the same amount to eat?—*A little more on this one* (B_1) *because it's all over* (i.e. continuous).—Why does that make it more?—*Oh, no, it's the same because what hides it* (i.e. the bricks) *is the same, so what's left is the same too.*"

There is a marked difference between these intuitive articulations and the more limited mobility of level IIA. Here we see how operations themselves grow out of progressive articulations. Thus, Vin begins no differently from children at level IIA in that he, too, thinks the remainders are unequal because their perceptual appearance is dissimilar. Then he discovers that two rectangular areas each made up of six squares are equal although three squares in one rectangle are slightly spaced. Yet he is not wholly convinced, as is shown by his cautious, but contradictory, attempt to reconcile the illusion with the reality, for his comment is: "It's really the same, but there's still more space here." The re-introduction of the meadows and houses now produces a new departure. Instead of being dominated by perceptual appearances as soon as the spaced houses seem to take up more of the grass, he now oscillates between the two till the end of the enquiry. One alternative is to make a direct perceptual comparison, but this is now balanced by the other, which is to judge the remaining areas as equal because the number of houses is equal: "It's the same because it's always three houses. You just put them that way." With Vin, the issue between intuitive composition in decline and operational composition in infancy is unresolved. The latter grows out of the former, but the filiation is hidden by the fact that intuition would have him compose the remaining areas as they stand while, in so far as he can think operationally, he begins to compare the houses and deduce from their congruence the equality of the meadowland. Lou's case is similar, the issue between intuition and operation is still unresolved, but Lou is more prepared to recognize the force of operational composition. With Hex, however, there is no conflict but a continuous evolution of intuitive composition tending towards the operational form. He studies the changes in the position of the houses together with the corresponding changes in the shape of the remaining grassland, and the ever-present compensations lead him to admit that the remainders are equal. Yet even after admitting their equality for three houses, he has to reason it out from the beginning when the same problem is presented with four, and again with five. Here there is a continuous progression in the system of intuitive regulations so that they verge on operational composition, but the generalization which this implies is absent. However, with Jos, operational composition finally prevails over intuitive articulation. Jos has almost attained stage III and the only trace of the previous stage is the slight hesitancy shown at the end of the enquiry.

Finally, here are two examples of stage III (level IIIA):

MAR (7; 6). The first question involves three houses on B_1 which are close together and three on B_2 which are spaced: *"There's the same amount of green left, because the houses are the same size and there are just as many of them.*— And like this (with ten objects in different arrangements)?—*It's still the same.*—But can you tell that by looking at them?—*No, it looks as if there's more green there* (B_1 with the houses close up to one side), *but it isn't true because there's the same number of houses.*—If I cut out all these little bits of green (B_2) could I put them all together and make this large bit (B_1)?—*Sure. If the houses are the same, then what's left is bound to be the same.*—But won't the cow have more green to eat on this big meadow (B_1) than on these little bits (B_2)?—*'Course not."*

AUG (7; 8) is presented with twelve bricks on each card straight off. Those on B_1 are arranged close together around the edge while those on B_2 are scattered: "Is there the same amount of green left on each?—(He laughs.) *Of course there is. If there are twelve houses on each field there's bound to be the same left over.*—But there's a lot of room left on this one, while there, there are only these little bits.— *Yes, but all together they take up the same room."*

These replies are quite different from those of level IIB. Perceptual evaluation has disappeared altogether and in its place we find immediate operational composition: the areas forming the subtrahend are grouped together (nA) and their sum is taken from the minuend ($B - nA = A'$), whence the remaining areas are found to be equal $B_1 - nA_1 (= A_1') = B_2 - nA_2 (= A_2')$. At the same time the subject conceives of their equality as a necessary ("Sure", "Of course") and general implication ("It's still [or 'always': Fr. 'toujours'] the same").

The entire sequence forms a particularly clear example of the way in which intuitive, and even perceptual, regulations evolve towards mobile and reversible operational composition. Whatever their age, all our subjects are agreed that when the two areas are diminished by

n bricks the remaining areas are equal, but only if the lay-out is identical for both. But this is a special case since they have no need to deduce the equality as they can perceive it immediately. On the other hand, the slightest change of position, involving one or two houses only, is enough for the youngest subjects to deny the equality. A little later, they learn to anticipate compensatory changes of position so long as these are slight (for there is always compensation of the area covered by bricks by the area left uncovered). Nevertheless, when the implied compositions are more complex, the anticipations are of no avail. Later there is generalization which extends to three elements, then four, etc., until finally the set of anticipations, together with the adjustments which follow, attains generalized and reversible mobility, that is, operational composition.

In conclusion we may ask why the end-stage is reached at level IIIA. The answer is that the same is true of the composition of lengths in one or two dimensions, so that the finding is not unexpected, since the present problem involves only a parallel operation with areas without any fundamental complication. Grouping partial areas (the areas taken up by the bricks or houses) and subtracting these from a larger area involves the same kind of operation as grouping and subtracting parts of a line. In both cases the composition consists of adding and subtracting parts which are subdivisions of a whole (cf. C.C.S., ch. V).

The subject discovers that n houses occupy a definite area in a given field, and moving these houses to another part of the field simply means that they will now occupy the same area elsewhere: the area left free is comparable although its shape may be different. His discovery is identical with that which he made when dealing with lengths and distances. In other words, he learns that any object conserves its dimensions when it undergoes a change of position and that fixed sites are identical whether or not they are occupied. Above all, he learns the fundamental principle which underlies both the composition of lengths and distances (chs. III, IV) and that of areas; the principle of reciprocal compensation whereby the spaces left free and those which are newly occupied mutually compensate one another.[1]

Finally, the solution of this problem, simple though it is, implies the conservation of area. Children of level IIA (and *a fortiori* those of stage I) cannot master a problem of additive composition, which is why they cannot subtract equal parts from equal wholes, but this is because the areas of houses are not conserved when their position is changed and the areas of empty spaces are thought to alter when they alter in shape. Older children are more successful and achieve reversible compositions because they master the relevant 'groupings'. Such

---

[1] At any rate the principle of reciprocal compensation is understood for a simple problem like the present. A more complex instance occurs later, para. 8.

groupings precede metric operations, both here and elsewhere, but they are sufficient to ensure the conservation of areas, including the areas of empty sites. The next section deals more directly with the conservation of area.

SECTION II. THE CONSERVATION AND MEASUREMENT OF AREAS

There is conservation of area as soon as there is operational grouping in the addition and subtraction of areas, but measurement of areas becomes effective only when these processes are fused with change of position. We will now study both these developments.

§4. *Outline of method and results*

From the purely technical point of view, the analysis of conservation is much more difficult in regard to area than it was in regard to length (chs. III–V). In spite of the difficulty, the reason for which will soon be apparent, after comparing the results which follow with the clear-cut evidence of section I, we have no doubt of the validity of our interpretation.

To discover what sort of notions little children might possess with regard to the conservation of areas, we used two complementary techniques. For method 1, the experimenter presented an area composed of several separate sections and modified the arrangement of these parts to see whether or not the subject considered that the whole remained constant. Thus he might use two cardboard rectangles, each made up of 6 squares. There were twelve such squares, all equal, and each of the rectangles was two squares wide and three squares high. After producing these rectangles, the experimenter transferred the top right-hand square on one of them to the bottom right-hand corner, which gave a pyramid made up of three squares in the bottom row, two in the second, and one in the top. The child was asked whether this figure had the same area as the other rectangle which was left intact. It was found that subjects frequently recognized that there was an equal number of elements, i.e. six squares in each figure, yet refused to admit that the areas were equal, or that there was "the same amount of room" (the formulation being similar to that used in section 1). In order to dissociate these two aspects and avoid any verbal misunderstanding, the experimenter took 96 little wooden cubes or a few sheets of cardboard which covered the rectangle exactly and asked the child whether these would exactly cover the second shape as well. (The cubes recall the 'houses' of section 1, but their number was purposely made large so that the child should be unable to count them.) However, this technique led to the strange result that some children correctly predicted

273

that the same number of cubes could be used to cover the second figure without necessarily admitting that the areas were equal. This rather paradoxical finding gives a useful pointer to the way in which children develop the notion of area.

Because the results of method 1 were not unequivocal, we also used method 2, in which the child was simply shown two rectangles recognized as congruent and the experimenter then cut a portion off one and moved it to another part of the same figure. Thus he cut the rectangle diagonally in half and put the two sections together in the shape of a triangle, or he cut off the four corners and put them against the sides to produce an irregular polygon, etc. Any congruent figures could be used instead of rectangles if desired. The question was always: "Are these the same size?" "Is there the same amount of room?" etc. These were varied and repeated to be certain that the answer was a judgment of area as such. But once again, interpretation is a delicate matter because physically an area cannot be dissociated from the third dimension (however thin the paper one uses), which means that there is always a danger that the child will confuse the conservation of area with that of matter, which we know is not achieved until the age of 7 or 8.[1] At the same time, failure to differentiate area from solid matter is interesting in itself, because it shows how young children cannot dissociate the notion of a 'site' on a plane from objects which occupy such positions but may be moved from one 'site' to another.

Nevertheless, taken by themselves, the results yielded by these two methods could not be interpreted theoretically without serious misgivings, if these were all we had to go by. But, in the first place, they are in complete agreement with the findings of section 1, where there was no doubt at all that the children were making judgments about an area as such, but there was a clear development from non-conservation through partial and intuitive conservation to necessary and operational conservation. In the second place, they also agree with what may be deduced from a careful analysis of the measurement of areas, when carried out as in method 1 by superposing partial areas (whether or not the partial areas are unit-squares). Hence we are confident in proposing the following developmental scheme. It is identical with that found to govern the conservation and measurement of lengths in one or two dimensions.

Even at level IIA (as at level I) children confine themselves to perceptual judgments and the areas are not conserved when their appearance is modified. Again, they cannot measure areas because they lack conservation of the moving middle term so that there is no transitivity. Children at level IIB gradually come to make a number of true judgments, but their success is the product of intuitive adjustments

[1] Piaget and Inhelder, *Le développment des quantités chez l'enfant*, chs. 1–III.

274

and so is lacking in generality. Likewise we now find some degree of transitivity, so that measurement as such begins to be seen at level IIB, but to this there are many limitations. At level IIIA there is operational conservation of areas when their shape is altered (although the conservation is limited to the area enclosed by a given perimeter and does not extend to the complementary area outside). Middle terms now serve as common measures because congruence is recognized as a transitive relation. But children still fail to understand the concept of a unit so that when calculating the total extent of an area they count all its parts as equivalent regardless of their size. Finally, at level IIIB conservation is generalized to cover complementary areas and this level marks the beginning of true measurement, involving unit iteration.

§5. Conservation of area. Level IIA: No conservation

There is little gain in dwelling on stage I since very young children cannot understand the problem. But at level IIA, they understand the question well enough, but their answers reveal a complete lack of conservation. They realize that the two areas were equal to begin with and they appreciate that the modified shape is solely the result of an altered arrangement of parts. Yet they will not admit that the areas are still equal to one another. Hence, with method I, they will not agree that the cubes or cards which cover the rectangle exactly could be rearranged so as to cover the modified figure. Following are a few examples, illustrating the two methods.

BRAU (4; 6). Method 2. The experimenter presents two large squares and the subject recognizes their congruence. The experimenter then cuts one of the squares to form two rectangles and arranges them perpendicularly to one another: "Is there still the same amount of room on there (two rectangles) as there is on here (square)?—*No, it's not the same any more because you've cut it.*—Is there more room on one side?—*Yes, there's more room here* (two rectangles).—But didn't these bits have the same room to start with?—*Yes.*— Well haven't they the same now?—*No, you've cut it.*"

The experimenter now presents two identical rectangles and cuts one of these to form a square and a small rectangle, but he leaves the two sections together so that the form of the initial rectangle is not distorted. "Is there still the same amount of room?—*Yes.*—Is it exactly the same?—*Yes.*—What about these two (leaving the cut rectangle as it is, with the long sides vertical and rotating the intact rectangle so that the long sides are now horizontal)?— *That one* (intact) *is larger.*—Why?—*Because you've turned it round the wrong way.*—What about these two (another pair of congruent rectangles both standing breadthwise)?—*They're the same.*—Now watch. (The experimenter cuts one of the rectangles diagonally and re-arranges the two halves in the form of a triangle.)—*That one* (triangle) *is much bigger.*—Why?—*Because it isn't cut the same way.*—What about like this (cutting the rectangle out into six little squares)? Is there the same amount of room on this one as there is on all these together?—*There's much more room here* (six sections) *because there's a lot of them.*—And like this (re-arranging the two halves of the triangle to give a rectangle)?—*You've put it so that it's the same as before!*—Yes, well?—*There's more room here* (six sections).—(The sections are now put together in the form of a rectangle.)—*Oh! Now it's the same!*—And like this (spreading the sections a little but keeping them in pairs)?—*There's more room on here* (three small rectangles)."

CRI (5; 6). Method 2: He recognizes two rectangles as identical. The experimenter cuts a small rectangle out of the top of one and puts it alongside its base so that the two shapes are in direct prolongation. "*No, it's not the same anymore. There's more room on here* (rectangle left intact).—And like this (replacing the small rectangle, and cutting out a little triangle which is placed against a side and near the base)?—*There's more room there* (the irregular figure).—Why?—*Because it's bigger.*—And like this (displacing it)?—*No, there's more room on here* (intact rectangle) *because there* (the other figure) *it's thin.*—Well, could I re-arrange the bits and put one over the other exactly? —*No.*"

PEL (5; 6). Method 2. Two equal squares: "*There's the same amount of room*—And like this (with one square cut in four)?—*There's more room there because it's all in one piece. You never cut it. Here you cut it, so it's less.*—(The experimenter re-arranges the sections in their original form.) What about like this?—*There's more room on the real square.*—Why?—*Because you haven't cut it.*—(The experimenter now cuts the 'real' square and transforms it into a rectangle.) And now?—*There's more room there* (the rectangle) *because it's bigger.*—(The four sections of the second square are spaced.)—*There's more room there* (the four sections), *because there's more of them.*"

GAI (5; 2). Method 1. Two rectangles, one red the other blue, each composed of six squares, are superposed, and Gai recognizes that they're "*the same size.*—Watch what I can put on this one (putting the 96 cubes on the blue rectangle). Could I put them on the red one as well if I wanted to?—*Yes.* —Why?—*Because there's the same amount of room.*—Good. (The experimenter puts the cubes on the red rectangle.) What about like this (the six squares being spaced a little for both rectangles)?—*Also.*" The experimenter now puts the blue squares together again to form a rectangle and takes off the top right-hand square of the red rectangle, putting it at the bottom to form a pyramid: AB–CD–EF has now become A–CD–EFB. "Will there be the same amount of room like this?—*No, there'll be less room.*—Why?—*Because it's like this* (indicating irregular outline).—What about the little squares which were on before? Could we put them on now?—*No. It would take less squares.* —Why?—*Because it's like this* (pointing to the irregularity on the right as if the deficiency lay there).—And now (re-forming the rectangle)?—*It's the same.*—And like this (putting the six red squares in line: ABCDEF)?—*No. There's less room here. It's a line.*—(The blue rectangle is covered with two sheets of card, one over ACE, the other over BDF.) Could we put these sheets on there (ABCDEF)?—(He looks at them carefully.) *Yes.*—Then there's the same amount of room?—(Unconvinced.)—Well, watch this. (Three cards are put over the blue rectangle, covering AB, CD and EF respectively.) Could we put these sheets exactly over there (row ABCDEF)?—

No, you could only put two of them there.—(The 96 cubes are now placed over the row of red squares.) If we put these on there (blue rectangle) would they cover it all?—*No, you couldn't cover it. There's too much space.*—And these three cards (on the blue rectangle, over AB, CD and EF), you tell me I couldn't put them over here (on the red)?—*No, there isn't enough room.*—Watch (the experimenter moves the cards over the red row).—*Oh, yes!*—Why?—*There's the same room.*—Now could I put the bricks (96 cubes) on this (pyramid), the ones I had on before (when it was a row ABCDEF)?—*No, it's not the same size.*—Count the squares.—*One, two, three . . . six.*—And before?—*Six.*—And here (the blue rectangle)?—*Six.*—Is there the same amount of room? —*No.*"

MUT (5; 9). Method 1. He compares the red and blue rectangles: "*They're the same size.*—(Experimenter places the cardboard sheets over the blue one. Would these go over the red just as well?—*Yes, there's just the same amount of room.*—And like this (moving square B on the rectangle to the right of EF to form a pyramid)?—*No, there isn't the same room any more.*—Why?—*It's bigger here* (indicating the base of the pyramid).—And supposing we covered it over with these pieces of card (left on the blue rectangle)?—*It wouldn't work. It's bigger here* (again indicating the base).—What if I do this (arranging the six red squares in a row ABCDEF)?—*That makes it bigger. There's more room because it's a line.*—Could I cover it with the same little squares (96 cubes previously placed over the blue rectangle)?—*No, you'd need more little squares.*—What about these cards?—*There isn't enough card to cover it all. It's too big.*—Watch (the experimenter puts the cards over the red row).— *Oh, it's the same space!*—And like this (three separate rectangles each made up of two squares)?—*It's not the same. You'd need more cards* (than those which cover the blue rectangle).—Could I cover them with the little squares (96 cubes)?—*No. There are too many squares and there won't be room for some of them* (evidently revising his judgment).—Why?—*There's less room on the red.*—Let's try (beginning to place the cubes).—*No, they won't go just right.*— (The arrangement is completed.)—*Oh, they do!*—And like this? (He is asked to compare a square made up of four blue squares with a row of four red squares.)—*No, there isn't the same amount of room: here* (row ABCD) *there's more.*"

GER (5; 11). Method 2. He is asked to compare two large squares: "Are they the same size or not?—*Yes the same.*—Why?—(He puts one over the other to prove it.) *Because I can do this.*—And now (cutting one of the squares to form two rectangles which are then laid at right angles)?—*There's more room there* (rectangles). *No there* (square), *because you haven't cut it.*—What difference does it make when I cut it?—*That makes it smaller.*—(The two rectangles are put in line.)—*Here it's bigger, because it's bigger this way* (lengthways)."

LUD (6; 0). Method 2. He superposes two equal squares, like Ger, and notes their congruence. The experimenter cuts off a corner on one square and arranges the triangle so that it projects from one side. "*It's bigger here* (where the square is intact) *because it's all square: that makes more room.*—Could you put them one over the other again?—*Yes* (he replaces the triangular cut-out and superposes the two squares), *that's all right.*—Then isn't there the same

277

room now (putting the triangle back on top of the figure)?—*No, there's more room here* (changing his mind).—And like this?—..." He continues to replace the cut-out piece and superpose the squares, while maintaining that the figure is larger when its parts are transposed. *"It's bigger here because you've made a turning.*—Could I put one over the other?—*Yes.*—Then there must be the same amount of room on both.—*No.*"

The general trend of these replies is familiar enough. A similar lack of conservation was found to obtain with distances and lengths (chs. III, IV and V), with continuous quantities in general (matter, etc.)[1] and with discontinuous collections,[2] etc. Nevertheless we feel that transformations of areas seem to possess a specific quality. The reason for non-conservation is still the same. Because the child lacks the relevant operations together with the reversible composition they permit, he cannot mentally compensate for the various modifications. Therefore each arrangement is judged perceptually on its own merits without reference to those that preceded. Often, indeed, he is perceptually convinced that the modification in form produces a change in area, even where he cannot fully decide whether this is now greater or less. But from the standpoint of perception, the squares, rectangles, pyramids and irregular polygons presented in a bewildering series of transformations have nothing in common. At the present level these shapes are so 'abstract' that the experimenter is always a little uncertain as to the meaning which the words used might have for the subject, and seldom wholly sure that the child is making an estimate of the area as against some other dimension. That is why the present experiments are somewhat different from all other studies of conservation, both those presented in chs. III–V and those published elsewhere. The difference warrants closer inspection.

In any domain whatever, the discovery of conservation implies the construction of a logical or sub-logical 'grouping' or else of a (mathematical) 'group' of operations, which is why the study of these invariants and their first appearance is important. The degree to which their invariance is recognized is also the measure of how the corresponding concepts are composed. For the concept of area, composition is a matter of the grouping or addition of parts to form a whole, and conservation is simply the expression of the fact that the arrangement of parts does not affect their sum. So far there is no difference between the concept of area and the other concepts we have studied. As regards the addition and subtraction of parts, we know from section 1 (in which houses were used to reduce the area of grassland in a meadow) that children at level IIA are quite unable to group a set of parts,

[1] Vide Piaget and Inhelder, *Le développement des quantités chez l'enfant*, chs. I–III, and Piaget and Szeminska, *The Child's Conception of Number*, ch. I.
[2] Ibid., ch. II.

because they cannot construct the invariants which form our main concern in this section. However, when we study the conservation of area as such, we are faced with the fact that every re-arrangement of parts implies a figure which is qualitatively new (although its quantitative value remains unaltered). When we transform a rectangle into a triangle and ask the child whether there is the same amount of 'room', we wish to know whether the area is conserved, the term 'area' being a geometrician's abstraction from the shape enclosed by the perimeter. This complication applies far less to the conservation of weight, while where the collections are logical or numerical it is almost wholly absent. Thus, when the experimeter alters the arrangement of a 'heap' of counters and transforms them in a straight line, their perceptual appearance is altered for the subject whose judgment is intuitive. But it seems far easier to abstract the number of elements from their visual appearance than it is to abstract the area from a triangular or rectangular shape. Moreover, by altering the form of an area we automatically extend or reduce its perimeter, and this in turn affects the topological intuitions which form the starting-point for children's thinking in the realm of space.

A similar problem arose in our study of the conservation of distances and more especially of lengths (chs. III–V), but there the problem was less acute. Thus, by altering a rectilinear path to a series of segments at angles to one another (zigzags and right angles, etc.) and asking our subjects whether or not there was conservation of length, we automatically introduced an opposition between the length of the path, which is invariant, and its qualitative shape, which is obviously changed (ch. V). But then we were able to use the child's intuition of movement to help create the notion of a path, so that at the very least the question itself was understood.

The difficulty with area is that to the intuitive judgment there is no means of equating the figure as initially given with the transformation since the two shapes are not congruent. They are equal in area only because there is compensation between the space (or 'site') which is excluded in one arrangement and included in the other and those for which these properties are reversed. This compensation is a necessary relationship but its recognition, like the additive composition of parts which it implies, depends on an abstract form of reasoning. The difficulty of the problem at level IIA is particularly interesting because at level IIIA it is overcome. In other words, the conservation of area is achieved at precisely the same level as the various other invariances (discontinuous collections, etc.). We may conclude that the perceptual appearance of a collection is far more important for young children, whose reasoning is intuitive, than is realized by their elders, who reason logically. Moreover it appears that there is no difference in principle between the opposition of the invariance of area to the qualitative heterogencity of geometrical figures on the one hand and the less striking contrast between the perceptual forms of logical or numerical collections and their intensive quantity or 'power' on the other.

We may therefore go on to a closer study of why our young subjects refuse to recognize that the area of a figure remains constant when the arrangement of its parts is modified.[1] The reasons which they give should throw considerable light on the first steps from simple congruence to what might be called composed congruence. When two squares are congruent Brau admits their equivalence and Ger and Lud prove it spontaneously by superposition. Simple congruence derives from superposition and it applies when the figures being compared are identical. It is a special case of a kind of behaviour which was discussed in ch. II under the heading of "manual transfer", and is therefore one of the earliest manifestations of what will eventually appear as measurement (although it comes later than "visual transfer" when comparison is perceptual and there is no change of position). However, when two identical rectangles are differently oriented, one of our subjects, Brau, claims that one "is larger because you've turned it round the wrong way", as though altering the inclination of a figure affects its congruence with another. When one of two squares is cut into rectangular sections and placed at right angles, Brau is prepared to admit that "the bits had the same room to start with" but not that their total area remains unaltered for, he says: "You've cut it!" Later, when the sections are re-assembled, Brau is amazed to find that the total area is the same (Oh! Now it's the same!), but spreading the sections again leads him to conclude that "there's more room". Cri goes so far as to deny that the sections can be reassembled in their original form and Pel, seeing four sections of a square re-assembled in their original form, denies that this square is the same size as the one which is intact: "There's more room on the real square because you haven't cut it." In other words the whole does not equal the sum of its parts even when their original arrangement is reconstituted. Lud recognizes that the sections can always be re-assembled in their original form and superposed but still believes that modifications in form will produce greater or smaller areas because they involve 'turnings' or longer perimeters. Finally, Gai and Mut refuse to believe that the 96 cubes or the sheets of card which cover the original shape could be made to cover the modified figure (which is hardly surprising in view of all that has been said), and even the complete demonstration leaves them unconvinced that the areas are equal. The use of a common measure does not prove

[1] The study is not without historical interest, for, as is known, Greek mathematicians were suspicious of any construction which was too dependent on change of position, as if the latter might modify the displaced elements themselves.

congruence for these subjects because their thinking lacks transitivity. Gai even denies the equality of two sets of six squares when their arrangement is different.

We must conclude that composed congruence, i.e. a judgment of equality between two wholes based on the equality of their parts, is out of the question at this level for a variety of reasons: (1) When a whole is sectioned into parts, it ceases to be the same as before because its continuity is lost (cf. C.C.S., ch. V). (2) A change of position on the part of any section must affect the total area, because the 'site' to which it is moved is not accurately compensated by the 'site' from which it is taken (cf. ch. IV, for the same faulty reasoning as applied to lengths). (3) When parts of a whole are spaced, a confusion arises between the overall area which includes the spaces between them and the total area of the parts which does not. (4) When a shape is transformed, both its form and the length of the perimeter are changed (cf. Lud's reference to 'turnings'). (5) Children cannot make use of a common measure because their thinking lacks transitivity—which follows from the reasons already given. (6) Even where they recognize that the number of units is identical in two figures they do not conclude that they are equal in area if the arrangement of units is not identical—again for the same reasons.

These six reasons can be reduced to two principal factors: children cannot add parts operationally and they cannot coordinate movable parts by using fixed 'sites' as references.

§6. *Conservation of area. Level IIB: Intermediate responses*

As usual, at level IIB, children answer some of our questions correctly, but their successes are the fruit of trial-and-error. They proceed by articulated adjustments and lack generalization and operational composition.

PIR (5; 10). Method 2. One of two squares recognized as equal is cut into three rectangles and then reassembled. *"There's the same amount of room.— Why?—Because you took them away but you put the same thing back again.—* And like this (cutting it further)?—*There it's more* (the square which is intact). —Why?—*Because those are a little less.*—Well, supposing I add this little bit (a piece of card not taken from the original square).— *Yes, now it's the same.—* (The additional piece is removed.) Supposing I put these bits together again to make up a square, will it be the same as before?—*No, it will be smaller.—* And if I used this bit as well?— *Yes, then you'd have enough."*

CHAT (5; 11). Method 1. The rectangle is transformed into a pyramid. *"There's more room here* (the pyramid).—*Why?—Because of the shape* (indicating the base).—What if I covered it over with the little cubes?— *There'll be more room left.*—(The squares are re-assembled to form a rectangle but the three squares on the right are placed slightly higher than those on the left.) And like this?— *Yes, there'll be the same number of cubes.*—Then there's the same amount of room as on the rectangle, is there?—*No, there's more room* (looking at the square which projects at the bottom of the figure). —What if I covered it with cubes?—*There'd be more cubes.*—What about these (three blue squares one above the other compared with three red squares in a horizontal line)?—*It's the same. There's the same amount of room.*—And like this (with the red squares spaced)?—*No, there isn't the same space any more.*—And if I put the cubes on it?—*They won't all go on it.*—Try it.—(He does so.) *Oh, yes! It's just right. It looked smaller.*—Well, what about like this (three blues in line compared with three reds in the shape of a triangle)?—*It's not the same. Here there's more room* (in line).—Why?—*It's longer.*—Try it with the cubes.—(He places them over the row.) *Oh, yes. There'll be the same number both sides.*—And like this (four blue squares in a row compared with four red squares in a square).—*Here it's bigger* (the large square).—What if I put the cubes over them?—(He studies it carefully.) *They'll all go on it: there's the same amount of room.*—(Six blue squares in a rectangle are compared with six red squares in a pyramid.) And like this?— *No, there's more room here* (pyramid: indicating the perimeter and the angles). And if I used the (96) wooden cubes?—*They'll go just the same, because the number's the same: six squares.*"

Bos (6; 0). Method 1. The rectangle is transformed into a pyramid (with square B alongside the base EF): "Shall I be able to put all the little cubes on there?—*No, you can't anymore. There are too many of them.*—Well, is there the same amount of room?—*No, because of this turning* (where the square was removed).—What about like this (the pieces being re-assembled as a rectangle and the three right hand squares being slightly staggered)? *Like that you can do it.*—(The cubes are set out.) You're right. What about like this (returning to the pyramid)?—*No, it won't work because you've got this as well* (pointing to B, now moved alongside EF, and forgetting the empty space from which it was taken).—Where is there more room, here (rectangle) or there (pyramid)?—(He considers.) *There's the same amount of room.*— Would the cubes cover all of it?—*No.* (He tries it.) *Oh yes.*—And like this (arranged as a triangle)?—*Like this too.*—Now we'll put them like this. (In a single row A . . . F).—*There'll be more cubes on the red* (row).—Try it.—*Oh, it's the same!*" Various other arrangements are proposed, including a circle, different angles, and so on, but now he is convinced each time that the areas are equal and that the 96 cubes will just cover them whatever their arrangement. But when the thin cardboard pieces are used as the common term instead of the cubes, he has his doubts. Finally, he admits that these are also unaffected. The experimenter goes on to separate the squares: again he is doubtful whether, between them, they have the same room, and also whether the 96 cubes will cover them. He convinces himself that the separated parts and the whole are equal by spontaneously putting them together, then moving them slowly apart.

Gui (6; 2). The red rectangle is transformed into a row A . . . F: "*They won't cover it all. The red is bigger.*—(The experimenter re-assembles the red rectangle and then moves one half a little so that ACE and BDF are staggered). Will they go like this?—*No, it's bigger here* (indicating square F which projects at the base of the figure but ignoring square A which projects at the top).

—Try it.—*Oh, yes.*—And like this (increasing the stagger)?—*Like that too.*— And like this (arranged as a pyramid)?—*No. They won't cover it all. There's one up there, then two, then three down there, so there's not the same room.*— Try it.—*Oh, yes.*—What about like this (with two rows at right angles)?— *They're the same.*—And like this (three pairs, these being staggered)?—*It's still the same.*—(The squares are separated.)—*Still.*—(A zigzag arrangement.)— (He thinks a moment.) *Yes, they'll just go.*"

BOR (6; 3). Method 2. Two equal squares: one corner is cut off and placed against a side: "Is there the same amount of red space as there is of blue?— *No, it's a smaller block because you've taken that bit off.*—Could we put one exactly over the other?—(He tries.) *Yes.*—What about like this (with a strip cut out of the square and moved to transform it into a rectangle.[1])?—*Yes, there's the same amount of room, because that strip there goes there* (where it was originally).—(Once more the experimenter cuts off a corner and places it so that it projects from one side.)—*Yes, it's the same* (and this time he indicates how the area is compensated)."

DEL (6; 3). Method 1. The red rectangle is transformed to a pyramid. "Is there the same amount of room?—*No, it's smaller.*—If I tried putting these (96) cubes over it, should I be able to put all the cubes on this one as well as that?—*Yes.*—Why?—*Because there'll be a space for each one.*—And like this (with the six squares all separate)?—*No, now there won't be a space for all of the cubes.*—Why?—*Because there's less room.*—Let's try it (putting 16 cubes over one of the squares).—*Oh, yes. There's room for all of them.*—Why?— *Because there's the same space as there is here* (blue rectangle).—Why is that?—*Oh, no. There's less space.*—(Cubes placed over the second square.)— *They won't all go.*—(The remaining squares are covered.)—*Oh, they do!*— And now (with the squares in pairs)?—*It's the same thing.*—(The squares are separated again and widely spaced.)—*The same.*—And this (drawing an outline round the rectangle and another round the pyramid)?—*No, there's more room here* (rectangle).—Why?—*Oh, no! It's the same as before.*"

MAY (6; 3). Method 2. Two squares are recognized as congruent. "Supposing I cut off this corner and put it over here?—*That makes it less.*—Why?— *Because it's not the same any more.*—What if I put it back?—*Oh, yes! It is the same.*—And this way (with one square cut in pieces and the pieces spread out)?—*It's the same.*"

ELI (6; 10). Method 2. The experimenter shows him two squares and then cuts out a triangle from one of them. The triangle extends over the whole of the base but its upper angle is very obtuse. This triangle is now placed over the top of the square, which makes it look like a house with a roof: "*There's more room now.*—Why?—*Because it's bigger there* (the roof).—What about this (re-entrant angle)?—*Oh, yes, it's the same.*—And like this (with the square cut in strips, these being so placed as to give a crenellated edge)?—*They're both the same.*—Why?—*Because you simply cut it that way.*—Are you sure there's the same amount of room?—*Exactly the same.*"

MON (7; 11). Method 2. He is asked to compare an intact square with another which is cut up into pieces. He still thinks "*it's bigger and it's wider as well*", but later he changes his mind.

---

[1] Presumably the square is cut in half (EL).

Here we find a check on the reasons given earlier to account for non-conservation. These same factors are partially at work at level IIB, but now they are counterbalanced by the more advanced and articulated intuition so that incorrect judgments are corrected in the course of the enquiry. Because children have a clearer intuitive understanding of sub-division, we no longer find them arguing that two identical shapes differ in area simply because one has been cut, even though the pieces have been left in their original positions (cf. Pir's first reply). But if the break-up of the original shape is carried too far, we again find that the child's powers of composition, still in their infancy, cannot cope with it (cf. the entire sequel of the interview with Pir: he goes so far as to agree that only when an extra piece is added to the original pieces will they be equal to the whole with which he started!). Again, if the sections are moved considerably from their original position, our subjects find a systematic difficulty in equating the area (or 'site') which they now occupy with the area which they have left free. On the other hand, we note once more the gain in articulated intuitions, for these subjects learn to understand this compensation fairly quickly (cf. Eli) and their subsequent generalizations take it into account. Thus they gradually free their judgment from a false impression created by the shape of the figure and the length of its perimeter and so come to understand that its area remains constant. Their progress is particularly marked in their handling of middle terms or common measures (this in spite of Del's initial uncertainty) and we begin to see transitivity being recognized.

To sum up, the composition of sections or subdivisions and the co-ordination of 'sites' are both furthered by the growth of articulations. At stage III these latter are generalized and attain an operational form which means that they are strictly reversible.

§7. *Conservation of area. Level IIIA: Operational conservation*

Only when he reaches the beginning of stage III can a child resolve problems involving the conservation of area, for now he ignores any alteration in the shape of the area, relying only on his understanding of transformation as such, which means that he no longer needs to compare the two figures resulting from such transformations.

DUT (6; 7). Method 1. The red rectangle is transformed to a pyramid by moving square B from the top right hand corner adjoining square A to the base of the rectangle alongside EF: *"There's exactly the same space.—*And if I tried to cover it with the (96) cubes?—*There'd be room for all of them.—*And like this (with a row of four BCDE and one square, A, above B, another, F, below E)?—*It's the same thing. There's the same amount of space.—*What about this way (with the six squares spaced)? Will all the little cubes go on there?—(He looks at it and is at first a little unsure.) *They'll all go on there,* *because there's the same space.*—Why?—*Because you've got all the squares there; they're always the same.*" The experimenter now takes a piece of paper and draws outlines round the blue rectangle and a pyramid made from the red squares: "Can I put all the cubes which go on this drawing into that one as well?—*Yes, they'll go into it. It's the same thing.*"

PIA (6; 10). Method 2. One of two equal rectangles is cut up in various ways and the sections variously disposed (a triangle etc.). Whatever the transformation, Pia immediately replies: "*It's the same thing. You've simply turned it round differently but it's the same size as before.*—And if I hid the paper?—*It'd still be the same.*"

GIN (7; 0). Method 1. The red rectangle is transformed to a pyramid. "*You'll have more cubes. Oh, no! It'll be just the same.*—Why?—*You've got the same number of squares.*—And like this (squares arranged in a single row A . . . F)?—*It's the same space. It's still six squares.*—And like this (spacing the squares)?—*It's the same space because it's the same squares.*—(Outline drawings of rectangle and pyramid)?—*The same.*—Then what made you go wrong to start with?—*I saw it was bigger at the bottom and I forgot it was the same squares.*"

KIP (7; 2). Method 2. A square is transformed to give a variety of shapes: "*It's the same. You just cut it, that's all.*—(The experimenter continues cutting.)—*It's still the same* (quite certain, almost without looking)."

LAM (7; 6). Method 2. "*It's the same, You keep cutting the same squares.*— But that changes the shape, doesn't it?—*Yes, but not the space.*"

RIG (7; 9). Method 2. "*Yes, it's the same space, because if you put them together it would be the same.*"

Even when a child shows a momentary lapse at the beginning, like Gin, his answers at this stage are quite different from those at the preceding level. He no longer compares the area of the new shape with that of the figure used as a control, and instead he reasons from the transformation itself. He regards the new shape simply as the outcome of such a transformation rather than a new area to be compared with the original. Consequently, he takes it for granted that the transformation is simply a re-arrangement of identical parts, and has no need to examine it in order to know that the whole is conserved (cf. Kip).

What is most striking about the operational conservation of area is that it appears at the same time as that of distance and length (chs. III–V) in spite of the specific difficulties of "composed congruence" when entirely new shapes appear in place of the old (cf. §5). Again, the conservation of area results quite simply from the coordination of qualitative operations, and here as in the case of one-dimensional lengths, their operational synthesis eventually leads to metric operations. The relevant operations are on the one hand subdivision and the addition of parts (considered by itself in section 1) which enables the subject to conceive of a whole as an invariant total whatever the disposition of parts, and, on the other, operations which govern position and change of position, involving their systematic coordination with reference to

285

fixed 'sites'. The second operation allows the subject to realize the necessary compensation between newly occupied positions and positions newly vacated, which is a feature of all change of position. Both operations are at work in ensuring operational conservation at level IIIA, but at this level they simply complement one another. §§9 and 10 show how later they are fused to give a single operation, the measurement of area, combining change of position and subdivision.

§8. *Conservation of the area outside a closed perimeter*

The conservation of area like that of length involves compensation between newly occupied and newly vacated 'sites' resulting from changes in the position of parts. Such is the conclusion to which we are led from the observations just reported and it suggests that there cannot be conservation of area without some coordination of the relevant plane. But how complete is that coordination? An earlier study (CCS, chs. XIII and XIV) proved that coordinate systems do not appear spontaneously before level IIIB although conservation as treated in the foregoing pages appears at level IIIA. On the other hand, we saw in section 1 how children at level IIIA correctly subtract partial areas which are equal (houses) from total areas which are also equal (meadows), finding that the remainders are also equal. Yet the correct solution carries with it not only the conservation of the area being subtracted (houses) but also that of the remaining grasslands, which are complementary areas in the sense that they lie outside the perimeter of the others, being simply those positions which are not occupied by them. These must also be coordinated and are coordinated at level IIIA. It seems therefore that the results of the experiments on conservation do not agree with those of the earlier study of coordinate systems.

Faced with this apparent contradiction, we undertook an investigation not unlike that of section I of this chapter in that this too deals with the conservation of an area within a closed figure but also involves the coordination of the plane of which that figure is a part. The question is whether the conservation of complementary areas always appears at the same time as that of enclosed areas or whether this is true only when the areas seen first are all alike and all the same size (like the houses in section I), and not when these are composed of dissimilar elements. It was hoped that this question would tie up the problem of conservation of area and that of coordinates without leaving any ragged ends. The result fully confirmed our expectations: the conservation of the area within a closed figure appears at level IIIA while the invariance of complementary areas, being those outside the closed figure is a construction of level IIIB, so long as the interior shape is transformed in a variety of ways like the squares and rectangles of the previous § instead of being a matter of disposing equal parts in several ways as in section I.

Our method was as follows. The child is shown two identical green meadows, B_1 and B_2, and asked to superpose them to convince himself that they are equal. The experimenter then places a brown square, A_1, inside B_1 calling it a ploughed field or a 'potato plot'. He puts a similar plot, A_2, in B_2, but A_2 is cut into movable sections. When the subject has verified that $B_1 = B_2$ and $A_1 = A_2$ and satisfied himself that the remainders are also congruent, i.e. $A_1 \, (= B_1 - A_1) = A_2' \, (= B_2 - A_2)$, the experimenter alters the shape of plot A_2 by separating the sections (which are not all alike) or by transforming the original square to a more or less elongated rectangle, etc. Occasionally we vary the form of the remaining areas A_1 and A_2 instead of the plots themselves A_1 and A_2 which is easy enough as the two fields B_1 and B_2 are irregular in form although congruent. Either way, the child is asked the following two questions: (1) do the two areas A_1 and A_2 remain equal although their distribution is different ("Is there the same space for potatoes on both fields?") and (2) do the complementary areas remain equal as well ("Is there still as much grass, or green, for each of the two cows?"). The two equalities can be checked with pieces of card which are brown for the 'plots' A and green for the 'meadows' A'.

We found three levels in answers to these questions. Up to and including stage II (i.e. about the age of 7) there is no conservation either of the interior areas (A_1 and A_2) or of the complementary areas (A_1' and A_2'), i.e. there is no conservation either of the potato-plots or of the meadowland. Occasionally we find so little conservation that a child will claim that both the interior area and the complementary area have increased! At level IIIA the interior area A is conserved whatever the modification in form, but the subject does not deduce that the complementary area A' is also invariant. The deduction is made only at level IIIB when both areas are conserved, whatever the transformations.

Following are examples of stage II:

WIR (5; 7) is at sub-stage IIA. With the forms as originally presented he recognizes the equality of the whole ($B_1 = B_2$), of the 'potato-plots' ($A_1 = A_2$) and of the remaining 'pastureland' ($A_1' = A_2'$). A_2 is then transformed to an elongated rectangle, while A_1 remains square (like A_2 at the beginning): "Is there as much space for potatoes here (A_1) and here (A_2)?—*Oh, no. You can put more potatoes in here* (A_2) *and less in the other.*—Could one change the patch back to what it was like before?—*Yes* (he re-makes the square A_2 with which we started).—But surely, doesn't it mean there's the same amount of room this way (A_2 changed back to a rectangle)?—*No. There's more potatoes here* (A_2) *than there is there* (A_1).—What about the meadow (drawing his attention to the grass on A_1' and A_2')?—*There's much more here* (A_2', which means there is more grass left by the rectangle which is thinner).—What about this way (transforming A_2 to an even more elongated rectangle)? Is there the same amount of space for potatoes?—*Now there's much more room than this way* (alluding to the previous rectangle of which a copy has been left purposely for comparison).—*What about the meadowland* (A_2')? —*It's bigger than in both the others* (i.e. the two previous forms of A_2')."

GEO (6; 11) is at the transitional level, IIB. Where the transformation is slight, as when square A_2 is altered to a squarish rectangle, he grants the equality of the interior areas, though not that of the complementary areas: "*They're both the same. It's the same border* (arranged differently).—Is there the same amount of space for potatoes?—*Yes, it's the same.*—What about the grassland (A_1' and A_2')? Is there the same there?—*No, there's more here* (A_1')."

However, when the transformation is greater, as when A_2 is transformed to a more elongated rectangle, Geo refuses to admit the conservation either of the interior or of the complementary area: "Is this patch (A_2) still the same? —*No, it's longer.*—But is there the same amount of room for planting potatoes, etc.?—*No, there's more room.*—What about the grass for the cows? —*There's a little less grass left* (in A_2') *because the potato plot takes up too much room.*"

These stage II responses tell us nothing new about conservation itself: at this level children do not understand the invariance of an area when its parts are re-arranged (but this we know already from §§5 and 6) nor can they realize that two complementary areas remain equal when the areas which they complement are differently disposed (but this also we know from section 1). The only fresh piece of information arises out of the fact that both questions are put simultaneously, and is provided by Wir at sub-stage IIA. Although he admits that the total area B_2 is unaltered and equal to B_1, Wir claims both that the internal area A_2 is greater than A_1 and also that its complementary A_2' ($= B_2 - A_2$) is greater than A_1'. In other words he is quite unperturbed by the glaring contradiction arising from the fact that B_2 remains unaltered while both its parts A_2 and A_2' are deemed to have increased in size. This contradiction disappears at level IIB (cf. Geo), i.e. even at the transitional stage which precedes conservation.

Sub-stage IIIA brings us as usual to the level of conservation of area. But in this experiment conservation is limited to the interior areas A_1 and A_2 (the 'potato plots') and is not yet extended to the two complementary areas A_1' and A_2' (the 'grassland' around the plots). This result is new and worthy of a closer analysis. Following are a number of clear-cut instances.

PIC (7; 9) begins by replying in a way which is intermediate between levels IIB and IIIA. When the square field A_2 is altered to a squarish rectangle he first says, "*There's less room now: it isn't as wide* . . . Can we make it the way it was again?—*Yes* (altering A_2 back to the original square). *Oh, I see! It's the same: there's no more cardboard and no less either.*—And the grassland (A_2')?—*That isn't the same as before: there's more than there was.*—You mean that by putting the potato plot (A_2) this way we make it the same but not the meadow A_2'?—*Yes, because there's more room when we put it this way.*—

288

And like this (A_2 transformed to a more elongated rectangle) is there the same amount of room on the potato plot?—*Yes, because there's the same amount of cardboard.*—And the grassland (A_2')?—*There's more grassland.* —So the potato-plot is the same but there's more grassland?—*Yes.*—Show me where there's more.— . . . —And the potato-plot?—*It's the same. It isn't more and it isn't less.*—And the grassland?—*It's more.*—Can we measure it?—*Yes. It's bigger here* (putting the green cards first over A_1', then over A_2'). *No. There's the same amount of grass on both.*—And this way (with the sections of A_2 all in different corners of B_2)?—*The potato plots are the same: it isn't more and it isn't less.*—And the grassland (A_2')?—*There's more than there was.*"

DAN (7; 6), having noted the congruence of A_1 and A_2 and also of B_1 and B_2, sees A_2 transformed to a rectangle: "Is there just as much room here (A_2) as there is there (A_1)?—*Yes, there'll be the same, because it was a square to start with just like the other.*—What about the meadowland (A_2')?—*That's the same, too. No, there'd be less grass than there* (A_1').—Why?—*Because it's longer.*—What about the potato plot (A_2)?—*There's as much space here* (A_2) *because the plots can be put round like that* (A_1).—And the grassland also?— *No, there's more space left here* (A_1').—What about this way (altering A_2 to a more elongated rectangle). Is there still the same amount of space left in the potato-plot?—*Yes. There's the same space, but it's longer now.*—Doesn't that mean it's bigger?—*No, because it's thinner.*—What about the grassland?— *There's more grass here* (A_2'), *but the potato plots are the same size.*—And this way (with the sections of A_2 dispersed in different corners of B_2)?—*There's the same amount of space there as there is here* (A_2), *because all these plots* (A_2) *taken together are the same size as* (A_2).—What about the grassland (A_2')?— *There's more grass because the plot* (A_2) *is all split up.*"

MIN (8; 2). The second square (A_2) is transformed to a rectangle. "Will there be as much room now as there was?—*Yes, because it was the same* (as A_1) *before. You've changed its shape round but you haven't changed its size.*— What about the grassland (A_2')?—*There's less here* (A_2').—And this way (with A_2 as a more elongated rectangle)?—*There's more grass there* (A_2').—What about the plot (A_2)?—*They're both the same* (A_1 and A_2).—And the grassland as well?—*No, there's less of that because you've changed the shape of the potato plot.*" Other transformations again produce similar replies.

All the above subjects realize that the areas within the plots A_1 and A_2 are constant however A_2 is modified and however remote its appearance from the original square shape. This much is in line with the finding of §7 that conservation of area is achieved at level IIIA. Even Pil, who begins like a child at level IIB by denying conservation, discovers quite soon that alterations in shape are reversible and so becomes convinced of the conservation of area. Dan explains the conservation by pointing out the compensation between the altered relations involved (longer × thinner), etc. On the other hand, unlike the subjects studied in section I these IIIA subjects fail to recognize the conservation of the remaining area ($A_2' = A_1'$) although they know that $A_1 = A_2$ and that these are subtracted from B_1 and B_2 which are also equal to yield A' ($B_1 - A_1 = A_1$; $B_2 - A_2 = A'_2$). This contradiction raises two questions: why are these replies different from those given in section I, and why is conservation of complementary areas harder to construct than that of an area circumscribed by a closed line like the two plots A_1 and A_2?

The answer to the first question is easy. In section I children were shown a number of houses each of which occupied the same area and the conservation of the total area of the houses (A) was no problem to them, since its invariance was pointed out in the first place and was also intuitively obvious even at level IIB:[1] hence those children had only one problem and that was to decide whether or not the remaining area (A') was conserved (i.e. whether there was the same amount of grassland left by the houses). As a consequence the relevant operations bore immediately on the remaining area which was immediately recognized as a complementary area and which was throughout in the forefront of the subject's attention. But in the present experiment he is faced with two complications. First, the area of the plot (A) is no longer divided into homogeneous parts but into unequal sections which are then grouped in different ways (more or less elongated rectangles, etc.). Therefore the conservation of area A itself is a problem which the subject must solve first of all. Secondly, the question of the invariance of the remaining area (A') is asked only when this question has been answered. This means that the experimenter does not provide the subject with the key to its correct solution, that it is complementary to area A_1, which he did in section 1. The subject must now make the discovery on his own. Thus the present task is harder than that of section 1 for two reasons: it involves two separate problems of conservation, each dealing with separate areas, and the child must find out for himself that these complement one another, while in section I there was only one problem of conservation since the child was told right from the start that one of the areas was invariant and the other was complementary to it.

However, the essential problem is why it is more difficult to realize the conservation of a complementary area (like that of the meadow A') than that of the first area (plot A) which is bounded by a perimeter. We may note that the conservation of area, like that of length and distance, involves compensation between positions (or 'sites') which are vacated and others which are taken up in the process of transformation, since this always involves changes in the positions of the various parts. All conservation entails some measure of coordination between these 'sites' which is why its appearance is relatively tardy. However, such coordination does not appear all at once, and earlier studies (C.C.S., chs. XIII and XIV) have shown that the overall coordination of a plane is not

[1] So long as the same number of houses was arranged in various ways.

achieved until level IIIB. At level IIIA children realize coordination only when they can use a perimeter, albeit one which changes, to help their reasoning, and the coordination is limited to the area which it encloses. Hence the conservation of complementary areas is a much harder problem. Here the child must not only understand the compensation between 'sites' which are occupied and those which are vacated but also the reciprocal relation between the area within an inner perimeter and the area outside. He must recognize that the latter is complementary with reference to a second outer perimeter. This reciprocal relation implies not a limited but an overall coordination of plane surfaces. Thus we should not be surprised to find that children who are quite convinced of the conservation of plot A and are perfectly aware that its parts will always add to the same total, are yet unable to reason logically regarding the complementary area A'. They fail to realize that the same reasoning applies to the whole area B (and the experimenter himself deliberately refrains from mentioning the latter) for if they did, they would surely reason that the remainder A' is also invariant. They ignore the whole (B) because so long as they are thinking about the inner area (A) they fail to draw any inferences bearing on the outer area (A'). This is because they lack an overall coordination of plane surfaces which means that they do not think of (A') as complementary to (A) in terms of the whole (B).

The fact that the grassland (A') complements the area of the plot (A) as judged in terms of the whole (B) is one which is understood at level IIIB. Children at stage II first thought that both the areas involved could be simultaneously enlarged, and later at level IIIA, they understood that area A was conserved but failed to grasp that A' is complementary to it. But at level IIIB, they reason in terms of the whole from the beginning which means that since they can recognize the invariance of A they can automatically deduce that of its complementary A'.

MAR (8; 3). Plot A_2 is altered to a rectangle. *"It's the same. That one (A_1) is put out in a square while that one (A_2) is made long. What's lost here* (in height) *is gained there* (in length).—What about the meadow (A_2')?—*It's the same. Here there's more room left and there there's less, so it's the same."* Other transformations are tried but the replies are similar. "But why is there the same space left in the grassland (A_2')?—*Because where there wasn't any grass there's grass now, and where there was grass there isn't any any more* (indicating the compensations as between A_2 and A_2')."

MIC (8; 4). Plot A_2: *"It's the same. You've just moved the cards round, that's all.*—And the grassland (A_2')?—*It's the same both sides* (A_1' and A_2').—Why?—*I can't explain, it's because the plots are the same* ($A_1 = A_2$)."

CEL (8; 4): *"The plot's the same, and so is the meadow* (A_2 and A_2') *because the plot always takes up the same amount of space."*

These replies are totally different from those of level IIIA. These subjects are immediately aware that the area of the plot A_2 is constant because, as the positions of the parts are changed, so those 'sites' which are vacated are compensated by others which are occupied. But they no longer limit their reasoning to the interior area A_2 but extend it to the larger whole B_2 (even though the latter may be irregular in outline). Hence they immediately think of the area of the meadow (A_2') as complementary to the plot A_2 ($A_2' = B_2 - A_2$) and it follows that A_2' remains constant by virtue of the same principle of compensation. Thus, as Mar puts it: "Where there wasn't any grass, there's grass now, and where there was there isn't any any more."

The difference between level IIIA and level IIIB is that children at the first level are just beginning to coordinate plane surfaces while those at the second level generalize the coordination to include the plane as a whole, so that when a question is asked about one delimited section the area outside its perimeter is immediately conceived as being complementary to it, and therefore subject to conservation by the very same principle. The ability to generalize the coordination of vacated 'sites' and occupied 'sites' with that of inner and outer areas is itself but one expression of the power to construct comprehensive reference systems or systems of coordinates, and this is achieved at level IIIB, as we know from C.C.S., chs. XIII and XIV.

The ability to coordinate spatial relations as revealed in this section is also the starting point for operations of measurement, since these imply a synthesis between operations of subdivision and operations of order and change of position. The next section therefore deals with the development of areal measurement.

§9. *Measurement of areas.* 1. *Measurement by superposition*

To study the measurement of area we used two separate techniques. Each of these taken by itself produced interesting results, but the comparison between them is particularly instructive. The second method is described more fully in §10. Briefly it consists in presenting the subject with a limited number of square unit cards which he must then move by successive iteration from one part of the surface being measured to the next. But with the first method the number of measuring cards is greater and there are enough or nearly enough to cover the whole of. the area being measured.

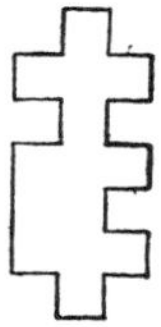

FIG. 18.

The test objects are a large right-angled triangle (which we shall call A), an irregular figure (called B, and shown in Fig. 18), and a number of smaller squares, rectangles (made up of two squares) and triangles (squares cut diagonally in half). There are enough of these smaller shapes to cover the whole of B and more than enough to cover A, which is somewhat smaller. One problem is simply to discover the age at which children will use the smaller cut-outs as a middle term or common measure. Usually, this implies only qualitative transitivity, and an understanding of unit measurement is not involved. Unit measurement may however occur if the subject chooses to move only one cut-out to measure the larger area, or if he counts the measuring units and uses them according to their respective sizes. In some cases this experiment was carried out before the investigation of §10 on unit measurement, but more often the latter was carried out before this.

The first level covers stage I and level IIA. There is no transitivity:

BRAU (4; 6): "*I think that one* (B) *is bigger.*—Would these cards help you?—*Yes* (he starts to cover B). *Oh dear, it's difficult, but I'm going to do it even if it is difficult.* (Eventually he just about manages it, but he takes no notice of the triangle A.)—What about this one A? I'd like to know whether this one is bigger.—(He covers A.)—Well, which one is bigger?—*I don't know.*—Well, why don't you need all the little cards to go over (A)?—*You can put all the little squares on there* (showing no understanding of the relation)."

REN (5; 0). "*This one* (A) *is bigger because it's got these points.*—Would these cards help you to measure?—*Oh, yes, let's try.* (He puts the cards in the spaces outside Figure B. The experimenter then shows him how to place his cards and the child then covers both B and A.)—Well, which of them is bigger?—*I think this one* (B) *is like the stairs in a chalet.*—But tell me, did these cards help you to decide which one was bigger?— . . . —Let's pretend these cards were made of chocolate. Which one would have more to eat?—*Oh, that one* (A)! *If you ate that you'd have a tummy-ache.*—But what do the little cards tell you? . . ."

PEL (5; 6) puts his fingers over the two figures: "*They're both the same.*—Would these cards help you?—*Yes. You can put this one here* (filling in the gaps on B) *and then it's the same.*—Try again (helping him with B). Did you manage to cover it all?—*Yes.*—Well, what can you do about this one (A)?—*I can cover this one the same way* (he does so).—Did you need all the little cards?—*No.*—Well which one is bigger?—*This one* (A) *is bigger and that one* (B) *is smaller.*"—The experimenter points first to card A and then to the small cards which cover it exactly: "Let's pretend these were all made of chocolate. Which lot would have more to eat, that one by itself (A) or these little bits?—*That one* (A) *because it's bigger.*" Clearly Pel cannot even see equality as between a whole and a number of pieces which cover it.

FAN (6; 10): "*That ore* (triangle A) *is bigger because this* (hypotenuse) *is longer.*—See if you can find some way of knowing whether you're right or not (handing him the small cards).—(He takes one card only and puts it over A in several positions one after the other.)—(The experimenter shows him what to do and he then covers A.) Did you use all of them?—*No, not all.*—What else can one do?—(He covers B.)—Were you able to put all the little cards on there?—*Yes.*—Then which one is bigger?—*This one* (A).—Is there exactly the same lot of bits here as there?—*No, it isn't the same. There's more bits when the bits are little, because there's more of them* (ignoring the fact that B takes all the pieces and A only a part)."

Although there are obvious similarities between these replies and those made by children at level IIA when asked to measure lengths, they are different in one respect. It is that these children can apply one area to another to make sure of their congruence when both areas are undivided (Ger and Lud in §5), but cannot understand composed congruence (i.e. that a number of sections taken together equal the whole which they cover). Needless to say, they cannot combine composed congruence with the transitivity of a common measuring term. The lack of such transitivity echoes a similar failure in problems of length.

Hence these children make no attempt on their own to cover the two areas A and B. Even when the experimenter suggests that they try covering one area they do not repeat the process with the other until specifically asked to do so. Moreover, when trying to cover B, they find this difficult because the figure is irregular, which is why they want to fill in the gaps and to make it perceptually comparable with A. However, the main point is that when the children have covered both areas under guidance, using all the pieces for B and only a part of them for A, they do not conclude that A is smaller—even after the experimenter has drawn their attention to the fact that all the pieces went on B and not all of them went on A. Brau, for instance, does not understand the question. Ren first says that B is bigger (a perceptual judgment which owes nothing to the measuring cards) but claims that A would make a larger slab of chocolate. Pel and Fan think that their measurement shows A to be bigger. Altogether, there is no transitivity: $A < M$; $M = B \ A > B$ is the logic of the last three subjects!

Nevertheless, the thing is self-explanatory in view of the non-conservation of area by children at this level (§5). In the first place they are ignorant of the composition of parts which means that they cannot understand that the set of cards taken together equals the total area B, and that a part of that set alone is equal to the total area A, so that $A < B$ because the part $<$ the whole. In the second place they cannot see that the sections taken together equal the intact whole. This is partly because the composition of parts is not yet mastered but it is also due in part to the fact that they cannot compare order and changes of position by strict reference to 'sites' which are vacated or taken up. Hence they do not realize what they are doing when they move the common measure from one object to another. Since both kinds of composition are lacking there can be no question of fusing the two to produce metric operations. But even the more limited coordination involved in qualitative comparison eschews them since both its components are wanting, so that a number of sections covering a whole are deemed to be less than that whole as soon as they are moved (Pel and Fan). If the measuring term itself is thought to alter in the course of movement, there can be neither measurement nor even logical transitivity. The first essential to either is the conservation of the middle term.

The first replies at level IIB are similar but later replies by the same children show how gradually by trial-and-error they discover that if all the cards are required to go over B while A can be covered by only some, A must be less than B.

PIR (5; 10). *"That one (B) is bigger, because there's this square, and this square, etc. and then there's all this* (portions which jut out).—Why is (A) smaller?—*Because it's like a roof and it's smaller. I don't know. I can see it is.*— Try measuring it."—(He takes the cards and covers A.)—Well, which one is bigger?—*Now it's that one (A) because it's got all the little cards on it.*—Have you tried putting them on the other one?—(He covers B.) Did you manage to go all over it?—*Yes, there are no more left.*—(The measuring cards are removed.) Which is bigger?—*That one (B) because I could put all the cards on it."*—The experimenter asks him to compare the measuring cards with B, remembering that, altogether, they just covered it earlier on. *"This* (the pieces) *is bigger because there's more of them.*—Why?—*Oh, no. It's the same."*

ROS (6; 10) begins by covering B and says: *"It's bigger.*—Well, what do you do next?—*I need more to go on there* (A).—You can use the same cards again.—(He covers A.) *Oh, it's smaller because all the cards wouldn't go on it."* Asked to compare the area B with the small cards put separately: *"It's the same."*

BRU (7; 2) first ignores the cards and covers B only when invited to do so. *"That's the one which is bigger.*—What can you do to find out if (A) isn't bigger after all?—*I can take them off and put them on there* (he places them over A).—Well?—*That one (B) is bigger because I needed all the cards for it but I didn't on that one* (A). (B compared with the smaller cards:) *The little bits make more. Oh, no! It's the same."*

PAU (8; 0, backward) illustrates the oscillations which are such a feature of this level. He first makes a perceptual judgment that A is bigger. Then, prompted by the experimenter, he covers A and B: "What happened?— *I can put all the cards on that one* (B) *but not on this one* (A).—Well, is (B) bigger or smaller?—*It's the same because I measured it with these cards. Oh, no! Because on this one* (B) *I put those on as well* (which would not fit over A). —Supposing they were both made of chocolate, which one would have more to eat?—*The same.*—Isn't one of them bigger?—*No . . . Yes, one is smaller, because I put more squares there* (B) *than here* (A)."

In short, we see the beginnings of a common measure, but only after prodding (as if perceptual judgments were good enough by themselves). Again, we see the beginnings of transitivity because there is better conservation. In other words the composition of parts within a whole and the composition of positions and changes of position are more coordinated.

At stage III the use of the common measure and the recognition of its transitivity are both immediate. Nevertheless we still find two substages: at level IIIA, children use their composite common term to compare A and B but in doing so they simply count all the cards as if they were equal units and ignore their inequality; but at level IIIB they understand the notion of a unit and so they take the size of the measuring elements into account. Here are two examples of level IIIA:

LAM (7; 6) covers A without being told and then counts the number of cards he used: *"That's seven. Now I'll try it with this one* (B. He covers it and again counts:) *That's thirteen. It's bigger.*—Are there any cards left when you cover this one (A)?—*Yes, because it's smaller."*

LAP (7; 7) covers B straight off and says: *"There's nine squares.* (He then covers A:) *It's smaller. There are only seven* (having counted all the pieces on B and only the squares on A).—Well, which is bigger?—*That one* (B), *because I counted more squares there."*

This kind of reply is reproduced in more detail in §10. Finally, here are two examples of level IIIB:

NAG (7; 6, advanced) takes a square and places it over B, then moves it stepwise over the entire figure, counting how many times its position is changed to cover the area as a whole. But the square is too big to go into all parts of the figure and he ignores these: "You can use the others.—*Well, I'll take all the cards, then I'll count them, and I'll use one to measure with.* (He studies the rectangular cards.) *That's two squares. This big bit* (on B) *is easy. I can tell that's four squares.* (He covers it all.) *I can count sixteen little squares.* (He covers A:) *It's smaller* (counting the squares and taking the triangles as half each)."

MOG (8; 8) covers both areas but instead of counting the pieces as such he counts the unit squares: *"That one* (B) *is bigger because it's sixteen squares and that one's only twelve* (A). *And you can't put all the pieces on there* (A), *so it's smaller."*

§10. *Measurement of Areas. 2. Unit Iteration*

The child is shown a number of shapes which are equal in area but which differ markedly in shape. One (A) is a square which can be composed out of nine smaller squares. The others (B and C) are irregular

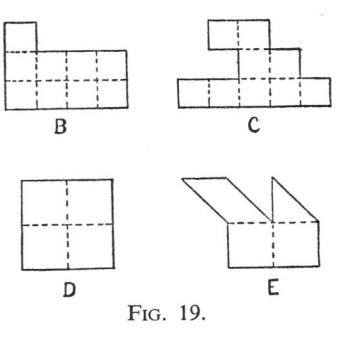

FIG. 19.

figures made up of the same number of small squares, as illustrated in Fig. 19. The child is given a cardboard square representing one unit together with a pencil. He is free to examine the material and draw on it, the cards being plain, white, without dotted lines. If he does not know what to do, the experimenter shows him how to step the unit-square to cover the large square by doing it for him two or three times and telling him to carry on by himself. When we have finished with A, B and C, we pass on to two more shapes which are more heterogeneous and not equal (D and E). The child is offered a choice of three counters to measure these. One is a square which is a quarter of D (so that E is worth three and a half such squares). The second is a rectangle worth two such squares, so that two would fit into D. Finally, there is a triangle equal to a square cut diagonally in half. If the triangle is used as the unit, D is worth eight units and E is worth seven.

The stages we found were similar to those noted in §9. The following responses belong to Level IIA:

REN (5; 0): *"This one* (A, large square) *is bigger.*—Why?—*Because there are some bits missing on that one* (B).—Can you tell any better by using this (the unit card)?— ... —(The experimenter draws nine small squares inside A.) —*Oh, I see how to do it now. This card goes in there* (gaps in figure B, i.e. outside the area itself).—Well?—*This* (one side of A) *is bigger and that* (one side of B) *is smaller.*—(The experimenter demonstrates how the card fits over the unit squares drawn on A.) What's this I'm doing?—*You've put squares on. I've got to put some in as well* (drawing squares on B, but adding more squares outside the figure, making it into a rectangle 3 × 4). *I see how to measure it: this makes it a square.*—So?—*It's the same size* (which is not true for the extended figure)."

PEL (5; 6, comparing A and B): *"It's a little bit the same size.*—Here you are (unit card). Can you tell by using this?— ... —(The experimenter draws a few unit squares in A and Pel continues them but does not draw any on B.) What about that one (B)?—(He draws squares in the gaps turning the figure into a square.) *It's the same as that one* (A).—Could you put any in there (C)? —*Yes* (drawing squares inside the figure).—Does that help you to tell which is bigger?—*No.*—Well, did you count them?—(He counts them, but fails to understand how the number can be compared with that in A.)—(Figs. D and E.) What about these?—*That one* (E) *is bigger, it's got an extra point."* He has no idea of measuring, even when the 'extra point' is transferred to the triangular gap at the top right.

FAN (6; 10). Comparing A and B: *"This one* (B) *is bigger. It's got this bit extra.*—(Squares drawn in both figures.)—*That's right. Now I know* (B) *is bigger: it's longer.*—Try counting the squares. How many in here (B)?— *Nine.*—And here (A)?—*Nine.*—Well?—*It's the same. No: this one* (B) *is bigger!"* So the perceptual disparity outweighs the numerical identity.

These subjects were taken deliberately because they figured earlier in the experiments on conservation and measurement by superposition. The replies they give in these situations explain the responses made here. One is immediately struck by their manifest unwillingness to compare two figures which differ markedly in appearance. Sooner or later, the subject tries to convert the figures so that they are similar in form. That is natural enough from the intuitive standpoint, and the same type of transformation could lead to rational demonstration if it were brought about by changes in the positions of actual parts. However, instead of confining himself to compensatory transformations, the subject simply puts in additional elements in order to arrive at a rectangle or a square, which is an odd way to go about measuring. Ren is quite satisfied: "I see how to measure it: this makes it a square." Conversely, when the experimenter introduces a legitimate compensation, for instance when the parallelogram at the top left of E is transposed to the top right, the subject is immune to persuasion, and acts as if the experimenter had no right to alter the figure once he has made his judgment perceptually (Pel).

However, the essential lesson to be drawn is that while subdivision into squares can sometimes make perceptual comparison easier for the children, they have no operational insight into its significance because they lack both additive composition and conservation of area. This means that when the experimenter tells them to count the unit sections, they have no idea why they are doing so. Even Fan who discovers that the numbers are equal refuses to deduce that the two areas are virtually congruent because each is composed of nine squares. Clearly, he believes the two questions are quite unconnected,—as indeed they are until the connexion is secured by composition of order and change of position. For unless the position of the unit squares can be altered in thought, each of them is bound to assume a unique value by virtue of its position within the configuration as perceptually given, so that it cannot be compared with other squares in different positions.

At level IIB, the replies made by children are transitional. They stand midway between this initial incomprehension and a real understanding of measurement.

PIR (5; 10). A and B: *"There's more room on that one* (B) *because it's bigger.* —Watch (drawing two unit-squares on A). In which of these could we draw more squares?—*This one* (B).—Try it.—(After several attempts he changes his mind and points to A:) *No, more here.*—Can you tell better by using this (unit) square?—*No.*—(The experimenter finishes the drawings.)—*They're the same size.*—Why?—*Because you've made these squares.*—But what makes them the same size?— . . . —Would counting them help you?—(He counts.) *Yes, because there's nine and nine.*—Supposing they were both made of chocolate, which would you choose?—*This one* (B) *because it's got more chocolate."*

GIS (5; 10) begins the same way: "Do you know why I've drawn these squares?—*No.*—Count them.—*Oh! nine and nine: they're both the same.*— D and E: What about these two?—*They're the same.*—Why?—*This corner*

298

bit goes there (pointing to the triangular projection and the similar incision but forgetting the missing triangle on the right).—Would these little cards help you?—(He applies the square stepwise on E twice and the triangle also twice, while on D he applies the square four times.) *That's four and four: so it's the same.*—But are the square and the triangle the same?—*No.*—Well?—..."

SAN (6; 8). A and B: *"This one* (B) *is bigger because it's got extra bits.*— (The experimenter begins to draw squares on B and San continues, also on B.) *Oh, that's right! There are more squares.*—Are you sure?—*No, wait. I've got to do them on this one.* (A: he does so.—Well?—He counts the squares.) *Nine and nine: they're the same."*

D and E: *That one* (E) *is bigger because it's got an extra bit.*—Try these cards.—(He applies the square and the triangle when measuring E and only the square when measuring D, and then counts the superpositions without regard to the difference between the units:) *Four and four: it's the same.*—But tell me. Is this triangle the same as this square?—*No* (he compares them). *The triangle is half.*—Well, how many squares does that make this one (E)? —(San does not understand.)—Well, divide up all the squares to make sure.— (He draws in the diagonals which gives him two sets of triangles.)—Well?— (He counts the triangles.) *Eight and seven. This one is bigger* (D) *because it's got eight, but that one is still bigger because it's got a bit which juts out."*

ROS (6; 10). A and B: *"That one* (B) *is bigger.*—(The experimenter shows him how to draw the squares and he puts them in, first on A then on B, putting additional squares outside the second figure.) *Yes, that makes it bigger.*— But isn't that because you've put in extra squares?—(He laughs and draws them inside the figure only.) *Nine and nine: it's the same."* The experimenter shows him D and E: *"Can I draw in them?*—Yes of course (offering him the three measuring cards).—(He draws in the squares, inserting the cards and counts the number of superpositions:) *Four and four.*—But are the squares and the triangle the same size?—*No.*—Well?— ..." The rest of his interview is similar to that of San.

Apart from the uncertainty shown by Pir, these subjects all eventually convince themselves that A and B are equal in area because each is composed of nine squares. But the same children all persist in treating squares and triangles as equivalent units when comparing D and E. Thus taken as a whole the level shows an improvement in the composition of subdivision and also in that of positions as given and changes in these positions (cf. the compensation between a projection and an incision in figure E as indicated by Gis), but the two articulations are not fully coordinated, and above all the notion of a metric unit is still unformed.

Levels IIIA and IIIB are respectively characterized by better co-ordination and synthesis of the two operations leading to the construction of a measuring unit. Following are examples of level IIIA:

MAY (6; 3). A and C: *"That one* (C) *looks bigger because it's got lots of bends.*—You find a way of making sure (giving him a pencil together with the unit squares).—(He draws nine squares on A and nine on C.) *It's the*

same because there are nine on both of them.—What about these (D and E)?—
(He takes the three measuring cards and reproduces squares and triangles
on both figures.)—*That's four here and four there. I'm counting the squares.*—
Are these cards all the same?—*No, this one* (rectangle) *is two squares and this
one* (triangle) *is half a square.*—Well? . . ." He counts the squares again until
he is specifically told to divide them all into triangles.

LAM (7; 6) first takes the unit square and moves it stepwise all round the
perimeter of A and B which tells him nothing. Then he does the same inside
figure A and counts the superpositions: "*Nine. I must see if there are nine here
as well.* (B. He draws the squares and counts them.) *Yes, it's the same.*—
What about these (D and E)?—(He applies the squares and triangles correctly
but simply counts the number of elements:) *Four and four. It's the same.*—
But you look at these two (square and triangle). Are they worth the same?—
No (and without further telling he draws eight triangles on D and seven on E).
That one (E) *is smaller.*"

And here are two examples of level IIIB.

MAG (7; 6, advanced) looks at A and B and immediately says: "*They're
the same size. If you folded it here and here* (projecting portions of B) *and put
the pieces here* (top right) *you get the same.*—And using this card?—(He steps
the card outside A marking three intervals on each side and counting twelve;
then, using these marks, he applies the card to successive sections of the
inside, counting nine. He draws the squares the same way for B.) *It's nine and
nine, so it's the same.*—What about these (D and E)?—*I'll try measuring them.*
—(He superposes the two shapes and shows how the projecting triangle would
fit the triangular incision, then points to the cut-off portion at the top right,
saying:) *It's smaller.*—And supposing you measured it?—(He measures in
squares and triangles but counts the steps in triangular units without being
told.) *It's eight and seven.*"

MOG (8; 10) says not a word, but decomposes A and B first into rectangles
then into squares and says: "*The same.*—And these (D and E)?—(He draws
a rectangle on D and divides it first into two squares, then into four triangles.
Then he says of D:) *It's four.* (After which he draws squares and triangles
on E, finally saying:) *That's eight on this one* (D) *and seven on this one* (E)."

Thus the development of conservation and measurement runs exactly
parallel whether the objects are lengths or whether they are areas and
the level at which they are finally grasped is the same for both. Conservation is always the outcome of complementarity between the two groupings: that of additive subdivision and that of ordered positions and
changes of position. The subject who mentally transfers irregular pro-
jections in figure B to places where he sees gaps and arrives back at
square A merely makes use of the reversibility of operations governing
the order of position and the addition of parts. But that reversibility
which is perfected at level IIIA is not enough for true measurement.
Likewise, since he can effect a twofold qualitative composition (adding
parts and ordering positions and changes of position) he can also use a

middle term to verify the composed congruence of any two wholes by virtue of the transitivity of the common term. But, here again, the mastery of common measures, like that of conservation, is achieved at level IIIA, and neither constitutes a system of metric operations.

The latter arises only when there is unit iteration, i.e. at level IIIB. Children at level IIIA all count the squares and triangles as equivalent units until they are reminded of their error. Now to construct a unit of area which will go into a given figure n times implies more than mere complementarity between the operational groupings of which we spoke: it implies the synthesis of the two, so that they are fused into a single operation which governs unit iteration. The argument is identical with that presented earlier when we were dealing with length.

But measuring areas can be undertaken in two different ways, involving different operations. San and Mag begin by applying the unit square to the perimeter which tells them that the larger square measures 3 units along either axis. But it is only when they have measured the area directly that they know that the square is composed of nine unit squares. Now they might easily have deduced this result from their linear measurements since $3 \times 3 = 9$. However children at level IIIB simply measure length in two or three dimensions and area by successive applications of an areal unit inside a larger area. The latter operation involves no more than the logical multiplication of lengths in two dimensions. What children cannot do before stage IV is to make a direct transition from length to area by a process of arithmetical multiplication (or the reverse transition by arithmetical division). This point is examined in more detail in ch. XIII, but before going on to it, we must first complete our study of subdivision.

Chapter Twelve

SUBDIVISION OF AREAS AND
THE CONCEPT OF FRACTIONS [1]

IN the last chapter we studied operations of adding and subtracting areas and saw how the ability to effect an additive composition of the set of parts brought about conservation of the whole. We saw too how that conservation preceded measurement, which involves a synthesis of subdivision and change of position. Here we shall carry that analysis one stage further by studying the beginnings of division in the field of area, using concrete models, like cakes to be divided among a number of children. This should enable us to see once more how part-whole relations are constructed and also how they are quantified as fractions. Here again we will meet the key problems of subdivision and conservation of the whole, but we shall also be dealing with metrical phenomena since the subdivision we require is particularly conducive to such quantification.

§1. *Outline of method and results*

Each of the children (whose ages range from 4 to around 7) is shown a circular slab of modelling clay together with two little dolls. He is told that the clay is a cake and the dolls are going "to eat it all up, but they've each got to have exactly the same amount as the other: how shall we do it?" To help him cut the 'cake' he is given a wooden knife. When he has solved the problem of dividing the cake in two equal halves, we bring on another cake together with a third little doll and this time we tell him to divide it into three, but to be sure that each doll has as much to eat as any other. Many of the younger children have considerable difficulty in dividing the cake into halves and thirds, and so we offer them a selection of circles, rectangles and squares, all made of paper, telling them to cut these into three equal parts, using a pair of scissors. This task can be easier as they are also provided with a pencil and told to mark the paper where they intend to cut it. [2]

Following these experiments, we pass on to division into quarters, fifths, or sixths, still using the same procedure. One possible variation is to ask the child to put matchsticks along the boundaries between

---

[1] Written with the collaboration of Miss M. Muller.

[2] Dividing the cake into three often begins by division into two; and so, with alternate subjects, we deliberately ask for division into three first of all, to counter the effects of perseveration (and sometimes, when bisection is too easy, we omit this part of the problem altogether).

fractions either before or instead of drawing and cutting. Where this method is used, we usually reach an approximately correct result more quickly, as the child is then able to attack the problem of subdivision more directly since all the matches can be adjusted almost simultaneously.

Finally, each time the child has divided a whole, we ask him whether the sum of the parts is equal to the original whole: "Would all these bits taken together (illustrating by a sweep of the hand) make up as much as the whole cake?" or "Supposing we stuck all these bits together again, how many whole cakes would we have?"

We found the following stages. During stage I (i.e. up to around 4 ; 0 or 4 : 6) children still find real difficulty in dividing a cake in two halves; the earliest solution is no more than a general fragmentation, that is, the children do not stop at two; next we find either that each doll is given an approximately equal share, but only a small one, leaving a large part undivided, or else the entire cake is shared out but in unequal portions; in the latter event we occasionally find a child dividing the cake into three because he confuses the number of cuts with the number of parts (cutting the cake twice gives three parts).

Usually the problem of dichotomy is solved at sub-stage IIA, at least when the wholes are small and regular, but when the original shape is large or irregular, children still find residual difficulties, and this is particularly true when they are required to carry out two successive dichotomies, so dividing into quarters. At this level, cutting a cake in three produces one of two solutions: sometimes a child cuts out three little slivers (usually somewhat unequal) leaving a part of the cake undivided; but others carry out two dichotomies and then leave out the last quarter, or they may even divide this into three tiny parts.

Dividing a rectangle into three is easier and dichotomy is less frequent, but otherwise the same kinds of reactions occur at this level. Trisecting a square is a little harder than trisecting a rectangle and a little easier than trisecting a circle. As for division into fifths, we noted the same kinds of responses, but each type of solution appeared somewhat later than it had done for trichotomy. Finally, at level IIA, children do not realize that the sum of all its parts must necessarily equal the original whole.

At sub-stage IIB, dichotomy no longer presents any problem. Trichotomy is also resolved but more gradually. Dividing a whole into fifths is still difficult, as suggested in the last paragraph. But conservation of the whole is realized, albeit intuitively and not operationally.

At level IIIA, trichotomy is governed by an anticipatory schema, so that there is an *a priori* understanding of the relations between the fractions to be realized and the original whole. Consequently there is operational conservation of the whole, that is, its equality with the sum of its parts is understood as a necessary relation.

Finally, at level IIIB, the anticipatory schema extends to division by five and six.

§2. *Stage I: Problems of division into two equal parts*

Up to the age of 4 : 0 or even 4 : 6, children still find systematic difficulties in halving. Either they cannot even divide the whole into two (irrespective of the equality of the two halves) and simply share the cake out in little pieces without using up the whole, or else they divide it all into unequal halves, or even into three parts. If we ignore the reactions of children of two or less, who frequently cannot understand what is meant by sharing until they are shown, and therefore refuse to cut at all, the earliest response is cutting out little pieces without knowing when to stop. When children do this, the business of cutting pieces becomes an end in itself, and this fact is interesting because it shows that there cannot have been any anticipation of the aim, or if there was, it was not the sort of anticipatory schema which enables a child to know in advance that he must cut two pieces, using up the whole cake.

BOC (2; 10) is given a paper 'cake' and asked to show with a pencil how he would "divide it up so that the man and the woman will both have the same amount of cake to eat". He covers the circle with pencilled scrawlings. When asked to cut it, he first takes out a piece: "*This is for the lady,*" and then another: "*This is for the man.*" He goes on the same way for six pieces, but gives an extra piece to the man, forgetting all about the sharing.—When asked to divide a rectangle he behaves the same way: first a little piece: "*This one is for him,*" following by more pieces which seem to be cut for the pleasure of cutting: "What about this?—*That's paper.*"

This undirected or unarrested cutting is succeeded by the cutting out of a small piece for the first eater (and often the child stops there as if there were no preliminary coordination between this section and the next), usually followed by a similar slice for the other, the rest of the whole being neglected altogether:

MIC (3; 0), like Boc, shows how he would cut the cake by making several pencil marks suggesting that he has in mind more than just two pieces. Then, being reminded of what he must do ("You take these scissors and give them half each"), Mic tears out a small piece and gives it to one of the dolls: "Divide it up into two.—(He gives a piece to the other doll and pushes the rest aside.)"

MAD (2; 5) is told to divide a cake in two halves but to show first where he will cut it, using sticks (which avoid the difficulties of drawing). He puts two sticks on the circle in such a way that they cut the circumference like cords. In other words, he indicates two pieces which together make up less than the whole, ignoring the remainder.

DRO (3; 10) behaves in a similar manner when asked to show how he would

304

cut a rectangular cake. He puts down two sticks parallel with each other but both on one side of the rectangle (which would result in two successive small sections accounting for no more than a quarter of the whole). When asked to cut a clay cake he simply cuts two little slices and forgets about the rest. The experimenter therefore produces a sausage made of modelling clay: "Now where must we cut this if we're to share it between us?—*Here and here* (cutting off two successive little pieces).—Who are these for?—*You and me.* —And the rest?—*It's for nobody.*"

FRAN (4; 2) is a little more advanced and his final replies are at level IIA. Nevertheless, he begins by cutting two small pieces out of a clay cake and handing them to the two dolls—this in spite of the fact that the experimenter had warned him: "The mummy says that they can have all the cake." As he stops short after cutting those two small bits, the experimenter remarks: "Now don't cut such tiny bits. You divide up the whole cake." He is given another cake and cuts off first two pieces, then two more, and finally divides the rest in two. With a third cake he again cuts out little pieces and goes on to give as many as fifteen such bits to each doll. But with a rectangle, he immediately divides the 'cake' into two pieces (unequal but leaving no remainder). A square cake is cut into four and each doll is given two quarters. Finally, when given another round cake, he cuts it in two.

Here the two dolls are each given a part of the whole which the child is told to share, which argues a more developed anticipatory schema than when the whole was broken up into bits without any restraint. But in spite of the instructions these children fail to realize that the pieces ought to account for the whole. Hence we cannot yet speak of halves but only of subdivision in general, and that too without much care for the equality of shares.

Before this kind of behaviour gives way to dichotomy we find an interesting transitional response. Children think they need to cut the whole twice to produce two sections, because they imagine that the number of intersections must equal the number of divisions. However, usually the response is of short duration, and is soon replaced by true dichotomy, although this does not mean that the child is immediately able to make the two parts equal. The next examples all illustrate dichotomy except for the first two, in which we show the transitional response which gives three sections instead of two because the subject makes two cuts instead of one.

LEI (2; 10), when sharing the cake between two dolls, indicates two parallel cords which would result in three unequal fractions although these would leave no remainder. Lei refuses to discuss the matter further.

GUET (3; 2) does the same, but says one third is for the lady and the other two thirds are for the man, forgetting all about the need to make their shares equal.

GIL (3; 0), however, after some hesitation, manages to cut a sausage into no more than two parts, although one is bigger than the other.

Top (4; 2), likewise, cuts a cake in two parts, although one is much bigger. When reminded to give each doll the same, he cuts off the larger a piece equal to the smaller and then does not know what to do with the remainder: "What about the rest?—*That's a cake, too.*"

Jea (4; 4) succeeds in cutting the cake in two in a somewhat peculiar way[1]: he separates the central portion from the outside so that he ends up with a ring and a circle. But when asked to cut the cake by a straight line he cuts two slices in two cuts which leaves him unexpectedly with a part left over: "*Shall I cut some more?*"

Pie (4; 6) cuts the cake in two straight off, with a single cut, but his two parts are unequal: "But they should both have the same amount to eat.— *That's right* (cutting the smaller section in two).—What about this (larger) piece?—*That's the table.*—Try again (with a fresh cake).—(Like Jea he cuts out a ring.) *That's for you and this* (interior circle) *is for me.*—Are you satisfied?—*You've got more.*—Well, try it with this (rectangle). You give exactly the same amount to this lady and this gentleman.—*I'll draw a line* (marking the longitudinal median). *That's for the man* (he now marks the transverse median) *and that's for the lady.* (He obviously began by thinking that to obtain two halves he must make two cuts, but he soon realizes that this gives him four pieces instead of two.) *Oh, I know! This one is for the man and this one is for the lady and these two are for the other two men who've gone* (!)— But these two are very sad that they can't eat it all. Now you try sharing this one (another rectangle) just for the man and the woman who are here.— (Once again, he cuts the cake twice, thus producing four sections. He then divides the third quarter, leaving the fourth.)—Well, look. This time we've got four men with one (round) cake. You give them each the same.—(He divides it into four.)"

Mey (4; 8) has no difficulty in cutting the round cake in two (unequal) parts, but when asked to do the same with the rectangle he cuts a narrow slice off either end which leaves him with the central portion: "What about the bit that's left?—*That's nothing what's left.*—Well, all right, you take this (long ribbon). Here are two little girls who want you to give them half each and what's more they don't want tiny bits. What will you do about it?— (He cuts a length off each end and hides the rest in the palm of his hand.)"

Dividing a whole into four first produces the same kind of response as dividing it in two; the subject simply cuts out an indefinite number of little sections but does not know how to stop at four because he cannot anticipate precisely the number of sections required. This solution is followed by cutting out four little pieces and ignoring the remainder. Finally we have an attempt at double dichotomy, but there is a curious paradox to this. Some children (like Pie, mentioned above) arrive at quartering in spite of themselves when their aim is to effect a simple dichotomy, yet others who want to quarter a whole are unable to do so. The reason is the same for both; they lack an operational anticipatory schema. The first two types of response need not detain us here as they

[1] No doubt suggested by the way in which cream cakes are sometimes cut in real life.

are the same for quarters and halves. The last kind of solution is shown in the following examples:

PRE (4; 7), wishing to share the cake among four dolls, begins by cutting it in two. He then cuts one half in four (making three successive cuts instead of two transverse cuts), and the other in five, which leaves him with nine pieces. These he shares out among the four dolls as best he can with an eye to their size. With a second cake he does exactly the same except that both halves are cut into four sections (again without using a double dichotomy) so that he now has eight pieces and deals them out in separate fours.

SOM (4; 8) cuts the cake in five (successive) parts, gives each doll one, and cuts the fifth part in four, again giving one to each doll. If the parts had been equal each doll would have had $\frac{1}{5} + \frac{1}{20} = \frac{1}{4}$, but in fact they are not.

At stage I, even simple dichotomy is failed, while double dichotomy as a form of quartering is still difficult at the beginning of level IIA. However, it is the reasons for lack of insight which are most instructive. To us, dichotomy is the easiest form of subdivision. From the qualitative point of view there can be no more elementary operation than the recognition of two parts in a whole, for such dichotomy underlies even the logical relation of complementary classes within a higher order class: $B = A + A'$. Moreover, to quantify the dichotomy so that A and A' become true halves involves no more than a single equation $A = A'$. We might well expect qualitative dichotomy, if not halving, to be precisely understood even at an intuitive level. But the simplicity of these notions is deceptive, as is often the case, and behind it lies all that complex elaboration which precedes both operations and articulated, but pre-operational, intuitions.

Dichotomy is a simple notion if and only if the two parts are thought of as functions of an invariant whole, one which is not altered either by subdivision or by the separation of its parts. We think of one half (or sub-class) by reference to the other half (or the complementary subclass) and of both as functions of the whole which comprises them whether or not they are sectioned off and separated. Little children, on the other hand, as is quite clear from the illustrations, do nothing of the kind. Instead they cut off one section after another so that the parts are thought of as independent rather than as fractions of the whole. Their attitude is so foreign to our own that we can hardly understand their point of view without considerable effort.

We are apt to be misled by our constant inclination to think of the successive levels of development as monolithic because they are also hierarchical strata of mental functioning in the adult. We therefore think of intelligence as a unique entity which ranges from perception and sensori-motor adaptation to verbal and formal thinking. But the unity of intelligence is only functional while from the structural point of view it entails a progressive series of different and heterogeneous structures. The relation of part to whole (and of half to whole) can be a perceptual experience, as it is when we see a pair of double doors; what we perceive is a rectangular shape together with another which is similar in shape and size. We see each door as a part of the whole, i.e. the closed double doors. The same is true of a baby who pushes one door open. Even a baby who cannot yet speak may realize that by so doing he achieves only a part of his purpose, and may therefore go on to push open the other door. In so doing he behaves in relation to this as the complementary portion of the whole upon which he is acting. But it is a far cry from such perceptual or sensori-motor part-whole relations to operational subdivision. There are systematic difficulties in understanding part-whole relations on the plane of verbal thinking, as we demonstrated long since.[1] When we used phrases like "a part of my bunch of flowers is yellow", or "half of this bunch is yellow", etc., we found that even children of nine or ten thought of the whole bunch as yellow because they thought of the part (or half) as something absolute rather than as being necessarily relative both to the other part (or half) and to the whole. Typical replies were these: "What's a half?—Something you've cut off.—What about the other half?—The other is gone." Obviously the half that is cut off and thought of as a thing apart without reference either to the whole or to the other half echoes the little pieces which are cut off in actual fact by children of two to four, as reported in this section. The wide difference in ages is due to the fact that quite early on children elaborate means of dealing with reality at the level of action, and even at the level of concrete operations, but these solutions still need to be re-worked at the level of verbal thinking by means of formal schemata. The very earliest intuitive representations of part-whole relations are still linked to real actions but even they are greatly different from the corresponding perceptual and sensori-motor relations, for the latter are foreign to any form of representation and can exist only when an object is already sectioned into parts. Again, our earlier investigations showed that the part-whole relation, even as a qualitative notion, was not mastered at this level of concrete operation until the age of seven, for only then did it exhibit reversibility and logical composition.[2] Thus, when shown a large number of brown beads alongside two white beads, all these beads being made of wood, the child under seven could not understand that there were more wooden beads than brown beads for he persisted in forgetting about the collection as a whole when concentrating on the brown beads and therefore came to the conclusion: "There are more brown beads than wooden beads because there are only two white beads." The present enquiry is again concerned with the

[1] *Judgment and Reasoning*, ch. III, para. 7.   [2] *The Child's Conception of Number*, ch. VII.

beginnings of subdivision at the level of representation. Here, as in *The Child's Conception of Number*, subdivision must be reconstructed in thought—but only with reference to a concrete situation. The problem is therefore solved later than perceptual and sensori-motor part-whole relationships but before subdivision is understood in a purely formal sense.

From about 2 to $4\frac{1}{2}$, the most striking feature in the illustrations given above is the absence of any relation between the pieces and the whole. The relation between parts is one of juxtaposition and not of a nesting series. The child first thinks of a 'part' (ignoring its quantitative aspect, that it is a half and therefore equal to the other part) simply as a piece removed from the whole. He does not think of it as a nesting element within a larger whole, from which it may be parted in fact but to which it still relates in thought. The notion of a fraction depends on two fundamental relations: the relation of part to whole (which is intensive and logical), and the relation of part to part, where the sizes of all other parts of a single whole are compared to that of the first part (a relation which is extensive or metric).

There can be no thought of a fraction unless there is a divisible whole, one which is composed of separable elements. This is the first aspect of the notion which is ignored by very young children (i.e. those about 2 years old). They regard the cake or the paper they are given as an inviolable object and refuse altogether to cut it, being put off by its continuous and closed shape (or *gestalt*). At $2\frac{1}{2}$ or 3, these inhibitions are overcome and children are quite prepared to share and to cut out, but now the act of cutting makes the object lose its character of wholeness (cf. C.C.S., ch. V, for the opposition of continuity to subdivision).

The next characteristic of a fraction is that it implies a determinate number of parts. Qualitatively we might say that sharing presupposes that the parts must correspond with the recipients. The youngest subjects, if they cut the whole at all, forget about this correspondence. Boc, for instance, simply breaks the paper up into little bits, and although he gives the first bit to one doll and the second to the other, the number of pieces far exceeds the number of fractions required (two halves) although they do not exhaust the whole. He goes on to share out the rectangle by giving one piece to the first doll, leaving the second to find his own salvation; yet he goes on cutting the paper without sharing the pieces and without even counting them when they have been cut.

The third characteristic of a determinate fraction is that subdivision is exhaustive, i.e. there is no remainder. Children who respect the first and second characteristics, giving the right number of pieces to the dolls, begin by cutting out two small sections for the two dolls, leaving the rest of the cake or paper untouched. The remainder is not thought of as a third fraction; it is either forgotten, or pushed to one side, or it is given another name: "That's paper", "That's the table", etc.; one subject even resorts to sleight of hand (Mey who hides it on his knees). What is interesting is that these children refuse to share out the remainder, apparently satisfied that when they have made up the two parts they were asked for, anything left over is neither part nor whole and has nothing to do with the two real parts: these alone are real because these alone go to make up their idea of a fraction.

In the fourth place, there is a fixed relationship between the number of parts into which a continuous whole is to be divided and the number of intersections. A single cut will suffice to split a line in two halves, or if the existing extremities of the line are taken as cuts too, three cuts are needed to mark off the two sections. But the little children who cut off small sections and ignore the unused portion of the whole (i.e. the third condition mentioned in the last paragraph) think of one cut in conjunction with one part. At the same time, because children at this level fail to discriminate Euclidean shapes, being concerned only with topological relations'(C.C.S., chs. I and II), they naturally look on the perimeter of a closed shape as a single line, so that, to them, the number of areas and the number of boundary lines correspond exactly. A child at this level, therefore, if he is aware of the need to use up the original whole in its entirety when constructing fractional parts, begins by thinking that the two halves require two cuts. Thus both Lei and Guet make two cuts in order to obtain one half for each of the two dolls, which gives them the unexpected total of three parts (yet if they had wanted to divide the cake into three, they could not have done so).[1]

Fifth, the concept of an arithmetical fraction implies over and above purely qualitative subdivision, that all of these parts are equal. If there is any equalization of parts during the actual sharing in the above illustrations, it is very approximate, and if we go on to insist that each dolly should have the same, we usually find that in making the portions equal after the original sharing children again leave undistributed remainders.

Sixth, when subdivision is operational and gives rise to true fractions, by which we imply a nesting system and not just a lot of juxtaposed pieces, the fractions themselves take on a dual character. They are parts of the original whole and they are also wholes in their own right, and as such they too can be subdivided further. The most advanced cases at this stage show some awareness of this, but the others ignore the point entirely. The youngest children who break off one piece after

---

[1] The non-correspondence between the number of parts and the number of intersections recalls the earlier problem of hurdles and mats (*The Child's Conception of Number*, ch. VI, para. 3): given a series of hurdles for athletes to jump over, with mats in between the hurdles and at both ends of the tracks, so that for n hurdles there will be $n + 1$ mats, children were asked to find the right number of mats for x hurdles, or vice versa. The problem was solved only at about the age of 7.

another show that they have no understanding of nesting series and know only juxtaposition, while others who ignore the unused remainder provide a clear illustration that the sharing out of a remainder into smaller parts involves an added difficulty.

In the seventh place, since fractions of an area relate to the whole from which they are drawn, that whole remains invariant; in other words, the sum of fractions equals the original whole. Conservation of a whole is an essential condition of operational subdivision, and applies with equal force to qualitative and quantitative subdivision. Later (§6) we shall find that children at the earlier stages do not appreciate this necessary conservation.

We should add that from the psychological point of view, the subject cannot comply with these seven conditions unless they form part of a general structure. Whether the latter is perfected and therefore operational or whether it exists only in outline in the form of a more or less articulated intuition, it must give rise to an anticipatory schema which directs the sharing throughout the actual behaviour. In the above examples, the reader must surely be struck by the fact that our youngest subjects cannot mentally anticipate even qualitative dichotomy, let alone equal division by two. They act as if they have no preliminary plan to guide their behaviour, which is why the seven conditions remain separate for them. Later on, subdividing a whole into two equal halves becomes a simple matter, but now children proceed by trial-and-error and (if they remember what they are about) they hit against a succession of unexpected difficulties which correspond with the seven characteristics of fractions. When the subject tries to cut the whole in two parts without remainder, his anticipation is more adequate and we should be justified in postulating an intuitive anticipatory schema. For although the schema is incomplete it still signifies that at least the first five characteristics of fractions are coordinated to a degree, even if the coordination is confined to sharing in two halves.

The accomplishment of sharing out two equal halves is usually achieved at the beginning of sub-stage II, between the ages of 4 and 4½. However, although the schema is worked out at this age when objects are small and their shape is simple (circles, squares or rectangles), any of the following three complications renders the schema ineffective until well into stage II (or even, in some subjects, until stage III):

Increasing the size of the original whole postpones sharing in equal halves. This is clear from the work of A. Rey who carried out the following experiment with some 50 children. The subject was given a slip of paper 18 cm. long × 1 cm. wide and asked to divide it into "two equal pieces", or "two strips the same length". On the table in front of him were a ruler, a pencil and string. If his first attempt was unsuccessful in that the strips were unequal, the test was repeated with a fresh strip of paper and this went on until he had given the best solution he could. Rey found the same four types of response as we did: (1) The strip is cut into several lengths, i.e. more than three, suggesting that the action of splitting was pursued for its own sake to the neglect of halving. Of the 48 subjects this response was made by 3 aged between 4; 6 and 5; 6, one between 5; 6 and 6; and one backward child between 7; 6 and 8; 6. (2) Two pieces are taken from the whole and the remainder is ignored or eliminated. This solution was given by 5 subjects between 4; 6 and 5; 6 and two between 5; 6 and 6; 6. (3) The original strip is split into two unequal lengths without remainder. This solution was given by 3 at age 4; 6 to 5; 6, 4 at 5; 6 to 6; 6 and 2 at 6; 6 to 7; 6. (4) Two equal halves (6 under 5; 6 and 21 over 5; 6 but under 8; 6).

Altering the shape of the whole can also postpone the solution. Thus if rectilinear strips, circles and oblongs are replaced by complex shapes (undulating lines, zigzags, triangles, etc.) the subject cannot determine the mid-point or the median by a simple intuitive anticipatory schema and must therefore use deductions and measurements. Under these circumstances the problem may not be solved before stage III (one gifted child of 6; 2 said of an undulating line: "Well, if we stretched it it would go that far, so the half is there", revealing intuitive articulation not far short of the operational level).

Finally, the correct solution is delayed when the subject is asked to divide a whole into quarters, implying two successive dichotomies. Thus Pre and Som are able to halve but cannot quarter. The former starts by halving and then cuts one half in four and the other in five, while the latter starts by cutting the whole in five and goes on to cut the last fifth in four. Thus those very same difficulties which have been overcome in problems of halving re-appear when the halves need to be halved in turn. The problem becomes even more complex when the object to be quartered is large or when its shape is difficult. The reasons for delay are now twofold which explains why in Rey's experiment accurate quartering was not realized until 6; 6 – 7; 6, i.e. stage III.

§3. Sub-stage IIA: Problems of trichotomy

For regular and small scale areas, halving appears at the beginning of sub-stage IIA (4; 0 – 4; 6). But tri-secting such an area involves added complications and these are well worth examining, since the solutions to which they give rise are not always the same as those we saw earlier. Only the first type recalls the replies of §2, although it is by no means identical with them: it consists in deducting small portions from the whole, but there is a difference in that the remainder is usually again divided into three. The other solution draws on the child's success in accurate halving; he tries to achieve trichotomy by way of one or more

312

dichotomies which leaves him with an extra quarter, and this he may apportion as best he can.

Following are examples of the first type of solution (which is probably less advanced than trichotomy via dichotomy):

Hoc (4; 2) stands midway between stages I and IIA. When asked to halve, he begins by cutting out two small portions and giving them to the two dolls, forgetting about the remainder. Told to give out "the whole cake" with a fresh whole, he again cuts out two small portions but now he goes on to divide the remainder into two large portions.—The experimenter goes on to the problem of trichotomy, using a fresh 'cake' and three dolls: he cuts a small triangular slice for each doll and looks at what is left, which is much more than what has been taken. He cuts off three more triangular slices, but these are even smaller so that he is still left with more than half the cake, now in a mangled condition; but he refuses to touch it.

Gis (5; 6) is more advanced in that he eventually uses up the whole. To begin with he divides the cake into unequal slices of which three are large and four are small. After giving each doll one of the large pieces he comments: "*There, now I've shared it out.*—What about the rest?—(He deals three of the four little slices to the three dolls A, B and C and the fourth to B.)—Have they all had the same?—*No.*—Well, you should be fair.—(He takes back the extra portion from B and cuts it in two giving one portion to A and the other back to B. He notes that there is still some unevenness, and therefore takes the smaller slice which he gave to C and cuts it in two, then hands both pieces back to C. As a result, each doll now has one large piece and two small pieces although there are appreciable differences between them.)—Is that right now?—*Yes, they've all got the same.*"

Geo (6; 1) is not far removed from level IIB. He starts by cutting three small slices from the cake and sharing them among the three dolls, ignoring the remainder. "But they've got to eat it all.—(He deals out three more slices followed by another three, but even then is left with a tenth piece.)—What about that bit?—*That's for the mummy.*—No, she's had hers. What are we going to do about it?—*I don't know.*" The experiment is repeated with a fresh cake but this time he is told to be sure that the dolls "eat it all up, they must all have the same and all in one bit.—(Geo cuts the cake into four successive slices, without first cutting it in half, his lack of success being due only to the fact that he failed to estimate a third part correctly.)—Is that right?—*No, it's too much. They've got to have that* (fourth) *piece tomorrow.*—No they don't. They want it all now.—(He divides the last quarter into three and shares it out.)—Have another go with this new cake.—(Once more he cuts four slices and divides the last into three.)—Now try it with this cake.—(This time he succeeds in cutting the cake into three parts but the first part is about half the cake while the other two are only a quarter each.)" The experimenter now hands him a sheet of paper and lets him draw the cutting lines with a pencil. His first attempt gives him four pieces and the next attempt as many as seven (because he made his pieces smaller instead of larger to reach three instead of four!). In the end he produces three sections but these are worth about $\frac{9}{20}$, $\frac{7}{20}$ and $\frac{4}{20}$: "*I made the first bit too big: otherwise I'd have four pieces.*"

In other words what he did was to use up two quarters to make his first part to avoid producing four sections!

These replies recall those cited in §2 where children tried to construct two parts by cutting small slices two at a time. However, some of the seven characteristics of fractions are more faithfully adhered to. This applies in particular to the topological attributes of trisection, for there are no longer any difficulties over the first (breaking up a continuous whole) or over the fourth (lack of correspondence between the number of cuts and the number of parts). The second condition also is fulfilled, remembering how many parts are required, although there may be a breakdown in its execution. But the equalization of parts (fifth attribute) is less successful because it is harder to reconcile with the third (using up the original whole) in the case of trisection. Finally, the nesting of parts within the whole and the conservation of the latter (attributes six and seven) are still neglected.

In general, trichotomy is more difficult than simple dichotomy (halving) and even twofold dichotomy (quartering), so that the anticipatory schemata to which it gives rise are less satisfactory. We can see why this is by analysing the replies of children who try to reduce trichotomy to dichotomy, as if one could obtain thirds by continued bisection (!):

PIE (4; 8) is asked to share a cake in equal portions for the three dolls A, B and C. He first halves it and gives one half to A, then he halves the remainder and gives one quarter each to B and C: "Are they all happy about this?—*This one's got half* (A) *and these two have got two halves* (halves of a half!) *That's two halves and one half.*—But will they all be eating the same? —*This one's got most.*—Well, try to be fair: give them all the same!— (Pie halves another cake, then quarters it and gives one quarter to each of the three dolls:) *There you are. There's one bit left over.*—But these children are greedy. They want to eat it all up. What shall we do about the bit that's left over?—*That's for the mummy.*—That's very sweet of you but the mummy doesn't want any.—*It's for daddy.*—He's away.—*It's for aunty.*—She isn't there.—*Well, then there's nothing we can do.*" The experimenter hands Pie a fresh cake and again tells him that it must all be eaten by the three dolls, and they must all have the same: "*I'll take the knife.*—Good. How many pieces will you want?—*Three.*" He divides the cake into four by first cutting it in two vertical halves, and then slicing it horizontally below the diagonal but perpendicular to the first cut. This gives him two large pieces and two smaller. Pie gives one small piece each to A and B, and a large piece to C leaving the other larger piece to one side. "How many is that?—*Three, but there's one missing* (i.e. one too many). *There should be only three.*" Given a fresh cake, he does exactly the same again and then says: "*There's still one missing!*" Pie is then given a round piece of paper with a pencil and a pair of scissors. He draws the sections and cuts them out exactly as before, adding: "*There's one missing just the same!*" The experimenter passes on to the trichotomy of squares and rectangles, to be reported below. He finally succeeds in trisecting a rectangle by uint of much suggestion and a little luck, and is then given another circle with the words: "That's excellent. You see you've done it. Now try doing the same with the round one.—(He cuts the circle in two halves and halves one of these, sharing the three unequal parts among A, B and C as he counts:) *One, two, three.*—Is that right?—*This one* (A = ½) *is too big but I don't want to cut it, else I'll have a bit over.*—I don't want any left. You think about it." Pie is given another circle: he cuts it in two halves and hides one half in his pocket, then he takes it out again and cuts both halves in two. He gives one quarter each to A, B and C and hides the fourth in his pocket: "Have you managed it?—*Yes.*"

JEN (4; 2) is a little more advanced in that he uses the remainder instead of looking on it as irreducible. He cuts the cake in two and hands one half to A, then divides the other half in two giving one quarter each to B and C. "Have they all got the same?—*No, this one* (A) *has more.*—What can you do to make sure they all have the same (with a new cake)?—(He cuts this into halves and then into quarters and deals three of these to A, B and C leaving the last to one side.)—What about this one? What are you going to do about it?—*I don't know . . . I have to cut it!* (and he cuts it into two giving two additional eighths to A and B which leaves C short by ⅛).—Are they all happy about that?—*Yes.*—What about this poor doll (C)?—(Jen now takes C's own quarter and cuts it in two so that C now has two eighths)." And now Jen is satisfied because each doll has two bits although they are unequal (¼ + ⅛ for A and B and ⅛ + ⅛ for C).

ROG (4; 11) proceeds very gradually towards equalization of his thirds. To begin with, he cuts the cake in two halves, one of which is halved again. Doll A is given a half while dolls B and C receive only a quarter: "Is that right now?—*No, that one is bigger* (A's share, which he now cuts into quarters giving one quarter to A again and dividing the other into eighths for B and C). —Which one has more now?—*Those two* (B and C who each have ¼ + ⅛).— Well, make it right.—*I'll do it this way* (halving the quarters and eighths and giving the three dolls what looks like the same number of pieces arrived at by successive dichotomy)." After asking a few questions about the conservation of the whole (see below, §6), the experimenter gives him another whole cake: Rog cuts it in two and gives half each to A and B with nothing for C; then he takes these halves back and cuts them into quarters of which three are shared among the dolls. Of the fourth quarter he says *"There's a bit left over.*— But there shouldn't be any left over.—(He quarters the last quarter and gives A and B $\frac{1}{16}$ each while C is given $\frac{2}{16}$ so that A and B now have ¼ + $\frac{1}{16}$ while C has ¼ + $\frac{2}{16}$).—Have they all got the same?—*Yes.*"

SCHO (5; 6) finds the best answer of any at this level among those who proceed by dichotomy. First, he halves the cake and gives one half to A, then he halves the other half and gives a quarter each to B and C. But he takes back the half he gave to A and halves that too. One quarter is now returned to A while the other is put aside. Finally he picks up the last quarter and cuts it in three straight off, sharing the three (unequal) pieces among the three dolls: "Jolly good! You've got it right now. There you are, take this new cake and see if you can get it right first time.—(But Scho still starts off by cutting it in two, exactly as he did before and immediate trichotomy continues to elude him.)''

These children are more advanced than those who break off one slice after another because they try from the start to discover a solution which will use up the entire whole. As a result their portions are unequal, because they cannot achieve trichotomy directly. Instead they proceed by successive dichotomy, but they do so only because they want to use up the whole cake from the start. To divide a quantity in three is in fact more difficult than dividing it in two because in order to use up the whole in the first subdivision one must anticipate the relation between the first part and its complementary. This relation is easy enough for halving because the first part and its complementary are equal, but for trichotomy it is more difficult because the first part needs to be only half its complementary. Therefore those children who try to achieve trichotomy while using up the whole take the line of least resistance and anticipate a first part equal to its complementary, repeating the process when they divide the second half. It should be added that dichotomy is the natural form of logical subdivision (i.e. irrespective of the equality of two complementary classes) so that children automatically tend to use it whenever they want to subdivide a whole, even though they then find themselves faced with an inequality among their three portions.

To sum up, these children we have instanced either begin by cutting three equal shares without anticipating the need to use up the whole (and then arrive at unequal shares as the fragmentation is continued), or alternatively they anticipate the need to use all the cake, in which case they use the method of dichotomy because they cannot anticipate equal thirds (implying a relation of 1 to 2 between the first part and its complementary). We add a number of examples in which children oscillate between the two procedures.

ANT (4; 5) begins by cutting the cake in two and halving the second half so that A and C each have a quarter while B has half, which satisfies him. But the experimenter hands him another cake and asks him to share it out 'fairly'. Ant first cuts it into four parallel strips which are approximately equal, then cuts the two outside strips into eighths. A is given two of these eighths, B one quarter, and C one quarter and the last two eighths as well: "Is that fair now?—Yes . . . no (he cuts B's quarter into four sixteenths which gives B four pieces like C, A still has two, and even now the shares are grossly unequal).—Try it with a new cake, but don't cut your pieces too small. —(He cuts three segments by cutting along three cords of the circular cake and distributes these, ignoring the remainder.)—All right, take another whole cake and cut it so that there's nothing left over.—(Ant cuts this cake in half and then divides one half into three unequal slices, the other into five, which gives him eight portions. These are shared out among the three dolls in arbitrary fashion.)''

316

WEB (5; 2) begins by dividing his cake in two and halving one of the halves. C is given half while A and B each have a quarter: "Is that fair?—*No, one of them has the whole piece* (he cuts C's half into quarters and leaves him a quarter, whereupon he points to the remaining quarter and says:) *We've got to eat this up, or else we have to bring along another doll.*—There aren't any more. Try again with this cake.—(He quarters by successive dichotomy and again gives A and B one quarter while C is given two.)—Try and make a drawing on this round bit of paper to show me how you'd cut it up for three dolls.—(He does the same again.)—Now try it with this one.—(This time he cuts off three small slices and shares them among the three dolls, whereupon he says of the irregularly shaped remainder:) *That piece stays.*—But we mustn't leave any over. Try again with this one.—(He cuts it in four and gives the three dolls one quarter each. Then he cuts the last quarter in three and gives each doll another piece.)"

LEO (5; 7) begins as Web ended, by first quartering then trisecting the fourth quarter. The experiment is repeated with another cake to see whether the trisection was planned or merely accidental. But this time Leo first cuts three small slices, leaving a large remainder, then cuts three more slices leaving a smaller remainder, and finally cuts this in half for dolls A and B. Finding that A and B now have three pieces each while C has only two, he simply cuts one of C's pieces in half. The solution is not improved on with a third cake. Leo reverts to the method of twofold dichotomy but ignores the fourth quarter.

It is true that these subjects find various ways of alternating the method of dichotomy with that of successive slicing but they show no more insight than either of the two previous groups because they are unable to combine the two requirements in a single act of anticipation. These, it will be recalled, were (1) the parts must be equal and (2) their number must correspond to the recipients (and there must be no remainder).

Before concluding this section we must see how children at level IIA set about trisecting a rectangle and a square. For it might otherwise be thought that the trisection of a circular cake is rather a special case. While halving a circle is accomplished by means of one straight line cut and corresponds to an elementary type of symmetry, its trisection requires three straight lines radiating from a common centre. Trisecting a rectangle or a square is easier because the section follows parallel lines and the final outcome is symmetrical about the median section. It should therefore be interesting to see whether the solutions given for a circle are still given when the cake is square or rectangular.

We deliberately avoided beginning with rectangular shapes because their simplicity can easily be misleading inasmuch as children more easily hit upon the correct solution by accident. This is almost bound to happen when a subject cuts a first portion which is a third but only by chance (he may have intended a qualitative dichotomy or simply to cut a slice without worrying about its size). When he now goes on to halve the remainder, it looks as if he anticipated exact trisection from the start.

The first examples are of successive fragmentation:

BoG (4; 5) cuts the rectangle into parallel strips. He ends with eight such strips and deals these to the three dolls which leaves A with three slices while B and C have only two. At his second attempt he ends with seven pieces, and the third yields four (cut successively). This time he simply puts the fourth quarter aside. When told to use up the whole, he simply reverts to smaller slices.

MAR (5; 11) divides the rectangle into five: "How many parts have you made?—(He counts the knife cuts like children at stage I.) *Four*.—Try again (with a fresh rectangle).—He cuts three small strips and gives one to each of the dolls, leaving the remainder.—Try again (third rectangle) and this time don't leave any over." He ends with eight slices but he thinks he has only seven because he counts the cuts. Another rectangle is cut into seven and the three dolls are each given two pieces while the seventh is ignored. The square is dealt with in a similar manner.

Later, he is given a piece of modelling clay shaped like a sausage and asked to divide it into three. Mar first cuts off three small pieces which he hands round, and then cuts seven more pieces, distributing them as he goes along. On his second attempt, he cuts the sausage into four and deals out three, ignoring the last quarter. For a third sausage he cuts three equal slices straight off but this successful trisection is due to chance, since it is not repeated with yet another sausage, for this last is again cut into four.

The next set of examples illustrate the method of successive dichotomies:

RoG (4; 11) quarters the rectangle (by twofold dichotomy) and shares out three of the quarters. The fourth quarter leaves him guessing: "*There's still some left*.—Is that right?—*No, it's wrong*." But he is no more successful at his next attempt. When he is given the square, he still cuts it into four but he pushes the fourth quarter to one side: "*It works* (counting three, but the experimenter replaces the last quarter). *Oh, no! It was wrong. It doesn't work*."

GIS (5; 6) is an interesting case of a subject who succeeds with the sausage but not with the rectangle. The latter is first divided into two halves of which one is given to A while the other is reserved intact for B and C. But the sausage is cut into successive thirds. A second rectangle is again cut into two, although this time the second half is divided into two for B and C. The same response is made to the square.

AM (6; 0) is limited to quartering both the sausage and the rectangle, and each time he simply finds that there is one piece too many. With a second rectangle he declares that he intends to divide it into three. But all he does is to halve it and then cut one half into two. He fails to break himself from this schema. A square is also quartered in the same way and he gives out the first three quarters, but then he has the idea of dividing the last quarter into three and does this successfully.

Finally, here are a number of mixed solutions (figuring both methods together):

JAN (4; 8) cuts his rectangle into four following the two perpendicular bisectors and puts away the fourth quarter. His second attempt is identical, but his third is different for he now cuts three narrow slices ignoring the remainder. He continues to oscillate between the two methods up to the moment when with every intention of halving he happens to cut one slice which is less than half. He cuts the other into two and so, quite by chance, he ends with almost equal thirds! He himself is so surprised that he counts these over several times: *"One, two, three"* as he gives them to the three dolls. But he cannot repeat his exploit at his next attempt.

OL (5; 8) cuts three corners off a square and hands them round to the dolls, leaving more than half the total area unused. He divides a second square into four and shares the first three quarters. He begins to cut pieces off the last quarter, but because he wants to give the same number of pieces to each doll he is left with a tiny remainder: *"There's still too much. This bit is left just the same."*

GEO (6; 0) prepares to quarter the square following the two axes, but just as he is about to cut the second half into two, having already halved it, he stops and says: *"No, I'd have four again"* (as with the rectangle). He then takes another square and cuts off three triangular sections at three corners, leaving the remainder.

It is obvious that trisecting a rectangle is a little easier than trisecting a circle; trisecting a square, which is harder, is still easier than the circle, while the sausage is the easiest of all (because it is like an elongated rectangle). Nevertheless the solutions we saw are the same for all the models. Even when the sections to be made are parallel instead of radiating from a common centre (as they would if a circular cake were cut in triangular slices), the fact remains that dichotomy affords a simpler behavioural schema because it involves only two complementary parts. Trisection implies a more complex anticipatory schema because the complementary to the first third must be re-divided while this first portion itself must not, and this is difficult if the various conditions listed earlier are respected (equality of parts, dividing without remainder, etc.).

§4. Sub-stage IIB and Stage III. Successful trisection, gradual at Level IIB, immediate at Stage III

Division into three equal parts is successfully performed at about the age of 6 or 7, when success is not preceded by trial-and-error and is not a matter of luck but is assured by operational anticipation. Thus, whereas halving is mastered at stage II and involves only intuitive anticipation, trisection is completed at the beginning of the level of concrete operations and not before. However, progress in this

319

performance is not sudden, and between the level IIA responses of §3 and those of stage III, we find behaviour which is intermediate in that the problem is solved but only by gradual stages. In general, this level, IIB, occurs between 6 and 7 years of age, but some brighter children reach it as early as 4 or 5. Following are a few examples in which the model is circular.

Rob (4; 3) starts by cutting the cake in two halves by means of a horizontal section with the lower half a little smaller than the upper. He then makes an oblique cut across the upper portion so that he finishes with three pieces. These are unequal but the differences are not gross (they range from $> \frac{1}{4}$ to $< \frac{1}{2}$) and there is no remainder. A second cake is sectioned off following two horizontal lines. Again the three parts are very roughly similar in size. But the paper circle is cut three times so that there are four portions in all, the last of which is subdivided into little strips with an unused remainder. A second paper circle is trisected more successfully by means of two vertical cuts. Thus, in spite of his tender age, Rob's responses are midway between level IIA and the correct solution.

Col (5; 6) begins by dividing the cake into four (twofold dichotomy) and then cutting the last quarter into three. A second cake is simply halved, whereupon each half is again subdivided into three parts for the three dolls. But a third cake is immediately sectioned off into three almost equal parts and the success is repeated with a paper circle, after a momentary confusion between the number of cuts (three) and the number of parts (four).

Hu (5; 8) begins by cutting one half and two quarters but a second cake is cut into three approximately equal vertical sections. The paper circle is first cut in four owing to confusion between the number of portions and the number of cuts.

Sim (5; 9) begins with double dichotomy but finishes with trisection and repeats these two stages for the paper circle.

Max (6; 0) begins with one half and two quarters but he, too, goes on to trisection with the parts about equal.

Ses (6; 2) starts off by cutting several series of small pieces and distributing these as he goes along. For the next cake he cuts off three large slices and leaves the remainder. Finally, he succeeds in cutting a third cake into three almost equal parts.

Laur (6; 2) first quarters a cake by twofold dichotomy, ignoring the fourth quarter. But at his second attempt, he makes his first cut below the horizontal diameter and then divides the upper portion in two, so that in the end his three parts are about equal. The process is repeated for a third cake. But a fourth cake is divided into three almost equal triangular slices with cuts radiating from the centre, and this method is again followed with the paper circle.

Next we present a number of examples of attempts at trisecting the rectangle and the square at the same level. It may be noted that the greater ease of this task as compared with the trisection of a circle is most apparent at level IIB. While it's true that some children solve the problem only at their second or third attempt, as they did that of the circle, others trisect the rectangle or the square immediately:

ROB (4; 3) is asked to trisect a square. (His response to the circle appears just above.) He removes a strip from one side and then halves the remainder, leaving himself with three pieces all about the same size although different in shape.

BOL (5; 6) divides the first square into four rectangles and cuts the fourth into three. At his next attempt he cuts three equal rectangular sections.

SCHO (5; 6) begins by cutting a rectangle into five and distributing three of these parts, leaving two. His next attempt produces six parts and the dolls are now given two each. The third attempt yields four parts and the fourth is further subdivided into three. Finally, he realizes the trisection immediately.

WEB (5; 8) cuts his first rectangle into four and his second into thirds.

COL (5; 9) is slightly more advanced: he cuts a rectangle into three parts at his first attempt although the parts are unequal. On his second attempt the parts are made equal, and a square is divided immediately into three equal rectangles.

HU (5; 8) took a long while before he succeeded in trisecting a circular cake but he trisects the rectangle at his first attempt.

MON (6; 4) fails completely to trisect the circle but cuts the rectangle into thirds straight off.

GID (6; 5), whose case is identical, says of the rectangle: "*This is easier because it's long. The others* (circles) *are too wide.*"

For the most part, these children first pass through a preliminary trial-and-error phase reminiscent of those at level IIA, before they finally achieve adequate trisection. Most of them begin by the method of dichotomy which is a trifle more advanced than fragmentation since it implies from the start that there should be no remainder. They then adapt their schema until it conforms approximately to the required trisection. But others begin by cutting three slices off the whole and then gradually increase their size until they eventually achieve trisection directly. While the portions these children construct are not perfect thirds, they are aware from the start that they should be equal and they know that they must leave no remainder.

As for the difference between the problem of trisecting a circle which is never solved at level IIB without preliminary trial-and-error, and that of the square or rectangle which are trisected immediately by the more advanced children at the same level, we need only refer to the comment made by Gid: the 'longer' the rectangle, the easier it is to anticipate trisection in successive thirds. Nevertheless, the evolutionary process is identical for the square and the rectangle even though it may be accelerated. We must therefore rule out the hypothesis that the difficulties of trisection are particular to any one shape of the whole to be divided. Trisection is always more difficult to anticipate than

321

dichotomy if the seven characteristics of fractions are adhered to (§2) for the simple reason that it is further removed from qualitative dichotomy implying only two complementary parts. That this view of the matter must be correct is amply demonstrated by the systematic attempts of so many subjects to reach trisection by way of successive dichotomies, having overcome the level of arbitrary fragmentation.

One final remark may be added concerning the difference between trisection of a circle and trisection of a square or rectangle. It is that cases of transfer of correct solutions from the latter to the former were found to be very rare. On the other hand transfer from the rectangle to the square and vice versa, depending on which figure was presented first, is the rule rather than the exception. Evidently transfer is limited by the perceptual configuration of the object, and this in itself proves that even when trisection of a rectangle is immediate it is still not operational because it is not generalized to all cases, especially to a circle.

Lastly, by way of comparison, we present three typical examples of trisecting a circle at stage III (level IIIA). These subjects are the youngest from whom we obtained the direct solution which is the distinctive feature of this level:

ROS (6; 8) immediately achieves trisection into about equal parts although these are parallel.

CAR (6; 8) cuts both the cake and the paper immediately into three triangular sections with straight-line radial incisions.

VERT (7; 6) begins by cutting the circular cake into three horizontal strips. When the experimenter asks him whether he could cut his pieces differently, he starts from the centre making as if to cut four slices. But he corrects himself at once and ends with three equal slices.

It is remarkable that although children continually see cakes being sliced (and there would be nothing unusual about cutting a cake into three slices), it is only at level IIIA that they achieve what might seem the easy feat of the last two subjects. Here as elsewhere, example is of no use unless it is accompanied by genuine initiative on the part of the child, and actions or operations which look simple enough nearly always conceal a preliminary process of elaboration which is highly complex.

§5. *Division into five or six equal parts* (*Level IIIB*)

To complete the foregoing studies we may well ask whether the achievement of trisection, implying, as it does, an operational anticipation of the necessary equality, brings with it an equal facility at sharing into fifths or, more especially, into sixths, which is essentially nothing more than trisection and dichotomy combined. Our account will be brief, and we may state at once that both division into five and division

322

into six are rather difficult and the correct solution is not achieved until level IIIB. Nevertheless the stages leading up to that solution are identical with those which precede trisection.

To begin with, here are a number of examples of stage II, when simple fragmentation is dominant:

CHRI (5; 6) is told to put matches on the cake first of all, to show how he will cut it into six equal parts: he places his matches so that they start from the circumference but do not meet at the centre. Then he cuts a series of little pieces following the lines previously occupied by his matches (having marked them with a pencil). He does the same three times in succession with three separate cakes, each time leaving an unused portion: "*I'll give the rest to the cat.*"

SIM (5; 9), it will be recalled, was successful in the long run when the problem was of trisection only (§4). In division by five he fails: what he does is to cut a series of small slices and deal them out as he goes along, leaving an unused remainder. When given another cake and told to finish it all, he cuts it into seven successive slices and distributes the first five only. Later, he finishes with six parts, but he never succeeds in dividing into five.

MAX (6; 0) also succeeded in trisection after a preliminary failure (§4) and he, too, fails to divide into fifths; he cuts a series of little pieces (eight in all) and only tries to make them correspond with the dolls after they have been cut: "*Three too many!*" He divides the next cake into four (by double dichotomy), then draws an oblique line bisecting the first and third quarters (which gives him six pieces), and finally bisects the fourth quarter, making a total of seven pieces. He divides the next circle into six. A third cake is first narrowed by drawing a smaller concentric circle, no doubt in the belief that reducing the size of the circle will reduce the number of parts. Max then divides the inner ring into six, ignoring the outer ring. The last cake he cuts into parallel and unequal strips, and even then he finishes with seven!

ERN (6; 6) is asked to divide the cake into six. First he draws six small circles on the paper circle opposite the six dolls, leaving more than half the paper unused. Even the number of little circles fails to correspond with the number of dolls, for he draws two more than are wanted. But he goes on to an interesting piece of behaviour: he draws smaller circles inside some of his little circles for no apparent reason and then divides the space between these two concentric circles into six tiny portions. Because the ring is so small, he has no difficulty in doing this. The experimenter then tells him to divide the whole cake into six, using matches to indicate where it will be cut: this time he uses the method of dichotomy, finishing with two quarters and four eighths, i.e. six parts but unequal. When told to make his portions equal, he cuts another cake into two parts amounting to little less than half each, and four more amounting to a little more than a quarter between them! He does not progress beyond this solution. Following this, he is told to divide a cake into three: his first attempt is one half and two quarters but he achieves the correct solution by stages (level IIB). However, he fails to draw any relevant conclusions for dividing into six!

THO (6; 10) cuts out a series of little triangles with their base lines touching.

He does this all round the cake so that the final outcome is like a star, with the centre of the circle still intact. However, he finishes with seven little slices instead of six. His later efforts are all similar except for the number of slices, which is increased, first to eight, then to nine, whereas only six were intended. RHYS (6; 10) simply cuts out six little bits at random from different portions of the total area and leaves the remainder. Asked to share it all, he too, like Tho, produces a star with eight triangular slices cut out of the periphery and the centre unused.

Because division into fifths or sixths is more difficult than trisection, the method of successive fragmentation re-appears as late as level IIB. Nevertheless it is seldom that older children revert to that method in its pure form. More often they construct some sort of overall configuration like the star of Thor and Rys, or else they turn to dichotomy. The latter is the second type of solution to the problem of sharing among five or six which we encounter at level IIB.

SCHO (5; 6), asked to share the cake among five dolls, confines himself to two dichotomies and is very surprised to find that the resulting quarters do not correspond with the number of dolls: *"There aren't enough."* Nevertheless he repeats his strategy two or three times: "Will that work out right like that?— *No* (but he tries it all the same just in case!)"

CYR (5; 6), when told to share among six, divides the cake into four first of all, and then divides two of his quarters into eighths, which gives him six unequal portions. He is told to remember that the portions must be equal and promptly divides his next cake into fifths, which he would not have achieved had he set out to do so in the first place! Now, the last fifth is simply divided into half. A third cake is divided into six portions straight off, but this success is accidental, for it is not repeated. Asked to share a fourth cake, Cyr executes what is almost a threefold dichotomy: two quarters and four eighths.

ELI (5; 6), again dividing by six, uses the method of dichotomy as did Cyr: first four quarters by twofold dichotomy, then two quarters and four eighths. "Is that quite fair now you've corrected it?—(He increases the size of the two eighths nearest to the quarters by taking some off the latter, but leaves the other two eighths as they were.)—Try again (with another cake).—(He again produces two quarters and four eighths.)"

LIA (5; 7) produces four quarters and halves the last quarter, his task being to construct fifths.

LEO (5; 7), for the same problem, divides the cake into two first of all, and then subdivides one half in two and the other in three, so that the five portions are still unequal. "Is that quite fair?—*No, because some of them have got more than others.*"

MAR (5; 11), sharing among five, cuts his circle into halves, and then divides one half in two parallel strips. He does the same with the other half and then goes on to cut the last strip in half perpendicularly to the previous sections.

MIC (6; 1) starts by responding in a way which is more advanced than the foregoing, and heralds the onset of stage III. To cut the cake into six, he first halves it and then divides each half into three unequal portions. But when he tries, at his next attempt, to correct the inequality, he succeeds in making the fractions equal only by increasing their number to eight. His third attempt is the same. Next he succeeds in returning to the number of six, but the parts are again unequal and bear no relation to a diameter as did the first dichotomy.

Finally, here is a mixed example:

CHEV (6; 7) is told to divide the cake into six. He ranges the six dolls at equal intervals round the cake but instead of foreseeing that the position of the dolls now gives him six portions, he draws a great many lines (14) perhaps believing that if each individual is given several thin slices the final portions are more likely to be equal. "How many pieces did I ask for?—*Six. I've done too many.*—All right. Have another go.—(He quarters the cake and halves two of the quarters.)—Are all your pieces the same size?—(He halves the other two quarters, but finds that he now has eight portions in all.)—Very well, take this new cake. Do you think the middle might help you?—*Yes* (he cuts it in two and then cuts each half in three parts all about the same size)."

The solutions given to the problem of finding fifths or sixths are identical with those given to halving and quartering and later to trisection. The sole difference is that primitive (incomplete and erroneous) solutions persist longer than they do for trisection, covering the whole of sub-stage IIB. This is only to be expected since the difficulty of anticipating the action increases with the number of fractional parts required (with the exception that quarters are easier than thirds). What is more striking, however, is that the added difficulty makes children revert to fragmentation with an unused remainder, or more often to various forms of dichotomy, when we might easily have expected them to cut five or six portions by trial-and-error with some inequality between the parts.

What we may infer is that whenever children are impressed by the need to leave no remainder, they automatically turn back to dichotomy as the most natural form of subdivision.

On the other hand, at level IIIA, the problem of trisection is solved at once and we now find that children can also divide into fifths or sixths. Yet even here there is an element of delay: the examples to be given are all cases of children who can trisect without preliminary trial-and-error while avoiding gross differences between the sizes of their thirds; yet these same children cannot divide into five or six without trial-and-error.

ROS (6; 8), whose responses to trisection is given in §4, is asked to divide the cake into fifths. He begins by constructing a series of successive parts which together account for all the cake but which number seven instead of five. He therefore tries twofold dichotomy but soon rejects that hypothesis. Eventually the cake is divided into five approximately equal pieces, but these are parallel sections as were his thirds.

CAR (6; 8) starts by dividing the cake into five triangular sections but these are unequal: the first two account for about half (although not preceded by dichotomy) instead of only two fifths. But at his second attempt he has little difficulty in constructing five approximately equal sectors.

VET (7; 6) also succeeded in trisecting the circle at his first attempt. Now he unhesitatingly bisects the circle and trisects each half, giving himself six equal parts. Unfortunately he was trying to construct five! On his second attempt he takes successive slices until there is none left, but this time he finishes with seven! Finally, he succeeds in anticipating the required number with a third cake by increasing the size of his slices so that he finishes with five equal portions. Dividing into sixths is successfully realized by repeating the strategy with which he began.

MARI (7; 2), for division into sixths, halves the cake and then divides one half into three and the other into four (without dichotomy, the error being one of faulty correspondence). His second attempt is successful.

ERV (8; 2), also dividing into sixths, begins by obtaining five unequal parts. With a second cake he first draws the vertical diameter and then two oblique diameters (forming the letter X) which gives him six equal parts.

GUN (8; 2) begins by ranging the six dolls at equal distances all round the cake and cutting six small slices against each doll. Because the slices are discontinuous one is reminded of the fragmentation of stage II. But Gun increases their size until he attains six equal portions leaving no remainder.

BUR (9; 2) is still at the stage of trial-and-error and goes so far as to make seven unequal portions before discovering the method of drawing three diameters shown by Erv.

While everyone of these subjects is eventually successful in dividing into five or six equal fractions, they all begin with a certain amount of experimentation although this is no longer necessary to them when trisecting. Only at level IIIB do we find division into fifths or sixths carried out with the same assurance as trisection.

BOU (9; 7) divides the circle into three equal sections which he then bisects. Division into fifths is carried out with considerable accuracy (with only one inequality) right from the start.

It is nevertheless surprising that division into sixths should appear appreciably later than trisection.

§6. *Part-whole relations and conservation of the whole*

As mentioned in §2, part-whole relations have recurred again and again in earlier studies like those dealing with nesting[1] logical classes or subdivision of a continuous whole (C.C.S., ch. V). Whatever the content, children who are still at an intuitive and pre-operational level fail to understand that a discontinuous whole when divided into sub-classes, or a continuous whole when subdivided into fractions, is none-

[1] = hierarchical (E. L.).

theless conserved as a whole of parts. Conversely, when the child has learnt to perform concrete operations, whether these bear on logical 'groupings' or on the composition of parts, he automatically realizes that the parts are logically mobile, and the whole is therefore conserved because it corresponds to the (real or virtual) collection of its parts. There can be no doubt that this question of conservation of the whole plays a decisive part in the problems of subdividing areas which are our present concern. In particular, those solutions which rely on simple fragmentation without using up the entire original whole argue a failure to establish a necessary relation between the sections as constructed and the whole conceived as an invariant. The only question is how far-reaching is the influence of that relation? In §2 we intimated that the part-whole relation was an essential feature of only one out of the seven attributes of fractions. In order to know more precisely just what part is played by this relation, we asked every child at the end of the enquiry whether all the pieces of cake taken together amounted to the same as the original cake. Our first example is of a child who was unable to bisect the cake at his first attempt:

SOM (4; 8, see §2) achieved bisection only after considerable trial-and-error: "How many cakes did the two dollies' mummy bring them?—*One.*—And how many cakes do we have here (the two halves)?—*Two, two half-cakes. Here* (indicating what was left over from another cake after he had removed two little slices, amounting to about ⅔) *there is only little because it's been cut.*— That's right. But how many big cakes are there here (the two halves), like the one we had to start with?—*We had one whole cake and now we've got two.*— That's quite true, but watch: is there the same amount of cake here (a whole cake) and here (the two halves)?—*No, there's more* (the two halves)." Later, when Som has cut out three small slices for three dolls, leaving an unused remainder, the experimenter puts all four sections together and compares them with another whole cake similar to the one with which they started: "Is there the same amount to eat on this whole cake and on these pieces together?—*Oh, no! This is more* (the pieces).—How many whole cakes could we make with these?—*It's more.*—But how many cakes is this (the whole)?— *One cake.*—But these, they're not more to eat, are they?—*Yes, of course they are, because there are more.*"

Next, we present examples taken from subjects who succeeded in halving but failed in trisection:

JEN (4; 2) first cuts a cake in two. The two halves are put before one of the dolls and a whole cake in front of the other: "This doll will eat these and that doll will eat this. Will they be eating the same amount?—*No.*—Don't they make up the same?—*No, it isn't the same thing.*—Which one will have more? —*That one* (whole cake).—Why?—*Because it isn't cut up.*—Well, look. Suppose I have this (the two halves) and you have that (the whole cake): haven't we both got the same amount to eat?—*I've got more.*—Why?—

327

Mine's all round and yours is cut up.—How many cakes did this mummy bring before we cut it (indicating the two halves)?—*One.*—Well, how many cakes could we get back from them?—*Two.*"

On the other hand, when Jen has cut a cake into six pieces (to share among three dolls), these six pieces are then put all together in front of one doll, while another doll is given two halves and the third doll one whole: "Have they all got the same amount to eat?—*No, this one has more* (the six pieces). —Why?—*Because there are more.*—What about the other two?—*This one has more* (the whole cake)." Jen is of the opinion that a whole is more than two halves but less than a collection of smaller fractions.

PIE (4; 8) has tried to trisect by the method of dichotomy (§3) and is now asked to compare one half and two quarters with four quarters: "Will these two dolls be eating the same amount of cake?—(He counts.) *One has four bits and the other has three. It isn't the same. This one has more* ($\frac{4}{4}$).—Think of the two mummies. How many big round cakes did this mummy bring and how many did that one bring to share among the children?—*Two.*—Well, how many cakes could you make out of this lot ($\frac{1}{2} + \frac{2}{4}$)?—*One.*—And with this lot ($\frac{4}{4}$)?—*One.*—Well, then, the two dolls are eating the same!—*No, that one has four bits and this one has only three.*—But how many cakes can we make up out of these pieces ($\frac{1}{2} + \frac{2}{4}$)?—*One.*—And out of those ($\frac{4}{4}, -\frac{1}{4}$) which accidentally rolls off the table at that precise moment)?—*One, no . . . two, no . . . one* (he collects the three remaining pieces and says:) *There's one bit missing. Now they've both got three bits, they've got the same amount to eat.*" Pie lacks the notion of a unit, which leads him to treat all the pieces as if they were strictly comparable irrespective of their sizes, so that he refuses to admit that $\frac{4}{4} = \frac{1}{2} + \frac{2}{4}$ although he is perfectly aware that either collection could be refashioned into one cake!

HOC (4; 2) is another instance of a certain duality of approach. He is shown three dolls. The first doll is given the ten pieces into which he has just cut one of the cakes, the second doll is given two half-cakes, also cut by Hoc himself, and the third is given a whole cake. "Well, now watch. The dollies' mummy gave one doll this lot, and one doll this lot, and one doll this lot. Are they all going to eat up the cake they've been given?—*Yes, if you eat a lot of cake you grow big, and if you eat too much you get a tummy-ache.*— That's right. Well, tell me what will happen to these three little dolls?—*That one* (ten pieces) *will have a tummy-ache, that one* (two halves) *will grow into a big girl, but that one won't. She hasn't had much, just this one bit* (the whole!).'" Hoc is then asked to choose between a whole bar of chocolate and two half-bars: without hesitating, he takes the two half-bars, to have more. But a moment later, he admits that 17 pieces into which a cake has been broken amount to the same as another cake which is intact: "*Yes, it's the same.*—Why? —*Because.*—Is there the same amount to eat?—*No.*—Which would you choose?—*That* (the whole cake). *It's more.*" Thus, for Hoc, the total quantity increases with the number of fractions until these are too small. In other words, there is no operational conservation of the whole, but a series of intuitive adjustments which are similar to perceptual adjustments, the two illusions cancelling one another at that point where the transition is made from one false estimate to the reverse.

ANT (4; 5) is aware that the slices into which the cake has been cut could be remade into a whole. He is asked about three pieces into which he cut a cake; "How many round cakes do these amount to?—*Three.*—What, three round cakes like the one we started with?—*No, it's the same.*" Yet he refuses to admit that the various collections of parts are equivalent to wholes. For instance, one doll is given a whole cake, another is given one half and two quarters, and a third is given two quarters and four eighths (these fractions being those into which Ant himself has previously split two of his cakes). "Have they all got the same?—*No, that one has the most* (whole cake) *because it's quite round.*—But they have the same amount to eat, haven't they?—*No. Here* (whole cake) *there's a lot to eat, and that one* (the third doll) *has little.*— But watch this (the experimenter cuts a cake in two). Is this the same amount of cake to eat as that (a whole cake)?—*No, that's more* (the whole)." A little later when sharing a rectangle, he again claims that a whole is greater than two halves.

ROG (4; 11) thinks that a cake cut into seven pieces represents more than one cut into two. "*That one* (the doll with seven pieces) *ate more.*" On the other hand, he also holds that one whole cake contains more to eat than two halves. Yet he admits that either of these collections ($\frac{7}{7}$; $\frac{2}{2}$; etc.) could be remade into one whole, but he will not allow that they are equivalent as they stand because they are wholes broken up.

GIS (5; 6) also says of fractions and a whole "*They're the same*", but when asked to choose between one whole cake and two halves, she chooses the whole, because "*I get more to eat this way.*"

We see how paradoxical are these replies. Subjects know that the whole cake can be reconstructed from the set of fractional parts into which it has been cut: Hoc, Ant and Gis go so far as to assert that "they're the same", in the sense that a return to the starting-point is always possible. But at the same time, they are all equally adamant that the sum of the slices, taken as they are, is not equal to the whole: "No. It isn't the same thing," says Jen. What is more the lack of equality is particularly manifest if attention is centred on some characteristic which directly concerns the realm of action (i.e. action in its utilitarian or egocentric aspect and not in its operational character). What all children are most sure about is that there is not the same amount to eat in the whole as there is in the collection of parts.

The very lack of agreement in children's judgments shows that their mode of thought is not operational as yet, but intuitive, so that its direction is a matter of simple articulations or adjustments, comparable with perceptual adjustments. The same was found at stage II when equal partial areas were subtracted from equal wholes (ch. XI). Sometimes subjects argue that an intact whole cake contains more to eat than two halves or three slices, etc., "because it isn't cut up" (Jen). At other times we learn that the collection of pieces contains more to eat, because there are many of them: "Yes of course they are (more to eat) because there are a lot of them" (Som). But even when this occurs it ceases to hold when the pieces are too small, which is a clear instance of the analogy with perception. When the fractions are tiny, they are thought to amount to less to eat than the whole, probably because the mouthfuls grow increasingly smaller. Between the two modes of judgment, we even find a momentary recognition of equality because the two opposing factors, the number of fractions and their diminutive size, compensate one another. Thus Hoc, for one brief moment, asserts that 17 pieces are worth the same as one whole similar to that out of which they were broken.

We need to understand the reason for this contradiction: on the one hand subjects assert that a return to the initial whole from the set of parts is possible, but on the other hand they deny that the sum of parts is therefore equal to the whole. This particular contradiction, together with numerous others which occur at the same level in all problems of conservation, might easily be resolved along the lines suggested by E. Meyerson, who states that children may be aware of reversibility yet lack identification: they admit that state A can be transformed into state B and state B can return to A, and at the same time fail to identify the quantities A and B. But in truth this solution is little more than a play on words, using these ambiguously, for there are two kinds of reversibility and also two kinds of identification and these correspond to two quite different ways of thinking. Operational reversibility is the inverse of the direct (or thetic) operation. Corresponding to this form of reversibility, we have operational identity which is the product of a direct operation and its inverse (e.g. $+ 1 - 1 = 0$). Operational identity and reversibility depend on logical 'groupings' or mathematical 'groups'. Before these structures have been elaborated we may find intuitive insights into the (empirical) possibility of a return to the starting-point. These pre-operational intuitions imply a certain reversibility which is incomplete and they too have their counterpart in pre-operational identifications implying some sort of generative source; thus the parts might be held to spring from the whole in the same way as clouds, to little children, spring from smoke, etc.

The paradox is now clear. There is no conservation of the whole in the sense of equality between the intact whole and the sum of any set of parts to which it might give rise, but this is because there is no true reversibility either, in the sense of an inverse operation corresponding the direct operation in a precise and necessary fashion—nor can there be for there is no direct operation as yet in any real sense! The whole of this chapter has shown how the earliest kinds of subdivision carried out by little children do not derive from an anticipatory schema which governs the behaviour as a whole, is operational in character, and conforms with the various conditions surrounding the notion of fractions.

Whether the behaviour takes the form of successive and empirical fragmentation, or whether it consists in a more or less crude attempt to
adapt the method of dichotomy to trisection or division into fifths and
sixths, its invariable hallmark is trial-and-error. Such actions cannot
therefore be called true operations, for this term implies a definite
character which allows of reversibility, i.e. of negation by the corresponding inverse operations. Here, the regrouping of dissociated parts
is not the inverse of the action whereby the sections were made in the
first place, or if it is, it is highly approximative, since the initial cutting-
out lacked an overall plan and was done bit by bit alongside the actual
sharing, without accounting for the whole of the original cake, etc.
Re-grouping the pieces to form a unique whole is the inverse of cutting-
out only if the latter operation follows a fixed and pre-ordered path,
for only then can that path be unambiguously reversed. Such is the
condition of true reversibility, and hence of the conservation of the
whole and the qualitative identity of the whole and the sum of its parts.

The replies we have cited can be evaluated in terms of two different
kinds of quantification. The first is 'intensive' and draws only on part-
whole relations. Where it exists in operational form there is conservation of the whole, conceived as the sum of its parts. The operation is
purely qualitative and as such it takes account of the first six only of
the attributes of fractions (§2), omitting the seventh, i.e. the equality of
fractional parts. Where there is non-conservation of the whole, it
follows that these intensive reversible operations have not yet appeared;
where there is conservation, it is their 'grouping' which assures the
invariance. The other kind of quantification is extensive and takes the
form of quantitative comparisons among the parts themselves. Such
comparisons are metrical inasmuch as the parts are made equal, which
implies the construction of a variety of unit concepts together with
corresponding fractions. The latter qualification is dependent on the
former; for where there is no conservation of the whole the notion of
a unit is ruled out *a fortiori*. The example of Pie is particularly instruc-
tive: comparing three pieces $(\frac{1}{2} + \frac{1}{4} + \frac{1}{4})$ with four $(\frac{4}{4})$, he is relieved
when one of the latter drops to the floor: "There's a bit missing. Now
they've both got three bits: they've got the same amount to eat,"
i.e. $\frac{3}{4} = \frac{1}{2} + \frac{1}{4} + \frac{1}{4}$ since all the pieces are regarded as equivalent as
though they were homogeneous units.

Conversely, the more precise and operational the subdivision
(whether intensive or whether it includes metric quantification), the
clearer to the child is the necessary relation between the sum of parts
and the whole, and also the conservation of the whole itself. We begin
with a few cases which are transitional:

Hu (5; 8) for instance: "Then these pieces here, and that whole cake over
there, do they contain the same amount to eat?—*No, that's more* $(\frac{3}{3})$ *because*

there are three of them." But when asked the same question a little later on, he replies: "*Yes, it's the same.*—And what were you thinking before?—*I thought it made three cakes.*"

Ros (6; 8), likewise, comparing five fifths, three threes and one whole, first asserts: "*That one* ($\frac{5}{5}$) *will eat the biggest lot and that one* ($\frac{1}{1}$) *a lot.*—What about this one ($\frac{1}{1}$) and that one ($\frac{3}{3}$)?—*This one has more* ($\frac{1}{1}$) *because that's very little* ($\frac{3}{3}$). *Oh, no! They both eat the same, because that's* ($\frac{3}{3}$) *the same thing, only cut up.*"

The remaining cases show well-defined conservation:

Mog (5; 11) comparing the three thirds which he has cut with a whole cake: "I've got this ($\frac{1}{1}$) and you have that ($\frac{3}{3}$). Have we got the same amount to eat? —*It's the same, because I've cut it.*—Is it exactly the same?—*Yes.*" Later, he divides a cake into four: "How many cakes did the mummy bring?—*One.*— And how many cakes could you make out of these bits?—*One only, because there was only one* (before cutting)."

Lau (6; 2) comparing four quarters with a whole: "*It's the same amount to eat because it's the same cake; they're the same size. There, there are four bits and here there's only one. Only that one, I've made it into bits and given them out. But it's still the same cake and it's round. It's the same thing if I put it together.*" He is asked to compare a whole with sixteen sixteenths resulting from successive dichotomies: "And who has more to eat now, you with all these bits, or me with my cake?—*It's the same thing all together! You put all these together and you have the cake. You can put them all together and it's the same thing.*—How many can you make out of all these?—*One.*"

Car (6; 8), comparing three thirds with a whole: "Who has more to eat?— *It's the same thing.*—Why?—*Because if you take them all together, you've got one the same.*—And these ($\frac{9}{9}$ and $\frac{1}{1}$)?—*It's the same thing because we've shared it.*—But why is it the same?—*If you stick them together you'll get one. If you put them back it's the same thing.*"

Vet (7; 6). $\frac{3}{3}$ v. $\frac{1}{1}$: "*It's the same thing because I've cut it in bits.*"

Even the young Rob, whose sharing was at level IIB, is convinced of the invariance of the whole (although he cannot explain it).

Rob (4; 3): "I'm going to eat this ($\frac{1}{1}$) and you can have that ($\frac{3}{3}$). Shall we be eating the same, or will one of us have more?—(He laughs.) *It's the same thing.*—Why?—*Because.*" The same reply for five fifths.

We see at once how, for all these children, the whole equals the sum of its parts, and hence that its quantity is invariant whatever the number of parts, and whatever their arrangement or dispersion: to eat one whole cake is the same as eating three-thirds or sixteen-sixteenths. All the above subjects were at level IIB or III when dividing into thirds or into fifths, etc. (although the level of the subdivision does not always correspond exactly with the level of conservation). Because they have either an anticipatory schema for subdivision (level III) or intuitive articulations which are almost operational, their actions and operations have sufficient reversibility to ensure the existence of invariants, and these are recognized in the most explicit manner by children like Lau and Car.

§7. *Conclusion. Subdividing areas and the notion of fractional parts*

The various findings of this chapter are important in three ways. They bear on the question of subdivision of space as a whole, on the parallel between subdivision of continuous quantities and nesting logical classes and on the quantification of parts in the shape of fractions.

It might seem reasonable to think of subdivision of continuous spatial quantities as involving a far more elementary process than understanding the relations involved in a complex of discontinuous logical or numerical elements. Thus, when a class or a collection is divided into sub-classes, it cannot be easy to remember the initial whole and its reconstruction must imply a precise operation of logical addition or of re-assembly. Subdivision separates the sub-classes from the whole class and the former then acquire a certain degree of independence, so that it becomes easy to overlook that they are still relative to the whole from which they were taken. But when a cake is divided into pieces, it still has all the appearance of a cake in bits, so that each piece should bring to mind irresistibly the thought of the whole from which it came and of the pieces which are complementary. We might even say that the subdivision and re-uniting of classes and sub-classes are somewhat abstract operations while sharing a cake and re-assembling the pieces is intuitive and concrete.

Yet in the event, the subdivision of an area even when it takes the form of a circular cake or of a square or rectangular sheet of paper is fraught with considerable difficulty for young children and its complications compare in every respect with those pertaining to logical subdivision or the nesting of partial classes within an inclusive class. Above all these difficulties are not peculiar to this or that fraction, be it thirds or fifths, but are evident even in halving and dichotomy (i.e. cutting two complementary parts irrespective of the equality of those parts which is implicit in the notion of halving).

Thus children fail altogether in their efforts at subdivision because they do not anticipate the possible relations between the parts and the whole. They begin with simple fragmentation, with the several parts juxtaposed, without any preconceived link subsisting between the parts, and without the relation of part to whole. Indeed, the whole is ignored insofar as it consists in the integration of virtual parts, which is why children cannot exhaust it, and do not think of doing so. When asked to share a whole between two, little children at stage I are content, as we remember, to cut out two small unequal slices, leaving a large remainder intact. The method recurs in problems of trisection and, later, of division into fifths.

It is obvious that the difficulty to which we point arises only because there is no anticipatory schema in which the desired fraction or part is recognized beforehand as something bound up with a divisible whole equal to the sum of its parts. In this field, as in every other domain which we have studied, the facts are clear: thought alone cannot give rise to anticipatory schemata, because representation cannot foresee the possible unless it is guided by action. Only when a child has reached the level where his actions are coordinated and form reversible operational groupings do we find operational anticipatory schemata. These are the psychological counterparts of systems of composition peculiar to grouping as such. Before these groupings are constructed, action is thrust upon its own resources, which means that it is reduced to all kinds of trial-and-error behaviour. In the present case, as we saw, it begins with successive fragmentation in which there is no overall plan.

We may conclude that the operations required for subdivision of areas or continuous wholes are identical with those which enter into the subdivision of classes or discontinuous collections. In both cases, there is a reciprocal relation between subdivision itself and re-assembly, or, for logical classes, the nesting of sub-classes within a hierarchical total structure. (By reciprocity is meant the interdependence of direct and inverse operations.) The sole difference is that for classes and discontinuous collections the subdivision and nesting of parts depend on proximity.[1] Apart from this distinction between the logical and the sub-logical[2] the operations are not only similar, but they appear at the same age in concrete situations (i.e. at the beginning of stage III). Moreover, dichotomy, as one variety of subdivision, occupies a privileged position both in the sub-logical subdivision of continuous wholes and in the logical subdivision of classes. For in the logic of classes, the simplest kind of sub-division consists in splitting a class B into two complementary sub-classes: A and A'. Additive grouping of classes depends, in the first instance, on re-uniting these sub-classes, for that grouping corresponds to a series of dichotomous subdivisions in which $A + A' = B$; $B + B' = C$; $C + C' = D$; etc. So too in the realm of fractions, dichotomy is the preferred type of subdivision: it appears at the beginning of stage II and older children frequently revert to successive dichotomy in their attempts at trisection or later, division into fifths (and indeed, however erroneous, the method is more advanced than the earlier empirical fragmentation).

The facts studied in this chapter show not merely that there is a clear parallel between the subdivision of continuous areas and that of

---

[1] Whether spatial or conceptual, and not on perceptual continuity (E. L.).
[2] i.e. spatial, see C.C.S., ch. XV, §§2, 3 (E. L.).

logical classes, but also that notions of fractions and even of halves depend on a qualitative or intensive substructure. Before parts can be equated in conformity with the extensive characteristics of fractions, they must first be constructed as integral parts of a whole which can be de-composed and also re-assembled. Once that notion of part has been constructed it is comparatively easy to equate the several parts. Therefore, while the elaboration of operations of subdivision is a lengthy process, the concept of a fraction follows closely on that of a part. For parts which are subordinated to the whole can also be related to one another, and when this has been achieved, the notion of a fraction is complete.

Chapter Thirteen

DOUBLING AN AREA OR A VOLUME[1]

THE operations considered so far in relation to areas or plane measurement, and likewise those relating to volume or three-dimensional space, were of two kinds only. Either they were reducible to logical addition and subtraction or else they were logical but not numerical multiplications. Frequently, the elements and relations involved were such as could be expressed in quantitative terms, but the problem of calculating an area in such terms is one which we have not yet considered. This question involves mathematical multiplication, which goes beyond logical multiplication: a rectangle measuring 2×3 linear units gives six *square* units.

In ch. VIII, for instance, we studied problems of measurement in two or three dimensions. The measurement consisted in successive applications of units along each of the rectangular axes concerned, but it did not include mathematical multiplication of these units. Instead, the units were arranged in linear fashion following a matrix with two or three entries, which means that the operative schema drew only on logical multiplication, not numerical. The construction of coordinate axes is similar, for these axes are a means of representing such a matrix in a quantitative fashion without mathematical multiplication. In ch. XI, we studied the conservation and measurement of areas, but here our questions were such that all the subject had to do was to apply ready-made units of area (squares, rectangles, half-squares, equilateral triangles, etc.) instead of calculating the area as a function of linear measurements, so that, once again, mathematical multiplication was unnecessary. Finally, ch. XII dealt with the subdivision of areas, but the process consisted in dividing whole areas into partial areas so that the units involved were all square units and the numerical relation between area and length of side was irrelevant.

We must now consider the problem of measuring areas and volumes insofar as it involves numerical multiplication. In other words, we shall analyse the relations between measurement of the sides of a figure and that of their area or volume. This problem is much harder than those just mentioned (chs. VIII, XI and XII) and consequently we do not find correct solutions until children reach the age when geometry is normally introduced into the school curriculum. The reasons for the increased difficulty will be made clear in the course of our analysis.

[1] Written with the collaboration of Mlle U. Galusser.

This does not mean that we shall examine the way in which children's thinking is adapted to academic instruction. That would be a highly interesting topic to analyse, but it concerns educational psychology rather than genetic psychology and, as such, has no place in the present work. Hence, we shall not ask how children come to understand that a rectangle measuring 2 cm. by 3 cm. has an area of 6 cm.[2]: In point of fact, they do not seem[1] to acquire that understanding until stage IV, which is when the topic is introduced in the school curriculum, while the problems dealt with earlier, like those of ch. XI, are resolved much more spontaneously.

However, although the application of arithmetical multiplication to calculations of area lies outside our field, the problem of intelligence which it raises can be analysed in a way which reduces associations with the classroom to a minimum. Our method should pinpoint the underlying operational mechanisms without stressing the final answer in its numerical form. Accordingly, subjects are asked simply to double an area or a volume. We do not insist on precise determination because that would involve not only arithmetical multiplication and division but square roots and cube roots as well. Nevertheless we should find it relatively easy to answer the single question with which we are concerned: how does the subject establish a relation between length and area or volume, and how does he come to substitute mathematical multiplication for logical multiplication?

§1. *Outline of method and results*

The subject is first shown a straight line measuring 2 or 3 cm., and asked to draw another twice as long. He is provided with a two-decimetre ruler and strips of paper but the experimenter avoids any verbal suggestions as to their use.

He is then given a square measuring 3 cm. × 3 cm. and told to draw another square twice as big. Here the experimenter must insist that what is wanted is another square, for otherwise the child can simply draw two squares together or a rectangle. Moreover, he makes it quite clear that it is the area which must be twice as great (rather than some other dimension like the sides, etc.) by making up a story like the one in ch. XI (§I), telling the child that the model represents a square field with enough grass for one cow and that he must draw another square field big enough for two cows each of which will have exactly the same amount of grass as the first. As a counter-experiment, the experimenter places a unit field (a square which is congruent with the model) over the big one with one angle superposed exactly and asks the subject whether the part of his field which is not covered really contains as

---

[1] See note at the end of this chapter.

much grass as the unit field. If necessary the portion left uncovered can be cut out with scissors and the child is then told to re-group its elements to see whether it is equal to the unit field.

But drawing and construction are not enough: the child is also shown a selection of ready-made squares and asked to choose the one he thinks is double the 3 cm. square model. There are four such squares in all and their sides measure 4, 4·25, 5 and 6 cm. respectively (the 4·25 cm. square being approximately twice 9 cm.^{2} since its area is 18·0625 cm.^{2}). The questions asked about the drawings are repeated for these ready-made squares.

Next we go on to a similar enquiry dealing with circular and triangular fields and with an irregular field consisting of a 4 cm. square less a 2·5 cm. square removed from one corner.

For doubling the cube no drawing is required and the child is simply shown a model which is a 3 cm. cube together with a range of larger cubes of which the largest is a 6 cm. cube. The child is asked to choose which cube will hold just twice as much as the model and the counter-check consists in asking the child how many unit-volumes will go into the cube he has chosen: the initial cube (or unit-cube) is filled with sand or with little wooden cubes and then emptied into the one chosen by the subject to help him understand the question.

Accepting the stages which have been described already, we noted the following responses to these questions. At stage I the experiment is ruled out altogether. During stage II, from the age of 4 or 5 to 7 or 7; 6, doubling is a matter of a slight but arbitrary increase in size. This is true even of doubling a length of 2 or 3 cm.: instead of re-applying the straight line, using it as a unit of measurement, the subject merely draws another straight line which projects a little further, without imposing any precise relationship. Needless to say, these children are totally unsuccessful at doubling a square. They try to draw a square a little larger than the model, but they cannot even do this because they lack an anticipatory schema for seriation (see C.C.S., ch. V, and the experiment of the largest possible square). When asked to choose the right square out of four already given, they make what amounts to a random choice (so that sometimes they choose correctly by accident) and are unable to establish a serial correspondence between successively greater areas and the number of cows which might be put to graze on these square fields. This is true also of the other two-dimensional shapes and of the cubes.

At level IIIA, children do one of two things. Either they juxtapose two areas or two volumes both of which are equal to that given as a model and overlook the requirement of shape (a doubled square becoming a rectangle, etc.) or they simply double all the dimensions. In other words they succeed only with the straight line, although even then they do no measuring (re-applying a unit of measurement precisely) but simply form an intuitive judgment based on visual transfer. When doubling a square they either produce a rectangle consisting of two squares in juxtaposition or they draw a large square four times the size of the original because they simply double the four sides. Triangles are dealt with in the same way (either they draw two triangles touching or they simply double the three sides), and when doubling the circle they try to double its diameter. When asked to choose from several models that square (or triangle, etc.) which is twice the size of the one first shown, children at this level refuse to accept the correct size, even when the experimenter tries to make them recompose the elements which project beyond the second unit-model (placed over a corner of the larger shape) to prove that the remaining area is itself worth one unit. When finding a cube with twice the capacity, children at this level invariably choose one larger because they will not believe that one which is in fact twice the size will take twice the quantity of sand or of small wooden cubes as that contained in the unit model.

Level IIIB, which is when measurement in one or more dimensions is finally realized (see chs. II and V–VIII), is an interesting turning-point in the development of the present behaviour, doubling an area or a volume, but the problem is not solved operationally at this level and efforts at solution are still empirical. Doubling a straight line is, of course, an exception. The child can measure in one dimension and therefore re-applies the unit length accurately. But when doubling a square, he makes the same preliminary trials as he did at level IIIA: he doubles the sides or he juxtaposes two squares to form a rectangle. However, once he has doubled the sides, he now realizes that the final product is not what he wanted and goes on to try various other ways of establishing a relation between the length of side and the area. Even so, he does not solve the problem because he has not evolved the operation necessary to its solution. The same applies to triangles and circles; the subject doubles the diameter or raises its value arbitrarily but at the same time he is aware of the discrepancy between the product of his effort and the doubled area which he wants. Doubling a cube is solved in an approximate fashion, with some beginning of composition, but the behaviour is still empirical and not deductive.

Finally, at the level of formal operations (stage IV) the child tries to calculate the relation of length of sides to the area or of that the edges to the volume and is no longer satisfied with merely empirical calculations.

§2. *Stage II. No doubling even of length*

Even at stage II, children cannot begin to double areas and volumes for the good reason that they cannot even double lengths, since they

339

lack the ability to measure operationally and, more especially, they cannot carry out unit iteration.

ERI (5; 2): "Here is a little road (straight line, 2 cm.), you draw me another road twice as long as this one.—(He draws a 3 cm. line.)—How did you do it?—*I went like this and made a bigger line.*—Can I put my road in your road twice over?—*Yes.*—Well, now, here's a square field with enough grass for one cow. You draw me one twice as large which will do for two cows.— *We'd need a bigger square.*—Yes that's right. Here are some to choose from. Which will you have?—(He takes the 4 cm. square, i.e. the next in size to the 3 cm. square.)—Would this one (4·25 cm.) do as well?—*Yes.*—And this one (5 cm.)?—*Yes.* And this one (6 cm.)?—*No, too big.*—Well you draw one better, twice as big as that one (3 cm.).—(He draws a square measuring a little less than 4 cm. square.)—All right, this time we have a round field. Show me which one is twice as big.—(By chance, he selects the right circle. This is hardly surprising since whatever he doubles, including the straight line, he simply constructs a figure which looks a little bigger to him.) Now we'll take a field like this (triangular). Show me one twice as big.—(The one he chooses has three times the area.)—Can you draw one?—(He draws an outline corresponding to two juxtaposed triangles, having heard the first triangle compared to a piece of cake; then he draws a line down the centre to divide it in two.)"

BEA (5; 4) draws a line 2·4 cm. as twice a 2 cm. line, and one 3·6 cm. as twice the 3 cm. When asked to double the 3 cm. square Bea tries to comply but the square he draws is actually a little smaller; at the second attempt he does draw one a little larger. When asked to choose one of the models Bea puts two cows on the 5 cm. square which he takes to be twice the 3 cm. square, while on the 6 cm. square he puts three cows. He is no more successful at seriation when dealing with the sets of triangles and circles. To draw a triangle twice as big as the model, he simply draws one a little longer.

LIL (6; 6) is at level IIB while the two previous subjects were at level IIA. His responses are midway between theirs and those of stage III. To draw "a road twice as long" as the 2 cm. line, he draws one just a little longer (2·5 cm.). "But it's only a little bit bigger.—*Like this* (drawing another line about 5 cm. long).—Watch (measuring his line and the original). It's too long.—*Well, then, like this* (the third line being too short, about 3·3 cm.)." But when doubling the square, Lil replies almost at level IIIA: he first draws a square equal to the original then he draws another one in juxtaposition to form a rectangle. When asked to choose one of the graded set, he points to a square four times the size. The triangle and the circle are simply enlarged a little, but the experimenter introduces the former problem as a question of slices of cake. Lil draws two slices adjoining one another (although the division is poor and his section line does not pass through the centre).

These three examples are sufficient to show the various aspects of responses obtained at stage II. Most interesting among these is the fact that children cannot double the length of a straight line, in view of their success at halving such a line (ch. XII) with a fair measure of accuracy. That success at halving has no reciprocal counterpart in success at doubling is proof that both responses are intuitive rather than operational. From the standpoint of intuition, it is a relatively simple matter to cut a line in two and to gauge perceptually the equality of the two halves, which is why it is accomplished right at the beginning of stage II (level IIA, see ch. XII, §3). Conversely, to double a line involves a true operation because the original line must be re-applied twice over, which is the key operational mechanism of measurement— iteration of a given length treated as a measuring unit. The difficulty of doubling a segment of a straight line is not an isolated finding, for all that it may seem surprising. It occurs throughout stage II, as was shown in an earlier experiment[1] when children were required to mark off sections in a road corresponding to the distances travelled each day by a vehicle travelling at a constant speed. At this level, their segments were either arbitrary or grew progressively longer (the implication being that because they reached a 'further' distance, their daily lap also grew longer), etc. They did not know how to iterate the unit segment. Non-conservation of length and distance, taken together with the problems encountered in linear measurement (chs. III–VI, above), account for their failure to carry out unit iteration.

The question remains why children who cannot draw a line twice as long as a given model and simply draw one a little longer are yet perfectly able to double a piece of cake (just as they can halve a cake or a large slice of cake). The reason is that a slice of cake is a perceptual whole whose shape is intimately bound up with its dimensions, which is not true of a straight line. In other words, copying the same shape twice is not psychologically equivalent to iterating a metric unit, although repeating actions is the starting-point for the development of unit-iteration. The fact that there was never any measurement at this level even when children divided cakes successfully (ch. XII) supports this interpretation.

When the subject at stage II is required to reproduce the form of the original (square, circle or triangle, which in the last instance means producing a similar triangle) while doubling its area, instead of merely drawing two slices of cake together or one slice twice as big, he is again unsuccessful, as he is at doubling a straight line. In all cases we find that he draws or chooses a figure which is only a shade larger. This is in marked contrast to the behaviour shown at stage III when children double each side of the square or triangle or the diameter of the circle and may suggest that these younger subjects have a keener sense of what is meant by doubling an area, the more so if we recall that sometimes they happen on the correct double by chance. In fact, however, this is not a case when intuition is more precise than the corresponding

[1] *Les notions de mouvement et de vitesse chez l'enfant*, ch. X.

operational or near-operational behaviour which follows, although such instances do occur in other spheres. What lies behind these stage II responses is the complete failure to differentiate doubling linear segments and doubling an area: because straight lines are increased only slightly, this behaviour recurs when these form a part of a plane figure so that the slight increase in the lengths of its sides (or in the diameter of a circle) inevitably produces an area more nearly twice the original, although the subject does not think of the area when he lengthens the side. As soon as he finds how to double a straight line exactly, he begins to double the sides of squares and triangles or the diameters of circles. This development can be seen even at level IIB, when the doubling of lines is more successful, and that of areas comes correspondingly nearer to the level of sub-stage IIIA.

§3. *Sub-stage IIIA: Areas are doubled by simply doubling their sides (or diameter) but lengths are doubled correctly*

At level IIIA, children can double straight line segments (although they cannot measure these accurately), but because they still do not differentiate increase in area from increase in length of side (or diameter), they either ignore the requirement that they must reproduce a similar shape, or else they simply double the relevant lengths. If they fail to reproduce the original shape, they draw a 2 : 1 rectangle for a square, or they draw a triangle with twice the base of the original, etc. In the latter case, their solution represents a half-way house between unit-iteration and reproducing a given shape twice over (like the double slices of cake drawn at stage II):

GLAS (6; 11) has no difficulty in doubling a segment of a straight line (although the session did not begin with this question for fear that it might influence his other replies). When asked to select a square from the graded series, he chooses first the 5 cm. then the 6 cm. square. The experimenter then places the 9 cm.² square over the lower right-hand quarter of the 36 cm.² square, asking him if the L-shaped 27 cm.² has the same area as the smaller square. He agrees that it is larger. The same procedure is repeated with the square measuring 18 cm.² instead of the largest, and he agrees that the L-shaped strip now looks to be the same size as the smaller squares. "Good. Now draw me a square twice as big as that one (9 cm.²).—*There* (having drawn one about four times the size).—Try again.—(He draws a rectangle about 6 cm. × 3 cm., showing that he understands the question but has given up hope of solving it without altering the original shapes.)" When asked to find a triangle twice the size of the model, he chooses one the sides of which are double those of the original, and again recognizes his mistake when the two are superposed. "What about this one (which is correct)?—*It's too small.* (He superposes it and examines the non-overlapping portion:) *Yes, too small.*—All right, draw me one the right size.—(He draws two triangles base to base, forming a diamond.)" For the circle, he immediately selects one with

342

twice the original diameter: "Look (superposing:)—*It's too big.*—And that one (the correct choice with the original superposed)?—*It's too small.*—Well, draw it.—(He draws a circle approximately four times the size of the model.)" JAN. (7; 2) draws a 4 cm. line for a 2 cm. line at his first attempt. "What sort of a drawing is this?—*It's a square.*—Draw it twice as big (the square being 9 cm.^{2}).—He draws a square 36 cm.^{2} and points to one of the sides saying:) *I can put two there.*—(The experimenter hands him the 3 cm. square and places it over his drawing.)—*I can put four on here.*—How come?— *If it were only two it would be long* (drawing a rectangle 6 cm. × 3 cm.).— Well, draw a square twice as big as that one (3 × 3).—(He draws a double square)."

Jan is shown two small cubes (with edges measuring 3 cm.), both full of sand, together with a graded series of larger cubes and asked to choose the one which will take both lots of sand. He chooses a cube with 6 cm. edges and is surprised to find that the sand does not begin to fill it. He is shown the cube with twice the capacity and is sure that it will not hold all the sand. On discovering that he is wrong, he is amazed and thinks the experimenter must have compressed the sand. "*I can't understand it. It must be because the sand isn't fragile. You can squeeze it.*"

ROL (7; 7) draws a double line by eye: "How did you do it?—*I looked carefully.*—What about this (square) field? Can you draw one for two cows, the same shape as this?—(He draws two squares together forming a rect-angle.)—But I want it the same shape.—(He doubles the sides by eye.)—Can you get just two little squares like mine in yours?—*Yes.* (He tries:) *Oh, no! Four.*—All right. Let's try again. Here's a square: now do one twice as big.— (Once more he starts by doubling the sides, but then he divides the large square into two rectangles to cover the error.) *There, that's two.*—Watch (the unit-square placed over one corner).—*Oh, no, four!*" The experimenter switches to the volumes asking Rol to choose a box to hold the sand from two 3 cm. cubes. He selects the 6 cm. cube and tries it, then goes on to the 5 cm. cube. "How many of these cubefuls of sand could I get into the big box (the 6 cm. cube)?—*Four.*—Try it.—(He does.) *Oh, no! eight!*"

LIO (8; 9) doubles a straight line segment by eye. Square: he doubles the sides by eye and finds it holds four of the original, so he draws a double square, i.e. a rectangle. The experimenter shows him the irregular card (see outline of method): he increases all its dimensions in arbitrary fashion: "But I want it just twice the size.—*You have to draw all the sides twice as big.*— Watch (superposing the model over his enlargement).—*No, it's too big.*" Finally he is shown the two sand-filled cubes and asked to choose the right box to hold all the sand: he chooses the cube with edges twice as long, and then says it is too big. He is sure the correct cube is too small, and surprised when he finds that it does hold all the sand: "Supposing we put both cubefuls of sand into the very big one, would that be full?—*No, the sand would come up to here* (quite close to the top!)."

MIC (9; 4), wishing to double a square, draws each side twice the length. "Will the little one go in it twice?—*Not quite* (and is amazed to find that it goes in four times). *I've to take this bit away* (one half, leaving a rectangle consisting of two unit-squares).—But what shape is it?—*A rectangle.*—How will you change it into a square?—*That's impossible. Even a grown-up couldn't do it.*—Well, look at these squares and choose which one is twice the size of that one (3 cm.).—(He points to the 6 cm. square.)—(The 3 cm. square is placed over one quarter of the 6 cm. square.) Is that right?—*Oh, no. Four times again.*—What about this one (which is correct, with the 3 cm. square placed over one corner)? Will this piece left over make up a small square?—*No.*—Try it (cutting up the L shape).—(He has no idea of how to reconstruct a square.)—Well, take that field (triangle). Can you draw me one twice as big?—*It can't be done.*—Why?—*You can make it bigger if you like* (doubling the sides).—Well, take that field (circle). Draw me one twice as big as that.—*It won't be right* (he draws a circle with just under twice the original diameter). —Choose one of the models.—(He selects one three times the original.)"

"In which one of these cubes could you empty these two little (3 cm.) cubes?—(He chooses the middle cube, then says:) *It's too big. Oh, no, it's too small because you can't put these two little cubes in it.*—Well, which is right?— (He points to the 6 cm. cube.)"

These level IIIA responses are instructive. In principle, they differ from stage IIA in only one respect: the subject can now double lengths or straight line segments. He can do so by eye even though he cannot as yet measure by using unit-iteration. Nevertheless the straight line segment is correctly drawn as twice the original length. But when dealing with areas and volumes, the subject reasons at the same level as he did at stage II: he thinks of doubling these higher power quantities as a matter of doubling length, and so he tends to double the sides of squares and triangles, the edges of cubes or the diameter of a circle. Because he can now double lengths correctly, his enlargement of areas and volumes is much greater than at stage II, when doubling straight-line segments was reduced to a fractional increase in length.

Level IIIA provides the clearest illustration of the paradox in the early responses of childhood. The subject cannot establish correct relations between areas or volumes and the length of sides or edges which determine them. Instead he confines himself to a kind of direct proportionality and imagines that if a square A^2 corresponds to side length A, then a square worth $2A^2$ will correspond to a side length $2A$; and similarly, because a cube with capacity A^3 has edges of length A, one of $2A^3$ will have edges equal to $2A$. The underlying principle is the same as that found at stage II (and *a fortiori* at stage I). It recalls the difficulties encountered by young children when coordinates are required or when they would need to measure in two or three dimensions to solve a problem. (But we shall see later how the primitive type of correspondence persists in problems of doubling areas and volumes even when difficulties in logical coordination have been outgrown.) Because these children cannot orient the elements which they see in the figures correctly in terms of two or three rectangular dimensions, using as common medium a developed concept of space, they inevitably think in linear terms only. This is not to deny that they have an intuition of an area as bounded by a line or of a volume as enveloped by plane surfaces. Such primitive topological intuitions form the starting-point for the discovery of dimensions (see C.C.S., ch. IV). But precisely because areas and volumes are thought of in terms of their boundaries, the linear factor is still uppermost in children's minds. Therefore, when they are required to construct a Euclidean structure by establishing precise relations between such higher order figures (relations which may govern linear elements but which do so in terms of the structure as a whole), they try to construct these in terms of linear dimensions only, i.e. lengths. The figures bounded by those lengths are then thought of as depending on them directly. When children reach the level at which their conception of length is controlled by qualitative operations (conservation of length and distance), they are well on the way to operational measurement of lines, but their notions of areas and volumes are still almost entirely dependent on considerations of a linear order. True, subtraction of areas, conservation of area, and subdivision into elementary fractional parts are problems correctly answered at level IIIA, as was shown in chs. XI and XII. But in all these problems the areas were thought of exclusively in terms of boundary lines or section lines and did not involve the relations between the lengths of the lines and the areal quantities which they determined. The problem of doubling areas and volumes demands such relations, and its difficulty springs from the fact that these children cannot construct them because they still think in linear terms.

These level IIIA responses show why the mathematical multiplication required in the calculation of area and volumes is a more difficult process than either addition and subtraction, or logical multiplication, which, together, governed the problems of chs. VII, VIII, XI and XII. Not that arithmetical multiplication is intrinsically more difficult than logical multiplication of classes and relations. It is its application to the geometry of area and volume which is difficult, because it involves the working-out of precise relations between perimeter lines and areas or between boundary surfaces and volumes. These relations do not enter into the child's primitive topological intuitions. They are based on a Euclidean structurization of space in terms of a coordinate system and they also involve measurement in two or three dimensions. Neither coordinate axes nor measurement have been elaborated at level IIIA. Even at level IIIB, when they have, they still form an operational schema which entails only logical multiplication of relations, even though the linear relations themselves are expressed in metric terms. Mathematical multiplication is still not necessary to measurement. Turning now to the study of responses at sub-stage IIIB, we shall see whether the construction of two- and three-dimensional coordinates and operations of measurement are sufficient to ensure successful calculation of areas and volumes.

§4. *Sub-stage IIIB. Experimentation in the establishment of relations between length of boundary lines and the areas or volumes which they enclose*

We may remind the reader that at level IIIB the measurement of length has been mastered both in one dimension (chs. V–VI), and in two or three dimensions (chs. VII–VIII). At the same time, the newly constructed coordinate axes (C.C.S., chs. XIII, XIV) govern not only the relations between one figure and another but also the elements included in their perimeters. That is why multidimensional measurement is now possible. These developments are quite sufficient to shatter the child's former belief in direct proportionality between the lengths of boundary lines and the areas or volumes which they enclose. This explains why level IIIB is a turning point which leads away from the responses of levels II–IIIA to those of stage IV. However, although two- and three-dimensional coordination produces a critical advance as compared with earlier attempts at doubling areas and volumes, that coordination is by no means enough to ensure the correct solution of the problem.

RoG (8; 6) measures the 2 cm. line when asked to double it and then applies his measurement twice over. On being told to double the 3 cm. square he begins by doubling its sides, but says at once: "*This will be too big.*" He therefore divides the 6 cm. square into two 6 cm. × 3 cm. rectangles and tries to cut one of them and re-compose it to make up a square twice the size of the original. He is unsuccessful. Doubling the 3 cm. cube, he first chooses the 5 cm. cube and pours in the sand. Bit by bit, he finally discovers the correct size, although he is still surprised to find that it will hold all the sand from both the 3 cm. cubes.

Luc (9; 3). 3 cm. line: "*I measured it to 3, then I went on to 6. So it's twice as long.*—Well, here's a square. You draw me another square twice the size of this one.—(He measures its side:) *It's 3: I'll go as far as 6.* (He draws a 6 cm. square then places the 3 cm. square over it.)—Do you think that space all round is the same as this (9 cm.²)?—*Yes . . . No, it's a little too much. You could put this one in four times.*—Well?—*I'll make one a little smaller. You can do it 1 cm. less, 5 cm. all round.*" Next, he is given the irregular figure the sides of which measure 4, 1·5 and 2·5 cm. He measures these sides, but instead of doubling them, he profits by his discovery with the square, saying: "*For this side which is 4 I'll go to 6 because that's 4 + 2; for 1·5 I'll take 2·5 and for 2·5, 3·5.*—Could we tell whether it's exactly twice the size?—*Well, you could. You could put one of the fields all in a line: then what's left would be the length of the other side* (the perpendicular portion).—All right. Now here are two boxes full of sand. I'd like to empty all the sand into one box just twice the size of one of these. Choose one of these boxes.—(He takes the 5 cm. cube and empties the sand into it.) *It only goes half-way.*—Well?—(He chooses the right box and verifies his selection.)"

346

CLAU (9; 8) also profits from his experiences as he goes along. To double a 3 cm. square, he first chooses a 6 cm. square. The smaller square is placed over it: "*It will go four times.*" He chooses a smaller square but doubts if it will be big enough. Instead he finds that the square is larger than necessary to take two 3 cm. squares because, when they are superposed, the two limbs of the L shape left uncovered can be re-composed in a way which makes this obvious. His third choice is correct: "Now draw me one twice the size of this one.—(He draws one approximately the right size, but without measuring it.) —Now the circle. Choose the one twice its size from among the others.—(The one he chooses is a little too big, but the one he draws is a little smaller. He places the original over his drawing.)—How did you do it?—*I thought about the ring round it* (the circumference!) *and made it a little bigger.*—What would have happened if you'd made this (the diameter) twice the size?—*It would have been too big.*"

CHAP (9; 8) measures the square and doubles its sides: "*No, that's wrong. I could get four squares in it.*" He draws a rectangle 6 cm. × 3 cm. "But you want to keep to the square shape.—*Well, like this then* (drawing a square a little larger without measuring it).—You can check it with these paper strips (placing the model over the drawing and handing to him the paper).—(He decomposes the remaining portion and superposes an equivalent area over the square:) *That's too much.* (For the cubes, he chooses the correct one straight away, having profited from previous experiences, but, looking at it he says:) *This one is too small, but the other is too big.*" He measures and finds the answer by trial-and-error.

SIM (9; 11) measures the line to double it. In order to double the 3 cm. square, he first draws a rectangle 6 × 3 cm. "But you are forgetting to keep to the same shape.—(He draws another rectangle, but this time about 5·5 × 3·5 cm.) *No, it's still a bit too big.* (He corrects it again, and gradually arrives at a square which he accepts as being twice the 3 cm. square by increasing the width of his rectangles as he decreases their length. Cubes: successive approximations. Pointing out the excess volume of one cube, he says: "You could empty another cube of sand in there," etc.

BRAS (10; 3) also draws a rectangle to double the square and goes on to take strips off its short side and put them over the long sides until he arrives at a shape which is square and about the right size. For the cubes, he chooses the correct box almost at once.

These solutions are clearly more advanced than those offered at level IIIA. These children begin like the others by doubling the lengths at issue, but they are immediately aware that a square having double the sides of the original has more than twice its area, etc. This increased awareness is shown in two ways. First, the error is discovered more quickly, the subject discovers either while he is drawing or immediately thereafter that the relation between the areas of two squares and the lengths of their sides is something other than one of simple proportionality, and that the same must be true of volumes and their edges. Secondly, and perhaps more important, the child now profits by his experience as the questions follow one another, so that his later constructions show increasing evidence of exact intuitive anticipations. Also, at this level, the child tries to reconstruct or decompose the whole (area or volume) by altering the disposition of its parts, which is in line with the findings of ch. XI on the conservation and measurement of area. We see him recompose the L shaped portion of a larger square to form a smaller square or he may mentally transform an irregular shape into an elongated rectangle, etc. Sim and Bras both transform a rectangle into a square, and so, starting with two squares side by side, they manage by successive approximations to construct a square twice the size of the original. In the problem of the cubes, these subjects study the empty portion. In other words, having chosen one as twice the size of the original they note how much it differs in volume from the sand, etc.

It would seem that the child now has all he needs in order to discover the correct relationships between length and area or volume, at least for simple shapes like squares. He can find out for himself that a square with twice the sides of another has far more than double the area, and should therefore realize that area can only be a multiple of the side. In other words, he could discover that the relation between side and area is one of mathematical multiplication and not one of simple proportion. Yet he cannot do so. And this, in spite of the fact that he has at his disposal the schema for quantifying relations and applying logical multiplication to them, so constructing a coordinate system. Yet the transition from logical to mathematical multiplication would not appear unduly difficult.

If we take a 3-cm. square like the one used in these experiments and draw a series of parallel lines at 1 cm. intervals horizontally and vertically, we have a matrix of 9 squares each 1 cm.^{2} (Fig. 20). Such a matrix can be a schema for logical multiplications, in which case it is a double-entry table and the entries are asymmetrical relations (order of position, etc.) or classes (parts). But it can also serve as a schema for mathematical multiplication governing the relations between the sides of the square and its area: 3 cm. $\times$ 3 cm. = 9 cm.^{2} The subjects quoted above all possess the necessary operational mechanisms to carry out the logical multiplications involved in the matrix. Thus, in dealing with its relations, they can coordinate the nine cells with one another because they possess coordinate systems (C.C.S., chs. XIII and XIV), and can therefore orient elements in accordance with the two axes, length and width. They can even quantify the relations of distance or length, characterizing the intervals between these ordered points. Again, considering the matrix in terms of subdivision, they understand perfectly that it breaks the square into parts, and would have no difficulty in quantifying these parts and realizing that they are equal. In short, they can construct the matrix shown in Fig. 20, which allows for the logical multiplication of relations and parts, both of which are expressed in quantitative form.

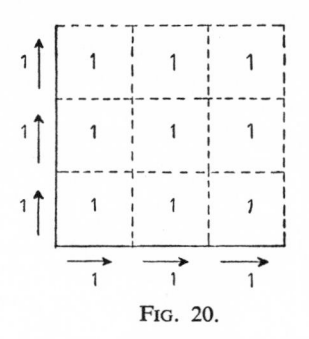

FIG. 20.

If it were merely a matter of dealing with elements whose quantitative form is given in advance, and moving from logical to arithmetical multiplication, there would be no difficulty since these children know that $3 \times 3 = 9$. Arithmetical multiplication is no more than the fusion into a single operation of logical multiplication of classes and relations, which means that it can be reduced to a system of associations or correspondences between ordered units. The principle of arithmetical multiplication is understood immediately that of logical multiplication is mastered, as has been demonstrated elsewhere.[1] But to find the relation between the sides of a square and its area is not a matter of simple mathematical multiplication, or even of its application to space. It involves the calculation of area as a function of linear elements, and, as we have shown in this chapter, what the child finds difficult is moving from one to the other (or from linear dimensions to measures of capacity). The question still remains why the child at level IIIB cannot perform that transition although he has mastered arithmetical multiplication as well as logical or sub-logical multiplication (i.e. that which bears on coordinated spatial relations).

Since stage IV is the level of formal operations, it looks as if calculating an area or a volume from linear dimensions involves a more 'formal' mechanism than arithmetical multiplication. In other words, it could be that 3 cm. × 3 cm. = 9 cm.² involves an operation of a higher order than $3 \times 3 = 9$. In our study of the subdivision of a continuous whole (C.C.S., ch. V), we found that between stages III and IV there is a fundamental transformation in children's representations of continuous space, both in one dimension and in several. Up to and

---

[1] Piaget and Szeminska, *The Child's conception of Number*, chs. IX and X, and Piaget, *Classes, relations et nombres*, ch. XI.

including level IIIB, that which is continuous is thought to comprise no more than a limited number of finite elements, but at stage IV subdivision tends in the direction of infinity and continuity.

It happens that the step from the arithmetical multiplication of discontinuous wholes to its use in the calculation of an area or a volume is closely related to the subdivision of continuous dimensions. Given two lengths of 3 cm. each, perpendicular to one another but starting from the same point of origin, the calculation of an area 9 cm.^{2} amounts to reducing that area to an infinite set of lines infinitesimally close to one another, just as a line at stage IV becomes an infinite series of neighbouring points. Hence the systematic difficulty found by children at earlier levels when trying to relate areas and volumes with linear quantities. The child thinks of the area as a space bounded by a line which is why he cannot understand how lines produce areas. We know that the area of a square is given by the length of its sides, but such a statement is intelligible only if it is understood that the area itself is reducible to lines, because a two-dimensional continuum amounts to an uninterrupted matrix of one-dimensional continua.

We can now understand why it is that to generate an area by multiplying lengths is a vastly different matter from the construction of a matrix or coordinate system like the one shown in Fig. 18. The difference between the two operational mechanisms is the difference between a matrix which is made up of a limited number of elements and one which is thought of as a continuous structure with an infinite number of elements.

Viewed in this way the decisive turning-point shown at level IIIB in attempting to solve the present problem agrees with the transformations known to hold at the same level in every other problem which concerns the representation of space.

§5. *Stage IV: The multiplicative relation between length and area or volume is understood*

The problem of doubling areas and volumes was such as to elicit interesting responses from children at earlier levels precisely because they failed to grasp the relation between lengths and two- or three-dimensional continua, but the responses given at the stage of formal operations, beginning at the age of 11 or 12, raise certain problems of their own. These arise out of the fact that the true solution involves the use of square roots and therefore demands specific academic instruction. On the other hand we are less interested in whether the solution is correct than in whether the subject is beginning to find a relation between sides or lines and multidimensional continua bounded by these lines. If the child can understand that the calculation of an area or a volume involves mathematical multiplication, he can construct such a relation without instruction. But it so happens that, as soon as the child can understand such calculations, and often before, he is taught how to do them in school. We must therefore forego our aim of tracing the evolution through to its final conclusion, and instead we will examine the responses made by children of 11–12 who have just started geometry in school.

Following are a number of examples given in order of increasing complexity:

DOE (11; 3) stands midway between levels IIIB and IV. Like children at the former level, he still recomposes linear elements, but he introduces calculation like those at stage IV. He begins by doubling the sides of the 3 cm. square and finds that he ends with four times the area he started with. But he then decides to try making the sides 4·5 cm. because that is half-way between 3 and 6: "*It's still a little too much. I worked out the perimeter which is 18 cm.*"

SCHNEI (11; 7) begins drawing a square with sides twice as long as the original (a 6 cm. square for a 3 cm. square) but half-way there he stops and says: "*No, that would give me an area of 36 cm.^{2} That's wrong.* (He considers the matter carefully and says at last:) *I must make the side 4·5 cm.*—How did you work that out?—*This square is 9 cm.^{2}, so twice that is 18 cm.^{2} Then I divided that by 4 and that gives me 4·5 cm.* (He thinks a little, then adds:) *No, that would be too much. I've got to make it 4 cm.* (an empirical guess)."

KIS (12; 5): "I want you to draw me a square twice as big as this one. How will you do it?—*I can work out the area by multiplying, and then multiply that by two, then I can divide that by the side to get the area. This one is 9 cm.^{2}. Twice that is 18 cm.^{2}. I divide that by 4 because there are 4 sides, which gives me 4·5 cm., but that's still not quite right.*—Why not?—*That won't give me the 4 sides. No, 4·5 × 4·5 is too much. You can't possibly work it out: you'd need to know how long the side has got to be.*—What would happen if you took twice 3 cm.?—*That's wrong. You'd have four times the area.* (!)—Well, have a look at this little cube which is full of sand. How would you get a cube which would take twice as much sand?—*I'd have to weigh how much there is and double that. Or else I could take the area of the 6 little sides and double that, then divide that by six again to find the area of the new sides: 9 cm.^{2} × 6 = 54 cm.^{2}. Twice that is 108 cm.^{2}. I divide that by six which is 18 cm.^{2}. I divide 18 cm.^{2} by ... by ... four. No, that won't do either.*—What if you took a cube with each edge twice as long?—*No, that would be four times the big one as well.*—Choose one of these cubes.—*Well, I know it isn't the big one* (with edges at 6 cm.): *The sand will go eight times into that.*—And that one (54 cm.^{3})?—*Yes, I think you could get two lots in there.*"

RAY (12; 10) tries making the side 6 cm. in order to get a square twice the size of a 4 cm. square: "*I make each side 2 cm. longer because that's half four. I know how to work out an area: 4 × 4 = 16 cm.^{2}. A square twice as big would be 32 cm.^{2}. Mine is 6 × 6 = 36 cm.^{2}. So it's wrong. 36 − 32 = 4 cm.^{2}. You ought really to take a little square of 4 cm.^{2} off one corner.*—But it's got to stay a square.—*Let's try 5·5 cm. That's 30·25 cm.^{2} so it's not enough. Try 5·6.*" In the end he produces a square of about 5·7 cm.

To double a 3 cm. cube he works out $3 \times 3 \times 3 = 27$ cm.³. *"You find twice that which is 54 cm.³."* He tries $4 \times 4 \times 4 = 64$ cm.³, then gives up.

Avo (11; 11). "Here's a square. You draw me one twice the area.—*If I double the sides I get a square four times as big.*—Yes, but I want one twice as big.—*I work out the area of the square: $3 \times 3 = 9$; I multiply that by two: $2 \times 9 = 18$; then I find the square root of 18; $4 \times 4 = 16$. There isn't a square root of 18. If I made it 16 it would be too small, and $5 \times 5 = 25$ which is too big. The side won't be far off 4.*—Here's a cube; make a cube which will hold twice as much sand.—*I work out the volume of the $3 \times 3 \times 3 = 27$ cm.³. I could multiply it by 6 because there are six sides* (he thinks). *No, that's wrong. Then I multiply by 2: $27 \times 2 = 54$ cm.³. I then divide by 3 to find its height or its width or its depth and $54 \div 3 = 18$. No, that doesn't seem right: 18 cm.² would be too big."*

None of these solutions is perfect and all are influenced by schooling. Nevertheless, they are interesting from our present standpoint. The first subject, Doc, still thinks in linear terms and concentrates on the perimeter of the figure, but unlike earlier subjects, he uses calculations instead of trial-and-error. Schnei, who comes next, has learned at school that the area is a product of linear dimensions raised to the second power. Moreover he shows a partial understanding of the relation between linear and areal measurements as he shows when, just as he starts to make the sides twice as long, he discovers by multiplying it out that his square would be too big ($6 \times 6 = 36$ cm.²). But that understanding is still incomplete because, after going on to double the area (2×9 cm.² $= 18$ cm.²), he simply divides his answer by four to find the length of side without apparently realizing that a square is not 4 times the side but the side multiplied by itself. Kis makes the same mistake, but he says immediately: "That's still not quite right." Unlike these, Ray has fully grasped the relation between the side of a square and its area, and it is only because he does not know how to work out square roots that he is forced to grope for the answer by squaring one length after another; in the end, his answer is not far out. Finally, Avo talks about "the square root", but in practice, his method is no different.

As for the cube, there is a certain time lag between the understanding of relations pertaining to area and those which govern volume. Thus, Kis, who decides that dividing the area of a square by 4 to find the length of its side is "still not quite right", is perfectly happy about first working out the volume then doubling it and dividing the answer by 6 to find the area of each face. Avo, for his part, divides the obtained volume by 3, because he is impressed by the fact that there are three dimensions. Only Ray uses the same method for the cube as he does for the square.

It is true that every one of these solutions falls short of the correct one. Nevertheless they show how children at stage IV understand that the relation between length and area or volume is different in kind from relations between dimensions of the same power. This realization coincides with the beginnings of formal operations and the consequent understanding of continuity.

Supplementary Note: The relation of linear measurement to the measurement of area in areal units

In order to study the difference between measurements of length and measurements of area expressed in square units, we suggested the following technique to Mlle Princigalli. (We had in mind both the difficulties of areal measurements and its psychological mechanism.) The subject was given a rectangle together with a number of little squares which could be made to cover it exactly. He was also given a number of matchsticks to measure the sides of the rectangle and of the unit squares. He was asked to make a forecast as to how many squares would be needed to cover the rectangle, using only the matches. The full account of this experiment is to be published in Italy by Mlle Princigalli, and we need only indicate that her results confirm the difficulty of the transition from linear measurements to squared measurements, as noted throughout this chapter. At sub-stage IIIA children either reproduce the arrangement of the squares on the rectangle by indicating a matrix with spaced matches, or else they cover the whole of the area with matches by packing them tightly together. In other words, they do not use the matches as measuring units and they fail to understand the relation between area and length of side. If they are not allowed to put the matches inside the rectangle they are completely at a loss. At level IIIB they achieve two-dimensional coordination, but they still use logical multiplication instead of numerical. The method most favoured is to divide the rectangle into a series of rows, which can be done either by constructing an interior matrix, as at level IIIA, or by putting squares all round the rectangle, or matches, which stand for the sides of the squares, and then counting the number of rows and the number of squares in each row, which is a form of arithmetical addition and does not involve arithmetical multiplication.

Only as children move from stage IIIB to IV, is there some hint of the use of multiplication as a shortened method of addition. Even then, there is little understanding of the relation between area and length of side (a conclusion which is particularly safe in view of the fact that the apparatus included ready-made units of area as well as linear units). We may therefore safely say that that relation is not properly mastered until stage IV itself.

353

Chapter Fourteen

THE CONSERVATION AND
MEASUREMENT OF VOLUME[1]

THE conservation and measurement of distance and length were studied in part II, while in part III we examined linear measurements in two or three dimensions. Ch. XI was devoted to the conservation and measurement of area. The ground has been further prepared by ch. XIII, in which we studied how children double areas and volumes. We now turn to the conservation and measurement of volume.

From the standpoint of geometry, area and volume are closely related, but from that of psychology, the question of volume raises many problems of its own, whence the need to prepare ourselves for this final study by means of the various discussions which precede it. Both lengths and areas are abstractions in a certain sense (abstractions both from the object and from the subject's own actions). But the notion of volume corresponds more closely with the physical structure of objects because there can be no macroscopic object without three-dimensional characteristics. At the same time, our study of the conservation of the physical properties of objects[2] has shown that we need to distinguish two invariants where the geometrician would recognize only one. These invariants are elaborated separately and at quite different developmental levels: the conservation of a quantity of matter appears as early as level IIIA, but the conservation of volume as a physical concept is not elaborated until stage IV, being the level of formal operations. For instance, when we showed children a ball made of modelling-clay and then rolled it out into a sausage shape, all those above level IIIA agreed that it was just as 'big', but it was found that they meant two very different things, depending on their level of maturity. The child at stage III, and that includes level IIIB, means no more than that the quantity of clay remains the same, and is prepared to allow that the substance might have expanded or contracted while still being the same clay as it was. He therefore contends that if you immerse the clay in water after elongating it to see whether it will displace the same amount of water, the clay will "take up more (or less) space" than it did when its shape was spherical. But the child at stage IV means that the object is as 'big' as it was both in the sense that the amount of matter is constant and in the further sense that its

---

[1] Written with the collaboration of M. H. Aebli and Mlle F. Pitsou.
[2] Piaget and Inhelder, *Le développement des quantités chez l'enfan)t.*

volume is invariant. In other words, he recognizes that it occupies the same space because it does not expand or contract. Obviously, that distinction raises a delicate problem in our present geometrical study.

We must allow for the fact that we cannot ask children questions about the conservation of volume without introducing physical objects like bricks or cubes filled with sand, etc., and this applies particularly to those at the level of concrete intelligence (stage III). We could say that the conservation of volume is not recognized in its geometrical sense until there is conservation of physical volume, that is, until the object is seen as being a true solid which cannot be made to expand or contract. In a sense this is true, but only in a sense, because we should be looking for a geometrical concept of volume which, like the physical concept, is based on the relations between the object itself and all the other objects round about. That concept presupposes the construction of a spatial continuum, and its quantification by means of multiplicative matrices, as already explained in our last chapter where we showed how essential these were to the calculation of area and volume. That construction belongs to stage IV, but it may be that there is also conservation of volume in a simpler form, one which does not entail the calculation of volume together with the elaboration of metrical relations between the volume under consideration and the surfaces by which it is bounded. Because that notion would be merely qualitative, it might well appear at level IIIA, together with the conservation of length (chs. III–IV), and area (ch. XI). This would be in line with the observation made in ch. XIII that children attain a certain kind of conservation of area at level IIIA, based on the primitive conception of area (and volume) as that which is bounded by lines (or faces). That understanding comes long before the ability to calculate areas and volumes by mathematical multiplication, involving relations between units of different powers, and at the same time as other elementary forms of conservation.

We shall try to answer these questions in this chapter, the last in part IV, and we shall see how they link up with our study in general.

§1. *Outline of method and results* (see Fig. 21)

The child is shown a block which is quite solid, and measures 4 cm. in height against a square base 3 cm. × 3 cm. so that its volume is 36 cm.³. He is told that the block is an old house built on a little island, a square piece of cardboard measuring 3 cm. × 3 cm. and pasted onto a large sheet of corrugated card meant to stand for the lake or sea. It seems that this house is threatened, and so the inhabitants decide to build another in its place. The new house is to have exactly as much room as the old, although it is being built on another island. The child is shown these other islands which are also pieces of card but which differ from the first in size or shape or in both, their measurements being 2 × 2 cm., 2 × 3 cm., 1 ×2 cm., 1 × 1 cm. and 3 × 4 cm. The problem consists in reproducing the volume of the first block while altering its form to comply with the base which is given. A further point of difference lies in that the equal volume must be built out of little wooden cubes each of which is 1 cm.³, while the original is a solid block. There is a good deal to be gained in avoiding the use of discontinuous elements in the model as well as the copy, but this is only with older children who would otherwise be able to solve the problem by arithmetical correspondence without considering the volume as such.

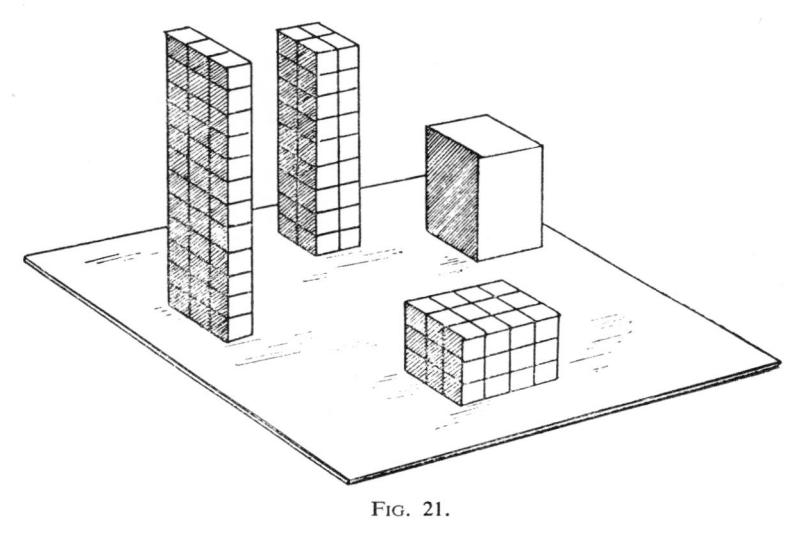

FIG. 21.

Younger children are more likely to be put off by the difference in construction, since they are apt to think "there are more bricks, rooms, wood, etc." where there are a large number of small elements than in one solid block. With little children, therefore, we have the first house made of unit-cubes as well, as we are less worried about arithmetical correspondence, since their counting is still poor. We may add that it is often useful to work with units greater than 1 cm.³, in which case the several proportions involved are kept the same.

Equality of volume is expressed by the words: "as much room". Should the child fail to understand what is meant, he may be told that every inmate is to have a room of his own, just like in the other house, etc. Little children try very hard to keep the shape of the house the same, and we then have to insist that the house cannot be built over the sea, and that it must be built on the island. Often, the successive constructions made in response to the enquiry are all left standing to the end, because they can then be used in the final discussion.

Alongside this, our principal technique, we used a number of other subsidiary techniques. The most revealing of these was to ask the child quite simply to reproduce the model itself, using either similar bricks, or bricks which differed only in size, or bricks which differed in shape also: cubes and a variety of parallelipipeds. The child may be asked to reproduce the model some distance away, or he may be told to build his alongside. When the last of these methods is used, we frequently find a type of behaviour which is most significant: the subject builds walls all round the model on five, or even on six, sides. In effect, he tries to reproduce not the object itself, *qua* solid object, but only the volume of that object in so far as it consists in so much empty space bounded by those surfaces. This response brings out the topological character of the first intuitions of volume, and shows how gradual is the construction of Euclidean notions, and why metrical calculation does not appear until very late.

Another auxiliary method consisted in showing children various cubes and parallelipipeds (there were a dozen of these altogether, all different) and comparing them two at a time: "Are these two as big as one another? Is there as much wood in each of them?" These objects are all of solid painted wood, and the experimenter must be careful in the way he chooses his words, in order to avoid any suggestion of one-dimensional comparisons. Indeed the child is helped to make a three-dimensional comparison by being offered a set of unit-cubes, which he can use in order to measure with, or alternatively, to reconstruct the objects. Another variant is to hand the subject a large block of wood, asking him to find another having the same volume out of a number of alternatives which differ in shape. Whatever the question being asked, the experimenter seeks to establish the way in which the subject organizes his comparisons, since the method he adopts is no less revealing than the answer he obtains.

Finally, whatever preliminary questioning is made, the enquiry always finishes with questions about the conservation of volume. To this end, the experimenter starts from the original model of 36 cm.^{3} (or more, as the case may be), that shape having been faithfully reproduced by the child out of unit-cubes, with or without the help of the adult. The latter now builds various other constructions out of these same bricks by changing the form of the bottom or base layer. The child watches him this while, and is then asked: (*a*) whether there is as much room in the new 'house' as there was in the old, or whether there is more or less, and (*b*) could one use the self-same bricks which now go to form the new house in order to re-make one like the original and exactly the same size. Needless to say, this question of conservation of volume is not easy to be certain about, as is clear from our introductory remarks. The experimenter must try to discover whether the subject relies solely on the conservation of the actual number of bricks being used, or whether he thinks in terms of their total volume and its conservation also. The fact that some subjects accept the first kind of conservation but reject the second proves that the two notions are distinct. Nevertheless, the experimenter must use considerable skill in order to know which of these is operative in any given case.

We thought it advisable to check our results by repeating with the present subjects the experiment which dealt with the conservation of volume when a solid object is immersed in water,[1] adapting the procedure to the present experimental situation. The child is shown a set of 1 cm. metal cubes which are then put at the bottom of a bowl of water. The experimenter builds a block out of 36 units ($3 \times 3 \times 4$) while the subject notes how the level of the water rises in the bowl. He is then asked if he thinks the level will change if the arrangement of the bricks is modified, by making constructions of $2 \times 1 \times 18$ or $2 \times 2 \times 2 \times 9$, etc. This makes it easy to question him concerning three different kinds of volume: internal volume, or the conservation of the 36 bricks (this can be analysed quite easily with the methods described in earlier paragraphs), volume as 'occupied' space, being the amount of 'room' taken up by the 36 bricks in the water, and finally, the complementary volume, i.e. the volume of the water. Both the last two volumes are measured by the level of the water, and where the subject recognizes their conservation, this is shown by the fact that he anticipates that the level remains unaltered. In addition to questions about the level, the child may be asked whether the bricks will continue to "take up the same amount of space in the water", or whether "there will be as much room for the water as before", etc.

We observed the following types of response at the various developmental stages. Since our techniques were impracticable below the age of 4 or 5, there was little to be gained from analysing responses at stage I. A different experiment might be made in order to discover when children first notice large differences in volume, and results would be more clear-cut if only one of the three dimensions were varied at a time. However, that problem hardly concerns us at present, since it is one of perception rather than representation.

Stage II usually lasts from about 4; 6 until between 5 and 7. There is first a sub-stage IIA when any transformations, reconstructions or comparisons of volume are made entirely in terms of one dimension only, usually the largest. Inevitably, such transformations lead to alterations in the volume of the object. However, the child of this level, although he is well aware of the difference in volume, still refuses to build a taller

[1] See Piaget and Inhelder, *Le développement des quantités chez l'enfant.*

building than the model to allow for a decrease in the size of the base. Even older children may at times find it difficult to dissociate height (and to some extent form) from volume, but when children are older they quickly understand what is meant if the experimenter goes on to explain that all he wants is a house with as much room in it but that its shape can be different if need be. But with younger children, the problem cannot be circumvented: irrespective of the size of the base of his own building, the subject will always stop when he has reached the height of the model. Turning to their attempts at reproducing a given volume, we find children at this level tend to follow the boundary surfaces as such. In particular, we often see them building curtain walls all round the visible faces of the volume which they have been asked to reproduce. Again, when asked to make comparisons between volumes, they do so without using common measures, and in one-dimensional terms. Finally, there is no conservation of volume as yet. During sub-stage IIB the responses given by children are intermediate between those just described and those which belong to stage III. The most notable advance occurs in their attempts to reproduce an equivalent volume on a different base. If necessary, children now make their own building higher than the model (which means that they are beginning to use logical multiplication in their handling of relations between dimensions).

Stage III begins around the age of 6; 6 or 7; 6 and continues until 11 or 12. Children at sub-stage IIIA work out the relations between the three dimensions (although to begin with, they cannot handle more than two and the third is progressively adjusted to these two), using only logical multiplication, that is, without measuring or making more exact compensations based on a unit system. When faced with problems of transformations in the shapes of houses (as in the principal technique), children at this stage can dissociate the three notions of height, shape and volume. So, when told to build his house on a small island, the child now builds a taller house, but he is still unable to determine just how much taller it should be, because he cannot make the differences equal and compensatory by using metrical decomposition and recomposition. In simply reconstructing the original model using different bricks, children are completely successful in regard to the first two dimensions, height and width, while the third, depth, is made to agree empirically. Comparison between one volume and another may be made by way of qualitative common measuring terms (implying only transitivity, without unit-iteration), or alternatively, the subject may effect mental changes of position (implying compensations based on logical rather than mathematical multiplication). Turning now to the conservation of volume, we find that such conservation exists only in regard to "interior volume", in other words the subject recognizes the invariance of the amount of matter which is contained within the boundary surfaces (in this case, the number of unit bricks in the construction). But that conservation does not extend as yet to what has been termed "occupied volume", meaning the amount of space occupied by the object as a whole in relation to other objects round about. Accordingly, if we ask our subjects whether a long row of 36 bricks will take up the same amount of room in a basinful of water as any other arrangement of the selfsame bricks, the answer will be in the negative.

Sub-stage IIIB usually begins around the age of 8–9, although we occasionally find children who are more precocious. In addition to the developments already noted, children now begin to measure correctly, using the unit-cubes as units, but they still do not carry out mathematical multiplication, which means that they cannot establish numerical relations between lengths or areas and volumes as such. What we usually find is a compromise between logical multiplication of the relations involved (these being expressed in quantitative terms because the subject can now measure) and attempts at using methematical calculation by treating volume as if it were the outcome of a process of addition of areas. The result is that these subjects are successful only where they can reconstruct the required volume by simply doubling one dimension while in all other cases they fail.

Finally, stage IV is marked by two decisive but related developments. First there is the discovery of the mathematical relation between area and volume; that two volumes are equal if the products of their respective elements (or lengths in three dimensions) are the same. Second is the discovery of the conservation of volume, in the sense of "volume occupied" by the object as a whole in a setting of other objects, as against its "interior volume" (volume as defined by boundary surfaces).

§2. *Sub-stage IIA: Non-conservation of volume together with one-dimensional comparisons*

A number of geometricians believe that instruction in elementary notions of space should begin with the idea of volume, because that idea is less abstract, since all the objects we encounter in our everyday experience are in fact three-dimensional rather than two-dimensional or linear. There is some justification for their point of view where the argument is limited to early topological intuitions of space (although, it should be borne in mind that volumes are always bounded by areas and areas in turn are bounded by lines, so that even at the earliest levels of representation, linear considerations are far more important than they are in perception). However, at the level of Euclidean intuitions, their position is quite indefensible. Representations of areas and lengths during stages I and II may be far from adequate, yet they are much easier to construct than those of volume, perhaps because not all the parts of a three-dimensional object can be seen at the same time. Hence, even at level IIA, children cannot transform the appearance of a solid while holding its volume constant, and cannot make any comparisons between volumes beyond one-dimensional relations. Following are a number of examples illustrating this primitive mode of response:

FLU (5; 0).The child is told to rebuild the model of $3 \times 3 \times 4$ units on an island measuring 2×3: the house which he builds is $2 \times 3 \times 4$, i.e. its height is the same as that of the model.[1] "Is that enough?—*Yes, that's enough.* —Which of these two houses is bigger?—*That one* (the model).—Well, what are you going to do about it? (He adds another storey to his building which makes it $2 \times 3 \times 5$ units or a total of 30 against 36 on the model.)—Is that right now?—*No. Here there are more bricks* ($2 \times 3 \times 5$).—Well, I want you to build me a house using the same number of bricks.—(He changes his house back to $2 \times 3 \times 4$ by removing the top storey.)—Is yours the same size now?—*Yes.*—How do you know?—*Because I put the bricks there.*— Is there the same amount of room inside it?—*It's the same because it's the same height.*" He is given a model half the size of the first, measuring $3 \times 3 \times 2$ units, so that it has 18 units in all and is built up of two layers. Once again he is asked to build another the same size on an 'island' measuring 2×3 units: immediately, Flu builds a house $2 \times 3 \times 2$ units, i.e. the same height as the model: "Are there the same amount of rooms in both houses?—*Yes, because it has these bricks.*—Have you measured it?—*Yes* (indicating that the two heights are the same).—But what about that (pointing to the difference in breadth, 2 in the copy, 3 in the model)?—*Oh, yes!* (and he adds a third storey).—Is that right now?—*No, that* ($2 \times 3 \times 3$) *is bigger than that* ($3 \times 3 \times 2$).—Where is there more room?—*There* (pointing to the higher construction).—Well—(He takes the top storey off again.)—Well, let's try and build a house with as much room as that one (18 bricks) on that little island (1×1).—(He puts two bricks together, one above the other, giving the same height as the model.)—Is there the same amount of room in that one?— *No, it's tiny.*—Well, what are you going to do about it?—(He adds a third brick.)—Is that enough?—(He adds a fourth.)—Is that right now?—*No, this* ($1 \times 1 \times 4$) *is bigger than that* ($3 \times 3 \times 2$!) *because I've put a lot of bricks to it.*"

MAY (5; 1). The model is $3 \times 3 \times 4 = 36$ units. "I'd like you to build it here (on a base of 2×3 units).—(He build his house $2 \times 3 \times 4 = 24$ units.) —Is there just as much room in both?—*Yes.*—I'm not so sure; it looks to me as if there's much less room on your island.—(He adds another storey to his house making it $2 \times 3 \times 5 = 30$.)—Is there the same amount of room now?—*Yes . . . a little bit more because it's bigger.*—Why?—*Because I put more bricks to it* (removing the top storey so that now it is only $2 \times 3 \times 4$).— *It's the same size* (putting the two together).—Is there as much room in it?— *Yes, because they're the same size.*—Well, what if we wanted to build a house with as much room as this one (36 elements) on this island (2×2)?—(He

[1] The first figure represents the depth of the building, the second its breadth, and the last its height.

builds a house of $2 \times 2 \times 4 = 16$ units.)—Is that right?—*Yes, it's the same size.*—Can I go on adding more bricks?—*No, there are more bricks here.*— And on that island (1×1)?—(He builds a tower 4 bricks high.)—Has this as much room as that (the 36 unit model)?—*No, there's more room there because it's thicker.*—And like this (adding a brick to the tower making 5 in all)?—*Here there's more (5) because it's higher.*"

Jos (5; 2). A model of $3 \times 3 \times 4 = 36$ bricks to be transformed and built on an island 2×2: "*It won't work. That one's too thick and it's too small here.*—Try.—(He builds a house $2 \times 2 \times 4$).—Has yours the same amount of room?—*No, there's more room there (36) because it's thicker.*—Can you get round that any way?—*Yes, I must build mine higher* (building it $2 \times 2 \times 5 = 20$).—Where is there more room, here (36) or here (20)?—*In mine ($2 \times 2 \times 5$), because it's bigger* (= higher).—Couldn't we make yours so that there will be the same amount of room on each?—*No, it just can't be done.*—Try making one exactly the same as this one (i.e. repeating the model on a base of 3×3).—*I just measure the sides with the bricks* (he copies it correctly and then checks to see that its height is the same).—Well, what if I ask you to build it again on this island (2×3) but keeping the same amount of room?—(He builds it $2 \times 3 \times 4$).—Is there the same amount of room in yours as in mine? Show me.—*Yes, it's the same height and the same thickness* (indicating its breadth and its height).—Watch. I'll do it myself. (The experimenter first makes a model $3 \times 3 \times 4$ exactly like the one shown to the subject, and then moves all his bricks to an island 2×2; on this island he rebuilds his house so that it now measures $2 \times 2 \times 9$.)—*Yours is bigger but there's less room than before* (because it is thinner). *No, there's more room, because it's bigger.*— Which one has less room?—*That one, because it's smaller* (36).—What about these ($2 \times 2 \times 9$ compared with $2 \times 6 \times 3$)?—*There's more room here ($2 \times 6 \times 3$) because it's longer.*—And this way (transforming $2 \times 6 \times 3$ to $2 \times 18 \times 1$).—*There's much more room in this one because it's much longer.*—Could we use these bricks (2×18) in order to make one like this again (the original $3 \times 3 \times 4$ model)?—*It's going to be a bit big . . . no, the same . . . I've got to find out if it's really the same* (building the structure and then comparing its height with the model). *Oh, yes! It is the same!*—And this way (transforming $3 \times 3 \times 4$ to $2 \times 3 \times 6$)?—*Here it's bigger* (with a height of six).—But is there the same amount of room?—*No, there's more room there ($2 \times 3 \times 6$) because that one is bigger.*"

Amb (5; 3) is asked to make a number of paired comparisons between volumes ready-made, and also to reconstruct some of them. "Have a look at these two ($1 \times 2 \times 1$ and $1 \times 1 \times 2$)?—*They're the same.*—And these ($1 \times 3 \times 1$ and $1 \times 1 \times 3$)?—*They're the same too.*—And these ($4 \times 1 \times 1$ and $1 \times 2 \times 2$)?—*That one ($4 \times 1 \times 1$) is bigger.*—Can you make this one yourself ($4 \times 1 \times 1$)?—*Yes* (doing so correctly).—And this one ($1 \times 2 \times 2$)? —*I can't do that one, it's too hard.* You try building an easier one.—*All right* (building a tower $1 \times 1 \times 2$ as his copy. Then he lays the original on its side, $2 \times 2 \times 1$, and constructs a single layer of bricks all round it).—And can you make that one when it's standing up ($1 \times 2 \times 2$)?—*No, I can't do that.*—And this ($2 \times 2 \times 3$)?—(He builds his $1 \times 1 \times 3$.)—Are they both the same?—*I don't know, I can't do them except for the long ones.*"

TON (6; 1). The technique is the same as that used for Amb. "Is there the same amount of room in these two ($1 \times 1 \times 2$ and $1 \times 2 \times 1$)?—*They're both the same.*—And these two ($1 \times 3 \times 1$ and $1 \times 2 \times 2$)?—*That one* ($1 \times 2 \times 2$) *is bigger.*—Good. You try and make one just like it.—(He builds a wall of bricks all round it.)—And now this one ($1 \times 1 \times 3$).—(He copies that exactly.)—What about these two ($2 \times 2 \times 2$ and $1 \times 4 \times 2$)? Have they the same amount of room?—*Oh, no!*—Which one has more wood in it? *That one* ($2 \times 2 \times 2$).—Can you make one just like it?—(He builds a layer of bricks round it.)"

CYR (6; 5) is told to make a copy of the standard model ($3 \times 3 \times 4 = 36$ bricks) and does so quite correctly. The experimenter alters his copy, making it $2 \times 3 \times 6 = 36$; "Is there the same amount of room in this one and in that?—(He thinks.) *There's more room there* ($3 \times 3 \times 4$) *because it's wider.*—And this way (altering $2 \times 3 \times 6$ back to its original proportions)?—*Now they're the same again.*—And this way (altering one of the two to $3 \times 4 \times 3$)? —*It's still the same.*—And this way ($2 \times 2 \times 9$)?—*No, there's less room here* ($2 \times 2 \times 9$) *because there's nothing in the middle* (= the breadth and depth are 2×2 only).—Could we make this again ($3 \times 3 \times 4$) out of this ($2 \times 2 \times 9$)?—*Yes, I think so.*—But you still say there's less room?—*Yes* ... *I don't know.* (He tries altering one to the other and succeeds.)—What about this way (transforming it to $2 \times 18 \times 1$)?—*That's not the same. This one is bigger* ($3 \times 3 \times 4$) *and that one is smaller.*"

GAU (6; 6) is an example of the sort of response obtained at this level when the technique adopted is to carry out the construction under water so that the subject can be questioned simultaneously about the 'interior' volume, the 'occupied volume', and the complementary volume. Gau is shown a structure underwater made up of $3 \times 3 \times 4$ bricks. He notes the level of the water. "Supposing I stood them up this way (vertically), what would happen to the water?—*It will go up. It's going to be higher.*—Watch and see what happens (making the experiment).—*Oh, no!*—Well, supposing I put them round like this ($3 \times 1 \times 12$), will both houses have the same amount of room or will one of them have more room than the other?—*There's more room here* (3×12 than $3 \times 3 \times 4$).—And is there the same amount of room for the water, or is there more or less?—*There's more room for the water.*— Why?—*Because it's flatter*", etc. We must infer that Gau holds both that the interior volume of the bricks is greater in the new arrangement and that the complementary volume, that of the water, is greater also—in exactly the same way as subjects at this same level argued concerning circumscribed and complementary areas (see the example of Wir, cited in ch. XI, §8).

The responses given at level IIA are interesting because they tell us a good deal about the early intuition of volume. It is quite clear that every one of the subjects quoted possesses such an intuition. In other words, he understands perfectly what is meant by the question: "Is there more or less room in one house than in another?", and similarly, he can tell what the experimenter means when he asks whether there is more or less wood in one structure than in another. Moreover, his replies are not uniformly incorrect: thus Flu understands that a house made up of $3 \times 3 \times 4$ units is bigger than one of $2 \times 3 \times 4$ units, etc. Nevertheless, it is abundantly clear that at this level notions of volume are predominantly topological: volume is that which is bounded by a set of surfaces, those which are visible from outside, and these in turn are chiefly defined by the lines which form their perimeters. These subjects are as yet unable to conceive of the idea that the interior of these boundaries can be evaluated in its own right by a multiplicative operation. So much is true even of logical multiplication which should govern the coordination of relations of height, of breadth and of depth. It is even more true of the mathematical multiplication which is required to generate a quantitative notion of volume as a triple product of length, breadth and height, all of these being expressed in quantitative terms. Consequently, their judgments of volume are no more than estimates of volume as bounded by surfaces, and these estimates are made in terms of what appears to them as the most important or the most striking of these surfaces.

Here we find a link between topological and Euclidean notions of volume. The child is asked to compare two volumes which are not parts of a nesting series and are not even homeomorphic and is therefore compelled to draw on whatever Euclidean notions he can to help answer the question. But what are these notions? In ch. XI we saw how, when dealing with areas, children at level IIA were quite unable to make comparisons between one area and another if they were dissimilar, even though they could see how both were made up of the same number of isomorphic elements (like the six squares which were arranged in the shape of a rectangle and rearranged in a pyramid). They were handicapped by their failure to coordinate the dimensions involved in terms of the two axes of the plane. So, in ch. VII, we saw how measurement at this level is always one-dimensional, even when it is applied to a plane surface or a solid. Even linear measurement is far from adequate, as was amply demonstrated in chs. IV–VI. Estimates of distance and length are still made with reference to isolated extremities, that is, having regard only to the point of arrival. Consequently, when the child at this level compares two volumes, he thinks of volume as a matter of boundary surfaces, and here too his frame of reference is limited to that dimension in which one of the two volumes projects most obviously.

In the event, we find that the subjects quoted, when asked to estimate the amount of 'room' in a house, whether or not they are required to build it themselves, show a marked tendency to go by the height alone. Sometimes we find a judgment which is based on breadth or on depth, but this does not alter the fact that only one dimension enters into consideration, this being whichever features most prominently (cf. Jos when considering a line of 18 bricks). Usually that dimension is height because where one building is taller than another the difference between them stands out clearly. Nevertheless, differences whereby one object projects beyond another are important because it is from their consideration that children make the crucial step in passing from topological intuitions of volume to the first Euclidean coordinations.

But it is here that we find a conflict between topological intuitions of volume which are based on boundary surfaces and Euclidean estimates which depend on one dimension only. Thus a child may set out to build a house on another island having the same height as the model, but even while doing so, he becomes aware that what is contained within its boundary surfaces is by no means the same. He therefore tries to correct his attempt by increasing the number of storeys. When he does this, he is put off as soon as his copy is made higher than the model, because he falls back on his limited criterion. So now, in spite of himself, he finds himself once more arguing from height to volume. Flu is a case in point. First he argues that a house measuring $3 \times 3 \times 4$ units will be equal to another consisting of $2 \times 3 \times 4$ units, but when he sees what they look like he decides that $3 \times 3 \times 4$ gives a bigger house, so he builds a fifth storey onto the other. But that second solution does not satisfy him either, which is why he says there is more 'room' in the $2 \times 3 \times 5$ house, ignoring the fact that it contains only 30 bricks as compared with 36 on the model. Later, he goes so far as to assure us that a tower of four bricks ($1 \times 1 \times 4$) "is bigger (than a house made up of $3 \times 3 \times 2 = 18$ bricks) because I kept putting more bricks on". The next subject, May, recognizes that the four brick tower is less in volume than a house of $3 \times 3 \times 4$ bricks, because the latter is 'thicker', but after adding a fifth brick to his tower, he tells us with perfect assurance that "there's more room here ($1 \times 1 \times 5$) because it's higher". What happens is that the child starts out by considering only one dimension and builds a house which has a lesser volume than the model. He then compares their remaining dimensions and sees that the model is larger ("bigger", "thicker", "thinner", "Nothing in the middle", etc.), but he cannot cross-multiply these dimensions since he cannot carry out mathematical multiplication or even logical multiplication (i.e. using a system of qualitative compensations). Accordingly he reverts to the comparison in terms of one dimension only, forcing himself to believe that this alone must determine volume in the sense of the space contained within boundary surfaces.

This interpretation is confirmed in striking fashion by the responses which are made to our alternative situation, where the subject is free to make an exact copy of the model instead of being asked to reproduce an equivalent volume on a different base. Topological notions of volume dictate the child's replies unmistakeably: instead of making another construction similar to the model, he simply builds a wall all round it so as to cover all its visible faces. Evidently, he believes that by so doing he is coming to grips with the essential characteristic of volumes, that of being contained within a set of boundary surfaces. This is true even though the child is not told stories about houses and walls but simply asked to do something with bricks (and these subjects had not previously been questioned by the technique of houses on islands). Thus Amb, who cannot copy a parallelipiped consisting of $1 \times 2 \times 2$ bricks, "I can't do them except the long ones", builds a layer of bricks around the model if this is too complicated! Ton, who is six years old and could copy the models quite easily if directly told to do so, still prefers to build a curtain wall round them like Amb. At least a third of the subjects at level IIA did the same.

Needless to say, under these conditions the construction of volume in the Euclidean sense is out of the question since the child has not acquired the essential preliminary to all Euclidean construction, conservation—here, the conservation of volume when shape is altered. Both Jos and Cyr deny that there is the same amount of 'room' inside two alternative models, made out of the same collection of bricks. This is hardly surprising inasmuch as the boundary surfaces do in fact differ (not only in shape, but quantitatively too). The linear relations between the elements in the two cases are likewise different, and so the subject is bound to feel that they differ in volume, since to him, volume depends on limits or boundaries. A subject may go so far as to doubt that he could, if desired, retrace the steps whereby the model has been transformed into a different shape, and so arrive back to his starting-point, using exactly the same bricks (which have not been added to or taken from, although it is true that they have not been counted either). And so we hear Jos saying: "It's going to be a bit big . . . no, the same . . . I've got to find out if it's really the same."

§3. *Sub-stage IIB: Intermediate responses*

As is usual, the main characteristic of level IIB is that it is transitional between stages II and III. In the present experimental situations, the level is marked by the recognition that a building erected on a narrower base must be higher if it is to retain the same volume, but while the height is increased a little, it is not increased sufficiently. Where the child is asked simply to reproduce the model, at this level he makes a number of successive approximations before reaching an exact replica. Either way, he is beginning to establish relations between the three dimensions instead of focusing his attention on one dimension only.

CHAP (5; 4). He is shown a model $2 \times 6 \times 2$ and an alternative base of 1×3. Placing the model over the base, he says: "*That one* (island) *is smaller* (and he goes on to make the second house $1 \times 3 \times 2$).—What was it that I asked you to do for me?—*A house with the same amount of room.*—Well?—*There's more room in this one* (indicating the model and its greater width).—

Well, what about it?—*I'll make it higher, I won't make it any thicker* (and he makes his 1 × 3 × 4).—Is there the same amount of room now?—. . . (He extends his building, going off the island, using the corrugated cardboard which is meant to stand for the water.)—That won't do; you must keep to the island.—*There isn't enough room here. That house* (1 × 3 × 4) *is bigger this way* (height = 4), *but this one is bigger that way* (breadth = 6).—Well, what shall we do about it?—(He gives up because he dare not raise the height above 4.)—Try doing it with this house (3 × 3 × 4) on that island (2 × 2).— (He makes his 2 × 2 × 5.)—Which one has more room?—(He makes his house wider by building it out into the 'water', but changes his mind as he remembers what he was told. Instead, he now adds a further storey, making it 2 × 2 × 6.) *This one is higher.*—Which of the two has more room?—*That one* (36) *because it's thicker.*—(He is now asked to make an exact copy of the model, 3 × 3 × 4 = 36.)—(To begin with, he makes his 2 × 3 × 4, but then he suddenly cries.) *I know the secret now* (comparing the depth of the two houses and altering his to 3 × 3 × 4).—Now watch carefully (introducing the problem of conservation). I'm going to take your bricks and put them together like this (2 × 2 × 9). Is there still as much room as in the other (3 × 3 × 4)?—(He puts the two together and says:) *One is wide and the other is long. There's more room in that one* (3 × 3 × 4 *because it has three rows* (i.e. its width is three)."

CHRI (5; 10), told to make an equivalent to a 3 × 3 × 4 house on a base of 2 × 2: "*I don't think I'll be able to build such a big house on a tiny island like this. I can* (only) *make it the same height* (making it 2 × 2 × 4). *No, I must make it a little bit higher* (and he makes it 2 × 2 × 5). *Now there's the same amount of room because this one's a bit higher than that one* (36).— Try building one just like this model (on the table without any restriction on the size of the base).—(He first builds round two sides of the model and then takes the model away and makes his own copy inside the boundary he has constructed. Then he puts the model and the copy together and so in the end he arrives at an exact copy.)—(The experimenter transforms Chri's copy to 2 × 3 × 6.) Is there still as much room as in that house (3 × 3 × 4)?— *No, there's more room in this one* (2 × 3 × 6) *because it's higher.*—And this way (transforming it to 2 × 18 × 1)?—*This one's much longer only it isn't as high.*—Could we make this one (3 × 3 × 4) again out of this one (2 × 18 × 1)?—*Yes, because this one's longer.*"

GEO (6; 11) asked to transform a 3 × 3 × 4 house and reconstruct it on a base of 2 × 2, begins by making it 2 × 2 × 4, but then he says: "*I don't know how to go on. Oh, yes! I've got to make it higher* (building it up to 2 × 2 × 7). *Now there's enough.*—Look at them carefully.—(He compares the two houses, then adds a further storey to his own, making it 2 × 2 × 8.) *This time I think it's right.*—Why?—*I can't explain.*" Told simply to copy the 3 × 3 × 4 model which is on the table in front of him, he makes his copy 3 × 4 × 4. "Are they both the same?—*Yes.*—Look at them carefully.—(He corrects his copy.)—(The experimenter now alters it to 2 × 2 × 9.) Is there still the same amount of room?—*It's the same because you've used the same bricks.*—(It is further transformed to 2 × 18 × 1.)—*Oh, this time there's more room here* (2 × 18 × 1) *because it's longer.*—Why?—*Oh, no! There's the same amount of room because they're the same bricks.*)—What about like this (1 × 36 × 1)?—*This time it isn't the same anymore because it's very very long.*—But they're still the same bricks, aren't they?—*Yes, that's simple. This one was only three bricks wide while the new one has all the bricks in the width.*—Well, can you make this one again (3 × 3 × 4) using these bricks (1 × 36 × 1)?—*Yes. They're the same bricks.*—But if the bricks are the same, can you still have more or less room?—*Yes, because the other one is very long.*—Well?—*It's the same bricks, but there's more room.*"

Luc (6; 2) is questioned by the alternative method, comparing structures and reconstructing them. The first comparison he makes is between two cubes in line (1 × 2 × 1) and the same two cubes in a tower (1 × 1 × 2). First he claims that they take up more room when vertical than when horizontal, but he thinks better of this. Next, he is asked to compare a cubic structure of 2 × 2 × 2 with eight bricks in line (1 × 8 × 1): "*They're the same, because if you cut this one up (2 × 2 × 2) and put the bits together you'd have the same as this* (1 × 8 × 1). (It should be borne in mind that where this method is used the models are solid blocks instead of being made up out of small bricks.)— Can you measure them so as to be sure?—(Luc takes a number of bricks and lays them end to end along the 1 × 1 × 8 model; but when he turns to the 2 × 2 × 2 model, he simply covers two of its faces.)—What about these two (2 × 2 × 2 and 1 × 4 × 3)?—*They're the same.*—Why?—*Here it's thinner but longer and there it's thick all round.*—You try copying them.—(He reconstructs the two models, finding that they are not equal.)—And these (1 × 8 × 1 and 1 × 4 × 3)?—*The second one is bigger* (and he begins to reconstruct them). *No, I'm wrong* (completing his reconstructions), *I'm right after all.*—And these (1 × 6 × 2 and 1 × 4 × 3), are they equal?—*This one* (1 × 4 × 3) *is bigger.* (But he goes on to reconstruct them, and finds in the end that he can transform one into the other:) *No, they're the same.*"

Pel (6; 7). Method as above. Pel's comparisons are correct for the smaller models which measure no more than 2 or 3 elements. But he goes on to assert that (1 × 3 × 1) has a greater volume than (1 × 2 × 2), "*because there are three bricks.*—Try making them yourself.—(He does so correctly.) *No, it's that one* (1 × 2 × 2), *because there was one brick missing on the other one.*— What about these (2 × 2 × 2 and 1 × 8 × 1)?—*That one* (the cube) *is bigger.*—Try copying them.—(He begins with 1 × 8 × 1 and does it correctly, but when he comes to 2 × 2 × 2 he says:) *I can't do that one* (and does not get beyond a curtain wall all round the visible faces of the model).—Try again.—(He begins once more to build round the visible faces.)—Start with the bottom.—(He finally manages it by putting one lot of 2 × 2 bricks on top of another.)—What about these (1 × 4 × 3 and 2 × 2 × 3)?—*That one* (2 × 2 × 3) *is bigger.*—Why?—(He counts 4 + 4 + 4 and 3 + 3 + 3 + 3.) *They're the same.*—Can you make them yourself?—(But once again he first covers the existing surfaces before he succeeds in constructing them correctly.)"

Building round the visible faces of the model as presented instead of reproducing it is not uncommon at this level, as is evident from the example of Pel. We must infer that the intuitions which guide the behaviour of these subjects are still topological in character. Nevertheless, these responses differ from those which were made at sub-stage IIA in that children now begin to establish relations between the several dimensions of the two objects being compared. Thus, on being asked to transform a given model, Chap remarks almost immediately: "I'm going to make mine higher because I can't make it any thicker," and later: "This one is thicker but that one is longer," or we may cite Chri's remark: "This one's much longer only it isn't as high," or Luc who tells us: "Here it's thinner but longer and there it's thick all round." Likewise, in their constructions these subjects show the same awareness of the three dimensions, usually one after the other rather than simultaneously, which shows that they are beginning to think in terms of logical multiplication, although their thinking still lacks the operational rigour of stage III.

The progress in relating the three dimensions is perhaps most clearly evident in the way children now transform a given volume by altering the height of the structure. Unlike those at level IIA who were not prepared to exceed the height of the model even when told to make their copy on a narrower base, children at level IIB try to compensate the loss in breadth and depth by increasing the height. Just the same, their audacity has its limits, which is why they never make their constructions more than two or three storeys higher than the model at the outside.

Progress in coordinating relations is equally apparent when these subjects are asked to compare two volumes which differ in form. Thus both Luc and Pel are able to make a number of comparisons without error, although one of the two shapes is elongated while the other is more nearly cubical. However, here too, their progress is still only relative, since their comparisons lack precision unless the objects being compared contain very few elements or the children are specifically told to reconstruct them out of unit-elements. (To succeed where the number of elements exceeds three or four without trial-and-error would imply decomposition and operational measurement.)

In all these trends, there is growth in the articulation of Euclidean intuitions of volume. It is through that increasing articulation that notions of volume lose their topological character and come to conform with Euclidean notions of length and area which are elaborated at this level. However, although these articulations pave the way for the operational handling of the various relations together with their logical multiplication, they are insufficient to enable children to effect those reversible compositions which mark the operational level proper. Thus these responses are intermediate in character, and this fact appears most clearly in the answers given to our questions about conservation. Where the transformation of the original model is limited in character, conservation of volume is practically complete, but the conservation is not generalized to all transformations. The example of Geo is particularly clear-cut. A figure made up of 3 × 3 × 4 (by Geo himself when copying the model) is altered to 2 × 2 × 9 and Geo is convinced that "it's the same, because you've used the same bricks". Then the transformation is carried further by making the construction 2 × 18 × 1 and Geo is uncertain ("Oh, this time there's more room here because it's longer."), but changes his mind: "Oh, no! There's the same amount of room because it's the same bricks". The difference in the look of the two structures is considerable, which shows that Geo is not far short of stage III. Nevertheless when that difference is further increased by making the longer figure 1 × 1 × 36, Geo is won over by appearances: "This time it isn't the same anymore because it's very very long." Yet he understands perfectly that the bricks are still the same and even explains in the clearest terms how a construction of 3 × 3 × 4 can be altered to one of 1 × 36 × 1 by putting all the rows in one continuous line. Nevertheless, although his intuitive grasp of relations is considerable he still denies that the two volumes are equal on the grounds that "the other one is very long". His final conclusion may seem contradictory and surprising, yet it is typical of pre-operational intuitions of Euclidean volume: "It's the same bricks, but there's more room." These difficulties can be overcome, but only by multiplicative operations which belong to stage III.

§4. *Sub-stage IIIA: Logical multiplication of relations together with conservation limited to interior volume*

The conservation of volume throughout the various modifications in the shape of the experimental model is assured at stage III and that discovery therefore provides an excellent criterion whereby the student can distinguish stage III from level IIA, when conservation is wholly absent, and also from level IIB, when, as we saw in the case of Geo, it is present but not complete. But the conservation of level IIIA is only one kind of conservation and therefore limited. It stands in marked contrast to the overall conservation of stage IV. The difference illustrates very clearly the difficulties in the way of the construction of Euclidean notions of volume and indeed of space in general. The conservation of level IIIA is as much topological as it is Euclidean; it is heralded by the behaviour shown at level IIB, since both derive from the same idea of volume as that which is contained within boundary surfaces, which comes to be translated in practice by the idea that the bricks which make up the objects being compared are identical. Looking at it from the physical point of view, we may say that the conservation is based on the invariance of a quantity of matter instead of that of volume in the sense of the amount of space taken up by solid or liquid matter. This means that from the geometrical standpoint, the volume which is conserved is "interior volume", which relates only to a content and not to a container. The volume of the latter could have meaning only in relation to an external spatial framework and therefore implies the recognition of a coordinate continuum which is unlimited by virtue of the fact that it is metrical. The conservation of length is a relatively uncomplicated matter while that of area may imply one additional variation: variation in the constituent lengths, and especially in the perimeter. But modification of form in three dimensions entails variation both in length and in area while the volume remains constant; thus a 2-cm. cube has a surface area of 24 cm.², but, when transformed into an elongated parallelipiped, $1 \times 8 \times 1$ cm., its area becomes 34 cm.² although the volume is the same in both cases, 8 cm.³. This explains why the child who is trying to build up invariant systems for the conceptualization of reality begins by recognizing the invariance of the content of a cube in the sense of the number of smaller cubes from which it is made, while the recognition that its volume is invariant in the sense that it occupies a fixed amount of space in relation to its surroundings comes a good deal later. The latter understanding demands more than the merely qualitative operations underlying the invariance of content or "interior volume". The child needs to establish the correct relations between the space which is contained and the faces or areas which bound it, and this involves not merely logical but mathematical multiplication. These operations are known to be impossible before the level of formal thinking, as we saw in ch. XIII, because they imply the infinite subdivision of continuous space.

However, even the limited discovery of level IIIA merits our attention. There is evidence that children think in terms of lines before they attach any importance to surfaces and of surfaces before they consider how these surfaces are filled. Conservation of 'interior' volume marks the final stage in that transition. The point is well brought out in a series of experiments carried out by Marc Lambercier in which children of various ages were asked to copy a clay cube. The youngest of his subjects simply made the outline of a square out of clay threads; older children, those who might be said to belong to one or other level of stage II, went on to build a sort of a carcase out of these clay threads, and later still, to fill out the boundary surfaces (by making some kind of a grille in between), but it was only at about eight years of age, i.e. at level IIIA, that children copied the cube as a filled solid; in other words, it was only then that they began to think of the content or 'interior' volume. The complete agreement of Lambercier's findings with our own provides a remarkable confirmation of that gradual coordination which forms the object of our study.

What is the operational schema which enables the subject to recognize the conservation of 'interior' volume and hence to think of space

371

correctly in three-dimensional terms? To begin with it is one of logical multiplication only, since this is sufficient to enable the child to understand how the various relations compensate one another when the form of an object is modified and its volume remains constant.

RYS (5; 1), young as he is represents a level somewhere between substages IIB and IIIA. Asked to reconstruct a 3 × 3 × 4 house on an island measuring only 2 × 2, he begins by keeping it the same height and measuring it with his finger to make sure: "Is there still the same amount of room?— *No* (and he puts his house which is 2 × 2 × 4 against the other. Seeing that the latter is broader by one layer of bricks, he makes his 3 × 2 × 4).—Try doing it without building in the water.—(He adds more storeys until it reaches 2 × 2 × 7.) *There you are.*—Now do me a house which has as much room as this one (2 × 2 × 5) but on this tiny island (1 × 1).—*It's difficult because all I can make is a tower* (making it 1 × 1 × 11).—Is that right?— *No, because you've got to have the same number in both.* (He counts the bricks in his tower and those in the 2 × 2 × 5 model.)—Is there the same amount of room?—*No, there's less here* (in the tower).—Now this one (3 × 3 × 4 = 36) on this island (2 × 3).—(He starts by making his 2 × 3 × 4.) *No, this house is thinner* (so he brings in another island and makes his 3 × 3 × 4, which is an exact replica of the model).—Supposing I change your house round and make it like this (2 × 3 × 6), will it still have the same amount of room?— *Yes, because they're the same bricks.*—And this way (2 × 9 × 2)?—*It's still the same.*—And like this (2 × 18 × 1)?—*Like that too.*"

WAG (6; 7) asked to transform 3 × 3 × 4 on to a base of only 2 × 2, begins by looking at its height and comments: "*Must be higher still* (making his 2 × 3 × 6 = 36).—Are you sure now?—*Yes.*—Why?—*I'll measure them.* (He removes the upper two storeys consisting of 12 bricks and builds them alongside the rest, copying the model which is 3 × 3 × 4; then he replaces them above the others as before 2 × 3 × 6.)—And can you have the same amount of room on this one (2 × 2)?—*I've got to make it really big* (making it 2 × 2 × 8 = 32).—Is that right?—*Yes, I've made mine two storeys higher than that one.*—And it works?—*Yes, I've measured it.*—Could we start out from your house and make that one (3 × 3 × 4) out of it?—*Yes* (trying it). *I must have been wrong. I'm four short!*—Well, what do you have to do to get the same amount of room (3 × 3 × 4) onto that little island over there (1 × 1)?—*I've got an idea* (and he builds a house of 3 × 3 × 4 on the table before proceeding to take them one at a time and put them on the 1 × 1 island—needless to say, his structure topples over before it is finally completed, but not before he has given a clear indication of his intention which is correct)."

ER (6; 7) asked to transform the 3 × 3 × 4 to go on a base of 2 × 2, starts by comparing the two heights and so builds his house 2 × 2 × 4; but he goes on to compare the remaining two dimensions and therefore alters his to 2 × 2 × 6; "What made you build yours higher?—*Because mine isn't as thick as yours* (adding a seventh storey).—What do you do to decide how many storeys you've got to put on?—*I know that this is what's missing* (indicating the difference in breadth).—See if you can copy this one (3 × 3

372

× 4) as it is.—(He does this correctly.)—Now watch (transforming the structure to 2 × 2 × 9). Which of these has more room?—*It's the same because you've taken the same bricks and you haven't used any others.*—What about this way (1 × 1 × 36)?—*I don't think that's the same. Oh, yes! There's still the same amount of room because they're the same bricks as before. This one* (3 × 3 × 4) *has all this* (putting his hand over it to suggest the size of its exterior faces). *The other one is high, but if you put them round the way they were that makes it lower again.*"

RUT (6; 9), told to transform a house of 3 × 3 × 4 onto a base of 2 × 3, says at first: "*You can't do it because it's smaller* (and he goes on to make his 2 × 3 × 2). *No, must have another storey. That's it, no another one* (and he goes on until finally he reaches 2 × 3 × 7 = 42). *Mine may have a little more room, because I've put so many storeys on it. Only its thinner, so you've got to make it higher.*—And on that one (2 × 2)?—*Oh, I know, I've got to make it higher still* (and he makes it 2 × 2 × 13 = 52!)"

MIC (7; 2) builds a house of 2 × 3 × 6 in order to reproduce one of 3 × 3 × 4 on a base of 2 × 3: "*That makes it the same, but it isn't the same height. Instead of putting the bricks in the water you simply put more storeys on.*—And on that one (1 × 1)?—(He tries to measure how many bricks go into the four lateral faces, but doesn't succeed.)"

STE (7; 0) is asked to compare 2 × 4 × 1 and 2 × 2 × 2: "Have these two got the same amount of room as one another or not?—(He looks at them both very carefully, then measures them with his fingers.) *It's the same.*—How do you know?—*You've got to cut them* (in order to transform one into the other).—Can't you use these little (unit-size) bricks to measure them?—*No, I don't know what to do.*—What about these (1 × 4 × 3 and 2 × 2 × 3)?—*They're the same.*—How do you know?—*I'll try it* (using 12 bricks to reconstruct a house of 1 × 4 × 3, and then transforming the structure to 2 × 2 × 3).—How can you be quite sure?—*I'll count them* (counting 12 in both)."

MAR (7; 4) compares 2 × 6 × 1 and 1 × 8 × 1: "*The second one is bigger but it's narrower. If you cut it in half* (2 × 4 × 1) *it would be shorter* (than 2 × 6 × 1).—What about these (1 × 8 × 1 and 2 × 2 × 3)?—*If you cut this one* (1 × 8 × 1) *into four* (making 2 × 2 × 2, i.e. 4 columns each 2 units high) *the other one would be bigger.*—Would these bricks help you to decide? —(He reconstructs the models and first compares them then counts the bricks in each.)"

MEY (7; 7) compares 2 × 2 × 3 and 1 × 6 × 2: "*They're both the same because if you cut this one* (2 × 2 × 3) *in half and put the two bits together* (breadthways) *it would be exactly the same as the other one.*—Can you make sure that's right by using these little bricks?—(He builds the unit-bricks up around the upright faces of the models like a child at stage II, and as a result he finds that the number of bricks he uses is different in the two cases.) *Just the same, they are the same.*—Find me one the same size as this one (2 × 4 × 1).—*That one* (2 × 2 × 2). *It's four little blocks of two. It's the same as the other one really, but here the little blocks are one on top of the other.*"

BUR (7; 7), comparing 1 × 8 × 1 and 2 × 2 × 2, puts the two side by side, saying: "*It's the same. If you could saw that one at the right height you'd have four pieces. We'll see right away if it is* (and he reconstructs the 2 × 2 × 2 structure out of unit-bricks, checking the congruence of each dimension, whereupon he transforms it to 1 × 8 × 1). *It's the same. It's got the same amount of room.*"

The above responses are typical of level IIIA. Clearly, these subjects require no assistance in establishing relations between the relevant dimensions, although to begin with only two dimensions are handled successfully. At first the coordination is qualitative, which means that it consists in the logical multiplication of relationships of 'more' and 'less'.[1] There is no measurement of any kind, and certainly no use of measuring units. Nevertheless, although to begin with this kind of coordination gives rise to compensations which are no better than approximations, with no equalization of the differences (as shown by Rys and by Wag in his first replies), and indeed with the differences being exaggerated on occasion (Rut), we soon find that our subjects make two important discoveries which make their compensations more adequate. First, there is a beginning of spontaneous measurement, involving logical transitivity as between two or more equations although unit-iteration is not yet mastered. Second, the compensations are determined with accuracy, albeit by reconstruction. A good example is the case of Wag who succeeds in duplicating the volume of a model consisting of 3 × 3 × 4 bricks on a base of 1 × 1 by first reconstructing the model as he finds it and then transforming it by altering the position of its bricks. Ste and Bur do the same.

The conservation of interior volume (i.e. of the amount of matter contained within an object) is something which children acquire by the same process as those of length and area. Qualitative coordination of subdivisions and changes of position occurs without their operational fusion, i.e. without a true metrical operation. Every one of these subjects recognizes conservation as self-evident as he shows when making transformations of his own in the arrangement of bricks, or in answering questions about transformations made deliberately by the experimenter, or finally, as with Mar and Mey, in making purely mental transformations without prompting in order to compare two differently shaped models.

However, conservation is still limited to interior volume and does not as yet extend to the spatial relations between the object and its surroundings. Bur and Er are explicit: "It's the same. It's got the same amount of room", or "There's still the same amount of room because they're the same bricks as before". Mey illustrates the point further in his attempt to reconstruct the two models by building bricks all round them, when, finding that the number of bricks he uses is not the

[1] "The second one is bigger (i.e. longer) but it's narrow." (Mar), or "It's thinner, so you've got to make it higher." (Rut), etc.

same for both, he still tells us: "Just the same they are the same." Mey is not the only subject who persists in trying to surround the given volume in order to reproduce it, but who nevertheless understands clearly that the number of elementary bricks is invariant: children like Mic and Mey argue correctly about volume as matter enveloped by boundary surfaces, but they get into difficulties when they try to compare the number of bricks they put against the upright faces of the two models.

That the two kinds of conservation are in fact different can be shown experimentally. Conservation relating to interior volume appears at level IIIA, but conservation of volume in relation to neighbouring objects in space is not achieved until stage IV. The subjects just quoted can tell us correctly and explicitly that a cube made up of $2 \times 2 \times 2$ compares with a parallelipiped which is eight units in length and only 1×1 in depth and height: "It's the same. It's got the same amount of room." (Moreover, they anticipate this kind of equality, as we found when they predicted that two boxes having these very distinct dimensions would hold the same amount of sand.) However, if we ask them questions about volumes immersed in water, their replies are similar to those given by children of 7 to 11 when we first made that experiment;[1] the volume taken up by a ball of modelling clay or by a cylinder will vary, depending on whether they are put in the water in one piece or whether they are first cut in two or four, etc., and even depending on whether the cylinder is put in flat or upright. According as it changes in form or even in position, the clay cylinder changes in volume— in the sense of occupied volume as determined by the displacement of water. But all the while its interior volume remains invariant, being determined by the amount of clay of which it is composed.

The following cases are fully representative of stage III (although they include some at level IIIB as well as those at level IIIA). They show clearly that the conservation of interior volume which is acquired at level IIIA is independent both of 'occupied' volume and of its complementary displacement volume.

SALZ (7; 10) anticipates that the level of the water will rise when we put in a tower of $3 \times 3 \times 4$ bricks, and this we do: "*You see I was right.*—Well, supposing I put the tower this way round so that it's lying down, will there still be exactly the same amount of room for the water?—*No, there'll be more room because the bricks will be right at the bottom.*—Well, now supposing we change it this way ($3 \times 1 \times 12$), will there be the same amount of room in the two houses?—*Yes, exactly the same. You've got the same bricks.*—And will they both take up the same amount of room in the water?—*No, it will take up more room. Oh, no! That's wrong! It will take up less room because the house is stretched out lengthways.*"

[1] Piaget and Inhelder, *Le développement des quantités chez l'enfant*, chs. III and XI.

JAQ (8; 2) realizes that the water level will rise on the immersion of the tower of 3 × 3 × 4: "Now what will happen if I turn it over?—*The water will go down a bit, because the house is at the bottom now.*—Well, will there be the same amount of room in the house itself if I put the bricks at the bottom?—*Yes. There'll be the same amount of room.*—And that means it's the same for the water?—*No, that's not the same.*—Well, supposing I split the house into two parts, will there still be the same amount of room inside?—*Yes, there'll be just the same amount, but in two parts.*—And then there'll be the same amount of space left for the water, eh?—*No, that changes. There'll be less room. No, more.*"

ETI (8; 5) also thinks the water level will differ according as the block is laid vertically or horizontally. The experiment is tried: "*I was wrong. The water stayed the same height because there are the same number of bricks.*— Does that mean I can put these bricks whichever way I like and the water will always stay the same?—*Yes, always.*—And then will the house always take up the same amount of room in the water?—*No.*—(The arrangement of bricks is transformed from 3 × 3 × 4 to 3 × 1 × 12.) Is there the same amount of room in this house now as there was before?—*Yes. It's got the same bricks.*—And will it take up the same amount of room in the basin?— *No, this way it's less* (3 × 1 × 12).—How do you explain that?—*It's the same number of bricks, but they take up less room.*"

JUI (9; 6) is another who thinks that a block of 3 × 1 × 12 when compared with another of 3 × 3 × 4 "*takes up less room that way.*—Well, is there the same amount of room inside the house or not?—*Yes, because there are always the same number of bricks whether the house is put upright or lengthwise.*—How does that affect the amount of space which it takes up in the water?—*It takes up more room when it's lying down.*"

GAL (13; 4) also thinks there is the same amount of room inside a block of 3 × 3 × 4 and in one of 3 × 1 × 12, but "*the bricks take up more space like this because now it's lower and wider. Before it was higher and narrower. That makes the space less.*"

For all these subjects then, the fact that when the block of bricks is immersed in a basin of water it conserves its interior volume does not ensure conservation of the volume of water which is complementary. Even more strangely, the volume which the block itself occupies in relation to the water is not invariant! "It's got the same number of bricks," is the sage comment of Eti, implying the invariance of its interior volume, "but they take up less room ", which proves that, to him, the volume which the bricks occupy in the water is not identical with their interior volume. The paradox is not resolved until stage IV. Its explanation will be apparent when we come to see how it is resolved (§6).

§5. *Sub-stage IIIB: First appearance of metrical relations*

There is little difference between the responses given at level IIIB and those of level IIIA in regard to the conservation of interior volume. On the other hand, there is a marked gain in the handling of relations in the course of real or mental transformations of the object. Where, previously, the coordination of these relations was achieved simply by logical multiplication, the relations themselves are now expressed in metrical terms. This does not mean that the subject knows how to calculate volume from linear measurements. It means only that he takes the trouble to measure lengths in three dimensions, making full use of the concept of a unit of measurement or, alternatively, that he equates his measurements of boundary sides with his notion of volume.

CAS (6; 7) is remarkably advanced. In spite of her tender age, her response borders on level IIIB. To transform a volume of 3 × 3 × 4 to occupy a base of 2 × 2, she first builds her structure to a height of 4, then says: "*No, that's not enough. I must make it higher.*" She adds a further two storeys and seems satisfied. But when asked to copy the house on a base of 1 × 1 she is not altogether happy having made her copy 1 × 1 × 13, and she tries to express the transformation in metrical terms: "*I must make mine higher because that one is wider. I've made it twice as high, nearly three times as high.*" The next task is to transform the model of 3 × 3 × 4 on a base of 2 × 3: she begins by noting that the breadth is equal: "*It's the same thing this way but that way* (i.e. in depth) *it's smaller.*—Is there any way in which you can tell just how high to make it?—*I'll see. I'm going to measure it.* (She puts a single layer of bricks on the 2 × 3 base and then compares it with the model, noting that one row of bricks is missing in one dimension. Her comment is: *It's no good making it twice as high because there's only one missing.*—(The experimenter asks her simply to copy the model of 3 × 3 × 4.)—(She puts three bricks side by side along one face and builds one of them only to a height of four. These measurements suffice to enable her to copy the model without difficulty:) *Each time I've got to make three rows and each row has three bricks.* (Again, she has no difficulty in transforming her structure to 2 × 3 × 6, for she merely removes one vertical layer of twelve bricks leaving her structure at 2 × 3 × 4, and then re-arranges the bricks to make two additional storeys, each 2 × 3.)—Will there still be the same amount of room if I put them this way round (2 × 18 × 1)?—*Of course. There's bound to be the same amount of room because you're using the same bricks.*—Can I make this again (3 × 3 × 4) out of this one (2 × 18 × 1)?—*Yes, since you've taken my bricks, there'll be enough!*"

GER (8; 4) is asked to transform the model of 3 × 3 × 4 onto a base of 2 × 2 and begins by making a guess like the children at level IIIA, simply adding an extra storey. After making his copy 2 × 2 × 5 he comments: "*The thinner we make this* (the base) *the higher the house.*—Has yours the same amount of room now?—*Yes. You can say they're both 100.*—How can you be sure?—(He counts the bricks on the copy which is 2 × 2 × 5, all of which are visible from the outside.) *That's 20 here.* There (3 × 3 × 4), *I've got three rows . . .*[1] (not knowing how to calculate from there, he suddenly calls out:) *I've got to take this one* (2 × 2 × 5) *and use the bricks to make that one* (3 × 3 × 4). He finds that he needs more bricks and takes enough to

---

[1] It should be remembered that the model is in one piece and the units are not marked.

make his structure equal to the model; then he carries them back to the 2 × 2 'island' and builds them to a height of 2 × 2 × 9.) *Now it's right.*"

EDU (9; 2) is also asked to transform 3 × 3 × 4 onto a base of 2 × 2. At first, he makes the two heights equal by building his bricks 2 × 2 × 4: "*No. That one is wider. It's got three rooms*[1] *and this one has only got two! I must make it higher.* (He makes it 2 × 2 × 6. Having done so, he looks down on the model from above and studies its upper face which is equivalent to 3 × 3 = 9 bricks. Counting the bricks which might form the boundary of their surface, he falls into the error of counting each corner brick twice over, which leads him to suppose that the total would be 12 instead of 8:) *It's four bricks three times over.*—Well then, is your house right (2 × 2 × 6)?—*Yes.* (He studies one of its upright faces and decomposes the twelve bricks into four sets of three, showing how these would fall into one-one correspondence with the four sides of the uppermost storey of the model.) *This one's for this, and this one's for this, and this one's for this, etc.*" Edu is clearly committing more than one error in measurement, since he tries to equate the whole of a lateral surface with part of a horizontal surface and miscounts the latter!

Later he is told to copy the model as it stands and his copy is then transformed to 1 × 36 × 1. "Is there exactly the same amount of room in this house as in that?—*Yes.*—Is there anything you could do to be quite certain that there is the same amount of room in both?—*Change this one* (1 × 36 × 1) *back to that one* (the model)."

BAR (9; 6), told to build a house on a base of 2 × 2 to equal the model of 3 × 3 × 4, makes his 2 × 2 × 8: "*I've made it twice the height, because this one* (the model) *is less high but it's wider, and that one is thinner and narrower but it's higher.*—But why twice?—*Because here there's this left* (a difference of 1 brick in breadth, 3 — 2) *and here there's this left* (a difference of 1 brick in depth), *so I made it twice that* (because 1 + 1 = 2!)."

NIC (9; 5) also tries to calculate the required height by finding the difference between the rows forming each boundary. In order to build a structure equal to the 3 × 3 × 4 model on a base of 2 × 2, he first puts 2 × 2 = 4 bricks over one corner of the top storey (3 × 3 = 9) of the model, and then counts the bricks which might make up the difference, i.e. five: "*This way I have five too few, so I need another storey* (4 + 1 = 5, the five storeys corresponding to the five bricks so that he now has 2 × 2 × 5 bricks in his structure).— How can you make sure?—*I'll see if I can fill up all round here* (i.e. build up a single layer of bricks all round the model to form a boundary! He now goes on to build such a layer, but only round the vertical faces of the model, ignoring the base and top. He uses 64 bricks in all, each of the four sides being 3 × 4 = 12 while the four corners each require an additional column of four bricks: 48 + 16 = 64). *It's going to be very high on here* (the base of 2 × 2!)" It is clear that Nic has little thought of using the 64 bricks to make a boundary layer round his previous copy (which was 2 × 2 × 5 and would have required 60 bricks). Instead, he believes that by putting these 64 bricks one above the other he can reproduce the volume of 3 × 3 × 4. However, he is a little doubtful, as we saw, and the reason is that there are so many of them: "Do you think there are too many or too few?—*I don't know. It will*

[1] See previous footnote.

378

be too big." He now takes the 64 bricks and tries to use them to make a copy of exactly $3 \times 3 \times 4$. He is amazed to find that there are far too many of them, but he tries again and again before finally exclaiming: "*I can't understand it. Did I count one of the sides twice* (when building bricks around the model)?" Nic obviously expected that the bricks he has used to build a wall all round the given volume must necessarily constitute the same volume!

UDE (9; 5) adopts the same method when measuring, yet his qualitative estimates are substantially correct. When asked to build a volume equal to $3 \times 3 \times 4$ on a base of 2×6, he arrives at $2 \times 6 \times 3$, which is correct. What he did was to make certain compensatory adjustments similar to those used at level IIIA. (After mentally splitting $3 \times 3 \times 4$ as if to go on a base of 3×6, he removed one layer from a side and converted it into an additional storey.) However, when asked to make sure that the construction is correct, he builds a layer of bricks against each of the 4 vertical faces of the model, each layer consisting of $3 \times 4 = 12$ bricks. (Ude shows a trifle more insight than Nic, in that he does not fill in the four corners.) "*I counted 4×12 because one side* (of the model) *is 12 and there are 4 sides which makes 12 and $12 = 24$, and another 24 which is 48. And this* ($2 \times 6 \times 3$) *is 48 as well.* (He demolishes his copy.) *Oh, no! There are some missing* (and he adds another 12). Try building a copy of this model ($3 \times 3 \times 4$).—(He does so correctly and finds that it uses less than 48 bricks.) *Oh, it's three times 12 bricks and not four times! Then we must have 36 bricks here as well* ($2 \times 6 \times 3$)!"

The first responses we observe at level IIIB often begin like those of level IIIA. So, with Cas and Ger, there is logical multiplication of spatial relations which gives rise to compensations when these are modified. The sole indication of progress is the fact that children use numbers or metrical relations to substantiate their successive estimates. Cas speaks of "twice as high, nearly three times as high", and, rightly refuses to make her copy twice the height of the original, since it is only one layer less in depth. Ger counts the 20 bricks he uses in his structure of $2 \times 2 \times 5$. Although measurement intervenes as a kind of an after-thought, to help in a process of construction which derives from intuition or from qualitative operational grouping in the first instance, the measurement itself is accurate enough. The reason is that it is applied only to linear quantities ("twice as high"), or, alternatively, to multi-plication of relations between ready-made, visible units: "Each time I've got to make three rows and each row has three bricks," is the formula used by Cas who is less than 7 years old. It is when the problem is one of volume as such that these children are lost. Thus Ger simply counts the 20 bricks in his own structure of $2 \times 2 \times 5$, all of which he can see, but when he turns to the model he stops short at: "I've got three rows . . ." and abandons measurement in favour of qualitative methods of compensation (i.e. the use of change of position to transfer bricks from one dimension which is reduced to another which is increased).

At the beginning of sub-stage IIIB, we may say, measurement, being a synthesis of subdivision and change of position, is not limited to one dimension but may occur in two or three (as we saw in ch. VII), but children have not yet begun to calculate the interior volume itself.

Later responses show an attempt to arrive at the volume itself by the use of measurement. But the attempt brings in its train a reappearance of the kind of behaviour shown at stage II when children tried to construct a volume by enveloping it. When they were told to reproduce a given volume, using a set of small bricks, they frequently used the bricks to build curtain walls around the visible faces of the model, as though by "surrounding" the thing they could seize the interior volume itself. Having reached level IIIB, our subjects are quite capable of copying a volume as it stands, using a set of bricks, but when they are required to measure it, or, more correctly, to calculate its interior volume starting from the lengths or areas seen in its boundaries, they tend to fall back on arbitrary measures taken on these boundaries, or they surround them like children at stage II. The explanation of their behaviour is that they are still unable to use mathematical multiplication in calculating areas and volumes as products of linear measurements taken in different dimensions. However, unlike children at stage II, they now measure the enveloping surfaces by counting the bricks used in constructing them! This is how Edu tries to establish a correspondence between one of the vertical faces on his own tower and the eight bricks corresponding to the outer portion of the upper horizontal face in the model (conveniently ignoring the ninth brick which would be in the middle, but perfectly visible!). Similarly, Bar makes his structure twice the height of the model because the latter is one unit greater in two dimensions (the model having a base of 3 × 3 while Bar's reconstruction is on a base of 2 × 2). Nic places four bricks corresponding with the base of his copy (2 × 2) on top of the model (which has an upper surface of 3 × 3), and by fitting them carefully over one corner, he notes that the model is greater by five bricks (9 − 4 = 5): this leads him to the remarkable conclusion that his construction should be five storeys high! Finally, he falls back on the kind of response which marked stage II: he surrounds the model with curtain walls using a total of 64 bricks (which he calls "filling it up all round") and prepares to construct a tower of 64 bricks on his 2 × 2 base in the belief that he will be constructing the same volume as that of the model! He is amazed to find that the 64 bricks do not even yield the 3 × 3 × 4 model itself when he tries to copy it as it stands—as though because a parallelipiped requires 64 bricks to build a continuous wall round four of its sides it must itself consist of 64 bricks rather than 36! Ude's reasoning is exactly the same, apart from the fact that Ude leaves the corners as they are and therefore estimates that the model of 3 × 3 × 4 = 36 must be worth 48 bricks because its four lateral faces compared with the four walls each $3 \times 4 = 12$ which he himself has put against them.

These first attempts at calculating interior volume may be summed up as follows. Either children equate the volume with a given number of unit cubes in which case the number is taken from one of the boundary surfaces (and may even correspond with a linear perimeter like the 8 bricks on the upper face which surround the single inside brick which is visible to Edu), or else they equate it with the number of unit cubes which it takes to surround the model. It is hardly surprising that throughout stage III (A and B) the conservation of volume is limited to interior volume and children cannot yet appreciate the invariance of volume relative to the surrounding space simply because they can neither measure it nor calculate it. Children at this stage are still dominated by topological notions of envelopment and of boundaries because they lack the operational understanding with which to construct Euclidean volume by measurement and calculation. Measurements in terms of units of length are made in three dimensions, but they cannot understand how by multiplying these lengths they would arrive at products in terms of square or cubic units. We saw in ch. XIII how this understanding presupposes formal operations which belong to stage IV, and this conclusion is borne out in the following section.

§6. *Stage IV: Mathematical multiplication of three-dimensional measurements together with conservation of true volume*

Knowledge learned in school increasingly interferes with the spontaneous development of geometrical notions as children grow older. Nevertheless we may discern the fact that stage IV marks the appearance of two correlative gains in understanding. On the one hand, children now establish relations between the lines and areas which form the boundaries of a solid and the volume itself, and on the other hand the conservation of volume now extends to the volume which an object occupies in relation to the surrounding space. To begin with we may introduce two examples which are intermediate between levels IIIB and IV.

MAU (10; 10) asked to transform a model made up of $3 \times 3 \times 4$ bricks to stand on a base of 2×3: "*The island isn't the same, so I've got to make the house higher* (counting the number of bricks required to cover the base and finding it to be 6).—Why did you count that?—*To find out how many more I need. The area is 6 and the height is 4. So I need 4 more . . . If only I knew how much that volume is* (the model)!—See if you can find out.—*The volume? I've got to put 4 more* (rows one above the other) *all over this space* (being the difference between the two bases). *So I need 12 more bricks* (making it $2 \times 3 \times 6$). *Now this one has the same amount of room as that one* ($3 \times 3 \times 4$)."

"All right. Try it on this island (2×2).—(He begins with $2 \times 2 \times 4$.) *Now*

381

I need 16 more. No, 12 more this way like before and another 7, no 8, that's 12 and 8 counting both ways, so that's 20 more (which would give $2 \times 2 \times 4 = 16 + 20 = 36$ and is therefore correct). *That means the height must be 10. No, that's all wrong. I've got to find the volume.*—Can't you find that?—*Well, it depends on the length. I have to count it: the breadth is 12* (having counted the bricks in the area of 3×4), *then it's 4 high and 3 long . . .*" (and he gets no further although he knows that he needs twenty more).

COR (11; 11) is told to transform $3 \times 3 \times 4$ to go on a base of 2×3. He says he must make his the same volume: "Do you know what we mean by volume?—*How many times the little brick goes into it.*—All right. Can you make that the same here (2×3)?—*You need $9 \times 4 = 36$.*—How did you work that out?—*It's 4 high and each row is 3 and that's $4 \times 3 = 12$ and I multiply by nine because that's the area on top.*"

Both these children try to determine the volume and say so: "If only I knew how much that volume is!" But although they realize that volume is a product of mathematical multiplication, they tend to multiply two lengths and an area: height and depth by a lateral surface $(4 \times 3 \times 12$, Mau) or height and breadth by the upper surface $(4 \times 3 \times 9$, Cor). In spite of this they both reason with competence when finding how many storeys to make this structure to allow for the modification in its base.

The interest in volume as such coincides with another development which we were able to note at this same intermediate level between stages IIIB and IV. The invariance of interior volume has been known since level IIIA, but only now do children think of interior volume as identical with the volume occupied by an object in relation to the surrounding space, which means that conservation of 'occupied' space is deferred until now. The kind of measurement shown in the two examples given implies that three-dimensional space has begun to take on a certain continuity, and it is this development which enables our subjects to think in terms of 'occupied' volume instead of 'interior' volume, recognizing that conservation still holds:

MAU (10; 10). The block of $3 \times 3 \times 4$ bricks is stood upright in the water: "*The water rises because the bricks take up space in the water.*—Supposing I laid the thing on its side?—*The water would still be the same, because it still takes up the same amount of room.*—And if I change its shape $(2 \times 1 \times 18)$?—*The water still comes up to the same level because it takes up the same amount of room.*"

DRO (11; 4) replied like Mau when called on to measure the blocks: "Supposing I take these bricks and put them up this way $(3 \times 3 \times 4)$ into the water, what will happen to the water?—*It rises. It's just the same if you put your hand in the water. It takes up a lot of room and so the water rises.*—And when I put them in this way $(3 \times 1 \times 12)$ are they going to take up the same amount of space in the water?—*No.*—Why not?—*Oh yes! I was wrong, it stays the same.*—What about the space taken by the water all round? Is that the same too?—*Of course.*—Well supposing we spread the bricks around? —*It's still the same. They'll always take up the same amount of room."*

One of our subjects (Dro) is a little hesitant at times but in the main we see the beginnings of conservation of volume as applied to occupied volume and even to the complementary displacement volume.

Finally, we present three instances which belong unmistakeably to stage IV:

GRA (9; 6) has apparently found out for himself how to evaluate volume, for bright as he is, he is in the same class at school as others of his own age, and geometry has not yet been touched: "See if you can build me a house with the same amount of room as mine (3 × 3 × 4) but on this island (2 × 3). —*I can see it's a bit small* (having built 2 × 3 × 4). *It's different in width, so I've got to put more on top.*—How would you do it?—*I count the bricks first* (those bricks on the model which project beyond the copy): *there are twelve of them in the row, so I simply put them over the top* (2 × 3 × 6).—All right. Now how would you build a house like this one (2 × 3 × 6) on this island (2 × 2)?—*If you take the bricks in this house* (2 × 3 × 6) *there are 36 of them: here* (on the 2 × 2 island) *you'll have 4 for each storey, so there are 9 storeys* (2 × 2 × 9). What about rebuilding this (3 × 3 × 4) on this island (3 × 4)? —*I count them* (on the model). *All the sides are 3 which makes 9 in each storey. Then there are 4 storeys and that's 4 × 9 = 36, since each storey is 9, 3 × 3, and there are 4 altogether.* (Whereupon he constructs 3 × 4 × 3). *There, now the house is finished.*—Has it the same amount of room?—*Yes."*

SCI (11; 8): "See if you can build a tower on this island (2 × 2) with the same volume as that one (3 × 3 × 4).—*I'd have to make it higher* (measuring the height of the model). *This one has four storeys. I'm working out the number of bricks in this model. I think it's 36. So . . .* (He assembles 2 × 2 × 4 = 16 bricks, then adds a further twelve, and finally adds eight more which gives him 2 × 2 × 9).—Supposing I put this model (3 × 3 × 4) in the water, what would the water do?—*It would rise.*—Why?—*Because this takes up space when it's in the water.*—What if I change this (3 × 3 × 4) to this (3 × 1 × 12)?—*The water still goes up just the same amount.*—Why?—*It takes up the same space because it's the same size.*—Why?—*Because there's the same quantity.*—One of your friends told me it takes up more room lying down than standing upright.—*He must have been thinking of the ground. He forgot about the height."*

GIS (12; 6) with a 3 × 3 × 4 model to equal on a base of 2 × 2: "*It's bound to be different in height, then* (counting). *It's got to be 36 bricks in all, and that makes 9 storeys.*—How did you work it out at 36?—*It's 3 long and 3 wide which is 9, and it's 4 high: 4 × 9 = 36."*

These responses may seem paradoxical when compared with those given at stage III. Until stage IV volume is always thought of as that which is contained within a set of boundary surfaces, and these in turn are thought of in terms of the lengths of their sides. Even at level IIIA (but not at stage II) children recognized the conservation of this interior volume when the shape of the object as a whole was modified. They did so by simply coordinating subdivision and change of position in a qualitative way: certain bricks might previously have been placed as extensions to the whole either in length or in depth and these bricks are now placed above the others: hence the increase in height compensates for the decrease in breadth or in depth. Nevertheless it was only at level IIIB that any attempt was made at measuring a volume, and even now measurements were limited to lengths in three dimensions and interior volume, although understood, was not measured or calculated. Sometimes children went so far as to surround the volume with a curtain wall formed of one layer of bricks and counted these instead. The volume occupied by an object in relation to the surrounding spatial medium was far from invariant at stage III: that is because a volume which is transformed is apt to change in surface area and therefore seems to occupy more space or less space in relation to neighbouring objects. Yet at stage IV children start from boundary lines and surfaces and are able to calculate volume as a function of these measurements, and it is now that they are assured of its conservation not merely as interior volume but in the sense that the total space which it occupies in relation to its surroundings is invariant. The paradox is clear: at stage III conservation is limited to interior volume but children cannot measure it and measure something outside it (the curtain walls), at stage IV they appreciate the relation between a volume and its boundaries and are thereby able to measure these and calculate the interior volume, yet it is only now that they extend its conservation to the relation between itself and objects outside of itself!

But in truth if at this stage children finally discover how to measure interior volume this is only the end of a lengthy development throughout which boundaries were being progressively filled. Stage III which brought with it the qualitative conservation of matter was a penultimate stage in the same development. When the process is complete, there is a clear relation between the boundaries of a volume and the volume itself, and that is why the conservation now extends to the space occupied by an object instead of being limited to the contents of its boundaries. At stage IV the understanding of volume is more advanced in two ways: volume is now conceived as completely filled and its relation to the surrounding space is understood. In effect this is no more than a synthesis of notions which previously were not coordinated.

As we saw in ch. XIII, this new construction becomes possible because children have elaborated the notion of a continuum: because at the level of formal operations (stage IV) children are able to decompose and recompose a spatial continuum indefinitely, the matrix of linear coordinates established at level IIIB now leads to the conception of areas and volumes which are entirely filled. Because this conception of continuity was not present at stage III, our subjects could not calculate volume itself by mathematical multiplication, although ·they could perfectly well measure boundary lines in two and three dimensions. The fact that at stage IV the linear matrix becomes a continuum which fills the whole of a solid explains why children can calculate areas and volumes by simply multiplying their sides. Mathematical multiplication assumes a transition from boundary lines to the interior which they contain whereas logical multiplication does not.

Having understood the relation between boundary lines (or areas) and interior volume, children inevitably deepen their sense of the conservation of volume. They discover for the first time that it is not merely the interior 'contained' which is invariant but the space occupied in a wider context. The relation between the lengths of sides and volume remains invariant when the whole shape is transformed, and this is the essential truth which is seized upon at stage IV and expressed in the form of mathematical multiplication: $3 \times 3 \times 4 = 2 \times 3 \times 6 = 2 \times 2 \times 9 = 36$, etc. Because interior volume can be measured and calculated from now on, its invariance now extends to the surrounding space. This explains why the conservation of occupied volume (in the sense in which the concept is understood by the physicist) is not achieved until the level of formal operations, for it is only now that interior volume can be measured by virtue of the new found concept of metrical continuity. The fact itself was apparent in the last chapter but its explanation had to be delayed to the present. It has frequently been suggested that measurement would have been impossible were it not for the existence of indeformable solids: we may now add that this concept of solidity is one which is impossible at the level of topological intuition which marks the beginning of children's spatial representation; it is a by-product of the metrical invariance of solids.

PART FIVE

CONCLUSIONS

Chapter Fifteen

THE CONSTRUCTION OF EUCLIDEAN SPACE: THREE LEVELS

THE whole of this volume has been concerned with Euclidean notions and with measurement. That study has now been the subject of fourteen chapters in this book and of chs. XIII and XIV in C.C.S., where we analysed the growth of reference systems and coordinates. In conclusion, we will try to outline the construction of Euclidean space at the level of representation. The last chapter of C.C.S. (ch. XV) contains an attempt to classify the various kinds of operation entering into the elaboration first of topological, then of projective and finally of Euclidean notions. But metric operations as such are only touched on in that chapter. Hence the need to describe their evolution in brief synoptic outline. The details of the many operations involved need not detain us any longer, and instead we will concentrate our attention on operations involved in the two fundamental mechanisms of Euclidean thinking as revealed throughout the present work: the conservation of size and its measurement.

We may distinguish three levels of achievement in the construction of Euclidean space. The first level is represented by the qualitative operations involved in various kinds of conservation, the majority of which are elaborated in the course of sub-stage IIIA: conservation of distance and of length, of area and interior volume, and conservation of congruences in the process of transitive comparisons, etc. The second level might be called the achievement of simple metrical operations. It occurs at level IIIB: the measurement of length in one, two or three dimensions, the construction of metric coordinate systems, and a first beginning in the measurement of angles and areas. The final level is reached when areas and volumes are calculated and delayed to stage IV, being the level of formal operations. Only now do we find mathematical multiplication being used to coordinate the results of logical multiplication and simple measurement and only at stage IV is there conservation of volume relative to the surrounding spatial medium.

SECTION I. THE TRANSITION FROM TOPOLOGICAL RELATIONS TO ELEMENTARY EUCLIDEAN NOTIONS OF CONSERVATION (level IIIA)

In our earlier volume (C.C.S.) we saw how the development of the child's conception of space implies a transition from topological relations to Euclidean relations, having studied the development of projective notions, affinitive transformations and similarity of shape. Thus, when the child learns to use systematic points of view, he can construct projective straight lines out of topological notions of order (C.C.S., ch. VI). This development is followed by the conservation first of parallelism (ch. XI) and then of angles (ch. XII). The construction of projective notions, affine relations and similarities paves the way for the subsequent elaboration of comprehensive coordinate-systems which is implied by Euclidean space (C.C.S., chs. XIII and XIV).

However the transition from topological to Euclidean relations may be studied more directly, as in the present work. Here we note the transition from the first recognition of relations of order of position and of topological subdivision to Euclidean notions of change of position and subdivision. It is the elaboration of these Euclidean notions which gives rise to the more elementary conservations like those of distance and length or of area and interior volume. We will try to summarize this transition in the present section.

Let us take a series of elements disposed in a topological line (as opposed to a nesting topological series involving two or three dimensions): A precedes B, B precedes C, C precedes D, etc., as we follow the line in one direction; we note that between A and B there is an interval AB and this interval is smaller than, say, AD; likewise the interval BC is smaller than AC or BD, etc. The order of elements can be reversed, simply by proceeding in the reverse direction, DCBA; but the order of its elements cannot be permuted by substituting ACB for ABC, etc. Similarly, the relative size of intervals is invariant, i.e. AB < AC < AD, etc., but the absolute size of the line is not. This topological series therefore takes no account of possible changes in the position of objects (although it allows for changes in that of the subject who is free to move along the line in both directions, as he must when constructing the direct and inverse order of elements). Similarly, the series does not imply conservation of distances or of lengths: the only relations which are held invariant are, first, those of 'betweenness' (B is between C and A and also between A and C) and, second, nesting relations which determine the relative values of intervals to one another. These elementary topological relationships form the starting point for the child's construction of Euclidean notions of change of position and, simultaneously with it, his recognition of the conservation of distance and length (see C.C.S., chs. XIII and XV).

To begin with, the child sees changes of position as no more than changes in rank order,[1] which differs from inversion only in that the change is due to permutations in the order of the objects instead of to a reversal in the direction taken by the subject as he imposes an order

[1] See *Les notions de mouvement et de vitesse chez l'enfant*, chs. III–V.

on them. Thus if B began by being situated between A and C and is subsequently found after C (ACB), the child is aware that the order of B has altered relative to C. But this primitive intuition of change in the order of elements is far from sufficient to allow the child to construct a representative grouping of changes of position. Even in its more elementary form, the latter development does not occur until level IIIA, as we saw again in ch. I of the present volume: it implies the use of a system of fixed references and the conservation of distance, these being essential preconditions for the construction of Euclidean space. The elaboration of reference systems, the conservation of distance, and the grouping of changes of position all occur at the same level of development, and together they bring about the transition from topological to Euclidean notions of space.

The matter may be expressed quite precisely if we say that just as projective straight lines are an outgrowth of topological order, but linked to a systematization of viewpoints, so that same elementary notion of order, when linked to a system of references (however incomplete in its beginnings) engenders Euclidean notions of distance and change of position.

If we take a series presenting the order ABC, the series contains two partial intervals AB, BC and an overall interval AC. These intervals may be recognized as distances between the ordered points A, B, and C, but only upon two conditions. First, it must be assumed that the three points A, B and C do not draw together or apart when the distances between them are evaluated. In other words, the line ABC, must be seen as rigid and not elastic. Either the three points themselves are fixed, or it must be understood that if their position is changed, the place which they formerly occupied can still be determined in relation to fixed reference-points. Thus the first precondition of the notion of distance already implies both the notion of change of position (because in postulating the relative fixity of limits of distance we are asserting that their change of position is zero) and that of reference-element, since only so can the child distinguish, where necessary, between sites, which maintain a constant relation with these reference elements, and moveable objects, which change their position. The second precondition of the notion of distance is the transformation of the topological series ABC . . . into a Euclidean straight line. The projective notion of a straight line is the result of a relation recognized to exist between a set of ordered points and one "point of view" in particular (that which is used in aiming). Likewise, the correlative Euclidean notion of a straight line which is evolved at the same time is the result of a similar relation recognized to hold between a set of ordered points and a movement taking place in a constant direction. In order to maintain a constant direction of movement, the subject must determine successive positions by fixed references. Thus we are forced back once more on our original contention that distance in the sense of a straight-line interval between two stationary points implies both the notion of change of position and the use of reference elements.

While the notion of change of position begins as a change in rank order, that conception itself later implies both the use of reference elements, and the recognition of determinate distances. To establish that the position of an object has altered relative to its neighbours is by no means the same as to note the fact that there has been a change in the rank order of these objects. It is essential that the subject should establish relations between the successive stationary 'sites' occupied by the object in the course of its motion, including those it vacates and those it occupies; he must be aware of fixed distances between these various stationary points. Thus because the concept of change of position implies an understanding of what is meant by a path of motion, it demands notions of distance and of reference elements, just as the reverse is also true.

We may therefore say that the transition from topological relations to Euclidean relations cannot be effected without the elaboration of the twin concepts of distance and change of position. These developments are simultaneous in their occurrence. Although they are separate qualitative operations, the two complement one another and both imply some relation to fixed reference elements.[1] The operation which constitutes distance is the subdivision of straight line intervals between fixed reference points, while that which constitutes change of position is a change in rank order conceived in terms of such distances. Nesting relations between successive distances and serial relations between changes of position are both dependent on the elaboration of reference systems. Psychologically speaking, we may say that space becomes Euclidean when topological space is structured by reference elements, since the use of such elements brings about the distinction between two kinds of spatial reality, these being fixed 'sites' and space taken up by movable objects. In topological space, no distinction is drawn between container (fixed 'sites') and contained (movable object), but in Euclidean space that distinction is constantly to the fore.

These two operations have been shown to underlie the elaboration of the conservation both of distance and of length in chs. III–VI. Both are intimately linked with the fundamental relation between fixed spatial container and movable content. In ch. III, analysing the growth of the notion of distance, we saw how the child at stages I and II would not allow that the linear intervals in empty space were strictly comparable with the lengths of solid objects. The operational concept of distance did not appear until stage III and it rested on a subdivision

[1] These operations are defined in C.C.S., ch. XV.

and recomposition of space which was comprehensive in that it included both kinds of elements. Again, in ch. IV, we studied the replies given by children when two equal straight sticks were first laid end to end and then slightly staggered in relation to one another. At stages I and II our subjects denied that their lengths were still equal, but at stage III they were convinced that they were because they could now equate the interval previously occupied by the rear portion of a stick which has been advanced with the interval now occupied by its forward portion. Here too, the conservation of length as seen in this particular situation could not be assured in the absence of homogeneity as between empty space as container and solid movable objects as contained. We went on to study the conservation of length when a straight line was transformed by being bent at various angles into a continuous series of shorter rectilinear segments. Here we found we could control the construction of invariance and see how it came about as the child coordinated two complementary qualitative operations, addition of parts and change of position. By adding the parts the subject can gather the set of partial segments and subsume them within a single whole; by changing their position operationally, he can modify their arrangement without altering their total length (ch. V). Finally, in studying children's responses when asked to effect equivalent changes of position along two rectilinear paths which were staggered (ch. VI), we were able to confirm what we knew of the representation of journeys from ch. I: the systematic coordination of movements at the sensori-motor level does not suffice to ensure their adequate elaboration at the level of representation, for this requires that operations governing order and change of position are linked to reference elements which alone allow the subject to subsume empty 'sites' and occupied 'sites' within a single framework of thought.

But it should be added that in spite of the relations recognized to exist between objects and reference elements or between filled 'sites' and empty 'sites', these being the spatial contained and the spatial container, comprehensive systems of coordinates do not appear in this early phase of Euclidean representation and must await the construction of metrical schemata. Not only do such systems involve more than one dimension, a complication to be reviewed below, but at first even linear distance is recognized only as a qualitative nesting series, so that comparisons between distances are restricted to a limited range of possibilities. These are: (1) the elements to be compared are in the linear order ABC when the child knows that $AB < AC$, or (2) the position of an object $A_1 B_1$ is altered to $A_2 B_2$, but the movement is rectilinear and stops short of B_1 (the order of points being $A_1 A_2 B_1 B_2$): the child knows that the interval $A_1 A_2 =$ the interval $B_1 B_2$ because the conservation of length $A_1 B_1 = A_2 B_2$ helps him to see the compensation of $A_1 A_2$ (vacated interval) and $B_1 B_2$ (newly occupied interval) and vice versa. But without measurement, which is reserved for the next level of development (sub-stage IIIB), there can be no complete coordinate or reference systems, because only by measuring distances can a subject compare distances irrespective of their extent, their location and their orientation, as against comparisons between the length of an object and the empty distance in its immediate prolongation.

We may turn next to the conservation of area and volume during this first qualitative phase (level IIIA). Both the processes themselves and the mode of transition from topological to Euclidean space are identical except that the content is now two- or three-dimensional. From the topological point of view, an area is a portion of space bounded by a closed line while a volume is simply a portion of space bounded by one or more areas, these being closed also. It follows that, topologically, one may speak of a nesting series of areas, each being enclosed by those members of the series which are greater than itself, and, similarly, of a nesting series of volumes. Here again we find the notion of order since the series may be looked at, from the inside outwards or from the outside inwards. As in the case of linear order, we are faced with a series of nesting intervals the relative sizes of which are given by the relation of enclosure. Thus we may say in general that areas begin as two-dimensional intervals bounded by closed lines (the areas are two-dimensional because the lines are one-dimensional), and volumes are three-dimensional intervals bounded by closed areas (the volumes in turn being three-dimensional because their boundary surfaces are two-dimensional). From the psychological point of view, we need only consider how children effect the transition from these simple topological notions to Euclidean constructions of area and volume.

The answer given by our research is that the transition is completed in three phases, unlike the construction of linear structures which is accomplished in two. The first level is again represented by elementary conservations. It allows children to think of areas and volumes as invariant in size in spite of transformation in shape, for it should be remembered that topological space is essentially elastic in size. Once more the achievement of conservation is dependent on the recognition of fixed (or relatively fixed) reference elements together with the distinction between a fixed spatial 'container' and a movable 'contained' (level IIIA). This is followed by measurement in two or three dimensions (level IIIB), but the measurement is still linear. As such it is inadequate to the measurement of areas and volumes themselves although it enables the child to quantify the linear elements which bound them. Finally, at stage IV, children come to calculate areas and volumes, which means that they are now able to apply metrical procedures to the spatial continuum itself and not merely to the lines which mark it off. In passing from topological to Euclidean notions of space in regard to two- and three-dimensional continua, children may be said to begin at the outside and work their way to the inside, since they start from the limiting lines of a figure and only later do they calculate the space contained within these lines. During the first phase, although there is elementary conservation of areas and volumes, both are still thought of in topological terms as something contained within a boundary. Nevertheless these dimensions show a greater stability because children are beginning to think of the spatial container itself as something fixed and the latter is now their reference term. But it is only with the second phase that area and volume become Euclidean because until then there is no measurement of their linear framework in two or three dimensions. The interior as such is not calculated until the third phase. Nevertheless, qualitative conservation of area and of volume is a feature of the very first level (IIIA), and presents a close analogy with conservation of length and distance.

The mechanism of both is almost identical, the sole difference being that in the one case conservation is attributed to lines themselves while in the other it bears on parts of space which are contained within lines or faces. The difference lies not in the process of conservation but in its object. In both cases, the essential mechanism consists in coordinating subdivisions and changes of position, and thereby recognizing that newly occupied 'sites' compensate for places left empty through change in position. The kind of conservation of area and volume which is realized at level IIIA is still qualitative. There is no question of measuring areas and volumes, just as the invariance of distance and length does not imply that these must have been measured. Children's conceptions of areas and volumes are little different from earlier topological intuitions, and the only new development is the recognition of change of position in its operational sense with reference to parts of areas and volumes. Henceforward children are aware that the space vacated by one part is exactly compensated by that newly occupied by another. This awareness of compensation rests on the discovery that parts of areas or volumes remain invariant when their position is changed. But that discovery in turn depends on the knowledge that when an object undergoes a slight change of position the space left unoccupied by its rear portion is exactly equivalent to the space newly occupied by its front portion. The argument is circular, since compensation between empty spaces and newly-occupied spaces depends on the invariance of area and volume despite change in position and the latter depends on the awareness of compensation. But although circular (and the same is true of the conservation of length), it is this reasoning which enables the child to coordinate subdivision and change of position and hence to recognize the conservation of area and volume when objects are subjected to modifications of shape (chs. XI, XIV).

The establishment of relations between empty spaces and filled spaces as they occur in the course of changes of position is no more than a beginning, and the child still lacks a comprehensive reference system just as he lacks coordinate axes. The reference system is limited to those parts of space immediately adjacent to an object, since these alone figure in the compensatory relations constructed where there is a slight change of position. At the same time, since there is neither measurement of areas and volumes, nor even linear measurement in one, two or three dimensions, the coordination is necessarily limited. It cannot be applied to distances in general and therefore it cannot affect the whole of the surrounding area or space. It follows that the first notions of conservation applied to areas and volumes refer only to the area or volume interior to a boundary and do not extend to area and volume in the sense of occupied space, implying a relationship with the whole set of shapes or of objects round about (and also with the empty spaces in two or three dimensions). Apart from this distinction, the analogy with conservation of length is complete. The invariance of interior area or volume is constructed in precisely the same way as the invariance of length. But the conservation of area and volume as occupied space implies a further relationship with the whole set of spatial containers and of objects (contained) of which the particular object or shape under consideration forms but one part. It also implies that the subject knows how to measure the lines surrounding a two- or three-dimensional object and establish metrical relations between these measurements and its interior area or volume.

It is true that at level IIIA children cannot measure because they simply coordinate subdivision and change of position, treating them as complementary operations, and cannot fuse them into a single operation to carry out unit iteration. Nevertheless they can quite well manipulate additions and subtractions of parts from wholes, since the composition of parts is a factor in the conservation of area and volume, where it takes the form of compensations between empty space and filled spaces. In particular, when equal parts are subtracted from congruent wholes the child at this level is aware that the remaining areas are equal also (ch. XI, section I). In that experiment, despite all appearance to the contrary, the areas of the fields themselves are not conserved, since these are areas in the sense of space occupied: only the area of houses built on these fields is subject to conservation, since these are looked on as interior areas bounded by lines.

There are three major consequences for geometrical reasoning all of which derive from the appearance at level IIIA of the operations of subdivision and change of position, and hence of the conservation of Euclidean size. The first concerns measurement itself. Although children cannot yet measure in the full sense of the word, they can use common measures in a qualitative way. In other words although they cannot yet use units of measurement, they can transfer congruences by using qualitative transitivity (A = B, B = C, therefore A = C), implying the conservation of a middle term B which is transferred from A to C. This is true alike of lengths (chs. II, V–VIII), of area (ch. XI) and of volumes (ch. XIV).

Secondly, the fact that relations of equality or congruence can b transferred is sufficient to ensure the generalization of equidistances in the operational construction of 'loci'. Therefore, in constructing a circle (chs. IX and X) children now appreciate the equality of its radii. It is a recognition which antecedes the construction of units of measurement.

Finally, the realization of transitivity enables children to reason by the elementary principle of recurrence. It is this kind of reasoning which underlies the generalization of other instances of equidistance. Thus we saw in ch. IX how at 7–8 years of age, children first discover a number of points which are equidistant from two given points A and B, and then reason that the same will be true of all points on the straight line which passes through these few initial points. Moreover, they appreciate that the line can be drawn in either direction: A ↑ B or A ↓ B.

Hence it is reasonable to conclude that although subdivision and change of position are still qualitative operations because their coordination is still a function of the immediate spatial neighbourhood rather than a generalized system of coordinates, these operations lie at the basis of the child's first notions of conservation and thereby help to form all those fundamental kinds of reasoning which constitute Euclidean space.

SECTION II. THE GROWTH OF MEASUREMENT
(LEVEL IIIB)

The possibility of measurement, and by this we mean unit iteration, depends on the construction of lengths, areas and volumes in forms which allow of elementary conservation. It depends, too, on qualitative operations of subdivision and change of position, and these are intimately linked with conservation. Thus the relation of measurement to the sub-logical operations of subdivision and change of position is an exact parallel to that of number in regard to the logical operations of nesting class hierarchies and seriations. But there is a difference. The construction of number appears at the same time as that of the logical operations of which number is a synthesis (level IIIA), but that of measurement appears later than its constituent operations (i.e. not until level IIIB).

To begin with, we may remind ourselves of the precise relations between the measurement of lengths and operations of subdivision and change of position (chs. V, VI). Let us suppose a straight line C with a given length. By operational subdivision and composition we understand the process whereby the line may be broken into a number of contiguous parts and these in turn can be re-united to recompose the original whole. Such parts may be represented by one length A which, together with another A′ to which it is contiguous, yields a more inclusive part B (= A + A′), while B in turn is completed by a final part B′, so that together they yield the whole line (B + B′ = C). A child at level IIIA understands composition and can therefore deduce the following relations: A + A′ + B′ = C; B − A = A′; B − A′ = A; C − B = B′; C − B′ = B; C − B′ − A′ = A; C − B′ − B = O; etc. He can even go on to quantify these relations, but only 'intensively'. In other words, the quantification is derived only from part-whole relations and not from relations between one part and another: our subject will be aware that A < C; A′ < C; B < C; B′ < C; A < B; etc., without needing to know the precise lengths of A, A′ and B′. Between these elementary parts, A, A′ and B′, there can be no relation other than that of qualitative equivalence which is derived from their common membership of C. Thus operations of subdivision may be quite independent of metrical operations, as indeed they are, when used in the conservation of length.

We find the same when we turn to qualitative operations of change of position. If we think once more of the linear series envisaged above, we may note that the initial order of its three elementary parts is A A′ B′. Any change in their relative position is simply a matter of altering that order to A′ A B or A B′ A′, etc. Similarly, to change the position of the total line C amounts to an alteration in the order of C relative to a series of reference elements. On the other hand any change in the order of its own parts will not affect the total length C because A′ + A + B′ = B′ + A + A′ = A + A′ + B′ = C. Likewise, the forward movement of the line C no longer affects its length. This is because of the compensation as between newly filled spaces and vacated spaces described earlier. But that compensation can also be expressed in the language of qualitative subdivision: by moving forward, the stick C is increased by a new element C′ at its forward end; at the same time it loses a part C″ which it leaves behind, which may be expressed as D − C″. But since change of position is a change in the order of things, the new part C′ and the old part C″ are regarded as equivalent, i.e. C′ = C″, and the child argues C + C′ − C″ = C just as C + C′ − C′ = C.

These qualitative operations of subdivision and change of position can be applied to several objects at once just as easily as they can to one object alone, so that they readily give rise to multiplicative correspondences. What this means is that a child can recognize relations of congruence between objects or between parts of objects without using measurement and without going beyond the level of qualitative operations. Thus we may take a straight stick C composed of parts A, A′ and B′, and apply it alongside another stick C_2: we can recognize the congruence of the two wholes $C_2 = C$, and also that of their parts: $A_2 = A$; $A_2 = A′$ and $B_2′ = B′$; these parts $(A_2 + A_2′ + B_2′)$ might even be applied to a third length C_3 $(= A_3 + A_3′ + B_3)$ to give $C_3 = C_2 = C_1$, etc. But all this involves no more than changes of position and transitive correspondences between subdivisions. In other words, the operations are still qualitative and intensive, because they do not entail the notion of a unit. They do not entail a quantitative relation between one part and the next, but only the recognition that any part is less than the whole. Partial changes of position cannot generate units since all we know of them is that they are less than total changes of position, and we cannot know how they stand in relation to other partial changes of position. Similarly, relations of congruence between two wholes or their respective parts do not involve units so long as we are concerned only with correspondences between elements, without uniting the two collections in metrical terms by the formula $C + C_2 = 2C$. Finally, the use of a common term or common measure C_2 to link C and C_3 by means of the three relations $C = C_2$, $C_2 = C_3$, therefore $C = C_3$ does not involve the notion of unit either and depends only on the transitivity of these correspondences.

Measurement begins when one part A belonging to a whole C is compared with the remaining parts of the same whole by change of position (either its own or that of a common measure, used transitively) so that A (or its equivalent) is superposed on these other parts. This implies that subdivision and change of position are fused into one single operation and no longer simply complementary. That operation is unit iteration. The operations to which we alluded above involve the alternate use of subdivision and change of position and not the two together: thus, subdivision antecedes change of position and is not its consequence, but change of position itself is also quite independent of subdivision. This fact may be seen in the conservation of an overall size, where there is always an initial subdivision of the whole into parts and their relative position is then changed so that the various parts take one another's positions. The operation does not involve any direct or indirect comparison between the several parts.[1] But when one part A is applied to the remainder of the whole C (i.e. $C - A$), the subdivision is not independently given: it is generated by the change of position effected either by A itself or by its transitive equivalent. Thus what happens is that A is moved stepwise along $C - A$, giving

---

[1] Elsewhere we have termed this operation 'vicariance'. See *Classes, relations et nombres*, ch. IV.

first A = A' (so that B = 2A), then A = A' = B' (so that C = 3A), and here the subdivision cannot be dissociated from the corresponding changes of position. So also in measurement we find change of position being used in a highly specific manner: a length A is first put in one position, then stepped so that it begins where it ended, and so on. The subdivision depends wholly on change of position, but the reverse is also true, and it is this synthesis of qualitative operations which gives rise to unit iteration and so constitutes measurement. By applying one section over and over until the whole has been covered completely, we effectively reduce the whole to a multiple of that section and the section becomes a unit. Since the unit can be subdivided in turn, using one of its fractional elements as a sub-unit, it follows that any size whatever can be compared with any other by means of whole and fractional units.

It is perfectly clear that, by stage IIIB the subjects cited in chs. II, V and VI have finally achieved the construction of measurement by fusing or synthesizing the operations of subdivision and change of position. Both operations were required at level IIIA for the notion of conservation, but there they were still complementary to one another instead of being fused into a single operation. There is a parallel to this elaboration of measurement out of two qualitative operations which are at first distinct but which must be synthesized to yield one integral operation. The parallel is in the elaboration of number. This cannot surprise us since there are isomorphic relations between the iteration of metrical units and the series of whole numbers (as also between the fractioning of metrical units and fractional numbers), likewise between subdivison and composition of parts on the one hand and nesting class hierarchies on the other, and finally, between change of position and seriation of asymmetrical relations. Thus measurement, in the field of sublogical operations is the exact equivalent to number in that of logical operations, since number is a synthesis involving the logical grouping of nesting classes and the seriation of asymmetrical relations. The only difference is that the whole-number series is constructed at level IIIA, and so follows immediately on these two logical groupings, while measurement is delayed for some while after notions of conservation have been mastered—although these are similarly dependent on its constituent operations: subdivision and change of position. We have tried to show how that delay is not unexpected, since numerical unity is something which may be perceived intuitively because any collection of discontinuous items consists of such unique elements, while choosing a unit of length within an overall length is to make an arbitrary fragmentation of a whole which is continuous.

Children at level IIIB are by no means limited to linear measurement and we soon find them using the same process to measure areas: they choose one area to act as unit and effect changes in the position of

400

that unit (ch. XI, section II). But there is a distinction between this kind of areal measurement and that which is yet to come. When children are aware of the relation between an area and the lengths of its sides (e.g. for a rectangle, that 2×3 cm. $= 6$ cm.²) they can measure these sides and calculate the area. But this awareness does not come about until stage IV. At level IIIB children understand linear measurement in two or three dimensions (which means that they can fix a point in a plane or in a volume by taking two or three linear measurements perpendicular to one another). They can also measure an area as such—but only if they use two-dimensional units. They cannot start from linear units and arrive at an areal measurement. The child at level IIIA discovers that an area remains invariant when the arrangement of its parts is modified. At level IIIB he discovers how to apply one part over each of the others in turn and can therefore measure the total area as a function of a smaller area if this is handed to him as a ready-made unit: thus we saw how he measured a rectangle, using a little square which went into it without remainders and, again, how he measured triangular shapes, etc. using a little triangle formed by halving a square. But to the child at this level the unit-square is by no means the same thing as a unit of length raised to the second power or "squared", it is simply a flat object suitably shaped to allow him to carry out subdivisions by changes of position and as a result he uses it as a unit of measurement.

At this same level, we find that children can divide an area into any number of equal parts: a cake, for instance, can be shared out evenly among five or six. But this behaviour can only be understood correctly if we make these two provisos. First, we may remember from ch. XII that even at stage IIIA, children divide correctly into thirds, while halving is successfully accomplished as early as stage II. At the same time we saw how subjects at sub-stage IIIA could divide a cake into three but were nevertheless unable to divide one into six although they might have done so with the greatest of ease by simply halving the three thirds, which in itself presented no difficulty, since bisection is far easier than trisection. We are forced to the conclusion that dividing an area into two or three equal parts is operational only in a qualitative sense. Thus the subject makes use of anticipatory schemata to direct the process of subdivision, but the equalization of parts is governed by intuition rather than by metrical considerations. Therefore he cannot divide into fifths or sixths, since this would require combining relations derived from measurement. In the second place, we may note that dividing an area in this way is not the inverse operation of doubling an area (ch. XIII). The latter problem required the conservation of shape and therefore implied a relation between the boundary lines of the square and its area which could be established only by mathematical multiplication. Here we did not ask that the child retain the shape of the whole cake when dividing it into equal parts, and so there is no multiplicative relation between boundary lines and areas. The number of parts is simply given by adding 1 to the number of cuts and the equality of parts is a judgment based on one side only (e.g. for a slice of cake it is the arc or the cord, etc.). This explains why dividing an area into a number of equal parts which differ in shape from the whole is successfully accomplished at level IIIB.

However, the measurement of volume is impossible at this level. The reason is not far to seek. We cannot measure a volume directly by congruence. We can establish the congruence of lines and surfaces with those which form the boundaries of a given volume, but, because there is no fourth dimension, we cannot reach inside the volume from without. Thus the child at level IIIA discovers that volumes remain invariant although the arrangement of their parts is modified. He does so by coordinating qualitative operations, subdivision and change of position, which enables him to rediscover the original elements in their new positions. Yet he cannot proceed to synthesize the two operations at level IIIB and measure volume directly, as he can for length and for area, because he cannot apply one unit-volume over the remainder of the volume under consideration. He can do so effectively only if the total volume consists of a number of similar elements all of which are visible (like a single or double row of cubes in juxtaposition), but he fails as soon as any elements are hidden from view, as in our model of 3 × 3 × 4 units. The protracted interval between conservation of interior volume (level IIIA) and calculation of measured volume (level IV) is an excellent pointer to the very real differences between qualitative conservation of a whole and operations of measuring. The answer given by children at level IIIB, as illustrated in ch. XIV, is most interesting: children measure the boundary walls (because they alone can be measured by congruence) and argue as though the relative sizes of these faces exactly parallelled those of the volumes enclosed by them (which is tantamount to assuming that the thickness is always one unit).

In effect, the responses of level IIIB are all of a piece. Measurement is carried out correctly but only where congruence can be established directly, that is, when linear units are used to measure lengths and areal units to measure areas. Calculations of area or volume based on linear measurements are still unrealized. However the structurization of Euclidean space depends to a considerable degree on other procedures. Here we refer to a series of linear measurements in two or three dimensions involving one-one correspondence or one-many correspondence. In the first case the result is a measurable systematization of space in terms of rectangular coordinates, in the latter, it marks the beginning of the measurement of angles.

The child who can measure lengths in one dimension can do so auto-

402

matically in several dimensions. The difference between one length and many is essentially the same as that between additive and multiplicative compositions (whether these be logical or sub-logical). Wherever this problem has been studied, we have always found that the child who can add can also multiply because logical multiplication is simply a matter of combining two or more additions and establishing the resultant correspondences. So in constructing a square, or a rectangle, or even a parallelogram, the child simply establishes correspondences beween a number of equal straight lines. When copying one of these models, he pairs the lines of his copy with the corresponding lines of the model, taking them either singly or two at a time which is easier since there are always two pairs of parallel lines. This construction is perceived intuitively at stage II before being translated into operational terms at level IIIA. It is a case of effecting a multiplicative composition of relations which are still only qualitative, and as such it is no more difficult than the addition of parts.[1] And so we find that almost as soon as he can take linear measurements in one dimension, the child can coordinate measures in two or three. At sub-stage IIIB, children can determine the exact position of a point situated in a two or three dimensional framework by taking two or three linear measurements at right angles to one another (ch. VII). Before that level, our subjects were unable to coordinate their measurements if they took two or three, or alternatively, they took only a single measurement parallel with one of the sides or running in an oblique direction from the point inside the area to one of its corners. These measurements, when successful, may determine the position of a point within an area or a volume, but they are by no means measurements of the area or volume as such, since they do not involve mathematical multiplication. They are no more than linear measurements which conform to the schema of a two entry table or a three entry table, which is one of logical multiplication. It is true that the measurements themselves are expressed in quantitative terms and are therefore metrical in character, but they are combined by means of logical (more precisely, sublogical) multiplication. In orienting their measurements in two or three rectangular dimensions, children follow a schema of one-one correspondence: the correspondence is one-one because the elements are paired horizontally and vertically which gives a lattice work effect to the system as a whole. However this is not the only kind of logical (or sub-logical) multiplication. The other involves one-many correspondences.[2] Yet it is a fact that children at sub-stage IIIB who can construct one-one correspondences are just as able to construct these. And so we found in ch. IX that children at this level

---

[1] See also ch. VI, §§3 and 4, illustrating the establishment of relations between two parallel lengths forming a parallelogram.
[2] See C.C.S., ch. XV, p. 480.

begin to measure angles by coordinating increase in height with increase in distance from the vertex. Measurement of angles corresponds to the elaboration of notions of similarity and it is successfully accomplished at the same time as the child decides by superposition whether or not two triangles are similar, i.e. at sub-stage IIIB (see C.C.S., ch. XII).

The fact that children at sub-stage IIIB are in a position to coordinate several measurements, using multiplicative schemata, is altogether fundamental to the structurization of Euclidean space. Thus quite apart from the striking coincidence of these developments with the qualitative construction of angles, their importance lies in that they enable the child to construct comprehensive rectangular coordinate systems. One cannot but be struck by the fact that at stage IIIB, when measurement first becomes possible in one or more dimensions, children are also beginning to use natural horizontal and vertical references in order to construct comprehensive systems of spatial relations which include both the dimensions and positions of natural and artificial objects and the spaces between them which may be empty. We may well ask whether these qualitative reference systems arise because measurements are being coordinated in terms of two- or three-dimensional frameworks or whether it is the other way about.

However, the truth is no different from what has been found in all similar dilemmas: the two kinds of construction are interdependent. There can be no metrical whole in the absence of a qualitative construction to support the measurements but at the same time the qualitative construction remains 'open' and therefore incomplete without the intervention of metrical relations. Systems of coordinates imply not only reference axes but also a comprehensive organization of relations. Their beginnings reach back as far as the earliest Euclidean operations; and as we remarked in section I the conservation of distance and of length implies not only fixed reference elements but also a firm distinction between movable objects or shapes and a stationary spatial 'container', this being the set of positions or 'sites' which are sometimes occupied and sometimes not. Precisely the same system is implied by the Euclidean notion of change of position. Indeed that system is also the precondition for the conservation of area and of interior volume and for measurement itself, since measurement involves change of position and presupposes the invariance both of wholes and of their subdivisions. But so long as the system is qualitative, it is no more than a beginning and it is limited to the immediate surroundings of objects. This is inevitable because the child cannot yet measure any distance which exceeds the length being used as a reference term. When he has worked out how to make linear measurements in one dimension and in two or three, he is in a position to extend the coordination. Hitherto, this was qualitative because it involved no more than the multiplication of order relations but now he can make precise measurements of distances and positions. The frame of reference therefore includes the whole of the spatial field under consideration. It is because the coordinate system is metrical in this sense that its function is general.

Throughout this work we have repeatedly stressed the fact that from the psychological standpoint, the question whether the representation of space is Euclidean or not depends on the construction of coordinate systems. Topological relations are concerned only with proximities within figures or configurations; projective space involves a coordination of points of view from which objects are observed; Euclidean space involves the coordination of the objects themselves. Now we know that objects are mobile. Their position is not immutable (and neither is that of the subject who creates projective space by virtue of his points of view but who is himself an object among others). It is for this reason that the coordination can be achieved only by connecting the positions and distances and changes of position to a fixed spatial 'container' which is so structured as to enable the mobile 'contents' to be accurately located within it. Thus the distinction between container and contained is essential to the representation of Euclidean space.[1] Out of it are born those coordinate systems which highlight the transition from topological to Euclidean space.

An additional feature of this study was an examination of the growth of various curves. Some of these, like certain mechanical curves, imply not one but two reference or coordinate systems combined. Here we find that, although our subjects at sub-stage IIIB achieved complete mastery of rectangular coordinate systems as such, they were only beginning to establish links between two such systems. At level IIIB the linkage was always the outcome of trial-and-error and not until stage IV, being the level of formal thought, were the solutions immediate. This brings us to the third level in the construction of Euclidean space, introducing the calculation of areas and volumes.

SECTION III. THE CALCULATION OF AREAS AND VOLUMES (LEVEL IV)

We saw how the notion of change of position, together with conservation of length and distance, introduces the beginnings of Euclidean space. Euclidean intuitions occur as early as stage II and the first Euclidean operations, implying links between moving objects and fixed reference 'sites', feature at level IIIA. Nevertheless, even at sub-stage IIIB, the development is far from complete. Throughout sub-stage IIIB

---

[1] This is particularly evident in children's responses to the problem of complementary areas, to be mentioned in section III.

there is a marked contrast between the success of Euclidean construction in linear measurement and the persistence of topological notions in the realm of area or volume. Children can coordinate linear measurements in several dimensions as soon as they learn how to carry out such measurements in one. We have already seen how the construction of comprehensive coordinate systems makes this possible by imposing a definite structure on Euclidean space. But these systems are still linear in character. Intersections of straight lines are sufficient for the accurate location of positions and for fixing orientations and distances. But even taken together, they are still lines in each of the three dimensions and do not constitute a continuum. That is why linear measurement and the representation of areas and volumes are heterogenous at sub-stage IIIB. These latter notions are still contaminated by topological residua which seem singularly resistant to Euclidean reconstruction.

It is indeed true that children can measure areas even at level IIIB In the same way, they can measure angles which are also plane surfaces, since an angle may be regarded as a plane sector delimited by its arms. But areas are measured only in terms of units which are themselves areas and angles only by the superposition of similar angles. Measurement does not yet involve areal dimensions which are worked out in terms of linear dimensions. Instead they are measured in terms of congruence combined with metrical composition. While the latter is derived from the metrical composition of length the two kinds of composition are always separate in the child's mind. It follows that area continues to be essentially topological: at level IIIB an area is a portion of space bounded by a boundary line. It is stable because it is subject to Euclidean conservation, and invarian. because it is linked to a stationary 'container', but it is not reducible to linear units. Hence these children cannot solve the problem of doubling an area while preserving its shape (ch. XIII). Usually, they try to double the lengths of its sides and are then surprised to find that they finish with an area four times the original. They have no idea why, precisely because they do not realize that areas must be measured in units of a higher power.

As for volumes, the facts are even more paradoxical. There is conservation of 'interior' volume in the sense that the child recognizes the invariance of the amount of matter or the number of elements (wooden cubes, etc.) contained within the boundary lines or surfaces. At the same time he begins to measure, but his measurements are confined to the boundary surfaces which enclose the interior volume. But what may seem strange is that the conservation of interior volume does not bring with it the invariance of true volume in the sense of the space occupied by the object with reference to its surroundings. The child recognizes that by re-arranging the blocks in a cube to form a long wall or a tower he does not alter its interior volume, but he still thinks that its volume in relation to the surrounding space is liable to be different. Interior volume, which is conserved, is simply the child's way of thinking of a certain amount of three-dimensional space contained within two-dimensional boundaries. He cannot conceive of any metrical relations between the boundaries and the volume itself. Here the position exactly parallels that which obtains in relation to area, and we find children thinking they can double a volume by simply doubling edges or faces.

Euclidean notions of space are completed in the course of stage IV and it is then that the duality of thinking in relation to area and volume is finally overcome. The first new discovery of stage IV is the conservation of volume in the sense of the physicist. Conservation of volume is no longer limited to 'interior' volume and divorced from the spatial context. The corresponding achievement in the construction of area belongs to sub-stage IIIB, because that is when we first find conservation of complementary areas as well as the areas which they circumscribe.

This raises the question why conservation in relation to the surrounding spatial medium does not occur at level IIIB in the case of volume, especially as that level sees the completion of comprehensive reference systems and coordinate axes. However, while it is true that the notion of 'occupied' volume is impossible without an overall structurization of space in terms of coordinate axes, that is not the only condition for its appearance. The child must find the true metric relationships between boundary lines and boundary surfaces and between surfaces and volumes. Alterations in the form of a line do not affect its overall length but transformation of areas and volumes do affect the total lengths or the total surfaces of their boundaries. It is because these perimeters are variable that children are led to believe that areas vary likewise and, in particular, they are long convinced that occupied volume does not remain constant in such transformations, since boundary faces and edges are key points of contact between a volume and the surrounding space. There is a similar staggering in the case of area since the conservation of interior areas is achieved at level IIIA while that of complementary areas is delayed until level IIIB. In the case of volume, the child cannot see all the elements simultaneously and hence he is quite unable to deduce the conservation of occupied volume from that of interior volume until he learns to establish definite relations between the sides of an object and its interior.

By definite relations we mean relations which are metrical rather than qualitative. They involve multiplication which is not merely logical but mathematical. In other words, by multiplying linear measurement of the side of a figure we arrive at products which are expressed in second and third power units. Taken by itself, the fact that the multiplication is mathematical would not constitute a serious obstacle even for younger children, since we know that the simplest kinds of mathematical multiplication are understood at level IIIA. Therefore we might reasonably expect that all that is needed for the elaboration of geometrically valid notions of area and volume is the structurization of space at level IIIB. But this is to forget that it is one thing to multiply two numbers together and quite another to multiply two lengths or three lengths and understand that their product is an area or a volume. The latter involves the continuity of space: surfaces can be reduced to lines only if they are thought of as infinite series of lines without lacunae. But the decomposition and recomposition of a continuum are operations which belong to the level of formal operations (C.C.S., ch. V). This explains why it is not until stage IV that children understand how they can arrive at an area or a volume simply by multiplying boundary edges. In a sense we may say that this form of multiplication is a prolongation of the use of metrical procedures together with logical multiplications in the construction of coordinate systems. But there is a clear difference in that now the matrix of coordinated lines is so packed in thought as to leave no lacunae. Continuity is therefore achieved by adding an infinite number of lines to the existing matrix. Having elaborated the notion of a continuum, children can now use mathematical multiplication to arrive at areas and volumes, and by so doing they reconstruct the notion in metric terms. Here we see the final phase in the reconstruction of Euclidean space. The level at which it is completed is also that at which topological notions themselves achieve an equilibrium of their own by virtue of formal operational thinking.

INDEX

409

International Library of Psychology, Philosophy & Scientific Method

Editor: C K Ogden

(Demy 8vo)

Philosophy

Psychology